ArtScroll History Series®

Rabbi Nosson Scherman / Rabbi Meir Zlotowitz
General Editors

Published by
Mesorah Publications, ltd

RABBI SHERER

The paramount Torah spokesman of our era

by Yonason Rosenblum
Foreword by Rabbi Shimshon Sherer

FIRST EDITION
First Impression ... November 2009

Published and Distributed by
MESORAH PUBLICATIONS, LTD.
4401 Second Avenue / Brooklyn, N.Y 11232

Distributed in Europe by
LEHMANNS
Unit E, Viking Business Park
Rolling Mill Road
Jarow, Tyne & Wear, NE32 3DP
England

Distributed in Australia and New Zealand
by **GOLDS WORLDS OF JUDAICA**
3-13 William Street
Balaclava, Melbourne 3183
Victoria, Australia

Distributed in Israel by
SIFRIATI / A. GITLER — BOOKS
6 Hayarkon Street
Bnei Brak 51127

Distributed in South Africa by
KOLLEL BOOKSHOP
Ivy Common
105 William Road
Norwood 2192, Johannesburg, South Africa

ARTSCROLL HISTORY SERIES®
RABBI SHERER
© *Copyright 2009, by* MESORAH PUBLICATIONS, Ltd.
4401 Second Avenue / Brooklyn, N.Y. 11232 / (718) 921-9000 / www.artscroll.com

---

ALL RIGHTS RESERVED
The text, prefatory and associated textual contents and introductions
— including the typographic layout, cover artwork and ornamental graphics —
have been designed, edited and revised as to content, form and style.

No part of this book may be reproduced
IN ANY FORM, PHOTOCOPYING, OR COMPUTER RETRIEVAL SYSTEMS
— even for personal use without written permission from
the copyright holder, Mesorah Publications Ltd.
except by a reviewer who wishes to quote brief passages
in connection with a review written for inclusion in magazines or newspapers.

THE RIGHTS OF THE COPYRIGHT HOLDER WILL BE STRICTLY ENFORCED.

ISBN 10: 1-4226-0944-8 / ISBN 13: 978-1-4226-0944-6

Typography by CompuScribe at ArtScroll Studios, Ltd.
Printed in Canada
Bound by Sefercraft, Quality Bookbinders, Ltd., Brooklyn N.Y. 11232

TABLE OF CONTENTS

Publishers' Preface   9
Foreword   15
Author's Preface   23
Introduction — Never Out of Character   29
A Note to the Reader   35

৵ Part I: EARLY YEARS

1 Foreshadowing
Basya Sherer / Zeirei Agudath Israel / Chinuch / Reb Elchonon Wasserman, Hy"d   39

2 Ner Israel
Rabbi Yaakov Yitzchak Halevi Ruderman / In the Eyes of His Contemporaries / Master of the Word / Young Idealist / Budding Activist / Preparing for the Next Step   64

3 Getting Started
Rescue Work / Reaching Out to the Survivors / Going National / Getting Out the Message / Hints of Discontent / On-the-Job Training   91

4 Marriage
Rabbi Shimshon Zelig HaKohen Fortman / The Ponevezher Rav   113

5 Laying the Foundations
Reb Aharon's Student / On Behalf of Eretz Yisrael / The Psak of Eleven Roshei Yeshivah / Battling Heterodoxy   126

6 Transition
Mike's Last Public Campaign / New Burdens / Different Times / Breakthrough / A New Political Activism / Charting the Future   147

≈§ Part II: THE VISION

7 Visions of Agudath Israel
Agudath Israel as an Ideological Movement / Agudath Israel Represents Klal Yisrael / The Image of Torah Jewry / A Clean Organization / Also a Social Service Organization / An Ideology of Activism   173

8 The Ideology of *Daas Torah*
Educating the Public / Serving the Yeshivos / Heeding the Gedolim / Strengthening the Moetzes Gedolei HaTorah / Shlucha D'Rachmana   197

9 *Baalebattim*
A Grassroots Organization / The Role of the Shearis Hapleitah / A New Cadre of Lay Leaders / A Relationship of Mutual Respect / The Contribution of Baalebattim   221

≈§ Part III: LEADERSHIP

10 The "People Thing"
In-Depth Relationships / A Source of Inspiration / A Holy Man / A Trusted Adviser / Wellsprings of Trust / Nurturing Relationships / Bridging the Gulf   251

11 Leader
Charisma / Many Levels of Leadership / Defender of Orthodoxy / Building Bridges / Alliance with the Catholics / Connecting the Dots / Knowing His Limits / Toughness   269

12 Advocate
Framing the Issues / Lawyer-like   301

13 Diplomacy in Action: A Case Study   314

≈§ Part IV: MODUS OPERANDI

14 Boss
Inspiration / Leading by Example / Good Enough Is Not Good Enough / Attracting Through Idealism / Mentor / Binding With Cords of Love   329

15 The Word
Homiletics / Bishtei Einayim / The Power of Persuasion / Getting Out the Message: Dos Yiddishe Vort and The Jewish Observer / Finding the Stalwarts / Siyum HaShas   345

16 Six Crises
SAVING THE DRAFT EXEMPTION: *A Crisis Brews / Putting the Pieces Together / The Battle in the House / The Battleground Shifts / Victory /* **PROTECTING THE ESROGIM:** *Quarantine! /* **THE HIJACKING OF RABBI HUTNER:** *Life Stops / Protecting the Jewish Passengers / Bringing Home the Harari-Raful Brothers /* **EXECUTIVE ORDER 50:** *A Brutal Choice / Agudath Israel Sues City Hall /* **THE SECOND NEW YORK STATE "GET LAW":** *Helping Protect Women /* **THE CROWN HEIGHTS RIOTS:** *Champion of the Urban Jews / A Modern-Day Pogrom / Support for the Rosenbaum Family / An Iron Fist in a Velvet Glove*   368

∾§ Part V: AGUDATH ISRAEL

17 An Independent Orthodoxy
A Painful Setback / Contempt for the Mainstream Leadership / Moving Ahead / Project COPE / The Southern Brooklyn Community Organization / AARTS   419

18 Expanding Capacities
Chief Executive Officer / The First New York State "Get Law" / Promoting Kiddush Hashem / Large Dividends   452

19 The Washington, D.C. Office
Achievements in the Halls of Power / Saving Shechitah / Working the Executive Branch   465

20 *Shtadlanus*: Theory and Practice
Setting Priorities / Assisting Jonathan Pollard / The Practice of Shtadlanus / End-of-Life Issues   482

21 On the International Scene
Iranian Rescue / Russian Jewry / Journey South / Forging a Foreign Policy   500

22 For the Land and Her People
Security for the Jews of Eretz Yisrael / Defending Religious Interests in Israel / Relations With the Israeli Agudah / The Am Echad Delegation 541

✥ Part VI: THE MAN

23 In Private
Tocho K'Boro / Protecting His Family / A Happy Home / Lessons of the Home / A Doting Grandfather / A Proud Father and Grandfather 567

24 Dealing With Adversity
Intimations of Mortality / A New Crisis / A Visit to the Agudah Camps / The Last Hurrah / His Last Pesach at Home 596

25 Farewell
A Speech Not Given / The Levayah / A Wish Fulfilled / Kasheh Preidasicha Aleinu 625

Index 647

PHOTO CREDITS

We express our appreciation to the following individuals and organizations who provided the photos that enhance this book:

Agudath Israel of America
Tsemach Glenn
Rabbi Yosef Chaim Golding
The Goldmark Group
Hamodia
Rebbetzin Fay Hollander
Mrs. Debby Jacobs
Mrs. Evelyn Kleinman
The Lakewood Shopper
Ner Israel Rabbinical College
Rabbi Boruch Neuberger
The Orthodox Jewish Archives of Agudath Israel of America,
    Rabbi Moshe Kolodny, Archivist
Frank Storch
The Shisgal and Greenfield Families
Trainer Studios
Rabbi Boruch Mordechai Wenger
Rabbi Dovid Yankelevitch
Zelman Studios

PUBLISHERS' PREFACE

IN SPEAKING ABOUT TESHUVAH, THE ALTER OF SLABODKA said, "It is not enough to make oneself better. One must make oneself different."

Rabbi Moshe Sherer made the Jewish world different. When his generation was growing up, secular Jews in America were convinced that Orthodox Judaism was moribund, shrinking, sinking into a generation gap. When Zeirei Agudath Israel, under the guidance of newly arrived refugee Torah sages, had the temerity to send food packages to the ghettoes of Nazi-occupied Poland, in defiance of the American and British governments' call for a boycott, a Jewish-American establishment leader wrote angrily that the rabbis were a "sickly weed, transplanted from Europe."

Who would have dared prophecy that the "sickly weed" would blossom into a luxuriant growth of kehillos and yeshivos, strong and confident, devoted to the timeless *Mesorah* of Judaism eternal? Who would have thought that Orthodox Jewry would become respected and heeded in the corridors of government and that it would produce a leader, Rabbi Moshe Sherer, who would eclipse those who were confident that Orthodox Judaism and Orthodox Jews would disappear from the American scene?

It happened. The American Jewish world is different.

Who made it happen? Many, many people. The hard-working men and women who refused to succumb to the blandishments and coercions of modern life, and who sent their children to the then handful of yeshivos. The courageous and principled rabbis who kept sparks alive from the 1880s to the Holocaust. The great Torah sages, yeshivish and chassidish, who came to America before, during, and shortly after the War — many of whom survived only through miracles — and threw themselves into the work of saving lives and building yeshivos and communities.

Anyone with an eye to peer below rationalizations that attempt to explain history can see that the survival of this small group of spiritual giants was a fulfillment of the Divine promise that despite the most intense suffering and persecution,

> ... while they will be in the land of their enemies, I will not have been revolted by them nor will I have rejected them to obliterate them, to annul my covenant with them — for I am Hashem, their God. I will remember for them the covenant of the ancients, those whom I have taken out of the land of Egypt before the eyes of the nations, to be God unto them — I am Hashem (Leviticus 26:44-45).

The *gedolim* provided direction and perspective, inspiration and example, and they motivated talmidim and followers. There were dedicated people — European and American-born — who refused to surrender to the once-prevalent feeling that the New World was a wasteland where the Torah of Europe could not thrive. They overcame history and opposition, and in the end they prevailed. It is one of the miracles of Jewish history.

If any one man can be credited with being the agent who brought Torah *hashkafah* and institutions to the forefront of public consciousness, from the 1960s onward, that man was Rabbi Moshe Sherer. From his teen years, he was imbued with a sense of responsibility to serve *gedolei Yisrael* and *Klal Yisrael*. His vehicle was Agudath Israel, and the man who recruited and mentored the young Moshe when he was still a a talmid of Yeshivah Ner Israel in Baltimore was the legendary

"Mike" Tress, whose drive and faith and courage ignited the zeal of a generation of activists for Torah. Even as a teenager, Rabbi Sherer was a talented writer, and his articles articulating the Torah view on current issues still read well.

When he joined Agudath Israel full time, it consumed his life. He called it his "fourth child," and over time the names Moshe Sherer and Agudath Israel became synonymous. But he was far, far more than an "organization man." His province was the Jewish people wherever they were and his masters were the great Torah sages, whatever their nominal affiliation. He was their loyal servant. They, especially Rabbi Aharon Kotler, molded him, and he projected their image as the only authentic leadership of *Klal Yisrael*. They had implicit faith in him and he rewarded them with service to Torah that was unparalleled in his era. He brought unprecedented prestige to Torah sages, Torah institutions, and the Torah community.

What made him unique?

Many words come to mind. One of them is "trust": his trust in Hashem and the *gedolim*, the trust they had in him, and the trust of all the people who dealt with him. People knew that Rabbi Sherer's word was inviolable. If he said something it was true. If he promised something he would deliver. If he warned someone against a course of action, it should be discarded. One of the darkest days of his life was when a tabloid insinuated that he had done something dishonorable. No one who knew him believed it, but he was tortured by the first blight on his reputation for integrity. A prominent investigative reporter followed up the story and called Rabbi Sherer to say that he had never encountered a public figure with such a reputation for probity.

Another word is "dedication." His "client" was the cause of Torah as represented and interpreted by the great Torah leaders, and to it he dedicated his every fiber. He was a brilliant tactician and strategist. Knowledgeable people said he could have been the CEO of a Fortune 500 company or become a wealthy entrepreneur, but he preferred to work for Hashem Yisbarach. More than that. Despite his extraordinary sophistication in analyzing what course of action would most benefit the Torah community, he gladly and totally deferred to the judgment of the *gedolim*.

This is best illustrated by an anecdote frequently related by Rabbi Chaim Dovid Zwiebel, an outstanding attorney whom Rabbi Sherer inspired to leave a major law firm and join the Agudah. At a meeting of the Moetzes Gedolei HaTorah, Rabbi Sherer presented his long thought-out plan for a course of action. After the Moetzes deliberated privately, they called him in to tell him that they had rejected his position. He left with a smile. Rabbi Zwiebel asked him why he wasn't disappointed. "Chaim Dovid," he said, "don't you understand? This is what we are here for — to follow *daas Torah*! If this is what *daas Torah* dictates, I am overjoyed to carry it out."

Indeed, he considered the greatest achievements of his long career that he established the primacy of *daas Torah* and that he won government recognition of yeshivos as institutions of higher learning, because their financial stability is indispensable to the staus of Torah study as the zenith of Jewish aspiration.

This biography tells the story of the greatest Jewish lay leader and advocate of the second half of the twentieth century. Rabbi Moshe Sherer strode the stage of history and was courted by dignitaries of every stripe. His list of accomplishments is endless.

To us, there was another dimension to the man. He was a friend, adviser, and confidant, even when we were young and raw. Somehow — we never understood how — he found time to be available to us, with encouragement and advice, whenever we called upon him. Often, an unsolicited complimentary note would come in his exquisite handwriting and graceful expression. It was a thrill. We were among the many who felt close to him and were flattered that he considered us and our work worthy of his attention.

For this reason alone we are proud to be the publishers of this volume that does justice to a great man. It is a textbook of self-sacrifice, wisdom, dedication to a cause, and the importance of integrity.

Rabbi Yonoson Rosenblum has spent years interviewing people who knew, worked with, and worked for Rabbi Sherer. He read thousands of pages documenting half a century of Klal work. And he had at his disposal Rabbi Sherer's voluminous treasure of *aides-mémoire* and personal accounts and impressions. He blended all these ingredients to create a biography that is not only the story of a beloved, respected, and effective leader, not only the story of a wise and loving family man, but also the story of the Torah community's emergence as the most dynamic and growing part of American Jewry. This book is a masterpiece and it will surely inspire many people to follow Rabbi Sherer's example and work to make the world different.

Rabbi Shimshon Sherer has put his *neshamah* into this tribute to his father. He was always available to read, review, correct, suggest, augment, refine, and offer information and perspectives. In addition, Rabbi Sherer's daughters and their families — the Langers and Goldschmidts — were invaluable contributors to the work. Reb Shimshie's participation was invaluable in providing a wealth of his father's broad repertoire of homiletic *"vertlach"* and stories. Master orator that he was, Rabbi Sherer always had an appropriate and thought-provoking Torah thought, and this book will be a handbook for speakers as well as thinkers.

Many thousands of readers will be grateful for this work. It is a study in greatness and the story how a great leader did so much to transform the New World into the host of a burgeoning Torah community under the aegis of the *gedolei Yisrael*.

Rabbi Meir Zlotowitz / Rabbi Nosson Scherman

FOREWORD
by Rabbi Shimshon Sherer

תִּפְאֶרֶת בָּנִים אֲבוֹתָם (משלי יז:ו)
The splendor of children is their parents (Mishlei 17:6)

SHLOMO HAMELECH STATES THAT PARENTS ARE THE splendor of their children. My father, *zt"l*, had a favorite *vort* that explains the inherent quality of *tiferes*, splendor, and the way it defines the role of parents.

Yaakov blessed his grandchildren, saying, "הַמַּלְאָךְ הַגֹּאֵל אֹתִי מִכָּל־רָע — יְבָרֵךְ אֶת הַנְּעָרִים וְיִקָּרֵא בָהֶם שְׁמִי וְשֵׁם אֲבֹתַי אַבְרָהָם וְיִצְחָק ... — *May the angel who redeems me from all evil bless the lads, and may my name be declared upon them, and the names of my forefathers, Avraham and Yitzchak ...*" (*Bereishis* 48:16). Strangely, Yaakov mentioned himself before his forefathers. In the name of an *adam gadol*, my father explained that each of the Patriarchs uniquely personified a different trait. Avraham exemplified *chesed*, kindness; Yitzchak exemplified *gevurah*, the twin characteristics of courage and fear; and Yaakov exemplified *tiferes*, splendor.

As the result of his perfection in *emes*, truth, and his complete immersion in Torah study, Yaakov was crowned with *tiferes*, a trait that is not a single, specific characteristic, but rather, one that fuses myriad qualities into a smooth and harmonious blend. The traits of *chesed* and *gevurah* can theoretically be in conflict; and — if uncontrolled — may even be harmful. To illustrate this, commentators point out that Avraham's *chesed* gave birth to the unbridled self-indulgence and lechery of Yishmael. The *gevurah* of Yitzchak gave birth to the selfish and bloody cruelty of Eisav. The *tiferes* of Yaakov is the synthesis of *chesed* and *gevurah*. It combines them in a perfect balance, so that each trait is manifested in the most constructive and beneficial way.

Thus, when Yaakov blessed his grandsons, he cautioned them to embrace his own trait first, to be guided by the "splendor" of having both kindness and strength, but balancing, controlling, and channeling them to achieve their maximum good.

The splendor of children is their parents. A child, with the impulsivity of youth, often acts with excessive kindness, in an unbridled, unrestrained fashion, perhaps even to the detriment of the recipient. A child, impetuously, may strive to be overly heroic and courageous, without contemplating the ramifications or repercussions of his strength. These are manifestations of a youthful lack of understanding or insufficient capacity to blend seemingly contradictory traits so that they complement one another and work in harmony. It is the father who provides the *tiferes,* splendor, to his children. Through his life and experience, he provides, not only by teaching but by his very example, the proper balance of different, even clashing, character traits. It is he who synthesizes and blends them together to form a perfect fusion for a child to emulate, in order to become a truly productive person.

My father passed away on the 21st day in *Iyar*, the 36th day of *Sefirah*. Kabbalah literature tells us that day 36 of the *Omer* corresponds to חֶסֶד שֶׁבִּיסוֹד, *Kindness of the Foundation*. Clearly, my father's יְסוֹד, his essence, was *chesed*. My father's *levayah* (funeral) took place on the 37th day of the Omer, which coincides with גְּבוּרָה שֶׁבִּיסוֹד, *Strength of the Foundation*. This underscores the unfathomable strength he needed to achieve his many heroic accomplishments. The first full day of *shivah*, our first opportunity to reflect on our tremendous loss, was the 38th day of the Omer, which corresponds to תִּפְאֶרֶת שֶׁבִּיסוֹד, *Splendor of the Foundation*. Indeed, my father's foundation was one of splendor. Within himself, he comprised the beautiful and seemingly conflicting qualities of *chesed* and *gevurah*, and he created a synthesis, a perfect balance — the ultimate *tiferes*.

יִשְׂמַח מֹשֶׁה בְּמַתְּנַת חֶלְקוֹ כִּי עֶבֶד נֶאֱמָן קָרָאתָ לּוֹ.
כְּלִיל תִּפְאֶרֶת בְּרֹאשׁוֹ נָתַתָּ לּוֹ (תְּפִלַּת שַׁחֲרִית לְשַׁבָּת קֹדֶשׁ)

Moshe rejoiced in the gift of his portion that You called him a faithful servant. A crown of splendor You placed on his head
(Shabbos Shacharis Shemoneh Esrei)

Moshe rejoiced in the great gift that was bestowed upon him — the privilege of being called an *eved ne'eman, a faithful servant of Hashem.* He was adorned with a כְּלִיל תִּפְאֶרֶת, *a crown of splendor,* the beautiful blend of traits that allowed him to be the consummate leader and servant. In order to properly be Hashem's faithful servant in leading *Klal Yisrael,* Moshe had to determine when it was important to act with humility and when to display strength. Moshe was the quintessential עָנָיו, *humble man,* but he was first and foremost a faithful servant. Thus, representing Hashem forcefully was not a contradiction to his humility; it was an expression of his sublime crown of splendor.

In his preface to *Bishtei Einayim,* my father expresses his profound gratitude to Hashem for blessing him and enabling him to dedicate his entire life to serve as an עֶבֶד לְעַבְדֵי ה', *a servant of the servants of Hashem.* Yes, it was his greatest joy to have devoted his every breath to the service of Hashem, to have toiled as a faithful servant. And the trait of *tiferes,* with which he was so brilliantly endowed, enabled him to be a true servant of the servants of Hashem, and to accomplish, with great *Siyata d'Shmaya* (Divine assistance), all that he did for *Klal Yisrael,* often achieving the seemingly impossible.

My father, by nature, was an unusually gentle, compassionate, and private man. Yet, whenever *k'vod Shamayim, kavod HaTorah,* or the honor of the Jewish people was at stake, he became uncompromisingly, unyieldingly firm, the fiercest of warriors. He loved all Jews but would fight with all his strength against those who attempted to falsify or misrepresent authentic Torah Judaism. When the honor of *Hashem* was not involved, he despised disputes and devoted every fiber of his being, at times with superhuman strength, to its eradication. He would say that the word מַחֲלוֹקֶת, *dissension,* is comprised of the same letters as the two words חֵלֶק מָוֶת, *portion of death.* Dissension is so destructive, he regarded it as a form of death; and, therefore, he devoted his life toward the pursuit of peace and unity in *Klal Yisrael.*

In our home, we constantly witnessed my father's total commitment and dedication to, as he always put it, "*Klal Yisrael* and Reb Yisrael," his unparalleled service to the Jewish people as a whole, and to each individual Jew. My father was a man of great vision, always driven by his mission in life and the fulfillment of the "huge agenda" that waited to be accomplished. Yet he never lost sight of the individual, and many an hour did he spend solving, not only the crises of an entire nation, but the problems of a single person.

We continually saw his brilliance, his exceptional ability, and the accumulated wisdom of his life's experiences. At the same time, we witnessed his אֱמוּנַת חֲכָמִים, *trust in Torah leaders*, his complete subservience, love of, and devotion to *gedolei Yisrael*, regardless of whether they were older or younger than he; and his total subjugation to *daas Torah*, no matter what his personal view might have been. So refined was his *tiferes* that no matter what the issue of the day — and there were many that were literally life and death — he maintained a serenity that emanated from a personality in which all parts were in complete harmony.

אֶשָּׂא עֵינַי אֶל הֶהָרִים (תהלים קכא:א) — אֶל הֶהוֹרִים (בראשית רבה סח:א)
I shall raise my eyes to the mountains (Tehillim 121:1) —
this means to the parents (Bereishis Rabbah 68:1)

The Sages use mountains as a metaphor for parents. My father explained, in the name of a great man, that just as the beauty of a mountain cannot be appreciated from close, and the entire breathtaking, majestic panorama can be appreciated only from afar, so too, the further removed a child is from his parents, the more majestic is his perspective.

As I pen these words more than a decade after his passing, I stand back, gazing in wonder and awe. There is much that we, as children, saw during his life. We saw his tremendous, boundless delight in life. Living with great faith and trust in Hashem, he always maintained an upbeat and positive attitude. He was the ultimate optimist who was never fazed by challenges; on the contrary, he would seek them out and exult in them as opportunities for growth.

In our home, we were privileged to be the beneficiaries of his exceptional devotion, both as a husband and as a father. Shabbos and Yom Tov were special times for us. During the Shabbos meals he enjoyed singing with us and sharing beautiful *vertlach*. He spoke about his *"heiliger mama"* and told us inspiring stories of *gedolei Yisrael*, many of which he witnessed personally. He shared with us various accomplishments of Agudas Yisrael, his "fourth child," and explained why he believed in its holy cause with all his heart. To me, his "third child," he was my father, rebbi, mentor, and truly my best friend. For the last 20 years of his life, as long as he was in town, no matter how busy he was, I had the privilege of speaking to him every single day. No decision that I ever made — big or small — was made without his input and understanding.

Those were joyous times, when we beheld our father from up close. And, yet, perhaps with the perspective that the distance of more than 10 years provides, the appreciation that we felt has grown to humble amazement at the privilege that we, his children, had.

In my father's daily learning of *Daf Yomi*, he very much enjoyed connecting the day's *daf* to current events. In fact, in many of his speeches, he incorporated and applied a pertinent lesson from that day's *daf* to the topic that he was addressing.

The daily *daf* on the day of my father's passing, 21 Iyar 5758, was *Eruvin* 13, where the Talmud records the famous two-and-a-half-year debate between Beis Shammai and Beis Hillel: Was it better for man to have been created or would it have been better had he not been created? Finally it was brought to a vote, and it was concluded that it would have been better for man not to have been created. *Tosafos* immediately qualifies this position, stating that this refers only to an average person, but regarding a *tzaddik*, we would clearly say: "אַשְׁרָיו וְאַשְׁרֵי דּוֹרוֹ — *Fortunate is he and fortunate is his generation*" that he was created. As was said by the Torah greats who eulogized him at his *levayah* and as was echoed countless times throughout the *shivah*, my father was a gift to his children and to his generation. To him, we can certainly apply the words of *Tosafos*: "Fortunate is he and fortunate is his generation."

וַיָּמָת שָׁם מֹשֶׁה עֶבֶד ה' ... מַה לְהַלָּן עוֹמֵד וּמְשַׁמֵּשׁ אַף כָּאן עוֹמֵד וּמְשַׁמֵּשׁ (סוטה יג)

> *Moshe, the servant of Hashem died there ...*
> *just as he served there, he still serves (Sotah 13b).*

When the Rosh Yeshivah of Lakewood, Rabbi Shneur Kotler, *zt"l*, passed away, my father obtained permission for his students to carry his *aron* (coffin) onto the plane to Eretz Yisrael. As we were waiting in the airport at El Al's cargo section for this to happen, a *talmid* approached the El Al official in charge. He had noticed that there was another *aron* waiting to be carried onto the same plane, and he requested, and received, permission for the *talmidim* to carry the second *aron* onto the plane as well. I commented to my father that now his *zechus* (merit), was doubled, because not only had he arranged this honor for Reb Shneur, but thanks to him, another Jew was receiving the very same honor. Typically, my father immediately responded, "This, my son, has nothing whatsoever to do with me." He explained that it was because of Reb Shneur, who was not only a *gaon* in Torah but also a *gaon* in *chesed*. Now, from heaven, he was continuing his life's work of *chesed*. It was Reb Shneur, he said, who had seen to it that his *talmid* honored the second Jew.

Based on this principle, I have no doubt that my father, the ultimate *meilitz* (advocate) for the Jewish people for over half a century, continues his life's work from heaven. He is surely serving as a מֵלִיץ יוֹשֶׁר for my mother, שתחי׳, whose entire being was devoted to him, for our family, and for all of *Klal Yisrael*. It is my fervent prayer that the lessons of my father's life, so beautifully portrayed in this book, will serve as a shining example for all to emulate. May we strive to fulfill his dream of peace and unity for all of our people.

Shimshon Zelig Sherer

עֶרֶב שַׁבָּת נַחֲמוּ, י׳ מְנַחֵם אָב תשס״ט, לס׳ כַּבֵּד אֶת אָבִיךְ וּלְס׳ וְשִׁנַּנְתָּם לְבָנֶיךָ
Erev Shabbos Nachamu, in the *parashah* of "Honor your father …, You should teach them diligently to your children."
10 Menachem Av, 5769

This biography has been over a decade in preparation. There were times in this period when we, as a family, were overwhelmed by the challenges inherent in the project. Yet, we were constantly encouraged by good and respected friends who insisted that *Klal Yisrael* would benefit greatly from this book. We know that only such a biography, one that would ultimately enhance the honor of Heaven, would have pleased our father. It is our sincere hope that this book brings glory to Hashem and benefits His people.

On behalf of my mother, my sisters and brothers-in-law, Yisroel and Rochy Langer, Moshe Yaakov (Robert) and Elky Goldschmidt, my wife Shifi and myself, I would like to express our heartfelt gratitude to Rabbi Yonoson Rosenblum. Only a writer of his caliber could do justice to the task of accurately presenting a biography of this scope. Perhaps the greatest tribute that we could give is to say that he has indeed written a work worthy of its subject. In so doing, he has recorded for posterity our father's place in Jewish history.

We are deeply grateful to Rabbi Meir Zlotowitz and Rabbi Nosson Scherman for their efforts in seeing this project to fruition. It is clear that for them this was a labor of love, a mirrored reflection of the love my father felt for them. Special thanks to Rabbi Avrohom Biderman for his extreme devotion to this project, and his constant courtesy and efficiency. We are also grateful to the entire ArtScroll staff for their help and cooperation.

I conclude this Foreword, as I began, with Yaakov's blessing to his grandsons, paraphrased now in the form of a prayer: "May *his* name be called upon them." May our homes, the homes of his children and grandchildren, be graced with the nobility, the *tiferes* that so characterized our father. זְכוּתוֹ יָגֵן עָלֵינוּ וְעַל כָּל יִשְׂרָאֵל.

SZS

AUTHOR'S PREFACE

THIS BIOGRAPHY OF RABBI MOSHE SHERER, ZT"L, HAS proven to be by far the most difficult that I have ever written. The principal reason for that difficulty might appear at first glance to be a great advantage to a biographer: I was the beneficiary of Rabbi Sherer's unparalleled ability to draw others close to him over the last 10 years of his life.

Why should my closeness to Rabbi Sherer have made this biography more difficult? Does not knowing one's subject constitute a great advantage to a biographer?

Not necessarily.

When I started working on the biography of Rabbi Yaakov Kamenetsky, zt"l, a number of people questioned my ability to write about a *gadol* whom I had not known personally. Rabbi Nosson Scherman took me to visit Rabbi Zelik Epstein, zt"l, to discuss the issue.

Rabbi Epstein explained to me that what others saw as a disadvantage was actually an advantage. Had I known Reb Yaakov, he said, I would have had my own view of him, and that would have dominated the biography. Because I did not know Reb Yaakov, however, I would be able to listen to every person whom I interviewed with an open mind. That would enable me to absorb a wide variety of views of Reb Yaakov, without unconsciously filtering out anything that did not agree with my own perspective, and thus allow me to capture all the many facets of Reb Yaakov's personality and the different ways he influenced others.

Another *gadol*, Rabbi Elya Svei, *zt"l*, offered a second reason why knowing one's subject is not always an advantage. When Rabbi Shimshon Sherer told Rabbi Svei, his rosh yeshivah, that I would be writing the biography of his father, Rabbi Svei offered his *berachah*. But he added a caveat: "Yonoson did not know Reb Yaakov or Rabbi Dessler, *zt"l*. They were exalted figures in his eyes. But he knew your father. And no matter how great his admiration and affection for your father, the mere fact that he knew him means that he sees him as a real person. And the danger is that he will reduce him from his true stature."

I admired Rabbi Sherer greatly in his lifetime, and nearly a decade of research has only added to that admiration. But I nevertheless feel the wisdom of both Rabbi Epstein's and Rabbi Svei's insights. I have tried to use their remarks as warnings against the pitfalls they described. But I recognize the existence of those traps nevertheless.

Rabbi Naftoli Neuberger, *zt"l*, Rabbi Sherer's closest partner in numerous major *Klal* projects over their more than 50-year friendship, pointed out to me a second challenge of a biography of Rabbi Sherer. At the outset of our first interview, Rabbi Neuberger told me, "Many of Rabbi Sherer's most important achievements cannot be written about." He mentioned, as an example, all the potential communal black-eyes that Rabbi Sherer managed to keep out of the media.

Certainly there is no purpose to revealing now that which Rabbi Sherer strove to keep out of the public eye. But restraint comes at a cost: Once again Rabbi Sherer's true stature can only be partially conveyed.

Every biographer seeks to present his subject in the most dramatic fashion possible, and would love nothing better than to turn his biography into an endless stream of events in which the protagonist single-handedly resolves one crisis after another with a passionate speech or a brilliant stratagem. There are, however, a number of pitfalls to that approach.

For one thing, what is gained in drama is often lost in verisimilitude. Most historic accomplishments are not achieved in one fell swoop, but entail a series of advances and retreats. A proper assessment of the magnitude of the achievement must include an account of the incremental steps that gave rise to that achievement.

To be sure, there was substantial drama in Rabbi Sherer's life. He was a man of great charisma and personal charm. The sheer force of his personality played a large role in his success. But he also paid meticulous attention to every detail. Most of the historic victories of Agudath Israel of America under his leadership resulted from hard work and determination as much as brilliance. An attempt to overly dramatize those victories by emphasizing the latter at the expense of the former would be both dishonest and a disservice to Rabbi Sherer.

An effort to portray Rabbi Sherer as acting single-handedly would result in another serious distortion of his achievement as well. Rabbi Elya Svei described Rabbi Sherer in his *hesped* (eulogy) as the general of Torah Jewry. One cannot write of a general without describing the battles fought by the army under his command. Victory depends not just on the strategic brilliance of the general, but also on the courage of the troops and the initiative of the other officers in the field. Those too are a reflection of the general who drilled the troops and selected and trained the officers, but all the glory does not belong to the general alone.

Rabbi Sherer's greatest pride was the influential, professional organization — Agudath Israel of America — that he forged. Everything that Agudath Israel achieved in his nearly 40 years of leadership can be rightly attributed to him. No one was hired, no department created or project undertaken, except at his initiative. He provided the animating vision. Without him, it is hard to imagine that American Orthodoxy would have had the benefit of such an organization, which has no parallel anywhere in the world.

But an organization, if it is to be successful, must draw on the talents of many people. Rabbi Sherer's ambitions for Agudath Israel went far beyond what any one person, no matter how talented or indefatigable, could achieve. He prided himself on the quality of people he convinced to work for Agudath Israel, and one of the secrets of his success was his ability to create an environment in which their talents could flourish.

In sum, it is impossible to separate Rabbi Sherer from the organization that he built. And that is what Rabbi Sherer would have wanted. His influence, and that of Agudath Israel under his direction, extended in dozens of directions.

That means that a full appreciation of how and why Rabbi Moshe Sherer became the most effective Jewish lay leader of the latter part of the 20th century will require the reader to attend to many details and follow a number of story lines. But it is important that we do so.

At the outset of this project, Rabbi Svei told Shimshon Sherer that one of the major purposes of this book should be to provide a handbook for all future *askanim* (community activists). If American Orthodoxy ever hopes to produce another leader of his stature, we will have to study well the best model available. That requires studying Rabbi Sherer in the institutional context in which he functioned. And it requires understanding both his passion and his thoughtfulness, his power over people, and the intellectual vision that moved him.

One of the great pleasures of finishing a book of this scope is the opportunity to publicly thank at least some of those who made it possible. Many people contributed to this book in significant ways. But there are a few of whom it can be truly said that without them it never would have appeared in its current form.

Over the past year, Rabbi Shimshon Sherer has become my full partner in this project, and the biography has been enriched immeasurably by virtue of his participation. Reb Shimshon is a living repository of his father's *divrei Torah*, which add an entirely new dimension to the biography. The *divrei Torah*, however, are but one aspect of the countless ways that Reb Shimshon has added to the book. I have never before had a *chavrusa* (study partner) with whom to work on a book, and having tasted that pleasure, it is hard to imagine doing without it in the future.

Rabbi Yonoson Rosenblum (l) and Rabbi Shimshon Sherer (r) at the grave of Rabbi Moshe Sherer

Rabbi Sherer's son-in-law, Robert (Moshe Yaakov) Goldschmidt, took charge of shepherding this project from the beginning. Without his complete calm even in the face of setbacks, attention to detail, and gentle prodding, it is doubtful that this project would have come to its successful conclusion.

Rabbi Nosson Scherman and Rabbi Meir Zlotowitz of ArtScroll/Mesorah Publications had a profound relationship with Rabbi Sherer extending over decades, and as a consequence both took a keen personal interest in this project. Reb Nosson edited every chapter in this book at least once, and in many cases two or three times. Every page of the book bears the stamp of his felicitous style, vast historical knowledge, and his eagle eye, able to discern at a glance the difference between a colon and a semicolon in the densest footnote. Reb Nosson is the writer in the Jewish world whom all others look up to. Yet he has that rare ability for one who writes so well not to impose his own style as an editor. I present this biography to the public with far-greater confidence by virtue of the fact that it has passed under Reb Nosson's quill.

Reb Meir volunteered to do the Index for this book, which will add greatly to its usefulness for future generations. The painstaking work involved was a true labor of love for Rabbi Sherer and for the entire Sherer family.

Rabbi Shmuel Bloom, the recently retired executive vice-president of Agudath Israel of America, worked side by side with Rabbi Sherer for a quarter of a century, and his institutional memory of those years is remarkable in its clarity. He made himself unfailingly available for every question, large or small, posed to him, and without him to guide the way, crucial parts of Rabbi Sherer's legacy might have been lost.

Jeff Bloom of Passaic, New Jersey did many of the initial interviews for the book, and spent two years combing through the voluminous archival material in the files of Agudath Israel of America. In sifting through the documents, he showed a keen eye both for what was historically relevant and that which cast light on Rabbi Sherer. His contribution has been inestimable.

Rabbi Moshe Kolodny, the veteran archivist of Agudath Israel of America, is a major resource for *Klal Yisrael*, and proved invaluable in writing this book. He uncovered hidden treasures probably known only to himself and was able to locate virtually every document sought from him.

Once again, Rabbi Avrohom Biderman has somehow pulled all the pieces together and shepherded this work to press with all the myriad details that entails.

Well over 100 people were interviewed for this book, some many times, and I am indebted to each and every one of them. Rabbi Yisroel Besser, my brother Rabbi Mattisyahu Rosenblum, and Stephanie (Pearson) Argamon read earlier versions of the manuscript and offered important insights, and, most important, encouragement. A healthy dose of the latter came also from my friend Shlomo Eisen of Bnei Brak.

Rabbi and Mrs. Nisson Wolpin provide my home away from home, and so much else as well. Chaskel Bennett, one of Rabbi Shimshon Sherer's most loyal congregants, made himself unfailingly available to do whatever he could to move this project toward completion.

I am personally indebted to Steven Rosedale of Cincinnati, Ohio, who provided me with an office — in which to complete the writing — capacious enough to accommodate dozens of piles of papers. I cannot imagine how I would have finished the book without the ability to employ such a "filing" system.

This will be the first major project of my life that I will not be able to bring to my father, Paul (Feivel Yisroel) Rosenblum, *a"h*, for approval at the end. The first draft of the chapter describing Rabbi Sherer's *yetzias neshamah* (departure of the soul; demise) was finished less than a day before my father, *a"h*, passed away unexpectedly. For both Reb Shimshon and me, this book has been part of the mourning process for greatly beloved fathers. That too has brought us closer.

Baruch Hashem, we still have our respective mothers, Mrs. Miriam Rosenblum and Mrs. Debby (Devorah) Sherer. May this work be a source of *nachas* to each of them, and to Mrs. Sherer a fitting tribute to a life to which she made such a large contribution.

I had hoped to complete this work prior to my 30th anniversary as a present to my wife Judith. Though I fell short by a few days, I still hope that the return of her husband after years of immersion in this project will serve as a welcome, albeit belated, present. All that is mine is hers, and this work is no exception. May we be *zocheh* to many more years rejoicing in each other and in our children — Micha David and Elisheva, Naama and Moshe, Elisha, Yechezkel Mordechai and Tova Rina, Chananya, Zechariah, Yaakov, and Elimelech Gavriel, שיחיו.

Finally, I wish to express my gratitude to the *Ribbono shel Olam* (Master of the Universe), Who has afforded me the opportunity to spend my days contemplating some of the greatest figures in the Torah world.

Yonoson Rosenblum

Introduction

NEVER OUT OF CHARACTER

THOSE WHO ATTEMPT TO DESCRIBE RABBI MOSHE SHERER almost invariably begin with a series of antinomies: lists of qualities not generally found in tandem. Thus he was a charismatic leader able to represent his cause with force and passion **and** a highly competent administrator. He was a powerful orator, who could weave a tableau of a glorious past and an equally glorious future, **and** a stickler for detail and master of the nuts and bolts of public policy. He was eloquent in Yiddish **and** English. He was a confidant of the greatest Torah leaders of the day **and** of presidents, governors, and senators.

Rabbi Yaakov Feitman's eulogy nicely captures Rabbi Sherer's ability to transcend the normal dichotomies:

> The visionary is not usually the detail man, the hard-driving perfectionist is rarely the compassionate father-figure, the experienced

elder-statesman never the self-abnegating agent of implementing the will of others. But Rabbi Sherer was all of these and more.

Nathan Lewin, a Washington, D.C. "superlawyer" and close adviser of Rabbi Sherer, was at his side in meetings with the world's greatest Torah scholars and with America's top elected officials. In his eulogy for Rabbi Sherer in the *Forward,* he pointed to Rabbi Sherer's role as a bridge figure between modern America and the eternal Jewish people. It was appropriate, wrote Lewin, that Rabbi Sherer's final public triumph was the 10th *Siyum HaShas* joining 20,000 Jews in Madison Square Garden to 50,000 more around the world by video hookup:

> He was a human bridge between American modernity, represented by Madison Square Garden and the video hookup, and total, principled commitment to the Jewish heritage, symbolized by the Talmudic text.

Who could have imagined when Rabbi Sherer began his more than 50 years of public service that the yeshivah perspective and total commitment to religious observance would have any influence whatever on American society? Lewin asked. And yet he lived to see that impossible dream come true. Indeed, more than any other figure he made that dream a reality. He was, in Lewin's words, a true *meilitz* (intermediary) between two worlds — interpreting and explaining one to the other — and ultimately persuading each to respect and value the other.

Yet for all that Rabbi Sherer embodied many traits not generally found together in one person and bridged many worlds, he was entirely of a piece. Everything about him fit together in one seamless whole. It is hard to think of another to whom the description of "acting out of character" so rarely applied. He was never out of character; he was the same Moshe Sherer when conversing with Torah giants and presidents and in the privacy of his home.

The source of Rabbi Sherer's essential unity lay in his intense consciousness that he was representing Hashem, the Torah, and the Jewish people in the world. That consciousness gave focus to everything he did. In his final tribute, Lewin pointed to Rabbi Sherer's absolute confidence that he was truly doing Hashem's work as one of the keys to his success. That confidence explained his optimism. No goal ever appeared permanently beyond reach because he knew that Hashem's power is unlimited.

He lived with a mission. In the summer of 1995, Rabbi Sherer had just finished his fifth round of chemotherapy for leukemia. His hair was gone, his immune system severely repressed, and he had not appeared in public in months. Yet he insisted on visiting the Agudah camps in the Catskills to deliver his annual message. By the end of the day, his voice could barely be heard, even with a microphone, and he could hardly stand.

What was the message — so important — that Rabbi Sherer felt he must put himself through such torture to deliver it? A very simple one: We are not put in the world to pursue our own pleasures, but to make the world a better place for our fellow human beings. On that trip, he and his message were one. He insisted on personally shaking hands with each one of the special-needs campers in one bunk, against his doctor's orders. When his son Shimshon protested, he replied, "You can't keep a father from hugging his children."

From an early age, Rabbi Sherer was imbued with a strong sense of mission. It never occurred to him that the purpose of life was to fill one's belly with life's various pleasures. Friends and classmates from his youth remember how he talked constantly of "doing for the Jewish people." And "doing for the Jewish people" in his lexicon meant helping to spread Torah ideals.

Rabbi Moshe Sherer was unquestionably the most influential Orthodox lay leader of the second half of the 20th century. It was he more than anyone who insisted that Orthodox Jewry be admitted to the communal table and be present whenever the fate of *Klal Yisrael* was on the agenda. He was recognized in the halls of power not just as a spokesman for Agudath Israel of America but for all Orthodox Jewry.

He acted as both Jews and gentiles imagine an Orthodox Jewish rabbi should. And by conducting himself with such dignity, he made us all look better. Since he was THE Orthodox Jew that many government figures knew best, they extrapolated from him to the whole community.

Dedication to the cause, fueled by his own intense faith, was Rabbi Sherer's greatest trump card. Much of what he achieved was as if with mirrors. He spoke with such passion and enthusiasm that secular politicians were sure that he must stand at the head of a movement of hundreds of thousands. And that, in turn, added to his clout.

He was the quintessential *osek b'tzarchei tzibbur b'emunah* (one faithfully involved with filling the needs of the community). The Skulener Rebbe, *zt"l*, once noted that there are three aspects of serving the community with *emunah* (faithfully).[1] The first is scrupulous honesty and integrity. *The New York Times* top investigative reporter once told Rabbi Sherer that he had never found anyone in public life with a higher reputation for honesty. Everyone who ever dealt with him knew that his word could be relied upon without qualification. Second, said the Rebbe, he must truly believe — i.e., have faith — in the cause which he serves. Rabbi Sherer always referred to Agudath Israel as a *davar she'be'kedushah*, a holy enterprise, and that belief was reflected in his total dedication to his work.

Finally, the faithful worker on behalf of the public must spread *emunah* wherever he goes. *Kiddush Hashem* (santification of G-d's Name) was Rabbi Sherer's life mission. He conducted himself at all times and in every place as Hashem's representative.

Rabbi Sherer serves as a model not only for Jewish *askanim*, but for each of us. We can all learn from his life, even if we have no aspirations to the mantle of communal leadership. The very qualities that made him so effective in a public context can serve each of us in our private lives as well.

The first of the lessons from his life is the power of treating every human being — Jew and gentile, friend and adversary — with dignity and respect. His willingness to build up those who worked under him and give them opportunities to shine on the public stage enabled him to join the talents and energies of hundreds. And his restraint from turning disagreements and even violent theological differences into personal vendettas gave him an ability to influence those far removed from a Torah viewpoint.

Reb Itche Meir Cymerman, a leading European Agudist, once commented, "Rabbi Sherer was far nicer to me than he had to be, and sought my opinion far more than he needed." The pages of this biography are full of examples of how his concern for others and sensitivity to their dignity was often rewarded with tangible benefit to the Jewish people.

The second lesson is the impact of conducting oneself with dignity. He dealt over the years with thousands of politicians and government

---

1. I'm indebted to Mordechai Friedman for calling my attention to this *vort* of the Skulener Rebbe, which Rabbi Sherer fully embodied.

officials without ever feeling a need to be "one of the boys," and they, in turn, felt elevated, more idealistic, in his presence and appreciative that he never acted as if he had to lower himself to speak to them.

Third, he taught the virtue of hard work and dedication to the task at hand. That dedication was fueled by a clear vision of a glorious future for Torah Judaism. But Rabbi Sherer's focus on the future was expressed not only in his vision but in day-to-day practical ways as well. He invested large amounts of time and energy cultivating connections with those who could provide no immediate benefit. He spent a lifetime developing relationships, thousands of them, often with those at the very first level of public service, because one could never know when a certain person would prove crucial.

Similarly, he invested heavily in the acquisition of information. He read voraciously and kept abreast of developments in many areas because one could never know when a particular piece of information would prove useful. If one waited until one needed a particular politician to develop a relationship or until he needed to know something in order to acquire that information, it was by then too late.

Rabbi Sherer once explained the secret of his success to a granddaughter: "When I'm working on something, I treat it as if the whole world depended upon it." That dedication allowed him to take an organization "lacking any natural constituency," in the Novominsker Rebbe's words, and build it into *Klal Yisrael's* most influential grassroots organization.

After his passing, his family found one of the many slips of paper on which he used to jot down quotations from his reading. This particular quotation came from Benjamin Franklin: "If you want to be remembered after you die, either write something worth reading or do things worth writing."

He did. This biography constitutes the proof.

A NOTE TO THE READER

THE PAGES TO FOLLOW CONTAIN MANY *DIVREI TORAH* that Rabbi Sherer said frequently. Where possible, we have identified the sources of these *divrei Torah*. With respect to the rest, some were said by Rabbi Sherer in the name of a specific *gadol*, whose identity has now been forgotten; others he simply offered in the name of an *"adam gadol"* (a man of stature). In most of the latter cases, we have not identified the source as an *"adam gadol"* because doing so would be stylistically awkward and quickly come to grate on the reader. The failure to identify a *vort* as having been said by a particular person or an *"adam gadol,"* however, does not mean that it was original with Rabbi Sherer. Such a claim would be anathema to him.

The *vertlach* are not offered to establish Rabbi Sherer's originality as a *darshan*, though he frequently employed *ma'amarei Chazal* in striking or interesting ways, but because the *divrei Torah* themselves were important to him, as evidenced by the fact that he repeated them often. They therefore help reveal the cast of his mind, his worldview, and his deep immersion in the world of *drush* (homiletics).

A second disclaimer is in order as well. As lengthy as this biography is, it makes no claim to being comprehensive. At the end of the day, it is no more than a series of "snapshots" of Rabbi Sherer's life. No one should make the mistake of counting entries in the Index to determine the depth of the relationship of any particular person to Rabbi Sherer. Many who enjoyed warm relationships with him are barely mentioned, or not mentioned at all. Some of those who played an important role in Zeirei Agudath Israel or Agudath Israel of America in the earlier decades, for instance, are not mentioned here because they were already discussed at length in *They Called Him Mike*, the biography of Reb Elimelech Gavriel ("Mike") Tress, *zt"l*. Others who interacted with Rabbi Sherer many times daily, like Rabbi Boruch B. Borchardt, *zt"l*, were in almost every "snapshot," so that mentioning them each time would have been superfluous.

One final disclaimer: Rabbi Sherer molded and led a large and sophisticated organization. A full appreciation of his achievements and those of Agudath Israel of America under his direction requires that certain complex policy issues be explained with some detail, both to clarify the issues and for the sake of the historical record. At the same time, we appreciate that there may be readers for whom the level of detail holds little interest. Such readers should not hesitate to skip ahead to the next topic. We are confident that they will find enough material just a little further down the road to engage them fully.

Part I
EARLY YEARS

Chapter One

FORESHADOWING

MOSHE (MORRIS) SHERER WAS BORN 12 SIVAN 5681/1921, nine years to the day from the founding conference of Agudath Israel at Kattowicz, Poland. In later years he made frequent mention of this sign that Providence had linked him from birth to the movement with which he will forever be associated.

Just as he attached significance to the date of his birth, so too did he draw inspiration from his name. He often quoted the Chasam Sofer's observation that since the name Moshe derives from Basya's words, "מִן הַמַּיִם מְשִׁיתִהוּ — From the water I drew him forth" (*Shemos* 2:10), his name should actually have been מָשׁוּי — he who was drawn forth. Pharaoh's daughter, Basya, sought to teach the Hebrew child, according to the Chasam Sofer, the lesson that if one is saved from drowning, he must himself become a מֹשֶׁה — one who saves others. Rabbi Sherer believed that his mother Basya had similarly wanted to teach him that he should live his life as a Moshe seeking to help others.[1]

---

1. In later years, Rabbi Sherer was acutely aware of himself as one who had been saved. Not a single relative from his extended family survived the Holocaust.

He was a *ben zekunim* to both his parents: his father Chaim Yehudah Sherer was already in his 60's at his birth, and his mother Basya Bluma (Moruchnik) in her mid-40's. According to family legend, Mrs. Sherer wrote to the Stoliner Rebbe when she was pregnant with Moshe, and he blessed her that she would have a child who "will light up the whole world."[2]

His mother would bring him as a young boy to the Stoliner *shtiebel* in Williamsburg, where she and her friends sat reciting *Tehillim*. Like any 4-year-old, he found ways to keep himself entertained. When he became too rambunctious, she would reprove him, "Moshele, the Rebbe promised me that you would light up the world, and you run around in shul. *Es past nisht* — It's not proper."[3]

Both parents had been widowed previously. Mr. Sherer had five

Mrs. Basya Bluma Sherer

Chaim Yehudah Sherer

---

2. Rabbi Sherer's son Shimshon once asked him whether the story of the Stoliner Rebbe's *berachah* was true. Rabbi Sherer laughed and told him, "I wasn't there. But I was once briefly in the lighting business."

3. Heard from Rabbi Yisrael Pilchik, and, *yblcht"a*, his brother Rabbi Meir Pilchik during the *shivah* for Rabbi Sherer. Their mother was a member of the same Chevrah Tehillim in the Stoliner *shtiebel* as Mrs. Sherer.

In later years, Rabbi Sherer used the same technique on his son Shimshon. When he would misbehave as a child, his father would tell him, "Shimshie! *Es past nisht* that a child for whom Rav Aharon Kotler was *sandek*, a child held in the arms of the holy Rav Aharon Kotler, should behave like that. *Es past nisht!*"

grown daughters, the youngest of whom was already 20 when Moshe was born. These five half-sisters played only a minimal role in his life thereafter. Mrs. Sherer too had a daughter, Jenny, from her previous marriage. Two full brothers, Harry, six years older, and Ruby, three years older, preceded Moshe into the world.

Mr. Sherer came from Odessa and Mrs. Sherer from the little town of Steppin, near Berditchev, in the Ukraine. Her family were followers of the Rebbes of Karlin-Stolin, and she maintained that loyalty her whole life. Yiddish was the language of the Sherer home. Speaking Yiddish in the home, Rabbi Sherer once said, "was not an accommodation; it was a belief …. You were supposed to speak Yiddish."[4] Rabbi Sherer often expressed gratitude that Yiddish was his mother tongue, and that he thereby gained the ability to speak and write eloquently in Yiddish. It was an ability that would serve him well.

Mr. Sherer had worked in the needle trades, like the majority of immigrants who arrived in America around the turn of the century, and at one time had even owned his own clothing store. But by the time Moshe was born, he was an invalid and unable to work. The Sherer boys had no idea where the money for food and rent, and to pay the rebbi with whom they learned every day after school, came from. Certainly money was never in plentiful supply. The family lived in a small two-bedroom apartment in a fourth-floor walk-up on Keap Street between Hooper and Rodney. Harry and Ruby shared one bed, and Moshe slept in a cot. Four other families shared the same landing.[5]

Yet, despite the lack of material plenty, there was no sense of deprivation. Five or six *pushkes* decorated the house, and on *Erev Shabbos* each boy would be given a penny to drop into each one. The Sherer home was filled with song. Both parents, but particularly Mrs. Sherer, loved to sing. The boys were awakened to the same *niggun* (tune) that the *vecker* (town crier) in Steppin used to arouse the townspeople as he rapped on the door and sang, "Awaken, awaken to do *avodas haBorei* (to serve the Creator), for that were you created."[6] The boys would sing, "*Modeh Ani*," upon awakening in the morning.

---

4. May 9, 1990 interview with Dr. David Kranzler [hereinafter Kranzler interview]. The subject of the interview was Michael G. Tress, Rabbi Sherer's older cousin and mentor. Mrs. Tress and Mrs. Sherer were sisters and very close. Rabbi Sherer's descriptions of his Aunt Henya, Mike Tress's mother, apply with equal force to his own mother.
5. Harry Sherer.
6. Quoted by Rabbi Sherer in his address at the 70th Convention of Agudath Israel of America in 1992.

There was no money for bicycles or skates, so the boys fashioned makeshift skateboards from discarded carriages. They made their own desks in the same fashion — from wood left in garbage cans. Neighbors went back and forth to one another — one day borrowing, the next day lending.

On Friday night (*Leil Shabbos*), Mr. Sherer joined the family at the table. After dinner, Mrs. Sherer would serve freshly baked cookies so that the boys' friends were always eager to climb the stairs to join the Sherer family in singing *zemiros* (Sabbath songs).

The cookies also provided a chance for the Sherers to get to know their sons' friends, something about which they were always very careful. When Mr. Sherer would see one of his sons going out on *Motza'ei Shabbos*, he would invariably ask him where he was going and with whom. Then he would ask to be introduced to the friends. If one of the boys showed any reluctance or complained that their friends did not want to climb up four flights of stairs just to meet their parents, Mr. Sherer's inevitable response was: "Are you ashamed of your friends?" In the end, the friends came upstairs to meet the boys' parents.[7]

Because of his health, Mr. Sherer was often unable to accompany his boys to shul on Shabbos morning, but when he did he always stressed showing *kavod* (honor) to the rabbi. He would tell the boys, "Stand up, the rabbi just came in." That quality of being a *mokir rabbanan* (one who honors Torah scholars) stayed with Rabbi Sherer his entire life.

One of those occasions when Mr. Sherer accompanied his youngest son to shul left an indelible impression on him. As Moshe and his father were entering the shul, those who had davened in the *vasikin* minyan were coming out. Moshe observed a number of the men come out of shul and head for the subway. And he remembered an older man crying in the back of the shul over the fact that he had to work on Shabbos.

Unable to comprehend how a Jew could work on Shabbos, Moshe turned to his father for guidance. His father could only answer him, "When you get older, you'll understand." Indeed when he got older he not only understood, but worked hard to ensure that the shame and pain he had seen on the faces of those Jews on their way to the subway not be forced on other Shabbos-observant Jews. Shortly before the 1970 New York gubernatorial election, Rabbi Sherer secured a written promise from Governor Nelson Rockefeller to do everything he could to pass

---

7. Harry Sherer.

Governor Nelson A. Rockefeller with Rabbi Sherer beside him, signing legislation protecting Sabbath observers. Standing l-r: Shimon Kwestel, State Senator Paul Bookson, Menachem Shayovich, State Senator Al Lewis.

a law banning discrimination by private employers against Sabbath-observant employees.[8] The pen used by the governor to sign the legislation was proudly displayed in Rabbi Sherer's office.

Basya Sherer

UNQUESTIONABLY BASYA SHERER WAS THE PRIMARY INFLUENCE on her son's formative years. His whole life he spoke about her frequently, and with great love and admiration.[9] When he wanted to express his affection for his daughter Rochel, the biggest compliment he could give was to tell her that she looked like her grandmother Basya. (She doesn't.)

Rabbi Sherer ascribed two qualities to his mother. The first was a deep piety of a type rarely seen today. Describing his mother and her sister Henya Tress, he recalled their "extraordinary piety — these people lived for G-d, with G-d." His mother would spend at least an

---

8. That promise was conveyed in a letter to Rabbi Sherer dated October 15, 1970, and it followed a series of legal setbacks for Shabbos-observant Jews in the courts. Governor Rockefeller states in the letter that he recognizes the importance to the Jewish community of such legislation. Such a bill was not actually passed, however, by the New York legislature until 1975. It became a model for other states and the federal government.
9. Rabbi Shmuel Dishon.

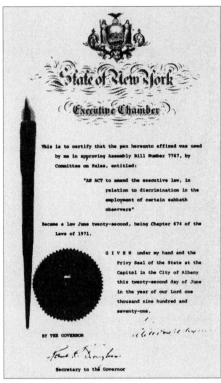

The pen used by Governor Rockefeller to sign the bill protecting Sabbath observers

hour every morning reciting *Tehillim* (*Psalms*).[10] In her last years, when she was dying of stomach cancer, the only thing that gave her any respite from her agony was the sing-song of Torah learning coming from nearby Yeshiva Torah Vodaath.[11]

One of Mrs. Sherer's *chesed* activities was the local *chevrah kadishah* (burial society). One time, she noticed the horrified look on the face of a young woman participating in her first *taharah* (cleansing of the body prior to burial). Mrs. Sherer told her, "Don't be scared. She is in a much better place." For Mrs. Sherer, those were not just words, but the way she lived her life.

Rabbi Sherer once told Mrs. Ruth Lichtenstein of *Hamodia* that his mother's prayers and tears were the basis for everything that he ever achieved. Without them, he said, he would have grown up to be just another American boy. The lighting of the Shabbos candles was a major production in the Sherer home. Mrs. Sherer retained her family's affiliation with the rebbes of the Karlin-Stolin dynasty, and frequently visited the Stoliner Rebbe in Williamsburg. Often he advised her to add another Shabbos candle. Eventually the Shabbos *licht* took up almost half the dining-room table.

When she lit the Shabbos candles, Mrs. Sherer would *daven* (pray) with great intensity. As a young boy, Moshe once hid under the

---

10. Kranzler interview.
11. During that period, her doctor was the legendary Williamsburg physician Dr. Isaac (Yitzchak) Diamond. Dr. Diamond recognized Mrs. Sherer as a rare *tzadekes* (holy woman) and rarely charged her or charged her only a minimal amount. The close connection between the Diamond and Sherer families has continued to this day. Dr. Diamond's son, Dr. David "Dudie" Diamond, was one of the last cadre of young *Klal* leaders trained by Rabbi Sherer, and after Rabbi Sherer's passing has emerged as one of the important lay leaders of the Agudah movement.

Shabbos table curious to know what his mother was *davening* for with such fervor. He heard her repeat again and again, "*Ribbono shel Olam*, light up my children's eyes with the light of Your holy Torah," until the tears began to fall. The realization that even when food was scarce in the house his mother's tears were only for her children's mitzvah observance and Torah learning left a deep impression on him. In later years, he would attribute his decision to dedicate his life to *Klal Yisrael* to the priorities he learned from his mother. Rabbi Sherer himself had no interest in money "almost to a fault," in the opinion of one friend.[12]

There was one story from his youth that Rabbi Sherer particularly enjoyed telling, for it encapsulated all the lessons in *emunah* and *bitachon* (trust in G-d) that he imbibed in his parents' home. As a young boy, he once fell ill and lay listlessly in bed. His mother called a doctor, who diagnosed his illness as a strep throat. In those days, before antibiotics, strep throats were far more worrisome than today. The infection could worsen into rheumatic fever and cause permanent heart damage and even death. The doctor explained all this to Mrs. Sherer.

The doctor prescribed medication, but warned the increasingly anxious mother that it was very expensive. Even after Mrs. Sherer had gathered all the money to be found in the house, she doubted that she had enough to pay for the medicine, but she nevertheless rushed to the pharmacy to plead her son's case. The owner was not in the store, so Mrs. Sherer begged his assistant to fill the prescription. The young man was moved by the concern of a frantic mother, and agreed to prepare the medicine in exchange for all the money Mrs. Sherer had.

After filling the prescription, the pharmacist's assistant handed Mrs. Sherer the precious medicine. In her eagerness to get home and hasten Moshe on his way to recovery, Mrs. Sherer tripped over a curb and watched in horror as the bottle flew from her hand and landed with the distinctive tinkle of breaking glass. Mrs. Sherer burst into tears as she crawled on the pavement to retrieve the paper bag in the hope of still saving some of the precious elixir. But by that time, it had seeped out of the bag and onto the street.

Her money and medicine gone, Mrs. Sherer rushed back to the pharmacy, still carrying the bag with the broken bottle inside, to once again plead for her Moshe's life. By that time, the storeowner had returned, and he listened to Mrs. Sherer's sobs and offers to clean the store after

---

12. Rabbi Lemel Ehrenreich.

hours if he would just refill the prescription. Unable to resist her pleas, the pharmacist went to the back of the store to refill the prescription. He returned a moment later, ashen faced. "Angels are watching over your son," he told her.

From the smell of the medicine absorbed by the bag, he realized that the original prescription had been incorrectly filled, and instead of the needed medication, Mrs. Sherer had received medicine that could have been life threatening to young Moshe. Shaken by the near disaster, he provided Mrs. Sherer with the proper medication and even returned the money she had originally paid.

Moshe heard the story of his miraculous salvation many times from his mother. She would tell him, "When I tripped and heard the bottle breaking, I thought my life was over. Little did I know that what I saw as an incomparable disaster was really the greatest *berachah* (blessing) from the *Ribbono shel Olam.*" [13] Throughout his life, Rabbi Sherer made frequent references to his mother's *fleshele* (bottle) of medicine.

Those closest to Rabbi Sherer often remark that it is impossible to fully understand the man without knowing the depth of his *emunah* in Hashem. That *emunah* and *bitachon* were the precondition for everything else he was able to achieve. Without it, he could not have spent so much of his life in the halls of power, interacting with politicians and bureaucrats, and still

Moshe Sherer as a teenager

---

13. Rabbi Sherer once told this story to the Bluzhover Rebbe. The latter applied to the incident a verse from *Tehillim* (118:13): "דָּחֹה דְחִיתַנִי לִנְפֹּל וַה׳ עֲזָרָנִי" — You pushed me hard that I might fall, but Hashem assisted me." The Bluzhover Rebbe interpreted the implicit subject of the verse not as the enemies of David HaMelech, but as Hashem. Thus he read the verse to mean: You [Hashem] pushed me and caused me to fall, and the very falling turned out to be Your means of bringing about my salvation.

remained the trusted confidant of *gedolei Yisrael*. The piety protected him and prevented him from being tarnished by his contact with the outside world. As Rabbi Eliezer Horowitz, the rabbi of the Fourteenth Avenue Agudah shul, where Rabbi Sherer *davened*, put it, "He knew all the *shticklach* and *dreidlach* [devious, unethical practices], but remained untouched by it. To know all the *dreidlach*, and yet remain apart is the truest test of *ehrlichkeit* [honesty]."

Each working day involved dozens of phone calls and letters: local, national, and international. But early every morning and again in the *evening*, Rabbi Sherer could always be found at his place when the *davening* started. He was careful to be on time to every *minyan* (quorum of 10 men) and every *shiur* (lecture), and to daven in a *makom kavua* (fixed place).[14] He never spoke during *davening*, even though there were always those eager to engage him in conversation. His prayer itself was quiet, heartfelt, with each word pronounced carefully and distinctly. Until the very end of his life, he always stood for *Krias HaTorah*.[15]

All this was a legacy from his mother. The other exceptional quality that Rabbi Sherer always mentioned in connection with his mother was the love of doing *chesed b'tzinah* (helping others in secret). She and her sister Henya Tress specialized in helping mothers who had just given birth. They would collect money for the new mother, and then early in the morning, they would slip an envelope with cash under her door. "I remember it so vividly," Rabbi Sherer once told historian David Kranzler, "because they would come back to my home and giggle while drinking coffee and wake me up .... I remember their glee that they had just fooled someone, that they had been able to make their way to a home and do some mitzvah."

Of his older cousin Mike Tress, Rabbi Sherer said, "His greatest thrill was when he helped people. He was happy .... It was an earthly pleasure of fulfillment, of satisfaction, of gratification when he was able to do something [for someone]." That earthly pleasure in doing *chesed*, said Rabbi Sherer, Mike inherited from his mother. And the same could be said of Rabbi Sherer: He inherited Basya Sherer's love of doing *chesed*.

---

14. Yet if a guest in shul was sitting in his place, he would not ask him to move. As he explained, we learn the importance of *davening* in a fixed place from Avraham Avinu (see *Berachos* 6b), whose primary character trait was *chesed*. One cannot benefit from emulating Avraham while acting in a manner that contravenes his entire essence by embarrassing the Jew who inadvertently sat in one's place.
15. Rabbi Eliezer Horowitz.

MOSHE GRAVITATED TOWARD THE ZEIREI AGUDATH ISRAEL *minyan* located next door to the Stoliner *shtiebel* at 157 Rodney Street.

Zeirei Agudath Israel From the age of 10 or 11, he was active in the Pirchei groups led by his cousin Mike Tress. Mike led the Williamsburg branch of Zeirei Agudath Israel (ZAI) from the early '30s. In a few short years, he transformed what had initially been a *minyan* and a social club into a budding national movement. His magnetic personality attracted people of all ages to him wherever he went. "Just knowing Mike was enough to make anyone in the world want to be an Agudist," recalls Harry Sherer.

Mike Tress was a constant presence in Moshe's life from an early age. Basya Sherer and Henya Tress were not only sisters, but extremely close. In his first years at Torah Vodaath, when he commuted from the Greenpoint neighborhood, Moshe used to eat his lunches at his Aunt Henya Tress home. After Mrs. Tress passed away and before Mike married, he lived in the Sherer apartment. And after Mrs. Sherer passed away Rabbi Sherer's half-sister Jenny lived with the Tress family.

Through the Zeirei Agudath Israel *minyan* at 157 Rodney, Moshe gained a lifelong mentor in Rabbi Gedaliah Schorr, who was the unofficial rav of the *minyan*, despite being younger than many of the Zeirei members. Rabbi Meir Shapiro, Rosh Yeshivas Chachmei Lublin and initiator of the *Daf HaYomi*, pronounced the young *ilui* (genius) to be the finest mind that he met in America and one of the finest he had met anywhere, when Rabbi Schorr was yet in his teens. By his early 20's, he combined a unique blend of Lithuanian *lomdus* (deep analysis) together with a thorough mastery of the depths of Chassidic thought. He knew many tractates of the Talmud by heart and was fluent in the works of the Maharal, Reb Tzadok HaKohen of Lublin, and the Sfas Emes. Rabbi Schorr was the inspiration for every young American yeshivah student, for he proved that even in America one could achieve greatness in Torah

Rabbi Gedaliah Schorr as a young man

Young Gedaliah Schorr (r) speaks with Rabbi Elchonon Wasserman (l) in Camp Mesivta

learning. Rabbi Aharon Kotler said of him, "He is the first American *gadol*."

Though few, if any, of those who came to his daily *daf yomi shiur* in the Zeirei *minyan* had any formal Torah learning past high-school age, Reb Gedaliah, with his natural modesty, had no sense of lowering himself. He viewed himself as just another *chaver* (member) of the Agudah *minyan*. The other members, even those much older than he, however, held him in awe, and he implanted in them the desire to learn Torah, *emunas chachamim* (faith in Torah scholars), and concern with the broader Jewish world.[16]

Reb Gedaliah also took part in the public activities of the Williamsburg Zeirei. He spoke at the Shabbos demonstrations against merchants who remained open on Shabbos, and even prepared the milk crates that served as the speakers' platform before Shabbos. He was one of

---

16. *They Called Him Mike*, pp. 66-67. See also Rabbi Sherer's eulogy in *Dos Yiddishe Vort, Tishrei 5740*, pp. 32-33. Rabbi Sherer once asked Rabbi Schorr to speak about his role in the early Zeirei movement as part of a history project on Zeirei Agudath Yisrael and the wartime rescue work, but he refused, citing a famous *vort* of the *"heiliger* Rizhiner." In the *Zichronos* section of the Rosh Hashanah *Amidah*, we describe Hashem as "He Who remembers all the forgotten matters." Rabbi Schorr told Rabbi Sherer that it was better that he should forget what he had done so that Hashem would remember.

Rabbi Gedaliah Schorr

the two American delegates[17] sent to the Second Knessiah Gedolah of Agudath Israel in Vienna in 1929, and he provided the members of the Williamsburg Zeirei with an Agudah perspective.

Rabbi Schorr exercised a major influence on the fledgling Agudah movement in America by virtue of his close relationship with Mike Tress. Rabbi Schorr and Mike Tress were the same age, and the two became close friends, despite the fact that the former was a world-class Torah scholar and the latter a product of public school and City College of New York. "My friend of the heart," is how Rabbi Schorr described Mike Tress. The two were like brothers.

Rabbi Schorr was the source of the *hashkafos* that Mike Tress was instilling in a younger generation of Pirchei groups. "If Mike had a *rebbi muvhak* whom he looked up to, it was Rav Gedaliah Schorr," Rabbi Sherer told David Kranzler. "Rabbi Schorr was the central figure in his life. He shaped him more than anyone else I know."[18]

Moshe Sherer, 10 years younger than Mike, inevitably had a very different relationship with Rabbi Schorr. Rabbi Schorr was a hero in his eyes, as he was for all American-born young men who had aspirations in Torah learning. In addition, he was Moshe's personal rav throughout his teenage years, and would remain one of the *rabbanim* with whom

---

17. The second delegate was Reb Yaakov Mordechai Gordon.
18. Kranzler interview.

Rabbi Anshel Fink and Rabbi Naftoli Neuberger serving as witnesses at the wedding of Rabbi Sherer's son, Shimshie. Standing, l-r, Rabbi Aharon Felder, Rabbi Sherer, Rabbi Anshel Fink, Rabbi Neuberger, Shimshon Sherer. Rabbi Moshe Feinstein is seated.

Rabbi Sherer consulted most frequently until Rabbi Schorr's passing in 1979.

Rabbi Yaakov Kraus of Los Angeles remembers an incident from the mid-1960s that conveys clearly the closeness that Rabbi Schorr felt for Rabbi Sherer. One day Rabbi Sherer came into the Torah Vodaath *beis medrash* looking for Rabbi Schorr. The latter rushed over to him and gave him a hug and a kiss. When some *talmidim* asked Rabbi Schorr how he could have kissed Rabbi Sherer in a *beis medrash*,[19] the latter replied, "If you had just seen me kiss a *Sefer Torah* would you ask the same question? Well, that's what I just did."

Another influence on the young man's development was Anshel Fink, who provided some of the ideological background that the young American Agudists were lacking. Fink, the son of Rabbi Yoel Fink, a rebbi in Torah Vodaath, was European born and had already been active in the Agudah movement in Europe. He too was a contemporary of Mike Tress and Rabbi Schorr. The latter described him as his "friend of the head." In later years, he became one of Rabbi Sherer's closest friends.

To be affiliated with Agudath Israel in the 1930s was to be part of a despised organization, both within the larger Jewish community and even within the Orthodox world. It was not uncommon, Rabbi Sherer

---

19. *Shulchan Aruch, Orach Chaim* 98.

L to r: Anshel Fink, Reb Shraga Feivel Mendlowitz, Rabbi Gedaliah Schorr

recalled, for Agudah events to be attacked by various Zionist groups, and the electricity cut or a rock thrown through the window. Most of the Orthodox rabbis in America were affiliated with the religious Zionist Mizrachi movement. The young men of Zeirei had difficulty even finding shuls in which they could run events. For the gala dedication of Zeirei headquarters at 616 Bedford Avenue, only one shul was prepared to let them use their facilities to launch the event and only a few rabbis were ready to march with them.[20]

The young Agudists were considered extremists and firebrands. One of Rabbi Sherer's fond teenage memories, for instance, was of the Shabbos morning that some of the older Zeirei members, led by Mike Tress and David Maryles, with Moshe tagging along, invaded the South

---

20. Kranzler interview.

The dispatch from "Moshe Sherer; Mesivta Torah Vodaath, Brooklyn" in *Dos Yiddishe Tagblatt*

Fifth Street shul. Moishe Oysher, a leading performer in the Yiddish theater, was serving as cantor. "He sings in shul in the morning, and he sings in the theater in the afternoon," the Zeirei members chanted, disrupting the *davening*, until the police came and threw them all out of the shul.[21]

Yet just as being hated by the nations of the world only caused the Jewish people to cling more stubbornly to their faith, so did the effect of being part of an outcast group only intensify Moshe's identification with Zeirei Agudath Israel. "When you are part of an embattled, persecuted minority, you have to believe more in the cause," Rabbi Sherer said of those years. That is why in those days there was much more discussion of Agudah ideology than there is today "when being religious is served on a platter and as easy as pie."

He was intoxicated with the idea of Agudath Israel from an early age. Already as a 16-year-old student in Torah Vodaath, he had an article published in *Dos Yiddishe Tagblatt* of Warsaw, the daily paper

---

21. Ibid. When he told this story, Rabbi Sherer would note with satisfaction that the phenomenon of a *mechalel Shabbos* (Shabbos desecrator) serving as a cantor in an Orthodox shul would never happen today.

of Agudath Israel. In it he enthusiastically described two meetings held for the purpose of creating an American branch of Agudath Israel World Organization, in addition to the already active Zeirei Agudath Israel.[22]

Chinuch

LIKE VIRTUALLY EVERY OTHER ORTHODOX BOY IN THE '20S, RABBI Sherer started out in public school and learned to read Hebrew and to *daven*, and studied a bit of *Chumash* with a *melamed* in an afternoon Talmud Torah. There were few yeshivos, and even when yeshivos were available, many parents could not afford the tuition. As a consequence, few children from *shomer Shabbos* (Sabbath-observant) homes in those days remained within the religious fold.[23]

Of the boys in his Talmud Torah class, Rabbi Sherer was the only one who stayed religious. In the '50s, a letter criticizing Agudath Israel of America arrived in the Agudath Israel office. Rabbi Sherer recognized the name of one of the signatories as that of his old Talmud Torah rebbi. He arranged to meet the man at a certain restaurant. When he walked in, he was surprised to see his old rebbi eating without a yarmulke. Rabbi Sherer told the man, "Now I understand why none of my classmates remained *frum* (observant). You didn't believe in what you were selling, and therefore were ineffective."

Rabbi Sherer repeated that story and the lesson he derived from it many times in later years. He learned from Noach that one cannot sell a cause unless his belief in that cause is absolute. Noach was given 120 years to build the Ark in the hope that he would thereby bring the wicked of his generation to repent. When the evildoers asked him what he was doing, Noach would respond that Hashem was going to bring a Flood and destroy the world on account of corruption of that generation. In effect, Noach spent 120 years giving *mussar shmuessen* to the people of his generation.

Yet, Rabbi Sherer pointed out, there is no indication that Noach had a positive effect on a single person in all those 120 years of daily *mus-*

---

22. The article appeared January 16, 1938. The first meeting described in the article was held in the Adas Yeshurun shul in Brooklyn, and the principal speakers were the Rosh Yeshivah of Torah Vodaath, Rabbi Shlomo Heiman, Rabbi Pinchos Teitz, and Rabbi Yehoshua Baumol, rav of the shul and an eminent *posek*. At a second meeting, which drew an overflow crowd to the Chasam Sofer shul on the Lower East Side, Rabbi Gedaliah Schorr and Rabbi Baumol were the main speakers.

23. Rabbi Sherer's firsthand knowledge of the failure of the Talmud Torah system and its inability to transmit a strong and vibrant *Yiddishkeit* to Jewish children fueled his lifelong devotion to the cause of yeshivah education.

Reb Shraga Feivel Mendlowitz (far left) and Rabbi Elchonon Wasserman (c) in Camp Mesivta

sar shmuessen, even though he was likely a polished orator. Why not? Because Noach was not fully convinced of the ultimate fulfillment of the prophecy that the *Ribbono shel Olam* intended to destroy the world. For that reason, he did not enter the Ark when first commanded to do so, but only after the rain began to fall. He was, in the words of *Chazal,* a *ma'amim ve'eino ma'amin* (literally, one who believes and does not believe), and with that attitude, Rabbi Sherer concluded, one cannot convince even a single person to join his side.

That *dvar Torah* captured the basis for Rabbi Sherer's great success in life. He was a superb salesman, and the product he sold was the vision of *Klal Yisrael* united around Torah and led by *gedolei Torah.* But only because he himself was so enraptured by that vision could he convey it so effectively to others.

He once told his son, "Shimshie, I believe in what I'm promoting. I believe in the *heiliger* [holy] Agudas Yisrael. I believe in what the Chofetz Chaim, and Tchortkover Rebbe, and the Gerrer Rebbe, and Reb Chaim Ozer — all of the *gedolei Yisrael* — established — this *heiliger mosad* [holy institution] Agudas Yisrael. If you believe in something with all your heart, you can indeed bring people over to your cause."[24]

Unlike his older brothers, who continued in public school and were working after school by the time they reached high school, Moshe did eventually study in yeshivah. Rabbi Gedaliah Schorr had taken note of his friend Mike Tress's younger cousin, and urged him to enroll at Yeshiva Torah Vodaath. Mrs. Sherer needed little convincing. Her youngest son was the apple of her eye, and she dreamed of seeing him as a rabbi one day. So at 12, he enrolled in Torah Vodaath, to which he commuted from the Greenpoint neighborhood where the family was then living.

Though Mrs. Sherer was delighted that Moshe was learning in yeshivah, even the 50-cent weekly tuition was often too much for the family. On at least one occasion, the oldest son Harry was dispatched to take Moshe out of the yeshivah. The *menahel*, the legendary Reb Shraga Feivel Mendlowitz, asked whether the reason was a lack of money for tuition. He then placed his hands across the entrance to the yeshivah and told Harry, "I won't let you take him. He'll be a leader one day."

As a young man

In those days in Torah Vodaath, remembers Louis Glick, a classmate of Rabbi Sherer's, there were two kinds of students. In the first group were those who already had an eye cocked on the outside world, and planned to attend college after finishing high school and then enter into business or the professions. These boys were usually identifiable by their attention to appearance and their fashionable dress. Then there were those who were fully involved in their learning.

Moshe Sherer, says Glick, was the

---

24. Rabbi Shimshon Zelig Sherer, "A Father to Me, A Father to *Klal Yisrael*," *Jewish Observer*, Summer 1998, p. 72.

L-r: Rabbi Elchonon Wasserman, Rabbi Aharon Kotler, and Rabbi Moshe Blau, leader of the Agudah in Eretz Yisrael until his passing in 1946

exception. He dressed stylishly like the more modern students, but was firmly planted in the yeshivah. He stood out not just by virtue of the care in his dress. He conducted himself with a certain air of royalty and precision in every action.

He had a sense of mission. And even in his teens, it was apparent that he was preparing to act on a broader stage. He worked hard on developing his oratorical abilities and looked for occasions to deliver sermons.[25]

The goal of these preparations was not money or the other accoutrements of success, but to represent Torah with honor and dignity to the outside world.

REB SHRAGA FEIVEL APPOINTED THE YOUNG MOSHE SHERER TO accompany Rabbi Elchonon Wasserman from his hotel to Mesivta Torah Vodaath for morning *davening* during Reb Elchonon's last visit to America in 1939. Even the older *bachurim* in Rabbi Shlomo Heiman's *shiur* were granted that privilege for only one or two days.[26] Yet Rabbi Sherer did so for two months just after Reb Elchonon's arrival in America.[27]

Reb Elchonon Wasserman, Hy"d

---

25. Mr. Louis Glick.
26. Rabbi Bernard Goldenberg.
27. Rabbi Elya Svei once told Rabbi Shimshon Sherer that Reb Shraga Feivel Mendlowitz had

Rabbi Sherer would later describe his contact with Reb Elchonon and the experience of being his attendant as a "turning point in my life in a very big way .... Reb Elchonon was the type of person who left a searing impact on the *neshamah* of any young person who met him."[28] Pictures of Reb Elchonon and of Rabbi Aharon Kotler had pride of place in Rabbi Sherer's *succah*, directly behind his seat, surrounded by a vast array of pictures of Torah giants from all circles in *Klal Yisrael*.

The first morning that the young yeshivah student showed up to accompany Reb Elchonon from the Broadway Central Hotel to the yeshivah, the great rabbi asked him to teach him how to say "*Gut Morgen* — Good Morning" in English. Reb Elchonon practiced saying "Good morning," until satisfied that he had gotten it right. Why? Because he wanted to be able to greet the gentile elevator operator in a pleasant fashion in accordance with the *Gemara* that describes Rabbi Yochanan ben Zakkai as having been the first to offer greetings to every person in the marketplace — even a gentile.[29] It was a lesson not lost on the young yeshivah student. His entire life he went out of his way not only to greet the doormen and cleaning ladies in the various buildings in which the Agudath Israel offices were located, but to engage them in conversation and inquire about their lives.

Rabbi Sherer emulated Reb Elchonon's example the rest of his life. While walking to shul in Boro Park with his young son in the early '60s, when Boro Park was still a largely gentile neighborhood, he would greet everyone he passed: complimenting this one on the car he was busy washing and another on the dog he was walking (even though Rabbi Sherer was terrified of dogs). When Shimshie asked him whether he was running for office, he would invariably reply with the story of his first encounter with Reb Elchonon.

The morning guard at 84 William Street, where Agudath Israel of America had its offices at the time of Rabbi Sherer's passing, started crying when his secretary Mrs. Debby Jacobs informed her of Rabbi Sherer's death. She related how every morning he would bound into the building, press the button to the elevator, and then cross the lobby to her desk to tell her, "Good morning, Lyla — don't forget to keep on smiling."[30]

Reb Elchonon provided a concrete example of the Torah's power to

---

foreseen that Rabbi Sherer would develop into an important Jewish leader and therefore wanted to provide him with maximum exposure to Reb Elchonon.
28. Kranzler interview.
29. *Berachos* 17a.
30. She subsequently told Rabbi Shimshon Sherer that she still "smiles every day" thinking of him.

Rabbi Shlomo Heiman (l) and Rabbi Shimshon Zelig Fortman (r), who would later become Rabbi Sherer's father-in-law

transform those who submit to its discipline to a different order of being. During his time in America, he almost always chose to walk rather than take a cab, lest he deprive his beloved students back in Baranovich of any of the fruits of his collecting. He would not cross the street against a red light because of the halachic principle *dina d'malchusa dina* (the law of the land is binding).[31]

One *Motza'ei Shabbos*, Moshe took notes at a meeting of rabbis with Reb Elchonon. One of the rabbis had a particularly sharp sense of humor, and succeeded in eliciting first smiles and then laughter from those present. Rabbi Shlomo Heiman, the Rosh Yeshiva of Torah Vodaath, tried hard to contain himself, but at some point he too succumbed and laughed. Meanwhile, Reb Elchonon just sat there with a strange half-smile on his face.

After the meeting, Moshe asked his rosh yeshivah how Reb Elchonon had been able to contain himself when even Reb Shlomo had not. Reb Shlomo explained to him, "It's really very simple. Reb Elchonon's every action is guided by Torah. The *Gemara* (*Berachos* 31a) states, '*Assur le'adam sheyemalei sechok piv b'olam hazeh* — until the coming

---

31. Yonoson Rosenblum, *They Called Him Mike* (Mesorah Publications 1995), p. 128.

of Mashiach when the Temple will be rebuilt, it is forbidden for a Jew to smile a full smile.' If the *Gemara* says it is forbidden, Reb Elchonon's limbs simply will not allow him to do otherwise. Everyone else was unable to control himself, and the *chashuv* [important] among them regret their inability to hold back. But Reb Elchonon cannot do what the *Gemara* forbids."[32]

Another lesson from Reb Elchonon would help Rabbi Sherer deal with the criticism that is the inevitable lot of any high-profile public figure. A woman once came to visit Reb Elchonon to complain bitterly that her husband and her friends were always criticizing her. Reb Elchonon quoted the verse, "בַּקָּמִים עָלַי מְרֵעִים תִּשְׁמַעְנָה אָזְנָי" — [W]hen my enemies arise against me, my ears will hear" (*Tehillim* 92:12). Then he offered a homiletic interpretation "When my enemies speak ill of me, tilt toward them an attentive ear, for perhaps there is a trace of truth in what they say." Reb Elchonon noted that the Hebrew word מְרֵעִים in the verse can also refer to close friends as well as enemies. If we should listen to criticism, even when it comes from enemies, he told her, how much more so when it comes from our closest friends.[33]

Reb Elchonon also taught the young yeshivah student that being a leader requires the ability to ignore criticism, and that leadership is not a popularity contest. In later years, Rabbi Sherer often repeated Reb Elchonon's interpretation of the *Gemara's* (*Sotah* 49b) statement that *"b'ikvesa d'Meshicha pnei hador k'pnei hakelev* — in the period just before Mashiach comes the face of the generation will resemble the face of a dog." The nature of a dog, explained Reb Elchonon, is to run in front of his master. But the dog constantly turns around to see if his master is following. Though he appears to be leading, he is still subject

---

32. Shimshon Sherer once repeated this story, which he had heard from his father, to Rabbi Tuvia Goldstein, who had been Reb Elchonon's student in Baranovich. Rabbi Goldstein added that Shimshon could confirm the truth of the description of Reb Elchonon from his own rebbi in the Talmudical Yeshiva of Philadelphia, Rabbi Mendel Kaplan. Rabbi Goldstein related that on the first day that he arrived in Baranovich, he was told to run to the dining room to see something he might never again witness: Reb Elchonon with a full smile on his face. The occasion was a *sheva berachos* for Rabbi Mendel Kaplan, and Reb Elchonon apparently felt that the mitzvah of causing the groom and bride to rejoice permitted a full smile.

33. Rabbi Sherer would often preface a bit of fatherly criticism to one of his children with this *vort* from Reb Elchonon.

Reb Elchonon also offered a second interpretation of the verse based on the fact that מְרֵעִים can mean both enemies and friends. According to the double meaning of the word, said Reb Elchonon, when we hear our enemies speaking ill of the Jewish people, we [our friends — i.e., fellow Jews] should pay attention and ask ourselves whether we are not guilty of similarly disparaging our fellow religious Jews. That second interpretation also left a profound impact on Rabbi Sherer, who was always extremely circumspect in criticism of other religious Jews in public.

to his master's will. So too, in the days prior to the arrival of Mashiach, the supposed leaders will be continually looking over their shoulders to ascertain whether their "followers" are content. If not, they will change direction.

Rabbi Sherer had the opportunity to observe firsthand how different Reb Elchonon was from the "leaders" he scorned. A rich man once came to visit Reb Elchonon at his hotel and offered him a very large sum to speak at a certain institution. The donation would have greatly hastened Reb Elchonon's return to his beloved students in Baranovich. Reb Elchonon remained looking down as the man spoke.[34] Then he told him that there was nothing that could persuade him to speak at the institution in question. The man threatened that unless Reb Elchonon complied with his request, his entire fund-raising endeavor in America would be severely damaged, but the rosh yeshivah would not yield.

By way of explanation, Reb Elchonon quoted his rebbi, the Chofetz Chaim. In every town, said the Chofetz Chaim, there must always be a town *meshugener* (literally, crazy person). That is the person who can be counted upon to do the right thing, even when everyone ridicules him as a *meshugener*. Being a leader, Rabbi Sherer learned, meant being prepared to be called a *meshugener*.

"I've been in America only a short while," continued Reb Elchonon, "and I have yet to see one 'town *meshugener*.' If I had to come to America to be the town *meshugener*, so be it."[35]

Years later, Rabbi Sherer would also have the term "*meshugener*" applied to him as an accolade by a great man. Five days before the passing of Rabbi Shneur Kotler, Rabbi Sherer went to visit him in the Boston hospital in which he was being treated. Both men knew they would never see each other again, and Rabbi Kotler sought to convey his great respect and love for Rabbi Sherer. Reb Shneur shared a *vort* of the Chofetz Chaim based on the verse in *Tehillim* (111:5): "טֶרֶף נָתַן לִירֵאָיו — He provided food for those who fear Him."

---

34. See the famous *Iggeres HaRamban* in which the Ramban instructs his son: "Your head should be bowed and your eyes directed downward to the ground *(Yevamos* 105b). And you should not look directly at any person when speaking to him." Rabbeinu Yonah in *Shaarei Teshuvah* (*Shaar* I: 29) writes in a similar vein: "His eyes must be constantly lowered, as it says, 'And He saves him whose eyes are lowered' (*Iyov* 22:29)."

35. Rabbi Sherer frequently quoted the Chasam Sofer's homiletical twist on the verse in *Hallel*: נְדָרַי לַה׳ אֲשַׁלֵּם נֶגְדָה נָּא לְכָל עַמּוֹ — My vows to Hashem I will pay, in the presence of His entire people." The Chasam Sofer read נֶגְדָה to mean "against" rather than "in the presence of," so that the meaning of the verse became: "I will pay my vows to Hashem [i.e., fulfill my duties toward Hashem], [even] against the entire nation" — even if everyone opposes me and calls me a *meshugener*.

With Rabbi Shneur Kotler

The Midrash (*Bereishis Rabbah, parashah* 40) reads the word טֶרֶף as *tiruf*, טֵרוּף (driven mad). The verse might then be loosely read as, "He drives mad those who fear Him." In every generation, Rabbi Kotler explained, Hashem inspires a few among those who fear Him to be driven mad with the desire to provide for the needs of *Klal Yisrael*. "You are that *meshugener* on behalf of *Klal Yisrael*," he told Rabbi Sherer.

In addition to the time spent as Reb Elchonon's *hoiz bachur* (attendant), Moshe also had a great deal of contact with Reb Elchonon through the Zeirei *minyan*. Reb Elchonon spoke frequently to both the Williamsburg Zeirei and to the Pirchei *minyan*, of which Moshe was first *gabbai* and later president. Though 1500 Jews packed the Clymer Street shul for Reb Elchonon's first address in America, he did not consider it beneath his dignity to address a Pirchei *Melaveh Malkah* of six teenagers two weeks later.

In his talks at 157 Rodney Street, Reb Elchonon provided much of the ideology for the fledgling Agudah movement in the United States. Reb Elchonon was, in Rabbi Sherer's words, "not only an Agudist in theory, he was *kulo* [entirely] Agudath Israel — the real thing, the real McCoy."

Reb Elchonon was closely identified with the concept of *daas Torah*: the principle that the Torah is the ultimate blueprint of the universe and for all that takes place, and that those who have immersed themselves in the Torah most fully have the deepest understanding of the Divine will, as revealed in the events of history. He wrote frequently in the Yiddish press on current events.

On Friday night at Rodney Street, Reb Elchonon made the concept of *daas Torah* come to life. He would stand at the front of the room, with a *Chumash* in hand, and tell the boys that everything is found in the Torah. "*Fregt a kasha* — Ask a question," he would tell them, and they would pepper him with questions about everything that was on their minds, such as Hitler's meteoric rise to power. To any question he was asked, he would jump up and say, "It's an explicit verse in the Torah," or "It's an explicit [statement of] *Chazal*." "He made me see that Torah is alive, and we are part of it, not that we are one thing and the Torah is something else," remembers Reuven Soloff, in whose home Reb Elchonon stayed for a brief time.

Ikvesa D'Meshicha (*The Footsteps of the Mashiach*), in which Reb Elchonon drew on all his vast knowledge of the Torah's prophecies and *Chazal's* descriptions of the final stages in Jewish history to interpret current events, was, in part, an outgrowth of the talks given at 157 Rodney Street.[36] Reb Elchonon's ability to read the events of the world through the eyes of the Torah provided a lesson in the meaning of *daas Torah* that would serve Rabbi Sherer well in his daily dealings with *gedolei Torah* in the years to come.[37]

---

36. *They Called Him Mike*, pp. 128-29.
37. The original hand-written manuscript of *Ikvesa D'Meshicha* was donated by Rabbi Simcha Wasserman to the archives of Agudath Israel of America, a fact in which Rabbi Sherer took great pride.

Chapter Two

NER ISRAEL

U UPON GRADUATING TORAH VODAATH HIGH SCHOOL, Rabbi Sherer decided to leave Brooklyn for Yeshiva Ner Israel in Baltimore. The immediate catalyst for that decision is unknown.

The wartime rescue activities of Zeirei Agudath Israel — at that point centered principally on the procurement of visas and affidavits of financial support — were just gearing up. Perhaps the young yeshivah student realized that were he to remain in New York he would be swept even further into the maelstrom of Zeirei activity and have little opportunity for serious Torah learning at an advanced level. Perhaps, too, he already saw that his long-term future lay in the public arena, and was concerned of the ill effects of too premature involvement in public affairs without first attending to his own spiritual growth.

According to Rabbi Ephraim (Freddy) Wolf, another active member of the Williamsburg Zeirei and a fellow student in Ner Yisrael, it was probably Reb Shraga Feivel Mendlowitz who directed Rabbi Sherer to Ner Israel. Such a step on Reb Shraga Feivel's part would have been consistent with his lifelong practice of sending students from Torah Vodaath to other institutions if he felt they could gain more from learning elsewhere.

After departing for Baltimore, Rabbi Sherer seldom returned to New York over the next two years. He threw himself into his Torah learning. In later years, he told his son Shimshie that he had been a *masmid* in Baltimore, and that the greatest personal sacrifice that he had made for a life of public service was the joy of being *mechadesh* in Torah that he had experienced in Ner Israel.

IN RABBI SHERER'S DAYS, NER ISRAEL WAS HOUSED IN A CONVERTed hotel on 3220 Garrison Boulevard, which had been purchased by the

Rabbi Yaakov Yitzchak Halevi Ruderman

Tifereth Israel shul. The Rosh Yeshivah, Rabbi Yaakov Yitzchak Halevi Ruderman, served as the rav of the downstairs *minyan* in exchange for the yeshivah being allowed to occupy the rest of the building. The yeshivah itself *davened* on the second floor, with boys being called downstairs from time to time to fill in the Shabbos *minyan*.

The Tifereth Israel shul

The caption from Ner Israel's yearbook appears on the facing page

> **Names of the Students**
>
> IN PICTURE OPPOSITE
>
> *First row from left to right:*
> Harry Liebb, Baltimore, Md., Oscar Kline, Lancaster, Pa., Joseph Pheterson, Rochester, N. Y., Samuel P .Mandelcorn, Montreal, Quebec, Canada, Samuel J. Labkovsky, Dallas, Texas, Benjamin Dinovitz, Baltimore, Md., Joseph Hirsch, Cleveland, Ohio, Walter Leibovitch, Ottawa, Ontario, Canada, Zelick Barnholtz, Toronto, Ontario, Canada, Albert Liff, Washington, D. C., Harold Shulman, Washington, D. C.
>
> *Second row:*
> Abraham Rudensky, New York, N. Y., Jacob D. Lieff, Ottawa, Ontario, Canada, Benno Eisenberg, Vienna, Austria, Sam Kamenetsky, Toronto, Ontario, Canada, Herbert Aron, Luxemburg, Luxemburg, Sam Silver, Ottawa, Ontario, Canada, Gerd Zwienicki, Bremen, Germany, Heinz Ney, Niederstetten, Germany, Israel Weinreb, Batavia, N. Y.
>
> *Third row:*
> Aaron Pernikoff, Baltimore, Md., Abraham Leibtag, Hamilton, Ontario, Canada, Mendel Silver, Ottawa, Ontario, Canada, Hyman Leibovitch, Ottawa, Ontario, Canada, Albert Pattaschnick, Baltimore, Md., Morris Shuvalsky, Baltimore, Md., Rudolph Weiss, Lancaster, Pa.
>
> *Fourth row:*
> David Roodman, Ottawa, Ontario, Canada, Abraham Krohn, Scranton, Pa., Yaakov Muskin, Chicago, Ill., Ephraim R. Wolf, Brooklyn, N. Y., Julius Hettleman, Baltimore, Md., Aaron Silver, Ottawa, Ontario, Canada, Scholom Kovalsky, Brooklyn, N. Y.
>
> *Fifth row:*
> Seymour Kreisler, Scranton, Pa., Milton Tittlebaum, Baltimore, Md., Ralph Berger, Cleveland, Ohio, David Leiter, Pittsburgh, Pa., Sidney Shulman, Washington, D. C., Manfred Hirschberg, Frankfurt, M., Germany, Sam Sager, Toronto, Ontario, Canada, Reuben Tailer, Ottawa, Ontario, Canada.
>
> *Sixth row:*
> Samson Krauss, Brooklyn, N. Y., Philip Krohn, Scranton, Pa., Emil Fischmann, Berlin, Germany, Morris J. Burok, Toronto, Ontario, Canada, Wilfred Wolfson, Sydney, N. S., Canada, Murray Halpern, Montreal, Quebec, Canada.
>
> *Seventh row:*
> Ludwig Bodenheimer, Darmstadt, Germany, Lawrence Cohen, New York, N. Y., Norman Kreistman, Baltimore, Md., Hillel Klavan, Washington, D. C., Joseph H. Shecter, Montreal, Quebec, Canada, Morris Bernstein, New York, N. Y.
>
> *Eighth row:*
> Jacob Mase, Baltimore, Md., Samuel Charney, New Brunswick, N. J., Jacob Konigsberg, Cleveland, Ohio, Harry Leibovitch, Ottawa, Ontario, Canada, Jacob Kurland, Rochester, N. Y., Moshe Bernholtz, Jerusalem, Palestine, Moshe Sherer, Brooklyn, N. Y.
>
> *Absentees:*
> Herbert Davis, Baltimore, Md., Rudolph Deutsch, Brooklyn, N. Y., Isidor Fisch, Debrezen, Hungaria, Wolfe Kellman, Toronto, Ontario, Canada, Ben Zion Krohn, Scranton, Pa., Isaac Sitren, Belloird, Ohio, Harry Mandelcorn, Montreal, Quebec, Canada, Schammai Zahn, Nuernberg, Germany

Certainly the pursuit of creature comfort had nothing to do with Rabbi Sherer's decision to study there. A municipal building inspector commented after one inspection that the building was so dangerous that he would not let his cat stay there, "but you're poor boys, and I don't want to kick you out."[1] The maintenance man for the building was an alcoholic, and when he went on one of his periodic drinking binges, the boys could be left without any hot water for days. Even in the best of circumstances, taking a shower was not without its hazards. Touching one of the metal sides of the shower invariably resulted in an electric shock. Most of the students preferred to shower at the local YMHA, where a shower cost 7 cents, but at least one did not have to worry about being electrocuted.

If Ner Israel provided few creature comforts, it offered something much more valuable and rare: close exposure to a major European-trained *gadol* in the person of the Rosh Yeshivah. Rabbi Ruderman was one of the leading products of Slabodka Yeshivah and the famed Kovno Kollel. By the age of 14 he had completed the entire Talmud, and immediately undertook to review it in its entirety between Succos and Pesach of that year. When his father passed away during that review, the Alter

---

1. Rabbi Shmuel Yosef Labkovsky.

of Slabodka, Rabbi Nosson Tzvi Finkel, withheld the information from the young *ilui* until he had completed his review. He explained that Kaddish is a *zechus* (merit) for the departed parent, but that the young genius's learning would be an even greater merit. The memory of the value that the Alter attached to his learning remained with Rabbi Ruderman his entire life.[2]

Rabbi Ruderman was known even in the European yeshivah world for his phenomenal memory. He once explained the rabbinic statement, "Be careful [of the honor] of the children of the poor, for from them will emanate Torah" (*Nedarim* 81a), to refer to the fact that poor students cannot afford their own *sefarim* so they have to memorize the yeshivah's library. When he first heard that explanation, Rabbi Sherer said to himself, "He is talking about himself."

Rabbi Ruderman's single-minded devotion to Torah learning is a constant refrain of all the Ner Israel students of that period. He had no interest whatsoever in politics of any type, and he sought to instill in his *talmidim* (students) the same thirst for Torah learning. While they were still in yeshivah, he insisted, any activity outside of the *beis medrash* was *bitul Torah* (wasting time from Torah Study).

Rabbi Sholom Kowalsky came to Ner Israel as an 18-year-old in 1940, just two years after arriving in America from Poland. At his initial interview with Rabbi Ruderman, Rabbi Ruderman commented, in his distinctly Lithuanian Yiddish, "*Ir zeit a Polisher* — You're Polish."

The young man answered, "Why? Is that a disadvantage?"

"Only if you can't learn," Rabbi Ruderman replied.[3]

The ability and desire to learn were the only things that counted for Rabbi Ruderman. One early *talmid* remembers, "The Rosh Yeshivah knew only learning. His entire conversation was in learning. He did not even have time for basic sociability. There was nothing in the yeshivah and no place for a boy who had any interest other than learning."[4]

A *vort* that Rabbi Sherer quoted many times in later years captures

---

2. "Rabbi Yaakov Yitzchak Ruderman, zt"l: The Late Rosh Hayeshivah of Ner Israel, *The Jewish Observer*, November 1987, pp. 12-13.
3. Rabbi Sholom B. Kowalsky, *From My Zaidy's House*, p. 124.
4. Rabbi Shmuel Yosef Labkovsky.

Rabbi Aharon Feldman, today the Rosh Hayeshivah of Ner Israel, notes that this was no longer true in his time in the yeshivah, and that in later years Rabbi Ruderman enjoyed reminiscing with *bachurim* about the Alter of Slabodka and other *gedolei Yisrael* of previous generations whom he had known.

With Rabbi Ruderman and the Gerrer Rosh Yeshivah (later Gerrer Rebbe), Rabbi Pinchas Menachem Alter

Rabbi Ruderman's single-minded devotion to learning and his conception of his role as Rosh Yeshivah. The *Gemara* (*Moed Kattan* 17a) states in the name of Rebbe Yochanan that one should only learn from a teacher who resembles a Divine angel. The question is: To which of the Heavenly angels is the *Gemara* referring?

Rabbi Ruderman answered that question by referring to the angel who visited Yehoshua on the eve of a decisive battle against the city of Ai, and who, according to the *Gemara* (*Megillah* 3a), reprimanded Yehoshua and the warriors with him for *bitul Torah*. The *Gemara*, however, says that they were not guilty of *bitul Torah* per se, but only of not having learned with sufficient depth — בְּעוֹמְקָהּ שֶׁל הֲלָכָה.[5] A rebbi, Rabbi Ruderman commented, must always be prepared to criticize in order to push his students to greater depths in *lomdus*, even if that criticism will not be well received. That is the kind of angel who came to Yehoshua and his men.[6]

Another statement that Rabbi Sherer heard frequently from Rabbi Ruderman would become one of the guiding principles of his life:

---

5. A play on the verse (*Yehoshua* 8:13) describing Yehoshua as spending that night in the valley — עֵמֶק.
6. Rabbi Sherer collected a number of homiletic explanations of precisely what angel the *Gemara* in *Moed Kattan* is referring to. He loved Reb Shraga Feivel Mendlowitz's explanation that the angel referred to by the *Gemara* is the same as those mentioned in the blessings of *Krias Shema* in the morning (in *Nusach Sefard*), who are described as "וְנוֹתְנִים בְּאַהֲבָה רְשׁוּת זֶה לָזֶה — giving permission one to another *with love*." The meaning of the *Gemara*, then, according to Reb Shraga Feivel, is that only one who teaches out of love of his students, and does not view his teaching as just another job, is fit to teach Torah. In Rabbi Sherer's mind, the *vort* perfectly described Reb Shraga Feivel himself.

Front row (l-r): Rabbi Naftoli Neuberger, Rabbi Yehoshua Klavan, Rabbi Yaakov Yitzchak Ruderman, Rabbi Isaac Baruchson, Rabbi Milton Titelbaum, Rabbi Gerd Wiener. Back row: Rabbi Dovid Roodman, Rabbi Moshe Sherer, Rabbi Sholom Kowalsky, Rabbi Avrohom Zelig Krohn, Rabbi Wilfred Wolfson, Rabbi Hershel Liebowitz, Rabbi Harry Mandelkorn

"מוּטָב לְהַעֲמִיד צֶלֶם בְּהֵיכָל וְאַל יַרְבֶּה מַחֲלוֹקֶת בְּיִשְׂרָאֵל" — Better to place an idol in the Sanctuary than to increase *machlokes* [strife] in Yisrael."[7] Much of the stress that Rabbi Sherer placed on preserving unity within *Klal Yisrael,* in general, and Agudath Israel, in particular, he attributed to Rabbi Ruderman's influence.

For the students from New York, who were used to the warmth and camaraderie of the Williamsburg Zeirei and the more Chassidic atmosphere created by Reb Shraga Feivel in Torah Vodaath, including as much as an hour of singing at *Shalosh Seudos,* the completely different atmosphere in Ner Israel required some adjustment.

During Rabbi Sherer's two years learning in Ner Israel, the number of students never exceeded several dozen, but that small close group included many of exceptional talent. Rabbi Abba Yaakov Liff, later a *maggid shiur* in Ner Israel, was sent to the yeshivah at the age of 13 by Rabbi Yehoshua Klavan, a rav in Washington, D.C. Rabbi Shmaryahu (Shmerl) Shulman was another of Rabbi Sherer's brilliant contemporaries. Rabbi Yaakov Kamenetsky, then a rav in Toronto, sent his two oldest sons, Rabbi Binyamin Kamenetsky and Rabbi Shmuel Kamenetsky, to learn under Rabbi Ruderman, his cousin and fellow native of Dohlinov.[8]

Other contemporaries of Rabbi Sherer in Ner Israel included: Rabbi Avraham Zelig Krohn, father of the famous *mohel,* author, and speaker Rabbi Paysach Krohn; Rabbi Hillel Klavan, who succeeded his father, Rabbi Yehoshua Klavan, as rav of Washington, D.C.; Rabbi Wilfred Wolfson, later the menahel of the Yeshivah of Greater Washington; Rabbi Shmuel Yosef Labkovsky, with whom Rabbi Sherer would work closely decades later on several major public projects in his capacity as

---

7. The statement is found in *Ein HaBedolach*, a work by Rabbi Yisrael Yonah Landau, the rav of Kampena. Rabbi Yitzchak Elchonon Spektor wrote of the work that it did not need his *haskamah* (approbation), as the author was "one of the greatest *geonim* of the generation." Rabbi Akiva Eiger referred to him in a letter as *"the pe'er hador, amud hayemini,"* and even asked him to write a *kemeiya* (amulet) for a sick person.

As rav in Kampena, Rabbi Landau once found himself in conflict with the community over firing a *chazzan* with a beautiful voice but whose religious observance left a great deal to be desired. He wrote to the nearby rav of Posen, known as Reb Yosef Hatzaddik, who was the son-in-law of the *Noda Bi'Yehudah,* about how to conduct himself in light of the community's refusal to fire the *chazzan*. The rav of Posen replied with the above-quoted phrase. See Rabbi Sherer's eulogy for Rabbi Ruderman published in *Bishtei Einayim*, pp. 425-26. Rabbi Dovid Kviat mentioned to Rabbi Shmuel Bloom that a basis for this may be found in the comment of *Daas Zekeinim MiBaalei HaTosafos* to *Shemos* 32:2.

8. Only Rabbi Binyamin Kamenetsky learned in Ner Israel during Rabbi Sherer's two years in the yeshivah.

Executive Vice President of Mesivta Tifereth Jerusalem, and two local boys, David and Rabbi Avraham (Vam) Schwartz.

Rabbi Sherer's *chavrusah* for *Yoreh Deah* was a young man, Hershel Leibowitz, the son of a captain in the Canadian Navy, who came to the yeshivah with little previous background in learning. Still, he managed to complete all of tractate *Yevamos*, generally considered one of the most difficult in the entire Talmud, his first year in Baltimore. On a visit to the yeshivah to test the students, Rabbi Eliezer Silver gave him an award as one of the outstanding *bachurim* in the yeshivah. Rabbi Sherer and Rabbi Leibowitz learned together with Rabbi Mordechai Rabinowitz, who was known as the Chofetz Chaim of Baltimore, and whose daughter Rabbi Leibowitz eventually married.

In the Eyes of His Contemporaries

ONE REMARKABLE ASPECT OF INTERVIEWS WITH RABBI SHERER'S contemporaries in the yeshivah is how closely their descriptions of him as a young man dovetail with the leader he would ultimately become. He already had the power to draw people to him. "He was always positive, never downcast," remembers Rabbi Shmaryahu (Shmerl) Shulman. "He commanded the attention of those around him," says Rabbi Vam Schwartz.

All his contemporaries from those years mention his wonderful singing voice, which he used to lead the singing of *zemiros* on Shabbos. He taught the other students "*A Succaleh a Kleiner,*" a *niggun* which Rabbi Dovid Leibowitz, the founder of Yeshivas Chofetz Chaim, had brought with him to America, and which was a favorite in Agudah circles in those days.[9] He was an all-American boy: a good athlete and smart dresser. Moshe Schwab, the son of Rabbi Shimon Schwab, in whose home Rabbi Sherer was a frequent visitor, remembers him as a very good handball player in the Friday games at the YMHA.

Rabbi Sherer's remarkable people skills were already firmly in place in his younger years. "Whoever met him liked him," remembers Rabbi Vam Schwartz. "He was very warm and gregarious." He was always eager to do a favor for someone. When Sholom Kowalsky, still a relatively new immigrant, decided to seek a rabbinical position, his friend Moshe Sherer was quick to offer to help him write and prepare several *derashos* (sermons) so that his deficiencies in English would be less noticeable.

---

9. Rabbi Avraham (Vam) Schwartz.

That readiness to do favors remained a trademark throughout his life. "If you needed a favor," says Rabbi Kowalsky, "he would consider whether he could do it. If he could, he would say, 'I can do it and I will do it,' and that was the end of the matter. You never had to call a second time to remind him or to find out whether it was done."

Yet for all his easy camaraderie with people, there remained a very private side as well. He did not share confidences easily or reveal his deepest thoughts to others. That too would never change. In later life, he invariably vacationed alone with just his wife in some remote hamlet in Connecticut or Maine, where he could be sure that no one would recognize him.

Master of the Word

ALREADY IN NER ISRAEL, RABBI SHERER'S MASTERY OF THE SPOKEN and written word stood out. Besides his singing voice, Rabbi Sherer is best remembered as the class orator, with a superb command of English and an excellent delivery.[10] His skill as a *darshan* and his ability to mine the Torah for *vertlach* to drive home the point he wished to make was already evident even at that young age.

He never spoke extemporaneously. He prepared each speech carefully and would write it out. That never changed. As a teacher of homi-

Speaking at Ner Israel's dinner in 1943. Rabbi Ruderman is second from right.

---

10. Rabbi Shmaryahu (Shmerl) Shulman.

With Rabbi Shimon Schwab in the 1980s. Rabbi Avrohom Pam is in the background

letics at Torah Vodaath in later years, the first rule he taught his students was: Never speak unless you are prepared. He left behind notes for hundreds of *derashos* he had given over the years.

On one occasion, while still in Ner Israel, he was asked to make a radio address. And Rabbi Ruderman used to send him to outlying communities as a Shabbos speaker in order to publicize the yeshivah and to help with fund-raising. Once he was sent to be the rav of a congregation in Richmond, Virginia for Yom Kippur. Just before *Ne'ilah* a group of congregants told him that he should make a fund-raising appeal to build a new sanctuary, something for which he was totally unprepared. During the break, he looked outside and noticed that it had rained and there was a rainbow in the sky. That rainbow served as the key metaphor for his hastily prepared speech. The colors of the rainbow represent all the various different talents and strengths of the members of the community, he began. When those individuals meld together in common cause, as in a rainbow, there is — to quote a popular proverb — a pot of gold to be found at the end of the rainbow. While that particular *derashah* will never be found in Rabbi Sherer's collected speeches, in later years he smiled with pride that he had come up with anything at all to say.

A speech given in Rabbi Shimon Schwab's shul Shearith Israel was inspired by stories he heard from Mike Tress about the frustration of pounding on the doors of officialdom in Washington, D.C., in an effort to save Jewish lives in Europe, and finding those doors locked.

The Torah recounts how Basya, Pharaoh's daughter, was walking along the river, and heard a baby crying. "וְהִנֵּה נַעַר בֹּכֶה ... וַתֹּאמֶר מִיַּלְדֵי הָעִבְרִים זֶה — Behold the child was crying, and she said: 'This is a Jewish child'" (*Shemos* 2:6). The commentators ask: How did Basya know that he was Jewish? They offer various explanations (e.g., the baby was circumcised; he was abandoned, when all Jewish babies were to be drowned, etc).

> I have another explanation: When Basya saw that a child was crying — a cry so piercing, so troubling — and yet his cries fell on deaf ears, she knew immediately he must be Jewish.
>
> By contrast, we find in the beginning of *Parashas Vayigash* that when Yehudah was protesting to Pharaoh's viceroy (actually Yehudah's brother, Yosef HaTzaddik) for taking Binyamin hostage, the *Midrash* tells us that Yehudah's cries were so strong that they were heard four hundred *parsa'os* away — a distance of hundreds of miles — by Yehudah's nephew, Chushim ben Dan, who immediately came to Egypt to assist his uncle. When he joined Yehudah, he too cried out, and not only did the palace shake, but the entire Mitzrayim trembled.
>
> According to the *Gemara* (*Sotah* 13a), Chushim was hard of hearing. If so, how could Chushim have responded to his uncle's cries? The answer is based on a simple truth. When a Jew cries from pain, another Jew is always able to hear the cry, even if he is otherwise hard of hearing. For this reason, Chushim heard the voice of his uncle Yehudah crying for the return of Binyamin. But as we see today, when a Jew cries out — even to one who is able to hear — all too often, the other person suddenly turns deaf.
>
> We here in the United States have an advantage over Chushim. Chushim was deaf, yet he heard the cry of his fellow Jews. We aren't deaf; we hear what's happening in Europe. Can we allow the cries of our fellow *Yidden* to fall on deaf ears, and be as guilty as the Egyptians were?

While at Ner Israel, Rabbi Sherer honed not only his oratorical skills but his writing skills as well. Under the pseudonyms Martin Nerl and Morris Moruchnik (his mother's maiden name), likely chosen to conceal his writing activity from Rabbi Ruderman's watchful eye, he wrote a column entitled "Reflections" for the Zeirei paper *Orthodox Youth* (subsequently changed to the *Orthodox Tribune*). Even at a distance of 60 years, it is hard not to marvel at the skill with which the young yeshivah student wielded his verbal rapier.

Sarcasm was his chief weapon, and in that sense the pieces reflect the author's relatively young age, despite his occasional efforts to affect the pose of an older observer looking back over the changes in American Jewry from his youth. Even in later years, Rabbi Sherer's speeches and writing could often be biting, especially when discussing the leadership of the mainline Jewish organizations or heterodox movements. But as the distinguished leader of a major organization, he did not give as full rein to his sarcasm as he did as a young man writing pseudonymously for a small, insular audience.

A frequent subject was the contrast between outward religious forms and the lack of inner conviction. In an early piece, he characterized the English-speaking rabbis beginning to be produced for Orthodox shuls as masters of the fine art of "how to win friends and not influence people." He accused these rabbis of a tendency "to mollycoddle every vital issue by murmuring platitudinous nothings about 'religion' and 'democracy' ... not to trample on the delicate feelings of their congregants."

Why were the young rabbis turned out by rabbinical seminaries unwilling to stand up for proper religious standards in their shuls? Martin Nerl had the answer: "[They view] the rabbinate either as a lucrative profession, a vocation, or a (shhh!) ... vacation. Hence ... dances, bingo, mixed pews, Zionist affiliation, clerical robe, book reviews, bas mitzvahs .... [N]ecessity, my boy, necessity."[11] That contempt for anyone who mixed pecuniary motives into any form of *avodas HaKodesh* (literally, holy work) remained lifelong.

The commercialization of Rosh Hashanah was the theme of another column. The holiday, in his view, had become "a devitalized and emasculated spectre of its former self, ... an occasion for pulling congregational budgets out of the red, family get-togethers, exasperating Post Office employees with tiny 'New Year's greeting' envelopes, and the earning of some wholesome cash by the members of the Jewish Tin Pan Alley, pseudo-cantors, choir boys and what have you."[12]

The worst part of all was the replacement of the *shaliach tzibbur* of old, who served as the spokesman of the congregation before G-d, by cantors who "mix some pianissimo with a bit of fortissimo, add some allegretto with a dash of andante, weave in some plagiarisms from Beethoven,

---

11. Martin Nerl, "Reflections," *Orthodox Youth,* March 1942, p. 4.
12. Ibid., September 1942, p. 4.

Sholom Secunda, and sepulchral music, [and] stir with raw eggs."[13]

Yet when it came to true repentance and heartfelt prayer, none was to be found. After the Struma tragedy, in which an overcrowded ship carrying 780 European Jews was denied haven in Palestine and sank at sea, Martin Nerl expected American Jewry to be roused "from the lethargic state to a wholehearted return to G-d." Instead there was only a mad rush to issue public statements and pass resolutions.[14]

Mizrachi dominated American Orthodoxy in the early '40s. Martin Nerl, however, was unintimidated, and did not waste an opportunity to heap scorn on the much larger organization. Those columns reveal a committed Agudah ideologue. When the Mizrachi leaders in Denver arranged for a renowned Zionist orator to speak on both the East Side and West Side of Denver on the same Shabbos, Martin Nerl was quick to call them to task for the manner in which "he was warmly received with great pomp, plaudits heaped upon him for his magnificent work, [praised for his dynamic speech] (some said he resembled a prophet — 'oh he was so inspiring') before he brazenly drove off to the next shul." The spiritual leaders of Mizrachi, wrote Nerl, were afraid to take a stand for Shabbos observance lest they engender "hostility and ill-feelings from their Zionist 'sugar daddy.'"

He was equally indignant when Mizrachi called for a *cherem* (ban of excommunication) against the Reform American Council of Judaism for its anti-Zionism. Why, he wondered, were "the pork-chop eating gentlemen from Park Avenue entitled to be recognized as 'rabbis' so long as they swear allegiance to the Shekel? The Shekel is their *semichah*." And, he asked, why did the Mizrachi leadership show no similar pain "when their pro-Zion Reform bedfellows declare themselves ... against G-d, against the whole Torah?"

Young Idealist

THOUGH HE HAD ALL THE SKILLS OF A SUCCESSFUL STUDENT politician, there was something much deeper in him. "He had a *bren*, a certain passion," recalls Rabbi Vam Schwartz. Above all he had a great desire "to do for *Yiddishkeit*." He and Sholom Kowalsky would stay up late at night discussing whether it was more important to dedicate oneself to working with individuals or for the entire *tzibbur* (community). Rabbi Sherer invariably came out on the side of working with the *tzibbur*.

---
13. Ibid.
14. Ibid., July 1942, p. 4.

He spoke of doing in America what Rabbi Samson Raphael Hirsch had done in his time in Germany: purify the air. Just as Rabbi Hirsch fought to establish his *Austritt* principle of no joint participation with Reform elements in communal organs, so the young yeshivah student looked forward to the day when it would no longer be acceptable for someone who was not a *shomer Shabbos* to serve as an officer of an Orthodox shul.[15] He also spoke to Kowalsky about his childhood memories of men coming out of an early Shabbos morning *minyan* only to enter the subway that would take them to work in the garment district. That scene continued to plague him.

Another fellow student with whom he discussed his dreams of public service on behalf of the Jewish people was Naftoli Neuberger, a recent refugee from Germany, who became a lifelong friend. It is a fascinating historical footnote that the two were contemporaries at Ner Israel. Over the next six decades Rabbi Neuberger would be the only other Orthodox *askan* who could be mentioned in the same breath as Rabbi Sherer in terms of his ability to navigate the halls of power and win the respect

A lifelong friendship with Rabbi Naftoli Neuberger

---

15. This was a big issue in those days. Rabbi Shimon Schwab, who was raised in Rabbi Hirsch's *Austritt* community in Frankfurt, lost a sizable portion of his congregation over his insistence on enforcing a congregational bylaw against non-Shabbos-observant members serving as officers of the shul.

of powerful politicians. To political leaders in Baltimore and Maryland, Rabbi Neuberger was the voice of Orthodox Jewry, and his web of contacts in Congress was very wide. As president of Ner Israel and the confidant of the Rosh Yeshivah Rabbi Ruderman, Rabbi Neuberger was the principal force behind Ner Israel's present-day suburban campus.

The extensive correspondence between Rabbi Sherer and Rabbi Neuberger, after the former's departure from Baltimore, testifies to the close relationship forged in Baltimore. It was a relationship that would only grow stronger with the passage of time as the two worked hand in hand on a wide array of crucial issues, including the rescue of Iranian Jews after the fall of the Shah, gaining academic accreditation for yeshivos, and preserving the draft exemption for yeshivah students.

Already in Ner Israel, Rabbi Sherer had established his lifelong habit of reading late into the night. Each night, he would pore over news magazines gaining the knowledge of world affairs that he would one day use for the benefit of *Klal Yisrael*. Sholom Kowalsky, who was in charge of waking the *talmidim* for *davening*, could always tell how late his friend had been up reading the night before by the difficulty that he had rousing him.

Rabbi Sherer engaged in *kiruv* long before the word was known. When he first met Avraham Robinson, the Buffalo native was working in Baltimore. Though he came from a *shomer Shabbos* home, Robinson had little learning background. Nevertheless he used to come into the Ner Israel *beis medrash* from time to time, and that is where Rabbi Sherer first met him. Robinson was not yet 20, and Moshe Sherer was only one or two years older.

Rabbi Sherer befriended Robinson and almost immediately went to work trying to convince him to go to Telshe Yeshivah, where, in those days, there were other students from weaker backgrounds. Eventually he succeeded in convincing him to enroll in Telshe, and sent him to Williamsburg for a Shabbos before traveling to Telshe. Robinson ended up spending eight years in Cleveland and receiving *semichah*. After marrying, he moved to Israel, where he lived for many years. Today, one of his sons is a rosh yeshivah. There is little question in Rabbi Robinson's mind that but for meeting the young Moshe Sherer he would never have studied in yeshivah.

Rabbi Emanuel Feldman was an even younger teenager when he came under Rabbi Sherer's spell. In a remembrance of Rabbi Sherer, published in his capacity as editor of *Tradition* magazine, Rabbi Feldman painted a moving picture of the young Moshe Sherer. It is worth quoting in full:

> There was once a 14-year-old boy in Baltimore whose major interests in life were tennis and the Baltimore Orioles. Those were the days before there were *yeshivot* beyond elementary school, so after graduating day school he attended a public high school. For his Torah studies, he participated in a special evening study program run by the local day school, and his father — a European *talmid hakham*, who was a *rav* in Baltimore — learned with him regularly. Although he gave grudging attention to his Torah studies, his teenage interests dominated his life.
>
> His father was concerned about him, especially with the long, hot Baltimore summer looming ahead. Since he was a good friend of the Rosh haYeshivah of Ner Israel, HaRav Yaakov Yitzchak Halevi Ruderman, z"l, the father called Rav Ruderman and asked him to recommend a student who might study with his son during the summer months. Without hesitation, Rav Ruderman recommended a 20-year-old who was spending the summer in the yeshivah.
>
> The young boy was reluctant to devote even part of his gloriously free summer days to anything but the baseball diamond, but when he finally met face to face with his putative teacher, there was an immediate rapport between the two. The older boy was very *frum*, but also very friendly, understanding, open, non-judgmental, enthusiastic — and he knew a lot about baseball. The younger boy enjoyed just being with him and with his infectious smile. They learned *Mishnah* and *Gemara* all summer long, and gradually the young boy discovered that Torah learning was not just for old men, but could be stimulating and challenging for youngsters as well. The Jewishness of that boy was invigorated, and he ultimately enrolled in Ner Israel. More: The 14-year-old and the 20-year-old remained lifelong friends.

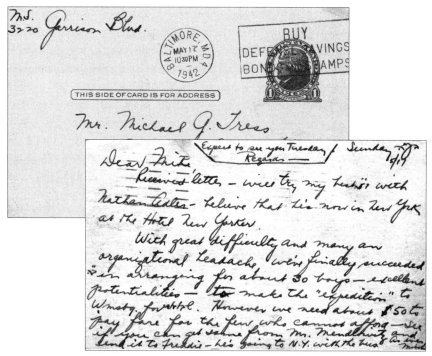

A postcard from Moshe Sherer at Ner Israel to Mike. "We've finally succeeded ב"ה in arranging for about 30 boys — excellent potentialities — to make the 'expedition' to Wmsbg. [Williamsburg] for Shavuos."

That 14-year-old boy whom the young Moshe Sherer did so much to influence went on to become one of the most successful communal rabbis in America, over nearly a half century of service in Atlanta, as well as one of the preeminent writers and editors in the Orthodox world.

WHILE IN BALTIMORE, RABBI SHERER REMAINED ACTIVELY involved in Agudah activities. That work had to be conducted without Rabbi Ruderman's noticing. The latter was both apolitical and opposed to *yeshivah bachurim* spending time on anything unconnected to their learning. He once told Freddy Wolf, "You are here to learn Torah, not to be involved in *askanus* (community activism)."

Budding Activist

Mr. Schwartz, who lived next door to Ner Israel and had two boys learning in the yeshivah, made available his basement with a telephone to Rabbi Sherer so that he could conduct his Agudah activities far removed from the Rosh Yeshivah's sharp gaze. Rabbi Sherer and Mike Tress were in frequent contact via letters and postcards, and an occasional phone

Chapter Two: Ner Israel □ 81

call. The former kept abreast of affairs at 616 Bedford Avenue from afar.

Despite the admonition that their sole purpose in Baltimore was to learn Torah, Rabbi Sherer and Freddy Wolf would sneak out of the yeshivah on Shabbos afternoon to lead Pirchei groups. They also organized "expeditions," led by Wolf, of 30 or so local boys to Torah Vodaath.[16] One local boy, Yitzchok Chinn, later the longtime rav of McKeesport, Pennsylvania, went to Torah Vodaath on one such an expedition. At that time, there was no yeshivah high school in Baltimore, and few parents were willing to send their teenage sons away from home. But after a Simchas Torah in Torah Vodaath, and a summer in Camp Agudah, Rabbi Chinn was hooked. "I owe Moshe Sherer a lot," Rabbi Chinn reflects, "Without him, I might not have gone to yeshivah."

Judging from his correspondence with Mike and others at 616 Bedford Avenue, the exercise of authority came naturally to Rabbi Sherer. From the beginning, he insisted on meticulous attention to detail, punctuality, and orderly record-keeping. In one letter to Gershon Kranzler, nearly a decade his senior and a veteran of the Agudah movement in Germany, the young yeshivah student set forth in great detail rules for the writing and submission of press releases: "(a) DON'T place headline on release; (b) DON'T put in such words as "SIVAN 5702 in release for Anglo-Jewish press; (c) DON'T use foreign words in release; (c) DO paragraph the release and explain it to the utmost; ... (d) Releases should be sent

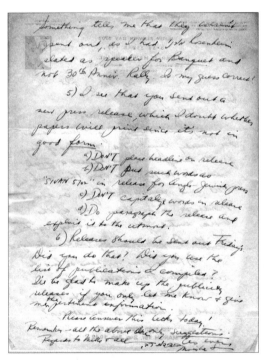

A missive to Gershon Kranzler

---

16. Moshe Sherer to Mike Tress, May 17, 1942.

out on Fridays." A letter to Mike contained a list of new Bnos members, and instructions on what should be in the letter sent to each member concerning an upcoming Bnos national convention and the ad journal being prepared in conjunction with it. "This should be done TODAY, so the girls receive the letters by Monday morning," Rabbi Sherer concluded.[17]

Mike used his younger cousin as the Zeirei representative in Baltimore. Many letters between the two dealt with solicitations of assistance from Mr. Nathan Adler, a leading member of the community and the most committed Agudist, for help in fund-raising for Zeirei's rescue activities.

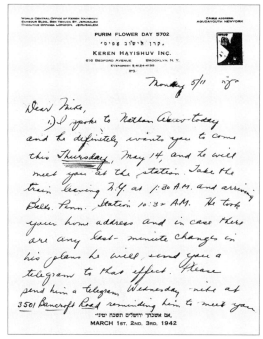

Arranging a meeting with Nathan Adler

Another frequent topic of communication was Camp Agudah, which opened its doors for the first time in the summer of 1942. Rabbi Sherer was a big booster of the undertaking, and constantly encouraged Mike, who was laboring under immense financial pressure due to the decision to open a camp in the middle of the war. "Our deficit for the camp is mounting and the financial headache is even greater than we thought," Mike wrote in one letter. "Nevertheless, we can always find room for any worthwhile boy, regardless of the ability to pay."[18] Rabbi Sherer actively recruited for the camp in Baltimore and tried to line up sponsors for camp scholarships to lighten Mike's burden.

---

17. Moshe Sherer to Mike Tress May 8, 1942.
Not only did the young yeshivah student insist that everything be done punctually, he also wanted a carbon copy of letters written upon his instructions. Moshe Sherer to Mike Tress, July 23, 1942.
18. Mike Tress to Moshe Sherer, June 17, 1942. Mike's answer was in response to an inquiry from Rabbi Sherer two days earlier in which he asked whether he could accept boys for the camp "with excellent potentialities for Mesivta" even though they could not pay.

Camp Agudah was just one expression of how much effort the young idealists of Zeirei Agudath Israel were willing to invest in any boy with potential for yeshivah studies. On occasion, Rabbi Sherer received letters from young men he had known in New York who were having difficulty in Torah Vodaath. After receiving one such "despondent card," he immediately wrote to Mike asking him to get in touch with the boy and "see what you can do for him." In the same letter, he mentions a 12-page missive he had received from another boy who had left Torah Vodaath, and who, in Rabbi Sherer's opinion, needed emotional therapy. He recommended to Mike that the boy be encouraged to return home for a few weeks until he regained his health, and that afterward Mike should "arrange his going back to Mesivta without loss of 'face.'"[19]

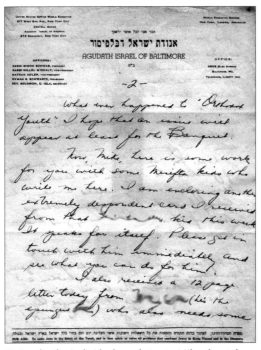

Caring for the individual — a letter to Mike about the needs of various boys

One of Rabbi Sherer's most important contributions to Zeirei Agudas Yisrael was his work on the 1941 Zeirei national convention in Baltimore. Rabbi Sherer played an active role in the preparations for the convention. Rabbi Shimon Schwab served as the unofficial host of the gathering. At that convention a number of recently arrived European *gedolim* were introduced to American Zeirei for the first time. Among the major figures attending their first convention were (in alphabetical order): Rabbi Eliyahu Meir Bloch, Rabbi Reuven Grozovsky, Rabbi Avraham Joffen, Rabbi Yisrael Chaim Kaplan, Rabbi Mordechai Katz, Rabbi Aharon Kotler, Rabbi Simchah Zissel Levovitz,

---

19. Moshe Sherer to Mike Tress, May 28, 1942.

Rabbi Moshe Shkop, and Rabbi Mendel Zaks. Rabbi Moshe Feinstein was also there, and, interestingly, Rabbi Yosef Ber Soloveitchik, later the chairman of American Mizrachi, chaired the Sunday-morning session. Moreinu Yaakov Rosenheim, the lay leader of the world movement of Agudath Israel from its inception, was also present. Notable by his absence was Rabbi Ruderman, who would one day join the Moetzes Gedolei HaTorah of Agudath Israel of America, but who in those years still resisted any trace of political affiliation.

Young Moshe Sherer came to the attention of Moreinu Yaakov Rosenheim — whom he would one day succeed as leader of the world Agudah movement — for the first time. The convention was also his first introduction to many of the *gedolim* with whom he would work closely in the years to come.

FROM THE TRESS-SHERER CORRESPONDENCE, THE CLOSENESS between the two cousins comes through clearly, as does the great

Preparing for the Next Step

admiration of the younger man for the older. The two met frequently at the Baltimore train station, on Mike's return trip to New York from one of his frequent visits to Washington, D.C. for the purpose of obtaining visas and other rescue activities. Mike was virtually the only family member that Rabbi Sherer saw face to face during his years in

The host committee for the 1941 Baltimore convention.
L-r, seated: Rabbi Shimon Schwab, Rev. Salomon Igla; standing: Moshe Sherer, Jacob Weiner, Efraim Wolf

Chapter Two: Ner Israel □ 85

AT THE 1941 CONVENTION

Rabbi Eliezer Silver addressing the audience. Seated, from the right, the Novominsker Rebbe, Moreinu Yaakov Rosenheim, the Boyaner Rebbe, Rabbi Moshe Feinstein, Rabbi Dov Leventhal

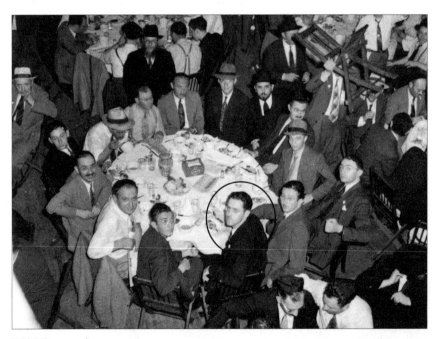

Rabbi Sherer at the convention

Mike Tress (center) with a group of convention delegates.

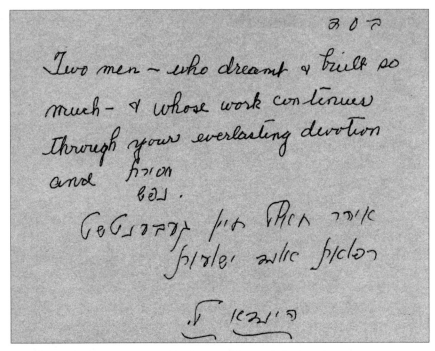

Mrs. Hinda Tress's inscription to Rabbi Sherer in *They Called Him Mike* (the biography of Mike Tress). She presented him with the book when he was recovering from treatments for lymphoma. It attests to the lifelong closeness between the two cousins.

Baltimore, and the latter looked forward with great anticipation to these meetings.

Occasionally Rabbi Sherer would write specifically asking his mentor to stop over for an hour in Baltimore before proceeding back to New York. In one such postcard, he is obviously a bit embarrassed to impose on his cousin, but explains his request: "Nothing really special — just that I would <u>very</u> much like to see you after such a long time .... Please try."[20] After one such visit, he wrote Mike, "I waited with bated breath for you to come yesterday, and you can't imagine how glad I was to spend several hours with you last night."[21]

As early as July 1942, the two began to discuss the possibility of Rabbi Sherer joining Mike in Zeirei. Rabbi Sherer wrote to Mike, "I'm sorry to see how run down you are — and I'm just rarin' to go to be in there beside you." Similar expressions of eagerness to be there "at

---

20. Moshe Sherer to Mike Tress, July 12, 1942.
21. Ibid., May 15, 1942.

> 19 days in Iyar 5702
> May 6, 1942
>
> Mr. Morris Sherer
> 3220 Garrison Blvd.
> Baltimore, Md.
>
> Dear Moishe:
>
> Received your letter and the application blanks for the camp. The camp may become a reality – we are trying to get the right place and we should definitely know where we stand within the next ten days – the enthusiasm is at the highest pitch. The difficulty lies in procuring the proper spot – a number of "camp"-sites have been offered, viewed and not found suitable for our purposes.
>
> What is new with you – I know that you are still learning and all goes well – About "Orthodox Youth", Heshy's father suddenly became very ill and things have been kept at a stand-still – however we hope that it will appear very soon.
>
> What is new in Baltimore? How is the Agudah, the board... really hate to trouble you so often, but you know that you are the only one with a will and capability to not only desire to do but also to realize that desire. Do let me know –
>
> Benjamin Hirsch wishes to go to Balt. on Sunday, something about somebody's Smicha. However he can't go (due to lack of funds) so he wants to know if he can be of any value either raising funds or organization work, then he would have the opportunity – the answer is dependent on your judgement.
>
> All right boy. Be well, regards to Freddie, Rev. Igla, the boys, Shwartss, Mr. Adler and anyone else you know.. Everyone sends their best regards.
>
> As ever,
>
> Michael G. Tress
>
> MGT:gk

[Mike's] side"[22] with "every ounce of strength I possess"[23] became the trademark conclusion of each of the rabbinic student's letters.

For his part, Mike was equally eager to have his cousin at his side. "[Y]ou are the only one with a will and capability to not only desire to do but also to realize that desire," Mike wrote.[24] In another letter, Mike wrote, "Camp business has as always reverted back on my shoulders. You have no idea how badly I need a strong hand here, and I am eagerly awaiting you."

In 1942, Rabbi Sherer completed his studies for *semichah* in both *Yoreh Deah* and *Choshen Mishpat*, and he received an effusive *semichah*

---

22. Moshe Sherer to Mike Tress, July 24, 1942.
23. Moshe Sherer to Mike Tress, May 28, 1942.
24. Mike Tress to Moshe Sherer, May 6, 1942.

Rabbi Sherer escorting Rabbi Ruderman at an Agudah convention in the 1980s

from Rabbi Ruderman.[25] The time had now come for Mike Tress and Moshe Sherer to realize their longstanding dream of working together on behalf of *Klal Yisrael*.

Rabbi Sherer's *semichah*

ב"ה

הנני להודיע בזה מעלת ידידי הרב הגדול והנעלה מופלא ומופלג
בתורה וי"ש חריף ובקי אור הברקי אוצר נחמד פה ספיק מרגליות
מו"ה משה שערער נ"י
אשר לפד בישיבתנו הקדושה נר ישראל ושקד על התורה ורכש לו
הרבה בגמרא ופוסקים בסברא בהבנה וישרות השכל והגיע להוראה
וכל מן דין סמוכו לנא
יורה יורה ידין ידין
והוא דגול ומצוין איש חי רב פעלים יקר ערך מאד והעדה אשר
ישכון כבוד בתוכה יהיה לה לנזר תפארה וישמחו וילכו לאור תורתו
ויראתו וינהלם על שבועי התורה והיראה בכחותיו הנדולים ובהשפעתו
הכבירה ותיכף לת"ח גדול ברכה הכו"ח למען התורה ולומדי'

ך סיון תש"ד באלטימאר

---

25. Longtime students of Ner Israel say that compliments chosen by Rabbi Ruderman in the *Yoreh-Yoreh / Yadin-Yadin semichah* — ... חריף ובקי אור הברקי were rare for Rabbi Ruderman.

Chapter Three

GETTING STARTED

RABBI SHERER RETURNED TO NEW YORK FROM BALTIMORE in January 1943. The offer from his cousin Mike Tress to join him in Zeirei Agudath Israel, or the Agudath Israel Youth Council as it was known in English, was still open. But he also interviewed for a number of rabbinical positions. The position of communal rabbi is where his classmates in Ner Israel had seen him headed. His love of learning, speaking skills, and ability to relate to people were tailor made for such a position.[1]

In a letter to his friend Rabbi Naftoli Neuberger in Baltimore, Rabbi Sherer related how he had met with the boards of a number of shuls in different neighborhoods of New York. In each case, the board had offered him the position. But the shuls were small, and none of them could pay a sufficient salary for a young man who was thinking of marrying and starting a family.[2]

---

1. Rabbi Lawrence Cohen. Rabbi Cohen, a classmate of Rabbi Sherer's from Ner Israel, later served as a day school principal in Newark, New Jersey.
2. Moshe Sherer to Naftoli Neuberger, January 27, 1943.

After a few weeks of indecision, Rabbi Sherer accepted Mike's offer to join him in Zeirei Agudath Israel. Mike wrote to the Zeirei branches on January 19 announcing Rabbi Sherer's appointment as Executive Director of Agudath Israel Youth Council. His salary was $35 per week. The subsequent press release described him as "a graduate of Ner Israel Rabbinical College, ... well known as an Orthodox orator and writer." The press release went on to note that a number of congratulatory notices had been received from Orthodox rabbis and laymen, including Moreinu Yaakov Rosenheim, president of the World Agudath Israel, who was then in New York.

Rabbi Sherer apparently did not view his acceptance of the position as a long-term commitment. He wrote to Rabbi Neuberger, "I consider this [position] temporary until a really good rabbinical position comes up."[3] He added, "I thank G-d that no matter how busy I am, I have my daily *seder* in *Mesechta Kiddushin*."

Announcing Rabbi Sherer's appointment

---

3. Ibid.

In time the offer of a prestigious rabbinical position did present itself. But by then Rabbi Sherer's commitment to *Klal* work was such that he did not accept the offer. The "temporary" position lasted over 55 years.

Shortly after beginning work, Rabbi Sherer wrote again to Rabbi Neuberger describing his duties as executive director: "[M]y duties are manifold. They consist of helping in the organization and strengthening of branches and the writing of literature about our work. Since our Council has several departments, and on top of that I try to keep up with 'learning,' you can readily imagine how occupied I am."

Minutes of a meeting of the Board of the Agudath Israel Youth Council from October 5, 1944 provide a detailed description of the post of executive director:

(1) Co-ordinate the various activities of the organization and implement its projects.

(2) Public relations work, i.e., propaganda pamphlets, educational work, press, general correspondence, etc.

(3) Co-ordinate branch activities, help organize branches and strengthen existing ones.

(4) Supervise the work of departments and sub-directors.

At the time Rabbi Sherer joined Zeirei Agudath Israel, the organization lacked stature within the larger Jewish world. Zeirei defied both

Addressing an Agudah dinner in 1943. Seated (l-r) Rabbi Michael Munk, Rabbi Yechiel Elbaum, Mike Tress

Chapter Three: Getting Started □ 93

the British government and the organized Jewish community in 1941 by organizing a campaign to send food packages to starving Jews in the ghettos of Nazi-occupied Poland. Outraged by the effrontery of the upstart organization, Dr. Joseph Tenenbaum, the chairman of the Joint Boycott Council, launched into a ferocious attack on Zeirei Agudath Israel. "It is to be deplored that Agudath Israel of America, *a sickly weed transplanted from foreign soil to the liberal American environment*, should continue to poison the atmosphere" (emphasis added), he bellowed. In the years to come, Rabbi Sherer never tired of referring to how the "sickly weed" had grown, while so many of those organizations that waxed powerful at the time had disappeared from the scene.

It did not take long for Rabbi Sherer to discover just how little status Zeirei commanded. One of his first assignments was to represent the Youth Council at a conference convened by Rabbi Yisrael Rosenberg of Agudas HaRabbonim to promote Shabbos observance. At one point, Rabbi Rosenberg called for a show of support. The 22-year-old Executive Director of the Agudath Israel Youth Council responded enthusiastically, with all the eagerness of youth.

The sight of the young Agudist taking the lead provoked a sneering response from Rabbi Aryeh Leib Gellman, the head of the American Mizrachi movement. "Who do you Agudah people think you are? You're nobodies. We won't join forces with nobodies like you."[4] While unkind, Gellman's remark was not totally off the mark. In terms of membership, Mizrachi was by far the dominant organization within American Orthodoxy in those days. Rabbi Sherer never forgot the sting of Gellman's insult, and whenever he repeated this story in later years, he always pointed out how Agudath Israel had grown into an organization with a staff of hundreds, while American Mizrachi no longer has even a handful of full-time employees.[5]

Money was in even shorter supply than prestige. The demands of the wartime rescue and relief work on the slim resources of the Agudath Israel Youth Council were such that the organization's motto might well have been, "Another day older and deeper in debt." Funds were in

---

4. Kranzler interview with Rabbi Sherer.
5. Rabbi Joseph Elias relates a similar incident involving him. At a meeting of Orthodox groups to fashion a joint position paper for the first meeting of the United Nations Relief and Rehabilitation Agency (UNRRA) in 1944, a great deal of time was devoted to find a way to append the signatures of the various groups without that of Agudath Israel coming first, as a purely alphabetical listing would have indicated. Yonoson Rosenblum, *They Called Him Mike*, p. 49, fn. 5.

such short supply that the Youth Council would send out multiple letters requesting remittance for the quarter spent on cables to American consulates abroad. Rabbi Sherer found himself writing many such letters himself, and countless solicitations of funds for the crucial wartime work of the Youth Council.

Something that Mike Tress told his "kid brother" on his very first day of work suggests how those pressures could take their toll on even the strongest of men. Mike began in a manner guaranteed to emphasize the importance of what he was about to impart: "I'm going to tell you something that, coming from me, will sound shocking and uncharacteristic, yet I feel that if you are going to survive serving the *Klal* you must hear. I'm going to tell you this once, and you will never hear it from me again." Then came the message: "When you work for the *Klal* or do a favor for an individual, never expect a thank-you. Just be happy if you don't get spit in the face."[6]

In the years to come, Rabbi Sherer fully understood why his "big brother" felt it was so important to impart that particular lesson. Not that the lack of appreciation ever stopped Mike Tress or Rabbi Sherer from doing countless favors for people. "Reb Elimelech Tress did favors for thousands of people," Rabbi Sherer once wrote, but few of the beneficiaries ever contributed to the building of Agudath Israel of America.[7]

Fortunately, Rabbi Sherer's introduction to *Klal* work was not all quite as ominous as the first lesson from Mike Tress. A few weeks after Rabbi Sherer began work for the Youth Council, Reb Shraga Feivel Mendlowitz came to visit his former *talmid*. His purpose was twofold: first, to give Rabbi Sherer a blessing for success in his new position and to express his admiration for the rescue work that the Youth Council was doing; second, to hand Rabbi Sherer a bundle of bills totaling $3,000, an almost unheard-of sum for the Youth Council in those days. "I know that your organization needs lots of money, and that without it you won't be able to do anything, so I took it upon myself to collect this for you," Rav Shraga Feivel said.[8]

Rabbi Gedaliah Schorr was another longtime mentor who offered guidance to Rabbi Sherer in his early days working for Zeirei. He told Rabbi Sherer that the key to his long-term survival in *Klal* work was

---

6. In fact, Mike's insightful warning reflected a paraphrase of a story oft-repeated in the name of Rebbe Shmelke of Nikolsburg. When doing favors for people, he would say, "I just did you a big favor, so when you throw stones at me, please use pebbles not rocks."
7. Rabbi Moshe Sherer to Rabbi Menachem Porush, January 1, 1970.
8. Surasky, Aharon, *Shlucha D'Rachmana* (Hebrew) (Feldheim Publications 1992), p. 287.

to maintain a feeling of being *glicklach* (fulfilled, blessed) in his work. To drive home his point, Reb Gedaliah cited the verse (*Bamidbar* 7:9), which describes how the *bnei Kehos* carried the *Aron* on their shoulders. Yet the *Gemara* (*Arachin* 11a) interprets the word for "carrying" (יִשָּׂאוּ) as an expression of *shirah* (song). From this Reb Gedaliah derived the lesson that to survive in *Klal* work — *avodas HaKodesh* (sacred service) in the language of the verse — one must not view that work as burden thrust upon one, but as a *glicklach* blessing worthy of joyous song. It was a lesson that Rabbi Sherer not only lived by for the next 55 years but frequently shared with new employees in Agudath Israel.⁹

Rescue Work

RABBI SHERER FREQUENTLY MENTIONED IN LATER YEARS THAT rescue work constituted his initiation into *Klal* work. The Agudath Israel Youth Council might have struck an outside observer as a small, insignificant organization. But in the little more than three years since the Zeirei opened its first office at 616 Bedford Avenue in Williamsburg, with only one employee besides Mike Tress (who took no salary) and a single typewriter, it had accomplished much. By the time Rabbi Sherer came to work for the Youth Council, it employed more than a dozen secretaries, most of whom were involved in processing visa requests and other activities connected to wartime rescue, and had moved to far-larger headquarters at 113 W. 42nd Street in Manhattan.¹⁰

"He Who Saveth a Soul in Israel Createth a World," was the motto of the Youth Council's Refugee and Immigration Division. In the first years of the war, before the gates had closed shut on the vast majority of Europe's Jews trapped by the Nazi war machine, the Refugee and Immigration Division hummed virtually around the clock. Within the first two years of its existence it advised 7,500 individuals on immigration matters. Each week, hundreds of letters and 50 or 60 cables

---

9. Rabbi Sherer once asked a question on a Rashi in *Bamidbar* to bring out Reb Gedaliah's message. The Torah relates that when Eldad and Medad began to prophesy in the encampment, Yehoshua urged Moshe Rabbeinu to "finish them" (כְּלָאֵם) (*Bamidbar* 11: 28). According to the first explanation of Rashi on the verse, Yehoshua's intention was that Moshe Rabbeinu should impose upon them public duties and as a consequence they would automatically be "consumed" by their duties. Rabbi Sherer joked that he appeared to be a living contradiction to the Rashi since he continued to thrive despite the multitude of public tasks on his shoulders. He answered, based on what he had learned from Rabbi Gedaliah Schorr many years earlier: Public responsibilities only consume a person if he views them as a burden imposed upon him, but not if he views them as a privilege and performs them with a sense of satisfaction.
10. *They Called Him Mike*, p. 179.

reached 616 Bedford Avenue from around the world. For those without a relative or friend to sponsor their visas, the Refugee and Immigration Division provided virtually the only American address to which they could turn for assistance.[11]

By April 1941, the Refugee and Immigration Division had obtained 1,300 affidavits of financial support, which were a prerequisite for any visa application. Almost all of those were collected from well-to-do Jews with no natural connection to Zeirei. By September 1941, 1,000 visas had been issued to families processed by the Refugee and Immigration Division, and 400 families had already entered the United States.[12] No exact figure can be given for the number of people saved on visas procured by the Refugee and Immigration Division, but it was certainly in the thousands.

The Refugee and Immigration Division also played a major role in bringing to America many of the Torah giants who would transform American Orthodoxy in the coming decades. Most of them came to America on above-quota Special Emergency Visitors Visas, which were reserved for people of singular distinction and did not count in the regular immigration quotas. Vaad Hatzalah was originally created for the express purpose of raising the funds to bring these leading Torah figures to America. But the immense paperwork involved in each visa request and making the case for the unique contribution that the applicant could make to the United States fell naturally to the Refugee and Immigration Division due to its experience in visa work.

The war years were one long fund-raising campaign by the Youth Council on behalf of Jews in Europe. "Sympathy Won't Help — Money Will," one of the Youth Council's fund-raising slogans, pretty much summarizes all these activities. The Youth Council did whatever it could to respond to the pleas for funds from the Sternbuchs in Switzerland, Rabbi Michoel Ber Weissmandl in Slovakia, and Dr. Jacob Griffel in Turkey for the various rescue plans they were continually hatching. The largest of the Youth Council fund-raising campaigns was launched in January 1944 in response to a series of telegrams from Rabbi Weissmandl, his father-in-law, the Nitra Rav, and the Satmar Rav describing the possibility of bringing thousands of Jews hiding in the

---

11. Ibid., p. 249.
12. Not every visa resulted in a family being saved. Obtaining a visa did not necessarily represent the end of a family's travails. There still remained the matter of securing passage to America. Too frequently by the time the visa was obtained it could no longer be used because of changing military circumstances.

> ORTHODOX TRIBUNE
>
> ## Sympathy Won't Help Them---Money Will!
>
> **THE CONSCIENCE OF EVERY JEW SPEAKS:**
>
> # "DO SOMETHING!"
>
> **Here is something practical that YOU can do:**
>
> The Refugee - Immigration Division of Agudath Israel Youth Council has since the outbreak of war been directly instrumental in the rescue of thousands of Jewish lives from Nazi extermination. The Refugee - Immigration Division is carrying on its titanic task of saving human souls despite the difficulties of war conditions, at a cost of tremendous sums of money.
>
> *YOU, Through a Contribution, Can Help Save Human Lives!*
>
> **DON'T WAIT! THE JEWS IN DANGER CANNOT WAIT!**
>
> **ACT IN TIME!**
>
> **ENDORSEMENTS**
>
> .... It is impossible to fully evaluate the wonderful life-saving work of the Refugee and Immigration Division of Agudath Israel Youth Council during the past few years. Their endeavours and accomplishments in redeeming the lives of our unfortunate brethren and sisters; their energetic intervention with the heads of governments; and their ever-ready helping hand to physically and spiritually rehabilitate those refugees who have reached safe shores are indeed most praiseworthy. It is the duty of every Jew to rally to their support in this hour of emergency....
> —The Union of Orthodox Rabbis of the United States and Canada
>
> .... I want to bring to public attention the extreme importance of the holy work of the Refugee and Immigration Division of Agudath Israel Youth Council. They have already saved many souls from the evil clutches of Naziism, and their self-sacrificing work in every field of refugee and immigration affairs today is a great light in this world of darkness. It is an all-important "mitzvah" to give them immediately the necessary financial means to continue their vital efforts, and all those who do so will be blessed by our Father in Heaven....
> RABBI ELIEZER SILVER, Chief Rabbi of Cincinnati, Ohio
>
> **THE REFUGEE - IMMIGRATION DIVISION**
>
> - Uses all the forces at its command to bring those who lurk in the shadow of death to a haven of refuge
> - Is in constant contact with government heads everywhere to rescue Jewish lives.
> - Brings aid and succor to those of our brethren fortunate enough to escape to neutral countries.
> - Helps in the rehabilitation of those whom G-d has brought to the safe shores of America.
> - Fills the physical and spiritual need of the many tormented Jewish men, women and children who have found temporary shelter in newly established settlements in far-flung corners of the globe.
> - Brings constant help and succor to our destitute brethren in danger zones throughout the world.
>
> **ENDORSEMENTS**
>
> .... In this tragic era in which our brethren are being slaughtered so innocently, you of the Refugee and Immigration Division of Agudath Israel Youth Council, were those who redeemed their blood, so much like angels of salvation. You are writing a page in Jewish history with your remarkable work in the field of refugees and immigration, and I trust that in this eventful hour American Jewry will fully realize its duty and come to your help substantially....
> RABBI SHLOMO HEIMAN, Dean of Mesifta Torah Vodaath
>
> .... It gives me great pleasure to endorse the work of the Refugee and Immigration Division of the Agudath Israel Yuoth Council. I have seen myself the very excellent work that you are doing. Your quiet but effective way has brought untold good on behalf of our refugee brethren and sisters.
> RABBI HERBERT S. GOLDSTEIN, West Side Institutional Synagogue
>
> *This Is a Race of Time Against Death! Minutes Count--Help NOW!*
>
> Send your generous contribution in check, cash, or money order to:
>
> **REFUGEE - IMMIGRATION DIVISION AGUDATH ISRAEL YOUTH COUNCIL OF AMERICA, Inc.**
>
> 113 West 42nd Street,   New York 18, N. Y.

forests on the Polish-Hungarian border to safety in Hungary. The price: $250 per person. In response to a tearful Shabbos morning plea from Rabbi Gedaliah Schorr in the Zeirei *minyan* at 616 Bedford Avenue, all the yeshivos and day schools in New York were closed for 72 hours, as youngsters fanned out all over the city in search of money. Within a few short weeks, the various Agudah groups in America transferred $100,000 to Rabbi Weissmandl via Isaac Sternbuch in Switzerland.

    Throughout the war, the Youth Council was the first address to contact for those who had managed to find refuge in far-flung places around the globe. In 1944, President Franklin Roosevelt signed a special order permitting 1,000 war refugees who had succeeded in reaching neutral territory to be interned in the United States in Fort Oswego, 35 miles north of Syracuse. A combined delegation of the Agudath Israel Youth Council and Agudath Israel of America, including Mike Tress and Rabbi Sherer, visited Fort Oswego to assess the needs of the refugees. The two organizations undertook to establish a kosher kitchen for more than 200 religious refugees.[13]

Reaching Out to the Survivors

ONE OF THE YOUTH COUNCIL'S MAJOR WARTIME PROJECTS WAS the Jewish Servicemen's Bureau, through which the organization had established contacts with hundreds of Orthodox servicemen fighting abroad. As soon as the war ended in Europe, that network of contacts was activated. On June 5, 1945, Mike Tress wrote to all those with whom the Servicemen's Bureau had been in contact urging them to send the names of survivors with whom they had met and the names of any known relatives the survivors had in America. He also sought detailed information on the physical and mental state of the *shearis hapleitah* (survivors).

Orthodox servicemen responded to that request for information with an outpouring of personal accounts of the bitterness of the *shearis hapleitah*. Three months after liberation, they reported, the major Jewish relief organizations had not yet established any presence in Europe. No food arrived to remedy the survivors terrible malnutrition, and as winter approached they lacked suitable clothes to keep themselves warm. Above all, the sense of having been abandoned by the Jewish world led to widespread depression among the survivors.

One group, however, did not abandon them: Zeirei Agudath Israel. The Orthodox servicemen were the means by which Zeirei was able to reassure the *shearis hapleitah* that there was at least one group in America that was profoundly concerned with them. The quickest way of demonstrating that concern was sending what the survivors needed most: food, *tashmishei kodesh,* and items that could be resold for high prices on the black market, such as cigarettes and nylon stockings. The Army Postal Office (APO) became the vehicle for Zeirei to reach the

---

13. The two groups were separate until 1948 when they finally merged. The name Agudath Israel Youth Council was something of a misnomer. By the time of the merger, for instance, Mike Tress, the head of the Youth Council, was already in his late 30's, as were most of the leading lay people in the organization. The Youth Council, which was primarily composed of American-born or American-raised Jews, was the far more dynamic of the two organizations.

shearis hapleitah long before the major Jewish relief organizations were able to set up their distribution networks.

Use of Jewish soldiers and chaplains to distribute foodstuffs and other vital necessities via the APO certainly put the army postal system to a use for which it was never intended, and may have been illegal, but the utter desperation of the survivors overcame such niceties. Within four months of the end of fighting in the European theater, the Youth Council had shipped 129,000 pounds of food and 155,000 pounds of clothing, together with 500 pairs of *tefillin*, 2,000 *Siddurim*, 1,200 *Chumashim*, and 20 *chalafim* (knives) for kosher *shechitah*. Lieutenant Meyer Birnbaum, who was stationed in the Munich area, where there were four large camps for displaced persons, received 3,000 packages in one month, and required a truck to distribute the contents among the four DP camps.

The Youth Council took over a rat-infested store on the Lower East Side to serve as a packaging headquarters. The packing center remained in use for two years after the war's end. Long tables were set up at which the packages were filled in conveyor-belt fashion. Five or six volunteers could in this fashion pack between 500 and 600 five-pound parcels a day for transmission through the APO. In addition, Mike Tress arranged with the Red Cross to deliver food to Jews behind the Iron Curtain from their relatives in the United States. The lines of Jews bringing packages for relatives in Hungary and Romania often stretched around the block on which the packing house was located.

In time, the volume of foodstuffs and other material distributed in Europe by the Joint Distribution Committee would dwarf anything the fledgling Youth Council could provide. But that did not diminish the pioneering achievement of the Youth Council: providing assurance to the Jewish survivors who had endured the unendurable that they were not forgotten.

Rabbi Sherer played an important role in conveying this message. Since he was an eloquent writer in Yiddish, as well as English, Mike Tress gave him the primary responsibility for communicating with the *shearis hapleitah* in the DP camps in the British and American zones. Mike Tress spent nearly two months in the Displaced Persons camps, in the uniform of the United Nations Relief and Rehabilitation Agency (UNRRA), from early December 1945 to late January 1946. He slept in the *lagers* (barracks) with the survivors, and became their great hero. But until Mike's arrival, Rabbi Sherer's name was, by virtue of his fre-

Survivors at the Feldafing DP camp send a Rosh Hashanah greeting to Rabbi Sherer and the Youth Council

quent letters, the best known to those who attempted to reconstitute Agudah groups in the various DP camps.

Above all, the survivors wanted to leave what they called the *farsholtenne land*, the accursed country. Most wanted to go to Palestine, but the gates were closed. Bringing as many Jews as possible to the United States became one of the Youth Council's major activities in the five years after the war. The Refugee and Immigration Division set up a special unit to compile the names of survivors and to connect them with relatives in the States. Within a few months of liberation, a list of 35,000 survivors in the various DP camps had already been compiled, and the Refugee and Immigration Division reunited 500 survivors with relatives in the States.

As the horror of the Holocaust began to sink in on American Jewry, the Youth Council found it much easier to garner support from the non-religious community than it had been during the war. Mike Tress took Lieutenant Meyer Birnbaum, still in uniform and sporting a chest full of combat medals, to secular Jewish groups to give a firsthand account of what he had witnessed in the liberation of Buchenwald and of the state of Jews in the DP camps. Such techniques netted over 4,000 affidavits of financial support in the first year after liberation, which was far more than the Youth Council ever managed to gather during the war.

Given the limited immigration slots available through the normal visa process, the Youth Council tried to bring in as many as possible under above-quota provisions, such as those for clergymen and academics. Congregations across the country were encouraged to send employment contracts for assistant rabbis languishing in Europe. And yeshivos did the same for newly created positions of professors of Talmud.

The Refugee and Immigration Division worked on the premise that it was much easier to secure permanent visas for survivors once they were already in the United States. To that end, student and visitors' visas were exploited for the purpose of bringing as many Jews from Europe as possible. Yeshivas Torah Vodaath, for instance, filed papers expressing its willingness to take in an additional 300 students, despite the fact that the entire student body at the time numbered no more than 200. Other post-high-school Bais Yaakov seminaries and yeshivos followed suit.

The Youth Council created events in order to have a plausible cover for applications for visitor's visas. One such stratagem involved inviting between 250 and 300 survivors to the United States as delegates to Agudah-sponsored conferences.

Many moving scenes took place as the survivors began arriving in America. One that Rabbi Sherer recounted frequently involved Beirach Rubinson, who came to America on the *SS Marine Flasher*, the first boat to bring survivors from the Displaced Persons camps. Rubinson appeared like an apparition one morning at the Youth Council offices, as Mike Tress and Rabbi Sherer sat discussing the tasks of the day. He entered — a 70-pound skeleton — and described how he had lost his wife and children to the gas chambers.

And then suddenly, he began singing in a low, haunting voice the words of *Tehillim* (119:49-51): "זְכָר דָּבָר לְעַבְדֶּךָ — Remember [Your] word to Your servant, עַל אֲשֶׁר יִחַלְתָּנִי — through which You have give me cause to hope. זֹאת נֶחָמָתִי בְעָנְיִי — This is my consolation in my affliction; כִּי אִמְרָתְךָ חִיָּתְנִי — for Your word has given me life. זֵדִים הֱלִיצֻנִי עַד מְאֹד — Insolent sinners have derided me greatly, מִתּוֹרָתְךָ לֹא נָטִיתִי — [but] from Your Torah I have not swerved."

He sang these words over and over again. And as he did, he took the

Mike Tress (center, seated) and Rabbi Sherer (left, second row) with a group of refugees. Beirach Rubinson is seated to the left of Mike.

hands of Mike Tress and Rabbi Sherer, and began dancing with them. Tears poured down their cheeks at the sight of a man who had lost everything, and yet could still rejoice in that he had not lost his connection to Torah.

Rabbi Sherer turned to his cousin and said, "With such *ruach* [spirit] these dry bones will yet live again." That was true of Mr. Rubinson, who eventually built a new family in America. He became, in time, a symbol as well for the rebirth of an entire generation of survivors.[14]

Going National

THOUGH THE DEMANDS OF WARTIME RESCUE AND RELIEF WORK drained most of the money and manpower of the Youth Council, the development of a national movement of Torah-true Jews was not ignored. In truth, the two could not be separated. From the beginning, the efforts of the Youth Council would have been impossible without a cadre of dedicated young volunteers. In the early years of visa work, for instance, virtually all the laborious typing of the four-foot-long visa forms that had to be filled out in sextuplicate was done by young women. The packing of food packages for trapped Polish the Jewish in the early days of the war, and the even

---

14. Rabbi Sherer related this incident in his Introduction to the Agudath Israel of America-produced volume, *Ashes to Renewal*.

Chapter Three: Getting Started □ 103

Rabbi Shimon Schwab addressing an Agudah dinner. Seated (l-r): Rabbi Sherer, Mike Tress, Nathan Hausman

larger packing operations for the Jewish *shearis hapleitah* (survivors) after the war, were also almost exclusively volunteer operations. All this would have been unthinkable without a movement producing a reservoir of committed youth.

Overseeing the many levels of organizational activities was one of Rabbi Sherer's primary tasks from his arrival in the Youth Council offices. That work flourished at every level. By 1944, for instance, the three-and-a-half-day convention on the sparse grounds of Camp Agudah in Ellenville, New York attracted 500 delegates. The conventions focused heavily on the work of the Youth Council and Agudah ideology. The main speeches at the 1943 convention, for instance, were all devoted to the fundamentals of Agudah ideology.

The ranks of Zeirei, Bnos, and Pirchei continued to swell during the war. A 1947 letter to the State Department, in support of an application for 75 special visas for immigrant rabbis to serve as teachers and field directors (though almost certainly a bit exaggerated), listed 13,000 members of the combined organizations: 3,700 Zeirei members (18-35); 2,600 Bnos members (18-35); 4,400 Pirchei members (6-18), and 2,300 Junior Bnos members.

The internal organizational work was relatively low budget, even for the perpetually stressed coffers of the Youth Council. That the Youth Council undertook the creation of a summer camp in the midst of the war, however, was nothing short of amazing. Rabbi Sherer was still studying in Baltimore when Camp Agudah opened its doors for the first time in the summer of 1942 in Ferndale, New York. But he was from the start one of the most ardent boosters of the camp. As he put it in a letter to Mike Tress on May 7, 1942, when a campsite had still not been found, "This Camp, at *all* costs, must become a reality — it is the *best* medium to 'save' scores of out-of-town boys." Rabbi Sherer avidly recruited campers from among the Pirchei boys with whom he had contact in Baltimore.

In its early years, Camp Agudah could have been justly called Camp Kiruv (before, of course, the latter term was even known). A very large percentage of the boys came from areas outside of New York City where there was as yet no yeshivah. At the most, they attended after-school Talmud Torahs, where they learned how to read Hebrew and a bit of *Chumash*. Approximately half the campers in those years did not come from *shomer Shabbos* homes.

Camp Agudah was explicitly conceived as a means of attracting boys to come study in yeshivah. As soon as camp was over, the counselors would disperse to different cities in an effort to convince parents to register their sons for yeshivah in the coming year. Those efforts bore fruit. A hundred boys were convinced to enroll in yeshivah from the 1943 session alone, and 200 overall from the first three years. Until at least 1956, it was still the practice for counselors to hit the road for two weeks after camp to recruit out-of-town boys to yeshivah.

Getting Out the Message

FROM THE BEGINNING, MIKE TRESS AND RABBI SHERER VIEWED Camp Agudah as a vehicle for instilling the Agudah ideology, which they saw as an essential element in creating a broad-based popular movement. In that regard, they were probably disappointed. Meanwhile the primary indoctrination in Agudah ideology came through *Orthodox Youth*, founded in 1940, and its successor *Orthodox Tribune*, whose first issue appeared in May-June 1943.

Though Rabbi Sherer did not write any signed articles for *Orthodox Tribune*, as he had for *Orthodox Youth*, he served as the de facto editor of the monthly journal. That experience was the beginning of a lifelong

The inaugural issue of the *Orthodox Tribune*, May-June 1943.

commitment to the crucial role of a magazine in any ideological movement, such as Agudath Israel of America.

In article after article, *Orthodox Tribune* hammered home the major points of Agudah ideology, and highlighted the differences between Mizrachi and Agudah. The ideals that *Orthodox Tribune* emphasized in countless ways were Rabbi Sherer's own: the unity of *Klal Yisrael*, the obligation of every individual Jew to commit him or herself to the *Klal*, fealty to *daas Torah*.

The Agudah ideologues in the *Orthodox Tribune*, most of them products of the pre-war German Agudah, emphasized that Judaism itself is based on a collective identity. As Rabbi Dr. Leo Breslauer put it:

> The Torah itself frowns upon anyone who dares to approach it singly, and refers him first to the community. It is G-d Himself Who

insists upon the foregoing affirmation by every Jew of our *collective trusteeship* of His will …. Not to individuals [was the Torah given], but to **a people**, to **His people**.

The duty of every Jew to *Klal Yisrael* was a frequently reiterated theme. Rabbi Shlomo Rottenberg, another immigrant from Europe, gave the idea its most forceful expression. In the wake of the destruction of European Jewry, he wrote: *"They died for our people! We have to live for our people! No more individual life! There is only Jewish life!* This is *our* duty!"[15]

That collective Jewish life must be based on Torah, and the leadership of the Jewish people vested in "those most learned in Torah," was another constant theme. On that point, Agudah could not make peace with Zionism in any form, for the Zionist vision was one in which Torah observance was reduced to a mere matter of individual taste. Zionism insisted on a political sphere independent of Torah, and outside its purview. That was anathema to Agudah thinkers such as Dr. Isaac Breuer, Rabbi Samson Raphael Hirsch's grandson:

> … The first aim of Zionism is the establishment of a secular sphere within the Jewish nation … Whether this sphere is great or small … is not the issue. The determining fact must be that the Jewish nation shall voluntarily get away from G-d and the Torah at some point.[16]

The singing of *Hatikvah* as a Jewish national anthem and the use of the Zionist flag were such burning issues in those days because they signaled acceptance or rejection of the Zionist conception of Jewish nationhood and the existence of a political realm independent of Torah. While still a yeshivah student in Baltimore, Rabbi Sherer wrote to *Orthodox Youth* to protest the way in which the Zionist flag, adopted by the Basel Convention, "an infamous gathering of [those] … for whom the very mention of *tefillin,* Shabbos …, *kashrus,* and *gedolei Yisrael* [were] anathema," had become "the symbol of the holy martyr people of Israel."[17]

Hints of Discontent

THE PRESSURES OF THE YOUTH COUNCIL WORK DURING THE WAR years were overwhelming. The organization labored under constant debts. Salaries were small and usually paid late.

Besides the financial pressures, there are indications that Rabbi Sherer did not feel that his talents

---

15. Rabbi Shlomo Rottenberg, "Their Inheritance — Our Goal," *Orthodox Youth,* April 1943, p. 3.
16. "Dr. Isaac Breuer on His Sixtieth Birthday," *Orthodox Tribune,* March 1944, p. 3.
17. Martin Nerl, letter in "What They Write," *Orthodox Youth,* February 1942, p. 3.

were being fully utilized in his first years in the Youth Council. Despite the rapid growth of the Youth Council office during the war years, most of the growth in staff was at the secretarial level. The Youth Council had little money to spend on professional employees. With Mike Tress bearing almost the entire load of fund-raising, it was left to Rabbi Sherer to oversee virtually all the office work.

The preponderance of routine administrative tasks was hard on the idealistic young man in a hurry to change the world. Minutes of an October 5, 1944 meeting of the Executive Board of the Youth Council hint to his dissatisfaction. From the minutes, it appears that he had noted his discontent and discussed resigning. Though the immediate crisis had already passed, the issue was far from dead. In the words of the minutes, "A committee met with Rabbi Sherer in reference to his remaining as Executive Director of the organization, and it seems that Rabbi Sherer would continue ... if an office manager would be employed to relieve him of managing the office detail work, and thus enable him to devote himself to work of a more organizational character."[18]

Three years later, the financial pressures of a growing family[19] persuaded Rabbi Sherer to resign and go into the lighting fixture and electric supply business under the name Genuine Electric. In a November 26, 1947 letter to Mr. Solomon Septimus, chairman of the Executive Board of the Agudath Israel Youth Council, Rabbi Sherer wrote, "In accordance with my notification of one-half year ago, I profoundly regret that reasons beyond my control compel my resignation from my position of Executive Director of our organization, effective Monday, December 1, 1947." Rabbi Sherer added that he had intended to leave earlier, but had put off doing so because of the "critical financial position of our organization." He concluded with expressions of his readiness to continue to "give of everything I possess for this organization — the best cause in Jewish life today."

Rabbi Sherer's presence in the Youth Council was missed greatly, especially by Mike Tress. Over the next year, the Youth Council and Agudath Israel of America finally merged into one organization, with Tress assuming leadership of the combined organization.[20] In an

---

18. Minutes of October 5, 1944.
19. See Chapter 4 — Marriage.
20. By the time of the merger, Mike Tress was already in his late 30's, as were most of the leaders of the organization, so the name Agudath Israel Youth Council was something of a misnomer.

> November 26, 1947
>
> Mr. Solomon Septimus, Chairman
> Executive Board
> Agudath Israel Youth Council
> 113 West 42nd Street
> New York 18, N.Y.
>
> Dear Chaver Septimus:
>
> In accordance with my notification of one-half year ago, I profoundly regret that reasons beyond my control compel my resignation from my position of Executive Director of our organization, effective Monday, December 1, 1947.
>
> As you know, I had intended to leave my position many months ago, but continued putting off the actual day of resignation because of the critical financial position of our organization. However, at this time, health reasons do not permit my continuing my duties beyond the above date.
>
> You understand, of course, that this action on my part does not in any fashion stem from my relations to the organization, which I humbly served to the best of my ability these past five years.
>
> I would appreciate your handing this resignation to the Executive Board at the meeting this Monday, December 1st and that you save me much distress and embarrassment by immediately accepting it without discussion.
>
> I trust that you will appreciate that I have no other choice in this matter and you may rest assured that I will always unstintingly give of everything I possess for this organization -- the best cause in Jewish life today.
>
> Very sincerely yours,
>
> Rabbi Morris Sherer

"... I profoundly regret that reasons beyond my control compel my resignation .... I will always unstintingly give of everything I possess for this organization —the best cause in Jewish life today."

October 1, 1948 letter to Mr. Herman Treisser, a leading member of the Executive Board, Mike wrote, "[W]e miss the efforts of Rabbi Sherer very, very much — more so now than ever before. The burden of reorganization and dealing with the different groups and committees is falling to a large extent on my shoulders and many times I am just about ready to 'throw in the sponge.'"

A few months in business convinced Rabbi Sherer that his family's financial future looked bright. After approximately a year in business, however, he was invited to a meeting at which a number of *gedolei Torah* were present. They informed him that *Klal Yisrael* needed him too much, and that he must leave his business. He requested a year to recoup his initial investment and to sell off his inventory, but they told him that his presence was too urgently needed. When he

---

The leadership of Agudath Israel consisted primarily of an older generation of European rabbis. Rabbi Eliezer Silver, the head of Agudath Israel, was also the head of Agudas HaRabbonim.

Relationships were frequently tense prior to the merger. The Youth Council, which was the more active organization of the two, commanded the support of most of the great European rabbis who arrived during the war, such as Rabbi Reuven Grozovsky and Rabbi Aharon Kotler. Thus after the merger, Mike Tress became president of the combined organization under the name Agudath Israel of America.

returned from the meeting, he told his wife, "Deb, it's back to bread and water."[21]

There was at least one tangible result from Rabbi Sherer's year in business. His secretary in Genuine Electric was a young woman named Mollie Bienstock from a *shomer Shabbos* home in the Bronx. Rabbi Sherer continually urged her to marry a *ben Torah*. Nothing in her public school background (which was the norm in those days) had prepared her for the idea, but she was so impressed with the way Rabbi Sherer conducted himself in every sphere that she decided that she wanted to marry a *"ben Torah"* like Rabbi Sherer.[22]

Four years after his brief time in business, Rabbi Sherer received the offer of the rabbinic position that he had hoped for when he first returned to New York from Baltimore. His father-in-law, Rabbi Fortman, had suffered a debilitating stroke, while still in his mid-50's. Rabbi Sherer assumed his duties for approximately six months. But Rabbi Fortman never recovered and passed away in February 1951 (27 *Shevat* 5711) at 55. The members of Congregation Kenesseth Israel, known as the White Shul, then one of the most prestigious shuls in the New York area, offered Rabbi Sherer the position of rabbi at the same salary his father-in-law had received.

At a time when his salary from Agudath Israel barely covered fish on Shabbos, Rabbi Sherer was greatly tempted by the offer. In addition, Rebbetzin Fortman was eager to see her son-in-law in the position that her husband had held. But Rabbi Sherer told her that he would have to first consult Rabbi Aharon Kotler, and that he would do whatever Reb Aharon instructed him.

Rabbi Aharon Kotler responded succinctly, *"Bishum oifen nisht* — not under any circumstances. No White Shul and no single shul. I have much bigger plans for you." And so he did.

Rebbetzin Fortman was sorely disappointed when Rabbi Sherer turned down the White Shul's offer. Not until 10 years later, when his picture appeared on the front page of the March 30, 1961 *The New York Times'* metropolitan section, with a long story about his congressional testimony the previous day, did Rebbetzin Fortman admit, "I saw what

---

21. Mrs. Chavie (Langer) Galinsky, Rabbi Sherer's granddaughter.
22. She married Rabbi Ephraim Kamin, who learned in Yeshivas Chaim Berlin under Rabbi Yitzchak Hutner and Rabbi Yaakov Moshe Shurkin. Their son Rabbi Dovid Kamin became a close *talmid* of Rabbi Shneur Kotler in Lakewood, and subsequently a highly respected ninth-grade rebbi in the Rabbi Jacob Joseph Mesivta in Edison, New Jersey, where he has taught three of Rabbi Sherer's grandsons.

a *Kiddush Hashem* you made. It seems Reb Aharon was right."

When retelling the story of his mother-in-law's change of heart after the appearance of *The New York Times'* article, Rabbi Sherer would always add wryly, "Never underestimate the power of the press. What Reb Aharon Kotler could not convince my mother-in-law of in 1951, the mighty *New York Times* succeeded in doing in 1961."

On-the-Job Training

DESPITE SOME DISCONTENT IN HIS EARLY YEARS IN AGUDATH Israel, Rabbi Sherer would acknowledge later that the experience he accumulated was invaluable. As a consequence of being forced to take on every task in the office, he knew how every single aspect of the organization functioned. As the organization grew, and new employees were added, he could always explain to each new employee exactly what his job entailed and how he should get started. When, for instance, Agudath Israel hired Rabbi Yitzchak Brandriss as its first full-time director of public relations in the early '80s, Rabbi Sherer could guide him step-by-step in his new role, since for more than 30 years he had personally written virtually every press release or other promotional material put out by Agudath Israel of America.

He was there at the beginning, when the organizational framework was being put in place; indeed, he created much of that framework. As

L-r: Rabbi Yaakov Kamenetsky, Rabbi Aharon Kotler, Rabbi Eliezer Silver, Mike Tress (speaking), Rabbi Sherer

a consequence, he knew every single person ever connected to Agudath Israel in any fashion. Every aspect of the organization was as familiar to him as the streets of Neharde'a and Pumbedisa were to the *Amoraim*.

In those early years in the Youth Council, he and Mike Tress could well have been called Mr. Inside and Mr. Outside. The latter was the public face of the Youth Council, the charismatic figure who first attracted most of the young people involved with the organization. Whenever there was an emergency fund-raising drive, Mike would be the one to make the appeals in meeting after meeting. At conventions and small gatherings, he was always the featured speaker, the one who aroused the latent idealism of his listeners and motivated them to work for the *Klal*.

In every picture of Mike Tress from that period, Moshe Sherer is invariably found near his side. The latter worked behind the scenes making sure that the office functioned smoothly and handling the administrative work, even as Mike bore the burden of spreading the organization's message and keeping its head above water financially. Those who dealt with the Youth Council were sure to know Rabbi Moshe Sherer, as well as Mike Tress.

All those who met Rabbi Sherer, even in his early 20's, recognized that they were in the presence of someone of considerable force of personality and talent, who was bound to make his mark in the coming years. When Yosef Friedenson, almost an exact contemporary of Rabbi Sherer, first met him in 1952, he was struck by both his unusual competence and his forcefulness as a speaker.

The *gedolim*, chief among them Rav Aharon Kotler, who had insisted that he return to the organization and subsequently prevented him from leaving, had no doubts as to how valuable a resource he was for *Klal Yisrael*.

The great leader of the Agudath Israel World Organization from its inception, Moreinu Yaakov Rosenheim, told David Turkel, a longtime associate and confidant, in one of their final conversations, "I met a young man by the name of Moshe Sherer .... He will put, I am convinced, Agudath Israel on the map of Jewish America. Sherer is capable and devoted. The kind of man we always needed."[23]

In time, Rabbi Sherer would become the great successor to Moreinu Yaakov Rosenheim, as the leader whose name is inevitably associated with Agudath Israel as an international movement.

---

23. Memoir of David Turkel, June 25, 1995.

Chapter Four

MARRIAGE

LESS THAN A YEAR AFTER COMMENCING HIS PUBLIC LIFE, Rabbi Sherer's personal life also entered a new stage. On *Rosh Chodesh Kislev* (Sunday, November 28, 1943), he married Debby (Devorah) Fortman, the daughter of Rabbi Shimshon Zelig Fortman, the rabbi of Congregation Kenesseth Israel ("The White Shul") in Far Rockaway. The *kallah* was working at the time as a secretary in the Zeirei offices. According to a longstanding family joke, she did not meet Rabbi Sherer's exacting standards as a secretary, but he was too kindhearted to fire her. The only alternative was to marry her and take advantage of the Youth Council's anti-nepotism policy.

For their more than 54 years of marriage, Mrs. Sherer provided her husband with the calm, well-run home in which he could find refuge from the pressures and people besieging him day and night. She adopted customs from his mother's home, such as always setting the Shabbos

ב"ה

הרב זעליג פּאַרטמאַן ורעיתו
מרת בתי' שערער

מתכבדים אנחנו בזה לבקש את קרובינו ומיודעינו לקחת חבל

בשמחתנו ביום כלולת בנינו היקרים שיחיו

החתן המהולל

הרב ר' משה שיחי'

עב"ג הכלה המהוללה

מרת דבורה תחי'

אשר תהי' אי"ה בשטו"מ

ביום א' פרשת ויצא, ראש חודש כסלו, תש"ד

בשעה 6:00 בערב

באולם עמפייר מענאַר

70 טהאַטפּאַרד עווניו

The only copy the Sherers had of their wedding invitation was the one Moreinu Yaakov Rosenheim had kept in his files.

Rabbi Moshe and Devorah (Debby) Sherer

table on Thursday night, to make him feel as comfortable as possible. Rabbi Sherer always took particular pains to stress in both private and public just how much he owed to his wife's support and to her devotion to doing everything she could do to assist him in his work.

In showing respect and appreciation for his wife's efforts, Rabbi

The *chassan* and *kallah* with Mrs. Basya Sherer during their engagement

Sherer had some excellent models. As a *bachur* in Ner Israel, he had once been at the Rosh Yeshiva's Shabbos table when the Rebbetzin served soup that had been somehow oversalted to the point of being inedible. Yet Rabbi Ruderman ate it with total composure and gave no indication that anything was amiss.

A few years later, shortly after their marriage, the Sherers were visiting her parents' home for Shabbos. Rabbi Yosef Shlomo Kahaneman, the Ponevezher Rav, was visiting that same Shabbos. Mrs. Sherer, still something of a novice in the kitchen, was assigned the task of preparing the cholent. Unfortunately, she burned it badly. The Ponevezher Rav, however, insisted on eating the burnt cholent and even praised it lavishly.[1]

---

1. To this day, Mrs. Sherer cannot help laughing when she thinks about the way the Ponevezher Rav went out of his way to praise the cholent.

Another Torah great who took the time to teach the young couple some of the basics of *"a Yiddishe shtub* — a Jewish home" was Rabbi Sherer's mentor from his youth, Rabbi Gedaliah Schorr. Rabbi Schorr had played a role in the *shidduch,* and he would frequently drop in on the young couple when he passed their apartment on the way home from Torah Vodaath at night.

The first time he did so was the day after *Sheva Berachos* were completed. Reb Gedaliah told the young couple that he wanted to inaugurate their new apartment with a *dvar Torah,* and asked Rabbi Sherer for a particular tractate. Rabbi Sherer replied that his *"chasan's Shas"* had just been delivered that day and was still in boxes. "A Jewish home already lived in, and the *Shas* is still in boxes?" Reb Gedaliah asked. He insisted on opening all the boxes until the volume he needed was found. When it was located, Reb Gedaliah opened it and found a few of the

With Rabbi Gedaliah Schorr in the 1970s

At the wedding of Rabbi Eliyahu Moshe Shisgal to Faye Feinstein in 1942. (L-r) Standing: Rabbi Avrohom Yitzchok Shisgal, Rabbi Eliyahu Moshe Shisgal, Rabbi Moshe Feinstein, Rabbi Nissan Waxman, Rabbi Shimshon Zelig Fortman, Rabbi Nechemia Katz, Rabbi Pesach Levovitz. Seated: Rabbi Reuven Levovitz, Yitzchok Katz, Rabbi Michel Feinstein, Rabbi Isaac Small, Reuven Feinstein

pages stuck together. Again he asked, as if in disbelief, "A *Yiddishe shtub* with *bletter* [pages] from *Shas tzugeklept* [stuck together]. It can't be — impossible." Once again the young *chassan* was forced to repeat that this was the first day after *Sheva Berachos* and the *Shas* had just arrived.

When Rabbi Sherer told this story, in later years, his reverence for Reb Gedaliah was unmistakable. He would invariably add, "I can assure you that there was never a day when Reb Gedaliah had a volume of *Shas* in his house in a box or with any pages still attached to one another."[2]

ALONG WITH A LIFE PARTNER, MARRIAGE BROUGHT RABBI SHERER into the family of a genuine *gadol b'Torah*. Mrs. Sherer often joked that

Rabbi Shimshon Zelig HaKohen Fortman

he had married her because he was so enamored of her father. Rabbi Fortman came from the Lithuanian *shtetl* of Starobin. Starobin was a town of *talmidei chachamim* — one local joke had it that the town derived its name from the fact that *Sta-Rabin* means "a hundred rabbis" in Russian. Rabbi Dovid Feinstein, the father of Rabbi Moshe Feinstein, was rav of the town from 1900 until his passing in 1927, and Rabbi Fortman and Reb Moshe were close boyhood friends.

Even among the scholars of Starobin, Shimshon Zelig and his older brother, Yisroel Tanchum, stood out. The Fortman brothers would go on to hold a number of important rabbinic positions in Lithuania, Latvia, and White Russia (Belarus). Shimshon Zelig learned in Yeshivah Eitz

Rabbi Shimshon Zelig Fortman

---

2. In his eulogy for Rabbi Schorr in *Dos Yiddishe Vort*, Rabbi Sherer emphasized that the same Reb Gedaliah who could not imagine a Jewish home without a *Shas* sold his own precious *Shas* in response to a desperate appeal from Rabbi Michoel Ber Weissmandl in Slovakia for funds to save Jewish lives during the Holocaust.

Chaim in Slutsk under Rabbi Isser Zalman Meltzer, where he was the *chavrusah* of the future *gadol hador* Rabbi Elazar Menachem Man Shach. The two continued to correspond after they began their respective rabbinic careers.

Rabbi Sherer's relationship with Rabbi Fortman would serve him well in later years when he had frequent occasion to be in contact with Rabbi Shach. From the first, Rabbi Shach treated him with special warmth as "Zelig Starobiner's *eidem* [son-in-law]."[3]

From an early age, the Fortman brothers were renowned as public speakers, and while they were still in their teens, they helped support their widowed mother by giving *derashos* in the shuls of nearby towns, during the yeshivah *bein hazemanim* (intersession) from their yeshivah

With Rabbi Elazar Menachem Man Shach

---

3. *Motza'ei Shabbos Chol HaMoed Succos* of 5732 (1971), Rabbi Sherer took his son Shimshon Zelig (who is named after his grandfather) to visit Rabbi Shach. The Rosh Yeshivah was already a widower at that time. Nevertheless, he asked the 17-year-old yeshivah student if he had eaten *Melaveh Malkah* yet, and when he heard that he had not, offered to make him scrambled eggs. Shimshon, of course, refused, at which point Rabbi Shach turned to Rabbi Sherer, and said, "He thinks I don't know how to cook." He then turned back to Shimshon and said, "Don't worry, I'm a good cook." His offer of scrambled eggs having been refused again, Rabbi Shach suggested that he would go downstairs to the *makolet* and buy Shimshon some cake and cookies, an offer that was quickly refused.

A conference of rabbis in Lithuania. Rabbi Yisroel Tanchum Fortman is in the front row, third from left.

studies. Their mother Henya Roshka eked out her livelihood selling fruits and vegetables. Once, while her sons were home from yeshivah, a relative of hers happened to be in the store, and noticed some of the local peasants slipping produce into their sacks. He asked her why she did not request her sons to help her in the store to prevent such theft. She replied sharply, "The fruit is mine, and if the peasants are going to steal it, let them steal it. But my husband left me my sons for safekeeping, in order that they should be Torah scholars, and not so they would stand around in my shop."

Rabbi Fortman's oratorical prowess served him well upon his arrival in America. Within six months of his arrival on May 18, 1930, he was offered the position of rabbi of Far Rockaway's Congregation Kenesseth Israel — popularly known as The White Shul — then one of the largest shuls in the New York area.[4] Subsequently, he also taught a homiletics class at Yeshiva Torah Vodaath that Rabbi Sherer would eventually inherit.

Though his abilities as a *darshan* (speaker) had been a major factor in securing the position, he did not content himself with his rhetorical talents in Yiddish. He realized that to maximize his influence on his congregants, particularly the younger generation, he would need to speak English well. He used to pay a Mr. Rabinowitz, the *ba'al korei* (Torah reader) in a nearby shul, to help him learn English. Much of the time, he would read *The New York Times* aloud and Mr. Rabinowitz would correct him. Rabbi Fortman attached so much importance to learning to speak English well that he paid Mr. Rabinowitz the princely sum (for those days) of $5 an hour.[5]

Because he was a Kohen, Rabbi Fortman's livelihood from the rabbinate was limited. In those days, payment for conducting funerals and unveilings constituted a significant part of a rabbi's earnings, and these sources of income were not available to him. In the words of one local wit, he was without "*shteiner* (literally, stones; figuratively, unveilings) and *beiner*" (literally, bones; figuratively, funerals.)

On at least one occasion, Rabbi Fortman's inability to attend funerals resulted in great embarrassment to another rabbi. At the *levayah* (funeral) of a prominent rabbi, a colleague saw Rabbi Fortman standing

---

4. Interestingly, in private conversation, Rabbi Fortman had a pronounced stutter, but as soon as he began to speak in public, it disappeared completely.
5. Rebbetzin Fay Hollander. Rebbetzin Hollander is Mrs. Sherer's younger sister and the wife of Rabbi David B. Hollander *zt"l*, a leader of the American Orthodox rabbinate and prominent activist for more than six decades.

Rabbi Fortman, assisted by Rabbi Sherer, officiating at the wedding of his youngest daughter, Evelyn, to Rabbi Yaakov Kleinman. Rabbi Fortman passed away seven weeks later.

outside Torah Vodaath and asked him what he would say if he were able to deliver a *hesped* (eulogy) inside. Rabbi Fortman offered a *vort* that he would have said about the *niftar* (deceased). As the *aron* (coffin) was being brought out, one of the children of the *niftar* saw Rabbi Fortman, and asked him to say a few words in honor of their father. He proceeded to repeat the *vort* that he had said earlier. What he did not know is that the other rabbi had delivered a *hesped* inside using Rabbi Fortman's *vort*, but failing to attribute it.

Though Rabbi Sherer was himself a gifted speaker by the time he married, he gained a great deal from his father-in-law, and frequently quoted *vertlach* that he had heard from his father-in-law. One *vort* of Rabbi Fortman's concerned the habit of certain rabbis of appropriating the *vertlach* of others without attribution, illustrated by the *maspid* described above.

It was a novel and witty interpretation of the *Gemara* (*Shabbos* 119b) that states that if *Klal Yisrael* would observe two consecutive Shabbasos, then *Klal Yisrael* would be redeemed immediately. According to Rabbi Fortman, those two Shabbasos referred to Shabbos HaGadol and Shabbos Shuvah, the traditional occasions for rabbis to deliver major *derashos* to the entire community. If on those Shabbasos, they would properly credit the *divrei Torah* they were quoting from others, in fulfillment of the rabbinic dictum (*Megillah* 15a) that one who says over *divrei Torah* in the name of the one who said it hastens the *geulah* (Redemption), then *Mashiach* would surely come.

Another *vort* that he heard from his father-in-law would become one of the pillars of Rabbi Sherer's worldview. The Mishnah in *Pesachim* (117b) specifies that one may not drink between the third and fourth cups of wine at the Seder — a proscription that does not apply between any of the other cups of wine. Citing the *Talmud Yerushalmi*, Rashi explains that the prohibition on drinking is in order that he not become drunk and rendered incapable of reciting *Hallel* over the fourth cup.

Each of the Four Cups, Rabbi Fortman pointed out, parallels one of the Torah's four descriptions of Hashem's redemption of the Jewish people from the Egypt. The Third Cup parallels וְגָאַלְתִּי (*I will redeem*) (*Shemos* 6:6), which refers to the actual exodus from Egypt. The Fourth Cup parallels וְלָקַחְתִּי אֶתְכֶם לִי לְעָם (*I will take you to Me as a nation*) (ibid. v. 7), which refers to the completion of the process of Redemption with the giving of the Torah at Sinai. Physical freedom, without using that freedom to connect to its Source, Hashem, is not only incomplete, but dangerous. Thus the Mishnah prohibits drinking between the Third and Fourth Cups out of concern that one will become intoxicated with one's new-found freedom and forget the last, most crucial stage in the process.

At the time he first heard this *vort* from his father-in-law, Rabbi Sherer thought it was a nice explanation of the Mishnah. But with the passage of time, he realized that it cast light on contemporary Jewish life, in which Jews had gained unprecedented levels of physical freedom but had failed to use that freedom to reconnect to Hashem. In modern-day Israel, for instance, the miraculous deliverance in successful wars had not led to a deepened connection to Hashem.[6]

The Ponevezher Rav

RABBI SHERER WAS AN AVID STUDENT OF JEWISH HISTORY AND eager to increase his knowledge of Torah Jewry in Europe prior to the war. As one of the outstanding products of some of the leading Lithuanian yeshivos, Rabbi Fortman provided a living link to a world that Rabbi Sherer could only imagine. Many Lithuanian-born roshei yeshivah naturally gravitated to the Fortman home on their travels to America, sometimes staying for weeks at a time. One of those was the Ponevezher Rav, Rabbi Yosef Shlomo Kahaneman, an old friend of Rabbi Fortman from Europe.

For Rabbi Sherer the opportunity to connect to a rav of the

---

6. *Bishtei Einayim*, p. 36.

At the Agudah Dinner in 1944 (l-r): Rabbi Sherer, Mike Tress, Rabbi Binyomin Zev Hendeles, Rabbi Eliezer Silver, Rabbi Herbert Goldstein, Dr. Isaac Lewin, Rabbi Shimshon Zelig Fortman, Rabbi Shabse Frankel

Ponevezher Rav's stature was a priceless opportunity. An insight from the Ponevezher Rav became one of his guiding lights. The Ponevezher Rav told him that an organization is like a *mentsch* (person). No person ever dies from a lack of money, as long as the animating *neshamah* (soul) is still strong, and so it is with organizations: No Torah institution ever collapses solely because of a lack of money. Only when something is lacking in the *neshamah* of the institution can it be destroyed by financial problems. He counseled Rabbi Sherer to always make sure that the Agudah movement never lost its "*shtarkeh neshamah.*"

In later years, Rabbi Sherer had many occasions to remember the Ponevezher Rav's words. And he always found that when a Torah institution floundered, even when financial problems were the ostensible cause, something else — internal *machlokes* (strife), poor leadership, an inferior staff — had been eating away at the institution first.

One piece of advice from the Ponevezher Rav could well have served as Rabbi Sherer's motto for life. Rabbi Fortman felt that perhaps his idealistic son-in-law's dreams about the future of American Jewry were unrealistic. He feared that Rabbi Sherer was setting impossibly high goals for himself, and would end up feeling himself a failure. But the Rav did not see it that way. He told Rabbi Sherer, "Dream all you want, but don't sleep (*chalem vifil du vilst, aber shlaf nisht*)."[7]

---

7. In later years, Rabbi Sherer would add to the Ponevezher Rav's words, "Dream but with your eyes open."

He never stopped dreaming himself, and enjoyed collecting homiletical gems on the subject. At his grandson Mendy Sherer's bar mitzvah, many decades later, Rabbi Sherer related the story with the Ponevezher Rav, and then added his own insight. The verb "to dream" in Hebrew is based on the same three letters — ח-ל-מ — as the verb "to fight or struggle" — לחם. Those same three letters also form the word for "bread — לֶחֶם." If you have a dream, Rabbi Sherer told his grandson, you must fight for it as if your entire life — your bread, your sustenance — depends upon it.

Rabbi Sherer offered a homiletic insight into why many insert a special supplication regarding dreams into *Bircas Kohanim*, the Priestly Blessing (see *Berachos* 55b and Rav Hai Gaon): Rabbi Sherer suggested that one of the greatest blessings a person can be granted is the ability to dream. *Bircas Kohanim* ends with the blessing that Hashem grant the person שָׁלוֹם, peace. The word שָׁלוֹם is related to שְׁלֵימוּת, completeness and fulfillment, because peace and fulfillment go together. One can only achieve his full potential if he "dreams big," and then prays to have those dreams fulfilled.

Chapter Five

LAYING THE FOUNDATIONS

Reb Aharon's Student

FROM THE TIME THAT RABBI SHERER RETURNED TO AGUDATH Israel until Reb Aharon passed away 13 years later, Reb Aharon took him under his wing and prepared him for future leadership. Rabbi Sherer once offered the following *mashal*: "Imagine that you had the greatest rebbi in the world give you a daily *shiur* for 13 years on the same *amud* of *Gemara*. Well, I was *zocheh* [privileged] to have the greatest rebbi in the world, Rav Aharon Kotler, give me a comprehensive *shiur in Meseches Avodas HaKlal* [Tractate Public Service] for thirteen straight years."

Rabbi Yaakov Kamenetsky once remarked that Reb Aharon was the most committed Agudist — an *emese Agudist* — of all the European-born roshei yeshivah who made their way to America. Reb Aharon had

Rebbi and *talmid*

been a member of the Moetzes Gedolei HaTorah even as a young rosh yeshivah in Kletsk.

Reb Yaakov was then asked: If Reb Aharon was such a committed Agudist, why didn't he educate his *talmidim* to be Agudists? Reb Yaakov answered: "In Reb Aharon's mind, the first great project for American Jewry was implanting the ideal of *Torah l'shmah*, of pure, unadulterated Torah study on the American firmament. Had he been granted more years, his next great project would have been the training of a cadre of committed Agudah activists."

But, Reb Yaakov added, "Reb Aharon did have the chance to train one *talmid* in how to be a devoted effective Agudist and devoted servant of the *Klal*. That *talmid* was Moshe Sherer. And he carried out his mission so well that he has become one of the greatest lay leaders of modern times."[1]

The name Rav Aharon Kotler was pronounced reverentially in the Sherer household. Once when Shimshie was about 5, Reb Aharon called the house and introduced himself only as "Kotler." Shimshie called out, "Daddy, Kotler's on the phone." The lecture he received on *kavod HaTorah* and who Reb Aharon was still rings in his ear.

---
1. Rabbi Kamenetsky told this to Rabbi Nosson Scherman.

A few years later, Rabbi Sherer took Shimshie along to the airport to see Reb Aharon off on a trip. Reb Aharon gave the young boy a *berachah* for success in learning. As soon as they returned home from the airport, Rabbi Sherer wrote out the *berachah* in the original Yiddish and handed the paper to Shimshie, with instructions to cherish it. At one of the biennial conventions of those years at the Pioneer Hotel, a bored Shimshie spent much of his time operating the elevators. Reb Aharon passed by, and after identifying the 6-year-old elevator operator, gave him a *glettel* (gentle caress) on the cheek. Shimshie immediately rushed into the main hall yelling, "Daddy, Daddy, guess what just happened?" Rabbi Sherer pulled his young son close to him on the front dais to hear his story. Then he whispered into his ear, "Don't tell Mommy I told you this, but if I were you, I wouldn't wash my face for a while."

Reb Aharon's guidance frequently drew on his own vast storehouse of experience. Rabbi Sherer never tired of telling stories that Reb Aharon had told him for the edification of a younger generation that never had the privilege of knowing the Rosh Yeshiva. At one Agudah-sponsored affair, one of the speakers spoke very sharply against a prominent public official. Reb Aharon knew that Rabbi Sherer would be writing a press release about the affair the next morning, and he called him to instruct him to omit any mention of that remark. (Rabbi Sherer's trademark care with respect to every public release or letter that went out on the stationery of Agudath Israel of America had its roots in the long hours spent weighing and sifting every word with Reb Aharon.) Rabbi Sherer had already decided to do so, but he was very relieved to receive confirmation from Reb Aharon.

Reb Aharon shared a story to explain his position. A rabbi in Lithuania once wrote an article that was considered to be insulting to the Chofetz Chaim. In response, a number of protest gatherings were held throughout Lithuania. At one of those protests, a speaker quoted a *Gemara*[2] that a particularly brazen person (עַז פָּנִים) is suspected of being a *mamzer*. As soon as the speaker said that, the rabbi who had criticized the Chofetz Chaim became the *nirdaf* (the one being pursued), and the issue of the Chofetz Chaim's *kavod* became secondary. The public dis-

---

2. The source is *Masechta Kallah* 1:15, but it is often cited as *Bava Metzia* (83b) where the *Gemara* states:

"מִדְחָצִיף כּוּלֵי הַאי שְׁמַע מִינָה דִּרְשִׁיעָא הוּא" — since this person acted so brazenly, we know that he is wicked."

cussion shifted to the harsh attack on the offending rabbi. And all the momentum went out of the protests. From this example, Reb Aharon illustrated the importance of always keeping one's language moderate and modulated in any public dispute.

It was a lesson that stuck with Rabbi Sherer, and which he was always careful to follow. In the early 1970s, an Agudath Israel Knesset member threw a Reform prayer book to the floor in the midst of a heated Knesset debate. Rabbi Sherer, who was left to deal with the fallout in the Anglo-Jewish press, wrote to the Knesset member in question "I would never have advised you to let your emotions force you to make such an unreasoned act ...." To another Agudah colleague in Israel, he added, "[A]nything so extreme always has the opposite effect ..." — just the lesson he had absorbed years before from Reb Aharon.

Reb Aharon conveyed to Rabbi Sherer one of the essential elements of a Jewish leader, employing a *vort* based on Rabbi Sherer's name — Moshe. The Talmud (*Sotah* 12b) relates that when Basya, the daughter of Pharaoh first saw a baby's basket floating in the river, she reached out her hand to grab it, even though it was far beyond her reach. Her hand miraculously extended far beyond its normal length, and she was able to grab the basket and pull the infant child to safety. From this incident Moshe derived his name — כִּי מִן הַמַּיִם מְשִׁיתִהוּ (*Shemos* 2:10). When a Jew is crying out for help, said Reb Aharon, we learn from Basya, who stretched out her hand farther than it could possibly reach, that we must try to help and cannot make the excuse that it is futile.[3]

Reb Aharon's closest *talmidim*, such as Rabbi Yitzchak Feigelstock, the Long Beach Rosh Yeshiva, testify to the great confidence that Reb Aharon placed in Rabbi Sherer. But it was Reb Aharon himself who put it best. When Rabbi Sherer visited *Eretz Yisrael* for the first time in 1954, as part of the American delegation to the Knessiah Gedolah of Agudath Israel, he brought with him a letter of introduction to the

---

3. Rabbi Sherer used to say a similar *vort* in the name of "an *adam gadol*." The Midrash (*Shemos Rabbah parashah* 1) states that although Moshe Rabbeinu had ten names, Moshe was the one most beloved by Hashem. Why was Moshe the favorite name? After all, some of the others, such as Yekusiel, refer specifically to Moshe Rabbeinu's special relationship with Hashem.

The "*adam gadol*" answered that the name Moshe embodied a lesson that a future leader of *Klal Yisrael* must always keep in mind. Throughout his life, whenever Moshe Rabbeinu heard his name called, it reminded him of the miracle that occurred when Basya reached out to do something impossible. The lesson for Moshe Rabbeinu and all subsequent generations of Jewish leaders was: When you hear Jews crying out, just as the infant Moshe was crying in the river, you must always try to help. Even when the situation seems utterly helpless, you must try and hope that Hashem will provide the necessary *Siyata d'Shmaya* (Divine assistance).

Brisker Rav from Reb Aharon. Reb Aharon described his young protégé to the Brisker Rav with these words: *"yado k'yadi* — his hand is like my hand."[4]

FROM THE MOMENT HE ARRIVED IN AMERICA, REB AHARON WAS A whirlwind of activity. Besides establishing Bais Medrash Govoha (Lakewood Yeshivah) and implanting the ideal of *kollel* learning, he was involved in a host of communal activities. While the war raged in Europe, saving every possible Jewish life was his constant focus. After the war, he directed himself to the building of Torah life in *Eretz Yisrael*, in particular to the establishment of an independent educational system. Reb Aharon's focus became that of Agudath Israel as well.

On Behalf of Eretz Yisrael

As the *shearis hapleitah* began to rebuild their lives in the years after the war, Agudath Israel of America's overseas activities shifted toward *Eretz Yisrael*. As Mike Tress wrote to Rabbi Yitzchak (Itche) Meyer Levin — the son-in-law of the Imrei Emes of Ger and head of Agudath Israel in Israel — in the fall of 1949, "I would also like you to know that we are reorganizing our work and all our efforts will be directed to practical and positive work in *Eretz Yisrael*."

With Rabbi Itche Meyer Levin (c) and Rabbi Menachem Porush (l)

---
4. Rabbi Sherer used to relate this story to his children with great pride.

The efforts on behalf of the religious community of *Eretz Yisrael* were connected to those on behalf of the survivors of the European inferno. For most of the *shearis hapleitah, Eretz Yisrael* was the preferred choice of places to start anew. From the end of the British Mandate in Palestine, the survivors of Europe, including tens of thousands of religious Jews, made their way to *Eretz Yisrael*. The needs of the newcomers in the late '40s, and of hundreds of thousands of religiously observant immigrants from Arab lands in the early '50s, were far beyond the capacity of the so-called Old *Yishuv* to meet.

The various Agudah groups in *Eretz Yisrael*, in the immediate pre-State period and the following five years, tried to do a great deal: build housing for new immigrants, establish trade schools, found agricultural settlements, and create drop-in centers in major cities for religious soldiers, many of them orphaned during the war. Dormitory educational facilities and youth villages were created for uprooted children from Arab lands and the younger orphans from Europe. The *chareidi* educational system nearly doubled in size in the space of a few years. While these efforts fell far short of the needs of the time, they were nevertheless remarkably ambitious, given the almost total lack of financial resources available for the task.

All of this required huge infusions of cash from North America, and frequent fund-raising trips to the United States by leaders of the Agudah movement in *Eretz Yisrael*. Rabbi Itche Meir Levin drew large

Greeting Israel's president, Zalman Shazar. Rabbi Menachem Porush, Rabbi Shlomo Lorincz and Rabbi Chaskel Besser are in the background.

Chapter Five: Laying the Foundations ☐ 131

crowds wherever he went. Rabbi Menachem Porush and Rabbi Shlomo Lorincz, the leading young activists in the Agudah movement in Israel, also came to America for months at a time to raise money for projects in the Holy Land. Their first stop on any visit was the headquarters of Agudath Israel of America, where they could count on a warm welcome and sound guidance. Agudah branches around the country received the visitors from Israel with open arms.

Rabbi Sherer's organizational skills played a crucial role in arranging the visitors' cross-country trips. Besides providing logistical support for these fund-raising trips, Agudath Israel of America often found itself left with the difficult task of collecting on the pledges. During those years, the basis was laid for the close relationship that Rabbi Sherer enjoyed with Rabbis Lorincz and Porush over nearly half a century. Both men represented Agudath Israel in the Knesset for over 30 years, and during that period they were often in daily contact with Rabbi Sherer.

Mike Tress made key introductions for Rabbis Lorincz and Porush, in particular to Rabbi Herbert Goldstein of the West Side Institutional Synagogue, whose contacts covered the full spectrum of American Orthodoxy and beyond. Rabbi Goldstein and Lester Udell, the long-time president of Rabbi Goldstein's shul, were among the incorporators of Children's Homes for Israel.

Though Children's Homes for Israel was not formally associated with Agudath Israel of America, in order to broaden its fund-raising appeal, most of the money raised went to youth villages founded by Zeirei Agudath Israel or Agudath Israel in Israel. Mike Tress and Rabbi Sherer were among the incorporators, and the day-to-day directors were Heshy Moskowitz, the first editor of *Orthodox Youth*, and Beirach Rubinson, the post-war immigrant who so inspired Rabbi Sherer on his first visit to the Youth Council office.

Nshei Agudath Israel of America was founded in 1947, and from the beginning its primary focus was on *Eretz Yisrael*. At the height of its activities, Nshei was supporting an entire network of 43 nursery schools and kindergartens. During Israel's War of Independence, Agudath Israel conducted a six-month campaign to send food to besieged Jerusalem. The Food for Jerusalem campaign raised $60,000, a large sum of money in those days, and sent over 60,000 pounds of food, including 13,000 pounds of meat.

But by far, the major project of Agudath Israel of America on behalf of the religious community of Israel was Torah Schools for Israel, the fund-raising arm of Chinuch Atzmai. The 1953 Israeli Education Law created a system of non-state but recognized schools. Those schools received approximately 60 percent of their operating budgets from the Israeli government. Besides covering the remaining 40 percent of the operating budget, the independent Chinuch Atzmai schools had to cover the entire cost for those school hours beyond what was offered in the state school system, which were far too little to provide an adequate Torah education. In addition, the cost of renting or purchasing all school premises was the responsibility of the schools themselves or Chinuch Atzmai.

Rabbi Aharon Kotler placed the funding of the Chinuch Atzmai system, which encompassed 268 schools and over 26,000 students, at the top of the agenda of American Orthodoxy. That project naturally became connected to Agudath Israel of America. Torah Schools for Israel shared premises at 5 Beekman Street with Agudath Israel of America, and it occupied a large percentage of both Mike and Rabbi Sherer's time.

In 1955, Reb Aharon decided that Chinuch Atzmai's fund-raising potential would be greater if it was not connected in the public mind with Agudath Israel, and Chinuch Atzmai became an entirely independent organization. Mike Tress and Rabbi Sherer, however, continued to work actively for Chinuch Atzmai.

The Psak of Eleven Roshei Yeshivah

IN TWO AREAS, RABBI SHERER PLAYED A LEADING ROLE FROM HIS earliest days in Agudath Israel of America. He took care of much of the contact with the Agudath Israel World Organization, most of which was handled through letters.[5] In 1954, *Eretz Yisrael* hosted the first Knessiah Gedolah of Agudath Israel since that held in Marienbad in 1937. Mike Tress led the American delegation to the Knessiah Gedolah, but Rabbi Sherer handled the lion's share of the organizational work for the Knessiah Gedolah and the preparations of the American delegation.[6] The extensive preparations for the Fourth Knessiah Gedolah and Rabbi Sherer's first visit to Israel further cemented his relationships with the leadership of the Israeli Agudah movement.

---

5. In a February 13, 1961 letter to Rabbi Jacob Mermelstein detailing the various pressures on him as a consequence of Mike Tress's illness, Rabbi Sherer lists his "previous burdens of helping to run an international movement," in addition to the new ones imposed by the necessity of taking over Mike's work as well. It would appear, then, that the international movement was already part of his bailiwick.

6. Interview with Mr. Yosef Friedenson.

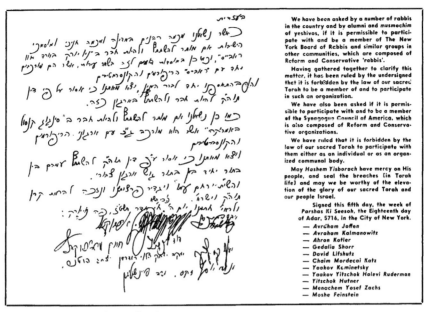

The *psak* of the 11 roshei yeshivah.

Together with Mike Tress, he played a major role in the ideological side of the movement. When, for instance, 11 leading American roshei yeshivah met to formulate their *psak din* of 18 *Adar* 5716 (1956) concerning participation in umbrella organizations which include Reform and Conservative clergymen or organizations, Rabbi Aharon Kotler invited Rabbi Sherer to the meeting and the *psak din* was written in Rabbi Sherer's hand.

The roshei yeshivah had been asked by *musmachim* of their yeshivos and other rabbis for their *psak* on two questions: (1) Is it permissible to participate with and be a member of The New York Board of Rabbis and similiar groups in other communities, which include Reform and Conservative "rabbis"? (2) Is it permissible to participate with and to be a member of the Synagogue Council of America, which include Reform and Conservative organizations? The roshei yeshivah gave the same unequivocal answer to both questions: Participation or membership in such organizations is "forbidden by the law of our sacred Torah."

It was left to Rabbi Sherer to promulgate the *psak din*, and to take all the necessary steps to maximize its impact. The key to the latter lay in convincing the Rabbinical Council of America (RCA), the largest organization of Orthodox rabbis, to formally adopt the *psak din* of the roshei yeshivah as the official policy of the organization. To that end, Rabbi

Sherer worked closely with the "separatist" wing within the RCA.[7]

The problem was that the RCA was already a member of the Synagogue Council of America at the time of the issuance of the *psak din*. The RCA never explicitly rejected the *psak din* of the roshei yeshivah. Rather it simply referred the matter to its Halachah Commission for consideration. More than a decade later the Halachah Commission had still not rendered a decision. In the meantime, the RCA and the Orthodox Union of America remained full members of the Synagogue Council.

Working together with a group of young rabbis within the RCA, Rabbi Sherer kept trying to force the hand of the RCA's Halachah Commission to rule one way or the other. In an October 1, 1956 letter to Rabbi Mordechai Gifter, Rabbi Sherer described how Rabbi Aharon Kotler had asked him to organize a petition to the Halachah Commission with as many signatures as possible, pressing for a decision by the coming Chanukah.

A fact sheet on the issue of affiliation of Orthodox rabbis and synagogues with umbrella organizations, including Reform and Conservative clergy and synagogues, was prepared by Rabbi Naftali Langsam and Rabbi Dr. Avraham Rappaport as part of this effort. It provides an excellent summary of the premises underlying the *psak din* of the roshei yeshivah. Above all, participation in such umbrella organizations, the fact sheet argues, provides religious legitimacy to clergymen and movements promoting a religion other than the Judaism of the Torah and the Talmud. It does not make a difference, the authors conclude, that Orthodox members of the Synagogue Council have a right to veto any pronouncements of a religious nature.

That veto power "is not and cannot be known and understood by the average Jewish layman. He judges, and quite rightly so, by the fact that rabbis of the three Jewish denominations … are united, meet together, issue frequent statements together, appear in the press together, officiate at marriages together, … exchange pulpits and all three talk on behalf of Judaism and against assimilation …. "

Rabbis Langsam and Rappaport took pains to refute the argument that the Synagogue Council and the New York Board of Rabbis were designed only to represent Jewish interests toward the outside world,

---

7. Of those Orthodox rabbis not affiliated with Agudath Israel, one of the most tenacious fighters against the Synagogue Council was Rabbi Sherer's brother-in-law, Rabbi David B. Hollander, a one-time president of the Rabbinical Council of America.

and thus would not be viewed as conferring an internal religious legitimacy on heterodox clergymen. The terms "synagogue" and "rabbis" in the names of these organizations was by itself sufficient to establish that they were concerned with internal Jewish matters. That conclusion was reinforced by the very constitution of the Synagogue Council, which listed, among the organization's purposes, the preservation and fostering of Judaism. Such activities as a "back to synagogue campaign" and a commission on Jewish information, made up of a Reform, a Conservative, and an Orthodox rabbi, all reinforced the internal nature of the organization, and thus led to the reinforcement of the notion that Judaism is comprised of three separate but equal "denominations." The religious activities of the New York Board of Rabbis — e.g., a Milah Board, training rabbis, promoting positive Judaism, and ministering to Jewish needs — even more clearly reflected the religious nature of the group.

Nor was the charge of conferring religious legitimacy on the Reform and Conservative movements, by reinforcing the view that there are three "streams" or "denominations" of Judaism, merely theoretical, Rabbis Langsam and Rappaport charged: "Today they [i.e, Conservative rabbis] insist on being included on Kashrus boards and Yeshivah boards," and Reform and Conservative rabbis minister as chaplains to Orthodox Jews in prisons and hospitals. The authors inveighed against the common practice of Orthodox rabbis co-officiating at weddings and other religious ceremonies with Conservative and Reform rabbis. Even when the Orthodox rabbi ensured that all the rituals were properly conducted, the impression of the average person in attendance was certainly that "two rabbis are carrying out a religious function and that the Orthodox rabbi is a colleague of the other rabbi."

At a time when the Conservative movement was growing rapidly, Rabbis Langsam and Rappaport claimed, the affiliation of Orthodox rabbis with Conservative colleagues had resulted in making it that much more difficult for Orthodoxy to "stress to our people the lines of demarcation" in a way that could reduce the loss of Orthodox Jews and synagogues to the Conservative movement. In addition, the affiliation of Orthodox rabbis as colleagues with Conservative and Reform clergy only weakened the case in Israel against recognition of the Reform and Conservative movements on an equal basis with Orthodoxy.

The refusal to join together in synagogue and rabbinical organizations, the fact sheet argued, need not drive a wedge between Jews or weaken the ability of the Jewish community to unite on matters of com-

L-r: Mike Tress, Rabbi Moshe Feinstein, Rabbi Sherer (speaker), Rabbi Yaakov Kamenetsky, Rabbi Aharon Kotler.

mon concern affecting the Jewish people. Permanent umbrella organizations were not needed in order for different Jewish groups to contact one another and act together in the context of a particular crisis. But in those situations, it still remained crucial to petition outside authorities as Jews, not as rabbis or synagogues, in order to avoid recognizing a multiplicity of Judaisms. Secular Jewish defense organizations, without the words rabbi or synagogue in the title raised no such problems. Opposition to membership in umbrella groups should not therefore be seen as dividing Jews from one another, but rather as separating Orthodox rabbis and synagogues from any others that sought to appropriate the name Judaism.

The *psak din* of the 11 roshei yeshivah was Rabbi Sherer's guiding light for the rest of his life. The battle against the legitimization of non-halachic Jewish movements was one from which he never desisted. He was frequently quoted describing the idea that Judaism has "three wings" as the single greatest threat to American Jewry. In March 1975, nearly 20 years after the *psak* of the 11 roshei yeshivah, he was still trying to wean the Rabbinical Council of America and the Orthodox Union away from the Synagogue Council. At a meeting with the heads of the RCA and the OU, Rabbi Sherer told them that as long as their organizations remained part of the Synagogue Council, their relations with Agudath Israel could never be on anything more than an ad hoc basis. And he expressed his frustration at their refusal to depart from the Synagogue Council, despite the fact that it was, in his opinion, "the most ineffectual and meaningless Jewish agency on the American scene."[8] In consultation with the Moetzes Gedolei HaTorah, he advised Avrohom Fruchthandler and Mendy Shayovich to remain on the OU board to try and fight the Synagogue Council from within.

Rabbi Sherer was constantly on the outlook for new breaches of the *psak*. When a prominent rabbi who was a close relative to a *gadol* who signed the *psak* participated on a Jewish Federation-sponsored symposium on Jewish medical ethics that included a Conservative and a Reform rabbi, Rabbi Sherer immediately asked him to reconsider his participation.[9] The rabbi, in reply, wondered whether Federation had now been added to the Synagogue Council and the New York Board of Rabbis as falling within the ambit of the *psak* of the roshei yeshivah.

To that Rabbi Sherer patiently explained that this rabbi's appearance on the same panel as Reform and Conservative clergymen might have the "unwitting but nevertheless devastating impact on many confused Jews" of suggesting that the others were also "halachic authorities that doctors might consult." "Precisely because you are a person of such stature and with such *yichus*, your actions carry a great deal of weight in many circles," Rabbi Sherer concluded his request for the rabbi to reconsider.

The *Jewish Observer*, the ideological organ of Agudath Israel of America, continually hammered away at violations of the *psak* of the roshei yeshivah, and highlighted every new evidence of the foresight of the roshei yeshivah in banning participation in the Synagogue Council or the New York Board of Rabbis.

An example of the latter was the Fortieth Anniversary dinner of the Synagogue Council on November 6, 1966, at which Arthur J. Goldberg, then the U.S. Ambassador to the United Nations, delivered the main address. Honored that evening were what one Jewish paper termed "the heads of America's great institutions of Jewish learning, Dr. Samuel Belkin, President of Yeshiva University, Dr. Louis Finkelstein of the Jewish Theological Seminary (Conservative), and Dr. Nelson Glueck, President of Hebrew Union College (Reform)." Also appearing on the

---

8. Aide-mémoire, March 20, 1975.
9. Letter on file; October 27, 1988.

program, which saluted, as Goldberg put it in his oration, "the religious statesmanship ... need[ed] to bring together the many divergent views in Jewish life," were the presidents of the three national rabbinic agencies affiliated with the Synagogue Council: the president of the Rabbinical Assembly (Conservative), the president of the RCA, and the president of the Central Conference of American Rabbis (Reform).

A more compelling proclamation of the equality of the three "branches" of American Judaism would have been hard to conceive. Describing the upcoming anniversary dinner of the Synagogue Council, *The New York Times'* religion correspondent wrote, "Leaders of the three branches of Judaism are expected on that occasion to sit side by side for the first time as a visible expression of Jewish unity,'" and he hailed the event as a harbinger of growing interdenominational dialogue within Judaism and a search for unity and commonality.

Four of the senior members of the Moetzes Gedolei HaTorah, Rabbi

בס״ד

**כב' אחינו האהובים, תלמידי הישיבות
די בכל אתר ואתר, שלומכם יסגי!**

הנה בימים הללו עומדת להתקיים „חגיגה של כבוד", אשר מטרתה לרומם את מעלתם של שלשת האנשים העומדים בראשם של „שלשת הסמינרים של יהודי אמריקה"., הלא הם: הסמינר לריפורמים דמתקרי HEBREW UNION COLLEGE והסמינר לקונסרבטיבים דמתקרי JEWISH THEOLOGICAL SEMINARY והסמינר לאורתודוקסים דמתקרי YESHIVA UNIVERSITY.

והנה משנה יתירה היא לפרש לפניכם את חומר האיסור ואת גדל השערורי' הכלולים בדרכי מות של השתתפות זו.

בעונותינו הרבים אין בידנו להעמיד הדת על תלה, ואזלת ידנו למנוע את ההשתתפות הזו.

אמנם, אי אפשר לנו לכלא את רוחנו ולהאנק דום מבלי להשמיע לכה״פ באהלי תורה זעקה גדולה ומרה על השבר הזה הבא בגבולנו.

וד' יגדור פרצותינו ברחמים.

— יעקב קמנצקי
— יעקב יצחק הלוי רודרמן
— יצחק הוטנר
— משה פיינשטיין

י' חשון, תשכ״ז

The statement of the roshei yeshivah regarding the 1966 Synagogue Council dinner

Yaakov Kamenetsky, Rabbi Yaakov Yitzchak Halevi Ruderman, Rabbi Yitzchak Hutner, and Rabbi Moshe Feinstein (in the order of their signatures) issued a brief statement on October 24, 1966, prior to the Synagogue Council Anniversary Dinner, in which they reaffirmed the severity of the prohibition against participation in the dinner honoring the three "centers of Jewish learning" and terming that participation "the way of death." The four roshei yeshivah bemoaned their inability to prevent the participation of Orthodox rabbis in the affair.

Subsequently, the *Jewish Observer* devoted a long editorial to the Synagogue Council dinner in its January 1967 issue. The article began by challenging the Yeshiva University public relations department to back up the claim made to the *Day-Morning Journal* that a number of roshei yeshivah at Yeshiva University had urged Dr. Belkin to attend, and name the roshei yeshivah in question. In the absence of such clarification, *The Jewish Observer* implied, it would have to credit "information from the faculty that such an incident never took place." Next, the editorial rebutted rumors circulated in a Yeshiva University's student publication that Rabbi Moshe Feinstein had not signed the condemnation of the Synagogue Council dinner, or alternatively, had signed the statement only under pressure.

In a letter dated 16 *Teves*, Rabbi Feinstein replied that the rumors were "nonsensical, and even those who have said these thing certainly know that they are absurd." The editorial asked pointedly, "How will *Klal Yisrael* ever, in the future, be able to benefit from the guidance of *Gedolei HaTorah* if their statements can be nullified, with impunity, by rumor and insinuation on the part of anyone not willing to accept their views?"

The editorial concluded with a sharp attack on those who defended Orthodox participation in the Synagogue Council on the grounds that it had no internal implications within the Jewish community and was only for the purpose of more efficient external representation. The editorial mentioned two illustrations of internal cooperation. The first was the announcement that *The American Rabbi*, a publication by and for rabbis, would resume publication with an editorial board consisting of Reform, Conservative, and Orthodox rabbis. The second was an invitation to the annual dinner of the Hebrew-language weekly *HaDoar* which would honor the "three branches of Judaism," with Rabbi Norman Lamm representing Orthodoxy.

Finally, the president of the Synagogue Council himself hailed the dinner as paving the way for the "long overdue unification of these three branches of Judaism." *The Jewish Observer* reported that shortly after the Synagogue Council dinner an Orthodox rabbi in Virginia was called by the local Conservative rabbi with the request that he join the local organization. When he repeated his previous refusal, the Conservative rabbi angrily declared: "Now that Dr. Belkin went through with the SCA dinner, I won't accept it that your refusal is a matter of principle."

Following immediately after the *Jewish Observer's* lead editorial was a statement by Rabbi Mordechai Gifter, one of the Telshe roshei yeshivah, in which he responded to those who criticized Agudath Israel and the roshei yeshivah for their "dull obsession" with the Synagogue Council. "It is the fundamental affirmation of the Jew of *Torah* and *Emunah* that there is not such a monstrosity as one tree of Judaism with three branches,' or 'one bird with three wings.' … Any understanding of Judaism contrary to Torah is not a branch or wing within Judaism; *it is not Judaism*," wrote Rabbi Gifter.

Battling Heterodoxy

ANNOUNCING THE CREATION OF AM ECHAD TO FIGHT AGAINST Reform and Conservative inroads in Israel, at the 59th Convention of Agudath Israel of America, in 1997, Rabbi Sherer quoted a famous question of the Kotzker Rebbe: Yisro suggested to Moshe Rabbeinu to appoint judges who are "*anshei emes* — men of truth." Thereafter, those selected are divided into those who are appointed over a thousand, those appointed over hundreds, those in charge of groups of 50, and those placed over groups of 10. If they are all men of truth, how can they be differentiated? After all, there is only one truth.

The Kotzker Rebbe answered that there are three levels of truth. The

Chapter Five: Laying the Foundations

lowest level is a person who does not lie. The second level is a person who always says the truth. At the highest level is the person who fights for the truth. When it came to combating the Reform and Conservative movements, Rabbi Sherer was that man. He devoted himself to preventing the growth of the heterodox movements in America and to ensuring that they gain no official recognition in Israel. Even when many of those who shared Rabbi Sherer's evaluation of the Reform and Conservative movements said, "Enough already," he never desisted. Every fresh departure from halachah by the heterodox movements was highlighted in *The Jewish Observer.*

He once told Mrs. Ruth Lichtenstein, then the American correspondent for *Hamodia* (and today the publisher and editor-in-chief of the English *Hamodia*), that he had devoted 15 years of his life to a close study of the Reform movement. Any time that she received a call from Rabbi Sherer early on a Sunday morning, Mrs. Lichtenstein recalls, she knew that it was in connection to some new action or resolution of one of the heterodox movements.

Rabbi Sherer forced himself to read the matrimonial notices in the Sunday *New York Times* every week — a form of self-inflicted torture — in order that he should never forget the scourge of intermarriage that the heterodox movements brought in their wake. Asked once whether he would meet with the leaders of the Conservative and Reform movements to discuss ways to lessen intermarriage, he replied, "Since when do the firemen invite the arsonists?" At one point, he even called on the phone a "rabbi," who advertised his availability to officiate at intermarriages in the *New York Post*, and engaged him in a lengthy conversation about his fees and qualifications as a "rabbi."[10]

He could be withering on the religious anarchy foisted upon American Jewry by the heterodox movements. At the November 1990 Agudath Israel convention, he read a report from the *New York Times* of the recent convention of the Council of Jewish Federations in San Francisco.

> They conducted five separate religious services. One was an Orthodox service; one a Conservative service where men and women "prayed in Hebrew shoulder to shoulder"; one a Reform service "conducted mostly in English; one a Reconstructionist service in which the "women wore yarmulkes." And then came

---

10. Aide-mémoire, March 6, 1973.

the last of the services, a service called Chai-Chi .... In this service the Jewish leaders "took off their shoes and chanted Hebrew mantras." Now, I looked up in Webster's Dictionary *vus meint,* "mantras," and it states "a mystical incantation as in Hinduism."

After surveying, with the help of the *Times,* the state of American Jewish religious life, Rabbi Sherer concluded, "In such an atmosphere of religious anarchy among those representing themselves as Jewish leaders, small wonder that they are losing their children to assimilation .... These secularist have lost their power of *'hemshech'* [continuity]."

He was constantly on the watch for any sign of a Reform or Conservative toehold in Israel. Indeed he was often the one to inform Agudath Israel's Knesset members of some new breach. Thus, he wrote to Education Minister Zevulun Hammer of the National Religious Party in June 1978 to protest the Education Ministry's official recognition of a Conservative school and the appointment as adviser for Diaspora Affairs in the Education Ministry of someone with ordination from the Jewish Theological Seminary (Conservative).[11]

"The Conservative movement is an even greater threat [than Reform] to classical Judaism because often times its outer garb and appearances tend to mislead the unwary into believing that this is indeed 'traditional Judaism,'" he wrote to Minister Hammer. And he warned that any laxity on the Minister's part "will be utilized by Conservative leaders in their plans to eventually become an officially recognized 'wing' of Judaism in Israel."

That letter to the Education Minister was followed by one to Rabbi Shlomo Lorincz, in which Rabbi Sherer expressed his opinion that the entry of the Conservative movement into Israeli schools was even more dangerous than the opening of Conservative synagogues. It made no difference that the school in question was small in numbers because the Conservatives have long followed a strategy of making "a very small beginning somewhere, and then build on these roots to develop larger and larger recognition." He also expressed his concerns to Rabbi Lorincz about the possibility of Mizrachi forging alliances with the Conservative or Masorti movement in Israel.[12]

When Rabbi Sherer was quoted in the American press as saying that Conservative education in the Israeli school system was worse than no

---

11. Rabbi Moshe Sherer to Zevulun Hammer, June 1, 1978. Minister Hammer's assistant replied that the facts were not exactly as reported in the press, but Rabbi Sherer's fears were not allayed.
12. Rabbi Moshe Sherer to Rabbi Shlomo Lorincz, June 1, 1978.

Jewish education at all, he received an outraged response from Professor Seymour Siegal of the Jewish Theological Seminary (Conservative). Rabbi Sherer did not mince words in his reply. He assured Professor Siegal that it was not only his personal view or that of Agudath Israel of America that Conservative teachings are "false" and "fraudulent," but that of all the foremost Torah scholars of past and previous generations. Every recognized Jewish authority in Halachah, he wrote, would agree with his statement, "It is preferable not to teach Jewish children anything about Torah rather than instill in them the concept that Torah is not Divinely revealed."[13]

No opening of any kind was too small to gain Rabbi Sherer's attention. In September 1975, he received a call from Rabbi Neuberger in Baltimore, who wanted to convey a disturbing report that he had received from a former student of Ner Israel, who was now a rabbi in Los Angeles. Chief Rabbi Ovadia Yosef was scheduled to speak at a large gathering of Sephardi Jews in Los Angeles, and the head of the Conservative movement's West Coast branch was to be the translator. In addition, Rabbi Yosef was also to appear at a youth rally to be held in a synagogue that had recently removed the *mechitzah*.

Rabbi Sherer went into overdrive to inform Rabbi Yosef and to make sure that he take another translator and demand another venue for the youth rally. He called his good friend Rabbi Menachem Porush in Jerusalem, and the latter agreed to go speak to Rav Ovadia. Immediately after Rabbi Porush met with Rav Ovadia, the Chief Rabbi telephoned Los Angeles to demand a new translator and a different venue for the youth rally. "Mission accomplished" was Rabbi Sherer's brief but accurate description of his intervention.

During the 1950s, the Conservative movement in America grew rapidly. As the population in many communities outside the New York area began to age, a number of formerly Orthodox congregations voted to affiliate with the Conservative movement. Others that did not formally affiliate with the Conservative movement nevertheless did away with the *mechitzah* and separate seating in an effort to appeal to the younger generation of American-born Jews.

The trend away from use of a *mechitzah* was arrested to some extent by two legal cases in the mid-to-late-1950s involving synagogues which had voted to do away with the *mechitzah*: one in New Orleans and the

---

13. Rabbi Moshe Sherer to Rabbi Seymour Siegal, October 27, 1978.

other in the summer resort community of Mount Clemens, Michigan. In both cases, members of the synagogue sued in state court to prevent the changes from being instituted on the grounds that the synagogues in question had been established as Orthodox houses of worship. They argued that all contributions made to the establishment of the synagogue and membership dues had been given on the condition of the synagogue remaining faithful to the halachos concerning the sanctity of a place of Jewish house of prayer and thereby created an irrevocable trust.

To support that claim, it was necessary to establish both that a *mechitzah* is a requirement of Orthodox Judaism, and that the only body qualified to determine those requirements is a *beis din* composed of Orthodox rabbinical authorities.

Rabbi Sherer took a keen interest in this litigation from the beginning, and became personally friendly with Baruch Litvin, the plaintiff in the Mount Clemens case. Eventually, the strategy developed by Samuel Lawrence Brennglass, a prominent Orthodox attorney in New York City, on behalf of the Katz family in New Orleans and Mr. Litvin in the Michigan litigation proved successful. The decision of the Michigan Supreme Court was particularly broad. The court held that the diversion of congregational property of a synagogue of a historically Orthodox character to another denomination violated the property rights of the Orthodox members of the synagogue, who could no longer continue to worship there.

The Michigan Supreme Court explicitly ruled that it made no difference that the synagogue's bylaws or constitution never described the synagogue as an Orthodox one or that the changes in the synagogue were effected by a majority vote — a "vote of a momentary majority," in the Court's words. Explicit in the decision was a finding that mixed seating is a violation of established Jewish law, and an observant Jew cannot in good conscience pray in such a synagogue.

Immediately after his victory in the Michigan Supreme Court, the victorious plaintiff Baruch Litvin began compiling a volume called *The Sanctity of the Synagogue,* which detailed the five-year litigation history leading up to his historic victory in the Michigan Supreme Court. The volume also included a wide variety of material from contemporary Jewish religious authorities, across the Orthodox spectrum, discussing issues connected to the halachic requirements for a synagogue, in general, and the requirement of a *mechitzah,* in particular.

Rabbi Sherer worked closely with Mr. Litvin in the preparation of the volume.[14] In one letter to Mr. Litvin, he even referred to it as "your (our) *sefer* ...." Subsequently, Rabbi Sherer served as Mr. Litvin's chief adviser on how to publicize and distribute the book as widely as possible. The two men carried on an extensive correspondence on the subject, with Rabbi Sherer providing a detailed list of every possible reviewer and publication to whom copies should be sent and offering to intercede with the various publications on Mr. Litvin's behalf. In another letter, he recommended that Mr. Litvin write a human-interest article about responses to the book, which Rabbi Sherer would then edit and try to have published in different Jewish periodicals.

The 1956 *psak* of the 11 roshei yeshivah and the *mechitzah* litigation were but the first two chapters of what would be Rabbi Sherer's lifelong battle against the Reform and Conservative movements. That battle would only end with his physical collapse after leading a delegation of American Orthodox leaders to *Eretz Yisrael*, against his doctor's orders, to fight against the spread of Reform and Conservative Judaism in the Holy Land.

---

14. Yosef Friedenson.

Chapter Six

TRANSITION

Mike's Last Public Campaign

THE HUNGARIAN REVOLUTION, WHICH BROKE OUT ON October 23, 1956, proved to be the occasion for Mike Tress's last great public campaign, with Rabbi Sherer at his side. The revolt against Soviet occupation provided Mike with a new opportunity to throw himself body and soul into an undertaking to save Jewish lives, or at the very least rescue from religious oblivion those thought to be permanently trapped behind the Iron Curtain from religious oblivion.

By mid-November, a Soviet-backed puppet regime was once more firmly ensconced in power. But in the less than a month between the outbreak of the revolution and its quelling by Soviet troops, 200,000 Hungarians, including 20,000 Jews, fled Hungary. Even after Soviet troops had succeeded in quelling the uprising, there were still opportunities in the resulting turmoil for brave individuals to flee over the

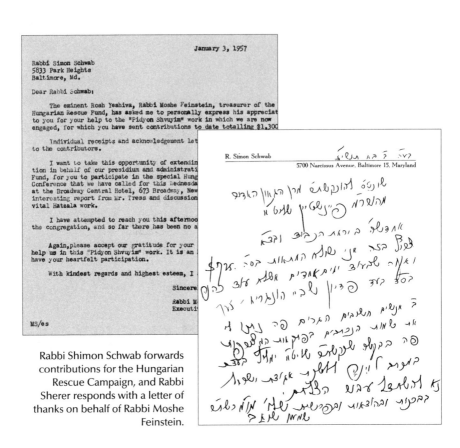

Rabbi Shimon Schwab forwards contributions for the Hungarian Rescue Campaign, and Rabbi Sherer responds with a letter of thanks on behalf of Rabbi Moshe Feinstein.

border into Austria. Smugglers now demanded $100, instead of the $60 charged in the immediate aftermath of the Revolution, for every person successfully transported across the border. With each passing day, the likelihood grew of Hungary's borders being once again sealed.

Just as during the Holocaust, here was a rare opportunity to perform the mitzvah of *pidyon sh'vuim*. Lives were at stake, and the regular bills and obligations coming due would just have to wait. Between December 5, 1956 and January 5, 1957, the heavily indebted Agudath Israel of America still managed to transfer $45,000 to the underground railroad ferrying Jews out of Hungary to Vienna.

In mid-December, Mike Tress flew to Vienna to supervise the operation of the underground railroad. While there, he purchased a 104-room hotel to house the refugees and established three kosher kitchens that provided kosher food for 1,000 Jews a day. That done, he returned to the United States to embark on one of those barnstorming fund-raising campaigns reminiscent of those he had undertaken upon the receipt of

Hungarian refugees in Vienna's Hotel Continental

Rabbi Michoel Ber Weissmandl's pleas for ransom money at the height of the Holocaust in Europe.

Meanwhile America waived many of its immigration quotas to allow in tens of thousands of Hungarian refugees. As commander in chief of the Allied forces in Europe, President Dwight D. Eisenhower had been among the first to view the liberated concentration camps. Perhaps the sight of Jewish corpses piled high inspired some guilt feelings over how little America had done to stop the slaughter of Jews or to waive immigrant quotas to allow more Jews to escape the clutches of the Nazis. In any event, this time, at least, President Eisenhower lifted the immigrant quotas.

Thousands of Hungarian refugees a day poured into Fort Kilmer in New Jersey. Rabbi Sherer convinced Heshy Leiser, who had run the Youth Council's packing operations for the DP camps after World War II, to take off from work for five months in order to offer assistance to religious refugees who found temporary accommodations at Fort Kilmer. Leiser recommended a woman named Judy Weinberger, who spoke Hungarian fluently, to the Hebrew Immigration and Aid Society (HIAS) for a secretarial job. HIAS was coordinating the absorption of all Jewish immigrants, and that placed Ms. Weinberger in a position to alert Leiser to the presence of any religious Jews on the sprawling army base. Jews with close relatives in America or who came from a well-organized religious community passed through Fort Kilmer in a matter of days. But those without relatives could remain there for months. In the meantime, a kosher kitchen was established for them, and Leiser would take them into Brooklyn and other Jewish communities to help them find jobs and locate housing.

Chapter Six: Transition ☐ 149

BY MID-1960, MIKE TRESS'S HEALTH HAD DETERIORATED TO THE point that Rabbi Sherer had effectively taken over the day-to-day running of Agudath Israel. Mike's health, and the new burdens placed upon him, is a recurrent theme in Rabbi Sherer's correspondence from 1960-61.[1]

New Burdens

Rabbi Sherer remained ever hopeful that his cousin would recover and return to his duties. In February 1961, he wrote to Rabbi Simon Schwartz, "Elimelech Tress is somewhat better and now comes into the office for about three hours a day." Four months later, he informed Rabbi Chaim Schmelczer, "Thank G-d, Reb Elimelech is feeling better than he did last year, and he is slowly getting back to work."

But Mike never recovered fully, and as a result the full responsibility for seeing through a major economic recovery program, begun in the late '50s when Mike was still near full strength, fell on Rabbi Sherer, who had until that point largely avoided fund-raising duties. It was not a task that he relished or for which he saw himself particularly well suited.

In a March 1961 memorandum to the Management Committee, which had been formed to resolve the perpetual financial crisis in which Agudath Israel found itself in the late '50s, Rabbi Sherer complained of his "enforced concentration on a one-track subject [i.e., finances and fund-raising]." And he warned that his "preoccupation with the dubious role of 'schnorrer'" to the exclusion of all else could lead "toward an Agudath movement which will be financially on the upgrade but spiritually out of sight and out of mind."

Rabbi Sherer had to spend a good deal of time just dealing with irate creditors, a task that drove him to the brink of despair. In one exchange that may sound amusing after the passage of more than four decades, but was surely anything but at the time, Rabbi Sherer wrote to the president of the First National Bank and Trust Company of Ellenville, New York thanking him for his patient understanding regarding a certain late payment. Four days later, came the bank president's response: "I am not understanding, and I am not very patient .... May we please have your check immediately."

About 1960, Agudath Israel had issued mortgage bonds to save Camp Agudah, which was the biggest financial drain on the organiza-

---

1. In a June 8, 1961 letter to Rabbi Chaim Schmelczer, Rabbi Sherer refers to Mike's "absence from actual work for almost a year." In response to a letter to an irate creditor of September 7, 1961, Rabbi Sherer describes Mike Tress as having been "incapacitated" for almost a year and a half. It emerges from these two letters that from sometime between May and June of 1960, Mike's health forced him to reduce his presence in the office to very part-time.

tion's resources at the time. Unfortunately, Agudath Israel was unable to redeem all the bonds as scheduled, and that led to a number of irate letters with which Rabbi Sherer found himself forced to deal. It was in response to many of those letters that much of the information concerning Mike Tress's ongoing health problems appears, as Rabbi Sherer pleaded Mike's prolonged absence from the office as a major cause for the delay.

Rabbi Sherer held out hope to those complaining of Agudath Israel's failure to make timely payment that the situation was turning around. "Our new Management Committee has succeeded in making tremendous progress in overhauling our entire financial structure, which is a major revolutionary improvement over the past 'impossible years,'" he wrote to the attorney for one charitable foundation holding the bonds.[2] To Rabbi Jacob Mermelstein, an Agudath Israel insider, he wrote, "Please believe me, my dear Jack, Mike and I are very appreciative of the big personal sacrifice that you made in [being] cooperative on this bond project. But it was worth all this effort, because it not only saved the Agudah and its camps from a catastrophic situation, but has enabled us to begin a new expansion program, whose effects we hope Torah Jewry will feel within the next few years."

There were times, however, when neither excuses concerning Mike's illness nor appeals to idealism of the bondholders availed. Occasionally the pressures piling up on Rabbi Sherer show through in his responses to the most importunate creditors. In response to one particularly pushy creditor, he wrote, "… [S]ometimes a creditor [sic] simply does not have the funds to pay his debt at the moment. I hope that you never were in such a position and never will be in such a position, but had you ever tasted such an unpleasant situation, you could understand the next person …. [S]ince you are the only person who is so persistent, I think you ought to … reconsider whether yours is the correct attitude…. Since you have been writing me so much 'mussar,' perhaps you too should do a little thinking."

Eventually the endless fending off of creditors and fund-raising, without the compensatory satisfactions of the tasks that he truly enjoyed, led Rabbi Sherer to resign. On March 18, 1961, he wrote to the Management Committee, consisting of Wolf Friedman, Herman Plagman, and David Turkel, tendering his resignation, with a curt note: "This decision is irrevocable, and I ask you to do me the personal

---

2. Rabbi Moshe Sherer to Albert Wald, January 11, 1961.

kindness of sparing me from the embarrassment and heartache of any discussions on this subject."

Had Rabbi Sherer's resignation remained in effect it is likely the American Agudah movement would have come to an end at that point. Writing two months later to Sam Feinberg, an accountant who had been very active in the financial reorganization of Agudath Israel, David Turkel described the "terrible crisis" into which Agudath Israel was plunged by Rabbi Sherer's resignation. The resignation, he wrote, threatened the organization with "a complete breakdown of all that we have been building up for the past year and a half."[3]

Fortunately the resignation was short-lived. Along with his letter of resignation to the Management Committee, Rabbi Sherer had also sent one to Rabbi Aharon Kotler, as chairman of the Moetzes Gedolei HaTorah. Predictably, Reb Aharon's first reaction was to summon Rabbi Sherer to a meeting. Rabbi Sherer knew that Reb Aharon would attempt to dissuade him from his decision, and he thoroughly prepared all his counterarguments.

Upon his arrival at Reb Aharon's Boro Park apartment, Rabbi Sherer was ushered into the living room to wait for Reb Aharon. While seated there, Rebbetzin Kotler suddenly came into the room sobbing. She looked at Rabbi Sherer, and through the tears, told him, "I read the letter that you wrote to the Rosh Yeshivah. How could you do this to him? How could you do this to my father, Reb Isser Zalman? How could you do this to *Klal Yisrael*?"

A few minutes later Reb Aharon entered the room, and motioned to Rabbi Sherer to join him at the table. Before Reb Aharon began to speak, however, Rabbi Sherer said to him, "Rosh Yeshiva, do me a favor, could I please have back my letter of resignation?" It was to be Rabbi Sherer's last attempt to resign from Agudath Israel.[4]

---

3. A check to Feinberg for $500 had apparently bounced, but Turkel expressed confidence that with Rabbi Sherer back at work the stage was set for a "final effort to normalize a situation which had gradually improved ... in great measure to your extremely able and self-sacrificing work." Feinberg's efforts, wrote Turkel, had rescued an entire movement and saved from "personal discredit the two men [Mike Tress and Rabbi Sherer] who had given their lives for its cause."

The personal discredit referred to by Mr. Turkel likely refers to the consequences if Agudath Israel had been forced to declare bankruptcy, though it is also possible that Mike Tress and Rabbi Sherer were guarantors on the bonds.

4. At the *seudas hodaah* (thanksgiving meal) the Agudath Israel staff arranged for Rabbi Sherer after his return to the office after open-heart surgery, he related the story of Rebbetzin Kotler's tears. At a Bais Yaakov D'Rav Meir dinner, he told the women present to never underestimate their power. Only due to the tears of two women — his mother and Rebbetzin Kotler — had he dedicated his life to *Klal Yisrael*.

Though Rabbi Sherer had retracted his resignation for the last time, the burden of fund-raising continued to weigh heavily upon him. In recognition that everything rested on his shoulders, he contemplated having Agudath Israel purchase a life insurance policy on his life, with Agudah as the beneficiary. He even underwent a physical exam for that purpose. The policy would have given Agudath Israel the ability to hire top-quality personnel in the event of his premature passing.

As the paperwork was being completed for the policy, however, Rabbi Sherer received a copy of Rabbi Aharon Sorasky's biography of Rabbi Meir Shapiro of Lublin. Like Rabbi Sherer, Rabbi Meir Shapiro was almost the sole fund-raiser for his Yeshivas Chachmei Lublin. And just as Rabbi Sherer was then contemplating doing, he had taken out a very large life insurance policy with Prudential Life Insurance Company on his own life, with his yeshivah as the beneficiary. Not long thereafter, Rabbi Shapiro, still only in his 40's, died from an illness that his doctors described as minor. Rabbi Sorasky records that when the Great Depression hit, and the financial situation of Chachmei Lublin declined precipitously, Rabbi Shapiro was heard to utter a bitter *"krechtz"* and comment, "It appears that only the death [of the insured] will be able to save the yeshivah from its debts."

When he read that, Rabbi Sherer decided to tear up the policy. He feared that Agudath Israel might also find itself in such dire financial straits one day, and such a *"krechtz"* might pass his lips. Unlike Rabbi Meir Shapiro, who had no children, Rabbi Sherer had three children of his own, and he felt he had no right for their sake to place himself in such a situation.[5]

Different Times

EVENTUALLY AGUDATH ISRAEL EMERGED FROM THE "IMPOSSIBLE years," during which it labored under debts of $500,000 (millions of dollars in today's terms). Rabbi Sherer resolved that henceforth incurring debt would be tantamount to "eating *chametz* on Pesach."[6] He had seen close up the price of living with perpetual debts in terms of the health of Mike Tress, and he had no desire to find himself in the same position over a period of years, much less decades.

Rabbi Shlomo Lorincz described the impact of those pressures on

---

5. Rabbi Shmuel Bloom.
6. Ibid.

Decades after withdrawing his resignation, Rabbi Sherer attends the *seudas hodaah* following his open-heart surgery. Seated (l-r): Rabbi Elya Svei; Rabbi Sherer; the Novominsker Rebbe, Rabbi Boruch B. Borchardt; standing: Rabbi Chaim Dovid Zweibel, Rabbi Shmuel Lefkowitz, and Rabbi Yosef Chaim Golding.

Mike Tress. On his first visit to the headquarters of Zeirei Agudath Israel in 1948, he watched Mike spend each day trying to cover the bills coming due that day. Not until the banks closed in the afternoon did he have a chance to sit back and turn his attention to the projects at hand. Many times Rabbi Lorincz witnessed him placing compresses on his head in an attempt to find relief from the pressures on him.

The modern Agudah movement in America was born in crisis in 1939. At a time when there was hope of ransoming Jewish lives for $50 or of purchasing a fake Latin American passport that might save an entire family, all calculations of financial wherewithal were beside the point.

During the war years, Zeirei Agudath Israel labored constantly under huge debts. And those debts only grew in the immediate post-war years. The debts of the war years remained long after the War was over, as did the crisis mode of action. And indeed much of the immediate post-war work of Agudath Israel — feeding and clothing refugees in the DP camps, obtaining entrance visas for them to America, seizing the opportunity to rescue thousands of Jews from a totalitarian and anti-religious government in the immediate aftermath of the 1956 Hungarian Revolution — had an immense and immediate impact on thousands of Jewish lives.

By the time that Rabbi Sherer took the helm of Agudath Israel, however, the life-and-death demands had ended, and it was possible to place the organization on an entirely different footing. Indeed if that were not done, Agudath Israel could not have survived, much less grown in influence on the American Jewish scene. Rabbi Sherer realized that Agudath Israel could not continue to labor indefinitely under crippling debt without eventually collapsing under its own weight. No organization can survive in the long run spending the better part of its energies servicing debt.

Rabbi Sherer's *modus operandi* was perfectly suited to the new circumstances. He was an enthusiast for new ideas and projects, but he never let his enthusiasm overcome his insistence on carefully preparing each step of every new initiative. He learned how to say of a particular project: This is important, but we cannot yet do it because we do not have the money. The fact that he did not plunge directly into a project did not mean that he was not interested or did not view it as important — only that the moment had not yet come. He would then file the idea away until such time as the proper people and the necessary funding was in place.

His approach to the establishment of Agudath Israel branches around the United States is an example of the way he deferred long-term goals. He did not attempt to turn his dream of many such branches into reality until he was sure that he had found the proper people to run the branches and the requisite local financial support.[7]

The ability to say "No" or at least "Not yet," and thereby serve as a brake on youthful enthusiasm, was, in Rabbi Sherer's view, one of the crucial tasks that the elders of the generation, the great Torah leaders, play. Often times when Rabbi Sherer had an idea for a new initiative, he would go to discuss the idea with the Bluzhover Rebbe, who was renowned for his sharp assessment of situations. More than once, the Rebbe would answer him with the Talmudic expression that when there is no clear, preferred course, "שֵׁב וְאַל תַּעֲשֶׂה עָדִיף — it's better to sit and do nothing." The Rebbe spiced his advice with a novel and wise interperetation of the Sages' adage: Sometimes a person is obsessed with an urge to "improve" an existing situation, without fully considering that the contemplated "improvement" may have unforeseen unpleasant consequences. To such a well-meaning person, the Talmud counsels, "שֵׁב sit; וְאַל תַּעֲשֶׂה עָדִיף, don't try to make things better."

So much importance did Rabbi Sherer place on the necessity of restraint in certain circumstances that he included a *vort* from the Chiddushei HaRim on the subject in his Introduction to *Bishtei Einayim*. The verse (*Bamidbar* 8:25) informs us that when the Levites reached the age of 50 they withdrew from physical labor in the Temple. And Rashi explains that upon reaching 50 they were assigned to lock the gates of the Temple. Why does Rashi mention only that they locked the gates but not that they also opened them in the morning?

The Chiddushei HaRim explains homiletically that "opening the gates" symbolizes the enthusiasm of youth, the desire to undertake new missions and blaze new trails. That is a positive trait, but not every initiative is wise. There are times when people with wisdom and experience must step in and "close the gates," saying that the newly embarked-upon course is wrong. That responsibility is placed on the Levites after a lifetime of service.

Once Rabbi Sherer had succeeded in extricating Agudath Israel from its crushing debts, he made sure that it would never again return to that predicament. One of his first major changes, upon assuming responsi-

---

7. Rabbi Shlomo Lorincz.

Rabbi Sherer greeting the Bluzhover Rebbe at Camp Agudah

bility for the day-to-day running of Agudath Israel of America, was to insist that salaries be paid on time. Until then, payment was haphazard and sporadic, with employees often going months without being paid. Under Rabbi Sherer, Agudath Israel became the first Orthodox organization to pay salaries on time. In his view, there was no other way to create the professional organization of which he dreamed.

In his efforts to institute a regime of financial stability, Rabbi Sherer was also aided by changing circumstances of the Orthodox community. Not only were the demands upon Agudath Israel's coffers no longer matters of life-and-death, but the resources available were far greater. During the war years, the Orthodox community in America included few people of substantial means. By the mid-'60s, many post-war immigrants and American-born yeshivah graduates had begun to earn comfortable livelihoods, and well-to-do Orthodox Jews were no longer a rarity.

That trend toward increasing affluence only accelerated in the decades to follow. At the 1971 Agudath Israel Convention in Atlantic City, for instance, $100,000 was raised — far more than at any previous convention. In addition, President Lyndon Johnson's Great Society generated a large number of new social programs which could be adapted to the needs of the Orthodox community, opening up an entire new source of funding for Agudath Israel and allowing the organization to expand its activities.

Breakthrough

THOUGH RABBI SHERER'S INITIAL FOCUS FROM THE TIME HE TOOK over the day-to-day running of Agudath Israel of America was on the organization's finances, he could never have been content to confine himself to fund-raising. Almost from the beginning, he began to establish connections in Washington, D.C. One of his first key contacts was Senator Jacob Javits, a four-term senator from New York (1957-1981) and for a period of time the only Jew in the Senate. Rabbi Sherer even opened his home to host receptions for Javits. The other was the powerful speaker of the House, John McCormack of Boston.

McCormack took a liking to Rabbi Sherer and wrote a number of letters of introduction for him to major charitable foundations. Initially, Rabbi Sherer approached them for scholarships for underprivileged children for Camp Agudah and Camp Bnos. In time, however, those contacts, in particular that with the Ford Foundation, would prove crucial to undertakings such as the Southern Brooklyn Community Organization (SBCO), the urban renewal project that helped preserve Boro Park as a Jewish neighborhood.

Rabbi Sherer's first major breakthrough in the corridors of power came in March 1961, when he was invited to address the House Education and Labor Subcommittee on public aid for parochial schools. Prior to his testimony, virtually everyone to whom he spoke about his hopes of gaining federal funding for Jewish education warned him that he was wasting his time and that the idea was a *gelechter* (a joke).

In the face of so much cynicism about his efforts, Rabbi Sherer went to discuss the matter with Reb Aharon. Reb Aharon pointed out that one of the *Avos* is Yitzchak, whose name derives from the Hebrew word for laughter. Most obviously that refers to the tremendous rejoicing that greeted his birth. But the name also reminds us of Sarah's dismissive laughter when she heard the angel tell Avraham that she would bear a son. Sarah believed that promise to be a *gelechter* — something that would never happen.

Reb Aharon explained that Hashem specifically wanted Yitzchak to bear a name that would recall Sarah's skepticism, and to serve as a permanent reminder that one of the pillars upon which *Klal Yisrael* rests was born from a *gelechter*, something that seemed impossible, but when Hashem wills it, nothing is impossible. "Let us hope your proposed *gelechter* will be like the one that greeted the promise of Yitzchak's birth." With that, Reb Aharon gave Rabbi Sherer a blessing for success.

Shortly after that meeting with Reb Aharon, but prior to his congressional testimony, Rabbi Sherer wrote to the Management Committee that the issue of both federal and state aid benefiting parochial schools was one "which we are not only duty-bound to speak up about, but which could also put Agudath Israel on the map as a spokesman for Orthodoxy." He added pointedly, "Unfortunately, my preoccupation with the dubious role of 'schnorrer' does not permit me to spend time on this type of activity, which is my first love .... We may be working toward an Agudah movement that will be financially on the upgrade, but spiritually out of sight and out of mind."

Readers of the March 30, 1961 *New York Times* opened the paper to find Rabbi Sherer's visage peering out at them above the fold of the cover page of the Metropolitan Section. The accompanying article consisted entirely of an extended excerpt from Rabbi Sherer's testimony, which filled the entire top half of the page. That testimony broke many of the stereotypes of Orthodox Jewry in America, and announced the arrival on the scene of a major new player, as Rabbi Sherer had predicted it would in his letter to the Management Committee four days prior to his testimony.

In his testimony, Rabbi Sherer described the extent of the Jewish parochial-school system and the heavy burden placed on Jewish par-

Rabbi Sherer hosting a reception in his home for Senator Javits.
Seated far left is Rabbi Chaim Twersky; at far right is Rabbi Leibel Cywiak

With Congressman John McCormack of Boston, Speaker of the House.

ents determined to provide their offspring with the "maximum religious education." He spoke of the sacrifices made over the millennia by Jewish parents, "even in the Nazi ghettos," to ensure that their children received a traditional Jewish education. And he called upon Congress to allow taxpaying citizens of the Orthodox Jewish faith "the benefit of their taxes to help defray the large expense of maintaining the Jewish parochial-school system."

Rabbi Sherer noted that it was necessary to bring to lawmakers' attention some basic facts about the extensive Jewish religious educational system in order to clear up the misconception "prevalent among the American public" that American Jews are opposed to parochial-school education. He attributed that misconception to statements made by "certain secularist Jewish leaders and the Reform clergy." Indeed, his congressional testimony pitted him against Leo Pfeiffer, general counsel of the American Jewish Congress and a nationally recognized authority on the separation of state and religion.

Rabbi Sherer's testimony was a breakthrough on many fronts. Rabbi

Aharon Kotler congratulated him on his return from Washington for having removed a serious *flek* (stain) from the Jewish community. No longer will people be able to say, Reb Aharon told him, that "Catholics are for religious education and Jews are against it." (When Rabbi Sherer entered the hearing room and sat down next to the Catholic representatives, the bailiff came over to him and told him, "Rabbi, you're sitting on the wrong side of the room." All the representatives of Jewish groups were on the other side.[8]) Removing that *chillul Hashem*, Reb Aharon assured him, was a major achievement whatever the practical consequences in terms of winning greater government funding that would benefit children in parochial schools and their parents.[9]

Finally, Rabbi Sherer's testimony served notice that a new era had dawned for Orthodox representation in the public sphere, and that the monopoly of the so-called Jewish defense organizations was a thing of the past. On *Tishah B'Av* of 5721 (1961), President John F. Kennedy invited Rabbi Sherer to the White House, along with 11 other leaders of major Jewish organizations, to hear his explanations of an American vote in the United Nations considered unfavorable to Israel. The inclusion of Agudath Israel in such a delegation was unprecedented and reinforced the message that American Orthodoxy had arrived.

Rabbi Aharon Kotler was emphatic that Rabbi Sherer must attend the Tishah B'Av meeting, and that he should shave and wear proper leather shoes (albeit with sand inside as a reminder of the mourning for the Temple) for the occasion.[10]

The night before the meeting, Reb Aharon spoke with Rabbi Sherer on the phone for an hour and a half to discuss Israel's security situation and all the issues that might arise in the discussions with President Kennedy. Reb Aharon instructed Rabbi Sherer as to how he should

---

8. Rabbi Sherer told this story to Rabbi Chaim Dovid Zwiebel.
9. Rabbi Shmuel Bloom, "Rabbi Moshe Sherer, זצ"ל: *Parnes HaDor*," *Jewish Observer*, Summer 1998, p. 42.
10. See *Mishnah Berurah* 554:33.
Years later Rabbi Sherer told Shimshon that shaving in preparation for the meeting had been one of the hardest things he ever had to do. He tried to think about Yosef HaTzaddik, who was removed from his cell and brought before Pharaoh on Rosh Hashanah after being given a haircut (Rosh Hashanah 10b; *Rashi, Bereishis* 41:14; see also *Chasam Sofer, Toras Moshe* ad loc.).

By the time he returned to New York from the meeting at the White House, it was almost time for Minchah. Rabbi Sherer traveled from the airport to Long Island in the hope of finding a *minyan* where no one would recognize him. Just before Minchah began, however, the rabbi announced to one and all that they had the honor of welcoming Rabbi Sherer. At that point, Rabbi Sherer had no choice but to ask the rabbi to announce that he had shaved for a meeting at the White House on the *psak* of Rabbi Aharon Kotler.

approach each issue. Though Reb Aharon did not read secular newspapers or listen to the radio, Rabbi Sherer attested later that he had fully anticipated the direction that the discussion with the president would take. At each turn, Rabbi Sherer presented the case for Israel as he had heard it from Reb Aharon, and the talking points that Reb Aharon asked him to present became the focal point of the discussion.[11]

Rabbi Sherer always referred to the Rosh Yeshiva's influence on the entire direction of the talks in the White House as a proof that the great

---

11. Rabbi Moshe Sherer (prepared for publication by Rabbi Shimon Finkelman), "True and Unwavering: the Proper Course for the Torah Jew and His Community," *The Jewish Observer*, Summer 1998, pp. 80-81.

talmidei chachamim are not only adept at unraveling the intricacies of difficult Talmudic subjects, but also possess a clarity of vision with respect to world events: "הֲפָךְ בָּהּ וְהֲפָךְ בָּהּ דְכֹלָּא בָהּ — Delve in it [the Torah] and continue to delve in it, for everything is in it" (*Pirkei Avos* 5:26).

A New Political Activism

IN A NOVEMBER 1966 ARTICLE IN *THE JEWISH OBSERVER* ENTITLED "Political Action: Orthodoxy's New Road," Rabbi Sherer described the new approach of Orthodox Jews to political action (which he distinguished from politics) that had commenced with his 1961 congressional testimony. He listed all the factors that had traditionally kept Orthodox Jews out of the public arena — "an innate fear of 'politics,' an enervating inferiority complex, and a distorted reverence for the powers of the *Yahudim* of non-Orthodox Jewry, who were assumed to have some mystical influence with the powers-that-be."[12]

Until the 1960s, Rabbi Sherer argued, Orthodox Jews "had relinquished their independence of action" in favor of "timidly and silently operat[ing] within the orbit of the non-Orthodox establishment, which had set up 'central agencies' to represent Jewish interests before governmental bodies."[13] Agudath Israel and the Agudas HaRabbonim had constituted the sole exceptions to this general pattern, dating back to the rescue work during World War II.

With the expansion of federal aid to parochial schools, however, the necessity of an independent Orthodox position was clear to all. While Agudath Israel had been the first to take up the cudgels for federal aid to Jewish parochial schools in 1961, President Johnson's Elementary and Secondary Education Act of 1965 had "catapulted American Orthodoxy into independent political action." "President Johnson," according to Rabbi Sherer, "did more with his education program to hammer out an independent Orthodox opinion in political affairs than reams of articles and decibels of convention speeches." Orthodox Jewry could no longer revert to its general dependence on central agencies who consistently adopted a "doctrinaire position on church-state separation, [which] undermined the position of the yeshivah day-school movement in the United States."[14]

---

12. Rabbi Moshe Sherer, "Political Action: Orthodoxy's New Road," *The Jewish Observer*, November 1966, p. 7.
13. Ibid.
14. Ibid., pp. 7-8.

Robert Kennedy recalls Rabbi Sherer's 1962 meeting with the president — and expresses support for goverment aid to private schools.

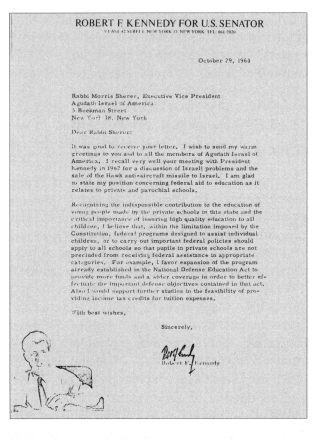

Rabbi Sherer could barely contain his bitterness at the American Jewish Congress and the Reform movement for their determination "not to budge one inch in their stubborn stand to deny federal-aid, not only to religious schools, but to their students as well."[15] Both groups had decried the proposed federal legislation due to the likelihood that it would encourage the creation of separate parochial-school systems in every denomination. Thus when it came to Jewish day schools, the Reform movement and the American Jewish Congress were on record as foursquare opposed. The Jewish agencies could save millions of dollars spent annually on creating good public relations for the Jewish community, Rabbi Sherer noted ironically, if the American Jewish Congress would cease and desist in its attacks on parochial schools chosen by millions of American parents.[16]

---

15. Morris Sherer, "The Great Society and Aid to Religious Schools," *The Jewish Observer,* January 1965, p. 3.
16. Ibid., p. 5.

Even as he decried Jewish opponents of federal aid to parochial-school students, Rabbi Sherer could also not contain his sarcasm when it came to the piddling aid offered Jewish education, in general, and day-school education, in particular, by Jewish federations. In 1963, only $5.5 million out of total Federation giving of $125 million went to any form of education. And of that amount only $633,131 was allocated to day-school education — nearly half of that amount in two cities, Chicago and Cleveland. In New York City, with total Federation fundraising of $20 million, not one penny went to day schools or yeshivos struggling to educate 50,000 Jewish children. During a decade in which federal aid to education increased over 2,000 percent, Federation support of Jewish education went up a measly 52 percent.[17]

By contrast, Jewish federations contributed $13 million nationwide to the building and operation of Jewish community centers. Only a sick Jewish society, in Rabbi Sherer's opinion, could give priority over *chinuch* to "recreation programs, sterile lectures, and social dancing."[18] Even Dr. Nachum Goldman, the most powerful figure in the Diaspora Jewish power structure, had warned that assimilation "threatens Jewish survival more than persecution, inquisition, pogroms and mass-murder of Jews in the past." How then, Rabbi Sherer wondered, did the federations condone the "starvation-diet offered to the pale and sickly *chinuch* plant ...."[19]

The major impact of the new political activism of American Orthodoxy described by Rabbi Sherer was felt in New York State, home to by far the largest Orthodox population of any state. The first success of abandoning the "hired-Kaddish" policy of relying on Jewish defense organizations came with the 1962 repeal of New York's Blue Law. The

---

17. Morris Sherer, "Education: The Step-Child of Jewish Budgeting," *The Jewish Observer*, September 1965, pp. 5-6.
18. Ibid., p. 6.
19. Ibid., p. 7.

    Ten years later, Rabbi Sherer was still beating the same drum about the lack of Federation support for Jewish education. At a time when the New York City Jewish Federation was allocating 27.4 percent of its budget to community centers and another 20 percent to "Jewish" hospitals, most of which did not even maintain a kosher kitchen, its contribution to Jewish education, of all denominations, constituted a mere 6 percent of its budget. The $700,000 given to the 92nd Street Y to maintain its "world-famous musical, dance, and dramatics program" was almost half of the total educational outlays. There could be no greater disgrace in the eyes of "our non-Jewish neighbors," Rabbi Sherer opined, than to demonstrate that Judaism has no viability in modern times due to a failure to provide Jewish children with a Jewish education sufficient to help them resist the assimilatory tides. Rabbi Moshe Sherer, "What is the Federation Doing With the Jewish Charity Dollar?," *The Jewish Observer*, February-March, 1977, pp. 4-6.

With President Lyndon B. Johnson

law required most stores to remain closed on Sunday and thus placed a great competitive disadvantage on *shomer Shabbos* merchants, who had to remain closed two days. The key to convincing the Catholic Church to abandon its opposition to repeal, according to Rabbi Sherer, was the Church's recognition that repeal was not part of an "on-going struggle to root out religion from public life, but rather a sincere demand by religious Jews … to be permitted to observe the religion to which they were personally committed."[20] That was something that the mainstream secular Jewish groups could never have done, and it was the beginning of a long cooperative relationship between Rabbi Sherer and the Catholic Church.

---

20. Ibid., p. 7.

Two other bills protected the rights of Shabbos-observant Jews. For years, *shomer Shabbos* Jews who wished to take civil service exams scheduled for Shabbos were forced to spend Shabbos locked in a room, until they took the exam on *Motza'ei Shabbos*. Under the Chananau Bill, both state and municipal bodies were required to arrange alternative dates for *shomrei Shabbos* when civil service exams were scheduled for Shabbos or Yom Tov. The DeSalvio Bill extended protection to *shomer Shabbos* students at state-funded educational institutions by requiring alternative arrangements for taking exams scheduled on Shabbos or Yom Tov. And on the national level, President Johnson signed into law a bill banning discrimination against Sabbath observers in federal employment.[21]

The other area where the newly released power of an independent Orthodoxy manifested itself was state aid to parochial schools. The New York State Textbook Bill of 1965 mandated the supply of textbooks to students in non-public schools from 7th-12th grades. Leaders of the New York State legislature told Rabbi Sherer that they had never been swamped by so much mail from Jewish constituents in support of any piece of legislation.[22] When the State Textbook Law was ruled unconstitutional by the lower state court, the Orthodox community moved quickly to have the decision overturned on appeal on the grounds that it benefits the student, not a religious entity. The various Orthodox organizations also successfully joined forces when the New York City Board of Education dragged its feet in implementing Title I of the 1965 Federal Education Act, which funded for the first time remedial services for parochial-school children.

Nor was Rabbi Sherer content with these successes. He had already trained his sites on the possibility of passing a Get Law that would encourage a husband to grant a religious *get* as a condition of obtaining a civil divorce. In cataloguing the Orthodox-friendly legislation enacted in New York State in the early 1960s, Rabbi Sherer did not take all the credit for Agudath Israel, other than to mention Agudath Israel's early calls for an independent political role for Orthodoxy. And he did not mention his own contributions to these successful legislative campaigns.

Nevertheless, it is clear that he had developed the closest legislative ties of any Orthodox figure, and was the de facto leader of campaigns

---

21. Menachem Lubinsky, "Rabbi Moshe Sherer, זצ"ל: A Life of … Is It Good for the Jews?" *The Jewish Observer*, Summer 1998, p. 61.
22. Ibid., p. 8.

in Albany. The quality of his political connections is attested to by the fact that he was chosen to head the national coalition representing five million children in non-public education in 1972, despite the fact that Jewish parochial schools constituted a small segment of the coalition.

In his legislative work, Rabbi Sherer demonstrated a mastery of political strategy from the start. When, for instance, certain members of the Catholic hierarchy began agitating for repeal of the Blaine Amendment, which outlawed any public financing for the benefit of private schools in New York, Rabbi Sherer urged them not to push the matter. The New York State textbook law, which provided textbooks to students in parochial schools, was then before the United States Supreme Court, and Rabbi Sherer felt that it would be preferable to allow the court to consider the issue in an atmosphere of calm and not in a "seething cauldron" of political activity. For that reason, he fully supported the refusal of the New York State Assembly Speaker Anthony Travia to bring up the repeal of the Blaine Amendment for discussion.[23] (The Supreme Court ultimately upheld the textbook law in *Board of Education v. Allen.*) Similarly, he opposed efforts to push new legislation to protect *shechitah* in New York State, which would have required extensive negotiations to reconcile the positions of various Orthodox groups. He had already secured Assembly Speaker Travia's promise that no humane slaughter bills would see the light of day in that legislative session, and therefore felt it preferable to leave the reconciliation of differences of Orthodox opinion to a later day when it became unavoidable. To one advocate of immediate legislation, he wrote, " All that you will create is to stir up a lot of ill-feeling which will not accrue to the benefit of Orthodoxy."[24]

In the summer of 1968, the New York Board of Education announced that it was ending the subsidized bus passes for children. When Rabbi Sherer learned of the decision from Rabbi Yehoshua Fishman of Torah Umesorah, he had only one question: Did the cancellation apply to all schoolchildren or only parochial-school children? Informed that it applied equally to all schoolchildren, Rabbi Sherer advised Rabbi Fishman against doing anything. Since there was no discrimination involved, there was no reason not to rely on parents of public-school children to raise an outcry. Given that Mayor John Lindsay was up for re-election that year, Rabbi Sherer estimated, there was every likeli-

---

23. Rabbi Sherer to Monsignor Eugene Molloy, February 26, 1968.
24. Rabbi Sherer to Judah Dick, February 12, 1968.

hood that he would intervene with the Board of Education to try to reverse the decision. And that is what eventually happened, without the Orthodox community having to use up any political credits.

EVEN AS HE DEALT WITH DAY-TO-DAY CRISES AND FUND-RAISING duties, Rabbi Sherer always had in front of him a long-range vision of

Charting the Future

what he wanted to do. As early as late 1962 he produced an eight-page document entitled Program of Activities for Agudath Israel of America, in which he set out his goals for the future — some short range and some further into the future. Reading through the document nearly half a century later, with the benefit of hindsight, one can see how Rabbi Sherer went down the extensive list he had given himself, ticking off one item after another.

One of the first items on his list was a creation of a "desperately needed" counterpart to *Dos Yiddishe Vort* to establish "a line of communication with the broad mass of English-reading Orthodox Jews." Such a journal was particularly needed, he noted, in light of the ingrained timidity of the larger Orthodox organizations to ever confront the Jewish establishment. That became *The Jewish Observer.*

Even then he dreamed of a "Torah Truth Squad" in every major city around the country that "would immediately react with a barrage of 'letters to the editor' whenever Torah views are distorted in the Anglo-Jewish and English press." That would become a large part of the Am Echad initiative 35 years later. When Daf Yomi was still virtually unheard of, he was thinking of how to "popularize the Daf Yomi project among America's Jews." And long before e-mail and the Internet provided access to Torah knowledge to Jews in faraway places, he was dreaming of "a national Torah-study correspondence course for adults residing in communities without proper facilities for genuine Torah education."

At a time when Agudath Israel of America could barely hold its head up financially, he called for an "all-out attempt to finance the opening of 50 Torah schools [in Israel] during the coming five years." And he had already anticipated the degree to which the "aroused views of American Orthodoxy" could be a potent force in the political/religious battles in Israel.

Despite the heavy fund-raising burden that weighed so heavily upon him, he stood prepared to engage in any "emergency fund-raising projects ... whenever the situation in any trouble-spot on the globe warrants it." And he was eager to establish "Agudist outposts in the entire Western hemisphere, by maintaining contact with Agudists in Latin American countries." Given the slender resources then at his command, the scope of his ambition is breathtaking. And all the more so in light of how many of his goals he realized in the coming years.

When Rabbi Sherer assumed the reins of Agudath Israel of America, the organization was tottering on the brink of bankruptcy. By the end of the decade, Agudath Israel was already functioning so successfully that it had become a model for emulation. Rabbi Aba Dunner wrote to Rabbi Sherer from London to compliment him on the recent growth of the American Agudah movement and to inquire as to the secret of his success. Rabbi Sherer felt confident enough of Agudath Israel's future by that point to answer:

> There is no secret method that helped the recent growth of the American Agudah movement. It requires a full measure of very hard work, deep commitment to the ideals, unswerving concentration on the goals and not the personalities, earning the confidence of the *Gedolei Torah*, demonstrating *ehrlichkeit* and honesty, running a democratic organization as a public trust, a basis of some talents — all stirred up, on a broad base of *Siyata d'Shmaya*. It's really not difficult at all, once Hashem gives that extra push.

He was clearly preparing to take Agudath Israel of America to the next level of growth, provided the *Siyata d'Shmaya* was there.

Part II
THE VISION

Chapter Seven

VISIONS OF AGUDATH ISRAEL

THE IMPORTANCE OF AN ANIMATING VISION WAS A CONstant theme of Rabbi Sherer's. The third essay in *Bishtei Einayim* begins with the well-known *Midrash* relating how Avraham asked his son Yitzchak, as they approached the mountain from afar, "Do you see what I see?" Yitzchak responded that he saw a "beautiful, stately mountain with a cloud connected to it." When Avraham posed the same question to the two servants accompanying him, they responded that they saw only an endless desert stretched before them.

The vision of the beautiful mountain from afar symbolized for Rabbi Sherer the secret of what a Jew needs to sanctify G-d's Name: "the ability to see the mountain .... Only one who is sensitized to the meaning of the true Torah ideal, someone whose gaze is firmly set on an ultimate goal, can possibly rise to the level of self-sacrifice. Perceiving the

grandeur of holiness gives one the ability to climb 'his personal Mount Moriah.'"

In a speech at the 1987 Agudath Israel convention, Rabbi Sherer referred to a puzzling passage in *Sefer Yehoshua*. On the eve of the fateful battle of Yericho, Yehoshua confronted an angel. To Yehoshua's request for guidance, the angel replied only, "Remove your shoe from your foot, for the place where you stand is holy" (*Yehoshua* 5:15). At first glance, the angel's words do not seem responsive to the request for guidance. But as interpreted by Rabbi Sherer, that angel's answer was: "When one realizes that 'the place where you are standing is holy' — i.e., that our misssion and ideals are holy — the walls of our enemies will come tumbling down."

But the vision of the ultimate goal and awareness of the sacred nature of our ideals are by themselves insufficient, unless accompanied by a commitment to action. The unique combination of vision and the ability to transform that vision into reality defined Rabbi Sherer.

"Why do we cover our eyes when we recite *Krias Shema*?" Rabbi Sherer once asked. He gave a novel answer: Because we can often see much more with our eyes closed. When our eyes are open we see only that which is immediately in front of us. But when our eyes are closed, we can imagine a much larger canvas: a canvas that encompasses all *Klal Yisrael* and its needs. One can think, for instance, about all those Jews around the world who need to be able to proclaim *Shema Yisrael*. That was the vision.

"But we not only cover our eyes," Rabbi Sherer continued. "We do so with our hands." The hand is the instrument of action, the means by which we take our thoughts and transform them into concrete deeds, he explained. Thus the covering of our eyes with our hands symbolizes our commitment to take our vision and do something about it.

That commitment to act on behalf of *Klal Yisrael*, Rabbi Sherer believed, had to start at an early age. He once pointed out that almost all the activists behind the creation of Agudath Israel in Europe, as well as the Bais Yaakov movement, and the religious press of Eastern Europe were in their 30's or even younger.

Agudath Israel as an Ideological Movement

SHORTLY AFTER ASSUMING HIS ROLE AS DIRECTOR OF AGUDATH Israel's Washington, D.C. office, Abba Cohen was summoned by Rabbi Sherer to New York for a meeting of all Agudath Israel senior staff. To his surprise, the meeting had nothing to do with any currently burning issues affecting the larger Jewish community or the Orthodox world. Rather, the subject of the meeting was how to stress the ideology of Agudath Israel and dispel the image of Agudath Israel as some kind of large social service agency on behalf of the Orthodox community.

If Cohen was shocked that Rabbi Sherer deemed enhancing Agudath Israel's image as an ideological movement to be of sufficient import to devote an entire meeting to the subject, he should not have been. Rabbi Sherer once wrote: [T]here is no greater misconception of the role of the American Agudath — *and no greater danger to its future as a vital force in American Orthodoxy* — than the myth that Agudath Israel of America is merely a "service agency." Rather, he insisted, "Agudas Yisroel is, first, and foremost, an *ideological movement,* a movement with a historical mission."[1]

That mission was enunciated by Moreinu Yaakov Rosenheim at Kattowicz: "to revive an ancient Jewish possession: the traditional con-

---

1. Rabbi Moshe Sherer, "Thinking Aloud: Candid Reflections on Agudath Israel of America as a 'Broad-based Grassroots Movement,'" *The Jewish Observer,* May 1992, p. 6.

cept of *Klal Yisrael* — Israel's collective body, animated and sustained by Torah as the organizing soul ...." The Kattowicz ideal animated everything Rabbi Sherer did, and he viewed Agudath Israel as its concrete embodiment.

The importance of instilling Agudah ideology was a recurrent theme for Rabbi Sherer. "There is no substitute for going out to woo the people," Rabbi Sherer told a *London Jewish Tribune* interviewer in 1981. That means, he continued, explaining to one's constituency what Agudath Israel is doing.

In his early years at the helm of Agudath Israel, he devoted a great deal of his time traveling to various branches. "During the next three weeks, I will be visiting five more areas for the sake of 'selling' Agudath Israel to the public, without any fund-raising involved. I'm convinced that we have to concentrate all our efforts on building a meaningful movement," he wrote to Rabbi Shlomo Lorincz.[2] The lack of fund-raising was crucial. Rabbi Sherer wanted the public to understand that Agudath Israel of America stood for a set of ideals, and was not just another self-perpetuating organization.

The yeshivos were central to the goal of spreading Agudah ideology, in Rabbi Sherer's eyes. "There is no other method of winning the *yeshivah bachurim* to our cause ... besides being exposed to Agudah leaders (and not regarding fund-raising)," he wrote to his protégé Rabbi Aba Dunner in London. In the same letter, he informed Rabbi Dunner that as a result of his concerns about the "lack of *bnei Torah* willing to offer their talents to *Klal* work," he had spent much time in recent months visiting a number of major yeshivos outside the New York area "talking to *bachurim* and winning them over to our ideals."[3]

After accepting an invitation to address a Melaveh Malkah from Dr. Shimon Askowitz, the president of the Philadelphia chapter of Agudath Israel of America, Rabbi Sherer requested that his schedule be arranged so that he could spend some time in the Talmudical Yeshiva of Philadelphia with the *bachurim*. He described "meetings with yeshivah students [as] of paramount importance in building our movement."[4] He spoke frequently with senior members of the Moetzes Gedolei HaTorah, particularly Rabbi Yaakov Kamenetsky, about encouraging *yeshivah bachurim* to identify with *Klal Yisrael* through Agudath Israel.

---

2. Rabbi Moshe Sherer to Rabbi Shlomo Lorincz, Nov. 25, 1968.
3. Rabbi Moshe Sherer to Aba Dunner, January 25, 1968.
4. Rabbi Moshe Sherer to Dr. Shimon Askowitz, Feb. 12, 1968.

Yet when he spoke in yeshivos, he primarily pushed Torah learning. On a 1967 visit to Telshe Yeshiva, which had an active Agudah chapter and whose roshei yeshivah, Rabbi Boruch Sorotzkin and Rabbi Mordechai Gifter, continually emphasized responsibility to the *Klal*, he told the *bachurim* that their sole focus at that stage in their lives should be *shteiging* in learning. "When ... you leave the walls of the *beis medrash* you should dedicate time to *askanus*, but until then, the best possible preparation of a life of *askanus* is learning Torah diligently," he told the *bachurim*.[5]

To bring out the obligation of those no longer in yeshivah to be involved in *Klal* work, Rabbi Sherer cited the *Gemara* in *Sanhedrin* (94b), which describes how Chizkiyahu HaMelech planted a sword at the entrance to the *beis hamedrash* and said, "כָּל מִי שֶׁאֵינוֹ עוֹסֵק בַּתּוֹרָה יִדָּקֵר בְּחֶרֶב זוּ — Anyone who is not involved in Torah, let him be pierced with this sword." Rabbi Sherer asked two questions. Why does the *Gemara* choose the odd term "involved," instead of the more obvious term "learning"? Second, why did Chizkiyahu HaMelech give over his message at the entrance to the *beis hamedrash* rather than inside? He answered that the *Gemara* is talking about one who has left the four walls of the *beis hamedrash* and is no longer learning full-time. (The entrance to the *beis hamedrash* is also the exit.) At that stage in a person's life, he must be "involved" in supplying the needs for a society based on Torah.

Rabbi Sherer sought to instill Agudah ideology from an early age. A memo to all head counselors at Camp Agudah and Camp Bnos in the early 1960s, for instance, stressed the "urgency of carrying through a planned program to inculcate our campers and counselor with the aims, accomplishments and history of Agudath Israel, both on the world scene and in America." He charged the head counselors — Rabbi Sysche Heschel, Rabbi Simcha Kaufman, and Rebbetzin Shonnie Perr — "to bear in mind that Camp Agudah and Camp Bnos are distinctive from other so-called Orthodox camps, not only in the depth of the religious fervor which we impart, but also in our duty to instill in our campers and counselors a love and appreciation of Agudath Israel as a world movement." The Zionist camps do an intensive job of brainwashing their campers to their ideals, he noted, and the Agudah camps should do no less.[6]

---
5. Rabbi Shlomo Mandel, Rosh Yeshivah of Yeshiva of Brooklyn.
6. Memo dated July 12, 1961.

"HE DEDICATED HIS LIFE TO *KLAL YISRAEL* AND EVERY INDIVIDUAL in it," says Rabbi Shlomo Lorincz. "Agudath Israel provided the ideological framework for his vision of *Klal Yisrael*. In recruiting new talent to work for Agudath Israel of America, Rabbi Sherer invariably emphasized the possibility of affecting thousands, and even tens of thousands, of Jewish lives for the good.

Agudath Israel Represents Klal Yisrael

Because Rabbi Sherer viewed Agudath Israel of America as the nearest approximation of the ideal declared at Kattowicz he constantly sought a leadership role for Agudath Israel of America in any matter of concern to the entire Orthodox world. Only the involvement of

With Rabbi Shlomo Lorincz

It frustrated Rabbi Sherer greatly when he would meet a young boy on Shabbos and the boy would tell him that he was going to Pirchei. "Pirchei what?" Rabbi Sherer would ask. Inevitably the boy would have no clue what he was asking. Then Rabbi Sherer would ask the boy his name. If the boy volunteered just his first name, Rabbi Sherer would ask, "Shmuli what?" in order to elicit the boy's last name. When that was forthcoming, Rabbi Sherer would explain, "Just as your last name is important because it describes your roots, so is it important to know that it is Pirchei Agudas Yisrael, a movement established by the greatest of *gedolim*."

Agudath Israel guided by the Moetzes Gedolei HaTorah insured, in his view, that the course charted would be that of *daas Torah*.

Yet he never confused the institutional needs of Agudath Israel with the larger concerns of *Klal Yisrael*. Looking over the program outline for an upcoming Agudath Israel convention, he once complained to Rabbi Labish Becker, "There is too much Agudath Israel and not enough *Klal Yisrael*."

"He knew when to wear the hat of Agudath Israel," says Professor Aaron Twerski, "and when not." In order to do battle with the American Jewish Congress on separation of state and religion issues, Rabbi Sherer saw the necessity of developing an Orthodox lawyers' group. Mendy Shayovich assumed that the new group would be under the aegis of Agudath Israel, particularly since Rabbi Sherer was one of the fathers of the concept.

Rabbi Sherer, however, disagreed. Most of the legal talent in the Orthodox world, he pointed out, consisted of graduates of Yeshiva University or those whose affiliations lean toward Modern Orthodoxy. Were the group to remain identified with Agudath Israel, Rabbi Sherer argued, it would not be able to attract many of the best Orthodox attorneys, and would, accordingly, be much less effective than it might be. Shayovich countered that if no institutional ties were preserved to Agudath Israel of America, within two years everyone would forget that Rabbi Sherer was one of the initiators of the idea and Agudath Israel would get no credit for its successes. So be it, Rabbi Sherer declared. It was far more important in his mind that the National Jewish Commission on Law and Public Affairs (COLPA) be effective.[7]

Driven by his vision of a united *Klal Yisrael*, Rabbi Sherer went to great lengths to bring as many divergent groups as possible into Agudath Israel. He always focused on the good points of every group in the Orthodox world, and honored each for its particular strengths. One result of his genuinely positive feeling toward each *chug* (subgroup) was that he was honored in turn by each group.[8]

The Syrian Jewish community of Flatbush constitutes a prime example of his efforts to broaden the Agudah coalition. Rabbi Sherer began his pursuit of the community by seeking to bring Chacham Yosef Harari-Raful, spiritual leader of the community, onto the Nesius

---

7. Among those involved in the early years of COLPA were Reuben Gross, Dr. Marvin Schick, and Julius Berman. Dennis Rapps later headed the organization for many years.
8. Rabbi Shlomo Lorincz.

Rabbi Raful addressing the
Ninth Siyum HaShas of Daf Yomi

of Agudath Israel of America. Before he embarked on his campaign, he called Rabbi David Ozeiry, Chacham Harari-Raful's brother-in-law. Rabbi Ozeiry told Rabbi Sherer that his efforts would be in vain: Chacham Harari-Raful never acts without considering every possible consequence at least a dozen times, and the answer is almost always no.

Not one to be easily discouraged, Rabbi Sherer persisted. He called Chacham Harari-Raful eight or nine times to pitch the idea. In the end, his perseverance simply wore down Chacham Harari-Raful's resistance. He told Rabbi Ozeiry, "Tell him — anything he wants, just don't call me again."

Thereafter Rabbi Sherer used every opportunity to thrust Chacham Harari-Raful into the limelight of the larger Agudah world so that the Halabi community would feel itself part of that world. Chacham Harari-Raful spoke at the *Siyum HaShas* in both 1990 and 1997, the last two of Rabbi Sherer's life.[9]

Rabbi Sherer devoted great energy to making the Syrian Jewish community feel welcome. After the first Agudath Israel convention attended by a large number of couples from the community, word got back to Rabbi Sherer that when speakers switched to Yiddish at crucial points in their speeches, and everyone else in the hall nodded or laughed, members of the community had no idea what the speaker had just said or what was so funny. At the post-convention meeting of senior staff that year, Rabbi Sherer spent considerable time discussing

---

9. In addition, Rabbi Sherer chose Rabbi David Ozeiry to be the 1996 recipient of the Rav Aharon Kotler Memorial Award at the Agudath Israel dinner.

their complaint and what could be done so that the problem not repeat itself the next year.

His eagerness to include the Syrian community, which until then had been an almost entirely self-enclosed subcommunity within the larger Orthodox world, was in part an expression of his view of the essential unity of Torah Jews. In addition, he wanted to do everything possible to avoid a reprise in America of the situation in *Eretz Yisrael* in the late '80s, in which the Torah community split into three separate political parties: Shas (Sephardi), Agudath Israel (primarily Chassidic), and Degel HaTorah (Lithuanian).[10]

Finally, Rabbi Sherer felt that identification with the larger Torah world would serve to strengthen the Syrian community itself. That latter assumption proved correct. For those who were growing rapidly in their religious observance under Chacham Harari-Raful's guidance, the knowledge of Agudath Israel's existence and that they were members of a much larger world of Torah Jews was an important step in their development. Prior to that, when Chacham Harari-Raful had urged members of his community to take opportunities to see great Torah authorities, like Rabbi Moshe Feinstein, they had not done so. But as they began to attend Agudath Israel events, their connection to *gedolei Yisrael* other than Chacham Harari-Raful developed.[11]

Rabbi Sherer's vision of Agudath Israel as the spokesman for *Klal Yisrael*, as we have seen, led him to seek as big a tent as possible under which divergent groups could gather. But it also meant that Agudath Israel would do everything possible to serve even those Torah communities which, for their own ideological reasons, chose not to affiliate with Agudath Israel. Agudath Israel, in his view, is a public trust, and as members of *Klal Yisrael*, it belonged to those groups no less than to those directly affiliated with the organization.

The largest of those communities is the Satmar community, centered in Williamsburg and Monroe, in upstate New York. Rabbi Yoel Teitelbaum, the Satmar Rav, was one of the most outspoken and frequent critics of Agudath Israel over the years. Yet Rabbi Sherer treated him as he did any other rosh yeshivah, and Satmar never doubted that their educational systems and yeshivos were as important to Rabbi Sherer as any other.[12] (Agudath Israel was equally at the service

---

10. Chacham Yosef Raful.
11. Chacham Yosef Raful.
12. Professor Aaron Twerski.

With Rabbi Ruderman (l) and the Bluzhover Rebbe (r).
Rabbi Shmuel Bloom is standing at left.

of the Yeshiva of Flatbush and Ramaz, at the left-wing of Modern Orthodoxy.)

Shortly after Reb Yoilish's successor, Rabbi Moshe Teitelbaum, was installed, he sent a message to Rabbi Sherer that he wanted to meet with him and Mendy Shayovich, who then held a high position in the administration of New York governor Hugh Carey. He asked, however, that Rabbi Sherer come to visit him at 5 a.m. on the Fast of Gedaliah, lest he be seen by some of the early-rising Satmar *Chassidim*. Shayovich asked Rabbi Sherer why he was even considering going to meet with someone who would not even be seen in public with him and who could be counted on to sharply criticize Agudath Israel in the future. Rabbi Sherer replied simply, "If a *Yid* asks you for a *tovah* [favor], you do it. I'll see you at 5 a.m."

Rabbi Sherer once found himself seated together with the Satmar Rebbe at a simchah of his close friend Eli Basch, who enjoyed a very close relationship with the Rebbe. The latter told Rabbi Sherer, "Reb Eli is Satmar's ambassador to Agudas Yisrael." To which Rabbi Sherer replied with mock hurt, "I thought I was your ambassador to Agudah."

His strong sense of Agudath Israel as a public trust led Rabbi Sherer to maintain a strict anti-nepotism policy in the Agudath Israel. On occasion, the ban on the hiring of spouses or children of those on staff created practical difficulties, but Rabbi Sherer felt that making clear that Agudath Israel is not a private fiefdom was more important than solving the immediate problem.

The Image of Torah Jewry

IN A SENSE, RABBI SHERER'S LIFE MISSION, SAYS MENACHEM Lubinsky, can be summarized in one word: image. For some the word conjures up Madison Avenue and media manipulation. But Rabbi Sherer saw it in a different context. He related his concern for public relations to Hashem's blessing to Avraham: "I will make your name great and you shall be a blessing." Publicity, said Rabbi Sherer, is a form of making "one's name great" in order to serve as a "source of blessing" to the Jewish people.[13]

Rabbi Sherer was a keen student of the power of the media and its uses. And he was meticulous about everything connected to the image he conveyed to those with whom he came into contact. "Rabbi Sherer," Rabbi Berel Wein, once famously remarked, "wore the whitest shirts of any man I knew." He was always impeccably tailored. Rarely was he seen without his suit jacket on, even in the office. He studied the great orators of his day and the most famous speeches, such as Martin Luther King Jr.'s "I Have a Dream" speech, because oratory was another skill that could be used in the service of *Klal Yisrael*.

At the White House signing of the Egyptian-Israel peace treaty in 1979, Israeli Prime Minister Menachem Begin made a "great *Kiddush Hashem*," in Rabbi Sherer's opinion, when he placed a yarmulke on his head before quoting from *Tehillim* in his speech. But the yarmulke itself, Rabbi Sherer wrote to Rabbis Porush and Lorincz, did not fit him and "looks as if were taken from the reception table at a bar mitzvah or wedding celebration."[14] He urged them to immediately present to

---
13. Rabbi Eliyahu Meir Klugman, "Portrait of a Leader: An Appreciation of Rabbi Moshe Sherer, zt"l," *The Jewish Observer*, Summer 1998, p. 27.
14. Rabbi Moshe Sherer to Rabbi Shlomo Lorincz and Rabbi Menachem Porush, March 26, 1979.

With Senator Joseph Lieberman

Prime Minister Begin a properly fitting yarmulke. Such details bothered him.

Rabbi Sherer sought to instill the same concern with self-presentation to other staffers of Agudath Israel. At one point, Rabbi Sherer even brought a shoeshine man into the office on a weekly basis.[15] Before Rabbi Nesanel Kasnett assumed his job as the first director of Agudath Israel's Washington, D.C. office, Rabbi Sherer made sure to teach him how to serve a business lunch, and even what socks to wear for a meeting.[16]

But all these details are merely expressions of a much deeper concern that guided his every waking moment: *Kiddush Hashem.*[17] As carriers of

---

15. Rabbi Chaim Dovid Zwiebel.
16. Rabbi Nesanel Kasnett, "The Yoseif of His Generation," *The Jewish Observer*, Summer 1998, p. 27.
17. On Rabbi Sherer's first *yahrtzeit* a special tribute was paid to him by the U.S. Senate, with close to 200 Agudah activists from all over the country present, as well as Senators John Ashcroft, Edward Kennedy, Joseph Lieberman, Trent Lott, Daniel Patrick Moynihan, Charles Schumer, Arlen Specter, and Strom Thurmond. Senator Lieberman began his remarks, "Rabbi Sherer's life can be summed up by two words: *Kiddush Hashem.*"

the banner of *Klal Yisrael*, united by Torah, the first and most important task of Agudath Israel was lifting the image of the Torah Jew. Agudath Israel as an organization, and each employee of the organization, he insisted, must always be guided by a consciousness of the *Kiddush Hashem* implications of every action. Every time they entered a meeting together, Mendy Shayovich remembers, Rabbi Sherer would say, "We are going into this meeting as *shluchim* [emissaries]. We have to make sure that a *Kiddush Hashem* comes out." That determination drove him constantly.¹⁸

Justice Cardozo's famous standard for fiduciaries — "not honesty alone, but the punctilio of an honor the most sensitive" — could have been written with Rabbi Sherer in mind. He epitomized the characteristic of being *n'ki kappaim u'bar lev* — of clean hands and a pure heart. Despite numerous offers, he refused to serve on the boards of any corporation or to accept any money other than his salary from Agudath Israel of America. Nor would he agree to be honored by any organization or institution. "I want to show that it is possible to serve *Klal Yisrael* without being repaid with honor or wealth," he once told his son. His refusal to benefit in any way from his public position was one of the factors that led the Steipler Gaon to support his choice as co-chairman of World Agudath Israel in 1980.¹⁹

Rabbi Meir Frischman, longtime director of Camp Agudah, had a close friend whose daughter had been put on the waiting list for medical school in Israel. The friend asked Frischman to see if Rabbi Sherer could use any of his contacts in Israel to get her in. As soon as Frischman explained the problem to Rabbi Sherer, the latter asked his secretary Mrs. Debby Jacobs to get Rabbi Shlomo Lorincz on the phone. While waiting for the call to go through, Frischman kept talking and told Rabbi Sherer that his friend had promised to donate $10,000 to Agudath Israel if Rabbi Sherer could help get her accepted. Rabbi Sherer immediately called out to Mrs. Jacobs, "Forget it." He then explained to the astounded camp director, "I don't want anyone to ever say that I did a favor for $10,000."

Nor was that an isolated story. Julius Klugman, a committed Agudist from his youth in Germany, once needed help obtaining an import

---

18. When the Hebrew year 5755 began, Rabbi Sherer began writing on his correspondence, under the date, שְׁנַת קדּוּשׁ ה׳, a reference to the gematria of *Kiddush Hashem* when written without the י.
19. Rabbi Eliyahu Meir Klugman, "Portrait of a Leader: An Appreciation of Rabbi Moshe Sherer, זצ״ל," *The Jewish Observer*, Summer 1998.

license for raw materials crucial to his human hair business. The matter required connections in the State Department, and, as so many did in such situations, Klugman turned to Rabbi Sherer, who put him in contact with the State Department official he needed. When Rabbi Sherer called Mr. Klugman to tell him of the arrangements, which he knew was worth a very large amount of money to the business, he did not forget to add, "If I see that your annual contribution this year was any larger than last year, I will send the check back to you."

That straightness in all monetary matters was one of the qualities that drew many of Agudath Israel's largest supporters to Rabbi Sherer.[20]

Rabbi Sherer was concerned not just with the image Agudath Israel projected to the outside world, but also the image of Agudath Israel in the eyes of its own constituency. One annual report to be distributed at an Agudath Israel convention contained a large 8½-inch by 11-inch photograph of Rabbi Sherer together with President George Bush at the White House. Shortly before the convention, when it was already too late to redo the report, Rabbi Sherer had second thoughts about the prominence given to that particular picture. He felt that an organization based on fealty to the direction of *gedolei Torah* should not act as if the greatest possible honor was to be on good terms with the president.

Rabbi Sherer spent a lifetime developing his connections with dozens of powerful politicians, and he was surely not ashamed of his relationship with the president of the United States. In addition, he knew the value of being known as one who was on intimate terms with many powerful people. One wall of the corner of his office where he sat with his most important guests was covered with pictures of himself with presidents and other political luminaries.

Nevertheless, those he chose to emphasize at the conventions were not political leaders but *gedolei Torah*. Accordingly, a day before the convention, he instructed the staff to post stickers over the photograph of himself with President Bush in over 1,000 annual reports, even though putting out a less than perfect product was anathema to him. But it would have been far worse, in his eyes, for Agudath Israel to promote itself by its association with the president rather than with *gedolei Yisrael*.[21]

That incident also reveals an important aspect of Rabbi Sherer's character: He was genuinely not star-struck by important people, even

---

20. Mordechai Friedman.
21. Rabbi Yosef Chaim Golding.

the president of the United States. Had he been he would not have been able to resist inclusion of that picture. Rabbis Meir Zlotowitz and Nosson Scherman explain this aspect of Rabbi Sherer: "If a person has been close to a real *gadol b'Torah*, as Rabbi Sherer was to Rabbi Aharon Kotler and others, they will never be awed by anyone else, no matter how powerful."[22]

A Clean Organization

NOTHING PAINED RABBI SHERER AS MUCH AS SCANDALS INVOLVing Orthodox Jews or institutions. The good name of religious Jews was an obsession with him, and any scandal hurt him personally.[23] He made it his highest priority to ensure that no whiff of scandal ever attached to Agudath Israel of America. None ever did.

If a religious Jew ran afoul of the law, Rabbi Sherer would do everything he could to make sure that every plausible argument was offered in his defense and that he was dealt with fairly by the authorities. And he worked tirelessly to make sure that any publicity was kept to the bare minimum. But he would never do anything that might suggest that either he or Agudath Israel condoned illegality of any kind. He never asked any government official to look the other way with respect to any corner cutting, and indeed always encouraged them to enforce their regulations equally with respect to Orthodox institutions.

On those occasions when Agudath Israel found it impossible to execute a contract for social or educational services with the government to the letter, the relevant government agency would be contacted and an explanation offered of Agudath Israel's difficulty with the contract as drafted. But if the government agency could not, or would not, waive or amend its regulations, Agudath Israel would terminate the contract and return to the government money already advanced.[24]

Based on Agudath Israel's success in managing other municipal programs, New York City once asked the organization to manage a multimil-

---

22. Rabbi Sherer once pointed out that when making a blessing on a Jewish king or a great Torah scholar, we use the verb חלק (shared) with respect to the Divine quality found in that person, whether it be glory or wisdom. By contrast, when making a blessing on a gentile king or a great gentile scientist, the verb employed is נתן (gave) (see *Berachos* 58a). Sharing implies that the relationship between the one providing the quality, Hashem, and the recipient is ongoing; whereas giving implies that the relationship is severed once the quality, whether glory or wisdom, is given. The great Torah leaders thus manifest their deep and ongoing connection with Hashem (*Magen Avraham Orach Chaim* 224:4). See Rabbi Yitzchak Hutner, *Pachad Yitzchak, Chanukah* 9.
23. Yosef Friedenson.
24. Rabbi Eliyahu Meir Klugman, "Portrait of a Leader: An Appreciation of Rabbi Moshe Sherer, זצ"ל," *The Jewish Observer*, Summer 1998, p. 21.

lion-dollar program. Under the program, the city would pay poor people to work as homemakers assisting housebound elderly people who were eligible for Medicaid benefits. The program would have brought money into Agudath Israel's coffers to assist struggling Russian immigrants and elderly Jews, though it would in no way be limited to the latter categories.

Rabbi Sherer recognized, however, that many of the "homemakers" and those they were assisting would not be *"shomer Shabbos,"* and thus Agudath Israel might be in the position of paying for work done on Shabbos. He turned down the grant without hesitation.

On another occasion, New York State approached Agudath Israel with an offer to sell it a nursing home facility for only $500,000. But Rabbi Sherer absolutely refused to become involved in an industry that had suffered from its share of scandals, no matter how much money Agudath Israel might bring in from the facility.[25]

Camp Agudah once had the opportunity to take over a government lunch program from another institution, and to earn a $5,000 administration fee in return. Meir Frischman presented the opportunity to Rabbi Sherer, who told him that he could go ahead, but with one crucial proviso: only if the institution's program was "100 percent kosher."

As a member of the board of AARTS, the accrediting organization for college-level yeshivos that he did so much to bring into existence, Rabbi Sherer insisted that all institutions fully comply with all the financial reporting requirements imposed by AARTS. Prior to one meeting with roshei yeshivah, he sent notice that he would resign "unless the meeting will formally decide that an institution cannot be accredited, or may not continue its accreditation, by AARTS unless it immediately opens its record-keeping files and all other materials to an audit by auditors hired by AARTS."

Richard Schifter, a partner in the prestigious law firm Fried and Frank and later an Assistant Secretary of State for Human Rights and Humanitarian Affairs in the Reagan and first Bush administrations, began working with Agudath Israel in the mid-'70s. He first heard of Agudath Israel when he read a *New York Times* article about the Southern Brooklyn Community Organization (SBCO). After hearing from Melvin Richey, an Orthodox partner in his firm, that Agudath Israel was a highly reputable organization, he approached Rabbi Sherer. Schifter's practice dealt primarily with government agencies, and he

---

25. Menachem Lubinsky.

explained to Rabbi Sherer that there were many government programs that might be of benefit to Agudath Israel's constituency, including housing for the elderly.[26]

At one of their first meetings, Rabbi Sherer told Schifter that there would be all kinds of individuals involved in some of the programs that Schifter had outlined. "If anyone ever suggests anything improper," he told Schifter, "I want you to come to me immediately." In his many years working together with Agudath Israel, Schifter recalls, no one ever did.

For Rabbi Sherer, the *kesser shem tov* (the crown of a good name) was truly above all. Because his good name was his most precious possession, the low moment of his entire public career was a front-page banner headline in the *New York Post* dealing with the scandals in the Orthodox community. The article alleged that a certain figure known to have "close links" to the yeshivos was the target of a government investigation in connection with scandals in the nursing home industry and might have been the intermediary in certain deals involving nursing homes. Though the article did not mention Rabbi Sherer by name, his identity was clear to any knowledgeable reader.

In a letter to Rabbi Mordechai Gifter, he poured out his anguish at the "'reward' that I receive for 33 years of working for Torah and *Yiddishkeit* — without ever having accepted a single penny in my entire life in 'side income' for anything I ever did for any institution or any individual …. [T]his is my 'reward' for having pleaded for so many years — as you yourself know so well — with all the [institutions] that they must do everything correctly and precisely."[27]

Rabbi Sherer described to Rabbi Gifter the long conversation that he had had with Dorothy Schiff, the publisher of the *New York Post*, and all the steps he was taking to press his case. But he expressed pessimism about the possibility of justice for a Torah Jew "from a woman who has already married three times out of the faith." He also poured out his wrath against the leader of one of the mainstream Jewish organizations who he was convinced had leaked his name to the *Post*. That man had been the executive director of the Synagogue Council at the time the eleven roshei yeshivah issued their famous *psak* against participation in the organization.

---

26. Eventually Mr. Schifter became the primary counsel for SBCO. He took only the attorney's fees allowed under the SBCO grant, a reduction of between 60-70 percent of his normal hourly rate.
27. Rabbi Sherer to Rabbi Mordechai Gifter, March 4, 1976.

Addressing the 1976 Agudath Israel convention. Seated at the dais (l-r): Rabbi Pinchas M. Teitz (partial view), the Bostoner Rebbe, Rabbi Gedaliah Schorr, Rabbi Chaskel Besser, Rabbi Yehudah Oelbaum, Rabbi Moshe Feinstein, Rabbi Yaakov Kamenetsky, Rabbi Yaakov Yitzchak Ruderman, Rabbi Boruch Sorotzkin, Rabbi Simcha Elberg

Rabbi Sherer's fear, as he expressed it in a subsequent letter to Rabbi Gifter, was that "the false newspaper smear could ruin my potential for doing good for Torah."[28] By the time of that second letter, that smear had passed without leaving its mark, though a still-shaken Rabbi Sherer wrote to Rabbi Gifter, "I am still not enough of a good Jew to have been able to live through my recent traumatic experience, without a sense of bitterness and rancor."

What had saved Rabbi Sherer in the end was precisely the reputation and reality for scrupulous honesty in which he had invested so much effort. When the story first broke, *The New York Times* assigned John Hess, its chief investigative reporter at the time, to cover it. Hess later told Rabbi Sherer that he had checked into the allegations, and he had never heard such undiluted praise for one man's integrity as he had for Rabbi Sherer's.[29]

Never again would Rabbi Sherer's personal reputation be impugned in any way. But 16 years after the infamous headline in the *New York Post*, another incident took place that must have aroused some of the same feelings of frustration and anger. The occasion was the publication of a book by Israeli journalist David Landau entitled *Piety and Power: The World of Jewish Fundamentalism*. The book contained an interview with Tom Dine, then the executive director of the America-Israel Public Affairs Committee (AIPAC), the powerful pro-Israel lobbying organization in Washington, D.C. in which Dine spoke derogatorily of "the ultra-Orthodox" (a term Rabbi Sherer detested for its implication that somehow the "ultras" are too religious).

Dine confided to Landau that since taking over AIPAC, he had never been to Brooklyn, and that "mainstream Jews [don't] feel very comfortable with the ultra-Orthodox. It's a class thing, I suppose. Their image is — smelly ... Hasid and New York diamond dealers." Dine went on to describe how United Jewish Appeal people, and the like, told him several times that "they don't want to fly El Al because of 'those people,'" and how he himself preferred Swissair and Luftansa. Dine summed up the image of the Orthodox as "low-class. Still the poor immigrant image. That's the perception of a lot of people I mix with."

One can well imagine Rabbi Sherer's anguish upon reading these words. He had spent his entire professional life of over 50 years molding Agudath Israel into the most highly professional organization in the Jewish world

---
28. Ibid., March 29, 1976.
29. Interview with Rabbis Nosson Scherman and Meir Zlotowitz.

only to have its entire constituency dismissed as "low-class" and "smelly" by one of the most influential Jewish professionals in America. Moreover, nothing in Dine's remarks indicated that he had ever heard of Agudath Israel of America, or that the high esteem in which Rabbi Sherer and his staff were held by a wide array of politicians and government officials had in any way affected his image of the "ultra-Orthodox."

In his letter to Dine, after reading *Piety and Power*, Rabbi Sherer described how he had to rub his eyes in amazement upon reading the Dine interview with Landau. His description of Dine's interview as "both shocking and heartbreaking" was not just for the public record, but surely described his personal feelings.[30]

But even Rabbi Sherer's "deep outrage" — at the exposure of the "raw nerve" that large numbers of non-Orthodox Jews view the *chareidi* world with "a scornful eye and muted disdain" or "resentment and embarrassment" — did not prevent him from attempting to draw lessons from the "Dine debacle" (as he called it). He did not give way to mere saber rattling and expressions of impotent rage. "Bias based upon ignorance," he wrote in the *Jewish Observer*, "is a malady that can be remedied."

Rabbi Sherer pointed out an interesting anomaly. When Hashem initially blesses Avraham Avinu, He tells him, "וַאֲבָרְכָה מְבָרְכֶיךָ וּמְקַלֶּלְךָ אָאֹר — Those that bless you, I will bless; and those that curse you, I will curse" (*Bereishis* 12:3). With respect to those who bless Avraham, Hashem uses the same verb to describe the blessing that He will provide them. But with respect to those who curse Avraham (מְקַלֶּלְךָ), the verb form does not remain constant. Instead of אֲקַלֵּל, which would have been the parallel verb to describe Hashem's cursing of those who curse Avraham, the Torah chooses another verb for cursing: אָאֹר. The latter verb is based on the same Hebrew root as light (אוֹר), and can be read as, "I will enlighten them: I will illuminate their eyes to see the real you."[31]

Rabbi Sherer urged a redoubling of efforts on the part of all Orthodox Jews to fulfill the role of enlightening their fellow Jews who are so "abysmally uninformed." "Let them see our *ahavas Yisrael* .... Let them visit Lakewood's Beth Medrash Govoha .... Let them experience the splendor of the chassidic courts .... Let them see how the study of the Daf Yomi has become a daily habit for tens of thousands of Jews ... and observe the state-of-the-art electronic systems created for this largest adult Jewish educational undertaking in our history .... Let them wit-

---

30. Rabbi Moshe Sherer, "Lessons of the 'Dine Debacle,'" *The Jewish Observer*, September 1993, p. 13.
31. Ibid., p. 14.

ness first-hand the effective, dignified broad range of global acitivities conducted by Agudath Israel, yes, conducted with 'class' (to borrow a word from the Dine interview)."[32]

As infuriating as Rabbi Sherer found the Dine interview, he did not dismiss the possibility that the Orthodox Jews "may at times be partially responsible for our negative image." That recognition provided an opportunity to return to one of his favorite themes — the need for the Torah community to dedicate itself to the cause of making Hashem beloved through our actions: "We must constantly review, through a high-powered magnifying glass, our business practices; our ethical standards; our public conduct; our speech; our good old-fashioned *'mentschlichkeit.'*"

He concluded his treatment of the Dine affair with an insight from Rabbi Moshe Feinstein. In the morning blessings preceding *Krias Shema*, we ask Hashem to intill in our hearts the capacity "to understand and elucidate, to listen, to learn, and to teach ...." How many of us, Rabbi Feinstein asked, actually aspire to teach Torah to others? He answered that each of us teaches Torah through the life that we live, and "we therefore beseech Hashem to enable us to plumb the depths of Torah, so that every move we make resonates with the rich inspiration of the Torah's teachings." Every Torah Jew, Rabbi Sherer stressed, is therefore a teacher of Torah: sometimes for better, and sometimes, unfortunately, for worse.[33]

Also a Social Service Organization

WHILE RABBI SHERER VEHEMENTLY REJECTED THE NOTION THAT Agudath Israel of America is "merely" or solely a social service organization, and felt that such a view was inimical to Agudath Israel. That was not to deny, however, that a large percentage of Agudath Israel's resources under his leadership were devoted to what might be classified as providing social services for the Orthodox community. Nor was Rabbi Sherer the slightest bit embarrassed about that fact.

On the contrary, providing help and sustenance to Jews was fully consonant, even required, by a proper understanding of the ideology of Agudath Israel. Rabbi Sherer liked to quote the *Gemara* (*Pesachim* 118a) that *Hallel HaGadol* (the Great Song of Praise) is thus named because it contains a verse of praise to Hashem for apportioning food to every

---
32. Ibid., p. 15.
33. Ibid., p. 18.

living creature. Accordingly, concern with the livelihood of Jews is fully consonant with the mission of Agudath Israel.[34]

In working to alleviate the problems and suffering of Jews, Agudath Israel was emulating the example of *HaKadosh Baruch Hu*. The *Midrash* (*Yalkut Shimoni, parashas Yisro*) asks why the Ten Commandments were not given at the very beginning of the Torah. The *Midrash* answers by comparing the situation to that of a king who descends upon a kingdom and announces, "I will rule over you." The people's natural response is to ask, "Have you ever bestowed anything good upon us that you should rule us?"

So, relates the *Midrash*, the king built a protective wall around their region, brought in water to drink, and fought their battles. When the king next said, "I will rule over you," the people replied, "Yes, yes."

Similarly, the *Midrash* concludes, "G-d took the Jews out of Egypt, split the Sea for them, provided them with manna, quail, and water from the well, and battled Amalek. Then He said, "I will rule over you!" And they replied, "Yes! Yes!"

That *Midrash*, commented Rabbi Sherer, teaches us that a leader must demonstrate that he is in touch with the community and knows its fundamental needs, and can address those needs. Otherwise his leadership will not be accepted.[35] In the same manner, said Rabbi Sherer, a dynamic program of action will attract people to the banner of Agudath Israel.

BY NATURE, RABBI SHERER WAS AN ACTIVIST CONSTANTLY SEEKING new challenges and vistas. He used to say, "When one's memories exceed his dreams, his end is near."[36] He never reached that point. When Yossi Feldman, for instance, first had the idea of establishing a career

An Ideology of Activism

---

34. To make the same point, Rabbi Sherer asked why, in *Bircas Hamazon* (the blessing after eating a meal), we pray for sustenance in conjunction with our prayer for the rebuilding of Jerusalem (וּבְנֵה יְרוּשָׁלַיִם); a more logical place for the prayer would seem to be in the blessing where we thank Hashem for food (נוֹדֶה לְךָ).

He answered that the placement of the prayer is meant to show a similarity between the Holy City and the *parnassah* (sustenance) of the Jewish people. The destruction of Yerushalayim, Hashem's home, is a *chillul Hashem* of monumental proportions. Similarly, it is a terrible *chillul Hashem* when Torah Jews — Hashem's children — are unable to adequately support themselves and their families. *Rabbi Shmuel Bloom.*

35. Rabbi Moshe Sherer, "An Ideology of Activism," *The Jewish Observer*, Summer 1997, p. 34.

36. Rabbi Meir Zlotowitz. Just as Rabbi Sherer was a collector of *vertlach* of all types, so did he collect pithy phrases, of which this was one. He was forever jotting down quotes from his voluminous reading. His longtime secretary, Mrs. Debby Jacobs, has piles of quotations scribbled quickly on scraps of paper.

counseling service for those entering the job market for the first time or those seeking a career change, he brought the idea to Rabbi Shmuel Lefkowitz, Agudath Israel's chief lobbyist in Albany. Rabbi Lefkowitz broached the idea with another member of the Agudah staff, who expressed reservations about taking on a new project. But when he mentioned the idea to Rabbi Sherer the instinctive reaction was very different: "If someone wants to do something about a communal problem, of course we want to help."

On more than one occasion, Rabbi Shimshon Sherer asked his father why he was constantly taking on new projects and putting himself under new pressure. The answer was always the same: "Agudas Yisrael is a *davar she'be'kedushah* [a holy undertaking]. It's *ruchniyus* [spiritual]. When it comes to spirituality, there is no leveling off. One might think he can reach a plateau and coast, but it's a false premise. In *ruchniyus*, if one does not constantly ascend, he will automatically drop."[37]

Rabbi Sherer was absolutely committed to the concept of *mesorah* (transmitted tradition) that has always guided *Klal Yisrael*, but he never lost sight of the fact that the *mesorah* of Torah through *gedolei Torah* provides guidance for addressing the emerging and changing needs of *Klal Yisrael* throughout the ages.

Rabbi Sherer's awareness of the inevitability of change is captured in one of his classic *vertlach* on the verse (*Devarim* 32:7) — "זְכֹר יְמוֹת עוֹלָם בִּינוּ שְׁנוֹת דֹּר וָדֹר שְׁאַל אָבִיךָ וְיַגֵּדְךָ זְקֵנֶיךָ וְיֹאמְרוּ לָךְ — Remember the days of old, understand the years of generation after generation. Ask your father and he will relate it to you; your elders and they will tell you." Rabbi Sherer noted that that word for years, שְׁנוֹת, is from the same Hebrew root as שִׁנּוּי, meaning "change." When one looks back at history, said Rabbi Sherer, one must also pay attention to how things have changed. In order to anticipate changes and know how to deal with them as they arise, one must seek guidance from our fathers and elders, the *gedolei hador*.

Activism, Rabbi Sherer argued, was part of the very ideology of Agudath Israel. The Talmud teaches, "Great is Torah study for it brings one to action" (*Baba Kamma* 17a), and thus the ideology of Agudath Israel necessarily leads to action on behalf of *Klal Yisrael*.[38] Certainly the activist streak ran deeply in him. While the Gates of Tears are never

---

37. Rabbi Shimshon Zelig Sherer, "A Father to Me, a Father to *Klal Yisrael*," *The Jewish Observer*, Summer 1998, p. 70.
38. Rabbi Moshe Sherer, "An Ideology of Activism," *The Jewish Observer*, Summer 1997, p. 35.

Heading a California delegation on a leadership mission to Washington.
L-r: Jeff Fishman, Marty Fishman, Rabbi Chaim Schnur, unknown, David Edelman, Isaac Weiss, Ira Handelsman, Bernie Weisel, Congressman Henry Waxman, Irving Lebovics, Sol Genuth, Senator Alan Cranston, Stanley Treitel, Dr. David Sherman, Rabbi Sherer, Eli Treitel, Peter Faber, Rabbi Shmuel Bloom

closed (*Berachos* 32b), he once said, they are locked for those who shed tears when they could be taking action. Hand-wringing and despair were luxuries that the Torah world cannot afford.[39]

Only through action is an ideology fully clarified. If the vision of Agudath Israel were never implemented in concrete actions, it would remain only a high-sounding abstraction, a bit of ivory tower philosophy, perhaps incapable of realization in the real world. Indeed, wrote Rabbi Sherer, all statements of Agudah ideology "pale in comparison to the profound message imparted by a dynamic organization actually functioning in accordance with Torah guidelines, as interpreted by Torah sages."[40]

Ideology and action were inextricably intertwined in Rabbi Sherer's mind. Action gives concrete expression to ideology, while, at the same time, ideology informs action and provides it with a more meaningful context. "A wondrous act of *chesed* performed by a *chesed* organization is just that: an act of *chesed*, but no more. When the same is discharged by an organization that embodies a sacred trust, this expression of kindness and concern is elevated to a higher plateau: it is a legacy of the sacred trust that conceived it ..." he wrote.[41]

---

39. Rabbi Eliyahu Meir Klugman, "An Appreciation of Rabbi Moshe Sherer, צז״ל: Portrait of a Leader," *The Jewish Observer*, Summer 1998, p. 27.
40. Rabbi Moshe Sherer, "An Ideology of Activism," *The Jewish Observer*, Summer 1997, p. 36.
41. Ibid., p. 36.

Chapter Eight

THE IDEOLOGY OF DAAS TORAH

"TOTAL SUBSERVIENCE ON ALL QUESTIONS OF POLICY TO THE *daas Torah* of *gedolei Yisrael*," Rabbi Sherer once wrote, "is the basic foundation block of Agudath Israel as an ideological movement." He constantly emphasized to the staff that Agudath Israel was a movement founded by the *gedolei Yisrael* of the previous generation to unite Torah Jews under the banner of Torah, and to ensure that all the problems facing the Jewish people, whether as individuals or as a collective, be confronted *b'derech HaTorah*.[1]

In an article entitled "Daas Torah," Rabbi Sherer once described the idea that the greatest Torah scholars should confine themselves to the *beis medrash* and not involve themselves in the leadership of the Jewish

---
1. Rabbi Shlomo Gertzulin, "A Great Leader ... A Master Teacher," *The Jewish Observer,* Summer 1998.

With *gedolei Yisrael* at Camp Agudah (l-r): Rabbi Sherer, the Bluzhover Rebbe (flanked by his grandsons), Rabbi Yaakov Yitzchak Ruderman, Rabbi Mordechai Gifter, Rabbi Chaim Dovid Zwiebel

people, as "a concept so foreign to Judaism it is difficult to imagine how it managed to spread from the Gentile world into the minds of even some Torah-observant Jews."[2]

There is no place for such a view among Jews, for whom Torah is not just "religion," but "everything, and encompasses not only the life of the Jewish individual but that of the nation as well." The concept of *daas Torah*, he explained, is fully rooted in the *Midrash* (*Bereishis Rabbah* 1:1) that describes Hashem as looking into the Torah and creating the world. Thus "the Torah provides history's agenda, past, present, and future, and encompasses the world's every secret."

As a consequence those who have merited to acquire the Torah "possess the best credentials for effectively addressing the world's problems." The wisest of men can still be blinded by their personal interests and human weaknesses. Not so the greatest Torah leaders, whose holiness allows them "to transcend all worldly concerns."

---

2. After a 1982 speech by Rav Shach aroused a furor in Israel over the fact that he dared to address topics considered "political," Rabbi Sherer sprung to the defense of the leader of the Torah world. The call for Torah scholars "to know their place," he noted, is an old one. The *Maskilim* did not begin with a frontal assault on the authority of Torah authorities. Rather they attempted to confine their place to the *daled amos* (four cubits) of the study hall.

In a witty reversal of the *Gemara's* (*Shabbos* 31a) phrase, "*Kavata itim l'Torah* — Did you fix times for Torah?" Rabbi Sherer used to say, "The Torah has to fix the times." Which times? Those mentioned in *Koheles* (3:1-8): a time to remain silent, a time to speak, and so on. That wordplay captured an entire worldview: Only the Torah giants of the generation can analyze the times and know what response is appropriate.

When Rabbi Sherer interviewed Rabbi Avi Shafran for the position of director of Public Affairs for Agudath Israel of America, a large part of the interview consisted of Rabbi Sherer's reflections on his own experiences with *gedolei Torah* over the years. He told Rabbi Shafran how on more than one occasion he had been convinced that the advice being given him by *gedolei Yisrael* was demonstrably wrong. But in each case he had subsequently discovered that the *gedolim* had been more farsighted than he. His most important question for Rabbi Shafran was: "Are you willing to bend your own will, whatever you might think, to that of the Torah authorities of the generation?"

A letter from Rabbi Sherer to one of the leading figures in the Orthodox Union and a one-time president of the organization, captures well Rabbi Sherer's philosophy of *daas Torah*. The Orthodox Union was one of the Orthodox organizations that did not heed the 1956 *psak din* of 11 leading roshei yeshivah against participation in the Synagogue Council. The issue remained a subject of great controversy within the OU itself over the years, and the OU leader had written to Rabbi Sherer seeking a further elaboration of the halachic reasoning and the sources in *poskim* upon which the *psak* was based.

Rabbi Sherer began his response with a discussion of what he had learned from his apprenticeship under Rabbi Aharon Kotler about such issues. "I recall that it was always his position that it would be inadvisable, in a matter that engendered so much controversy, for *gedolei Torah* to release the sources and reasoning behind their issuing a *psak din*," Rabbi Sherer wrote. All that would result, Reb Aharon felt, was that the public would be confused, as opponents "would pounce upon the sources and attempt to tear them down, while offering contradictory 'sources' to negate the *psak din*."

The issue, Rabbi Sherer insisted, ultimately boils down to one basic point: "Does one have faith and recognize the authority and dependability of the *gedolei Torah* who issue the *psak din* or not? If one lacks faith in their competence and sincerity, then all the halachic sources in the world are meaningless .... Instead of opening a debate between

Lilliputians and giants on halachic issues, the issue must be faced squarely ...: Does anyone have the right to refuse to accept a *psak din* in which all the *gedolei Torah* in the world concurred?"

RABBI SHERER VIEWED ONE OF THE CRUCIAL TASKS OF AGUDATH Israel as educating the Orthodox world in the concept of *daas Torah*.

Educating the Public

Agudath Israel conventions were used to instill the idea that *gedolei Torah* are the natural leaders of the Jewish people.[3] At every main session of the conventions, at least one major Torah figure spoke, and the speeches by venerable members of the Moetzes Gedolei Torah were presented as the substantive and emotional highlight of the program. Roshei yeshivah and *rabbanim* sat on the dais facing the audience during major sessions, with members of the Moetzes Gedolei HaTorah prominently seated toward the center.

A prominent leader of the British Agudah credits Rabbi Sherer with having educated an entire generation of American *baalebattim*. "We also had world-class *gedolim* in Britain in the '70s and '80s," he notes, "but we took *gedolim* and made them into rabbis. Rabbi Aryeh Leib Gurwicz, the Gateshead Rosh Yeshivah, could walk into a shul and stand at the back, and no one would even escort him to the front. That would never have happened in America."[4]

Rabbi Sherer's educational agenda was carried out in private as well as public, especially when the individual in question was someone whom he had tapped as a future *askan*. While he was still a *talmid* in yeshivah, Menachem Lubinsky was offered a free ticket to Jerusalem to attend a conference of the World Zionist Youth Foundation. As a national officer in Zeirei Agudath Israel, Lubinsky went to ask Rabbi Sherer what he should do. Rabbi Sherer sent him to Rabbi Moshe Feinstein, who in turn sent him to Rabbi Yitzchak Hutner.

Rabbi Hutner spent two-and-a-half hours talking to Lubinsky about responsibility to *Klal Yisrael*. As for the specific question he had posed, said Rabbi Hutner, he might just as well send two red yarmulkes, since all the sponsors wanted was two yarmulkes that would stand out in the crowd to show that they had Orthodox participation. Later Lubinsky asked Rabbi Sherer why he had sent him to ask the question when he had certainly known the answer in advance. Rabbi Sherer admitted that

---

3. Rabbi Shlomo Lorincz.
4. Rabbi Aba Dunner.

At a meeting of the Moetzes Gedolei HaTorah in the home of the Bluzhover Rebbe. L-r: Menachem Lubinsky, Rabbi Sherer, the Bluzhover Rebbe, Rabbi Yaakov Yitzchak Ruderman, Rabbi Yaakov Kamenetsky, Rabbi Yitzchak Hutner

he had known what Lubinsky would be told, but felt that it was important to educate him in the need to consult *daas Torah.*

Any public questioning of *daas Torah,* no matter how small the forum, was likely to draw a response from Rabbi Sherer. A former student in Rabbi Sherer's homiletics class wrote a letter to some obscure, long forgotten Orthodox weekly taking issue with the view of the Moetzes Gedolei HaTorah concerning participation in the 1968 Conference of World Synagogues in Jerusalem. (There appears to have been no publication with an Orthodox readership, no matter how small, that Rabbi Sherer did not view it as his duty to read.) Rabbi Sherer reprimanded him sharply for publicly taking a stand at variance with his own Rosh Yeshivah. "At the very least, "Rabbi Sherer suggested, "perhaps you should have thought twice about making a public demonstration of your refusing to accept his views."

The same young man had privately expressed to Rabbi Sherer his opinion that *daas Torah* is purely advisory when it comes to non-halachic issues, such as Orthodox participation in the New York Board of Rabbis. Rabbi Sherer begged to differ — and sharply. Whatever the limits of *daas Torah,* he wrote him, it had no applicability to the current case: "a clear-cut decision of Torah authorities, on live issues, in the form of a *psak din,* after their having duly considered the specific issue."

Though his reproof was sharp, Rabbi Sherer ended his letter — characteristically — by making it clear that his criticism was not personal, and that he looked forward to the recipient's *"teshuvah."* He even went so far as to predict that "there will come a time when you will sense the validity of our position, and that no individual, simply because he once attended a yeshivah and has *semichah,* has the right to make decisions for himself, in areas where the leading *gedolei hador* have issued a *psak din."* (In fact, the recipient of that letter went on to work closely with Rabbi Sherer on many matters in the years to come.)

Serving the Yeshivos

CLOSELY RELATED TO *DAAS TORAH*, IN RABBI SHERER'S MIND, WAS the status of the yeshivos. One of the key lessons he absorbed from Rabbi Aharon Kotler was that there is no *Klal Yisrael* without the yeshivos. He would not tolerate any public criticism of roshei yeshivah. A speaker at an Agudah event once expressed such criticism. Rabbi Sherer cut him off in the middle of his speech.[5]

On one occasion, Dr. Ernst Bodenheimer, the chairman of *The Jewish Observer* editorial board and the driving force behind the creation of the magazine, inadvertently made a remark that could have been understood as a criticism of the Moetzes Gedolei HaTorah. When Rabbi Sherer learned of the remark, he traveled to Hunter, New York, where Dr. Bodenheimer was staying, and insisted that he write a letter of apology to the Moetzes. Then Rabbi Sherer sat down with Dr. Bodenheimer and helped him draft his response.[6]

No project was closer to Rabbi Sherer's heart than *The Jewish Observer*. From the moment that he assumed the leadership of Agudath Israel of America, he dreamed of a magazine that would provide the Torah viewpoint on the great issues confronting *Klal Yisrael*. Without Dr. Bodenheimer, *The Jewish Observer* would never have come into existence when it did. He too had long been thinking about the importance of a magazine in English to show the true nature of Orthodox Judaism to a larger Jewish audience. Rabbi Sherer placed him in charge of creating *The Jewish Observer*. Over more than four decades, Dr. Bodenheimer contributed to the *The Jewish Observer,* through his astute editorial comments on every article, endless dedication, and his financial support.

In short, Rabbi Sherer had great respect for Dr. Bodenheimer. There

---

5. Rabbi Labish Becker.
6. Dr. Ernst Bodenheimer, "Remembering Rabbi Sherer," *The Jewish Observer,* Summer 1998, p. 31.

was no one else who could have taken his place and maintained *The Jewish Observer* afloat. At the same time, Agudath Israel of America obviously could not have its principal English-language ideological journal run by someone who did not enjoy the full confidence of the Moetzes Gedolei HaTorah. And that is why Rabbi Sherer made a beeline for the Catskills to immediately resolve any tension that might have been created.

A part of Rabbi Sherer always remained the Ner Israel *yeshivah bachur*. His reverence for Torah learning was real and deep. One prominent Orthodox professional to whom Rabbi Sherer was very close recalls how every time they spoke, Rabbi Sherer would ask, "Are you learning?" There was never a conversation where he did not mention the subject of how crucial regular Torah learning is to anyone who represents the Orthodox community.

Agudath Israel brought in large sums of money for the yeshivos, and, in addition, helped the yeshivos with the clerical work required by both state and local governments. On more than one occasion (usually in the midst of a financial crisis of some sort), it was suggested to Rabbi Sherer that Agudath Israel should ask the yeshivos to defray some of the costs of the organization's services on their behalf. Rabbi Sherer would never hear of it. "Agudath Israel exists to service the yeshivos," he would say. "Period. End of story."

On his summer "vacations," in the early 1970s, Rabbi Aba Dunner of the British Agudah used to spend a couple of weeks in Rabbi Sherer's office. He was sitting in the office one day when Rabbi Sherer arranged for free busing for New York City yeshivah students. When he put down the phone, Rabbi Dunner asked him what percentage fee Agudath Israel of America would take for having arranged the municipal subsidy.

Rabbi Sherer was visibly taken aback by the question. He rose from his seat, walked around his desk to where Rabbi Dunner was sitting, and looked at him directly. "Aba, don't ever talk to me that way. Either you understand what we are doing here or you don't. We are not in this business for the money."

Tightening the relationship between Agudath Israel and the yeshivos was one of Rabbi Sherer's constant goals. Rabbi Yaakov Kamenetsky served as the most important liason on this issue. Reb Yaakov, for instance, met with leaders of Zeirei Agudath Israel to discuss the philosophical justification for *yeshivah bachurim* participating in Zeirei and how to encourage such involvement. He pointed out that every individual has an obligation not only to learn Torah but to teach it. No one learns 24 hours a day. So the time given to *tzarchei tzibbur* (public needs) should never come at the expense of learning, but can take the place of exercise or some other form of relaxation. On the other hand, Reb Yaakov warned, Zeirei should avoid the participation of the type of *bachur* who will use his participation in Zeirei to make a name for himself at the expense of his learning *sedarim*.[7]

Reb Yaakov lamented the development among some *yeshivah bachurim* of an erroneous belief that Agudath Israel and its supporters are not *"frum"* enough. That derived in part, he explained, from the misconception that the Brisker Rav had opposed Agudath Israel. In truth, said Reb Yaakov, he supported Agudath Israel from the outside, but "unfortunately we lack a Reb Aharon today to argue and correct these errors."[8]

THOUGH RABBI AHARON KOTLER WOULD ALWAYS REMAIN RABBI Sherer's great hero, after Reb Aharon's *petirah,* Rabbi Sherer transferred his absolute allegiance to Reb Aharon's successors. "He would change his mind in a minute if the *gedolim* said otherwise; he was a *gevaldige ma'amin* (great believer) in *gedolim*," said Rabbi Boruch Borchardt, who worked

Heeding the Gedolim

Consulting with Rabbi Yaakov Kamenetsky

---

7. The meeting with Rabbi Kamenetsky took place at his home May 11, 1978. All citations are to the minutes of that meeting.
8. On the Brisker Rav's support for Agudath Israel, see Rabbi Shlomo Lorincz, *B'mechitzasam: In Their Shadow* (Feldheim Publishers 2008), pp. 189-195.

closely with him for nearly 50 years.

Rabbi Boruch Borchardt once asked him how he could take a particular position on an issue when just the day before he had expressed the opposite view. To Rabbi Sherer the explanation was obvious: "I heard differently from Reb Aharon."

Not only did Rabbi Sherer listen to the *gedolim*, he sought out their opinions, even in areas which others might have considered mundane.[9] Says Rabbi Shlomo Gertzulin, comptroller of Agudath Israel of America, "There was no subject of substance in which he regarded himself as sufficiently expert to make decisions without the advice of *gedolim*."

Rabbi Chaim Dovid Zwiebel recounts an incident from early in his career in Agudath Israel in which Rabbi Sherer was so confident that his recommendation to the Moetzes Gedolei HaTorah would be accepted that he had already begun planning for its implementation. Yet after listening to Rabbi Sherer's presentation, the Moetzes decided upon an alternative approach: one that had been considered and rejected by the experts with whom Rabbi Sherer had consulted.

Zwiebel was taken aback by the way that Rabbi Sherer left the meeting smiling from ear to ear, already busily planning how to execute the direc-

Greeting Rabbi Aharon Kotler with Rabbi Chaskel Besser. Rabbi Yaakov Kamenetsky is seated in the foreground

---

9. Rabbi Shlomo Gertzulin, "A Great Leader … A Master Teacher," *The Jewish Observer*, Summer 1998, p. 50.

Consulting with Rabbi Moshe Feinstein; Dr. Ernst Bodenheimer is in the background

tives of the Moetzes. Sensing Zwiebel's bewilderment at his reaction to the rejection of a proposal upon which he had lavished time and energy, Rabbi Sherer told him, "Don't you understand, Chaim Dovid? This is what Agudas Yisrael is all about. This is why I came here, for a day like today, when my own opinion would be rejected by the *gedolei Yisrael*."

That response, Zwiebel adds, had nothing to do with Rabbi Sherer having been persuaded that the *gedolim* were right and he was wrong. Rather it was a result of his deeply held belief that only the primacy of Torah leadership could secure the future of *Klal Yisrael*.[10]

Inevitably there were cynics who downplayed Rabbi Sherer's professions of subservience to the Moetzes Gedolei Torah, and who claimed that he manipulated the Moetzes. Such remarks grew more numerous over the years with the passing from the scene first of Rabbi Aharon Kotler, and two decades later of Rabbi Moshe Feinstein, Rabbi Yaakov Kamenetsky, and Rabbi Yaakov Yitzchak Ruderman, and their replacement on the Moetzes Gedolei HaTorah by roshei yeshivah, who were in many cases younger than Rabbi Sherer and who possessed nothing like his vast experience.[11]

---

10. Chaim Dovid Zwiebel, "Changing the Landscape of Torah Jewry in the United States: the Internal and External Legacies of Rabbi Moshe Sherer," *The Jewish Observer*, May 2008, p. 15.
11. Asked how he could display the same fealty to the younger roshei yeshivah of his later years, as to such legendary figures as Rabbi Reuven Grozovsky, Rabbi Aharon Kotler, Rabbi Moshe Feinstein, and Rabbi Yaakov Kamenetsky, Rabbi Sherer had a ready answer based on a *vort* from

Consulting with Rabbi Yaakov Yitzchak Ruderman

Whenever he heard such statements, relates his son, he would laugh out loud and say, "Shimshie, anyone foolish enough to say that has no concept of the *gedolei Yisrael*. Do they have even an inkling of who the *gedolim* are? Do they have any concept of their vision? Can they begin to comprehend the depth of their analysis of any issue? It is impossible to ever tell such giants what to do. They [i..e, the cynics] have no idea what true *gedolei Torah* are like if they can say something so foolish."

The cynics made a simple mistake: They confused influence with control. Undoubtedly, the members of the Moetzes Gedolei HaTorah placed great confidence in Rabbi Sherer's judgment and relied upon him for the most objective presentation of the facts possible. Whenever a decision required assessing the likely consequences of different courses of action, the Moetzes depended on him for that assessment. The members of the Moetzes knew that no one in the Jewish world possessed his experience in public affairs or his ability to foresee the outcomes of different courses of action: both the probable and the possible. They could rest assured that their decisions would be well informed because of the quality of information he provided them.

---

the Imrei Emes of Ger. *Chazal* state that Moshe Rabbeinu was ten *amos* tall (*Bechoros* 44a). And if so, Aharon HaKohen was also ten *amos* tall, because the *Midrash* says that they were "*shkulim*," equal in physical stature" (*Bereishis Rabbah* 1:21). That raises a problem: How then could Elazar have worn the same priestly vestments worn by his father Aharon HaKohen (*Bamidbar* 20:26)? Elazar was not ten *amos* tall (cf. *Shabbos* 92a). The Imrei Emes answered that somehow the priestly vestments worn by Aharon fit Elazar. So it is with the Moetzes, said Rabbi Sherer: The younger generation somehow fills the shoes of their illustrious predecessors.

With the Novominsker Rebbe and the Bostoner Rebbe

So unquestionably Rabbi Sherer's influence on the decision-making of the Moetzes Gedolei HaTorah was enormous. But the members of the Moetzes placed their confidence in him only because they trusted him so deeply. They knew that he viewed himself as nothing more than a *shlucha d'Rachmana* (an emissary of the Merciful One).

Thus they had no doubt in whose hands the final decision rested. The current Rosh Agudas Israel of America, the Novominsker Rebbe, Rabbi Yaakov Perlow, spoke for the Moetzes, when he said, "Members of the Moetzes had 100 percent confidence that he was not running the organization behind their backs. He could push an issue, but he honestly believed that his role was to execute the directives of the Moetzes. On any ideological issue, he was completely subservient, even to the members of the Moetzes who were younger than he."[12] Rabbi Yitzchak Feigelstock, another member of the Moetzes in Rabbi Sherer's later years, testifies to having witnessed numerous examples of instances in which Rabbi Sherer had offered his opinion and then changed it in light of the opinion of members of the Moetzes.

---

12. Rabbi Perlow is well situated to compare Rabbi Sherer's relationship to different generations of members of the Moetzes Gedolei HaTorah by virtue of the fact that his father, the previous Novominsker Rebbe, also served on the Moetzes.

In a beautiful personal letter to Rabbi Sherer, Rabbi Yitzchak Hutner, Rosh Yeshivas Chaim Berlin, wrote:

> Few, very few are the remaining *gedolei Torah* [after the Holocaust] of whom it can truly be said their *daas* is *daas Torah*. But far rarer still is the *askan* on behalf of the public who truly bows before the *daas* of those *gedolei Torah*. I know very well how many internal trials you have undergone to preserve that quality of submission that dwells in your soul. And I know the emotional price that you have paid for the point of light that derives from that quality of submission. But there is no price too high to pay for that point of light deeply embedded in your soul.[13]

Rabbi Sherer frequently expressed his joy that the final decision on the great issues facing *Klal Yisrael* lies with the *gedolei Yisrael* and not with lay leaders. "Their word is final. The *achrayus* [responsibility] is not on me. It is the *gedolei Yisrael* who are responsible," he used to say.

He once received a plea to use his connections to secure the release from a Soviet prison camp of a Prisoner of Zion. He realized that the most promising avenue was through a former high U.S. State Department official, who had excellent connections to the Soviet leadership. Rabbi Sherer knew the official well, but hesitated about approaching him. At the time, there were widespread news reports that the official in question was contemplating a run for the Senate from New York. Rabbi Sherer feared that the price of securing his assistance would be the promise of some form of political support at a later date. And that was problematic, since the official in question was Jewish and had just married a gentile woman. To support his candidacy in any way, Rabbi Sherer feared, would constitute a *chillul Hashem*.

Rabbi Sherer presented his dilemma to Rabbi Yaakov Kamenetsky. Reb Yaakov told him the question was a very difficult one, and he would have to think about it overnight. The next day, Reb Yaakov told Rabbi Sherer that while *pikuach nefesh* (saving a life) overrides every prohibition in the Torah, except for three, nowhere do we find that it takes precedence over *chillul Hashem*. Therefore, he said, Rabbi Sherer would have to confine himself to other avenues.[14]

Over a period of decades, Rabbi Sherer labored on end-of-life issues,

---

13. Rabbi Yitzchak Hutner to Rabbi Moshe Sherer, *Rosh Chodesh Iyar* 5730.
14. Some time after Reb Yaakov had *paskened* the *sheilah*, Rabbi Sherer had occasion to relate the story to Rabbi Elazar Menachem Man Shach, who responded in almost exactly the same words Reb Yaakov had.

such as the determination of the time of death, autopsies, and health-care proxies for patients no longer able to give informed consent to their own medical-care decisions. Those efforts required building up extensive contacts with the State Board of Health, with key legislators, and with representatives of other religious groups concerned with the same issues. In the early 1990s, the Commissioner of Health of New York State developed legislation on health proxies that was in many respects the answer to Agudath Israel's dreams. The legislation would have made it possible for Orthodox Jews to appoint health-care proxies for themselves in the event of being incapacitated to ensure that all medical decisions concerning their treatment were according to halachah. The Commissioner of Health no doubt expected both the gratitude and support of the Orthodox community for legislation that responded to the fears of Orthodox Jews that their lives would be terminated prematurely under non-halachic standards.

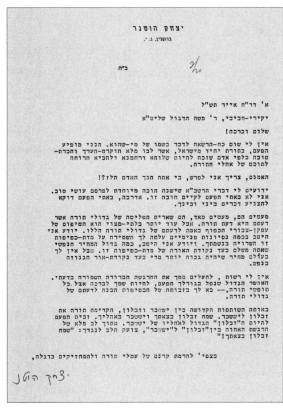

Rabbi Hutner's letter of admiration

At the same time, the legislation would have made it possible for duly appointed proxies to authorize the withholding of such necessities as food and water and medical care. The question for the Moetzes was: In a secular society, in which Orthodox Jews constitute a very small minority of the population, should Agudath Israel be content with legislation that protected the ability of Orthodox Jews to lead their lives in accordance with halachah? Or would it constitute a *chillul Hashem* for Orthodox Jews to support legislation that would allow health-care providers to carry out passive "euthanasia," something unacceptable in halachah? An additional factor was that there was almost no chance of securing legislation that would both ban the forms of passive euthanasia forbidden by halachah while providing Orthodox Jews with the ability to ensure that their end-of-life treatment would be according to halachah. In other words, by opposing the legislation, the Orthodox community might risk some very crucial protections.

The Moetzes Gedolei HaTorah ruled that Agudath Israel must oppose legislation that would have the effect of authorizing, and thereby condoning, euthanasia. Rabbi Sherer was left with the unenviable task of informing the Commissioner of Health that Agudath Israel had no choice but to oppose the legislation. He did not hesitate.

Strengthening the Moetzes Gedolei HaTorah

THE IDEOLOGY OF *KLAL YISRAEL* LED BY *GEDOLEI YISRAEL* WAS one that Rabbi Sherer inherited from the founders of Agudas Yisroel in Kattowicz. The institution of the Moetzes Gedolei HaTorah also existed long before he entered the movement. But he formalized the operations of the Moetzes Gedolei HaTorah in such a way as to increase the involvement of the Moetzes in the day-to-day operations of Agudath Israel.

Rabbi Sherer felt strongly that *daas Torah* is most fully experienced when the *gedolei Torah* sit together and discuss an issue together. Though the Moetzes had always met periodically, Rabbi Sherer worked actively to ensure that the meetings of the Moetzes Gedolei HaTorah took place on a regular scheduled basis, and that as many members as possible attended, whether in person or by conference call.[15] On certain occasions, when he wanted to make sure that both sides of an issue were presented as clearly as possible to the Moetzes, Rabbi Sherer would stage a debate for them, in which distinguished representatives of both positions would present their case.[16]

---

15. Rabbi Chaim Dovid Zwiebel.
16. In an aide-mémoire dated January 20, 1969, Rabbi Sherer describes a meeting with Dr. Joseph Kaminetsky, the National Director of Torah Umesorah. Part of the meeting was devoted to Rabbi Sherer explaining to his colleague why Agudath Israel of America enjoyed such a high level of confidence from the *gedolim*. Rabbi Sherer cited the practice of having spokesmen for opposing sides appear before the Moetzes as proof of Agudah's "honest approach" to the *gedolim*. Because Agudath Israel of America submits the minutest policy decisions to the Moetzes, Rabbi Sherer explained, the Moetzes members "sense the total reliance [upon their decisions and] they respond

The decision on whether Agudath Israel should join the newly formed Jewish Community Relations Council occasioned one such debate. George Klein, a prominent Orthodox businessman and a leading activist in local New York City affairs, made the initial approach to Rabbi Sherer about joining the Federation-sponsored JCRC. Rabbi Sherer felt that Agudah membership on the JCRC offered many potential benefits for the Orthdodox community, and immediately entered into lengthy negotiations with the JCRC about the terms of membership.

Before those negotiations even commenced, Rabbi Sherer made it clear that Agudath Israel's participation was contingent on approval of the Moetzes Gedolei HaTorah. But he wanted to secure the most favorable possible conditions prior to presenting the issue to the Moetzes for approval. To secure approval, Rabbi Sherer knew, it would have to be crystal clear that participation in the JCRC could not be compared in any respect to participation in multidenominational religious bodies, like the Synagogue Council or the New York Board of Rabbis, or be construed as conferring legitimacy on heterodox groups that were also members. He succeeded in extracting, in the course of negotiations, a major concession: If any constituent organization determined that a particular issue was religious in nature, it could demand that the issue be removed from the agenda.

When the issue was presented to the Moetzes, Rabbi Sherer and two others spoke in favor of joining the JCRC, and three other leading Agudath Israel insiders spoke against it. Despite Rabbi Sherer's efforts to secure Agudah membership, and the length of time he had invested in the proposal, the Moetzes decided that Agudath Israel should confine itself to observer status on the JCRC. Rabbi Sherer was left with the unenviable task of informing George Klein that the weeks of negotiations had proven futile, and the matter was closed for Agudath Israel in light of the Moetzes meeting. But he never flinched or second-guessed the decision.

Rabbi Sherer was always looking for ways to secure greater input from roshei yeshivah into the work of Agudath Israel. In the late 1970s, for instance, most of the members of the Moetzes — Rabbi Moshe Feinstein, Rabbi Yaakov Kamenetsky, Rabbi Yaakov Yitzchak Ruderman, and the Bluzhover Rebbe — were already well into their 80's. In addition, over

---

with total confidence."

L-r: Rabbi Shneur Kotler, Rabbi Boruch Sorotzkin, Rabbi Yaakov Yitzchak Ruderman, Rabbi Yaakov Kamenetsky, Rabbi Moshe Feinstein at Agudath Israel's 1968 dinner

a period of less than three years, two of the youngest members of the Moetzes, who were seen as leaders of the next generation, passed away: Rabbi Boruch Sorotzkin of Telshe Yeshiva, and Rabbi Shneur Kotler of Beis Medrash Govoha of Lakewood.

The loss of Rabbi Kotler and Rabbi Sorotzkin to Agudath Israel was immense. The former had inherited his father's commitment to Agudath Israel. Agudah was also in Rabbi Sorotzkin's blood; his father Rabbi Zalman Sorotzkin headed Agudath Israel in *Eretz Yisrael* for decades. He was often the member of the Moetzes pushing Agudah to set its sights even higher on any new project, e.g., for new immigrants from the Soviet Union.

The situation was doubly problematic. First, despite the elevation of Rabbi Elya Svei and Rabbi Avrohom Pam to the Moetzes, the majority of the members of the Moetzes could no longer be involved on a day-to-day basis with all the questions posed by the executive staff of Agudath Israel. Second, there was a critical need to train a new generation of roshei yeshivah to assume leadership roles.

In response to these challenges, Rabbi Sherer, in conjunction with the Moetzes, came up with a plan to restructure the Nesius of Agudath

With Rabbi Avrohom Pam

With Rabbi Elya Svei

Israel of America. In the early days of Zeirei Agudath Yisrael, the Nesius had consisted of one *gadol* (Rabbi Eliezer Silver), one *baalebos* (Louis Septimus), and one full-time Agudah executive (Mike Tress). The Nesius was later reconstituted with Rabbi Chaskel Besser and Rabbi Sherer assuming the roles originally filled by Louis Septimus and Mike Tress.

But now the Nesius added a large group of younger roshei yeshivah, many of whom ultimately ascended to the Moetzes: the Novominsker Rebbe, Rabbi Ahron Schechter, Rabbi Avrohom Chaim Levin, Rabbi Yitzchak Feigelstock, Rabbi Elya Fischer, and Rabbi Yosef Harari-Raful.[17] The task of the newly constituted body was to meet regularly with the executive staff of Agudath Israel to discuss issues and receive input from them. Twice a year, the Nesius directed questions, which the members were reluctant to resolve on their own, to the Moetzes for its determination. A special Nesius office was created at 5 Beekman Street at which members of the Nesius were to be present each month and available to discuss any *Klal* subject.[18]

The concept of the Nesius was taken one step further at a meeting between the senior staff of Agudath Israel and twenty roshei yeshivah on March 25, 1980. Again Rabbi Yaakov Kamenetsky took the lead in explaining the concept. Reb Yaakov pointed out that while the Moetzes ruled on issues brought to it, it was not a proactive body. What was needed was to involve roshei yeshivah more actively in the day-to-day workings of the organization.

Such an involvement of the roshei yeshivah in Agudath Israel would be highly beneficial since it would leave an impression with *yeshivah bachurim* of the importance of Agudath Israel that would remain long after their days in the *beis medrash*. That, said Reb Yaakov, was essential because without Agudath Israel, the Torah community would be "in

At the Agudah's 1956 dinner, honoring Rabbi Eliezer Silver.
L-r: Rabbi Yaakov Kamenetsky, Rabbi Aharon Kotler, Rabbi Eliezer Silver, Mike Tress, unknown, Rabbi Chaskel Besser, Rabbi Sherer, Louis J. Septimus

---

17. Rabbi Shmuel Bloom.
18. Aide-mémoire July 1979.

At a meeting of the Nesius of Agudath Israel of America, circa 1988. L-r: Rabbi Avrohom Chaim Levin, Rabbi Ahron Schechter, the Novominsker Rebbe, Rabbi Shmuel Kamenetsky, Rabbi Elya Fischer, Rabbi Shmuel Bloom, Rabbi Yosef Harari-Raful, Mr. Yosef Friedenson, Rabbi Shmuel Avigdor Faivelson, the Bostoner Rebbe (Boston), Rabbi Yitzchok Feigelstock, Rabbi Moshe Sherer.

terrible straits." Rabbi Shneur Kotler stressed how crucial it was for the roshei yeshiva*h* to respond positively to Agudath Israel's request for their guidance and thereby convey to their students the message: "I must have a link with *Klal* and that link is Agudath Israel." At that meeting, a committee was established to appoint a specific rosh yeshivah with oversight responsibility for each of the major divisions within Agudath Israel.

RABBI SHERER COMMANDED TREMENDOUS RESPECT FROM THE leading rabbinic figures in *Klal Yisrael.* In 5732 (1971), shortly after the passing of the Gerrer Rebbe's brother-in-law Rabbi Itche Meir Levin, Rabbi Sherer *davened* on Yom Kippur in the Gerrer *shtiebel* in Jerusalem. In the midst of the *shaliach tzibbur's* repetition of Mussaf, the Gerrer Rebbe, the Beis Yisrael, left his place and pointed to Rabbi Sherer at the words, *"Ve'yitnu lecha keser meluchah* — And they will give you the crown of royalty," an apparent indication that he wanted Rabbi Sherer to take over Rabbi Levin's position as chairman of the Agudath Israel World Organization (AIWO).

Shlucha D'Rachmana

At the outset of Rabbi Sherer's final illness, Menachem (Mendy)

Greeting the Vizhnitzer Rebbe of Bnei Brak

Chapter Eight: The Ideology of *Daas Torah* ☐ 217

Rabbi Itche Meir Levin addressing an international Agudah conference in 1963. Among those at the dais: Rabbi Sherer, Rabbi Yehudah Meir Abramowitz, Dr. Isaac Lewin, Rabbi Yaakov Kamenetsky, Rabbi Yosef Naftali Stern, and Rabbi Yosef Ferber.

With Rabbi Yaakov Kamenetsky

Shayovich went to the Vizhnitzer Rebbe in Bnei Brak, and asked him to pray for Moshe ben Basya Bluma. When the Vizhnitzer Rebbe learned that it was Rabbi Sherer for whom he was being asked to pray, he started crying. "*Klal Yisrael* needs Rav Moshe," he told Shayovich. "There is no one else like him in this generation, and I do not know if there was another like him in previous generations either."

After he turned 60, Rabbi Sherer mentioned to Rabbi Yaakov Kamenetsky that he did not feel old in any way, despite the fact that the mishnah in *Pirkei Avos* (5:25) describes 60 as the age of *ziknah* (the onset of old age). Reb Yaakov replied that *ziknah* can also refer to wisdom (*Kiddushin* 32b)), and that quality he surely possessed.

On another occasion, Rabbi Sherer went to see Reb Yaakov Kamenetsky, upset that he had perhaps erred in something he had done. Reb Yaakov comforted him with the words of the *Gemara* (*Horayos* 10b), which gives a homiletical twist to the words: "אֲשֶׁר נָשִׂיא יֶחֱטָא — When a leader will sin ..." (*Vayikra* 4:22). The *Gemara* says "אַשְׁרֵי, fortunate is

Chapter Eight: The Ideology of *Daas Torah* ☐ 219

the generation that has a leader who sins." Only one who never tries to achieve anything never makes a mistake, and no generation can afford such a leader, Reb Yaakov explained. He told Rabbi Sherer that the generation was fortunate (*glicklach*) to have someone with his drive to do great things, and he must not let the inevitable mistakes deter him or depress him; and he conveyed how important it is for a person, especially a leader, to be courageous enough to admit when he makes an error.

Perhaps no one expressed the love and respect of the *gedolim* better than Rabbi Hutner in the letter already quoted above. Rabbi Hutner begins by addressing Rabbi Sherer as "my beloved one":

> I have no authority to speak in the name of anyone else. In this case, I speak only as an individual in *Klal Yisrael*, whose heart is filled with great appreciation and *hakaros hatov* toward one who has merited to be the *shlucha d'Rachmana* [the emissary of the Torah] to bring relief to the tents of Torah.
>
> Need I explain myself? For you are that man.
>
> The words of the *Rashba* of the special obligation to publicize the deeds of those who do good are known to me. But I do not come in fulfillment of that obligation, Rather I have come at this time to speak privately between me and you ....
>
> I have no permission to hide from you the clear feeling that holds fast in my mind of the great rejoicing that has fallen to your lot at this time, so that your name is a blessing to all those who hold to the Torah — that comes to you on the merit of your submission to the judgment of the *gedolei haTorah*.
>
> With respect to the partnership between Zevulun and Yissachar, the Torah places Zevulun before Yissachar, "Rejoice Zevulun, in your going out and Yissachar in your tents [of Torah]. " You have merited to be the great Zevulun to all the tents of Yissachar. With a heart overflowing with the brotherhood of Zevulun and Yissachar, my heart cries out to you: Rejoice, Zevulun, in your going out"(*Devarim* 33:18).

Chapter Nine

BAALEBATTIM

A Grassroots Organization

RABBI SHERER'S DEVOTION TO *GEDOLEI YISRAEL* NEVER detracted from his respect for *baalebattim* (lay people). Just as he knew that *Klal Yisrael* depends upon the leadership of *gedolei Torah*, so did he know that there is no king without a nation.

Klal Yisrael, Rabbi Sherer recognized, depends for its survival on the development of committed, honest lay activists. From the first, Rabbi Sherer viewed the development of a group of such *baalebattim* as one of his most important tasks. His success in this regard must be rated as one of his greatest achievements.

In a series of letters to leading members of the British Agudath Israel occasioned by the passing of Mr. Simcha Unsdorfer, the head of the British organization, in late 1967, Rabbi Sherer expressed his views on the importance of a core of dedicated lay people to any successful Agudah movement. In a letter to Unsdorfer's son, Rabbi Sherer

Dancing with his son, Rabbi Shimshon Sherer, at an Agudah convention, surrounded by a circle of close associates. In the circle, clockwise from lower left: Asher Schonkopf, Benzion Fishoff, Zvi Ryzman, Yaakov Rajchenbach, Rabbi Chaim Dovid Zwiebel, Avrohom Halpern, Mordechai Friedman, Chaim Leshkowitz

described his father as one of the "very few *ehrliche* [honest] workers for *Klal* in the entire world." "*Ehrlich*," he explained, might seem like a "very simple characterization," lacking any particular distinction, but that is "so only if one does not appreciate how rare a quality it is and how much it encompasses."[1]

To another active member of the comparatively small British Agudah, Mr. Boruch Moshe Cymerman, he wrote, "It is a delight to have an Agudah activist without the prefix 'Rabbi' preceding his name, and I salute you as 'Mister.'" That ability to make clear to *baalebattim* that he respected and valued them, despite his own *semichah*, served Rabbi Sherer well over the years.

And he truly did not look down on those who dedicated themselves to the service of *Klal Yisrael*. "[A]ll our ideas [of Agudath Israel] will dissipate into thin air unless we are blessed with *askanim* who are ready to work hard to root these *hashkafos* [ideals] into solid earth," he added to Mr. Cymerman.[2] In the course of an exchange of letters with Aba Dunner, Mr. Unsdorfer's successor in the British Agudah, Rabbi Sherer remarked upon their agreement that "[W]e suffer from a ... dearth of *bnei Torah* willing to offer their talents to *Klal* work."

Two of Rabbi Sherer's favorite terms for describing Agudath Israel of America were "grassroots organization" and "democratic." His letters to public officials almost invariably mentioned that Agudath Israel of America is the largest grassroots Orthodox organization in America or that Agudath Israel has the largest number of individual dues-paying members of any Orthodox organization.

What did Rabbi Sherer mean when he described Agudath Israel of America as a "democratic organization [run] as a public trust?" Obviously he did not mean that the professional staff of Agudath Israel or the Moetzes Gedolei HaTorah were elected. Nor did he mean that major decisions were determined by vote. The ultimate decision-making authority of Agudath Israel rests with the Moetzes Gedolei HaTorah. Rather he meant that he always sought input from a wide group of people who were not part of the professional staff of the organization, and that *baalebattim* played a large consultative role in the organization.

Rabbi Sherer was fond of quoting a remark he once heard from Speaker of the House John McCormack. McCormack told him that the

---
1. Rabbi Sherer to Mr. Zalman Unsdorfer.
2. Rabbi Sherer to Mr. B.M. Cymerman, January 2, 1968.

Lower dais: Rabbi Shmuel Bloom, Shimon Kwestel, Governor Hugh Carey, Rabbi Sherer, Rabbi Yaakov Yitzchak Ruderman, Rabbi Shneur Kotler.
Upper dais: Aaron Seif, Benzion Fishoff, David Turkel, Volvie Friedman, Ephraim Klein, Chaim Hertz

only reason he was the Speaker of the House was that his constituents in Boston kept electing him to the House of Representatives every two years. The lesson for Rabbi Sherer was obvious: It did not matter how many politicians he hobnobbed with or how much influence he wielded in the corridors of power, if he did not retain the respect and confidence of the rank-and-file members of Agudath Israel. And that meant involving as many *baalebattim* as possible in different aspects of the organization.

In part the large role played by *baalebattim* in Agudath Israel of America was an outgrowth of the organization's humble beginnings as Zeirei Agudath Israel. Until 1939, Zeirei Agudath Israel was little more than a loose confederation of neighborhood chapters, of which the Williamsburg branch, led by Mike Tress, was the most active. These branches were largely social clubs where *frum* young men could gather.

Only with the outset of the war and Mike Tress's decision to leave his job as an executive at Lamport Brothers to work full-time for Zeirei Agudath Israel (albeit without a salary for the first few years) did it begin developing into something more than a social organization. Even then, the fledgling organization could afford no more than one or two part-time employees. Much of the most important work of Zeirei Agudath Israel — e.g., gathering the affidavits of financial support necessary for any immigration visa, fund-raising — fell upon the shoulders of a core of dedicated young *baalebattim*, who had grown up in the Williamsburg chapter of Zeirei or in one of the other local branches, such as Louis and Sol Septimus.

Over the next 20 years, neither Zeirei Agudath Israel nor its successor organization, Agudath Israel of America, ever employed much more than a handful of non-secretarial employees. And so the tradition of actively involved lay people continued. When, for instance, Agudath Israel faced a severe financial crisis in the late '50s, much of the work of reorganizing its finances fell upon a three-member Management Committee consisting of Wolf (Volvie) Friedman, David Turkel, and Herman Plagman. Without the efforts of the Management Committee, it is likely that Agudath Israel would have had to close its doors by the early '60s.

During the early to mid-'60s, Rabbi Aba Dunner, then one of the two professional employees of Agudath Israel of Great Britain, spent five or six weeks in America every summer. During those visits, he had an open invitation to spend as much time as he wanted in the Agudath

At a Pirchei event. L-r: Rabbi Malkiel Kotler, Rabbi Sherer, Rabbi Mordechai Mehlman, Rabbi Joshua Silbermintz, Rabbi Avrohom Pam, Rabbi Nosson Scherman

Israel offices on 5 Beekman Street. When in the office, Dunner would sit in Rabbi Sherer's office, soaking up everything he could learn about how to run a growing organization. The full-time professional staff of Agudath Israel then consisted almost entirely of Rabbi Sherer, Mr. Yosef Friedenson, and Rabbi Boruch Borchardt. (Of the part-time staff, none was so important or beloved as Rabbi Joshua Silbermintz, who led Pirchei Agudath Israel for decades.) Yet, Dunner recalls, the office was a beehive of activity. During the day, Volvie Friedman and others would often drop by to talk to Rabbi Sherer, sometimes staying for an hour or more.

Nor were the visitors only Rabbi Sherer's contemporaries. Two young men who would soon leave their mark on Agudath Israel of America, Menachem Lubinsky and Mendy Shayovich, were also frequent visitors. Though Rabbi Sherer was not yet the famous and revered figure of his later years, already then, Dunner remembers, "people believed in Moshe Sherer and wanted to be around him."

L-r: Eli Basch, unidentified, Rabbi Leibel Cywiak, Volvie Friedman, Mr. Geffen, Rabbi Sherer, David Turkel, Herman Plagman

The Role of the Shearis Hapleitah

THE CORE GROUP OF ACTIVE *BAALEBATTIM* ACTIVE IN AGUDATH Israel in the early years of of Zeirei Agudath Israel consisted of native English speakers who had come of age in one of the Zeirei Agudath Israel branches.[3] As the post-war refugees became more solidly established in America by the late '50s, they began to take on an increasingly large role in the organization. All three members of the Management Committee, which helped guide Agudath Israel through its difficult transition period in the early '60s, were European born. David Turkel was sent to America in the late '30s to assist in efforts to obtain visas for European Jews. Herman Plagman, too, was Viennese. And Wolf (Volvie) Friedman had been considered a promising young Torah scholar in Budapest before the war.

---

3. A number of refugees played vital roles in early Zeirei. Moshe Berger, a young refugee from Germany, was the only paid employee working on the immigration matters when Zeirei Agudath Israel opened its first national office at 616 Bedford Avenue in 1939. Gershon Kranzler, another German refugee, was placed in charge of national organization work at the same time. Yosef Rosenberger, a refugee from Vienna, though not an employee of Zeirei Agudath Israel, did his pioneering work in *shaatnez*-checking while living in the refugee dormitory at 616 Bedford Avenue. And Rabbi Joseph Elias began his lifelong association with Agudath Israel of America, working on the Jewish Pocketbook Series and other educational projects shortly after arriving in the United States from Germany via Montreal.

The Boyaner Rebbe and the Kopyczinitzer Rebbe

In time, the warm relationship that Rabbi Sherer established with the *shearis hapleitah* (survivors) played an important role in the development of Agudath Israel of America. Although Zeirei Agudath Israel helped bring over many of the individuals and families who arrived in America from Europe, both during the early years of the war and after the war, they had little time for *Klal* work. In general, the refugees spent their first decade in America adapting to a new country, learning the language, establishing families, and trying to earn a livelihood.

Nevertheless, from the late '40s on, Rabbi Sherer built up many friendships among the survivors. He had been raised on stories of the great figures of Eastern European Jewry. Through Agudath Israel's rescue work during the war, he had become well acquainted with the Boyaner Rebbe and the Kopyczinitzer Rebbe, two exemplars of the pre-war chassidic world. And he was eager to hear from the newcomers about the vibrant pre-war European Jewish life. The manner in which he treated the survivors as the invaluable repositories of knowledge contrasted sharply to their more typical experience of being looked down as "greeners," unable even to speak the language.

One of the newcomers with whom Rabbi Sherer developed a particularly close connection was Rabbi Chaskel Besser. The two men were almost exactly the same age, and first met at the Williamsburg *tisch* of the Bluzhover Rebbe in 1948. Rabbi Besser's cosmopolitan background and extensive travels in his youth made him an invaluable resource for

In Washington, D.C. with Pinchas Goldberg, Benzion Fishoff, and Mordechai Friedman

the young Yankee with a tremendous thirst to know about Jewish religious life before the war, especially the leading Polish Rebbes.[4] The two remained lifelong, intimate friends.

When many of the *shearis hapleitah* began to taste their first success in business in America in the '60s and '70s, they did not forget the respect that the young Rabbi Sherer had always shown them. Members of this group became not only the biggest financial supporters of the American Agudah, but also some of its most active members.

Throughout his life, Rabbi Sherer had a special *chein* (charm) in the eyes of the European-born *baalebattim*. Their association with someone who commanded such respect in Washington, D.C. and Albany gave them a sense of having arrived in their adopted country. They appreciated his "class," and were proud that Orthodox Jewry had such a representative.

Those closest to Rabbi Sherer among the *shearis hapleitah*, such as Benzion Fishoff and Mordechai Friedman, invariably mention the quality of *n'ki kapa'im* (financial rectitude) when discussing their attraction to Rabbi Sherer. A number of people were asked to make suggestions

---

4. Rabbi Besser was born in the Upper Silesian city of Kattowicz, the birthplace of the world Agudath Israel movement, to a family of Radomsker Chassidim. Kattowicz was under German control until 1922 when it reverted to Poland. As a young man, Rabbi Besser learned in the Radomsk Yeshivah in Lodz, home to Poland›s second-largest Jewish community and a major commercial city. He also accompanied his father, a well-to-do businessman, to Berlin to visit the Radomsker Rebbe, who was forced to stay in Berlin for more than half a year undergoing medical treatment. Rabbi Besser spent the war years together with his family in Palestine.

Rabbi Sherer's tombstone. The acrostic spells *Moshe eved ne'eman*, Moshe the faithful servant, and notes his attribute of *n'ki kapayim*.

for the language on Rabbi Sherer's *matzeivah* (tombstone). One quality was mentioned by every single one. *n'ki kapai'im*.

Louis (Leuchu) Glueck, a native of Hungary, who arrived in the United States from the Displaced Persons camps in 1948, explained Rabbi Sherer's attraction for him and other Hungarian Jews: "Hungarians are known as straight, hardworking people. Not only was he absolutely straight, but he sought out those who shared that quality with him."

Rabbi Sherer once told Mr. Glueck that one of the keys to running a successful organization is to avoid any temptation to get rich or to look for side income. He regularly turned down offers of positions on the boards of major corporations.

RABBI SHERER WAS NOT CONTENT, OF COURSE, TO REST UPON HIS relationship with the *shearis hapleitah*. He recognized early on that the future of Agudath Israel of America would depend on developing a new generation of American *baalebattim*. And indeed the core group of highly committed American-born *baalebattim* that he left behind was one of his most important legacies to his successors in the Agudah.

A New Cadre of Lay Leaders

He never tired of promoting the ideal of service to *Klal Yisrael*. Professor Larry Katz, today a national vice-president of Agudath Israel of America, was a young law professor, just starting to become active in the local Baltimore branch, when he spent a Sunday at Rabbi Sherer's office in the late '60s. Rabbi Sherer's goal that day was to educate the young man from Baltimore in the goals, history, and projects of Agudath Israel, and the techniques of communal service. He devoted three hours to the task, his enthusiasm never lagging. By the time he finished, there was no one else left at 5 Beekman Street, and it was left to Rabbi Sherer to lock up, as he did most Sundays.[5]

Rabbi Sherer would buttonhole the younger members of the Fourteenth Avenue Agudah *minyan* where he *davened* and talk to them about getting involved in Agudath Israel or other *Klal* activities. Why were you put on this earth? he would ask. And the answer was always the same: to serve *Klal Yisrael*.[6]

The *Gemara* (*Berachos* 6b) says that when Hashem comes to a *beis haknesses* and does not find 10 men there, "He immediately becomes angry." The Maharsha explains that this refers to a situation in which nine people are waiting for a tenth to arrive. To this comment, Rabbi Sherer would add a homiletical interpretation. What causes Hashem pain, he said, is to watch nine man waiting passively. They should go out and look for the tenth rather than just sitting around. Their problem is that they underestimate their own capacities. And that was precisely

---

5. Professor Lawrence Katz, "Rabbi Sherer — Never Off Duty," *The Jewish Observer,* Summer 1998, p. 24.
6. Shlomo Chaimovits.

the message that he conveyed to every young person of talent that he met: Don't underestimate your capacities to contribute to *Klal Yisrael* and to change it for the better.[7]

The theme of communal service was a staple of Rabbi Sherer's no matter what the forum, whether it was his homiletics class at Torah Vodaath or his annual summer addresses to younger audiences at Camp Agudah and Camp Bnos. He sought to instill at a young age the concept of service to the *Klal*.

In one of his last *derashos* at Camp Agudah, he quoted the Tchebiner Rav on a Mishnah in *Pirkei Avos*: "If you have learned much Torah, do not take [credit] for yourself, for you were created for that purpose"(2:9). The Tchebiner Rav explained, "Do not take the Torah only for yourself. And the same is true of every aspect of life. Everyone was created with the mission to share. That is true not only of the Torah you've learned, but with any talents that the *Ribbono shel Olam* grants you. You must share them with others."[8]

Presented with a tee shirt during his annual visit to Camp Agudah. The boy at the far left is his grandson, Levi Langer: seated next to him is Rabbi Rafael Andrusier, the camp's longtime head lifeguard

---

7. Ibid.
8. Ibid., p. 74.

Bonding through *zemiros* at the 1996 Agudah Convention. Seated at the table (l-r): Mordechai Friedman, Dovid Moskowitz, George Klein, Dr. David Diamond, Zev Schlesinger, Menachem Shayovich, Meyer Rosenbaum, Abish Brodt, Rabbi Sherer, Leuchu Glueck, Reuven Dessler, Rabbi Avrohom Yosef Laizerson.

Rabbi David Ozeiry, a brother-in-law of Chacham Harari-Raful, will never forget the first time he met Rabbi Sherer, in the Brooklyn office of then-congressman Chuck Schumer. Rabbi Ozeiry was there in connection with efforts to obtain visas for members of the Syrian Jewish community still stranded in Syria. Rabbi Sherer immediately struck up a conversation with the young rabbi, and began asking him about himself. Later, as they were standing outside together in the rain, Rabbi Sherer suddenly grabbed his new friend by the lapels and began talking to him as if they had been close for 20 years. "David, people are fools. They don't realize how many doors we can open, how much we have done, and how much we can do," he told him. The young rabbi was mesmerized by his fire and commitment.

That same passion attracted many to the service of *Klal Yisrael*. Rabbi Sherer gathered as many as he could to his banner. But he had one condition: He had to be sure that they would never do anything to embarrass *Klal Yisrael* or Agudath Israel in any way. He was a shrewd judge of character, and possessed a keen sense of who might be cutting corners in business or with the government.[9]

RABBI SHERER WAS A BUILDER OF PEOPLE. THAT BUILDING returned a twofold dividend. Those who were warmed by his encouragement were filled with the desire to ally themselves with his causes. And when they did so, they had the confidence necessary to put their talents to effective use.

A Relationship of Mutual Respect

Rabbi Sherer's eye for talent was ever sharp. He first met a young Torah educator when the latter was still in his early 30's, and had only recently started his first institution, with no more than 20 students. Rabbi Sherer immediately offered the young man a senior position in Agudath Israel. As always, he stressed the potential to achieve through the grand coalition that is Agudath Israel than one could achieve through a single institution. On that occasion, the persuasion failed, but Rabbi Sherer's judgment proved unerring. Over the next three decades, the educator in question built up one of the largest networks of Torah institutions in the world. [10]

---

9. Avrohom Biderman.
10. On his last trip to Israel, with the Am Echad mission, Rabbi Sherer arranged a long breakfast meeting with the educator in question. As usual, he kept the conversation focused on what the other person was doing. At one point, he told his friend that he was relieved that he had not succeeded

Mr. Yosef Friedenson addressing the 1969 Agudah dinner.
Seated (l-r): Rabbi Moshe Feinstein, the Bostoner Rebbe, Rabbi Sherer, Rabbi Shmuel Bloom

Rabbi Sherer's eye for talent paid greater dividends with another young man in his late 20's. After a visit to his alma mater, Yeshivas Ner Israel, in 1968, he wrote to a young rebbi in the yeshivah high school, "I look forward to working more closely with you in the future, as you develop into what I always predicted: one of the outstanding Orthodox leaders in this country." That rebbi was Rabbi Shmuel Bloom, the recently retired Executive Vice-President of Agudath Israel of America.

Rabbi Sherer first met Rabbi Avrohom Chaim Feuer when the latter was still learning in the Telshe Kollel in Cleveland. He told the young man, "If I were investing in futures, I would invest in you."[11] That prediction proved prescient; Rabbi Feuer has not only had a successful career in the rabbinate in Miami and Monsey, but is a well-known author and speaker as well. In the decades since that first meeting with Rabbi Sherer, he has never forgotten that early vote of confidence.

Such shots in the arm came naturally to Rabbi Sherer; he dispensed

---

in bringing him into the offices of Agudath Israel many years earlier, because that would have deprived *Klal Yisrael* of one of its leading disseminators of Torah.

11. Rabbi Shimshon Zelig Sherer, "A Father to Me; A Father to Klal Yisroel," *The Jewish Observer*, Summer 1998, p. 74.

them freely, but not indiscriminately. Hundreds of people whose talents had caught Rabbi Sherer's eye or who had performed some valuable service treasured the handwritten notes they received from him complimenting them on a job well done. Each note was individualized, written in a beautiful script, without any errors of spelling or grammar; just the type of memento that one would reach for to show one's children or grandchildren or to look at in hard times.[12] A note initially addressed to "Mr. So-and-So" might have the "Mr." crossed out and "Reb Shlomo" written in its place, as an indication that Rabbi Sherer considered their relationship to have reached a new level of closeness.

For Rabbi Meir Zlotowitz that first note came in response to a Pirchei

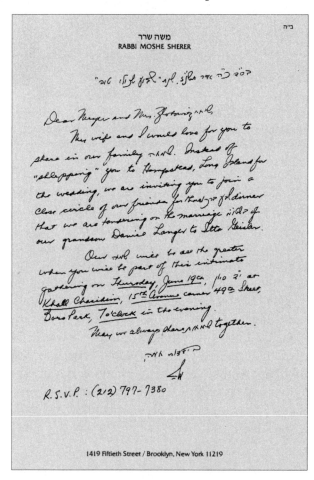

Rabbi Sherer's handwritten invitation to Rabbi and Mrs. Meir Zlotowitz to the *sheva berachos* of Daniel and Itta Langer

---

12. Rabbi Nosson Scherman and Rabbi Meir Zlotowitz, "The Man in the Corner," *The Jewish Observer*, Summer 1998, p. 45.

At Rabbi Sherer's surprise 70th birthday celebration. Clockwise from top: Rabbi Meir Zlotowitz, Rabbi Nosson Scherman, Professor Aaron Twerski, Rabbi Nisson Wolpin

Leadership Guide he had written; for Rabbi Nosson Scherman the note was in appreciation for a slide show prepared for an Agudah convention; for Rabbi Shlomo Gertzulin the occasion was a volunteer project he had undertaken for what was to become the Office of Government Affairs.

Those notes were worth their weight in gold in inspiring the recipient to new efforts. It is no accident that shortly after completing the volunteer project Rabbi Gertzulin joined the staff of Agudath Israel of America as comptroller, and later vice president, or that Mesorah/ArtScroll Publishing, headed by Rabbi Zlotowitz and Rabbi Scherman, would render so many services to Agudath Israel over the years.

Though Rabbi Sherer viewed doing favors for others as part of his job, he was particularly eager to do so for those who had dedicated themselves in any way to the *Klal*. In part, that was his way of expressing his *hakaras hatov* (gratitude) for those who bore some of the burden of *Klal* work with him. One time, for instance, Shlomo Chaimovits, one of the younger *baalebattim* in the Fourteenth Avenue Agudah *minyan* where Rabbi Sherer *davened*, told him that there was no room in Camp Agudah that summer for one of his children. Rabbi Sherer confirmed with Meir Frischman, the director of Camp Agudah, that there was not an extra bed in the entire camp. Rabbi Sherer asked Meir if he could find a bed for a Sherer grandchild. Frischman answered that of course he would. "Fine," said Rabbi Sherer, "think of this boy as my grandson."

Similarly, when the Chaimovits children were involved in *shidduchim*, Rabbi Sherer insisted that he be of assistance in obtaining information for them. As he explained, "The roshei yeshivah will tell me things that they wouldn't tell you." He did the same for many others.

Rabbi Sherer was extremely solicitous of the wives of those who devoted themselves to public activities. Many a wife was surprised to receive a call from him thanking her for all her support for her husband's activities and expressing his recognition of the burden that this often imposed on other members of the family. For a number of years, Rabbi Moshe Meir Weiss of Staten Island gave a 10 p.m. *daf hayomi shiur* in Boro Park, and as a consequence usually did not return home until around midnight. On Erev Yom Kippur, his wife received a call from Rabbi Sherer. He told her how much he appreciated her sacrifice so that her husband could give the *shiur* and how large was her share in his *harbatzas Torah* (dissemination of Torah).

A letter from Rabbi Sherer to Sarah Biderman — wife of one of Agudath Israel's leading *askanim* — on Erev Yom Kippur 5722 (1991) is typical of his solicitude for the wives of communal activists. Rabbi Sherer began by expressing his sympathy for the deprivations of "your own personal life" and the tests of patience, "including late suppers

Presenting an award to Avrohom Biderman as Rabbi Avrohom Pam looks on

and other large and small inconveniences" that are inevitable "when a woman has a husband such as Avrohom, who is so deeply involved in *Klal* concerns."

But he wanted her to derive satisfaction from her share in the wonderful mitzvos that her husband was doing to save Russian-speaking immigrant children in Israel through his tireless work for SHUVU (an entire school system created for such children). And Rabbi Sherer wanted to convey what Biderman meant to him personally:

> Lately when the skies seem very dark, when I think of what Avrohom is doing in his quiet way, it gives me renewed courage and faith that indeed there is a new, young generation growing up with a heartfelt understanding of *Klal achrayus*.
>
> Before you go shul for *Kol Nidrei*, I want these words to reach you and to give you a deeper sense of what your husband means not only to you as a life partner ..., but also to people like myself who are trying to build a new Torah society in a sick world.

Nor did that solicitude end after their husbands were no longer alive. Rabbi Shimshon Sherer relates how he once came into his parents' home on Erev Yom Kippur and found his father on the phone wishing one woman after another a *Gmar Chasima Tovah* and an easy fast with great wamth. His son asked him who these women were, and he replied that they were *almanos* (widows) who had recently lost their husbands. "If I call them and wish them a *gut yahr*, they realize that they have not been forgotten, and it lifts up their spirits going into the new year," he explained.

"During the *Aseres Yemei Teshuvah* [Ten Days of Repentance]," Rabbi Sherer pointed out, "we ask the *Ribbono shel Olam* to answer our prayers as the *Dayan Almanos* — He Who judges for the benefit of widows. How can I ask the *Ribbono shel Olam* to accept my prayer as *Dayan Almanos* if I do nothing to help Him in His task?"[13]

Rabbi Sherer treated people with respect and knew how to make them feel important. Telephone calls were returned, usually the same day. And if Rabbi Sherer could not get back to the caller quickly, he made sure that someone else did. One of the few new technological devices that Rabbi Sherer ever attempted to master was a car phone. He accepted the gift of an early-model car phone from a supporter because

---

13. Rabbi Shimshon Zelig Sherer, "A Father to Me; A Father to Klal Yisroel," *The Jewish Observer*, Summer 1998, p. 74.

it enabled him to use his driving time to return calls.

Above all, he solicited the opinions of others and listened carefully. Mr. Itche Meir Cymerman — one of the leading Agudah activists in Europe, and a member of the Vaad Hapoel of World Agudah during the period that Rabbi Sherer served as co-chairman of World Agudath Israel — once remarked upon the frequency with which Rabbi Sherer called to solicit his opinion on some matter or another. "A man like that did not need my advice," said Mr. Cymerman, "but he called nevertheless."

Rabbi Sherer called his closest *baalebattim* often, if only to speak for a few minutes. Until Volvie Friedman's passing, he and Rabbi Sherer spoke on the phone at least once every day. After Volvie Friedman's *levayah*, Leuchu Glueck, who had been a *yeshivah bachur* together with Volvie Friedman in Budapest, approached Rabbi Sherer. He told him, "I know I can't replace Volvie. But I want to help in any way I can." Rabbi Sherer would consult frequently with Glueck on practical matters, telling him, "You see things in a practical way."

The Contribution of *Baalebattim*

RABBI SHERER TOOK ENORMOUS PRIDE IN THE GROUP OF *BAALEbattim* who were active in Agudath Israel, and valued their contributions on a number of levels. For one thing, he saw any Orthodox Jew who achieved a position of high visibility as a *Kiddush Hashem*. He invested his political capital with the administration of New York Governor Hugh Carey to secure an appointment for Dr. Seymour Lachman to the New York Board of Regents. "A major reason for my strong push for Dr. Lachman is my conviction that, in the light of recent blemishes on the public Orthodox Jewish image, it is imperative for us to focus a spotlight on an openly Orthodox Jewish personality in high public office," he wrote in a 1975 aide-mémoire.

After Avrohom Biderman was appointed New York City Finance Commissioner, Rabbi Sherer wrote expressing his great pride in Biderman's attainment of the "highest position ever held by an Orthodox Jew in the administration of the City of New York." Rabbi Sherer proclaimed the mayor's recognition of Biderman's "talent and integrity ... a *Kiddush Hashem*."[14]

---

14. Two years later, Biderman was appointed New York City Housing Commissioner, a position in which he served until 1990.

Rabbi Sherer also drew on the experience of his close circle of *baalebattim*. His calls and solicitations of advice were not merely diplomatic. He took seriously the opinions of others. He knew that one man, no matter how indefatigable, cannot do everything himself. Only by unleashing the talents of others and giving them the opportunity to act could Agudath Israel maximize its achievements. Before any large event, such as the annual convention, he convened a large number of committees of *baalebattim* to take responsibility for various aspects of the planning.

Much of Agudath Israel's most important work in the later decades of Rabbi Sherer's life depended on committees of highly committed *baalebattim* willing to devote themselves to the task at hand. Once he had picked out the laymen that he thought were suitable to a particular task, Rabbi Sherer was not afraid to delegate responsibility to them. Thus the Iranian rescue work of the late '70s and '80s largely depended on a small group of lay volunteers who took responsibility for the fund-raising and worked intimately with Rabbi Shlomo Berger, who worked full-time on the Iranian rescue project out of the Agudah office. Similarly, almost all of Agudath Israel's work in the Soviet Union in the '80s and early '90s was based on the efforts of the efforts of Mordechai Neustadt under the banner of Vaad L'Hatzolas Nidchei Yisrael.

When Rabbi Sherer tapped Rabbi Shmuel Lefkowitz, a 31-year-old social worker, to head the Southern Brooklyn Community Organization (SBCO), with the goal of staving off urban blight on the perimeter of Boro Park, he promised him a board of *baalebattim* who would be able to carry much of the load. That group included the top young accountants and lawyers in the Agudah orbit, as well as some

At the Agudah's Orthodox Jewish Archives with Leuchu Glueck

of the older *baalebattim* closest to Rabbi Sherer. Once he had assembled a board with the proper mix, Rabbi Sherer contented himself with general oversight of the project and making the necessary connections at crucial moments.

SBCO was just one example of the way that Rabbi Sherer fit different individuals to whom he was close to the particular task at hand. He knew each person's strengths and where he would be most effective. Rabbi Chaskel Besser's fluency in Polish and other European languages, plus his broad knowledge of Polish high culture, made him the ideal representative for all matters involving dealing with Eastern European governments on such issues as the preservation of Jewish graves. Benzion Fishoff's courtly European manners and personal charm led Rabbi Sherer to call him his *"Malach HaShalom"* (Angel of Peace), and suited him to represent Agudath Israel on international bodies like the Memorial Foundation. Fishoff was also Rabbi Sherer's emissary to the Gerrer Rebbes.[15]

Sometimes Rabbi Sherer used trusted laymen to expand the reach and influence of the Agudah world. There came a time, for instance, when the YMHA of Boro Park ceased to represent the changing demo-

With the (future) Gerrer Rebbe

---

15. In his later years, Rabbi Sherer also cultivated younger emissaries to the Gerrer Rebbe. On his visits to *Eretz Yisrael*, Shlomo Werdiger would walk him from the Central Hotel to the Gerrer *beis medrash*. Werdiger also played a major role in bringing the Gerrer Rebbe to America, together with Rabbi Aharon Leib Shteinman in May 1998, a visit that began at the *beis olam* for Rabbi Sherer's burial.

graphics of the community, which had become increasingly *chareidi*. So Rabbi Sherer encouraged certain *baalebattim* to get involved in the YMHA. Eventually the board of the YMHA reflected the makeup of the community, and the institution's offering of activities grew much more suited to today's Boro Park. Those who imbibed Rabbi Sherer's philosophy of activism on behalf of *Klal Yisrael* naturally took lead roles in all forms of community institutions, such as yeshivos and Bais Yaakovs, as well as non-denominational institutions serving the Orthodox community, such as Brooklyn's Maimonides Medical Center. As president of the Bikur Cholim of Boro Park, Leuchu Glueck spearheaded a huge array of *chesed* activities. He was also deeply involved as vice chairman and life trustee of Maimonides Hospital.

The respect with which Rabbi Sherer treated others and the confidence that he showed in them was reciprocated with something akin to reverence. And nowhere was that clearer than at meetings of the organization's top *baalebattim*. Rabbi Sherer's control of those meetings was absolute. He was able to adhere to his carefully planned time schedule of agenda items. By his left hand on the boardroom table there was

At the *hachnasas Sefer Torah* for the *Sefer Torah* presented to Rabbi Sherer by a group of Agudah *baalebattim*. Foreground (l-r): Rabbi Sherer, Rabbi Elias Karp, Mordechai Friedman. Others in the background include Rabbi Avrohom Nissan Perl, Daniel Langer, Shlomo Rieder, Rabbi Levi Langer, Benzion Fishoff, Rabbi Meir Frischman, Rabbi Shimshon Sherer, and Rabbi Berish Rapaport

The surprise presentation of the *Sefer Torah* to Rabbi Sherer at the 1997 dinner. L-r: Rabbi Elya Svei; Benzion Fishoff, Chaim Gross, Rabbi Paysach Krohn, Avrohom Schonberger, Menachem Shayovich, Rabbi Shimshon Sherer, Mendel Berg, Rabbi Sherer, Mordechai Friedman, Leuchu Glueck, Senator Joseph Lieberman, Avrohom Halpern, Mayor Rudolph Giuliani

Rabbi Paysach Krohn and Rabbi Shimshon Sherer present the *Sefer Torah* as Menachem Shayovich, Mendel Berg, Rabbi Labish Becker, and Mordechai Friedman look on.

At the private celebration of the *hachnasas Sefer Torah* with (from left): Rabbi Shlomo Rottenberg, Rabbi Avrohom Pam, Rabbi Ahron Schechter, Rabbi Yitzchok Feigelstock, Rabbi Elya Svei

an alarm clock. He had to do no more than to tap the top of the alarm clock with his index finger and whoever was speaking would quickly wrap up.[16]

At those meetings, he did not mind constructive criticism, but he had no patience for negativity that would not generate results. Those present were invited to express their opinions freely, but only on condition that they were ready to back up their words with actions. The lesson, he would say, half-jokingly, can be learned from the description of the Heavenly angels in the blessings of *Krias Shema* in the morning. First they are described as "וְכֻלָּם עוֹשִׂים בְּאֵימָה וּבְיִרְאָה רְצוֹן קוֹנָם" — They all do the will of their Maker with dread and reverence." And only later do we recite, "וְכֻלָּם פּוֹתְחִים אֶת פִּיהֶם בִּקְדוּשָׁה וּבְטָהֳרָה" — And they all open their mouths in holiness and purity." First, one has to resolve to do, and then one can open his mouth, he would say.

The second condition he placed on criticism was that it be accompanied by constructive criticism. For this point, he quoted a certain rav who responded to some sharp criticism of the pre-war European Agudah for not doing more for *Eretz Yisrael*, at a gathering of *rabbanim* in Warsaw. That rav pointed out that one of the names of Moshe Rabbeinu's father-in-law Yisro was יֶתֶר (extra), in honor of the fact that an extra section was added to the Torah as a result of his suggestions to Moshe Rabbeinu. Rashi, in his commentary, identifies that extra section as starting with the words וְאַתָּה תֶחֱזֶה, in which Yisro counseled Moshe to appoint qualified men to assist him in judging the people (*Shemos* 18:21).

---

16. Moishe Zvi Reicher, who served as Director of International Affairs for Agudath Israel World Organization, in Rabbi Sherer's last few years.

But, the rav pointed out, those are not the first words in the section containing Yisro's suggestions. Rather the section begins four verses earlier, with the words, "וַיֹּאמֶר חֹתֵן מֹשֶׁה אֵלָיו לֹא טוֹב הַדָּבָר אֲשֶׁר אַתָּה עֹשֶׂה — And Moshe's father-in-law said to him, 'The thing that you do is not good'" (*Shemos* 18:17). It is noteworthy that Rashi does not identify those four verses of criticism as the added section of the Torah for which Yisro is commended. By stressing that Yisro is commended only for his constructive suggestions, not the preceding criticism, Rashi teaches us that criticism is cheap and easy, but unaccompanied by concrete suggestions it is not worth much.

Every one in public life must live with the fact that they thereby make themselves targets for criticism. And there will never be a shortage of Monday-morning quarterbacks eager to point out their failures to them. Yet, says Rabbi Aba Dunner, who was present at many meetings chaired by Rabbi Sherer, "I never once saw anyone speak disrespectfully to Rabbi Sherer, or even in a slightly confrontational fashion." In more than 40 years in professional leadership positions, notes Rabbi Dunner, he cannot think of another figure who commanded that kind of respect and awe.

Chapter Nine: *Baalebattim* □ 247

Part III
LEADERSHIP

Chapter Ten

THE "PEOPLE THING"

THE ACCOMPLISHMENTS OF AGUDATH ISRAEL OF AMERICA under Rabbi Sherer's leadership were to a very large extent a function of the web of personal relationships that he laboriously built over decades. He was close to presidents from John F. Kennedy on; leading senators on both sides of the aisle, in particular the four-term Republican senator from New York Jacob Javits and New York's popular Democratic senator Daniel Patrick Moynihan, longtime Speaker of the House John McCormack, dozens of congressmen; the governors of New York, from Nelson Rockefeller to George Pataki; and the mayors of New York City from Abe Beame through Rudolph Giuliani. No less important were the personal relationships he established with a host of government bureaucrats in both Albany and Washington, D.C.

Rabbi Sherer never lost sight of the importance of personal relations. The negotiations over a California autopsy bill illustrate the significance

With President Ronald Reagan

that Rabbi Sherer attached to forging long-lasting bonds with legislators. The fledgling Agudath Israel of California had proposed a religious exemption to those autopsies otherwise required by law. While the bill was in committee, the sponsors were asked to accept a number of amendments that significantly watered down the protections in the bill. It was clear that without those amendments the bill would die in committee, without any religious exemption.

A long-distance conference call was arranged between the Agudah activists in California and the New York headquarters. In the course of the conversation, Rabbi Sherer said, "Sometimes it is better to take no loaf than half a loaf." But Dr. Irving Lebovics, who had led the lobbying effort for the bill, was reluctant to do so. In response to Rabbi Sherer's request for his opinion, he argued that a number of prominent politicians had "gone to the mat" on behalf of Agudath Israel of California to negotiate a compromise in the State Senate Judiciary Committee and that it would be costly for a new organization like the California branch of Agudath Israel to turn its back on their efforts, even if it meant accepting half a loaf.

Rabbi Sherer immediately changed his previous opinion, over the objections of some members of his staff and other Jewish organizations, and adopted Dr. Lebovics's approach. He recognized the importance of the "people thing" and the forging of lasting relationships.[1]

---

1. Dr. Irving Lebovics, "Rabbi Sherer ז״ל and the 'People Thing,'" *The Jewish Observer,* Summer 1998, p. 26.

RABBI SHERER HAD THE ABILITY TO FORM DEEP PERSONAL connections far beyond the "hail fellow well met" variety, as attested to by the large numbers of public officials who considered him a close personal friend.

In-Depth Relationships

True, these connections served the interests of Orthodox Jewry and the Jewish people well, but there was a genuine element of personal closeness as well.

On many occasions, Rabbi Sherer expressed his admiration for various public officials in his private communications. In a July 1, 1975 aide-mémoire, Rabbi Sherer describes a Washington, D.C. meeting with John Proffitt, a senior official in the Department of Education. It was a "very hearty and intimate chat between friends, running a broad gamut of subjects too numerous to record," writes Rabbi Sherer. He goes on to describe Proffitt as "one of the most high-minded men I have ever met in all my years working with government officials."

"I never felt that my friendship with Rabbi Sherer was because I was Congressman Stephen Solarz's chief of staff or subsequently Senator Joseph Lieberman's," says Michael Lewan. His proof: Rabbi Sherer was special to many people from whom he needed nothing.

When he first met Rabbi Sherer, Lewan was the 23-year-old campaign manager for Stephen Solarz, in the latter's successful first bid for Congress. After Rabbi Sherer's passing, Lewan was honored at the Agudath Israel of America annual dinner for his work as Chairman of the U.S. Commission for the Preservation of America's Heritage Abroad, which deals in large part with the preservation of Jewish cemeteries in Eastern Europe. At that dinner, Lewan said, "Over 25 years, I made no major decision in my life without Rabbi Sherer." In private conversations, he went even further. A person has only a few friends in life on whom he can always count, Lewan observes. "Rabbi Sherer was one. He would tell me when I was wrong; he cared about me ...."

Shortly after the death of his father, Lewan accompanied Rabbi Sherer to a meeting with some important Ukranian government officials to discuss cemeteries in the Ukraine. After the meeting, they sat down to talk, and Lewan began to speak about his father. In the course of reminiscing, Lewan started to cry. It was the first time, he recalls, that he was able to cry and truly express his grief over the loss of his father. Only in the presence of a rabbi nearly 30 years his senior was the non-Jewish Lewan able to give full vent to his inner feelings.

Introducing Stuart Eizenstadt

THE ADMIRATION EXPRESSED BY THOSE WITH WHOM RABBI SHERER dealt over a period of years went far beyond his technical skills as an advocate and leader. Many public officials describe him as one of the seminal figures in their lives, a source of inspiration and uplift. Stuart Eizenstadt, President Jimmy Carter's Domestic Policy Adviser and subsequently Under Secretary of State in the Clinton Administration, says: "Let me be as clear as possible. I loved Rabbi Sherer. That is the only way to put it. I had an enormous respect and admiration for him that went beyond that for almost anyone I have ever known."

A Source of Inspiration

Though Rabbi Sherer's contact with Eizenstadt over the years touched many extremely complex and technical issues, such as European reparations work, the spiritual dimension was never far from the surface. "He touched a personal nerve because of his earnestness and spirituality," Eizenstadt recalls. "I admired his capacity to live in both worlds — the religious and the political — without losing his conviction for either."

When Eizenstadt's own son became Orthodox, and with Rabbi Sherer's encouragement took time off after law school to study in the Mirrer Yeshivah *kollel* in Jerusalem, Eizenstadt was comfortable with

With Leuchu Glueck and Stanley Brezenoff

his son's decision. Knowing that his son's "spiritual mentor" was someone "with his feet as firmly planted in the world as Rabbi Sherer" left Eizenstadt feeling secure about the path taken by his son.

Stanley Brezenoff first met Rabbi Sherer when he was a Deputy Mayor of New York in the Koch administration. "It was a blessing to have met Rabbi Sherer when I was still a young man," he says. The early introduction to a man of such idealism and honesty, Brezenoff feels, protected him from ever becoming jaded or cynical about public service. One of the few photographs hanging in Brezenoff's office when he was president and chief executive officer of Brooklyn's Maimonides Medical Center was of Brezenoff together with Rabbi Sherer and Louis (Leuchu) Glueck.

In a similar vein, former Congressman Stephen Solarz applies Jackie Kennedy's description of her husband — "an idealist without illusions" — to Rabbi Sherer. Rabbi Sherer, in Solarz's words, moved with "consummate grace" both within the Jewish world and on the larger public stage.

A Holy Man

FOR ALL HIS EASY FAMILIARITY WITH A HOST OF DIFFERENT TYPES of people and his ability to discuss virtually any topic, Rabbi Sherer never permitted himself the slightest deviation from his role as representative of Torah Judaism. No risqué remark or the slightest hint of vulgarity ever passed his lips. He had absolutely no need to show himself to be one of the boys. And he commanded even more respect as a consequence.

"A holy man" is a frequently recurring encomium even among those who dealt with Rabbi Sherer on the most technical issues of public policy. That aura of deep religious conviction facilitated his ability to function in any political or educational setting. Because those with whom he came into contact never doubted his religious sincerity, they were careful to conduct themselves in his presence in a manner that would not offend him or make him uncomfortable.

Even people of other faiths felt that knowing Rabbi Sherer deepened their own faith. Over the years, one of those with whom Rabbi Sherer worked most closely on a wide range of educational issues was Alan Davitt of the New York Catholic Conference. Asked to name those whose company he enjoyed most, Davitt could name only two outside of the Catholic Church, and one of them was Rabbi Sherer. Yet though Davitt considered Rabbi Sherer a friend, he never addressed him as anything other than "Rabbi Sherer," just as he would have addressed any Catholic clergyman by his title. Davitt credits Rabbi Sherer's devotion to his faith with having strengthened his own faith.

Michael Lewan is another Catholic who feels that he is a better person for having known Rabbi Sherer. Since his passing, says Lewan, he frequently asks himself the question: *What would Rabbi Sherer tell me in this situation?* And he has tried to pattern his treatment of others on the way that Rabbi Sherer treated him over the course of their 25-year relationship.

A Trusted Adviser

RABBI SHERER WAS AN INFORMAL ADVISER TO A WIDE VARIETY OF public officials. He had a unique ability to give advice untainted by any trace of his own interest. "His advice was never about Agudath Israel or Rabbi Sherer," recalls Lewan, but was individually tailored to the needs of the person he was advising. Rabbi Sherer often found himself advising opposing political candidates, giving each the advice best suited to him.[2]

---

2. Rabbi Chaim Dovid Zwiebel.

Rabbi Sherer became the guide for all sorts of politicians and public officials in their relationships with the Orthodox world. When Stephen Solarz was first elected to Congress at 33, he knew little about the Orthodox world, despite representing a Brooklyn district. Before any meeting with a chassidic rebbe or other important figure in the Orthodox community, he would have his chief of staff, Michael Lewan, call Rabbi Sherer for a thorough background briefing.

Though initially Rabbi Sherer served primarily as a guide to the Orthodox world for public figures with little personal knowledge of that world, in many cases the scope of his advice grew over the years. As a young deputy mayor, Stanley Brezenoff would join Rabbi Sherer for a lunch of tuna fish sandwiches at the Agudath Israel offices at 5 Beekman Street three or four times a year. Their conversation quickly expanded beyond the narrow confines of Agudah, or even Orthodox concerns, to general topics. Brezenoff would pick Rabbi Sherer's brain for insights into city politics and how to balance competing interests on sensitive issues.

The task of the deputy mayor, as described by Brezenoff, is to make the right connections and not to make any mistakes. Rabbi Sherer helped him with both these tasks. He introduced him to important contacts and helped him steer clear of any pitfalls. Those lunches, with the "urbane, witty, and insightful" Orthodox leader became, over time, a "sort of mini-vacation" for Brezenoff from the pressures of his job.

One of the most important officials with whom Rabbi Sherer dealt over many years was Gordon Ambach, the New York State Commissioner of Education in the early 1980s. On each visit to Albany, Rabbi Sherer always made it a point to stop by Ambach's office, even if it was only to exchange a few pleasantries. Rabbi Sherer offered numerous times to take Ambach to Israel "to meet some of the great rabbis there." Though that trip never took place, Ambach was impressed by Rabbi Sherer's absolute confidence that even a non-Jew, lacking Hebrew or Yiddish, would be moved by a meeting with great rabbinic figures.

From 1980 through 1984, the New York State Department of Education undertook a top-to-bottom review of all New York state educational requirements that would result in the 1984 Regents' Action Plan. The Plan was proceeded by regional meetings throughout the state. Rabbi Sherer was careful to attend these meetings because he knew what great store Ambach placed in his suggestions. When the Regents' Plan was eventually passed, it was with the full support of the non-public-school sector, in large part due to Rabbi Sherer's input. One outgrowth of the Plan was the establishment of a non-public-school advisory council to supervise the provision of state services to the non-public-school sector. Ambach consulted extensively with Rabbi Sherer as to who should be on the council.

Ambach was awarded the 1985 Agudath Israel Humanitarian Award at the annual Agudath Israel dinner, as acknowledgment of the crucial assistance that he had rendered to private and sectarian education as Commissioner of Education. For Ambach, it was the first time that he had ever been at a large gathering of Orthodox Jews, and he was not familiar with the customary protocol. As the guests left the pre-dinner reception to enter the hall, Ambach began to put his arm around the back of the woman to whom he had been speaking to escort her into the hall. Suddenly he felt his arm caught and restrained by Rabbi Sherer. He never did quite figure out what he did wrong. Remembering the incident with bemusement years later, Ambach could only conclude: "She must have been a rabbi or something."

Wellsprings of Trust

ONE KEY TO RABBI SHERER'S INFLUENCE WITH GOVERNMENTAL officials was that he never asked for anything for himself, and "himself" included Agudath Israel of America. As a consequence, government officials always knew that he was speaking on behalf of the public, not on behalf of himself or his institution. They, in turn, were more forthcoming than they might have been to someone less selfless.

New York Mayor Rudolph Giuliani picked Rabbi Sherer to deliver the invocation at his first inaugural. In response to a question from Rabbi Chaskel Besser, the mayor explained why he was so drawn to Rabbi Sherer: "In Rabbi Sherer, I met for the first time a pleasant but astute political leader with whom I had a very interesting conversation, but who left me without asking for anything. I immediately recognized him to be a man of character and high caliber."[3]

The trust of government officials placed in Rabbi Sherer redounded to the benefit of every legitimate yeshivah. Prior to coming to work for Agudath Israel, Rabbi Shmuel Bloom was the executive director of the Yeshiva Gedola of St. Louis. The yeshivah's application for accreditation from the Education Department was found wanting, and Rabbi Bloom

---

3. Rabbi Chaskel O. Besser, "My Last Flight With Rabbi Sherer," *The Jewish Observer*, Summer 1998, p. 33.

Mayor Giuliani thanking Rabbi Sherer for his invocation at the mayoral inauguration

had only 48 hours to get the matter straightened out before the deadline for that year passed. He prepared and submitted an entire new set of documents, but the official in charge of reviewing the material was out of town. As a consequence, the entire set of documents was forwarded to Dr. Leslie Ross, the special assistant to Dr. John Proffitt.

A frantic Rabbi Bloom called Rabbi Sherer and asked him to intervene on behalf of the Yeshiva Gedola. Rabbi Sherer telephoned Dr. Ross and informed him that he was well acquainted with the St. Louis yeshi-

Chapter Ten: The "People Thing"   □   259

vah, and told him that it would be a pity if the yeshivah were to lose the entire annual funding because of a few small technicalities in the paperwork. Dr. Ross replied that the paperwork had still not reached him, but that Rabbi Sherer's "word that everything is in order" would be sufficient, and that he would arrange the accreditation based on nothing more than Rabbi Sherer's say-so.[4]

Around the same time, Rabbi Binyamin Paler of Yeshivas M'kor Chaim also sought Rabbi Sherer's intervention in an accreditation matter. Rabbi Sherer called Dr. John Proffitt. As Rabbi Sherer recorded in an aide-mémoire, "[Dr. Proffitt's] warm response was that in view of my personal guarantee, he would not even have to obtain the file from his subordinate .... [H]e will immediately issue an order that the letter of approval ... be sent immediately."

The Pell grant scandals of the early 1990s and the public hearings conducted by Senator Sam Nunn (D.-Ga.) were, in the view of Rabbi Sherer's closest associates, the lowest point of his public career. Under the Pell grant program students in post-secondary institutions are eligible to receive government stipends. Among the beneficiaries under the programs were the *yeshivos gedolos* accredited through AARTS (Association of Advanced Rabbinical and Talmudic Schools), which Rabbi Sherer did so much to bring into existence.

In order for students in particular institutions to be eligible, however, the state in which the post-secondary institution is located must provide a letter that the institution in question was recognized by the state to offer post-secondary education. Because of the close relationships that Rabbi Sherer had built up with the New York State Education Department over the years, his say-so was all that was ever required for the issuance of such a letter.

After the scandals broke, however, a high-ranking official in the State Education Department called Rabbi Sherer and informed him that the old system could no longer continue because of a number of incidents involving Jewish institutions (albeit no *yeshivos gedolos* and no institution for which Rabbi Sherer had vouched). The official, who had a long relationship with Rabbi Sherer, was apologetic, but insistent:

"Rabbi, you know that I respect and trust you more than any other person in the world. In my eyes, your word is as good as gold. However, because of certain recent reports about abuses in the Pell grant program,

---
4. Aide-mémoire re: Accreditation accomplished for Yeshiva Gedola of St. Louis, June 13, 1973.

we have decided that we can no longer simply rely on your say-so in a letter of authorization to Jewish schools that want to enter into the Pell grant system. From now on, they will have to go through the formal process of submitting various documents and catalogues, and subject themselves to the full review of our office …. Please understand that it is nothing personal, Rabbi, but that is just the way it has to be."

As Rabbi Sherer related the conversation behind closed doors in his office, Chaim Dovid Zwiebel had never seen him look so broken. He saw his life's work in jeopardy. A handful of unscrupulous individuals had squandered the good name and reputation he had spent a lifetime cultivating. "Whatever we were able to accomplish all these years, was because of our *chezkas kashrus* [reputation for probity] at the highest levels. Now, I'm afraid, that *chezkas kashrus* had been lost because of a few bad apples," he told his young protégé.[5]

The Pell grant scandal and its repercussions constituted a poignant illustration of an insight Rabbi Sherer shared many times on a *Mishnah* in *Pirkei Avos* (4:17): "Rabbi Shimon said: There are three crowns — the crown of Torah, the crown of priesthood, and the crown of kingship; but the crown of a good name surpasses them all." Why, Rabbi Sherer asked, does Rabbi Shimon say that there are three crowns, when the crown of a good name constitutes a fourth? He answered that in truth there are only three crowns, but that if those crowns are not joined to a *shem tov* (good name), then they lose all their value.

Nurturing Relationships

PERSONAL RELATIONSHIPS, RABBI SHERER UNDERSTOOD, MUST BE constantly developed; they are not preserved through inertia. The countless notes that he sent to public officials over the years were one of his chief means of nurturing the friendships that he had built up. At one level, many of those notes were purely an expression of his highly developed *middos*, particularly *hakaras hatov*. A note of appreciation to Secretary of State Cyrus Vance, after his resignation from the Carter cabinet, for instance, carried little chance of any future payback. But

---

5. Rabbi Chaim Dovid Zwiebel, "Straightening Out the Pictures," *Hamodia,* May 22, 2008, pp. B6-7.
   Rabbi Yaakov Bender once came to visit Rabbi Elya Svei and found him looking downcast. When Rabbi Bender asked him why, Reb Elya just motioned to a newspaper headline relating to some financial improprieties involving a bogus yeshivah, and added, "This is a tragedy. These people are going to destroy what it took Reb Moshe Sherer 30 years of hard work to build."

Vance had been very helpful to Rabbi Sherer in Agudath Israel's efforts to ship matzos to the former Soviet Union, and Rabbi Sherer felt it important to express once again his appreciation.

There was nothing pro forma about Rabbi Sherer's notes and letters. A great deal of thought went into them, and that was obvious to the recipients, who often wrote back to thank Rabbi Sherer for his kind words. After Robert D. Stone, the longtime chief counsel of the New York State Education Department, found an expeditious solution to ensure that crucial funding reached its intended beneficiaries, Rabbi Sherer wrote him, "Believe me, Bob, it is rare to find someone in your position, who is snowed under with problems, to act so quickly and with such sensitivity to help find a solution for kids who have a problem." Stone wrote back that it was words like those in Rabbi Sherer's letter that "make public service rewarding."

Probably no elected official, in the last decades of the 20th century did so much to help save Jewish lives, in both Iran and Syria, as Congressman Stephen Solarz, and Rabbi Sherer made sure that Solarz always felt good about what he had done. After one such note, Solarz wrote back, "Your recent communication was one of the most meaningful and moving I've ever gotten. There is nothing more important to me than saving Jewish lives ... and I consider myself privileged to be in a position to lend a helping hand to you in your own enormously impressive and continuing efforts on behalf of the noble cause of rescue and relief."[6] In response to another missive from Rabbi Sherer, Solarz announced, tongue in cheek, that if he ever became president, "I'm going to insist that you finally leave the Agudah and come to work with me in the White House."[7]

The notes served many purposes. Some were for the purpose of introducing a newly appointed public official to Agudath Israel;[8] some offered congratulations on electoral victories or new appointments;[9] and others offered encouragement to those who had gone out on the limb to help Orthodox Jews. John Zuccotti, a non-Jewish lawyer and real estate developer, who had at Rabbi Sherer's request attempted to save Yeshiva Chofetz Chaim on the West Side, fell into the latter cat-

---

6. Congressman Stephen J. Solarz to Rabbi Sherer, November 15, 1986.
7. Ibid., October 7, 1981.
8. Rabbi Moshe Sherer to Dr. Hadley S. DePuy on the latter's appointment as Deputy State Commissioner of Higher and Professional Education, January 24, 1978.
9. New York State Attorney General Robert Abrams to Rabbi Sherer thanking him for his congratulatory note, November 30, 1978.

egory. He was being pilloried in the press for his efforts. Rabbi Sherer wrote him:

> In our Jewish tradition, we are taught that the more pain one suffers from doing a good deed, the more one receives from the One Above. In fact, from reading the Scriptures, it seems to have always been the fate of those who serve the public well, beginning with Moses, to suffer as a result of false rumors circulated by the public. The only difference is that in the days of Moses there was no mass media to fan the flames of untruth far and wide.[10]

"Prayers" for the recipients of his communications were common in Rabbi Sherer's communications. And what is more the recipients were inclined to believe in the efficacy of his prayers. During one of his visits to Israel, Rabbi Sherer sent Ewald (Joe) Nyquist, the State Educational Commissioner, a postcard with his prayers for an increase in the state educational budget. Nyquist wrote back, "Your prayers were successful. We did get more money." Senator Robert Packwood, then the ranking Republican on the Senate Finance Committee, which deals with tax legislation, wrote to Rabbi Sherer after one successful legislative battle in which they were on the same side, "I'm absolutely convinced your prayers made the difference."[11]

Rabbi Sherer was always on the lookout for some reason to compliment those with whom he had a long relationship. With few politicians did he enjoy a longer or more fruitful relationship than with Senator Daniel Patrick Moynihan of New York. The two worked closely on tuition tax credits and other initiatives to aid parents of children in non-public schools. After Moynihan introduced legislation to extend the Basic Educational Opportunity Grant, Rabbi Sherer was quick to congratulate him: "You have once again demonstrated how your brilliant, innovative mind works for the benefit of people."[12]

Written communications were only one of the means by which Rabbi Sherer cemented his personal relationships. Office "chats" or "lunches" were another. After newly elected New Jersey governor Thomas Kean dropped by the Agudah headquarters for a "chat" with Rabbi Sherer, the latter offered to make a reception for him — in his new home — for Jewish leaders from the tri-state area.[13] First-term Congressman

---
10. Rabbi Sherer to John Zuccotti, June 12, 1980.
11. Senator Robert Packwood to Rabbi Moshe Sherer, March 10, 1982.
12. Rabbi Moshe Sherer to Senator Patrick Moynihan, February 25, 1980.
13. Rabbi Moshe Sherer to Governor-elect Thomas Kean, December 31, 1981.

Senator Daniel Patrick Moynihan addressing an Agudah mission to Washington. Seated (l-r): Senator Joseph Lieberman, Rabbi Chaim Dovid Zwiebel, Rabbi Sherer, Rabbi Labish Becker.

Stephen Solarz replied to a breakfast invitation that such an invitation from Rabbi Sherer was "the functional equivalent of a command performance."[14] Another young Jewish congressman from Brooklyn, today the senior senator from New York, Charles Schumer wrote, after a lunch in Rabbi Sherer's office, "I can see one of the major reasons for Agudah's success — your leadership." [15]

Rabbi Sherer also liked to bring people together in ways that would both generate ideas and connections. Hosting a luncheon for UN Ambassador Jean Kirkpatrick at Agudah headquarters, with a lot of prominent people in attendance, was both a good way to impress Kirkpatrick with the reach of the Agudah and to demonstrate to the other guests the respect in which the Reagan administration held Agudath Israel. A leading member of the New York city council wrote to Rabbi Sherer after the luncheon, "You do things in the grand manner, and it always pleasure to be among those who share these events with you."

The birth of the Southern Brooklyn Community Organization (SBCO) was announced at Agudah's third annual breakfast on social concerns, and the resulting New York Times coverage of the event helped bring Agudah to the attention of Richard Schifter, a prominent attorney and later a top State Department official, who rendered crucial services to Agudath Israel in both capacities.

---

14. Congressman Stephen J. Solarz to Rabbi Moshe Sherer, November 4, 1977.
15. Congressman Charles Schumer to Rabbi Moshe Sherer, January 24, 1978.

Bridging the Gulf

IT IS COMMON FOR GENTILES AND NON-RELIGIOUS JEWS TO FEEL uncomfortable in the presence of religious Jews. The latter, in particular, are prone to feeling that they are looked down upon by religious Jews. Mayor Ed Koch put his finger on the key to Rabbi Sherer's success in this regard: "He exuded the attitude: Hate the sin but love the sinner." He did not make religious differences personal.

A large part of his success with Jewish politicians like Ed Koch, Charles Schumer, and Stephen Solarz was that they never perceived him as looking down on those who were not as religious as he was. Indeed he would still use their Judaism as a means of building a connection. With Schumer, for instance, whose great-grandfather was a Chortkover chassid, Rabbi Sherer was always prepared with a story or a *vort* from the Chortkover Rebbe.

One of the great paradoxes of Rabbi Sherer's career was that despite being the sharpest and most outspoken critic of the heterodox branches of Judaism on the American scene, he was still able to form working relations with some of the leaders of these movements in bodies like the Claims Conference. He conducted himself in such a way as to even win their grudging admiration. Alexander Schindler, longtime head of the American Reform movement, eulogized Rabbi Sherer in *The New York Times*.

Similarly, he knew how to use religion to draw non-Jews to him rather than cause them to feel a sense of distance. Alan Davitt of the New York State Catholic Conference once made a slightly teasing remark to Rabbi Sherer about the wearing of a yarmulke. He quickly apologized for having spoken with disrespect of a religious symbol. Rather than take umbrage, Rabbi Sherer simply explained that a yarmulke serves as a constant reminder of Hashem's presence. A few days later, he sent Davitt, who is Irish, a green yarmulke. That last little gesture is typical of the way he could not only defuse tension but also use someone else's embarrassment to further build the relationship.

Don Nolan, the Deputy State Commissioner of Education from 1982 to 1993, is a religious Christian. He and Rabbi Sherer would on occasion exchange their favorite verses from Psalms. Nolan's son married a Jewish girl, and he confided his disappointment to Rabbi Sherer. Rabbi Sherer was no doubt far more dismayed by the match than Nolan, but he nevertheless sent Nolan a copy of a Rabbi Haim Donin's *To Be a Jew*. Ostensibly his purpose was to provide Nolan with more information about his new daugher-in-law's faith, and that is how his gesture was interpreted. Nolan even quoted from the book in a letter to Chaim Dovid Zwiebel written after Rabbi Sherer's *petirah* (death). But anyone who knows the way that Rabbi Sherer always sought to salvage something positive from any situation cannot help but suspect that his main purpose was the hope that Nolan's Jewish daughter-in-law would herself pick up the book one day and learn something about her own Judaism.

Rabbi Sherer was always on the lookout for ways to render some form of assistance to public figures, and when the opportunity to do so presented itself he acted with alacrity. Former New York City Mayor Ed Koch remembers a time when he was in a deep depression over a corruption scandal in City Hall. Cardinal O'Connor called him and told him, "You don't have to be depressed. We all know that you are an honest man." Koch, who is Jewish, then complained to Cardinal O'Connor that he had not received a similar call from the Lubavitcher Rebbe.

Cardinal O'Connor must have called Rabbi Sherer, with whom he enjoyed an exceptionally close relationship, as soon as he put down the phone. The next day Mayor Koch received a call from Rabbi Sherer in which the latter began, "Well, I'm not the Lubavitcher Rebbe, but I want you to know that I'm concerned."

Rabbi Sherer knew how to find the point of commonality with each person. The father of Judah Gribetz, who served as deputy mayor of New York city under Mayor Abe Beame and later as chief counsel to Governor Hugh Carey, headed the Jewish Free Loan Society. Whenever Rabbi Sherer met Gribetz, he would tell him a story of the days when he and Mike Tress had been frequent recipients of loans from his father and how important those loans were to the survival of Agudath Israel of America in its early days.

In a similar vein, letters to Senator Edward (Ted) Kennedy often began with some reference to Rabbi Sherer's relationship with the senator's brothers. Senator Kennedy was once honored at Agudath Israel's annual dinner. Unbeknownst to him, his brother Senator Robert F. Kennedy had been slated to be honored at an Agudah dinner, but was assassinated shortly before the scheduled dinner. At the conclusion of his introduction of Ted Kennedy, Rabbi Sherer presented him with the plaque that had been prepared for his late brother. Senator Kennedy was visibly moved by the presentation, and had to compose himself prior to beginning his speech.

With Senator Robert Kennedy

Good *middos*, Rabbi Sherer understood, are both a religious imperative and the building blocks of a relationship. A bus loaded with children from Washington Heights was once involved in a traffic accident during a severe snowstorm in Pennsylvania. Governor Carey ordered a group of National Guardsmen to escort the children's parents to Pennsylvania during the treacherous weather conditions. Rabbi Sherer asked Rabbi Boruch Borchardt, who lived in Washington Heights, to have every important figure in the Washington Heights *kehillah* write a personal letter to Governor Carey expressing appreciation for the governor's quick response to the plight of the worried parents. With his customary eye for detail and for turning every situation to potential advantage, Rabbi Sherer instructed that each letter writer should be careful to mention specifically the crucial role played in making the arrangements by Mendy Shayovich, who was both a protégé of Rabbi Sherer and a top staffer in the Carey administration.

In his instructions to Rabbi Borchardt, Rabbi Sherer emphasized two points. The first was the crucial importance of showing *hakaras hatov* from a Jewish point of view. Only then did he add that the Jewish community could find itself in need of emergency assistance from Governor Carey in the future, and that expressions of gratitude for the assistance

Chapter Ten: The "People Thing"   □   267

rendered could help ensure that the governor would be eager to act if a similar situation were to arise.

As always, the building and preservation of relationships was at the forefront of his thoughts.

Chapter Eleven

LEADER

Charisma

RABBI SHERER POSSESSED A RARE ABILITY TO ATTRACT others to himself and his cause from an early age. He carried himself with a "certain élan" that announced his presence from the first moment he entered a room, says Seymour Lachman, a former president of the New York City Board of Education and New York State senator.

"He was a terrific human being, much nicer than he had to be," remembers Stanley Brezenoff. "Urbane, witty and insightful" are just a few of the qualities that Brezenoff came to associate with Rabbi Sherer. "He lit up a room with his effervescence and sparkling personality," recalls Stuart Eizenstadt. Yet, Eizenstadt is quick to add, that sparkle was never at the expense of his gravitas. His seriousness and depth of conviction were never in doubt.

In honor of a visit by Rabbi Sherer to Los Angeles to meet with the newly constituted chapter of Agudath Israel of America, a meeting was arranged with a number of prominent politicians. Prior to his arrival, the room was taut with nervous tension. The politicians had never been in a gathering of Orthodox Jews before, and their hosts lacked the experience to know how to put them at their ease. Then Rabbi Sherer walked in. The politicians had little idea of who he was, but from the way he carried himself, they instinctively understood that he was the one with whom they wanted to have their photograph taken.

When he arose to speak, Rabbi Sherer began with a joke: "The Jewish people have been compared to a teabag .... We don't get going until we are in hot water." From that moment, he had the politicians eating out of his palm. He then proceeded to explain how the new Agudath Israel of California was going to change the whole mind-set of Jews on the West Coast.[1]

It is impossible to ascertain precisely how much of what is commonly called charisma is due to a person's unique personal qualities and how much to the position that he occupies. What is clear, however, is that the two reinforce each other. The more a person accomplishes, the greater the aura that attaches to him. And the greater that aura the more he is able to achieve. With each concrete success, Rabbi Sherer's ability to rally others to his banner was reinforced.

For his part, Rabbi Sherer took little pride in being described as charismatic. It is a term that is often applied to politicians and movie stars, and the ability to move masses can be used as easily for great evil as great good. Shortly prior to his death, Rabbi Sherer told his son that he hoped instead to be remembered as one who possessed "*Yiddishe chein,*" a quality that derives from an inner connection to Hashem that radiates outward and is perceived by others, as the verse states, "and you will find favor (*chein*) and goodly wisdom in the eyes of G-d and man" (*Mishlei* 3:4).

Most leaders succeed by virtue of one or two qualities finely honed. Rabbi Sherer, however, possessed virtually all the qualities that make for effective leadership. He combined, to a rare degree, superb people skills with the ability to get things done. He was, says Lachman, that "rare combination of an eloquent speaker and a superb administrator." Senator Charles Schumer mentions another one of the usual dichotomies that Rabbi Sherer transcended: "He combined abstract wisdom with being very practical at the same time."

---

1. Dr. Irving Lebovics, "Rabbi Sherer זצ״ל and the 'People Thing,'" *The Jewish Observer*, Summer 1998, p. 26.

President George H. W. Bush meets with Jewish leaders.

DURING THE LAST DECADES OF HIS LIFE, RABBI SHERER WAS NOT only the most influential Orthodox leader, but one of the most influential Jewish leaders — period. At a meeting with Jewish leaders, President George H.W. Bush signaled to Rabbi Sherer that he should take the seat close to him.

Many Levels of Leadership

He functioned as a leader on many different levels. Within Agudath Israel, he was the unquestioned driving force, and it was his vision that set the direction for the organization. As the leader of Agudath Israel of America, he spoke on behalf of the Torah world to the outside world. When Daniel Tropper, an expatriate American working as an aide to Israel's Education Minister Zevulun Hammer, wanted to know whether the yeshivah world would participate in a world conference on Jewish education, he turned naturally to Rabbi Sherer. As he explained, "I know that you do not represent the entire yeshivah world, but if I had to single out one person who can sense the situation, size it up, and give an accurate recommendation, it is you."[2]

---
2. Dr. Daniel Tropper to Rabbi Moshe Sherer, October 22, 1981.

Not only did he represent Agudath Israel within American Orthodoxy, but over the years he came increasingly to be seen as the leading spokesman for Orthodoxy to the larger Jewish community. For example, in December 1975, he met with the leaders of the New York Federation for nearly three hours. Rabbi Sherer started the meeting with a 30-minute discussion of the various trends in American Orthodoxy and their respective leaders. He criticized the Federation for its lack of support of Jewish education, and pointed out that the Federation's spending priorities were often more the product of inertia than of an analysis of current communal needs. He described Agudath Israel's move into social service fields as, in part, a response to the Federation's inability to address itself to Orthodox needs.[3]

One of the Federation participants present subsequently wrote Rabbi Sherer, "I know that in your long career you have been 'up front' often enough to know when you are getting to the insides of the people you are talking to. I'm certain that you know you got to our insides ... We all had to examine old conceptions against the ideas and position you put forward."[4]

More than any other Jewish leader, Rabbi Sherer pushed the Orthodox to the communal table. After President Carter met with a group of American Jewish leaders to discuss American Mideast policy, and neglected to invite any Orthodox representatives, Rabbi Sherer wrote a sharp note to the president's top domestic affairs adviser, Stuart Eizenstadt. He described the omission as "unthinkable" and as betraying a lack of understanding of the "realities of the composition of the American Jewry in the 1970s." By omitting the Orthodox, Rabbi Sherer wrote, the president deprived himself of a "deeply rooted perspective that generates more profound insights."[5]

---

3. Aide Memoir, December 11, 1975.

Rabbi Sherer was ever on the alert for opportunities to present American Orthodoxy to the Jewish establishment. For instance, when Theodore Mann was appointed Chairman of the Conference of Presidents of Major Jewish Organizations, Rabbi Sherer wrote to invite him for lunch: "It struck me that you may want to get to know in depth the 'world' of Agudath Israel of America, which has radically changed since your early Torah Vodaas days." Rabbi Moshe Sherer to Theodore Mann, December 13, 1978.

Rabbi Sherer also initiated meetings between articulate Orthodox Jews and members of the secular media.

4. Dr. Melvin Mogulof to Rabbi Moshe Sherer, December 12, 1975.

5. Rabbi Moshe Sherer to Stuart Eizenstadt, March 15, 1978.

Later that year, Rabbi Sherer wrote to Matthew Nimetz, chief counsel to Secretary of State Cyrus Vance, in the same vein. President Carter's "benign neglect" of the Orthodox Jewish community that had grown over the last decade, Rabbi Sherer asserted, did not serve the country well because

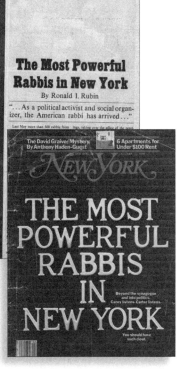

Featured among "the most powerful rabbis in New York," *New York Magazine*, January 22, 1979

When Alfred Moses took over as President Carter's Jewish liason in May 1980, Rabbi Sherer was quick to inform him of the existence of a "vibrant Orthodox Jewish community, growing by leaps and bounds, which is not represented on the Presidents Conference." As he always did, Rabbi Sherer invited Moses for a lunch meeting at Agudath Israel headquarters and a 20-minute tour of the Agudah offices, which he promised would be an "eye-opener."[6]

In his reply, Moses, who had in the intervening week met Rabbi Sherer personally at a meeting of the Presidents Conference, mentioned that he had heard a great deal about Rabbi Sherer and Agudath Israel from their mutual friend Richard Schifter, and that he shared Rabbi Sherer's views on "the new Orthodox in America."[7]

The so-called "Jewish establishment" was not always thrilled with

---

it deprived President Carter of "the unique perspective" the Orthodox would add to these meetings.
6. Rabbi Moshe Sherer to Alfred H. Moses, May 7, 1980.
7. Alfred H. Moses to Rabbi Moshe Sherer, May 14, 1980.

With President Jimmy Carter

the new prominence given Orthodoxy in Washington. After attending a Pentagon briefing with Secretary of Defense Donald Rumsfeld and the Joint Chiefs of Staff, together with other Jewish leaders, during the Ford administration, Rabbi Sherer noted that he and George Klein were the only "yarmulkes" in the room, and they were the only two names omitted from the Jewish Telegraph Agency story on the briefing.[8]

Defender of Orthodoxy

OVER TIME, RABBI SHERER DEVELOPED INTO THE PREMIER defender of Orthodoxy. His daily reading included the general press in both America and Israel,[9] the Anglo-Jewish press, and the religious press in Israel. As a consequence, he was often the first to know of media attacks against Orthodoxy anywhere in the world and to respond. Already by 1970, he had secured from the Jewish Telegraph Agency's news editor

---

8. Aide-mémoire, May 20, 1976.
9. When the Israeli tabloid *Maariv* published a completely false story that Agudath of Israel had set up a defense fund for nursing home owners under investigation, Rabbi Sherer wasted no time threatening a libel action if a full retraction did not appear on page one.

Murray Zuckoff a promise to drop the term "ultra-Orthodox," with its implication of somehow being too much. Unfortunately, that undertaking did not extend to JTA's Israel correspondent David Landau. The consequence, as Rabbi Sherer complained in a 1986 letter to Zuckoff, was that Agudath Israel found itself lumped together under one rubric with the pro-PLO Neturei Karta.

At the height of the "Who is a Jew" issue in Israel in 1988, Rabbi Sherer wrote to *New York Times* editor Max Frankel protesting the paper's coverage of the issue and the failure to quote even one Orthodox spokesperson. Again, he objected to the paper's use of terms like "ultra-Orthodox" and "fundamentalist" to characterize various Orthodox groups, including Agudath Israel in Israel. "Frankly, in my 45 years of public service, rarely have I seen such an outpouring of invective," Rabbi Sherer concluded. But characteristically, he did not burn his bridges and suggested a meeting with Frankel to discuss some of their differences.[10]

The same day *Newsday* published a cartoon showing then-Prime Minister Yitzchak Shamir being carried away by two bearded, black-hatted Jews over the caption, "Mein golly — I hope George Bush will not criticize me for allowing meinself to be carried away by some screwy, right-wing fundamentalists." In a letter to *Newsday* publisher, David Laventhol, Rabbi Sherer wrote that in all his public life he had never seen such a blatantly anti-Semitic cartoon and demanded a public apology.[11]

Having secured a place at the communal table for American Orthodoxy, Rabbi Sherer also became an important spokesman for American Jewry (and not just for the Orthodox world) on issues such as the security of Israel. Nor was his influence limited to the United States. As co-chairman of Agudath Israel World Organization from 1980, he kept constantly abreast of anything touching the lives of Jews anywhere in the world, and was a major player, on many levels, in Israel..

Rabbi Sherer once told his longtime secretary, Mrs. Debby Jacobs, that the mission of Agudath Israel was to do whatever it could for every Jewish man, woman, and child anywhere in the world. And to that end, he maintained an extensive web of contacts who served as his antennae to all corners of the Jewish world. None were more important in this respect than two Orthodox Jews who had risen to the

---

10. Rabbi Moshe Sherer to Max Frankel, November 22, 1988.
11. Rabbi Moshe Sherer to David Laventhol, Novermber 22, 1988.

Greeting Malcolm Hoenlein with Rabbi Mordechai Avigdor

very pinnacle of organized Jewish life: Malcolm Hoenlein, the longtime Executive Vice-Chairman of the Conference of Presidents of Major Jewish Organizations, and Israel Singer, former Secretary-General of the World Jewish Congress. Rabbi Sherer was in frequent, sometimes daily, contact with both men.

The connection to both Singer and Hoenlein went back a long way. Singer's grandfather came to America on a visa procured by Mike Tress, and his father was close to both Mike Tress and Rabbi Sherer. Singer had been a homiletics student of Rabbi Sherer in Torah Vodaath; he credits Rabbi Sherer with teaching him to speak on behalf of Jews. Hoenlein first met Rabbi Sherer while doing research for his Ph.D. thesis on the autopsy issue in the archives of Agudath Israel.

Both men viewed Rabbi Sherer as a mentor in organized Jewish life, who could give them sage advice about how to navigate the ever treacherous waters as publicly identified Orthodox Jews. Hoenlein knew he could always count on Rabbi Sherer for a non-judgmental, *Klal Yisrael* view of any situation. Rabbi Sherer would advise him as to which criticism to ignore and which had to be taken into account. "You could call him up out of the blue and get advice," Hoenlein remembers. "He would let you talk and hear the challenges of both sides. He did not have a personal agenda when he gave advice."

Singer learned from Rabbi Sherer to have the confidence to make decisions. He appreciated Rabbi Sherer's broad perspective on the crucial issues facing the Jewish community on the international scene. "When it comes to saving Jewish lives, Rabbi Sherer recognized you cannot act as if it were *'shtiebel* politics,' in deciding whom you will deal with and who you will not," says Singer.

For Singer, Rabbi Sherer personified what it meant to be a Jewish leader. Rabbi Sherer once shared with him a *vort* from Rebbe Dovid Lvov of Tarnopol on what it means to be a Jewish leader. In *parashas Ki Sisa*, Moshe Rabbeinu is described in one verse as standing "on the rock": "וַיֹּאמֶר ה׳ הִנֵּה מָקוֹם אִתִּי וְנִצַּבְתָּ עַל הַצּוּר — Hashem said, 'Behold! There is a place near Me; you may stand on the rock' " (*Shemos* 33:21). And in the very next verse, he is described as standing in the "cleft of the rock": "וְהָיָה בַּעֲבֹר כְּבֹדִי וְשַׂמְתִּיךָ בְּנִקְרַת הַצּוּר — When My glory passes by, I shall place you in a cleft of the rock ..." (ibid., v. 22).

The difference, Rabbi Sherer explained, is that in the first verse Moshe Rabbeinu is functioning as a leader of the Jewish people, standing near Hashem, and thus he must present himself proudly from the top of the rock. In the next verse, he is a private individual, and therefore must adopt a position of humility in the "cleft of the rock." That, says Singer, was Rabbi Sherer. In his personal life, he was selfless, seeking nothing for himself. But when representing Hashem and the Jewish people, he carried himself with great dignity. "He always looked like he was dressed out of the Brooks Brothers window .... He never came to a meeting late and when he spoke, he spoke with great care. People listened to him because they sensed something important was taking place. Because of him, *frum* Jews became recognized in New York City, the State of New York, and Washington, D.C. By the end of his life, there was not a president who did not recognize his name because they knew he spoke for an important segment of the Jewish people."

Rabbi Sherer's contacts with Hoenlein and Singer were informal. Agudath Israel was not an official member of the Presidents Conference or part of the structure of the World Jewish Congress. Singer did, however, appoint Rabbi Sherer as the major Orthodox representative on Holocaust restitution issues to the Claims Conference, because he spoke with an authority and in an unequivocal manner that no other Orthodox leader could muster.

Building Bridges

AS DEPUTY MAYOR OF NEW YORK CITY, STANLEY BREZENOFF found Rabbi Sherer to be a "bridge builder at a time of great divisiveness," someone capable of bringing the entire Orthodox community together — a feat, Brezenoff acknowledges, easier said than done. His bridge building, however, was not at the cost of the integrity of Agudath Israel. Rabbi Sherer's superb political skills allowed him to be an effective advocate for his own organization, but not just for his own organization, says Brezenoff.

Senator Charles Schumer offers an interesting example of Rabbi Sherer's ability to build coalitions, in this instance between the black and Jewish communities. A certain savings and loan association failed. Unfortunately, the Hebrew Academy for Special Children (HASC) had savings well above the FDIC-insured limits deposited in that savings and loan association. The loss of those savings would have been a severe, perhaps fatal, blow to HASC.

At almost the same time, the Freedom National Bank in Harlem failed. Rabbi Sherer had stored the information about the failure of Freedom National Bank, and he immediately recognized that the simultaneous failure of banks serving the black and Jewish communities provided an opportunity to pool political forces. He called then-Congressman Schumer and asked him whether he was making any efforts on behalf of Freedom National Bank. Schumer responded that he had been involved, but only tangentially.

Rabbi Sherer suggested that Schumer contact Harlem Congressman Charles Rangel to explore the possibility of combining their efforts on behalf of the two banks. They did, and were eventually able to recover much of the savings of depositors in both institutions. The impact of the two congressmen working together, in Schumer's opinion, was far greater than would have been the impact of either one working alone. As a result of their efforts, HASC was spared a major loss of funds. That success provides a clear example of Rabbi Sherer's great creative abilities as a "fixer, a problem-solver."[12]

In recognition of Schumer's efforts, Rabbi Sherer called him on behalf of HASC and told him that the organization wished to honor him at its annual benefit concert at Lincoln Center. Senator Schumer cites Rabbi Sherer's efforts on behalf of HASC as an example of the way that "he spoke for the community and everyone knew it."

---

12. Former Congressman Stephen Solarz.

NO ASPECT OF RABBI SHERER'S BRIDGE BUILDING PAID GREATER dividends than the alliance that he developed with the Catholic Church, on issues of common concern, over decades. Because of the far-greater numbers of Catholics and the resources of the church, that alliance magnified Rabbi Sherer's lobbying power exponentially.

Alliance With the Catholics

Close relations with the Catholic Church were a crucial element of Rabbi Sherer's *shtadlanus* strategy. He once referred to the Catholic Conference, a Catholic lobbying organization, as "my secret weapon all these years." And the church returned the high regard. Alan Davitt of the New York Catholic Conference reported to Rabbi Sherer an especially effusive compliment he had heard about Rabbi Sherer from Bishop McManus, the Vicar for Education in the Archdiocese of Chicago, and, according to Davitt, the church's "leading and most perceptive spokesman on non-public schools." In the bishop's opinion, "the finest hour in the history of relations between non-public schools and the government occurred on the day of your testimony before the House Ways and Means Committee."[13] When the Catholic hierarchy began lobbying for tuition tax credits in the early '70s, it tapped Rabbi Sherer to chair the non-denominational organization created to lead the battle.

In dealing with the church, Rabbi Sherer adhered to *shtadlanus* principles similar to those adopted with public officials. Thus he made a point of keeping disagreements private and avoiding public confrontations. One classic example followed the pope's 1987 public meeting with Austrian president Kurt Waldheim, after the latter had already been exposed as a former Nazi officer. The pope's warm comments after the visit caused a great deal of bitterness in the general Jewish community and a number of harsh condemnations of the pope by mainstream Jewish groups.[14]

Rabbi Sherer met privately with Cardinal John O'Connor on August 6 1984, more than a month after Pope John Paul II received Waldheim, and expressed his own strong dismay at the visit and the pope's "laudatory remarks" after the visit. But he explained that Agudath Israel had nevertheless issued no public statements because as "religionists

---

13. J. Alan Davitt to Rabbi Sherer, October 30, 1972.
14. The entire story is related by Rabbi Chaim Dovid Zwiebel in "A Model Lesson in 'Interfaith Relations,'" *Hamodia*, June 23, 2000, p. 85. Most of the material in the article consisted of excerpts from Rabbi Sherer's personal diary.

we do not use the newspapers and picketing and other rash methods to express our dismay with the heads of a religious faith community."

That meeting came about in response to a phone call from Mayor Koch to Rabbi Sherer. The mayor told him that he had met with Cardinal O'Connor, and that the cardinal had expressed his shock that his efforts to heal the breach between Catholics and Jews through an ecumenical prayer service of some kind, or if necessary by the cardinal going to a synagogue for a joint "meditation event," had been summarily rejected by the Orthodox rabbinate. The mayor called upon Rabbi Sherer to explain the Orthodox opinion to Cardinal O'Connor.

Cardinal O'Connor's proposal of an ecumenical service placed two of Rabbi Sherer's *shtadlanus* principles with respect to the church on a potential collision course. On the one hand, Rabbi Sherer strenuously opposed all forms of interfaith dialogue. Conservative leader Wolf Kelman once responded to Rabbi Sherer's criticisms of the Conservative movement for its sponsorship of interfaith dialogue by pointing out Rabbi Sherer's own extensive web of contacts with the Catholic Church. The latter responded sharply:

> I am baffled and perplexed how any logical person cannot see the clear distinction between engaging in interreligious discussions and the type of activity which I have been engaged in over the years .... I have never at any time discussed any topic of religion or theology, directly or indirectly, with any member of the Christian clergy, or for that matter with any non-Jew. I consider interreligious ecumenical dialogue an open passport to *shmad* [conversion from Judaism] .... [T]echnical contacts between qualified Orthodox Jewish leaders and Christian clergymen, to which the broad public is not privy ..., can never have the deleterious effects

of exposing the uninformed Jewish masses to the missionary messages implicit in interreligious dialogue.[15]

On the other hand, his good relations with Cardinal O'Connor personally and with the entire Catholic hierarchy were a crucial component of his *shtadlanus* efforts. How could he preserve those relationships without violating his absolute rejection of interfaith dialogue? But Rabbi Sherer did not shrink from a challenge, and he followed through immediately on Mayor Koch's request by scheduling a meeting with the cardinal the next day.

He began by pointing out to Cardinal O'Connor that Agudath Israel had issued no public condemnations of the pope's meeting with Waldheim. Next he described to Cardinal O'Connor the crisis facing the entire Jewish people as a result of rapid assimilation and intermarriage. In such a situation, "when we have such ignorant masses in the general population, " Rabbi Sherer explained, "in order to preserve our integrity, and not permit the lines of demarcation between various faiths to completely tumble down, we have to build fences around ourselves." Avoiding any form of joint prayer services, said Rabbi Sherer, was one of those fences.

Not only did Cardinal O'Connor accept the explanation, he expressed his admiration for Rabbi Sherer's candor. For good measure, the cardinal confessed that he considered himself the "Orthodox" within the Catholic Church on such matters, and added "in confidence that he ha[d] spent many hours in dozens of meetings of an ecumenical nature and [found] that they are of very little value. What is important is that people should strengthen their own religion, as long as they respect the next person's religion."

"Only in America," says Michael Lewan, the chairman of the U.S. Commission for the Preservation of America's Heritage Abroad, "would the way for a Catholic layman to get to the pope be through an Orthodox rabbi." Lewan drafted the legislation establishing the commission, which deals primarily with the preservation of Jewish graves in Eastern and Central Europe, while serving as an aide to Congressman Stephen Solarz, and he was appointed chairman of the commission by President Clinton in 1994.

In early 1997, Lewan read that pope John Paul would be visiting his native Poland. As the first Polish-born pope, his visit was guaranteed

---

15. Rabbi Sherer to Wolf Kelman, February 5, 1968.

to generate great interest in Poland. Lewan had the idea of asking the pope to use his visit to encourage the Catholic clergy in Poland to assist in the task of uncovering and preserving Jewish gravesites. The only problem was that he had no idea of how to reach the pope to broach the idea. He discussed his idea with Rabbi Chaskel Besser, who served with him on the commission, and Rabbi Besser told him that the best way to get the pope's attention was through the Archbishop of New York, Cardinal John O'Connor. And the best way to get to Cardinal O'Connor was through Rabbi Sherer.

Lewan arranged a meeting with Rabbi Sherer, at which he outlined his goals. Rabbi Sherer agreed to introduce him to Cardinal O'Connor. At that later meeting, Lewan was struck by the warmth and affection that Cardinal O'Connor showed Rabbi Sherer. Cardinal O'Connor agreed to place Lewan's request before Pope John Paul. That Easter he traveled to Rome, and met with the pontiff in the Vatican. Five weeks later, Pope John Paul delivered the following message to a gathering of Catholic priests in Kalisz, Poland: "These Jewish cemeteries are part of our common past. They are places of deep spiritual and historic significance. Let these places join Poles and Jews together .... "

The pope's words filtered down from the Catholic clergy to their flocks. Not long after the pope spoke, Rabbi Shmuel Bloom ran into a Polish-born Jew, who told him that he had just returned from Poland, where he had been able to bring his two brothers to *kever Yisrael* (Jewish burial) 55 years after they were murdered in a field by the Nazis. When Rabbi Bloom asked him how he had located their burial place after the passage of so many years, the man replied that an elderly Polish gentile had shown him the place.[16]

In its efforts to lesson the polluting and corrosive impact of societal moral decline, Agudath Israel often found a powerful ally in the Catholic Church. On more than one occasion, Cardinal John O'Connor referred to Rabbi Sherer as his guide in these matters. For instance, when the New York State educational authorities announced a required health curriculum dealing with AIDS and its prevention, one of Rabbi Sherer's first moves was to alert Cardinal O'Connor to the issue and enlist his support.

Cardinal O'Connor told Rabbi Sherer that he had not heard about this latest development, but that he fully concurred with the opposi-

---

16. "Rabbi Moshe Sherer ז״ל: *Parnes Hador*," *The Jewish Observer*, Summer 1998, p. 40.

tion to the proposed curriculum expressed by the Moetzes Gedolei HaTorah. He and Rabbi Sherer agreed that Chaim Dovid Zwiebel would work on the nitty-gritty details of strategy together with Bishop (today Cardinal) Edward M. Egan.

The same story repeated itself with respect to indecent advertising on New York City's public transportation. On May 4, 1993, Rabbi Sherer wrote to Peter Stangl, chairman of the Metropolitan Transport Authority (MTA), asking whether the MTA had any standards whatsoever in determining whether to accept ads. In response, he received a letter from Mr. Bernard Cohen, the MTA's director of policy and planning, in which Cohen explained that the First Amendment's protection of free speech from government interference required the MTA, a governmental body, to accept even highly offensive advertising.

Rabbi Sherer immediately requested Chaim Dovid Zwiebel to prepare a legal memorandum assessing Cohen's claim that the MTA had little discretion to reject ads on the grounds that they were offensive or indecent. Zwiebel concluded that the MTA, in fact, had the power to enunciate clear regulations as to what kinds of ads it would take. First, the ads are "commercial speech," which enjoys a lower level of protection than so-called "political speech." Second, courts have long recognized a compelling state interest in shielding impressionable children from inappropriate images. Such an interest underlies much of federal regulation of radio and TV broadcasters. And that interest is particularly strong when dealing with what is, in effect a captive audience: those who ride the subways regularly or who are exposed to the images on passing buses.

Rabbi Sherer hastened to send the memo to Mr. Cohen on July 12. Cohen responded on September 8 that the MTA was indeed investigating whether "it is possible to formulate improved objective and enforceable advertising standards." Having received no further response from the MTA in the next two months, Rabbi Sherer wrote to Cohen to urge him to place the issue on the "front burner ... because the issue is so important to our community and to other city residents who are profoundly offended by the moral assault perpetrated by these ads."

When that letter too received no response, Zwiebel was dispatched to testify before the New York City Council Committee on Transportation, and to urge the city to consider legislating in an area where the MTA had dillydallied not for want of authority but due to "a lack of will." Eventually, however, the MTA did adopt advertising standards in

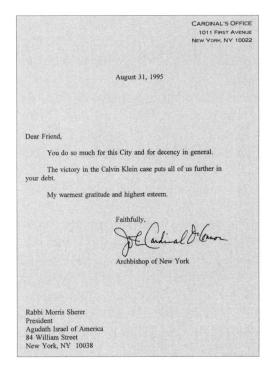

response to the concerns raised by Rabbi Sherer and others. In March 1994, it announced that it would no longer accept advertisements that are "obscene" or "indecent to minors." And those standards were strengthened in September 1997 to include other, similar advertisements or those that "contain images or information that would be deemed by a significant segment of the public to be patently offensive, improper, or in bad taste."

Writing in the September 30, 1993 issue of *Catholic New York*, Cardinal O'Connor described how the "rightfully [sic] revered" Rabbi Sherer had taken serious exception to the Metropolitan Transport Authority's indecent commercial advertising. Cardinal O'Connor related that he had not been surprised by Rabbi Sherer's leadership in this area, and noted that the two men "consistently shared the same moral values. If anything, he has been even more watchful than I, and unfailingly courageous," wrote the cardinal.

Cardinal O'Connor then proceeded to pay abundant tribute to both Rabbi Sherer and Chaim Dovid Zwiebel. "Sometimes we Catholics think we are alone when we wage these battles," Cardinal O'Connor wrote. "Frequently, I find Rabbi Sherer way ahead of me." Mr. Zwiebel's analysis of the MTA's claim that the First Amendment required them to accept the indecent advertising, Cardinal O'Connor wrote, "leaves that policy without a leg to stand on."[17] (For good measure, he added that

---

17. Unfortunately, the MTA's original claim that it had no discretion over the content of the advertisements it accepted gained some legal support from the Second Circuit Court of Appeals in *New York Magazine, v. The Metropolitan Transportation Authority* (1998), long after the MTA had adopted its own set of limitations on sexually provocative advertising material. The case involved an advertisement for *New York Magazine* that poked fun at New York City Mayor Rudolph Guiliani by describing the magazine "as perhaps the only good thing in New York for which Rudy had not

he had never read "clearer or more persuasive briefs on church-state constitutional issues than those written by Mr. Zwiebel.")[18]

On at least one occasion a prominent Catholic politician, who knew of Rabbi Sherer's influence with Cardinal O'Connor, begged Rabbi Sherer to intervene on his behalf. New York Governor Mario Cuomo, in a speech at Notre Dame University in South Bend, Indiana, had distinguished between his personal religious opposition to abortion, and his feeling that as governor of New York, he was bound not to impose his own religious views.

For that attempt to walk the tightrope between his church and the views of his Democratic Party, Cuomo found himself the subject of a sharp attack from Auxiliary Bishop Austin Vaughn, who compared Cuomo's position to that of a Nazi soldier who "may have objected to the Holocaust but nevertheless supported the German government's right to murder six million innocent Jews." The power of the metaphor hurt Cuomo deeply, and he called upon Rabbi Sherer, as perhaps the one person whose connections with the Catholic hierarchy were sufficient to convince the Catholic hierarchy to cease likening him to a Nazi.

Rabbi Sherer accepted the assignment and penned a letter to Cardinal O'Connor distinguishing between "responsible ways to express opposition to abortion on demand and irresponsible ways." The Nazi analogy, he argued, is of the latter kind. "For one thing," he wrote, "I deem it irresponsible to compare any public official in this great nation to a Nazi," no matter how resolute our disagreement with him on the abortion issue. Secondly, Rabbi Sherer noted "how emotionally sensitive the post-Holocaust generation of Jewish survivors and their descendants are to comparisons ... made between evils, lesser evils, and that which

---

taken credit." The MTA pulled the ad, citing a New York State Civil Rights Law prohibiting the unauthorized use of a living person's name for advertising purposes. The Second Circuit ruled that inside of MTA buses and trains had the status of a "public forum," and therefore the MTA did not have the discretion to reject the ad in question. Though the advertisement in question arguably involved political speech, which is entitled to the highest level of protection, and not commercial speech, which is entitled to far less, the Second Circuit's reasoning nevertheless cast a big question mark over the MTA's limitations on indecent advertising.

18. Rabbi Sherer also ordered his troops into action at the side of the church when public money was spent on "artistic" works and exhibits that made mockery of Christian religious icons. In doing so, he emphasized the common interest of "religionists" in protesting against public ridicule and humiliation of religion. That policy continued after his passing. Thus Agudath Israel filed an amicus brief in the Second Circuit supporting New York Mayor Rudy Guliani's right to cut city funding to the Brooklyn Art Museum in response to an appropriately labeled "Sensation" exhibit, whose own promotional materials warned that the contents of the exhibit, which included depictions of revered religious figures incorporating revolting, pornographic and lascivious elements, might cause "shock, vomiting, confusion, [or] panic."

Rabbi Sherer arranges a meeting between Governor Mario Cuomo and members of the Moetzes Gedolei HaTorah; l-r: Rabbi Elya Svei, Rabbi Avrohom Pam, the Novominsker Rebbe and Rabbi Ahron Schechter.

transpired at the hands of the Nazis."

The Holocaust analogy faded from the rhetoric of the pro-life movement to the great relief of both Governor Cuomo and the Jewish community, which has such a strong interest in protecting against the cheapening of the Holocaust by turning it into an all-purpose metaphor for all that one finds objectionable.

Connecting the Dots

THE FILES OF AGUDATH ISRAEL OF AMERICA UNDER RABBI Sherer's leadership are filled with hundreds of examples of his ability to solve problems, sometimes major ones, just by knowing whom to contact: a brief note to Howard Golden, president of the borough of Brooklyn, urging him to intercede with the Board of Estimate to prevent a zoning dispute over the Yeshivah of Brooklyn's expansion plans;[19] a call to Senator Jacob

---

19. Rabbi Sherer to Howard Golden, president of the borough of Brooklyn, May 20, 1986. "Howie, I cannot overemphasize the importance of this issue to our community... .," wrote Rabbi Sherer. "[T]he burgeoning Orthodox population in Brooklyn, which I'm sure you will agree is a positive development for the stability of the borough, has created a demand for yeshivah education that existing institutions are simply unable to meet because of logistical limitations." Rabbi Sherer informed Golden that the community viewed the case of the Yeshivah of Brooklyn as a precedent. Nine days later, Golden wrote back that the Board of Estimate had followed his advice not to intervene, and

With Senator Jacob Javits (l) and Moshe Braunfeld

Javits seeking his intervention with the Czechoslovakian authorities to protect and refurbish the grave of the Noda B'Yehudah;[20] another contact with Senator Javits about a dispute between *shochtim* (ritual slaughterers) and government inspectors in Iowa that threatened the supply of kosher meat;[21] a few weeks of intensive lobbying in Albany to restore a $350,000 grant to Torah Umesorah.[22]

Rabbi Sherer's effectiveness lay not only in the breadth of his connections, but in his ability to connect the dots between them in novel ways. One of the most significant examples of Rabbi Sherer's ability to utilize his vast web of connections involved the famed Bais Medrash Govoha

---

the yeshivah could go ahead with its plans.
20. Rabbi Moshe Sherer to Senator Jacob Javits, February 2, 1978, including three pages from the *Encyclopedia Judaica* on Rabbi Yechezkel Landau. Senator Javits promised to directly contact the Czechoslovakian ambassador to the United States. Rabbi Moshe Sherer to Senator Jacob Javits, December 8, 1975.
21. Rabbi Moshe Sherer to Senator Jacob Javits, December 8, 1975. *Shochtim* had reported to Rabbi Sherer that inspectors were threatening to prevent them from washing the necks of animals prior to *shechitah*, as is halachically required. Senator Javits investigated and reported back that the government inspectors had objected to the plant manager only about using a garden hose to wash large animal carcasses, and there was no objection to ritual washing of the neck or any intention to prevent it.
22. Telephone call from Rabbi Moshe (Murray) Friedman to Rabbi Sherer thanking Rabbi Sherer and Agudath Israel for weeks of lobbying of the New York State legislature for the restoration of a $350,000 "Counterforce" grant to provide guidance to students and their families.

of Lakewood. News reached the yeshivah in December 1977 that the Job Corps was planning to convert the former Irvington Hotel, a short walk from the yeshivah, into a dormitory for hundreds of male and female juvenile delinquents and school dropouts from South Bronx. By the time the Rosh Yeshivah, Rabbi Shneur Kotler, called Rabbi Sherer for guidance, the situation was grave because the United States government had already purchased the hotel for nearly $700,000, and might have no way of recouping its investment if it did not go ahead with the program.

Rabbi Sherer immediately went to work devising a multipronged strategy. The first involved assembling a multiethnic delegation from Lakewood to travel to Washington, D.C. to meet with New Jersey Senator Harrison Williams to express its opposition. Williams was the Chairman of the Senate Committee on Human Resources, which had jurisdiction over the Job Corps, and could exert a great deal of influence on the Job Corps bureaucrat in charge of the project. The same delegation, Rabbi Sherer instructed, should also meet with New Jersey Governor Brendan Byrne. At the same time, Rabbi Sherer urged Rabbi Kotler to hire a top lawyer — which, in his book, invariably meant Nathan Lewin[23] — to bring an injunctive action against the Job Corps, hopefully in conjunction with the New Jersey attorney general and the Lakewood town counsel.

Finally, Rabbi Sherer set up meetings for himself with key Labor Department officials. He called New York State Labor Commissioner Phil Ross, who agreed to call his friend Assistant Secretary of Labor Ernest Green in Washington, D.C. When Green proved unavailable to meet within the short time frame available, Ross set up a meeting between Rabbi Sherer and Thomas Komarek, the regional administrator of the Department of Labor, with responsibility for New York and New Jersey. At that meeting, Rabbi Sherer delivered a half-hour presentation, in which he described the importance of the Lakewood Yeshivah

---

23. Rabbi Sherer's respect for Lewin's abilities was virtually unlimited and he called upon him frequently. In late 1975, the Internal Revenue Service published a regulation that could have called into question the tax-exempt status of yeshivos because of a lack of black students. A team of tax experts assembled by The National Jewish Commission on Law and Public Affairs (COLPA) responded to the proposed regulation by noting that the reason for the underrepresentation of blacks was the small percentage of black Jews. When an IRS official replied that, in his opinion, yeshivos did not have the right to limit their student body to Jews, Rabbi Sherer called Lewin, 10 minutes before he was to teach a class at Harvard Law School. In those 10 minutes, Lewin, in Rabbi Sherer's words, managed "to set the entire issue straight in a beautiful manner," laying out with great clarity the legal basis for the yeshivah's position, which was subsequently incorporated in a memo to the IRS. Aide Memoir, March 20, 1975.

to the survival of the entire Jewish world due to its status as America's premier institution of Torah learning. Were the Job Corps to establish a dormitory in the immediate proximity to the yeshivah, it would have to close and move elsewhere, and that was clearly an impossibility, Rabbi Sherer pleaded. [24]

At the conclusion of the meeting, Komarek let Rabbi Sherer understand that he would never permit the government to harm such significant interests in so fundamental a fashion. But it was important, he told Rabbi Sherer, for the yeshivah to continue to wage its battles both in Washington and in Trenton. In the end, the Labor Department informed the yeshivah that it would not go ahead with the project, just as Komarek had promised.[25]

The letter of appreciation from Rabbi Yaakov Weisberg, the longtime administrator of Lakewood Yeshiva, and someone with whom Rabbi Sherer had worked closely for years, neatly summed up Rabbi Sherer's achievement, not only on the issue at hand but on hundreds of others over his long career:

> It is amazing how all the contacts you have cultivated and developed through years of work can be pyramided in a given situation to press the right button at the right time. Only those who are involved in this type of work on a small scale know how much effort, previous history, and experience go into setting up a meeting of a few hours that changes the course of an impending disaster.[26]

When Sheldon Silver, today the New York State Assembly Speaker, was first getting started in politics, he was asked to secure an early release from jail for a member of the Jewish Defense League, who was scheduled to be freed on the second day of Pesach. He quickly succeeded in lining up some prominent Democratic politicians to help him, but he felt he needed a powerful Republican to intercede as well. He

---

24. Rabbi Sherer's own contacts with New Jersey politicians may also have been part of that effort, though he did not mention it in his Aide Memoir. Rabbi Meir Frischman recalls a prominent New Jersey politician visiting Rabbi Sherer's office shortly before the Job Corps crisis broke. Rabbi Sherer noticed that the man seemed fascinated by a picture of Rabbi Aharon Kotler, and he seized the opportunity to describe who Rabbi Kotler was and the significance of Lakewood Yeshiva. That same politician turned out to be one of the principal sponsors of the Job Corps program. When Rabbi Sherer called him, he was able to draw on his description of the yeshivah of only a few weeks earlier to explain why a school for chronic truants would not be an appropriate neighbor for Beth Medrash Govoha.
25. Aide Memoir, December 13, 1977.
26. Rabbi Yaakov J. Weisberg to Rabbi Moshe Sherer, January 30, 1978.

went to the office of Senator Jacob Javits, whose secretary told him that it could take months to obtain a meeting with the senator and sent him away. He then called Rabbi Sherer and explained his problem. Rabbi Sherer told him to return the next day to Senator Javits's office. When Silver showed up the next morning at Senator Javits's office, however, the secretary curtly told him, "I told you yesterday that it will take you months to get an appointment."

Fortunately, Silver was not intimidated. He told the secretary that Rabbi Sherer had told him to come that morning, and asked her to check with the senator. A chagrined secretary came out a few moments later and told him, "The senator will be right with you. He was expecting you." When Senator Javits came out, he told Silver that Rabbi Sherer had instructed him to treat the problem as if it involved Rabbi Sherer's own son. And he proceeded to make several calls on the prisoner's behalf.

Late one Friday afternoon in January 1973, Rabbi Sherer received a call from a *gabbai* of the Belzer Rebbe in Jerusalem. The man explained that the Rebbe wished to visit the graves of his forebears in Belz, but as an Israeli citizen he could not travel behind the Iron Curtain. So he was applying for permanent residence in the United States. The Rebbe had been informed that Rabbi Sherer would be able to arrange for him to receive a green card shortly after his arrival in the United States. Rabbi Sherer tried to dissuade the *gabbai* from favoring him with this particular mitzvah, and explained that in his experience a minimum of two months would be required.

Rabbi Sherer, however, knew that Brooklyn Congressman John Rooney had been the one who sponsored the head of the Immigration and Naturalization Service for his position, and so he called Rooney. The congressman told Rabbi Sherer that if he received the Belzer Rebbe's papers on Monday morning, he would attempt to obtain some kind of special dispensation. Rabbi Sherer received the papers on Sunday, but he had no secretary to help him produce a cover letter. He had a typewriter and stationery delivered to his secretary's home on Sunday to type the letter he had dictated, and asked Mendy Shayovich to make sure that all the papers reached their proper destination when the offices reopened on Monday morning. Eleven days later, Congressman Rooney sent a telegram that he had arranged an immigration hearing for the Rebbe on February 14 (less than a month after the original call to Rabbi Sherer) and the Rebbe would receive his green card on the spot. Rooney shared with Rabbi Sherer that this was the first time the

Rabbi Sherer meeting with the Belzer Rebbe in New York.
In the backgound, l-r: Rabbi Shmuel Bloom, Yosef Neumann,
Yosef Friedenson, Chaim Gross, and Rabbi Nachman Elbaum.

Immigration and Nationalization Service had ever granted a green card on the day of the hearing on such short notice. The news was greeted euphorically by the Belzer Rebbe, who rejoiced in the fact that he had relied on Rabbi Sherer's reputation.

The sheer multitude of Rabbi Sherer's contacts ensured a certain amount of serendipity in his ability to resolve issues, as when the same government official he needed for one matter needed him to resolve another. In January 1973, Rabbi Sherer received a call from Rabbi Yerucham Gorelick, the founder of the Bais Yaakov of West Bronx. Rabbi Gorelick told him that the neighborhood in which the school was located had become intolerable due to the high crime rate. He was hoping to sell the building to the city school system, but so far nothing had come of the negotiations. He asked Rabbi Sherer if he could contact Dr. Seymour Lachman, then the president of the Board of Education.

The next day, Dr. Lachman called Rabbi Sherer out of the blue to seek his assistance on a totally unrelated matter. The issue of school busing had pitted the rabbis of East Flatbush, a racially changing neighborhood, against those of Canarsie, a relatively stable neighborhood. The former sought the forced busing of white students from Canarsie to East Flatbush schools, and the latter opposed it. Dr. Lachman felt that if the sharp dispute between the two groups of rabbis exploded in public it would constitute a *chillul Hashem*, and he enlisted Rabbi Sherer's help in setting up a meeting with Rabbi Moshe Feinstein. (One of Reb Moshe's close *talmidim* was a member of the East Flatbush school board, as well as a rabbi in the community.)

Rabbi Sherer and Dr. Lachman visited Rabbi Feinstein at his apartment, and the latter expressed his view that local rabbis should stay out of such controversial issues and promised to speak to his *talmid*. Lachman's request for Rabbi Sherer's help provided Rabbi Sherer with a perfect opportunity to raise the issue of the Bais Yaakov building in the Bronx, which the city, in fact, needed. Within hours Rabbi Gorelick called to say that the city had promised to quickly complete the negotiations.[27]

The breadth of Rabbi Sherer's connections reached into unlikely

At a meeting of *gedolei Torah* in the home of Rabbi Moshe Feinstein, Rabbi Feinstein greets the Bostoner Rebbe.

---

27. Aide Memoir, January 2, 1973.

places: everywhere from the pope to the longshoremen's union. In the midst of a longshoremen's strike, Rabbi Sherer received a desperate call from Telshe Yeshivah in Cleveland. A shipment of tens of thousands of boxes of Chanukah candles that the yeshivah needed for its annual mail solicitation was tied up on the New York docks. Rabbi Sherer called a well-connected friend in the New York State Labor Department, who called back a day later to say that everything had been taken care of.

An emissary from Telshe Yeshivah was dispatched to the docks. When he arrived at the pier, he was challenged by some burly longshoremen until he uttered the magic words, "Rabbi Sherer." With those words, the candles were instantly reclassified as perishables and unloaded. The Telshe emissary had brought with him a large wad of cash to pay the longshoremen for moving the candles. But the boss refused to take it. "We were told this is a favor for the Jewish godfather. It's on us," he said.[28]

ANOTHER ASPECT OF RABBI SHERER'S SUCCESS WITH PUBLIC officials was that he never asked them to do anything improper or that was beyond their authority. When, for instance, the state and federal governments began a massive investigation of Pell grants, under which students received subsidies for studies at accredited institutions, a number of Orthodox institutions found themselves under investigation. Don Nolan, then the Deputy Superintendent of Education for New York State was amazed that Rabbi Sherer never urged him to go easy on Orthodox institutions or to content himself with a less-than-thorough investigation of the institutions involved.

Knowing His Limits

With his keen sense of politics, Rabbi Sherer knew precisely what each politician could and could not do for him, and did not ask from them what he knew in advance they could not deliver. As Rabbi Shmuel Kamenetsky put it, in an appreciation of Rabbi Sherer, "He was not a politician ... , but he was one of the most politically astute people I have ever met. He fully comprehended each situation and had a keen instinct in terms of knowing when to persist and how far to push, as well as when to desist."

---

28. Rabbi Shmuel Bloom.
In a letter of thanks on behalf of Telshe Yeshiva, Rabbi Seymour (Abba Zalka) Gewirtz wrote to Rabbi Sherer that the entire financial viability of the yeshivah would have been at stake if the candles had not been moved off the docks. Rabbi Seymour Gewirtz to Rabbi Moshe Sherer, October 17, 1977.

With President Jimmy Carter (l) and Congressman Stephen Solarz

Consequently he never wasted time trying to convince a politician to do anything that he would view as political suicide, and avoided placing politicians in the uncomfortable position of having to refuse him.

His goal in any negotiation was always to make it as easy as possible for the other side to say yes. Thus he concentrated exclusively on points of potential agreement and avoided all discussions of philosophical issues about which he knew he had no chance of convincing the other side. Some of his most important relationships were with liberal Democrats, like Senator Teddy Kennedy, whose views on a host of social issues, such as abortion, could not have been further from Rabbi Sherer's.

"He did not push where he was not going to get anywhere," says Stephen Solarz, who represented a liberal Brooklyn constituency. "Rabbi Sherer had so many fish to fry, why endanger the relationship by forcing an issue like abortion?" By not pushing issues where agreement was impossible, Rabbi Sherer preserved an extremely fruitful relationship with Solarz.

As Solarz's stature in the House increased with seniority, he became an invaluable ally to Rabbi Sherer, both domestically and internationally. The two worked closely on legislation specifically tailored to the needs of Orthodox Jews. Solarz, for instance, introduced a bill to prevent Orthodox federal employees from losing their paid vacation days. Until then, employees who could not come to work because of Yom Tov had those days deducted from their paid vacation days. Thanks to

Solarz, an Orthodox worker did not have to lose his vacation days in order to observe Yom Tov.

As the powerful chairman of a crucial House Subcommittee on Foreign Affairs, Solarz played a vital role in helping Jews leave Syria, and at one point almost single-handedly assured that the major pipeline for Jews fleeing Iran remained open. He pressed President Jimmy Carter, who would be meeting with Syrian dictator Hafez al-Assad, to raise the issue of Syrian Jewish girls who were unable to find husbands in Syria. Under pressure from the president of the United States, Assad agreed to let any Jewish girls leave Syria, provided they had received marriage proposals from abroad. Solarz subsequently was able to arrange the proposals.

Rabbi Chaim Aron Weinberg, principal of Yeshivah Ateret Torah in Brooklyn, gives one poignant example of how valuable Solarz influence proved to be to the Jewish community. In September 1991, Mrs. Alfih, a mother of two children in the school, came to Rabbi Weinberg's office and shared a heartrending story. She and her husband had left Syria in 1986 with two children, who were now in Ateret Torah. But they had been forced to leave two other children hostage, in the care of two healthy grandmothers. At the time, they had assumed they would succeed in gaining permission for the other two children to leave. That had not happened, and now the grandmothers were ailing and no longer able to care for the children left behind. Mrs. Alfih, after consulting Rabbi Yosef Harari-Raful, had decided that she had no choice but to leave her husband and (now) three children and return to Syria to be with the two remaining children. Rabbi Weinberg told her to let him try one last avenue: a call to Rabbi Sherer.

Rabbi Sherer immediately went to work by contacting Congressman Solarz. The latter wrote to Assistant Secretary of State Edward Djerejian, asking him to put the fate of the two children on the agenda for his upcoming meeting, together with Secretary of State James Baker, with Syrian dictator Hafez al-Assad. Solarz had already made a request for the children's release on a visit to Syria a year earlier.

In mid-October, Assistant Secretary of State Richard Schifter, another longtime friend of Rabbi Sherer's, assured him that the request for the children's release had been put forward. Schifter wrote again on December 29 that the request had been granted. But the local secret police in Syria had still not granted exit permits. Rabbi Sherer wrote to Schifter asking him to "personally follow through on this mission of mercy to make sure it has a

Rabbi Chaim Aron Weinberg, Mrs. Alfih and the Alfih children visiting Rabbi Sherer in his office

happy ending." In January 1992, the family was reunited.[29]

Rabbi Sherer's relationship with Charles Schumer, another young congressman representing a liberal Brooklyn constituency, was, in many respects, similar to his relationship with Solarz. From Schumer's first election as a boyish 30-year-old, Rabbi Sherer reached out to him, even though his district did not have a large Jewish population at that time. Their first meeting, remembers Schumer, "established a bond that was never broken."

With respect to Schumer's liberal social agenda, they had a "respectful disagreement." Rabbi Sherer did not allow that "respectful disagreement" to stand in the way of enlisting Schumer as one of the major movers of legislation against discrimination in the workplace. From time to time, Rabbi Sherer would discuss with the young congressman social problems within the Orthodox community, such as "at-risk teens," and Schumer would try

---

29. Rabbi Weinberg subsequently brought the two children to Rabbi Sherer's office. After the meeting, Rabbi Sherer wrote to the parents: "Looking at the faces [of your son and daughter], as well as meeting your other children was the greatest reward that I could receive." He also told the family that he had arranged for one of New York's best immigration attorneys to work on the immigration case of the two younger children free of charge. Four years later, Rabbi Sherer shocked the parents by coming to the bar mitzvah of the boy he had helped to free from Syria. "I would not have missed it for the world," he wrote. The two oldest Alfih children were their class valedictorians at Ateret Torah's boys' and girls' branches, respectively. Rabbi Chaim Aron Weinberg, "The Story Behind the Picture," *The Jewish Observer*, November 1998, p. 48.

to get city social agencies involved in dealing with some of these problems within what he called Rabbi Sherer's *"mishpachah."*

Rabbi Sherer knew how to pay back such favors to the Orthodox community. When Schumer found himself in trouble with some of his Orthodox constituents over his vote against a congressional resolution authorizing the first Iraq war, Rabbi Sherer made the rounds of the Orthodox community to tell people of all that Congressman Schumer had done for the community.

His efforts on behalf of Schumer point to what was perhaps his greatest asset in public life: his reputation as someone in whose loyalty and honesty one could have full confidence. As Schumer puts it, "He was the kind of person you could trust. You could tell him what you thought. Absolutely everything." Bureaucrats knew that they could rely on the information that he supplied them, and would never end up looking bad as a consequence of that reliance. And because of this they showed him more flexibility than they would have to someone who did not inspire that confidence.

"You trusted him immediately. He was the kind of person you could live with on a handshake," remembers Stanley Brezenoff. He had a reputation "as someone whose word stuck — who would do exactly what he said he would do," according to former New York State Commissioner of Education Gordon Ambach.

Toughness

RABBI SHERER WAS PARTICULARLY FOND OF RABBI AKIVA EIGER'S explanation of the "veil" that Moshe Rabbeinu placed on his face, after he came down from the Mountain with the Second Tablets. The veil, according to Rabbi Akiva Eiger, was necessary to hide Moshe Rabbeinu's humility, for sometimes a leader needs to be tough.

Not everything that Rabbi Sherer achieved was exclusively a function of his easy charm and winning manner. When the occasion demanded, he could play hardball. Those who dealt with him knew that he would never compromise on principle for the purpose of ingratiating himself.[30]

Rabbi Sherer was a tiger when it came to defending the honor of the yeshivos. In the early '70s, before the major yeshivos had their own accrediting agency (AARTS), Rabbi Sherer engaged in lengthy negotiations with

---

30. Israel Singer, former chairman of the World Jewish Congress. Singer cites his former boss, Edgar Bronfman, longtime president of the WJC, as one of those who had a close working relationship with Rabbi Sherer, but knew that the latter would never budge on any ideological issue.

With Dr. Seymour Lachman

John Kneller, president of Brooklyn College, over the number of credits to be granted to yeshivah students. At one point, Rabbi Sherer wrote to Kneller, with whom he had met several times at length, that he better throw his full weight behind Rabbi Sherer's proposals and not let the faculty come up with a "totally demeaning and unacceptable compromise plan," under which Brooklyn College faculty would evaluate the quality of yeshivah education. The Orthodox Jewish community would not permit the academic discipline of the yeshivos to be denied "the full recognition it deserves from Brooklyn College, located in the heart of the largest Jewish community in the world."[31] During a subsequent phone conversation, President Kneller told him, "I read your message loud and clear."[32]

When a senior official in the office of civil rights of the Department of Health Education and Welfare had the temerity to seek an explanation of why yeshivos insisted on classes segregated by gender, even for courses not connected to ordination, Rabbi Sherer "forcefully and candidly told him" that when it comes to a bona fide religious faith community, such as Orthodox Jewry, the government is not entitled to any explanations. We do not have to explain to the government, for example as to why our religion forbids eating cheese with meat ..." He followed up that response with a warning that the official in question was treading on dangerous ground and could "suddenly find himself involved in a scandal of government interference in religion which would be very explosive."[33]

---

31. Rabbi Moshe Sherer to John Kneller, President of Brooklyn College, May 7, 1974.
32. Aide Memoir, May 15, 1974.
33. Aide Memoir, January 17, 1974.

It was not the only time that Rabbi Sherer brandished the threat of scandal. In the late '70s, Rabbi Sherer devoted a good deal of effort to improving relations with the Federation of Jewish Philanthropies of New York. At one point, he pushed the Federation to withdraw its official opposition to New York State legislation prohibiting the use of Medicaid funds for abortions. Rabbi Sherer reminded Federation head Sanford Solender of his previous commitment not to take public stands that the Orthodox community could not live with. (That commitment was given in the context of the Federation's previous opposition to all aid to non-public schools.)[34]

But when a patient at the Federation-sponsored Jewish Home and Hospital for the Aged complained that the home had refused to provide kosher food as required under state law, Rabbi Sherer wrote to Solender that he could not continue to sit on this story, and that when it went public, the shame of the Jewish community would be very great.[35]

Even with longtime friends, like New York Mayor Abe Beame, Rabbi Sherer knew how to deftly apply pressure when necessary. After the New York City board of Education cut nearly $3 million dollars in funding for remedial speech therapy for non-public schools, Rabbi Sherer wrote to Mayor Beame. He began solicitiously enough, telling Beame that he had purposely avoided writing for weeks during these "stressful and tense times" — the city was then in the midst of a major budget crisis — but felt it crucial to alert him that top Catholic and Jewish leaders were meeting to plan a legal suit against the city and huge public demonstrations.[36]

That letter was hand-delivered at 11 a.m. to the mayor's office, and within half an hour Mayor Beame was on the phone to Rabbi Sherer. First, he corrected Rabbi Sherer's information that the funding had been terminated because of a recent Supreme Court decision. General budget cuts were the explanation, and these would be made on an equitable basis between public and non-public-school students. Armed with the

---

34. Rabbi Moshe Sherer to Sanford Solender, Executive Vice-president of the New York Jewish Federation, January 9, 1978. Solender did not exactly commit himself to withdrawing the federation's memorandum of opposition to the bill in Albany, but he did express his commitment to ensuring that the Federation's actions are based upon the "utmost consideration for the concerns of every segment of the community." Solender to Rabbi Sherer, February 6, 1978.

That was enough to allow Rabbi Sherer to express his appreciation of the "stand you are now taking" and to express his hope that in this new spirit "we could solve some of the basic core issues which have strained relations between the Orthodox Jewish community and the Federation." Rabbi Sherer to Solender, February 8, 1978.

35. Rabbi Moshe Sherer to Sanford Solender, head of the Jewish Federation of New York, December 4, 1978.

36. Rabbi Moshe Sherer to Mayor Abraham Beame, June 26, 1975.

mayor's statement, Rabbi Sherer convened a meeting, together with Catholic representatives, with the Board of Education.

That meeting began heatedly, with the Board of Education officials still refusing to restore any of the funding cuts. But when Rabbi Sherer produced the written opinion of Robert Stone, the general counsel of the State Board of Education, that there was no constitutional objection to funding speech therapy for students in non-public schools, together with Mayor Beame's commitment to equitable cuts, the board officials, in Rabbi Sherer's words, "got the message loud and clear that we would literally sue the city to fulfill its obligations."[37]

Public officials were not the only ones whom Rabbi Sherer occasionally felt the need to reprimand sharply. When the relatively new head of a major Orthodox organization sent out a letter inviting other organizations to a conference on time-of-death legislation, Rabbi Sherer informed him that Agudath Israel would not attend. In light of Agudath Israel's long involvement in the issue, "simple etiquette and basic manners," Rabbi Sherer wrote, would have called for some prior consultation about the proper way to approach the issue. As the senior statesman of American Orthodoxy, Rabbi Sherer proceeded to explain that such unilateral invitations are not how things are done. Rather, the presidents of the major organizations hold informal telephone conversations in advance when there is a need for united action by the Orthodox community. Rabbi Sherer concluded with an expression of regret that his multiple invitations to the leader in question to join him for a private discussion on ways to prevent problems and establish a smooth working relationship had never been acted upon.

Skilled diplomat, superb advocate, trusted adviser: these were just a few of the qualities that elevated Rabbi Sherer above his contemporaries as a Jewish leader. Dr. Seymour Lachman, calls Rabbi Sherer, "my rebbi and mentor in how an Orthodox Jews should conduct himself in secular society." "I would call him my model," Lachman adds, "were the standard not so high."

Former congressman Stephen Solarz sums up the matter succinctly, describing Rabbi Sherer "as the absolute class of the field [among Jewish leaders]. He possessed a certain gravitas, and a deep wisdom concerning human nature."

---

37. Aide Memoir, June 26, 1976.

Chapter Twelve

ADVOCATE

Framing the Issues

"THE MARK OF A GREAT LEADER," ADDS STUART EIZENSTADT, "is the ability to represent your constituents to the outside world and the outside world to your constituents." Rabbi Sherer, in Eizenstadt's opinion, performed this dual function of educating the larger world about Orthodox Jews and Orthodox Jews about the outside world with "great aplomb and brilliance."

He had the ability, remembers Senator Schumer, not just to speak for the entire Orthodox community, but also to communicate effectively with the non-Orthodox world. "No one can do so nearly as well today," he adds. Former congressman Stephen Solarz makes a similar point: "He was an extremely effective advocate for a community unable to speak for itself. He knew how to frame an argument to appeal to people who were not part of his community as well."

Rabbi Sherer's ability to frame issues for secular politicians and bureaucrats paid frequent benefits to the Orthodox community. Under

New York law, each yeshivah must fill out a questionnaire in order to be eligible for certain state funding. One of the questions that yeshivos were required to answer was whether they provide AIDS education. Initially, the decision was taken by yeshivah principals to answer the question affirmatively on the grounds that the strict code of morality stressed by yeshivos is itself the best preventive for diseases like AIDS.

Subsequently, however, the State Education Department developed a mandatory AIDS curriculum. Now the question being asked the yeshivos was whether they were teaching the specific AIDS curriculum of the State, and that question could no longer be answered in the affirmative. Rabbi Sherer immediately began lobbying the State Regents. Bringing with him to Albany copies of *Mesilas Yesharim* and *Orchos Tzaddikim*, he argued that the teaching of Torah constitutes the best preventive for AIDS, an argument buttressed by the virtual non-existence of the disease in the Orthodox community. To the amazement of all those following the issue, Rabbi Sherer succeeded in convincing the State Board of Education that the Torah education in yeshivos and seminaries should be considered the functional equivalent of the AIDS curriculum developed by the state, and even obtained a written ruling to that effect. The next time that Rabbi Sherer had occasion to visit the Vizhnitzer Rebbe of Monsey, the latter stood up, walked around the table and kissed him in gratitude for his success in Albany.[1]

Rabbi Sherer's February 14, 1978 testimony before the House Committee on Ways and Means on tuition tax credits provides a good example of his advocate's ability to frame an issue in the most emotionally appealing fashion. A vote for tuition tax credits, he argued, would be a vote for freedom of conscience and against coercion. The absence of such credits, in his words, constituted a form of "pocketbook coercion, which propels a parent to the public schools against his will." That coercion, he argued, is "no less an evil than any other subtle restraint that denies an American the ability to live according to his conscience." To the argument that the credits would harm public education, Rabbi Sherer replied, that, on the contrary, they would benefit public schools by "providing salutary competition ... and promoting the vitality of cultural pluralism in America."

After Rabbi Sherer testified to a similar effect before the Senate Committee on Education, Senator Moynihan wrote him: "Your testi-

---

1. Mordechai Friedman; Rabbi Chaim Aron Weinberg.

With Leuchu Glueck and Senator Moynihan

mony was splendid — lucid, informative, and greatly helpful to the Committee."[2]

Rabbi Sherer's efforts over a period of more than a decade to protect religious families in Israel from nonconsensual autopsies on their loved ones offer another classic example of his ability to frame an issue in terms that everyone can understand. In the 1950s and '60s, Israel had the highest autopsy rate in the Western world. Doctors routinely ignored the wishes of the family, even where there was no question about the cause of death. Religious Jews were terrified to enter hospitals, lest they be subjected to autopsies, and families made sure that critically ill family members were never left unattended so that, in the event of death, the body could be immediately removed from the hospital. Bais Yaakov girls often joined in vigils around patients' beds.

All the political pressure brought to bear by Agudath Israel's Knesset members proved unavailing. But Rabbi Sherer found an unlikely pressure point on Israeli hospitals: the United States surgeon general. The United States government banned the funding of research at hospitals without proper protocols for ensuring the informed consent of patients or their next of kin in case of death. Rabbi Sherer suggested that the ban be extended to include hospitals anywhere in the world receiving United States government research funds. After a September 1968 meeting with Surgeon General Dr. William Stewart, Rabbi Sherer sent Dr. Stewart an elegantly written and argued memorandum on the issue.

---

2. Senator Daniel Patrick Moynihan to Rabbi Moshe Sherer, March 15, 1978.

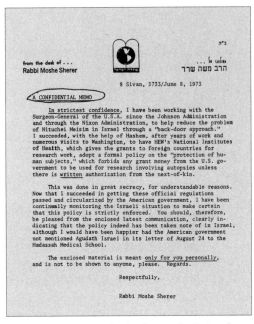

Working to stop unauthorized autopsies in Israel

The memorandum in question began by quoting Dr. Stewart's own testimony before a Senate Committee that year in which he described the requirement of informed consent as "deeply rooted in the basic principle that the individual has the right to control any use of his person." The same principle, the memo argued, applied equally to the post-mortem disposition of a person's body, and indeed the laws of every state in the United States and virtually every Western democracy recognize the decedent's right not to be subject to an autopsy without the consent of closest kin, in the absence of special circumstances.

And, as Dr. Stewart had testified in the case of informed consent to medical experimentation, "It makes no difference whether objections of the family or decedent are grounded upon religious belief, personal whims, superstitions or foibles or no reason at all." Again quoting Dr. Stewart, the memorandum concluded, the issue involves a basic human right — "the same one that condemns slavery and underlay the judgment at Nuremburg." "Your acceptance of this proposal," Rabbi Sherer wrote to Dr. Stewart in his cover letter, "will earn you the ... warm appreciation ... of all Americans of all faiths who cherish the hallowed principles of the dignity of man and the inviolate rights of man to determine the disposition of his body in death as in life."[3]

The threat of a cut-off of American funding to Israeli hospitals was neither idle nor insignificant. Rabbi Sherer asked Congressman Leonard Farbstein to write a letter to Israeli Ambassador to the United States Avraham Harman expressing his dismay over the indiscrimi-

---

3. Rabbi Moshe Sherer to Surgeon General Dr. William H. Stewart, September 18, 1968.

nate performance of autopsies in Israel. In that letter, Congressman Farbstein pointed out that he had a direct interest in the question, as the previous year he had sponsored legislation that resulted in a $1 million grant to Hadassah Hospital to construct a new wing.[4]

Hadassah Hospital in Jerusalem, one of Israel's major research hospitals, was particularly vulnerable to the public relations campaign that Rabbi Sherer mounted. Zeirei Agudath Israel conducted public demonstrations against Hadassah under the slogan "How long, Hadassah?" as in "How long will you refuse to grant your brothers and sisters in Israel the same basic right that you enjoy in America — the right to enter any hospital without fear that your body will become public property?" Spokesmen for ZAI took pains to emphasize that the group was neither anti-Israel nor anti-Hadassah. "All we want is that sick people in Israel should not die because of their fear of entering a hospital where an autopsy could be performed on their body without authorization."

After Hadassah removed organs, without familial consent, from a Jewish victim of terror to save a notoriously anti-Jewish Arab, Rabbi Sherer wrote to Hadassah President Bernice Tannenbaum that the incident in question only brought into more dramatic relief an ongoing human rights violation. "To perform an autopsy, ... without the family's authorization is a violation of the deceased's religious and human rights, that is not condoned in the United States." Nor should such violations of elementary human rights be permitted in Israel. Again, he made sure to avoid any religious argumentation, and put the issue in a manner that a secular person could

---

4. Congressman Leonard Farbstein to Ambassador Avraham Harman, April 13, 1967.

grasp and appreciate.[5]

Eventually Rabbi Sherer's "back-door approach" to the issue of autopsies in Israel bore fruit. The National Institutes of Health, which made grants to foreign countries, adopted regulations forbidding U.S. government grant money from being used for research involving autopsies, unless written authorization was first obtained from the next of kin.[6] A letter from NIH to Hadassah Medical School explaining the new policy went so far as to mention Agudath Israel's role in bringing about the new policy.

Rabbi Sherer's efforts to convince the Mormon Church not to proceed with plans to build a Mount Scopus campus of Brigham Young University provides another example of his ability to appeal to those starting from a completely different perspective. The proposed Mormon Center, adjacent to the Hebrew University and overlooking the Temple Mount, was already the subject of a fierce battle between Jerusalem Mayor Teddy Kollek and the *chareidi* public long before Rabbi Sherer became involved in the summer of 1985, at the urging of the Moetzes Gedolei HaTorah of both *Eretz Yisrael* and America.

Using his close connection with Dr. Terence Bell, a former Secretary of education in the Reagan Administration and a Mormon, Rabbi Sherer sought a meeting with the highest echelons of the Mormon Church. He called Dr. Bell in Salt Lake City on a Friday with his request, and that afternoon Dr. Bell called back with the news that he had made all the necessary arrangements. Rabbi Sherer hastened immediately to the public library where he took out four books on the Mormon Church, all of which he read before arriving in Salt Lake City.[7]

The following Monday he flew to Salt Lake City, Utah, where Dr. Bell picked him up at the airport. On the way from the airport to Dr. Bell's home, Rabbi Sherer learned that the next day's meetings would not be easy ones. He was heartened, however, to see hanging on Dr. Bell's living room wall the plaque presented to him at Agudath Israel's dinner a few years earlier.

Tuesday's meetings began at 8 a.m. with Dr. Jeffrey Holland, the Brigham Young official with responsibility for international operations.

---

5. Rabbi Moshe Sherer to Bernice Tannenbaum, February 11, 1980. The next year the Knesset finally passed legislation in Israel restricting autopsies without the written consent of next of kin or other appointed guardians.
6. Confidential Memo, May 24, 1973.
7. This account of Rabbi Sherer's trip to Salt Lake City is based on a document in the Agudath Israel of America's files entitled Confidential Memo re: Mission to Salt Lake City.

Dr. Holland told Rabbi Sherer that every Mormon student in Israel for the preceding 18 years had signed a statement in advance of his or her trip that they would not engage in any missionary activity on the threat of expulsion from the country.

Rabbi Sherer listened politely before launching into his presentation. The thrust of his argument was that nothing Dr. Holland could say or do would ever calm the fears of the Jewish people. "We lost a million and a half children in the Holocaust. And when we hear of the possibility of losing even one more, we go wild. Are we crazy? Perhaps. But we have a right to be crazy."

When he had finished, Rabbi Sherer urged Dr. Holland to make a dramatic gesture of compassion for the unspeakable horrors suffered by the Jewish people during the Holocaust. He assured Dr. Holland that the Mormon Church would suffer no loss as a consequence, as there were Jewish groups that would gladly purchase the site and half-completed campus for full price.

In the early afternoon, Rabbi Sherer, accompanied by Dr. Bell and Dr. Holland, was escorted to the world headquarters of the Mormon Church to meet the two oldest of the Council of Twelve Apostles that runs the church. The two church elders had been in Israel the previous month to study the problem and were more than a little irked by what they perceived as the "rough" treatment the Mormons were receiving. Once again, Rabbi Sherer attempted to explain the fierce reaction to the campus, and why nothing the church could do other than abandon the project would ever cool the determination of the demonstrators.

After that meeting, Rabbi Sherer was taken to meet Gordon Hinckley, the "prophet" of the Mormon Church. Scheduled to last 15 minutes, the meeting went over an hour. Dr. Bell's enthusiastic introduction of Rabbi Sherer guaranteed an attentive audience, and he did the rest. At the end of the meeting, President Hinckley told Rabbi Sherer that he would convene the Council of the Twelve Apostles in the near future to deliberate on Rabbi Sherer's presentation.

In his own assessment of the meetings, Rabbi Sherer held out little hope that he had done anything more than sensitize the Mormon leadership to what the Holocaust means to every Jew, and made clear to them that they would never enjoy a moment's peace in Jerusalem if they followed the "bad advice" of Jerusalem Mayor Teddy Kollek to proceed with the project.

Despite his pessimism, Rabbi Sherer's powerful presentation had made more of an impact than he thought. The Council of Apostles agreed to abandon the building site in Jerusalem in which the Mormon Church had invested so heavily. All the Mormons asked in return was another comparable plot of land somewhere in Israel.[8] (Ultimately, the Moetzes Gedolei HaTorah in *Eretz Yisrael* ruled that they had no right to offer land for a missionary center anywhere in *Eretz Yisrael*, and the center was built in Jerusalem, despite Rabbi Sherer's heartrending efforts.)

Lawyer-like

MANY OF THE PUBLIC OFFICIALS WITH WHOM HE DEALT ASSUMED that Rabbi Sherer had an extensive legal background. His "demeanor and style," remembers Gordon Ambach, were that of an expert advocate. His presentations were invariably well prepared and intelligent. Another state education official, Don Nolan, describes Rabbi Sherer as "very Talmudic" in the cogency of his arguments. After a meeting with Rabbi Sherer, he says, one could easily summarize every point that was discussed and what had been agreed upon. Though Rabbi Sherer himself never entered a meeting without preparing fully in advance, he never assumed the person to whom he was speaking was similarly prepared, and was always careful to lay out all the relevant background to the discussion.

Nolan had good reason to know based on a relationship with Rabbi Sherer that extended over nearly two decades. In early 1990, Mesivtha Tifereth Jerusalem of America received a letter from the State Education Department requesting that the yeshivah stop using the term "credit" in transcripts and other printed materials and use the term "clock hours" instead. Rabbi Sherer called Nolan, who was then the Deputy Commissioner of Higher and Continuing Education, and explained why the term "clock hours," which is generally associated with proprietary trade schools, would convey a totally inaccurate picture of the type of training provided by rabbinical schools. In a follow-up letter, summarizing the conversation, Rabbi Sherer wrote, "In every respect — the rigor of the program, the large number of hours devoted to independent research as opposed to classroom training, the number of years required to complete the course of study — the academic programs offered by rabbinical schools bear absolutely no resemblance to proprietary trade schools, but rather resemble those offered at accredited colleges and universities."

---

8. Rabbi Shmuel Bloom.

In his letter, Rabbi Sherer did not stint on the compliments to Nolan, as "somebody who had many years of exposure to our rabbinical schools and who understands the type of rigorous academic education" they provide. He concluded, "I look forward with relish — kosher relish, of course! — to our forthcoming lunch in my office, when we will once again celebrate our longstanding friendship and mutual respect .... I consider myself a fortunate man to count you as a friend." Appended in Rabbi Sherer's handwriting was a verse from Psalms, something

he typically did in correspondence with Nolan, who was a religious Christian.

Rabbi Sherer received from Nolan's office exactly what he sought: a letter that yeshivos could continue using the term *credit* in their brochures, as long as they included in those brochures a specific disclaimer that they were not offering academic degrees requiring registration with the State Education Department or its approval.[9]

In time, Rabbi Sherer's style as an advocate permeated the entire organization. Agudath Israel never tried to be flamboyant and flashy, like some other groups, recalls Stephen Solarz. But its representatives "always knew their brief, and came into every meeting with a very clear idea of what they wanted and how it needed to be done." As a congressman, Solarz appreciated the fact that if Agudath Israel needed his help with a regulatory matter, he was always furnished with the exact name of the governing statute, the intervention requested, the name of the government official in charge and his phone number, so that all that was left to do was to make the phone call.

This emphasis on detailed preparation was something Agudath Israel staffers learned directly from Rabbi Sherer. One could never be too prepared in his view. Rabbi Joel Kramer, who was then principal

---

9. Deputy Commissioner Donald Nolan to Rabbi Sherer, March 9, 1990.

of Prospect Park High School, once confided to Rabbi Sherer that some academic meetings had not gone well. Rabbi Sherer told him, without hesitation, if a meeting does not go well it's because "you didn't do your homework in advance."

Rabbi Shmuel Lefkowitz, the director of SBCO and later Agudath Israel's liason in Albany, describes the process that he went through every time he asked Rabbi Sherer to contact a particular government official. "He would pepper me with 62 questions about the project, and I would have to go back and do my research and bring him the answers. Only then would he make the call."

Once Rabbi Lefkowitz told Rabbi Sherer that he had a meeting scheduled with the president of a major foundation, and that this man had written a book on Southern Jewry. Rabbi Sherer instructed him to read that book cover to cover before the meeting. That advice was backed up with a story about Rabbi Michoel Ber Weissmandl, one of the great heroes of European rescue work during the Holocaust.

After the war, Rabbi Weissmandl reestablished the Nitra Yeshivah in Mount Kisco, New York. At one point, the yeshivah needed a zoning variance and encountered fierce opposition from the local planning board. The head of the planning board was the president of the New School for Social Research and the author of many academic articles and books. Rabbi Weissmandl requested a private meeting with this individual, and before the meeting he read every book and article of his that he could find. At the meeting itself, he seized the first opportunity to steer the conversation toward the subjects of the man's academic writing. As soon as the head of the planning board realized what an intellectual and scholarly person Rabbi Weissmandl was, he granted the yeshivah the requested variance.

Though Agudath Israel of America hired its first full-time attorney only in the early '80s, Rabbi Sherer was deeply involved in legal issues, particularly the constitutional law issues of separation of state and religion long before then. Chaim Dovid Zwiebel — Agudath Israel's longtime vice president for governmental affairs and one of the United States's foremost experts in this area — says that he never spoke to Rabbi Sherer as a layman when they discussed legal matters, but as another expert. Indeed the decision to hire legal talent of Zwiebel's stature reflected Rabbi Sherer's almost two-decade involvement in constitutional issues.

In a series of articles in *The Jewish Observer* beginning in 1963, Rabbi

Sherer demonstrated his mastery of constitutional analysis. As always he had done his homework. His first article on the subject, "Federal Aid: Fact and Fallacy" (*The Jewish Observer*, October 1963), begins with a quotation from a prominent Harvard historian on the vision of the Founding Fathers concerning education: "The modern conception of public education, the very conception of a clean line of separation between 'private' and 'public' was unknown before the end of the eighteenth century." There was nothing in that vision, Rabbi Sherer argued, that would prevent the sort of proposals to assist students in private schools that had been introduced into legislation by Senator Abraham Ribicoff (D.-Conn.), the former Secretary of Health, Education, and Welfare. And indeed many of those proposals were subsequently enacted in the Elementary and Secondary Education Act of 1965.

In the 1973 *Pearl v. Nyquist* decision, however, the Supreme Court struck down four basic types of assistance to non-public education: (1) tuition grants to parents of non-public-school children; (2) tuition tax credits; (3) payments to schools for maintaining health and safety facilities; and (4) reimbursement for state-mandated record-keeping. With a lawyer's scalpel, Rabbi Sherer dissected the majority opinion. The court had enunciated in a series of cases involving the constitutional prohibition against the establishment of religion two tests to determine if the Establishment Clause had been breached. The first test was that the statute should not have the "primary effect" of helping or hindering religion, and the second that it not lead to an "excessive entanglement of state and religion."

But, writes Rabbi Sherer, the court in *Nyquist* had ignored the plain meaning of its own test.[10] Rather than asking whether the primary impact of the statute was to further religion, it had introduced a new test: Did the statute "have the direct and immediate effect of advancing religion"? Under the former test, argued Rabbi Sherer, the statute under consideration should have been upheld since its "primary effect" had been to assist non-public schools in the performance of completely secular functions and to reduce some of the financial burden on parents of non-public-school children.

But Rabbi Sherer was even more scathing about the court's approach to the issue of excessive entanglement of the state with religion. Legislation concerning non-public schools, said the court, was particu-

---

10. "The 'Victors' and the 'Vanquished': Reflections on the Non-Public Schools' Day in Court," *The Jewish Observer*, September 1973.

The letter from Rabbi Hutner

larly problematic because of its potential for "political divisiveness." Political strife over aid to religious schools, in the court's view, could entail an excessive entanglement of state and religion.

Rabbi Sherer approached this doctrine, not like a lawyer considering its immediate application, but as a law professor taking into account all its future ramifications and applications. The attempt to remove a certain area of discussion from the democratic process, Rabbi Sherer argued, was nothing less than "incredible," and might "spell the death knell to *any* legislation on *any* issue … raised by minority religious groups to protect their religious interests or civil rights." The court's logic was, in his opinion, a "booby-trap, … which asserts that even if a statute is on its face constitutional, it could still be declared unconstitutional when [religious] citizens exercise their rights of free speech and petition …. "

Such an approach was fraught with implications for a whole laundry list of issues of vital concern to the Orthodox community, Rabbi Sherer pointed out, including: *shechitah* protection, fair Sabbath laws, and even aid to Israel. The court had not needed the "political divisiveness" reasoning to reach its decision, Rabbi Sherer asserted, and had only done so "to raise a scarecrow to silence religionists."

As disappointing as the court's decision was to Rabbi Sherer, he did have one consolation: a beautiful letter from Rabbi Yitzchak Hutner. The Rosh Yeshivah of Yeshiva Chaim Berlin reminded Rabbi Sherer of Rabbi Yisrael Salanter's three rules of *Klal* work: *nisht beiz verren, nisht farmattert verren, und nisht vellen oisfirren* — don't get angry, don't get tired, and don't be obsessed with prevailing. He pointed out that Avraham Avinu did not actually sacrifice Yitzchak Avinu at the *Akeidah*, but that did not detract one iota from the merit that accrued to him and all his descendants. *"Ah mentsh darf tun, nisht oiftun* — Man is commanded to do, not to accomplish," Rabbi Hutner reminded him; the rest is up to Hashem.[11]

---

11. Rabbi Eliyahu Meir Klugman, "Portrait of a Leader," *The Jewish Observer*, Summer 1998, p. 15.

Rabbi Sherer also thought of a *vort* he had once heard that related directly to his situation. The *Gemara* (*Berachos* 6a; *Kiddushin* 40a) states: If a man thinks to do a mitzvah, and he is prevented from doing so by circumstances beyond his control (ונאנס) and did not do it, it is accounted (מעלה עליו) by the Torah as if he did it." An "*adam gadol*" interpreted מעלה עליו to mean that the reward for the unfulfilled mitzvah is even higher (מעלה) because the person who sought to do the mitzvah does not even have the satisfaction of having performed it.

Chapter Thirteen

DIPLOMACY IN ACTION: A CASE STUDY

IN THE COURSE OF HIS NEARLY SIX DECADES IN PUBLIC LIFE, NO elected official was closer to Rabbi Sherer than New York Governor Hugh Carey.[1] Despite their vastly different backgrounds, there was

---

1. That is not to say that Governor Carey rendered greater service to the Orthodox community than any other politician. Such a judgment is beyond the scope of this book and the competence of the author. At least two other elected officials come immediately to mind as having worked very closely with Rabbi Sherer over a period of many years. The files of Agudath Israel of America are filled with hundreds of requests from Rabbi Sherer to Senator Javits for some type of intervention. (The author cannot remember seeing a single one where Senator Javits's response was not both prompt and positive.) So constant was the contact between Rabbi Sherer and Senator Javits that Rabbi Sherer enjoyed very friendly relationships with some of the senator's top aides as well, such as: Samuel Halperin, who went on to become a Deputy Assistant Secretary of the Department of Health, Education and Welfare, and Roy Millenson.

a personal chemistry between the two men that went far beyond the common political interests that initially brought them together. Rabbi Sherer's relationship with Governor Carey provides a case study of the way in which he developed relationships with government officials and how those relationships benefited the Orthodox community.

Congressman — later Governor — Hugh Carey at a reception in his honor at the Sherer home

From 1961 to 1974, Carey represented in Congress a district with one of the highest concentrations of Orthodox Jews in the country, including Rabbi Sherer's Boro Park neighborhood. That circumstance alone would have been enough to ensure plentiful contact between Congressman Carey and Rabbi Sherer. In addition, the two men were brought closer by their work together on the 1965 Elementary and Secondary Education Act, for which Carey was the House manager. Carey, an Irish Catholic, shared Rabbi Sherer's belief in the value of private sectarian schools, and that belief was reflected in a number of provisions of the act.

The value that Rabbi Sherer placed on Carey's assistance in Congress can be discerned from a February 8, 1968 letter from Rabbi Sherer, in which he informed Carey that he had convinced Brooklyn Borough President Howard Goldin to withdraw his opposition to a

---

Over Congressman Stephen Solarz's 18 years in the House, he and Rabbi Sherer worked together on a constant basis. Solarz introduced many pieces of legislation of great benefit to the Orthodox community, and, as a leading member of the House Foreign Affairs Committee, intervened frequently on behalf of Jews around the world, often in literally life-saving fashion.

When we describe Rabbi Sherer's relationship with Governor Carey as extremely close, we do not mean to downplay the closeness of his relationship to any other elected official. Certainly his relationship with Senator Javits and Congressman Solarz was personal as well as professional. During Senator Javits's debilitating final illness, Rabbi Sherer was one of the few visitors that he received.

We simply know more about the personal side of Rabbi Sherer's connection to Governor Carey. For that we have the testimony of Menachem (Mendy) Shayovich, who was not only a confidant of Rabbi Sherer for decades, but also a senior official in the Carey administration. In addition, there is a treasure trove of correspondence attesting to the personal aspect of the relationship.

Chapter Thirteen: Diplomacy in Action: a Case Study

redistricting proposal then before the New York State legislature that would have made Carey's seat more secure. Rabbi Sherer explains his efforts on Congressman Carey's behalf as an expression of the "huge debt of gratitude for your pioneering efforts on the House Education Committee."

The relationship between the two men, however, went far beyond the normal political expediency and mutuality of interests that naturally brought together a politician representing a large Orthodox enclave and the most important Orthodox leader in that district. Rabbi Sherer's high regard for Carey is attested to in a memo written while Carey was still a congressman. Rabbi Sherer describes him as "a *tzaddik*" for his willingness to fly up from Washington, D.C. to New York to join Rabbi Sherer for a meeting with officials of the Regional Manpower Division of the United States Department of Labor regarding a job-training grant for a company called Ezer Associates. Though the appointment was scheduled to last only half an hour, it stretched to two hours, thereby greatly delaying Congressman Carey's return to the bedside of his seriously ill wife.

The two men shared a number of traits: a sharp intelligence and scrupulous honesty being the two most obvious. Menachem (Mendy) Shayovich, who served as the Special Commissioner for Downstate for the entire eight years of the Carey administration, describes Carey as possessing a photographic memory. He would field questions from the press on the annual state budget for four hours without notes. Carey occasionally embarrassed Shayovich by referring to a memo that the latter had written weeks or months earlier and long forgotten.

Carey was secure enough in his intellectual abilities that he never felt threatened by other highly intelligent people. Indeed he made every effort to surround himself with highly capable advisers. In that, he had much in common with Rabbi Sherer, who was always on the lookout for highly talented and idealistic people to bring into Agudath Israel and took great pride in the quality of the staff that he had assembled.

Carey first ran for governor as a reform candidate in opposition to the Democratic machine of the time. Unlike many such reform candidates, he, in fact, maintained ethical standards far above the norm once in office. Judah Gribetz, the governor's chief counsel from 1975 to 1978, summed up his administration: "The governor always did the right thing." Such a remark is more remarkable given the typical hard-bitten cynicism of political operatives and the pride they tend to take in their tough-minded acceptance of the moral compromises that are often thought to be part and parcel of political life.

A large part of what drew Governor Carey to Rabbi Sherer was the recognition that Rabbi Sherer was cut from the same cloth when it came to probity. According to Mendy Shayovich, in the eight years of the Carey administration, Rabbi Sherer never once asked Carey for anything for himself or Agudath Israel of America. More, he refused to use his relationship with the governor to make any request that might ever reflect poorly on Carey. The most vitriolic and hurtful attacks on Rabbi Sherer in his entire public career were orchestrated by certain businessmen outraged that Rabbi Sherer had refused point-blank to use his influence with Governor Carey to attempt to short-circuit a criminal investigation.

Based on their natural affinities, the relationship between them became, in time, personal as well as political. Carey's first wife, Helen, was dying of cancer during his first campaign for governor. Though she was a devout Roman Catholic, Mrs. Carey found great solace in Rabbi Sherer's presence. During that extremely difficult time, Rabbi Sherer became, according to Seymour Lachman, a "personal friend and guide, almost a spiritual leader" for the Careys.

When Mrs. Carey passed away, Rabbi Sherer was faced with a difficult situation. On the one hand, he was halachically proscribed from entering the Park Slope church in which the memorial service was held. At the same time, in view of his special relationship with the Careys, he had to find some way to express his condolences. Through Tom Regan, one of Carey's close aides, Rabbi Sherer and Mendy Shayovich sent word that they would be outside on the street of the church in which the services were conducted during the funeral. On his way into the church, Carey came over to where Rabbi Sherer and Mendy Shayovich were standing. Rabbi Sherer explained, "We cannot go into the church, but we are with you in your time of sorrow."[2]

Rabbi Sherer gave the invocation at Governor Carey's first inauguration. The governor invited him to do so, remembers Judah Gribetz, not because he needed a representative of the Jewish community to give an invocation, but because of the special closeness he felt to Rabbi Sherer. That night, after the inauguration, Rabbi Sherer was one of the few friends to join Governor Carey in the Governor's Mansion.

Hints to the depth of the relationship that developed between

---

2. See *Shulchan Aruch, Yoreh Deah* 149.

Governor Carey and Rabbi Sherer in the period leading up to Carey's first successful campaign can be found in Rabbi Sherer's correspondence. In a note written shortly after Carey's election, Rabbi Sherer wrote, "Do you think it's time that we engage in some 'spiritual hand-holding' again? Just remember: 'Have Yarmulke — and will travel' — at least as far as Prospect Park West or Broadway and environs!" In a personal note asking the governor to set aside the evening of June 8, 1976 in order to attend the wedding of his son Shimshon, Rabbi Sherer made a special point of mentioning their "shared ... joys and sorrows for so many years."

Rabbi Sherer became one of Governor Carey's most trusted advisers. Carey knew that he could rely on Rabbi Sherer to give him advice that was absolutely untainted by any personal or institutional interest. For instance, Carey once asked Rabbi Sherer, via Mendy Shayovich, whether he should address the New York Board of Rabbis. The organization, comprised of both Orthodox and heterodox Jewish clergymen, was anathema to Rabbi Sherer, and had, in fact, been the subject of the famous 1956 *psak* of 11 roshei yeshivah banning participation of Orthodox rabbis in joint groups with heterodox clergymen.

At the wedding of Shimshon Sherer. L-r: Meyer Thurm (partially obscured), Governor Carey, Rabbi Sherer, Efraim Tepler, Rabbi Dovid Price, Shimshon Sherer, Yossi Ostreicher, Rabbi Elya Svei

Nevertheless, Rabbi Sherer understood that from Governor Carey's point of view, as a secular politician, it would make little sense to snub a prominent Jewish organization. He could not expect Governor Carey to grasp the fine points of Jewish theology raised by the New York Board of Rabbis. Nor was there any danger that an address by a secular politician would in anyway validate the Board. He therefore advised Governor Carey that he should address the group.

Governor Carey "venerated" Rabbi Sherer, in Seymour Lachman's words, as a symbol of American Orthodoxy, and Rabbi Sherer was to a very large extent his liason to the entire Orthodox community. On the eve of then-Congressman Carey's announcement of his candidacy for governor, Rabbi Sherer hosted a get-acquainted session for Carey in his own home for leaders across the spectrum of Orthodox Jewry. In attendance were leaders of the Chassidic community, officials of the Orthodox Union, and Rabbi Norman Lamm of Yeshiva University. Rabbi Sherer personally wrote, for Carey's signature, a letter to *The Jewish Press's* publisher Rabbi Sholom Klass, thanking him for the paper's editorial endorsement of Carey's candidacy. (In fact, Rabbi Sherer had also written *The Jewish Press's* endorsement.)

With Dr. Seymour Lachman and Governor Carey

Rabbi Sherer's assistance was not limited to the Jewish community. On a number of occasions, he used his excellent connections in the Catholic hierarchy to aid the governor. Nor was his advice necessarily political in nature. In an aide-mémoire, Rabbi Sherer describes a Washington, D.C. meeting with John Proffitt, a senior official in the Office of Education, devoted to eliciting from Proffitt a list of seven individuals who could serve as an educational think tank for the governor on the relationship between education and the general problems of society.

Governor Carey appreciated Rabbi Sherer's incisive take on events, and sought out his opinions on a wide variety of issues. Mendy Shayovich relates that Governor Carey would frequently tell him, "Mendy, find out what Morris thinks about this" or "Let's go up and have lunch with Morris, and see what he thinks." When Carey was in New York City, and his schedule was marked "personal," Shayovich knew that he was going to the Agudath Israel of America offices at 5 Beekman Street for a chat over lunch with Rabbi Sherer.

On any matter touching Jewish sensitivities, Rabbi Sherer's word was final as far as Governor Carey was concerned. In late January 1976, Israeli Prime Minister Yitzchak Rabin was in the United States, and the governor hosted a reception in his honor at a private home in New York City. The guest list was a veritable international Who's Who, and included UN Secretary General Kurt Waldheim, Senator Jacob Javits, New York City Mayor Abe Beame, Israel's ambassador to the United States, Simcha Dinitz, financier Felix Rohatyn, and a variety of other movers and shakers. Rabbi Sherer was among the distinguished invitees.

The hostess called the Israeli Embassy and asked whether the reception had to be kosher, and the embassy told her that it did not. In addition, the Israeli Embassy raised no objection to the 4 p.m. starting time, even though it was before the end of Shabbos. Mendy Shayovich, at Rabbi Sherer's insistence, called the Israeli ambassador and told him bluntly, "A Catholic governor is not going to invite Jews for a reception on Shabbos. It's not going to happen. Period." He then conveyed the same message concerning kosher food. Shayovich had full confidence that he would have the backing of Governor Carey because of the governor's closeness to Rabbi Sherer.

In the end, the event took place well after *Havdalah*, and afforded Rabbi Sherer an excellent opportunity to renew contacts with many highly influential people. (In his aide-mémoire on the event, he

Menachem Shayovich presents Rabbi Sherer with an award from Agudath Israel branch presidents as Volvie Friedman and Rabbi Chaskel Besser look on.

describes one of the participants favorably as a "real g*alitzyaner*.") Most importantly, Rabbi Sherer used the occasion to explain to Prime Minister Rabin the position of Agudath Israel of America toward the State of Israel. He assured Rabin, whom he described as looking "extremely haggard and dejected," that he could always count on Agudath Israel of America to be strongly supportive of Israel's security needs.

An even more significant example of Rabbi Sherer's influence on all matters pertaining to Orthodox sensitivities involved a bill to define the time of death submitted at the end of the legislative session in June 1975. Rabbi Sherer received a call from Judah Gribetz, the governor's chief counsel, that a bill to define death in terms of the "irreversible cessation of spontaneous respiratory and circulatory function" was up for consideration. There would be no time to get the legislation to the floor for a vote, Gribetz explained to Rabbi Sherer, unless the governor issued a "message of necessity," which he would do if Rabbi Sherer wanted.

Rabbi Sherer called Rabbi J. David Bleich, who pointed out that the

Rabbi Sherer greeting Rabbi Moshe Feinstein as Rabbi Boruch Borchardt looks on.

term "spontaneous" could allow for the pulling of the plug on a patient who was breathing with the help of a respirator. Rabbi Sherer called the *posek hador*, Rabbi Moshe Feinstein, who was in the Catskills. Reb Moshe confirmed that removing the plug from a patient already breathing with a respirator would constitute murder, and urged Rabbi Sherer to do everything possible to stop passage of the legislation.

Complicating the entire sequence of events was the fact that the Carey administration was hearing contrary advice from an Orthodox state assemblyman, who had earlier played a leading role in preventing passage of "time of death" legislation even more inimical to halachic concerns. And that assemblyman was basing his stance on the advice of a rabbi who felt that the legislation was a major improvement over one proposed by the medical establishment that would have made cessation of brain waves alone sufficient for a declaration of death. That rabbi too could plausibly argue that he was reflecting the opinion of Rabbi Feinstein. Nevertheless, in the end, Governor Carey informed the embarrassed state assemblyman that he would follow Rabbi Sherer's advice. Judah Gribetz called Rabbi Sherer with the news that the bill had been killed, and asked for permission to tell anyone who asked that the reason was "the opposition of the Orthodox Jewish community."

In relating these events to his old friend from Ner Israel Rabbi Naftoli Neuberger, Rabbi Sherer could not resist pointing out to Rabbi Neuberger that what the Orthodox community had failed to achieve in Maryland with a Jewish governor, Agudath Israel of America had achieved in New York with a Catholic governor. Rabbi Neuberger replied, with a twinkle, that the answer was simple. At the recent Agudath Israel dinner, where Governor Carey was honored with the 1975 Humanitarian Award, he had declared himself an Agudist.

From Rabbi Sherer's extensive correspondence with Governor Carey and other officials in the Carey administration a clear picture emerges of his modus operandi in developing a relationship. In each note one finds numerous intertwined strands: his enormous sensitivity to the needs of others and knowledge of human nature, the amount of thought that went into developing relationships with everyone from personal secretaries to the governor himself, and the genuine desire to be of service to others.

Rabbi Sherer's unique sensitivity to the needs of others can be discerned from a brief note to Governor Carey shortly after the latter's first inauguration. The death of his wife left the new governor with responsibility for raising a number of young children. Rabbi Sherer's note begins by assuring Governor Carey that he can have full confidence in the advice of Tom Heath, the official in the State Education Department with the portfolio for non-public education, when it comes to finding Catholic schools for his children. Then Rabbi Sherer adds that Gordon Ambach, the State Education Commissioner — "a fascinating fellow of high caliber" — lives a short distance from the Governor's Mansion and has young children about the age of the Carey children. It is hard to imagine that there were many others who were so solicitous of the well-being of the Carey children, or that the governor was not extremely grateful for that solicitude.[3]

The Talmud (*Beitzah* 16a) states when one does a favor for someone else, of which that person would not otherwise know, he should inform him.[4] Rabbi Sherer took this instruction very much to heart in all his public activity. On at least one occasion, Rabbi Sherer took it upon himself to run interference for Carey with the Catholic leadership. In an April 4, 1974 letter to Carey, written before he had even won the Democratic nomination, Rabbi Sherer describes how he turned his last two visits to the state capital in Albany into "Carey for Governor" happenings. At a private dinner hosted by Bishop Broderick, and attended

---

3. One familiar with Rabbi Sherer's methods could surmise that Tom Heath and Gordon Ambach also received brief notes from Rabbi Sherer mentioning that he had spoken favorably of them to their new boss.
4. Rashi explains that when the beneficiary learns of the benefactor's concern for him, feelings of friendship and closeness between them are strengthened.

by State Education Commissioner Ewald B. Nyquist and a number of his leading aides, he "needled the Catholic leaders present about their not really doing what they should for Hugh Carey in view of his record," and adds humorously, "I got them to the point where they were almost ready to enter a confessional booth and agree to repent."[5]

A week later, at an official meeting of the Advisery Council on non-public-school education, Nyquist related how Congressman Reid, another gubernatorial hopeful, had tried to impress him with his desire to do something for education. At that point, Rabbi Sherer recounts, "I exclaimed, 'But I know someone who'll do a thousandfold more than Reid for education.' Nyquist immediately took up the cue and said, 'I know whom you mean — Hugh Carey, and Carey really is the strongest and the best of the lot.'" Rabbi Sherer concluded this missive by advising Carey to follow up on this opening with the Catholic leadership, and offering to do whatever he could to be helpful in this direction: "Just let me know how and when, and I'll be there."

Rabbi Sherer carefully cultivated his relationship with various gatekeepers. He knew, for instance, how important secretaries could be to ensuring that a letter received the hoped-for attention from the governor. When, for instance, he wanted to make sure far in advance of the day that Governor Carey set aside time to share in the joy of his son Shimshon's wedding, he sent his personal note to the governor inside another note to the governor's personal secretary, Martha Golden. The latter sought her help in making sure the "boss" sets aside June 8 for a "family reunion" with me. A few weeks later, another note to Martha Golden expressed his "repentance" for having allowed too much time to pass since his last trip to Albany and expressing "eagerness to do retribution for my sins." One can be sure that Ms. Golden was charmed.

A brief handwritten note to Dr. Kevin Cahill shortly after meeting him for the first time at Governor Carey's inauguration captures in a few sentences all the thought that Rabbi Sherer put into such notes, which he dispensed by the multitudes. Dr. Cahill was perhaps

---

5. Nor was this the only time that Rabbi Sherer rendered Carey valuable help with the Catholic hierarchy. In June 1978, when Carey was in the midst of his second gubernatorial campaign, Alan Davitt of the New York State Catholic Conference complained to Rabbi Sherer that the Carey administration had not initiated legislation on school transportation for non-public-school children, and threatened that unless such legislation was forthcoming the Catholic community would campaign against Carey. Rabbi Sherer wrote on June 21 to Robert Morgado, Carey's chief of staff, that if Davitt was right "then someone has goofed, as this is a bread and butter issue for tens of thousands of concerned parents in New York State ... [O]n top of the justice of the issue, we don't need anymore headaches at this time."

Governor Carey's closest friend and the last person that he spoke to at night before going to sleep, and the governor subsequently appointed him State Public Health Commissioner. After meeting Cahill for the first time, Rabbi Sherer wrote, "I just want to express my delight that, after so many years of hearing about you from Helen, of blessed memory, and from Hugh, at long last I had the pleasure of meeting you. Above all, to meet under such happy circumstances was the frosting on the cake! I hope that our paths cross more often, and I pray that you succeed in all that you do."

That note was at once both very flattering to Dr. Cahill, for it informed him that his name was constantly on the lips of the soon-to-be governor and his late wife, and also served to alert him that Rabbi Sherer was an intimate of the Careys, on a first-name basis with both of them. Not surprisingly, after that excellent beginning, Dr. Cahill and Rabbi Sherer did, in fact, become friends. On several occasions, Dr. Cahill invited Rabbi Sherer to give invocations to meetings of the American-Irish society, and Dr. Cahill's excellent connections within the Catholic hierarchy were of frequent use to Rabbi Sherer. In one letter to Rabbi Sherer, Dr. Cahill informs him that he spoke to Cardinal O'Connor and his note was received. On a personal note, Dr. Cahill told Rabbi Sherer, "I miss our morning coffees, and when your hectic schedule permits, why don't you come by and we'll share some notes."

Rabbi Sherer also knew how to give Governor Carey the positive feedback that everyone, even those in high position — perhaps especially those in high position — likes to hear. Shortly after their first meeting subsequent to Carey taking office as governor, Rabbi Sherer sent him one of his short notes to let him know "it was a delight to see you bearing up so well under such heavy pressures." Rabbi Sherer adds he has received feedback from those in attendance at a recent speech by the governor to a Jewish group that it was obvious the speech "came from the heart and not from a ghost-written paper." In conclusion, Rabbi Sherer proffers his assistance whenever the governor may need his services: "Please continue to keep your balance — and if I can be of any help, just ring the bells and I'll walk across the street, gladly."

Rabbi Sherer's relationship with Governor Carey was surely one of the closest of his public career, but the way that he nurtured that relationship was typical of hundreds of others formed over the years.[6]

---

6. Dr. Kevin Cahill to Rabbi Moshe Sherer, June 16, 1980.

Part IV
MODUS OPERANDI

Chapter Fourteen

BOSS

THE FIRST MARK OF A SUCCESSFUL CHIEF EXECUTIVE IS his ability to extract the maximum possible from his staff. In that respect, Rabbi Sherer had few equals. Whatever a person's level of competence, Rabbi Sherer raised him or her to a higher level of performance.

Mr. Yosef Friedenson, one of Rabbi Sherer's two closest contemporaries (along with Rabbi Boruch Borchardt) in the Agudah office, applied to him the *Gemara's* (*Moed Kattan* 24a) praise of a great leader, "*Gavra d'mistafina minai* (literally, someone others feared)." In every organization, there must be someone who keeps people from taking it easy, comments Mr. Friedenson. That was Rabbi Sherer. Professor Moishe Zvi Reicher, Agudath Israel World Organizations director of international affairs in Rabbi Sherer's last three years, confirms Mr. Friedenson's observation:"As soon as I arrived in the office, I could tell immediately whether Rabbi Sherer was in town that day or not. When he was around there was electricity in the air."

Sharing in the *simchah* of a colleague. At the wedding of the daughter of Mr. Yosef Friedenson (standing, far left) to Yosef Chaim Golding (seated), a founder of Agudath Israel's Jewish Education Program and later a long-time employee of the Agudah

Inspiration

THE ABILITY TO INSPIRE OTHERS PLAYED A LARGE ROLE IN RABBI Sherer's success. From his early youth, Rabbi Sherer was intoxicated with the ideal of Agudath Israel: the Jewish nation united under the banner of the Torah. He worked hard to imbue every employee with that same excitement in serving *Klal Yisrael*. Rabbi Sherer once happened to come out of his office just as a new secretary on her first day of work was walking by. He greeted her, and asked her for whom she worked. The young woman replied with the name of one of the senior staff. But Rabbi Sherer corrected her: "No, you work for *Klal Yisrael*. All of us here work for *Klal Yisrael*."

When he interviewed Mrs. Rochel Miller for a secretarial job, at a time when Agudath Israel was still a relatively small organization, Rabbi Sherer was disappointed to learn that she knew nothing about the organization other than it sponsored Camp Agudah and Camp Bnos. He took the time to cure the deficits in her knowledge, and to fill her with a sense that it was a privilege to work for Agudath Israel. He succeeded beyond even his high expectations.

"I was so proud to be associated with Agudath Israel," Miller remembers. "I thought of myself as working for the public. We stood for something." That sense of doing something for *Klal Yisrael* compensated for working for "peanuts."

Mrs. Debby Jacobs, his secretary of nearly two decades, asked early in her tenure for some clarification of Agudah ideology. Rabbi Sherer replied, "Agudath Israel is an umbrella that embraces every Jew, in every walk of life. Our task is to do whatever we can for every Jewish man, woman, and child."

Rabbi Labish Becker had just received *semichah* (ordination) from Mirrer Yeshivah, and was planning on entering a career in *chinuch* (Torah education), when he happened to find himself sitting on a plane next to Benzion Fishoff, a member of Rabbi Sherer's inner circle of friends and advisers. Mr. Fishoff was impressed by the young man, and suggested that he should consider working for Agudath Israel.

Mr. Fishoff arranged an interview for Rabbi Becker with Rabbi Shmuel Bloom, and during the interview Rabbi Sherer came into the room. Rabbi Sherer sought to impress Rabbi Becker with what it meant to work for Agudath Israel: "As a rebbi, you'll be *mashpia* (influence) maybe 20 children a year. Working for Agudath Israel, you have a chance to influence 20,000."[1]

When Rabbi Becker later recounted this exchange to his wife, he had not adopted the view that helping thousands is necessarily more important than the intense impact that a rebbi can have on his *talmidim*, but the passion with which Rabbi Sherer had spoken had left its mark. "From anyone else it might have sounded corny," Rabbi Becker told his wife. "From him it had a certain grandeur."

In a hundred different ways, Rabbi Sherer emphasized what a privilege it was to be an employee of Agudath Israel. He wanted the staff to view working for Agudath Israel as a mission, not just a job. Once he saw Rabbi Becker moving a table at an Agudath Israel convention in full

---

1. Rabbi Sherer frequently used this line. Rabbi Yaakov Horowitz was already a principal at the time he came to Agudath Israel to head Project Y.E.S. (Youth Enrichment Service). On his first day in the office, Rabbi Sherer presented him with *Against All Odds: The Growth of an American Orthodox Jewish Movement*, a documentary history of Agudath Israel of American, to familiarize him with the organization he had joined. As he got up to leave the room, Rabbi Sherer put his hand on Rabbi Horowitz's shoulder and said, "As a rebbi, you were able to touch 25 lives a year — perhaps 1,000 over your teaching career. Working for Agudah Israel, you can help all of *Klal Yisrael*. I trust you can meet that challenge." Rabbi Yaakov Horowitz, "Basic Training," *The Jewish Observer*, Summer 1998, p. 56.

public view. He ordered him to stop immediately and to find a hotel employee to do the job. "You have to act with a certain *kavod* (dignity)," Rabbi Sherer explained. "An employee of Agudath Israel must not be seen as a *shlepper*." When a secretary had worked particularly hard that week, she would hear from Rabbi Sherer, "*Klal Yisrael* thanks you."[2]

Leading by Example

RABBI SHERER WAS PASSIONATE ABOUT HIS WORK. HE ONCE TOLD a close associate blessed with a naturally calm disposition, "I see everything in living color." But his passion was never allowed to detract from an image of dedicated professionalism or to call attention to itself. Rabbi Sherer looked for employees in his image: who put the mission of Agudath Israel above everything, but were devoid of anything pompous or attention seeking in their behavior or manner.

A letter from Rabbi Aharon Fried, principal of Chush, a school for special children, to Rabbi Sherer conveying his gratitude for the efforts of Shmuel Prager and Menachem Lubinsky on behalf of his handicapped children must have made him swell with pride. "Agudath Israel has kept our doors open," Rabbi Fried wrote. "Often it was difficult to tell whose problem they were working on — mine or theirs. This attitude of seeing the problems of the *Klal* as being the problems of Agudath Israel is one that I am certain you have inspired."[3]

Above all, Agudath Israel employees learned that working for *Klal Yisrael* is not a 9-to-5 job. That message was conveyed principally by example. Rabbi Sherer was usually the first one to arrive at the office in the morning and the last one to leave at night. Long after every one else had gone, he would be at his desk writing with a fountain pen all the personal notes that he used to build new relationships and to cement old ones, or arranging index cards for his files. No invitation to a simchah went without a response. Yet even when he finally went home it was invariably with a briefcase filled with reading for that night.

Sundays were spent in the office. In the winter, that required him to work wrapped in a heavy sweater in the unheated building. When his secretary arrived for work on Monday morning, she would invariably find two full cassettes filled with dictation with which to start the week. As remarkable as the length of his day was the efficiency with

---

2. Mrs. Chaya Lider.
3. Rabbi Aharon Fried to Rabbi Moshe Sherer, October 19, 1981.

which each minute was used. He kept two secretaries busy. As soon as his principal secretary had left the room, the second knew that it was a signal for her to rush in to take dictation or receive directions on filing documents.

Rabbi Sherer once shared with his granddaughter, Mrs. Chavie (Langer) Galinsky, his secrets of success. First, he said, begin every day by thinking about what you have to do that day, and then praying to Hashem for help doing it. People make the mistake of thinking that one only *davens* when things are going badly, he said.

The second key, Rabbi Sherer said, is to do everything as if one's whole life depends upon it. "Sometimes I give a person or a team a project to complete. After a week or two, they come back to me and tell me that they have tried their best but they just cannot complete the project in the allotted time. I go into my office and come out an hour later with the project done. No magic. You just have to look at it as the most important thing in the world, and as if your life depended upon it. You cannot imagine what it is possible to achieve with that attitude."

That attitude spilled over to others involved in far less monumental tasks. In her early years at Agudath Israel, Mrs. Miller's principal task was placing Rabbi Sherer's phone calls. She learned not to tell Rabbi Sherer that the line was busy or that she could not find a number. She just kept dialing until she reached his party or searched for the number in different places.

Agudath Israel employees knew that the intense workday they witnessed was only the tip of the iceberg. He told his secretary that he awakened every morning at 5 a.m., and spent the first hour of the day planning everything he had to do that day. They heard too about the many times that he arose in the middle of the night to make a call to *Eretz Yisrael.*

These details were not shared in order to boast, but so that employees would know what working for the *Klal* entailed. Rabbi Sherer did not expect his staff to work the same hours that he did. But he provided a model that they could keep in front of them, a standard against which they could measure themselves.

Workaholic is a term frequently used to describe Rabbi Sherer. He was aware of the charge, but denied it. "I'm not a workaholic. I just have a lot of work to do," he said.[4] His definition of required work, however,

---
4. Rabbi Shmuel Bloom.

was incredibly broad. That work might include studying the bureaucratic charts of every municipal, state or federal agency or department whose decisions could potentially have an impact on Jewish life.

When a young man with a yeshivah background, Abraham Biderman, began his meteoric rise in New York City government that would end with his appointment as Finance Commissioner and then as Housing Commissioner, Rabbi Sherer wasted no time turning to him as a source of information on the inner workings of the city bureaucracy.

Similarly, Menachem (Mendy) Shayovich, a top adviser to Governor Hugh Carey, served as Rabbi Sherer's antennae within the New York State government.

At home, he was constantly reading, often with classical music playing in the background. The reading, too, was theoretically unlimited, for one could never know when some apparently innocuous piece of general information could turn out to be important. Even as he read, Rabbi Sherer was contemplating the ways in which a news story might one day become relevant. Could a plan being mooted for a new sports complex for one of the New York area sports teams, for instance, prove relevant to the planning for the next *Siyum HaShas* (celebration of the completion of the cycle of Talmud learning)?

And it was the same with the writing of notes to those who came to Rabbi Sherer's attention. One never knew which newly elected young congressman might one day become the senior senator from New York, or which Jewish attorney general in Connecticut might one day come within a few hundred votes of being elected vice president of the United States. But if they did someday rise to great prominence, they surely would not forget the gracious handwritten congratulations they received from Rabbi Sherer early in their careers. Indeed, Chuck Schumer and Joseph Lieberman made mention in later years of the congratulatory notes they received at the outset of their political careers.

The same was true for a previously unheard-of *baal teshuvah* who had just started writing opinion pieces for a new English-language chareidi newspaper. Rabbi Sherer's discerning eye caught that the young man might have a future, perhaps even working for Agudath Israel. He was soon the surprised recipient of not only a personal note from Rabbi Sherer, but of a transatlantic phone call in which Rabbi Sherer gave him his "private phone line," if the editorialist ever wanted to discuss an issue of concern.

Not every bureaucratic flow chart studied, periodical read, or note

With Senator Joseph Lieberman at a reception in the *succah* of Barry Hertz

written paid immediate dividends; most never did. But over the years so many did that it was no wonder that Rabbi Sherer saw it all as part of the work that he had to do.

RABBI SHERER'S SENSE OF MISSION DROVE HIM TO PAY ATTENTION to every single detail. "Good enough is not good enough," was his

Good Enough Is Not Good Enough

motto, and he worked hard to instill that attitude in every employee.[5] He insisted that everything in the Agudath Israel offices be done with the highest level of professionalism, and no detail was too small for his attention. When he called into the office, for instance, he was always careful to note whether the phone was answered within two rings, as he had instructed.[6]

He strove for perfection himself and sought it from others as well. Nothing escaped his notice. If he noticed a picture hanging unevenly or

---

5. Yosef Friedenson relates one amusing incident when Rabbi Sherer was hoisted on the petard of his own favorite phrase. The two had been working on an article under Rabbi Sherer's byline for *Dos Yiddishe Vort* for some time, and Mr. Friedenson was still not satisfied. He insisted that Rabbi Sherer polish it one more time. The latter had many other matters on his mind at the time, and told Mr. Friedenson that the article was "good enough." Mr. Friedenson feigned shock. "But you always told us, 'Good enough is not good enough,'" he said. Rabbi Sherer realized he had been bested. He sank wearily into a chair in Mr. Friedenson's office to give the article another read.
6. Rabbi Ephraim Oratz.

Chapter Fourteen: Boss ☐ 335

a window shade not opened just as he liked it, as he made his rounds in the halls, he would enter the office and fix it. "I cannot stand a *krummeh zach* [something crooked]," he would say. When he discovered documents not filed in proper chronological order, it disturbed him and he would say, "If this is wrong, who knows what else is wrong."[7] Anything that detracted from the image of a professional organization that he sought to convey — e.g., a box of files in the hallway — was sure to provoke his ire.[8]

Rabbi Yaakov Horowitz learned what it meant to work for Rabbi Sherer shortly after being appointed to head Project Y.E.S., a program for at-risk teens. Debby Jacobs, Rabbi Sherer's personal secretary, called to relay a message from Rabbi Sherer, who was then hospitalized. Rabbi Sherer had noticed an ad in *Yated Ne'eman* for a speech by Rabbi Horowitz, and requested Rabbi Horowitz to make a number of changes before the ad appeared again. First, the ad gave the address for the speech, but failed to provide the cross streets. That piece of information, Rabbi Sherer felt, would be helpful for those coming from outside of Flatbush. The ad specifically noted that "all the proceeds will benefit Project Y.E.S." But since the checks would be made out to Agudath Israel, Rabbi Sherer wanted the ad to specify that the money collected would "exclusively benefit Project Y.E.S.," and not some other aspect of Agudath Israel's work.

This exchange took place only two weeks before Rabbi Sherer's *petirah* (passing). Even on his deathbed, he was still reading every newspaper ad put out under Agudath Israel's name with a metaphoric magnifying glass. And that is precisely the message he asked Mrs. Jacobs to convey to Rabbi Horowitz: "Rabbi Sherer asked me to tell you that Agudath Israel is the organization it is, because he personally checked every ad and every letter we sent out for the past 50 years."

Rabbi Labish Becker, head of Torah Projects, had a similar experience in his early days working for Agudath Israel. At that time, he was in charge of producing an internal youth magazine called Zeirei Forum. One day, Rabbi Sherer called him into his office and told him something was wrong with the cover of the most recent issue. He made Rabbi Becker look and look, until he found an extra י in the word לרעיך (which is usually spelled in the Torah without the י).

That perfectionism undoubtedly made Rabbi Sherer a demanding

---
7. Mrs. Chaya Lider.
8. Mrs. Rochel Miller.

New York Governor Mario Cuomo, New Jersey Governor Tom Kean, and Massachusetts Senator Ted Kennedy greet one another at an Agudah dinner as Rabbi Sherer and Menachem Lubinsky look on.

boss, but he controlled that tendency with his customary discipline. Mrs. Debby Jacobs would watch him count to 10 before speaking many times each day.

RABBI SHERER HAD THE ABILITY TO GET OTHERS TO SHARE HIS sense of mission. Beginning in the early '70s, he lured to Agudath Israel a series of high-quality young professionals, each of whom could have earned much larger salaries in the private sector. He invariably appealed to their idealism.

Attracting Through Idealism

The first of the young dynamos who helped transform Agudath Israel into the large, professional organization was Menachem Lubinsky. Rabbi Sherer recognized his potential from his work as a leader in Zeirei Agudath Israel. Lubinsky was still learning in *kollel* and taking accounting classes at night when Rabbi Sherer offered him a position as his assistant. Lubinsky eventually took over the day-to-day running of Government Affairs, the area closest to Rabbi Sherer's heart.

Rabbi Sherer's recruitment of the would-be accountant was straightforward: "How will you evaluate your life at the end of the day?

With Rabbi Shlomo Gertzulin on the Am Echad mission

Somehow it does not strike me that you will be satisfied just being a successful accountant." Rabbi Sherer could make this pitch with complete conviction because wealth held no attraction for him.

After Lubinsky came Rabbi Shmuel Bloom, upon whom Rabbi Sherer had set his eyes when the former was still a Zeirei leader in Ner Israel, and who was serving as the executive vice president of St. Louis Rabbinical College when Rabbi Sherer tapped him for Agudath Israel of America. Shlomo Gertzulin was Rabbi Sherer's next catch. He left a promising career as a certified public accountant to join Agudath Israel as comptroller and subsequently Executive Vice President for Finance and Administration. Chaim Dovid Zwiebel was on the fast track to becoming a litigation partner at Paul, Weiss, Rifkind, Wharton, and Garrison, one of the country's most prestigious law firms, when Rabbi Sherer convinced him to take over the entire Government Affairs portfolio, after Menachem Lubinsky's departure.

RABBI SHERER'S WAS A SUPERB MENTOR OF YOUNG TALENT. "I DID not feel I was just an employee of Agudath Israel, in his eyes," says Rabbi Becker, "but a work in progress, whom he took pride in fashioning."

Mentor

Staffers grew under his guidance in ways that neither they nor anyone else would have predicted. Deborah (Jacob) Zachai, for instance, started working for Agudath Israel without any special training, but Rabbi Sherer recognized her talents and watched her grow over the years into an extremely effective advocate on behalf of religious schools within the New York State Department of Education. Early in her career at Agudath Israel, he shared with her a Torah insight that always remained with her. He asked: Why is it considered a curse that the primordial Snake was told he would henceforth eat of the dust of the earth? After all, he was thereby guaranteed an inexhaustible supply of food. He answered, in the name of one of the Gerrer Rebbes, that the curse is that the Snake would never again be challenged to feed himself, and that lack of challenge is itself a curse. [9]

When Menachem Lubinsky entered the still-small Agudath Israel office straight out of *kollel*, Rabbi Sherer taught him how to do everything, right down to the correct way to staple papers and lick envelopes. He passed on to his young assistant the accumulated wisdom of 30 years.

During his first six months working for Governor Hugh Carey, Mendy Shayovich never sent a memo to the governor without first showing it to Rabbi Sherer for comment. That period was one extended tutorial in how to write a memo in such a way that a busy chief executive receives the information he needs in a concise and easily digested form.

Rabbi Sherer developed the confidence of staff members by showing them that he valued their opinion. In particular, he relied on the advice of Mr. Friedenson, who served as the unofficial ambassador of Agudath Israel to the whole community of the *shearis hapleitah* (post-war immigrants from Europe), and Rabbi Boruch Borchardt, who had come to work for Agudath Israel just a few years after Rabbi Sherer and whose devotion to the organization was total.

Senior staffers gained the feeling that they were important cogs in the organization from the frequency with which they gathered to discuss any new initiative or project. Rarely did he act without consulting widely in the office, both in formal meetings and individually with key staff members. He could "disagree, even strongly, and still listen," remembers one close aid. Despite the vast disparity in both age and experience from most of his senior staff in his later years, the words, "*kiblu da'ati* — accept my opinion," were infrequently on his lips.[10]

After the annual convention every year, he would gather the entire

---

9. To his children he gave another answer to the same question from the Kotzker. In giving the Snake a lifetime supply of food, as it were, Hashem was also severing His ties with him. Similarly, if a father were to give his child in one check a sum large enough to last a lifetime, but at the same time cut off all further relations, it would be a great curse.
10. Rabbi Shmuel Bloom.

With Rabbi Boruch Borchardt

senior staff to review every detail of the convention — what was successful, what needed improvement — with a fine-tooth comb.

The frequent consultations had two purposes: They raised the confidence of those consulted and encouraged them to learn to think strategically, and they offered Rabbi Sherer the benefit of another perspective. Even as his stature grew in the larger world and within the narrower Orthodox community, Rabbi Sherer did not let it go to his head. Once on a visit to Rabbi Sherer's office, Rabbi Yaakov Kamenetsky noticed Mrs. Debby Jacobs rising from her chair every time he passed. He asked her whether she showed the same *kavod* (honor) for Rabbi Sherer. The next day she did. Rabbi Sherer smiled and then told her, gesturing with his forefinger for emphasis, "You did it — now don't ever do it again."

Rabbi Sherer continued to take counsel, and even criticism, from staff members. Nor was he afraid to build up someone else's self-esteem at his own expense. A relatively young employee once made a couple of suggestions on a letter Rabbi Sherer had drafted. At the next staff meeting, Rabbi Sherer announced, "*Rabbosai*, I just want you to know this young man has improved my writing."[11]

---

11. Yosef Chaim Golding.

When he felt staff members were ready for it, he did not hesitate to give them responsibility. To the contrary, he pushed staffers to the forefront and gave them a chance to sink or swim. His judgment of people was so acute that they rarely sank. As he once told Rabbi Ephraim Oratz, "If you want to run an organization, you have to give up 20 percent of the authority to others. If you try to hold 100 percent, you will end up with nothing."

In his view, it was a positive reflection on Agudath Israel, and by extension Orthodox Jews, that it could field so many competent, articulate professionals. He looked for people whom he could entrust with important tasks. Thus he ardently pursued Rabbi Ephraim Oratz — who was roughly Rabbi Sherer's contemporary and then living in Israel — to head Project RISE (**R**ussian **I**mmigrants **S**eniors and **E**ducation).

He did not hoard the limelight for himself, as other leaders in his position might have. In the mid-'70s, Ted Koppel of ABC's Nightline was doing a show on tuition tax credits, and he called Agudath Israel to send a representative to be interviewed on national TV. There was no issue in which Rabbi Sherer was more intimately involved than that of education. (Senator Jacob Javits used to refer to him as Agudath Israel's Secretary of Education.) His testimony before the House Education Committee in 1961 was his first taste of national exposure, and through his alliance with the Catholic on issues of non-public school education, he had risen to national prominence as a leader in the fight for tuition tax credits.

Yet he told Menachem Lubinsky that he should represent Agudath Israel on Koppel's widely watched and influential program. Repeatedly Lubinsky suggested that Rabbi Sherer do the interview, but each time Rabbi Sherer insisted, "No, you're the one." To this day, Lubinsky marvels at the way a national leader of Rabbi Sherer's stature turned down such exposure. Rabbi Sherer made sure to tell Lubinsky, after the show had aired, that he had done a "fantastic job."

That praise was typical of Rabbi Sherer. As demanding as he could be, he never stinted on his praise. Indeed because he was so demanding his praise meant even more to employees. One of his secretaries could not hold back tears when he told her at the end of a particularly stressful week, "You worked so hard this week." "We tried very hard to please him," says another. "There was nothing like his praise."

With his intuitive knowledge of each person, he always knew how to show his appreciation in the most meaningful way. On the occa-

Rabbi Nisson Wolpin making a presentation to Rabbi Sherer on behalf of the Agudath Israel staff following Rabbi Sherer's recovery from open-heart surgery. Seated are Rabbi Boruch Borchardt (l) and Rabbi Yaakov Lebovics.

sion of the 50th anniversary of the liberation of the death camps, Yosef Chaim Golding worked for months on a video celebrating the survivors and their subsequent contributions to American Orthodoxy. Prior to the Agudath Israel convention, at which the video was to be shown, Golding held a private screening for Rabbi Sherer in a small room in the Agudath Israel offices. When the video was finished, Rabbi Sherer did not say anything. He just went over to Golding and kissed him on the top of the head and left the room.

NO INGREDIENT WAS MORE CENTRAL TO RABBI SHERER'S ABILITY to lift his staff to new heights of performance than love. Rabbi Sherer used to say that Agudath Israel of America was his fourth child, and to a large extent that atti-

Binding with Cords of Love

tude extended to the individual members of the staff. Shortly after Rabbi Labish Becker decided to join Agudath Israel, his father passed away. Even though Rabbi Becker had not yet begun working, Rabbi Sherer still flew out to Milwaukee to be *menachem avel* (offer his condolences). Mrs. Jacobs had only been working for Rabbi Sherer a short time when he flew to Detroit for her wedding. Such gestures conveyed the message that an employee was not just coming to work in an office, but joining a family.

His involvement in the personal lives of his staff was legendary. After he left Agudath Israel, Menachem Lubinsky kept up his close connection with Rabbi Sherer. The latter continued to take an intense interest in his life.. "He knew my business as well as I do," says Lubinsky.

He encouraged staff members to bring their problems to him, and was hurt when they did not. Rabbi Sherer once came into the office of Agudath Israel's comptroller, Shlomo Gertzulin, on an Erev Shabbos, and announced that he had a grievance. Somehow he had learned of a personal problem with which Rabbi Gertzulin was wrestling. The latter had not consulted Rabbi Sherer out of concern for the immense demands on his time and a desire not to mix his private affairs with his public duties with Agudath Israel.

Rabbi Sherer, however, remonstrated with him for his reluctance. "*Mein kind* [my child], do you realize how many individuals call me at all hours of the day and night for this and that …? I have already taken care of your matter, and it is fully resolved." And indeed when Rabbi Gertzulin arrived home that night, his wife related that she had received a phone call that the problem that had been troubling them had been put to rest.

Though Rabbi Sherer pushed his staff hard, he did not lose sight of the fact that each staffer was a human being with family and other commitments outside of his hours in the offices of Agudath Israel. Over the last two decades of Rabbi Sherer's life, Chaim Dovid Zwiebel, Vice President for Government and Public Affairs, was the staff member who most frequently stayed late at the office working together with Rabbi Sherer. One late night, Rabbi Sherer urged his young colleague to return home to his family. "Be a better father to your children than I was to mine," Rabbi Sherer told him.

That concern was not limited to senior staffers. Whenever the Moetzes Gedolei HaTorah met at the offices of Agudath Israel, Rabbi Sherer would call over all the single women in the office and anyone else who needed a *berachah* to the senior roshei yeshivah to receive their blessing. "He took care of me like I was his own child," remembers Mrs. Chaya Lider, one of his secretaries. "As meticulous as he was about his time, he would not begin dictation in the morning if he felt something was bothering me. And when I was involved in a *shidduch*, he always had all the time in the world to talk to me."

On her first day of work, Debby Jacobs was panic stricken when she sat down to transcribe Rabbi Sherer's dictation for the first time, and heard singing on the tape. She assumed that she had inadvertently erased Rabbi Sherer's dictation. She was about to throw herself on his mercy when she realized that the singer was none other than Rabbi Sherer himself, and he was welcoming her with an old Pirchei *niggun*.

Another secretary was married for a number of years without children. During that period, Rabbi Sherer gave her constant *chizuk* (encouragement). When she was blessed with a child, Rabbi and Mrs. Sherer came over to her house. "They were overjoyed," she remembers, "and helped me appreciate Hashem's *chesed* in a way I never would have imagined."

At one of their initial meetings, after Rabbi Nesanel Kasnett's appointment as the first director of Agudath Israel's new office in Washington, D.C., Rabbi Sherer asked him a completely unexpected question. Why, he wondered, is Yosef referred to as an "*ish matzliach*"? (*Bereishis* 39:12). Rabbi Kasnett gave the obvious and expected reply: because he was successful in all his endeavors. But Rabbi Sherer did not agree. In that case, he replied, the Torah would not have used the causative form, but rather described Yosef as an "*ish mutzlach*." Rather, said Rabbi Sherer, the Torah uses the active form to tell us that Yosef made *others* successful everywhere he went: in Potiphar's house, in the prison, and as viceroy of Egypt.[12] The measure of Yosef's success was that he helped everyone around him succeed in his assigned role.

In his ability to bring out the potential in others, Rabbi Sherer was the Yosef of his generation.

---

12. Rabbi Nesanel Kasnett, "The Yoseif of His Generation," *The Jewish Observer*, Summer 1998, p. 27.

At a convention of Agudath Israel, Rabbi Sherer once made a similar grammatical point. The verse (*Yirmiyahu* 31:14) describes Rachel Imeinu as crying over her children — רָחֵל מְבַכָּה עַל בָּנֶיהָ. He pointed out that the more typical grammatical usage would be to describe Rachel Imeinu as, בּוֹכָה, crying. The verb מְבַכָּה, means that she causes others to cry; she arouses within others a need to cry along with her. So it is with a leader, Rabbi Sherer said: A leader must not only cry out over Jewish suffering, he must bring others to cry with him and share his sense of urgency.

Chapter Fifteen

THE WORD

FROM A VERY EARLY AGE, MOSHE SHERER WAS ENAMORED with words. English words, Yiddish words, spoken words, written words: their power fascinated him. By high school, he was always the one called upon to give a speech or make a *derashah* when the occasion called for it.

He could, in the words of one colleague, speak "a Chassidishe Yiddish, a Litvishe Yiddish, and English beautifully," and he spoke Hebrew well enough to be interviewed on Israel TV and by the Israeli press. A collection of some of his important articles and speeches appeared in Hebrew under the title *Bishtei Einayim*, and he was at work on an English volume at the time of his death.

One of Rabbi Sherer's principal lifetime projects was to change the image of Torah-observant Jews: to imbue their image, in one of his favorite words, with a touch of class. He viewed every contact between a Torah Jew and a non-religious Jew or a gentile as a not-to-be-missed opportunity to change the perceptions the other held of Torah Jews.[1] And he knew that in every such encounter such things as the carriage and, above all, speech would determine the success or failure of that mission.[2]

Command of the English language provided, in his view, the quickest and most effective tool for changing perceptions of Torah Jews. In the 1970s, when yeshivah students who were about to enter the business world asked him whether they should wear a yarmulke or not to their initial job interviews, he would reply, "I think you should. If you are articulate and present yourself well, the yarmulke will cease to be a problem after a minute and a half. If you aren't, it will remain a problem the entire interview."[3]

Homiletics

RABBI SHERER STUDIED THE ART OF PUBLIC SPEAKING, DISTILLED its rules, and was eager to impart his knowledge to others. One of the reasons he taught homiletics at Torah Vodaath for so many years was to instill as many Orthodox young men as possible with the ability to present themselves well. Rabbi

---

1. Menachem Lubinsky.
2. Rabbi Sherer never missed an opportunity to convey a message, in one fashion or another, about Orthodox Jewry. He was once sitting on a plane next to Dovid Reidel, a grandson of Mike Tress. Reidel noticed that Rabbi Sherer had ordered a kosher meal, but did not touch it. Rabbi Sherer explained to him that he always ordered a kosher meal, even though he did not eat it, so that the airlines would know that there are Orthodox Jews interested in kosher meals and maintain that option.
3. Ibid.

Yitzchok Kerzner, the longtime rabbi of the Clanton Park shul in Toronto, was one of his homiletics students.[4] An acclaimed *darshan*, Rabbi Kerzner often expressed his gratitude over the years for Rabbi Sherer's homiletics classes.

But the beneficiaries of Rabbi Sherer's knowledge were not limited to his homiletics students. A young *baalebos* whom Rabbi Sherer had identified as having leadership potential knew that he would receive a full critique after any speech at which Rabbi Sherer was present.[5] While he was always prepared to give constructive criticism of a speech, Rabbi Sherer was no less eager to encourage promising young talent. After listening to a *derashah* by Eli Oelbaum, then a 17-year-old *bachur* in Telshe, at his younger brother's bar mitzvah, Rabbi Sherer asked the young speaker for a written copy.

Upon receiving the written copy, he wrote to Oelbaum that he had read the *derashah* twice and it was "a homiletical gem" — "effectively and professionally organized," without the usual "trite remarks heard at occasions of this sort." He offered only one little suggestion: that in the future Eli should try to recapitulate the thrust of his remarks at the end using the same verse with which he began. While adjuring the young *bachur* to concentrate all his *"kochos hanefesh"* in Torah learning while in yeshivah, Rabbi Sherer expressed the hope that he would one day use his "blessed talent to articulate Torah thoughts in order to inspire the masses to genuine *Yiddishkeit*."[6]

Among the other beneficiaries of Rabbi Sherer's expertise in public speaking were his children and grandchildren. He knew that many of his offspring would go into careers as *rabbanim*, or teachers, or as communal leaders, and that the ability to speak well would be a major asset in those roles. Even a *dvar Torah* at the Shabbos table might be interrupted if their grandfather had a particular pointer to share with them.

His grandchildren learned his rules for public speaking, and could recite them by heart. The first of his rules was: Never speak if you aren't prepared — a rule that could have been extended to include everything that Rabbi Sherer did. The stress on preparation reflected Rabbi Sherer's awareness of the awesome power of words and his sensitivity to their

---
4. Rabbi Kerzner had previously been a homiletics student of Rabbi Sherer's father-in-law, Rabbi Shimshon Zelig Fortman, from whom Rabbi Sherer inherited the class.
5. Shlomo Chaimovits.
6. Rabbi Sherer to Eli Oelbaum, June 2, 1977.

nuances.[7] A corollary of that first rule was: Look up every source that you intend to quote. Rabbi Sherer liked to tell the story of the homiletics student who could not figure out why his teacher appeared to laugh every time he quoted the words *al tishkach* in a *derashah*. Only after he finished the speech and looked up the verse in question, did the student realize that the Hebrew phrase is *lo tishkach* (see *Devarim* 25:19).[8]

Other basic rules included the maximum time allotted for each type of occasion — e.g, no more than five to ten minutes at a *Sheva Berachos*; the necessity of starting with a bit of salt and pepper — i.e., a good joke or story; "Always leave the audience thirsting for more, not wishing you had finished earlier"; "Never start until you know where you are going to park";[9] "If you have a good *vort*, find a way to use it."[10]

Many of the rules that Rabbi Sherer drilled into his homiletics class and his descendants concerned the importance of brevity in speaking — all concisely phrased:

(1) Preparing a good speech is like baking a cake: It requires lots of shortening;
(2) Never forget the 3B's: Be brief, be sincere, be seated;
(3) Learn from the *shochet's chalif* (the knife used for kosher slaughter): The shorter the *chalif* the less chance of a *p'gimah* (a nick that renders the knife unfit);
(4) A good speech is like drilling for oil: If you don't strike in the first five minutes, stop boring!

The *Gemara* in *Berachos* (63b) describes Rabbi Yehudah as the main speaker at every event. Rabbi Sherer wondered why he was so honored. Quoting his Rosh Yeshivah Rabbi Ruderman, he found the answer, not surprisingly, in Rabbi Yehudah's brevity. We find in the Haggadah of Pesach that Rabbi Yehudah compresses the Ten Plagues to just three words derived from the first letters of the Ten Plagues.[11]

His homiletics lessons went far deeper than pithy sayings on the vir-

---

7. Rabbi Nosson Scherman and Rabbi Meir Zlotowitz, "The Man in the Corner," *The Jewish Observer*, Summer 1998, p. 48.
8. Mrs. Chavie (Langer) Galinsky.
9. Gedaliah Weinberger.
10. Rabbi Levi Langer; Menachem Lubinsky.
11. Not only did an overly long speech deprive the speaker of his effectiveness, in Rabbi Sherer's view, it was a form of *tircha d'tziburah* (an imposition on the public), and at Agudath Israel conventions and dinners, he rigorously enforced time limits. As speakers approached their time limits, a note to that effect was inevitably slipped onto the podium. Rabbi Chaskel Besser once said, only half in jest, at the outset of a speech, "Rabbi Sherer asked to see my speech in advance. When I showed it to him, he ripped it in half and asked me which half I wanted to give."

tues of brevity. Rabbi Sherer made his homiletics students understand that a speech is judged by the impact it makes on the intended audience. Therefore it is crucial to identify that audience in advance and understand it. He half-humorously told his homiletics students at Torah Vodaath whom they should focus their attention on when trying out for rabbinical positions: "When you are giving a speech to try out for a position, there will be an elderly man with a *kamatz* [chin beard] somewhere in the shul, usually in one of the rear corners. He is the *mavin*, the *talmid chacham*; the rest of the membership will defer to his judgment. He is the one you must impress." The manner was humorous, but the message serious: Your job is to deliver the message of Torah so that it will be heard and respected.[12]

Some of the rules of speaking were technical. Rabbi Sherer always emphasized, for instance, the importance of eye contact. Once, while speaking, he became very frustrated by a spotlight that blinded him and made it impossible to see his audience. Eye contact helps to involve the listener in the speech. But it also allows the speaker to judge his audience's response to his words. Rabbi Sherer told Menachem Lubinsky that he had on more than one occasion changed a speech in the middle in response to the audience feedback he was receiving.

Speech has its rules, and writing its rules, and, Rabbi Sherer stressed, the two should not be equated. An elevated vocabulary might be impressive in writing. But it loses its impact in a speech. In speech, the simpler the words and the sentence structure the easier to follow and the more forceful the presentation. In order to avoid confusion between writing and speech, Rabbi Sherer did not write out his speeches, but rather relied on note cards on which were written the major points he wanted to make and the sources he would quote.

Writing allows the reader to review what he has read, to stop and ponder; speech does not afford that opportunity. For that reason, Rabbi Sherer taught his homiletics students that it is always better to develop one idea fully than to show off everything one knows. If the listener cannot follow the logical structure of a speech, and keep in mind the connections between the various points, he will be left at the end with nothing besides his confusion. For that reason a speech must always be focused on the development of one or two ideas.[13]

---

12. Rabbi Nosson Scherman and Rabbi Meir Zlotowitz, "The Man in the Corner," *The Jewish Observer*, Summer 1998, pp. 48-49.
13. Menachem Lubinsky.

Teaching the techniques of effective speaking, however, was only one of Rabbi Sherer's goals in his homiletics class — and not the most important one at that. Rabbi Shmuel Dishon — today the *menahel ruchani* of the Stolin Yeshivah and director of Yad Yisrael, Stolin's Torah projects in the former Soviet Union, and one of the most sought-after speakers in the Torah world — remembers Rabbi Sherer's *derashos* as polished from beginning to end. But the central message was always the same. He encouraged *askanus*, acting on behalf of *Klal Yisrael*, recognizing that a person is put in this world to help others. Every single class, he presented the same message in a new package. Testimony to the power of those *derashos* is the number of leading *askanim* in Agudath Israel who passed through Rabbi Sherer's homiletics class.

EVEN A CURSORY GLANCE AT *BISHTEI EINAYIM*,[14] THE HEBREW collection of some of Rabbi Sherer's speeches and articles, provides a sense of his mastery of the written and spoken word. (Many of the pieces are based on speeches.) In his introduction, Rabbi Sherer describes his work as the product of the second stage of Torah Jewry in America. Having succeeded in securing its own future, with the creation of yeshivos and Bais Yaakovs and Agudath Israel, the time had come for American Torah Jewry to look outward toward the broader Jewish world and to return to the entire Jewish people the crown of being the *Am Hashem* (G-d's Nation) and the *Am HaTorah* (the Nation of the Torah).[15]

Bishtei Einayim

Rabbi Sherer had the speechwriter's ability to coin memorable phrases. In one convention speech, for instance, he said of those Orthodox groups that pride themselves on their moderation and actively pursue

---

14. Dozens of *divrei Torah* from *Bishtei Einayim* are sprinkled throughout this biography.

15. The title *Bishtei Einayim* is drawn from an *Aggadah* (*Shabbos* 88b), based on a verse in *Shir HaShirim* (4:9): "לִבַּבְתִּנִי אֲחֹתִי כַלָּה לִבַּבְתִּנִי בְּאַחַד מֵעֵינָיִךְ — You have captured My heart, My sister, O bride; you have captured My heart with one of your eyes." The *Gemara* interprets the verse to refer to the Jewish people's having captured Hashem's favor with "one eye" when they accepted the Torah at Sinai, and with two eyes when they performed the mitzvos.

In the explanation of one of the *gedolim* on this *Aggadah*, "one eye" and "two eyes" refers to two stages in the development of a Jew. At the beginning of his path, a Jew must focus his eye primarily on himself and on his own self-development. When the task of self-perfection is well along, he can then turn his other eye outward to others. Rabbi Sherer took that explanation as applied to an individual Jew and applied it to the collective American Torah Jewry, in general, and Agudath Israel in particular. With his choice of titles, Rabbi Sherer described what he viewed as one of the key missions of Agudath Israel under his leadership: to contest for the leadership of American Jewry with the "grandees" of the mainstream organizations.

institutional connections with heterodox groups: "Those who make a principle of compromise will end up compromising principle."

He knew how to relate a vignette, and transform it into a metaphor for something much larger. Once while standing in Strauss Square on the Lower East Side, in the midst of a demonstration on behalf of Shabbos observance, Rabbi Sherer was approached by an elderly gentleman who asked him whose funeral it was. At first, Rabbi Sherer was bemused by the man's assumption that the only thing that could draw thousands of *yeshivah bachurim* together would be a funeral. But then he realized that the Shabbos demonstration was truly a funeral of sorts:

Bishtei Einayim

> To anyone who remembered the very different demonstrations of years past in the same square — the hordes of wayward Jews celebrating one or another of the myriad "isms" they had discovered and were anxious to share — this march was the perfect burial procession for all the hollow dreams that had polluted the minds of so many Jews for so long. Those revolutionaries back then would have regarded the prospect of a Strauss Square in honor of Shabbos observance to be about as likely as a return to the horse and buggy. They felt utterly secure in their belief that they had dealt the Jewish past a decisive deathblow.[16]

Rabbi Sherer was an expert at taking a *maamar Chazal* and giving it contemporary significance. "Two Sides of the Coin" takes as its starting point the *Midrash* that Mordechai minted a coin on one side of which was sackcloth and ashes and on the other a crown of gold. For Rabbi Sherer, the crown of gold represented the joy of a Jewish life. But even amidst that joy, and living in a free country that extends its Jewish citizens full equality, it is important, he noted, to prepare our children for times of sackcloth and ashes by teaching them "to feel Judaism's grandeur even when facing the hatred of vicious and powerful enemies and when targeted with curses, spit, and worse."

---

16. *Bishtei Einayim*, op. cit., "Funeral for an Era," p. 218.

In an article on Chanukah, Rabbi Sherer also began with a *Midrash* to discuss the opposite poles of exile (גָלָה) and redemption (גְאוּלָה). The *Midrash* is based on the vision of Zechariah read on Shabbos Chanukah: "וְהִנֵּה מְנוֹרַת זָהָב כֻּלָּהּ וְגֻלָּהּ עַל־רֹאשָׁהּ — And behold there was a golden Menorah, with a *guloh* [golden bowl] on its top" (*Zechariah* 4:2). The *Midrash* notes the similarity in sound between the *guloh* (golden bowl) and *golah* (exile) (which is written with the same three Hebrew letters) and *geulah* (redemption).[17]

How one views the bowl, Rabbi Sherer wrote, determines the path in life one will choose: the path of exile or that of redemption. The Hellenizers among the Jews saw only the external, the pure gold, while the Chashmonaim focused on the internal, the pure oil that burned within the bowl. The Greeks themselves understood that the source of Jewish strength was something internal. That is why they defiled and contaminated the pure oil of the Temple, rather than destroying it entirely. They knew that the best way to undermine the Torah, represented by the pure oil, would be to distort it and spread it from contaminated sources.

Just such a perversion of Torah takes place today "when Madison Avenue has developed a booming Chanukah industry in an effort to exploit the Menorah" as a purely external symbol, like an Xmas tree. The modern-day Hellenizers serve Jewish children nothing but "spiritual lollipops, instead of inspiring them with ... Torah." They perceive only the external aspect of the Menorah, and therefore have created a Judaism "based on slogans instead of sincerity, on theatrics instead of theology." The result is a generation that "has lost its belief in miracles, and placed its faith in studies, surveys, and resolutions," creating a Jewish community that is "glittering and dazzling on the outside, but eroded and cold on the inside." The distorted Judaism of the modern Hellenizers, based on contaminated oil, arouses no yearning for redemption.

In an essay on "the empty bowl of 'Holocaust Judaism,'"[18] Rabbi Sherer again lamented all the ersatz forms of Jewish identity being foisted on American Jewry as substitutes for a Judaism based on Torah and mitzvos. Rabbi Sherer never forgot the general apathy of American Jewry during the Holocaust and its failure to act more forcefully on

---

17. Moshe Sherer, "*Golah* or *Geulah*?: Reflections on Chanukah," *The Jewish Observer*, December 1968.
18. *Bishtei Einayim*, pp. 290-293.

behalf of the Jews trapped in Europe.[19] But he was no less indignant about the post-war development of an American Jewry of which Holocaust Remembrance was its major pillar — perhaps partly out of guilt over its earlier lack of action.

He found his critique of "Holocaust Jewry" encapsulated in just a few lines of *Midrash* (*Midrash Tanchuma, Ki Setzei*). The *Midrash* compares two commandments to remember: the commandment to remember the Shabbos day — זָכוֹר אֶת יוֹם הַשַּׁבָּת לְקַדְּשׁוֹ (Remember the Sabbath day to sanctify it) (*Shemos* 20:8) — and the commandment to remember Amalek — זָכוֹר אֵת אֲשֶׁר עָשָׂה לְךָ עֲמָלֵק (Remember what Amalek did to you) (*Devarim* 25:17). The two commandments are not the same, concludes the *Midrash*: The remembrance of the Shabbos is "over a bowl that is filled with all that is good"; that of Amalek is "over an empty bowl."

The first, wrote Rabbi Sherer, sustains; the second cannot. A Judaism based solely on sentiment and memory cannot provide the spiritual sustenance to preserve generations to come. He recalled the American Jewry of his youth, in which the primary connection for many Jews had been to come to synagogue three or four times a year to recite *Kaddish* on a *yahrtzeit* or for *Yizkor*. The children of those Jews did not even bother to come to synagogue to recite *Kaddish* for their parents.

And so, he predicted, would it be with the children of "Holocaust Jews," who base their whole connection with Judaism on Holocaust remembrance. Those children would not even remember the Holocaust. Only a Judaism based on Shabbos, the symbol of all 613 mitzvos, a Judaism rooted in the Tree of Life emanating from Sinai, could offer the spiritual food to sustain future generations.

RABBI SHERER HAD A DEEP FAITH IN THE POWER OF LOGICAL argument and moral suasion. His enchantment with the art of rhetoric was an outgrowth of his desire to convey ideas and change opinions. Without a command of language, he realized, one was permanently handicapped in the war of ideas.

The Power of Persuasion

Throughout his career, he showed a decided preference for reasoned argument over anything that smacked of strong-arm tactics. The controversy over the 1968 World Conference of Synagogues at Heichal Shlomo, the seat of the Israeli Chief Rabbinate, provides a case study

---
19. See Chapter 17 pp. 421 ff.

of that preference. The conference was strongly opposed by the *gedolei Yisrael*, who saw it as a possible precursor to the establishment of a quasi Sanhedrin under the dominance of the Chief Rabbinate. Yet the issues involved were little understood by the public, which largely viewed an international gathering bringing together Orthodox congregations across the religious spectrum as a positive step.

The question was how to combat that public perception. When Rabbi Yaakov Kamenetsky and Rabbi Yitzchak Hutner heard that plans were afoot for yeshivah students to picket the gathering, they asked Rabbi Sherer to convey to the roshei yeshivah in Israel their opinion that such demonstrations could only be harmful, even though they were "100 percent opposed to this World Conference." "[Picketing] does not convince or influence anyone, and will only put the *bnei yeshivos* in a bad light among the many Jews who innocently travel to the conference from different parts of the world," Rabbi Sherer wrote in their name. They recommended instead inviting small groups of visitors to the conference to meet with *gedolei Yisrael* to hear their perspective.[20]

When the Jewish Telegraph Agency published a (false) report, eight days later, that Agudath Israel in Israel had declared a *cherem* (ban of excommunication) on anyone who participated in the conference, Rabbi Sherer quickly wrote to Rabbi Menachem Porush to point out that *cheramim* had never been an instrument of Agudath Israel.[21]

With Rabbi Yitzchak Hutner and Rabbi Yaakov Kamenetsky

---

20. Rabbi Sherer to Rabbi Menachem Porush, January 2, 1968.
21. Ibid., January 10, 1968.

In a private letter, written after the conference, Rabbi Sherer lamented that in his meetings with American *yeshivah bachurim* in Ner Israel and Telshe Yeshiva few fully comprehended the opposition of the *gedolim*. And then he added what might have served as his credo:

> I wonder whether we spent enough time with the various individuals who attended the conference to explain the entire background of our opposition. **I also wonder whether we could have spent more time in reasoning with the people of the other camp who did not agree with us.** Above all, my primary concern is the ordinary, average Orthodox Jew of whom I assure you over 90 percent have viewed the entire controversy with amazement and complete lack of understanding …. **I am afraid too much time was spent on blanket *Kol Koreis*, instead of engaging in logical argumentation** …. (emphasis added).[22]

Effective persuasion, in Rabbi Sherer's view, required not only speaking the truth, but knowing how and when to do so. Once in his early years in the Philadelphia Yeshiva, Shimshon returned home for vacation filled with *kana'us* (zealotry) and a laundry list of criticisms of different aspects of the Jewish organizational world. After completing his earnest presentation, he said to his father, "And you know everything I'm saying is true, but you are too much of a diplomat to say it."

Rabbi Sherer asked him to please bring a *Chumash Bereishis* with the *Targum Yerushalmi*. The *Targum Yerushalmi* gives a non-literal translation of the first three words in the Torah: בְּרֵאשִׁית בָּרָא אֱלֹקִים. The *Targum* renders those words as, "With *chochmah* [wisdom] G-d created …. " Next, Rabbi Sherer showed his son that the last three letters of the first three words of the Torah are מ-א-ת, the same letters as the word truth, אֱמֶת, but not in the same order. The biggest *chochmah*, Rabbi Sherer told his son, lies in knowing that sometimes the truth is best left unspoken. And if it has to be said, one must know how and in what order.

A *vort* of the Kotzker Rebbe's of which Rabbi Sherer was very fond, brought home the same idea about knowing when and how to express the truth. If one were to recite the words, "שְׁמַע יִשְׂרָאֵל ה' אֱלֹקֵינוּ ה' אֱמֶת" — Hear O Israel, the L-ord Your G-d is True," said the Kotzer, one's declaration would be true. But if one substituted those words for the first verse of *Krias Shema*, by replacing the word אֶחָד with the word אֱמֶת, one would not only have failed to fulfill the mitzvah of *Krias Shema* but has

---

22. Rabbi Sherer to Fishel Gelernter, January 25, 1968.

also turned all the preceding blessings into *berachos l'vatalah* (blessings recited in vain).

One remarkable aspect of Rabbi Sherer's private correspondence is the amount of time he devoted to just such logical argumentation with individuals who wrote to him. And it made no difference whether those writing were public figures or teenage yeshivah students, Agudah constituents or far removed from Jewish observance.

When Rabbi Sherer read in the Anglo-Jewish press of a Reform convert who had complained to Peggy Tishman, the president of the United Jewish Appeal of Greater New York, of "religious ruffians" who told his children that he was not Jewish, Rabbi Sherer wrote an extremely sensitive letter to the children. He explained that the blame did not lie with the Orthodox community, but with those who converted their father without informing him that his conversion would not be recognized by large sections of the Jewish people. He pointed out that the way was still open for their father to become a full-fledged member of the Jewish people through a proper Orthodox conversion. But no matter what decision their father made, wrote Rabbi Sherer, they should always be proud of him.

After Rabbi Sherer was quoted in the Anglo-Jewish press on the tragedy of umbrella Jewish organizations that convey the impression that there are three equally valid "wings" of Judaism, the executive director of the Charleston, South Carolina Jewish Federation wrote to him that many non-Orthodox Jews in the Charleston community had asked why the Federation was generously funding the local Torah Umesorah school (or why an Orthodox school could accept money contributed by non-Orthodox Jews). Rabbi Sherer responded at length. He pointed out that the opposition to religious umbrella groups did not preclude Jews joining together on such issues as Israel's security or combating anti-Semitism. Federation support for a Torah Umesorah school that "saves Jewish children from assimilation," he argued, falls into that category of common interests.[23]

Communal support for Torah educational institutions and conversion were two hot-button public issues in the broader Jewish community about which Rabbi Sherer had obviously thought deeply. But he was equally quick to respond to private individuals on far more parochial issues. The son of a senior Agudath Israel employee, then

---

23. Rabbi Sherer to Steven Wendell, Executive Director of the Charleston, South Carolina Jewish Federation, December 11, 1981.

learning in Ponevezh Yeshiva, once wrote Rabbi Sherer questioning whether Agudath Israel had not strayed from its ideological roots in favor of social welfare programs, and wondering why Agudath Israel did not speak out against college. Rabbi Sherer expressed his delight "to see a young *ben Torah* think about problems of this nature, which others usually relegate to a cynical shrug of the shoulders." He then proceeded to explain in detail why his correspondent was not right in his general critique. As for the issue of college studies, Agudath Israel did not speak about it because the subject properly falls within the realm of the individual roshei yeshivah, who have somewhat varying approaches.[24]

And when another English-speaking *ben Torah* living in Israel questioned whether Agudath Israel's joining other Jewish groups to meet with Secretary of State Cyrus Vance was not a breach of the 1956 *psak* of the roshei yeshivah, Rabbi Sherer hastened to refer him to a recent speech by Rabbi Moshe Feinstein on the subject. Meetings over Israeli security concerns, Rabbi Sherer wrote, do not "diminish by a hairsbreadth our constant battle against recognition of Reform congregations as legitimate branches of Judaism."[25]

Getting Out the Message: Dos Yiddishe Vort and The Jewish Observer

WHILE STILL IN NER ISRAEL, RABBI SHERER WROTE FOR THE Zeirei Agudath Israel's monthly publication *Orthodox Youth*. And one of his first tasks upon joining the staff of Zeirei Agudath Israel was as unofficial editor of the *Orthodox Tribune*. Such publications were central to his vision of Agudath Israel as an ideological movement.

In the early '50s, when Yiddish was still the lingua franca of many American Jews and the Yiddish-speaking community had been bolstered by the arrival of post-war immigrants, all three of New York city's Yiddish papers were strongly anti-Agudah. Rabbi Sherer saw the need for Agudath Israel to have its own Yiddish publication to counter the jibes of the rest of the Yiddish press. When Yosef Friedenson arrived in New York from the Displaced Person camps in Germany, Rabbi Sherer quickly recognized the arrival of a remarkable writing talent, and set out to create the broadest possible forum for him. He viewed Mr.

---
24. Rabbi Sherer to Raphael Wolpin, December 15, 1978.
25. Rabbi Sherer to Rabbi Yosef Goodman, December 12, 1977.

Mr. Yosef Friedenson addressing an Agudah convention. Seated are Yaakov Schwebel, Rabbi Sherer, and Benzion Fishoff.

Friedenson as a rare treasure and an invaluable weapon in the ideological wars then raging.[26]

Friedenson had already put out the first issues of *Dos Yiddishe Vort* while still in Germany. And Rabbi Sherer was determined that it should continue in the United States. He approached Louis. J. Septimus, an old friend from the early Williamsburg Zeirei Agudath Israel, for a start-up loan. Within three issues, the publication was already bankrupt, but one way or another, Rabbi Sherer succeeded in keeping it going until the present day. Its appearance on the scene forced the other Yiddish publications to adopt a much more balanced approach on religious issues and to include more religious material.

Not by accident was the creation of a Torah magazine of ideas in English the first concrete goal that Rabbi Sherer set for himself upon assuming the helm of Agudath Israel. Already in 1960, he wrote to

---

26. Mrs. Ruth Lichtenstein, editor and publisher of the English-language *Hamodia*.

Rabbi Mordechai Gifter, "[O]ur greatest tragedy [is] that we have no public organ through which to speak to the masses .... I have always dreamed of putting aside all my other work and devoting myself exclusively to a large-scale English magazine, which will be devoted to frank Torah views on all subjects .... [B]y personal inclination I would prefer this task to any other."

In 1963, *The Jewish Observer* was born. Serving together with Rabbi Sherer as midwife at the birth was Dr. Ernst Bodenheimer, a product of the intensely ideological pre-war German Agudah movement, who fully shared Rabbi Sherer's vision of a contemporary journal of ideas from a Torah perspective. Dr. Bodenheimer served as chairman of the magazine's editorial board from its creation to his passing in 2000, when he was succeeded by his brother-in-law Rabbi Joseph Elias. *The Jewish Observer's* founding editor was Rabbi Nachman Bulman, whom Rabbi Sherer had long admired for his "unusual depth of Jewish thought." Both in terms of style and content, the new magazine was far above anything previously available to the Orthodox public.

The Jewish Observer was, in the words of Rabbi Nisson Wolpin, the magazine's editor for nearly four decades, very much Rabbi Sherer's "baby." Rabbi Wolpin explains that there were many tasks that Rabbi Sherer viewed as ones within Agudath Israel's ambit, but which he was only too happy to delegate to others. *The Jewish Observer*, however, was different. If Rabbi Sherer had had the time, he would have edited the magazine itself. As it was, he continually sent Rabbi Wolpin clippings from his voluminous reading. And he followed up to make sure that the gleanings from his reading had received their due consideration.

He read the magazine prior to publication, and then again after publication, frequently appending his comments to the finished product. He often suggested topics for upcoming issues, and weighed each issue in terms of his prescription that it should be a mix of the timely and the timeless. One of the magazine's central purposes, in Rabbi Sherer's view, was to provide readers with a thorough grounding in Agudah ideology: fealty to *gedolei Torah* as leaders of the Jewish people, the significance of the 1956 *psak* of 11 roshei yeshivah forbidding any participation in umbrella organizations with heterodox groups within the Jewish community, the falsifications and dangers of the heterodox movements. These were the timeless.

With Rabbi Nisson Wolpin

But even more important, in his view, was that *The Jewish Observer* examine the issues of the day through the lens of Torah — that was the timely. Rabbi Sherer's vision of an independent Orthodoxy required an organ that would allow the American world to freely express its own interpretation of contemporary Jewish life unfettered by the grandees of the mainstream organizations. The battle for the soul of American Jewry was above all a battle of ideas, and in that struggle Torah Judaism could not be left defenseless and unarmed.

The mission statement published in the first issue of *The Jewish Observer* in September 1963 clearly expressed his view:

> One segment of American Orthodoxy — to our mind its most vital segment — has to date "spoken" its mind and heart, to the remainder of American Jewry, almost entirely through the literary "mouths" of its critics and detractors .... Is it any wonder, then, that the vast majority of American Jewry has only the haziest notion of what they think and feel, to what they aspire and what their values are, over what they grieve and over what they rejoice?

Rabbi Sherer was determined to reverse that state of affairs, and *The Jewish Observer* was his chosen vehicle for doing so.

That mission statement quoted above explicitly linked the new journal to a vision of an independent Orthodoxy. That vision, the editors were careful to note, was today identified with Agudath Israel, but, in fact, historically antedated Agudath Israel. As the editors explained, the core principle of Agudath Israel, from which all else flows, is "an utter refusal to acknowledge the possible legitimacy of any organizing principle in the collective life of the people of Israel other than that of Torah — Torah as understood through all the ages of Jewish history."

And the necessary corollary of that principle is the refusal to "entrust the interests of [Torah] institutions to the tender mercies of Jewish organizations or agencies whose fundamental life-principle is not that of Torah." The historical experience of the previous 150 years convinced Torah Jews that whenever they failed to insist on their independence, their "strength of principle has been diluted and transformed beyond recognition ... or they have been paralyzed and crushed by the brutal force of their adversaries .... "

Just as the Agudah movement from its founding at Kattowicz had joined together diverse groups within Torah Jewry, so the editorial board of *The Jewish Observer* acknowledged that the new journal was not speaking to or on behalf of a monolithic community — but for *Chassidim, Misnagdim,* and those who espouse the Hirschian principle of *Torah im Derech Eretz* — and that these various group "often react differently to the events of contemporary Jewish history." But they all subscribed to one thing — the conviction "that Judaism's standards, its dictates and norms [are] objective," and that those norms and values must be defined "by reference to the written legacy of the Sages of Torah of all ages, or by addressing ... inquiries to the living repositories of Torah, to the great Torah scholars of the age."

Those sharing this view, wrote the editorial board, included the decisive majority of contemporary Torah sages, the decisive majority of students of the great mesivtas, and the decisive majority of laymen who are Torah scholars. The "independent" — or "separatist" in the eyes of their detractors — Orthodoxy that they advocated had constituted the majority, both qualitatively and quantitatively, of pre-war Eastern European Jewry.

With the proliferation of weekly newspapers and magazines over the past decade or so, it is possible to forget the impact of *The Jewish Observer's* appearance on the scene. But for more than 40 years, it was the authoritative voice of Torah Judaism: the source of Torah ideology for those outside of the community who sought to acquaint themselves with the Torah approach to contemporary issues, and to those within the community seeking to further clarify their thinking.

Finding the Stalwarts

IN HIS DETERMINATION TO WAGE A BATTLE OF IDEAS FOR THE hearts and minds of American Jewry, Rabbi Sherer kept a constant lookout for those with the rhetorical gifts to do so. In the mid-'80s, a number of Jerusalem bus stops were firebombed. Since most of them were located near the Meah Shearim neighborhood and had contained advertisements that were offensive to the residents of Meah Shearim, it was generally assumed that the perpetrators were from there.

Rabbi Avi Shafran, then a rebbi in the yeshivah high school in Providence RI, wrote a piece that ran in a number of Anglo-Jewish newspapers in which he invited the readers to imagine other types of advertisements that they might consider so deeply offensive to their values that they would feel justified in destroying the offending advertisements. The piece caught Rabbi Sherer's vigilant eye, and he promptly wrote a note to the young rebbi praising him for his imaginative use of analogies. At the same time, he advised the author that it had been a mistake to tacitly admit that *chareidim* were behind the bombings since those responsible had not yet been caught. That approach was vindicated when the perpetrators were caught and turned out to be secular youth eager to besmirch the reputation of the *chareidi* community. The author never forgot either the praise or the advice. And a few years later, he responded affirmatively to Rabbi Sherer's invitation to become Agudath Israel of America's Director of Public Affairs.

Rabbi Sherer began cultivating Yonoson Rosenblum from the moment that his second op-ed appeared in the fledgling English *Yated Ne'eman* (then a four-page weekly.) And when he first became a regular columnist for the *Jerusalem Post* in 1997, Rabbi Sherer was thrilled that for the first time the *chareidi* world had a regular spokesman "in the enemy camp," as he put it. One of the issues raging at that time in Israel was a bill that would have amended the Law of Return to limit recognition of converts to those converted "according to halachah," an issue particularly close to Rabbi Sherer's heart. The Torah view of *geirus* (conversion) as requiring a full acceptance of the yoke of mitzvos had until then never been presented in the mainstream Israeli press.

In one of their last conversations, Rabbi Sherer expressed his intention to raise tens of thousands of dollars to reprint the *Jerusalem Post* pieces as paid advertisements in the Anglo-Jewish press if the editors of the Jewish papers could not be prevailed upon to print them as op-eds. Though that plan never came to fruition, it is indicative of the primacy he put on presenting a reasoned view of Torah views to the broader public.

When the first ArtScroll translation and elucidation of a canonical text — *Megillas Esther* — appeared, Rabbi Sherer was among the first to both call and write Rabbi Meir Zlotowitz to congratulate him and encourage him to produce other such volumes. And he took enormous pride in the fact that the best-selling English-language Torah texts were being produced by products of traditional yeshivos.

Any project to strengthen religious Jews in their observance and learning of Torah or to draw non-observant Jews to Torah was close to Rabbi Sherer's heart. He made a general rule never to speak at a parlor meeting for the purpose of fund-raising. But in the late '70s, he spoke at five such parlor meetings on behalf of JEP (Jewish Educational Project), an outreach project founded by two young yeshivah products, Mordechai Katz and Yosef Chaim Golding. He explained to Golding why he made an exception for JEP: He had attended public-school as a boy and was the only one from his public-school class who remained religious. And he therefore personally felt the need for *kiruv*.

That lifelong commitment to bringing every single Jew closer to his heritage partly explains Rabbi Sherer's enthusiasm for the early ArtScroll translations with an English commentary.

RABBI SHERER QUICKLY SAW THE HUGE POTENTIAL OF THE ArtScroll English translation of the Talmud to greatly increase the numbers of those studying Talmud on a regular basis, including many for whom Talmud was previously a closed book. That explosion in Talmud learning was quickly reflected in the dramatic growth of the *Siyum HaShas* celebrating the completion of the seven-and-a-half-year *Daf Yomi* cycle.

Siyum HaShas

The idea of Jews all over the world learning the same *daf* (folio) of Talmud every day is inseparably identified with the Agudah movement. Rabbi Meir Shapiro, Rosh Yeshivah of Yeshivas Chachmei Lublin, announced the idea, after first gaining the approval of the Moetzes Gedolei Torah, at the first Knessiah Gedolah in Vienna in *Elul* of 5682 (1923). Yosef Friedenson, the editor of *Dos Yiddishe Vort* and a former *talmid* in Yeshivas Chachmei Lublin, remembers the conclusion of the second cycle in Lublin in 1938, which drew thousands of celebrants. Many of the *gedolei hador* of the pre-war generation were present.

But with the mass murder during the Holocaust of the vast majority of Jews who learned Talmud, the *Siyum HaShas* ceased to be a major event on the Jewish calendar. Friedenson celebrated the completion of the third cycle in 1946 with a few other broken survivors in a DP camp in Germany in 1946. For that occasion, they had only two volumes of Talmud.

Thereafter the *Siyum HaShas* remained a minor event, little noticed outside of the small and shrinking circle of those learning *Daf Yomi*. The fifth *Siyum HaShas* in 1961, for instance, was part of the annual convention of Zeirei Agudath Israel at the Glenwild Hotel in the Catskills. No more than a few hundred young Zeirei boys were present when Rabbi Aharon Kotler read the final words of Tractate *Niddah* and recited the *Hadran* upon the completion of *Shas*. And of those, it is safe to assume that none were celebrating their own completion of the *Daf Yomi* cycle.

Not until the completion of the seventh cycle in 1975 did Agudath Israel of America make a separate event of the *Siyum HaShas*. Manhattan Center with 1,200 seats was reserved for the event, and the Telshe Rosh Yeshiva, Rabbi Mordechai Gifter, delivered the main address. For the next *Siyum HaShas* in 1982, the 5,000 seats of the Felt Forum were completely taken.

Well before the 1990 *Siyum HaShas*, Shmuel Yosef (Ralph) Rieder approached Rabbi Sherer and told him that the next *Siyum HaShas* should fill Madison Square Garden. Rabbi Sherer replied that he would be delighted but he had two concerns: funding such a project and ensuring that the hall would be filled. Rieder said he would be responsible for the former, in the merit of his father Yaakov (Al) Rieder, one of Rabbi Sherer's closest friends and biggest supporters. Four days later, after consulting with the roshei yeshivah, Rabbi Sherer called Rieder back and told him he had a deal.[27]

The 1990 *Siyum HaShas* was the first after the start of publication of the ArtScroll Schottenstein Edition English-language Talmud, and the upsurge in learning of *Daf Yomi* that it inspired. When the 25,000 seats of Madison Square Garden were filled for the ninth *Siyum HaShas*, the secular media began to pay attention for the first time.

The *Siyum HaShas* serves many functions. It is a personal celebration for those who have completed the arduous cycle of more than

---

27. Yaakov (Al) Rieder and his brothers Shlomo and Harry were among the largest supporters of Agudath Israel of America during the 1980s. Rabbi Harry Rieder used to call Rabbi Sherer every Erev Shabbos and offer him a short *vort* on the *parashah* (weekly Torah reading). Rabbi Shmuel Bloom.

seven years and for their families. And even for those who have not completed the cycle, the experience of reciting *Shema Yisrael* together with tens of thousands of fellow Jews and rejoicing together over the Torah leaves a profound impression. The most recent, highly publicized *Siyumei HaShas* have motivated many to commit themselves to fixed, daily Torah study.

But apart from all the internal communal benefits from the *Siyum HaShas*, Rabbi Sherer quickly grasped that it could be a major tool in changing perceptions of Torah Jews, and even more importantly for creating an awareness of Talmud among millions of Jews who have never had the privilege of so much as seeing a page of Talmud. As the scope of the *Siyum HaShas* grew, the mainstream media could not help but notice. Suddenly Talmud study was on the front page of *The New York Times*, and readers of the *Times* learned that Talmud study was not just for yeshivah students and *Chassidim*, but for doctors, lawyers, accountants, and businessmen as well. Essays describing the "sea of Talmud" began appearing in leading secular papers and journals.

The tenth *Siyum HaShas*, Elul 5757 (1997), was the last of Rabbi Sherer's life. Years of planning at Agudath Israel headquarters went into the event. The 25,000 seats at Madison Square Garden sold out within two weeks of going on sale, and the Nassau Coliseum was taken as a second major venue. Another 35 locations around the world were linked by satellite to the two main venues. Rabbi Nosson Scherman, general editor of ArtScroll Publications, the chairman of the evening at Nassau Coliseum, pointed out that the gathering constituted the "largest celebration of the Torah study since the last *Hakhel* gathering in Yerushalayim some two thousand years ago." He related how his Rosh Yeshiva, Rabbi Gedaliah Schorr, used to speak of the dual identity of every Jew as an individual and a member of *Klal Yisrael*, and described the event as "80,000 individuals fused into one mighty *tzibbur*."

For Rabbi Sherer the event was a personal celebration — he had undertaken at the previous *Siyum HaShas* to complete the *Daf Yomi* cycle — and it was in a certain way a valedictory celebration of his lifework of building Torah in America. Addressing the largest audience of his career, he used the occasion to rejoice in the rebirth of Torah learning from the ashes:

> It was the goal of the Nazis, *yemach shemam*, not only to annihilate the Jews of Europe, but to destroy the Jews, the Talmud, and the *Talmud Lehrer* (those who taught Talmud), because they under-

Addressing the Tenth *Siyum HaShas*.

stood that this is the secret of Jewish continuity. After emerging from the Valley of Tears [*Churban* Europe in 1945], many entered a Valley of Fears that there was no future for Torah and Talmud in the entire world. Therefore ... [this event] when ... over 70,000 *Bnei Yisrael* gather to celebrate the daily study of Talmud ... is more than a celebration, it is a powerful demonstration of the *nitzchiyus* — the eternity — of Torah, and of Israel as the Torah nation.

Once Orthodox Jews were dismissed as a dying breed, "the last of the Mohicans," by mainstream American Jewish spokesmen, but the *Siyum HaShas* powerfully demonstrated that Orthodox Jewry is the most vibrant segment of world Jewry. And the man who had done more than any other to orchestrate that demonstration — Rabbi Moshe Sherer — was arguably the most influential Jewish leader in America.

Rabbi Sherer's vision of the *Siyum HaShas* as a means of lifting the image of Torah Jews in the eyes of their co-religionists and providing them with a sense of the centrality of Torah study to any pulsing Jewish life was fully vindicated by his final *Siyum*. Rabbi Yosef Wikler, the editor of *Kashrus Magazine,* related the following vignette in a letter to the *Jewish Observer* after the most recent *Siyum HaShas*, which brought together 120,000 Jews at 70 locations worldwide. Two days after the

Siyum, Rabbi Wikler found himself sitting next to two not-yet-religious relatives at a family *simchah*. One asked him, "Are you part of the Orthodox group that learns the 2,700 pages of the Talmud?"

Rabbi Wikler replied that Talmud study was not limited to just certain Orthodox Jews, and began to describe a bit of what *Gemara* is. He added, "If you want to learn *Gemara*, I'm available. We can do it by phone with telephone conferencing: you, and your brother, and I."

All his previous efforts to interest these non-religious brothers in any way had fallen on deaf ears. But to his amazement, they took him up on his offer: "[W]hen 100,000 Jews got together to celebrate the millions of *blatt* learned since the last *Siyum HaShas*, the media picked it up. A little national coverage of the *Siyum HaShas*, and two Jews bought their first ArtScroll *Gemaras*, cleared their Wednesday nights to learn Torah, and have committed to master at least a little bit of *Shas*." That confirmation of the power of the *Siyum HaShas* to arouse a thirst for Talmud learning would surely have made Rabbi Sherer beam.

Upon the completion of every tractate, Rabbi Sherer used to point out, we recite the *Hadran*, in which we mention Rav Pappa and his 10 sons. The commentators explain that we remember Rav Pappa because he used his great wealth to make a celebration at the end of every tractate to which he invited his 10 sons and many others, and thereby publicized the importance of Torah learning.[28] Rabbi Sherer similarly used the *Siyum HaShas* to glorify Torah learning, and, in this respect, became the Rav Pappa of our day.

---

28. *Yam Shel Shlomo, Bava Kamma,* end of the seventh *perek* (chapter); *Teshuvos HaRema.*

Chapter Sixteen

SIX CRISES

RABBI SHERER BEGAN HIS WRITTEN APPRECIATION OF Rabbi Aharon Kotler with the *Gemara's* description of Rabban Shimon ben Gamliel at the *Simchas Beis Hasho'eivah* celebrations in the Temple: "He would take eight lit torches, throwing one and catching another, without one touching the other" (*Succah* 53a). The *Gemara*, he explained, surely did not mean to describe Rabban Shimon ben Gamliel's physical prowess, but rather his ability to simultaneously lead Klal Yisrael in eight different respects, without any one of these areas interfering with the other.[1]

Rabbi Sherer too juggled a multitude of tasks and roles at the same time. He could keep his eyes directed toward a particular goal over a span of years, even decades. His battle against the spread of heterodoxy in both the United States and Israel was lifelong; the struggle to secure

---

1. Rabbi Sherer, *Bishtei Einayim*, "Sparks From the Holy Light: HaGaon Rabbi Aharon Kotler, *zt"l*," pp. 329-338.

tuition tax credits for parents of non-public-school children lasted 13 years in its first phase; the establishment of an academic accreditation agency for advanced yeshivos took nine years; and he was involved for decades in the complex end-of-life issues raised by modern technology. All these battles were waged while engaged in countless other tasks.

But when the need arose, he could also switch gears and focus all his energy on a particular problem, with laserlike intensity. Sometimes he was able to resolve the issue — such as the Department of Agriculture's decision to forbid the importation of *esrogim* from Israel — by himself; other times resolution of the crisis involved organizing a vast array of disparate forces, as in the campaign to preserve the draft exemption for rabbinical students. Sometimes, the crisis did not involve any particular action so much as standing up for a core principle, even at a heavy cost. Agudath Israel's actions in the controversy over the second New York State *Get* Law fall into this category.

On yet other occasions, it is hard to specify precisely what was achieved through the massive expenditure of time and energy. Rabbi Sherer's intense efforts during the three weeks that Rabbi Yitzchak Hutner, Rosh Yeshivas Chaim Berlin, was held hostage in Jordan by Palestinian terrorists, for instance, did nothing (demonstrably) to secure Rabbi Hutner's release. Ironically, it was Rabbi Hutner himself who on another occasion reminded Rabbi Sherer that the task of a worker for the *Klal* is to do not, to achieve.²

In this chapter, we examine Rabbi Sherer's actions during some of the most pressured moments of his long public career.

Saving the Draft Exemption

A Crisis Brews

THE LARGEST AND MOST COMPLICATED LOBBYING CAMPAIGN that Rabbi Sherer ever ran was that to preserve the draft exemption for divinity students, including yeshivah students. On January 28, 1971, President Nixon sent legislation to Congress to completely overhaul the selective service system. The President's call for the end of undergraduate deferments garnered the most attention. Barely noticed was the simultaneous call

---
2. See the end of Chapter 12.

for the end of divinity student exemptions, which was seen as only equitable in light of the proposed termination of undergraduate deferments. One person who did not miss President Nixon's reference to divinity students, however, was Rabbi Naftoli Neuberger of Ner Israel. He promptly called Rabbi Sherer to alert him to a potential crisis.

For the next two months, Rabbi Sherer and Rabbi Neuberger would devote themselves almost entirely to maintaining the divinity student exemption. After March 1, Rabbi Sherer completely set aside all other claims on his time for five weeks. His "loyal partner" in the whole battle, Rabbi Neuberger, did the same. Rabbi Sherer subsequently wrote a detailed, 12-page aide-mémoire on the struggle in the House of Representatives (for the sake of history), but, as he made clear, it barely scratched the surface of the "feverish activity," hundreds of phone calls, and contacts made.

Putting the Pieces Together

MANY PIECES HAD TO FALL INTO PLACE IF THE PROPOSED LEGISLATION was to be defeated. The first was alerting every yeshivah in America, from Satmar to Yeshiva University, to the potential threat. Beyond the yeshivos themselves, it was crucial that the rest of the Orthodox world be on board for the fight. Congregational rabbis would be critical to bringing constituent pressure on crucial lawmakers, and so the large rabbinical membership organizations, such as the Rabbinical Council of America and Orthodox Union were also crucial to the battle.

But even a fully unified Orthodox world would not be sufficient. In many districts with representatives on House Armed Services Committee or other key legislators, there were no Orthodox synagogues. The only Jewish clergymen who could possibly exert influence in certain districts were from the Conservative movement.[3] For the only time in his career, Rabbi Sherer joined forces with Conservative representatives in allocating lobbying responsibilities, and a top official of the Jewish Theological Seminary even attended a meeting at the offices of Agudath Israel for that purpose.[4]

---

3. Though the Reform movement also maintained its own seminary, it did not oppose the legislation. On the other hand, neither did it actively support it. That neutrality of the Reform movement may be chalked up as the only positive achievement of the Synagogue Council in its long history. Because the Synagogue Council as a whole opposed termination of the draft exemption, the Reform movement, as a member of the council, did not get actively involved in the issue.

4. Rabbi Sherer maintained good working relations with a number of major secular Jewish organizations, such as the Joint Distribution Committee (JDC) and the Hebrew Immigrant Aid Society

The ability to join forces with the Conservatives on an issue of mutual interest to both yeshivos and the Jewish Theological Seminary proved a complete rebuttal to one of the arguments most frequently made by proponents of Orthodox participation in the Synagogue Council of America. The proponents claimed that it would be impossible to form ad hoc alliances in cases of necessity, and therefore an ongoing structure involving representatives of all religious groups was necessary. The fight over draft exemptions for divinity students showed that was not true. Agudath Israel, which had always been the most vociferous opponent of the Synagogue Council, succeeded in creating precisely such an ad hoc alliance.[5]

Rabbi Sherer and Rabbi Neuberger immediately recognized that if the legislative battle were waged as a Jewish issue, defeat was assured. The number of Jews who felt strongly about the issue was simply not sufficient to sway more than a handful of legislators, especially with the president on the other side. Unquestionably, the Orthodox Jewish community felt more strongly about the issue than any other religious group, because of concerns that the armed services could not fully accommodate the needs of religious soldiers and that those services would be an inappropriate environment for Orthodox Jews. The former set of concerns clearly did not apply to Christian denominations, which do not have the same religious requirements.

The presentation of the issue as an interdenominational one of equal import to Jews, Catholics, and Protestants, was, in the words of the Rabbi Reuven Savitz, one of the leaders of the campaign, an act of "high political theater" on the part of Rabbi Sherer and Rabbi Neuberger.

Yet the only chance of success lay in convincing the organized Catholic community and certain Protestant denominations to join the battle at some level. Accordingly, Rabbi Sherer's first response after speaking to Rabbi Neuberger about the proposed legislation was to get on to the phone to his friends in the Conference of Catholic Bishops (Catholic Conference) in Washington, D.C.

What he heard was far from encouraging. Some in the hierarchy felt that army service was no longer as threatening now that seminarians were, in any event, no longer secluded from general society. Other

---

(HIAS), but never before or after did he join forces with the heterodox movements on an issue of mutual interest.

5. I am indebted to Rabbi Nota Koslowitz for this insight. While still a *bachur* in Beis Medrash Govoha of Lakewood, Rabbi Koslowitz played an active role in the Capitol Hill lobbying campaign.

bishops even expressed concerns that the seminaries were becoming filled with those seeking to evade the draft, not to pursue a life in the priesthood. By mid-February, however, the Catholic hierarchy had decided to join Agudath Israel in opposing the proposed termination of the 2-D deferment. There would, however, remain a certain ambiguity in the Catholic position and important differences between the Catholic Conference and the yeshivos at different stages in the legislative battle that required Rabbi Sherer's constant attention.

Even with the organized Catholic Church on board, there were many obstacles still to be overcome. For one thing, Congress was in a distinctly foul mood with respect to divinity students, many of whom had taken leading roles in the protests against the Vietnam War. In addition, the largest Protestant umbrella organization, the National Council of Churches, supported ending the draft exemption for divinity students and sent a memo to all congressmen and senators informing them of their position.

Eventually, an ad hoc Inter-Faith Committee on Selective Service Exemption of Seminarians was created to preserve the traditional exemption for divinity students. Its members included the Baptist Joint Commission on Public Affairs, the National Association of Evangelicals, the National Association of Jewish Theological Seminaries (itself an ad hoc group), the United Methodist Church, and the United States Catholic Conference.

Both the House Armed Service Committee and the Senate Armed Services Committee (SASC) were holding hearings on the legislation, and it was necessary to organize inter-religious delegations to visit the members of those committees. Rabbi Sherer and Rabbi Neuberger divided states between them in putting together the delegations to visit key legislators.

In the first days of

With the Bostoner Rebbe of Boston-Har Nof

With Rabbi Avrohom Chaim Levin (l) and Rabbi Avrohom Pam (center). Rabbi Shlomo Mandel and Rabbi Shmuel Bloom are in the background.

March, Rabbi Sherer was in contact with Rabbi Elya Svei in Philadelphia about meeting with Pennsylvania Senator Richard Schweiker of the Senate Armed Services Committee; with the Bostoner Rebbe about contacting Senator Edward Kennedy, who was also on the Senate committee;[6] with Rabbi Mordechai Gifter about meeting with Ohio Senator William Saxbe, another member of the Senate committee, and with Rabbi Avraham Chaim Levin in Chicago about speaking with Illinois congressmen on the House Armed Services committee.

Another interdenominational delegation consisting of Rabbi Herschel Schacter, an army chaplain during World War II, Dr. Pat Robertson of the National Association of Evangelicals, and a Catholic priest was assembled to meet with Selective Service Director Curtis Tarr on March 17. That meeting gave no cause for encouragement or hope that Tarr would soften his stance against the exemption. It did become clear in the course of the meeting that Tarr was the moving force behind efforts to end the divinity student exemption.

---

6. The Bostoner Rebbe did ultimately meet with Senator Kennedy together with the dean of the Boston University School of Theology and the Archbishop of Boston.

By March 18, Rabbis Sherer and Neuberger realized that they could not run the entire campaign by themselves, and they sought from the major roshei yeshivah authorization to create a wall-to-wall coalition of yeshivos from Yeshiva University to Satmar. The Yeshivah Emergency Committee met for the first time in New York's Statler Hilton Hotel on March 23, and each yeshivah agreed to contribute $400 to the coffers. Rabbis Sherer and Neuberger were appointed as treasurers, and Rabbi Reuven Savitz, the executive director of Bais Yaakov of Baltimore, was hired by the committee to work full-time out of Washington, D.C. until the end of the lobbying campaign.[7]

The Battle in the House

THE CAMPAIGN AGAINST TERMINATING THE EXEMPTION WAS dealt a severe setback when the House Armed Forces Committee voted 24-7 to support the legislation on March 19. Rabbi Sherer's Catholic contacts had assured him that the committee would likely vote for continuation of the exemption. The question that now had to be addressed was whether to abandon the fight in the House, in light of the overwhelmingly unfavorable vote in committee, and concentrate all efforts on the Senate, or to still try to win on the floor of the House.

On March 24, a strategy session of all religious groups was held at the offices of the United States Catholic Conference. In addition to the Orthodox Jewish delegates, two faculty members from JTS were present, and a number of Methodists, Baptists, and Evangelicals. The Catholics were in favor of concentrating all lobbying efforts on the Senate. Rabbi Sherer, however, had met that same day with Speaker of the House Carl Albert, who had until then not even known that the divinity student exemption was on the table. Albert urged him not to abandon the House as a lost cause, and expressed the opinion that a well-organized lobbying campaign might yet succeed in preserving the exemption.

Armed with that information, Rabbi Sherer succeeded in winning the agreement of the interdenominational group to continue the fight in the House. That decision, in many respects, determined the ultimate outcome of the campaign.

---

7. Rabbi Savitz had previously organized the four Jewish day schools of Baltimore into the Association of Jewish Day Schools of Greater Baltimore, and in that capacity he became the leading local Jewish spokesman for state and federal aid to non-public schools. That role brought him into close contact with the Catholic hierarchy, both lay and religious, of Baltimore.

While working the halls of the House together with Congressman Hugh Carey, Rabbi Sherer realized how little time remained to change the tide, and how ill informed congressmen were about the issue. He and Carey had run into three other New York representatives: Herman Badillo, Bella Abzug, and James Scheuer. While each expressed support for the continued exemption, Scheuer told Rabbi Sherer that he had been under the impression that all the religious denominations were agreeable to dropping the exemption.

The key now was to organize state caucuses of congressmen so that the interdenominational groups would be able to make their presentations to a number of representatives at one time. At the second meeting of the Yeshivah Emergency Group, in the offices of the Rabbinical Council of America, it was decided to contact influential rabbis in different states to influence their local congressmen to convene state caucuses on the issue. Rabbi Boruch Sorotzkin worked on the issue in Ohio; Rabbi Shneur Kotler, together with Rabbi Pinchos Teitz of Elizabeth and Rabbi Zev Segal of Newark, did the same for New Jersey; and Rabbi Elya Svei worked organizing lobbying committees to visit Pennsylvania congressmen the following week. After securing the promise of Rep. Emanuel Cellar to convene a New York conference for the next week, Rabbi Sherer contacted Congressman Hugh Carey and Charley Tobin of the New York Catholic Conference to seek their help in ensuring a large turnout. (Twenty New York representatives turned up at the caucus.)

Motza'ei Shabbos (March 28) of the week of the vote in the House everything swung into high gear. Shortly after Shabbos, Rabbi Sherer, Rabbi Neuberger, Rabbi Shmuel Yosef Labkovsky, Rabbi Yaakov Weisberg, and Rabbi Reuven Savitz held a conference call to plan a blitz phone campaign the next day.[8] Rabbi Labkovsky had drawn up lists of rabbis and phone numbers of rabbis across the United States to be contacted. The next day, Sunday, teams of *yeshivah bachurim* from Torah Vodaath and leaders of Zeirei Agudath Israel manned a bank of 10 phones in the offices of Agudath Israel calling rabbis across the country to contact their congressmen. Rabbi Sherer briefed the two crews on what to say and how to speak on the phone. In all, rabbis in 119 cities in 19 states were contacted.

For the next three days, the organizers, including Rabbi Sherer, took a suite of rooms in the Congressional Hotel just across from the Capitol

---

8. The first four were also the key early players in the creation of AARTS (See Chapter 17, pp. 440-451). Only Rabbi Weisberg had not learned with them in Ner Israel.

to be able to coordinate the campaign from the scene.⁹ *Talmidim* from Lakewood and Ner Israel joined them to provide technical support. Monday began with an early-morning meeting at the offices of the Catholic Conference to work out the composition of the delegations for the next day. Rabbi Sherer spent the rest of the day contacting rabbis to encourage them to fly to Washington for the next day's lobbying campaign. Simultaneously, Rabbi Neuberger worked the phones with Protestant ministers and Catholic priests, who were crucial to the success of the mission. Rabbi Labkovsky recalls the hotel owner saying, "We've had lots of lobbyists over the years, but I've never seen a group with such dedication."¹⁰

On Tuesday, interfaith delegations visited caucuses of the Kansas, Missouri, and Florida congressional delegations. All the congressmen from Pennsylvania were visited by delegations from Philadelphia or Pittsburgh, and similarly all Maryland congressmen were visited by an interfaith delegation. Rabbi Sherer personally participated in an interfaith meeting with Speaker Albert, who publicly credited Rabbi Sherer with bringing the issue to his attention; in the meeting with the New York caucus, most of whose members he knew well; and in a 4 p.m. meeting with House Minority Leader Gerald Ford,¹¹ who gave him the good news that the Nixon administration would not make any attempt to impose party discipline on the next day's vote.

Wednesday, the day of the vote, 30 freshly scrubbed, well-dressed *yeshivah bachurim* from Ner Israel arrived at 9 a.m. to hand-deliver a memorandum from the interfaith committee to each of the 435 representatives. After a briefing from Rabbi Sherer, they were off. By the day of the vote, Rabbi Sherer felt the tide shifting in their favor, but still expected a very close vote. The last-minute appearance of a relatively small rabbinic organization, which had not previously participated in any of the planning sessions, provided a last-minute scare. The

---

9. Until then, Rabbi Savitz had been working out of the offices of the U.S. Catholic Conference. No doubt a number of eyebrows were raised in congressional offices when Rabbi Savitz identified himself and said he was calling from the U.S. Catholic Conference. As the Catholic support cooled, however, it became necessary to find other headquarters. The Catholic Conference, for instance, refused to provide Catholic clergymen for the lobbying campaign, and insisted on using only paid lobbyists.
10. As an example of the dedication, Rabbi Labkovsky recalled personally pushing a 300-pound pastor up the steps of the Capitol.
11. After the successful House vote, Rabbi Sherer sent a letter of appreciation to Congressman Ford. The latter responded by asking Rabbi Sherer to inform the rabbis in his district of how helpful he had been. "Just shows how the big people do not forget about taking care of little items," Rabbi Sherer wrote in his aide-mémoire. It was a rule that fully described him as well.

With Senator Jacob Javits and President Gerald Ford

organization wanted to send telegrams to all the congressmen. When told by Rabbi Savitz that their telegrams would be superfluous at that point, and perhaps even counterproductive, the organization heads complained that they were "being held back from doing great things."[12]

At 1 p.m., Rabbi Sherer and his partners filed into the House gallery to watch the debate. "It was a beautiful sight," he wrote later, "to see how the various congressmen whom we had contacted were using the very language that we had used in speaking to them." (Rabbi Sherer was one of the principal draftsmen of the interfaith memorandum.) Following the advice of Hugh Carey, the decision was made not to ask for a roll call vote of all 435 representatives, with each vote recorded, but to rely on a simple division vote, where those on the floor of the House move to opposite sides of the room to be counted. The final count was 114 to 29 in favor of an amendment introduced by Philadelphia Congressman

---

12. By acting outside of the interdenominational framework, the group kept threatening to turn the exemption into a "Jewish" issue, which was just the opposite of the course Rabbi Sherer and Rabbi Neuberger had charted. Rabbi Neuberger commented, at one point, "The Conservatives are with us; the Reform are not against us; only this group threatens to destroy everything we have worked to build." At a later stage, the group managed to secure an appointment with a White House official through Nathan Lewin, who had not realized that they were acting outside the general framework. When Lewin was informed as to how damaging the organization's involvement might be, he made sure that they were given only five minutes of the official's time before being ushered out.

Byrnes to retain the 2-D draft exemption. "Our people quietly marched out of the gallery, and there was hardly a dry eye among us," Rabbi Sherer reported.

THERE WAS NO TIME, HOWEVER, FOR RABBI SHERER AND RABBI Neuberger to rest on their laurels from the victory in the House. They immediately trained their sites on the Senate Armed Services Committee (SASC). For if the Senate did not vote to maintain the draft exemption for divinity students, the final version of the bill would be hammered out in the House-Senate Conference, where anything could happen.

The Battleground Shifts

On April 4, four days after the House vote, Rabbi Sherer and Rabbi Neuberger met in New York City with most of the country's leading roshei yeshivah, including, Rabbi Moshe Feinstein, Rabbi Yaakov Kamenetsky, Rabbi Yaakov Yitzchak Ruderman, Rabbi Yitzchak Hutner, Rabbi Shneur Kotler, Rabbi Mordechai Gifter, Rabbi Gedaliah Schorr, and Rabbi Shraga Moshe Kalmanowitz to review each yeshiva's draft policies. Later the same day, they met together with Rabbi Savitz, Rabbi Louis Bernstein of Yeshiva University, and Neil Gilman, the dean of students at JTS to divide up assignments with respect to contacting the 16 members of the Senate Committee.

After flying down to Washington, D.C. on April 6 to meet with the military aide to Senator Peter Dominick of Colorado and the military aide to Senator Edward Kennedy of Massachusetts, Rabbi Sherer reported that he had secured commitments from seven of the 16 senators on the committee. By April 21, that number had grown to 10, with only one senator on the committee showing any hesitancy about the retention of the divinity student exemption.

Just as victory in the SASC seemed assured, the chief counsel to the committee dropped a bombshell in a private conversation with Rabbi Savitz. He asked him what his reaction would be to changing the exemption for divinity students to a deferment. (Under the existing exemption, anyone who studied in a recognized divinity school until the age of 26 was forever exempted from the draft.) Two days later, the committee took a preliminary vote to accept that change. The first consequence of the proposed change was to introduce tensions into the alliance between the yeshivos and the other religious groups forming part of the coalition.

Under the new proposal, a former *kollel* student who left *kollel* without taking a rabbinical position of some kind would be immediately subject to the draft. That did not bother the Catholics. The chief counsel of the Catholic Conference told Rabbi Sherer that the Catholics could not care less if a former seminarian who did not enter the priesthood was drafted. "Let them draft those clowns," he said.

At least prior to the Senate Armed Services Committee's final vote, Rabbi Sherer was able to hold the interfaith committee together. One day before the final Senate committee vote, on April 26, Rabbi Sherer argued at a meeting of the interfaith committee that it was important to insist on no change in the current exemption language because the Senate Armed Services Committee had acted improperly in not calling as witnesses any religious leaders before removing the historic exemption for divinity students. On that narrow basis, the interfaith committee sent a letter to the chairman of the SASC, Senator John Stennis, requesting that no change be made in the language of the historical exemption unless religious leaders were afforded the chance to be heard.

Even after Rabbi Neuberger had already placed 16 copies of the letter in his briefcase, the chief counsel of the Catholics still tried to rescind the agreement and have the letter withdrawn. Only after being told that it was impossible to rescind decisions taken at the meeting did he reluctantly agree to distribution of the letter.

That victory, however, was short lived. The next day the SASC voted to change the existing exemption to a deferment.[13] This time there was no hope of reversing the SASC vote on the floor of the Senate. The other members of the interfaith committee informed the Jewish representatives at a May 14 meeting that they had no intention of participating in a floor fight in the Senate.

Nevertheless, because of harsh language used by Curtis Tarr in his letter to the SASC, they would join in a memorandum explaining the committee's objection to any change in the traditional language of the exemption to be submitted to all 14 members of the House-Senate conference. In his testimony to the SASC, Selective Service Director Curtis Tarr had been outspoken in his criticism of divinity students. He had implied that many denominations had a surfeit of ministers and that

---

13. The roshei yeshivah viewed the loss of the divinity student exemption for those learning in a divinity school until 26 as "extremely harmful and potentially catastrophic."

As if to show how little the aforementioned rabbinical group understood of the issues involved, they took out a large advertisement in the *Jewish Press* that week "commending" the Senate Armed Service Committee for its vote, and taking credit for this historic development. "All the roshei yeshivah were crying, and [they] were rejoicing," Rabbi Sherer commented acidly in his aide-mémoire.

the divinity schools were being used to evade the draft. He went so far as to charge that the quality of the clergy was being diluted by the fact that divinity students were not moved by a pure religious calling but had ulterior movements for entering divinity school.

Tarr's sharp remarks provided another example of how particular sharp or harsh statements tend to harm the one uttering them more than the target. Rabbi Sherer was the main draftsman of the interfaith committee's memorandum for the House-Senate conference. Rather than undertake the difficult task of explaining the necessity of the traditional exemption, the memorandum focused on the impropriety of Tarr's remarks. It argued that Tarr's call for an end to any exemption for divinity students should be seen as a denial of the traditional importance the nation's founders had attached to the clergy, and a strengthening of the forces of secularism. Furthermore, by questioning the commitment of divinity students and reflecting on the diminished quality of the clergy, Tarr had opened the door for a dangerous and even unconstitutional intervention of the government in the affairs of different religions. To nip such trends in the bud, argued the memorandum, the traditional exemption must be retained.

The qualified support of the interfaith committee for a joint effort to persuade the House-Senate conference to adopt the House language on divinity student exemptions proved inadequate. That battle too was ultimately lost. The leading members of the Yeshivah Emergency Committee — Rabbi Sherer, Rabbi Neuberger, Rabbi Labkovsky, and Rabbi Weisberg — informed the roshei yeshivah in a July 20 meeting at the home of Rabbi Moshe Feinstein[14] that the battle over the draft exemption was over and the Senate version would prevail in conference. They received authorization at that meeting to keep the interfaith coalition together for future negotiations with Curtis Tarr over the Selective Service regulations pursuant to the newly enacted statute.

Victory

DESPITE THE FAILURE TO PRESERVE THE TRADITIONAL EXEMPTION, the legislative battle must be scored a decisive success overall. Had the legislation originally proposed by the Nixon administration passed, thousands of yeshivah students would have found themselves subject to the draft. Even though the traditional per-

---

14. Present at the meeting were Rabbi Moshe Feinstein, Rabbi Boruch Sorotzkin, Rabbi Yaakov Yitzchak Ruderman, Rabbi Gedaliah Schorr, and Rabbi Yosef Harari-Raful.

manent exemption for those who remained in divinity school until 26 was not retained, as a practical matter there was little chance of any 26-year-old being drafted, except in the event of a war on the scale of World War II. By that age, they would enter the lowest classification category employed by the Selective Service. The chief counsel of the SASC had made this point to Rabbi Savitz, and it was confirmed in subsequent meetings with the leading experts on the military draft.

One final threat, however, remained: the Selective Service regulations under the new legislation. In the initial regulations promulgated for comment, Curtis Tarr proposed that divinity students would have to sign up for a predetermined number of years at the outset of their studies and demonstrate that they were making proportionate progress every year. In addition, the new regulations eliminated any provision for graduate study after obtaining ordination — i.e., *semichah*, in the case of rabbinical students. Those regulations were obviously inimical to *kollelim*. This time, fortunately, complete unity prevailed at the November 16 meeting of the interfaith committee. Rabbi Sherer secured the full agreement of George Reed, chief counsel of the Catholic Conference, to oppose the new regulations. All the other groups at the meeting — Methodists, Baptists, Evangelicals — fully concurred. Thus, the religious groups were able to present a united front at the next days meeting with Tarr.

When the final regulations appeared, the exemption for those in a "full-time graduate program" had been restored. In addition, there was no mention of limitations on the length of the course to be pursued or the need to demonstrate "proportionate" progress. All that was required was "satisfactory progress in these studies as required by the school in which the registrant is enrolled." At the top of his copy of the regulations, Rabbi Sherer wrote two words: *Baruch Hashem*!

As a consequence of the battle over the draft, and particularly the decision to wage an all-out battle in the House, it is almost certain that not a single yeshivah student was drafted involuntarily into the army prior to the United States moving to a volunteer army in 1973.[15]

---

15. Even though the draft issue was rendered moot by the move to a volunteer army, Rabbi Sherer considered the investiture of his energies to have been fully justified, even in retrospect. He felt that the preservation of the draft exemption for divinity students also had significant implications for the preservation of the yeshivah student deferment in Israel.

Protecting the Esrogim

Quarantine!

A CASUAL READER OF THE NEW FEDERAL REGULATIONS PUBLISHED in the Federal Registrar of April 23, 1968 might have failed to notice anything of great import to observant Jews. Yet nestled away among the hundreds of pages of regulations promulgated that day was one issued by the Plant Quarantine Division of the Department of Agriculture dealing with the dreaded Mediterranean fruit fly and steps needed to prevent its entry into the United States. That regulation carried within it the potential to prevent hundreds of thousands of American Jews from fulfilling the Biblical command of the Four Species.

The Mediterranean fruit fly inhabits citrus fruits. Among the citrus fruits imported to the United States is the citron, or, as it is better known to Jews, the *esrog*. In the past, the Department of Agriculture had permitted *esrogim* to be imported to northern states, in which no citrus plants are grown, on the theory that the Mediterranean fruit fly could pose no danger where there were no citrus plants. Now, however, the Department had become aware that not all *esrogim* are consumed at their point of entry to the United States, and determined that more strenuous protections were needed. The new regulations therefore required fumigation with ethylene dibromide of all imported citrons.

The problem, as Rabbi Sherer pointed out in a June 13 Memorandum he prepared for officials in the Department of Agriculture, is that the fumigation might well render the *esrogim*, which possess a notoriously sensitive skin, *pasul* (unfit) for performance of the mitzvah. Moreover, there was no possibility of determining whether that would be the case. The Department of Agriculture had proposed preliminary testing of the fumigation, but that was impossible because *esrogim* grown in Israel do not ripen until late July, and must be shipped by late August to be in the United States in time for Succos. That did not allow enough time to determine the effect of ethylene dibromide or to test alternative fumigants. Treatment by extreme cold, the other method mentioned by the director of the Plant Quarantine Division, was also known to be injurious to *esrogim*.

Rabbi Sherer knew that there was no point in relying on the sympathy of Department of Agriculture bureaucrats to the religious requirements of observant Jews. The mandate of the department was to protect the American citrus industry from potential devastation by the Mediterranean fruit fly, not to ensure that observant Jews had access to *esrogim* for Succos. He would have to come up with a solution that would be fully responsive to the concerns of the bureaucrats of the Plant Quarantine Division before he could appeal to America's "time-honored tradition of religious freedom."

Rabbi Sherer's proposal, contained in the June 13 Memorandum, was for the *esrogim* grown in Israel to be quarantined for five days after cutting in warehouses far removed from the orchards in which they were grown. After five days, they would be inspected by the Israeli Agriculture Department. Because the presence of the Mediterranean fruit fly renders the fruit unfit for ritual use, and would be easily ascertainable to the trained eye, there could be no doubt that the proposed inspection would be adequate. In addition, the Israeli Agriculture Department agreed to sponsor an inspector from the Division of Plant Quarantine to come to Israel to supervise the inspection, packing, and shipping procedures. Rabbi Sherer emphasized that the plan would be temporary since there would be adequate time before the next year to test the effect of various types of fumigants on the *esrogim*.

With the memorandum in place, Rabbi Sherer called upon Senator Jacob Javits (as he did so many times over the years) to use his influence to arrange a meeting with the appropriate Agriculture Department officials and to attend himself so as to emphasize the importance of the issue. Two days later, Senator Javits sent a telegram that he had arranged a meeting for Rabbi Sherer with Dr. Ned Bayley, an assis-

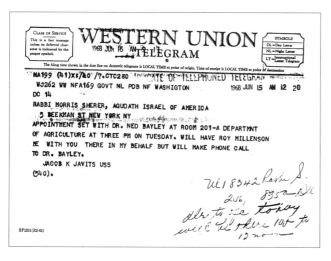

Senator Javits arranges an appointment with Dr. Ned Bayley, Assistant Secretary, Dept. of Agriculture

tant secretary in charge of scientific matters, for the first week of July. Though he could not personally attend, he promised Rabbi Sherer that his top aide Roy Millenson would be present, and the Department of Agriculture would fully understand the importance of the matter to Senator Javits.

At that meeting, Rabbi Sherer's proposal was accepted by Dr. Bayley in toto, and on July 30, 1968, Israel's Ethrog Center and the United States Department of Agriculture entered into a formal agreement, in which the former committed to covering the enumerated expenses in connection with bringing an inspector from the Division of Plant Quarantine to Israel and to deposit in escrow $4,000. With that agreement, the ability of Jews to observe the mitzvah of the Four Species was assured for 1968.

Rabbi Sherer did not, however, stop there. He feared that the one-year solution would not be allowed to remain in place indefinitely, and also wanted to avoid the higher cost to the consumer of *esrogim* entailed by the payment for a United States government official to spend several weeks in Israel.

To that end, he arranged a series of meetings between officials of the Israeli Department of Agriculture and those from the Division of Plant Quarantine. On May 6 1969, he received a phone call from Chaim Ouziel, the economic attaché at the Israeli Embassy in Washington, D.C., informing him that the Department of Agriculture had agreed to rely on the inspection of the Israeli Ministry of Agriculture, without any U.S. inspector being present. Ouziel thanked Rabbi Sherer for arranging the crucial meetings. The system put in place at that time has remained in place ever since.

THE HIJACKING OF RABBI HUTNER

SEPTEMBER 1970 IS REMEMBERED BY MOST OF THE WORLD AS Black September, the month that Jordan's King Hussein finally confronted the PLO, which had established itself as a semi-independent government within Jordan. The Torah world, however, remembers Sunday, September 6 for the hijacking of TWA Flight 741 from Tel Aviv to New York via Frankfurt. On board that flight were Rabbi Yitzchak Hutner, Rosh Yeshivas Chaim Berlin, Rebbetzin Hutner; Rabbi Hutner's son-in-law, Rabbi Yonoson

Life Stops

Time magazine, September 21, 1970

David; and his daughter, Rebbetzin David. Also on board were two of the major figures in the Syrian community of Flatbush: Chacham Yosef Harari-Raful and his brother Chacham Avraham Harari-Raful.

The TWA flight was one of four hijackings carried out that day over the skies of Europe by George Habash's Popular Front for the Liberation of Palestine (PFLP). Hijackers also took over Swissair, Pan Am, and El Al airliners.[16] Three days later, the PFLP also successfully hijacked a British Airways (then BOAC) airliner. The TWA, Swissair, and BOAC planes were all flown to Dawson Field, a dusty, isolated airfield in the Jordanian desert, with a baked-sand runway.

Word that Rabbi Hutner's plane had been hijacked spread rapidly throughout the Torah world. Even before the destination of the plane was known, the State Department had already cabled its legations in

---

16. Only the El Al hijacking was foiled by the quick-thinking pilot. He plunged the plane into a steep descent, which knocked the hijackers off their feet. The male hijacker was killed by El Al security guards, and the female hijacker, Leila Khaled, subdued, albeit not before she released a grenade from which the pin had been pulled. Miraculously, the grenade did not detonate.

With Rabbi Yitzchak Hutner

whatever cities the plane might land: "Among the passengers ... is Rabbi Isaac Hutner ... highly respected, elderly and ailing .... Insure to the extent possible, he is accorded appropriate treatment." President Richard Nixon was told that "one of the senior American rabbis is on board."[17]

A central command was immediately set up at Yeshivas Chaim Berlin, and another working group began to form in Washington D.C. One of the first things done by the group assembled at Chaim Berlin, under the direction of Avrohom Fruchthandler, was to call Rabbi Sherer. Only his daughter Elky was home. Her parents were on their annual summer vacation, and had told no one where they would be vacationing.[18]

Elky, however, had watched her parents planning the vacation using the American Automobile Association (AAA) travel guide, and she knew that they were likely somewhere in Connecticut, and probably in the Essex-Niantic area. She convinced AAA to give her a list of all the motels and hotels in the area, and began calling them one by one. Eventually she located her parents. Rabbi Sherer immediately began

---

17. David Raab, *Terror in Black September*, p. 54. Raab, together with his mother and four siblings, was a passenger on TWA Flight 741. He spent the entire three weeks in captivity together with the leading members of the Chaim Berlin community. The son of an Orthodox rabbi and day-school principal in Trenton, New Jersey, Rabb was 17 at the time of the hijacking.

18. From that time on, at least one child was always left with their contact information in case of emergency.

calling some of his key Washington contacts from his motel room, while Mrs. Sherer packed.[19] They then rushed back to Brooklyn.

The next three weeks were among the busiest of Rabbi Sherer's life, and for that reason among the most poorly documented. No matter how busy he was, he always carefully recorded and documented his activities, but, in this case, that proved impossible. He wrote in an aide-mémoire entitled "The Last Page of An Unwritten Diary: Operation Hostages":

> Life changed for me on Sunday, September 6th, when the TWA plane was hijacked and its passengers became hostages of the Arab guerrillas. What unfolded that afternoon was like a nightmare that lasted three weeks. All of my regular activities stopped, and working closely with a small team from Chaim Berlin, we literally worked around the clock for three full weeks, including Shabbosim, trying to devise many rescue schemes, at the same time that we sought to pressure various governments to act in accordance with the enormity of the problem. Because of the complexity of these activities and the immense amount to detailed work and overseas contacts involved (the Agudah's overseas phone bill for that period alone amounted to about $3,000), I could not keep a diary of the fast-moving events.

To describe the situation as complex does not begin to do it justice. Connections had to be established to the White House and the State Department, where Secretary of State William Rogers immediately set up a special Working Group to deal with the hostage situation. Lists of the hostages had to be compiled, and a determination made as to their nationalities and religion. Efforts had to be made on behalf of Rabbi Hutner's party and the numerous other observant passengers to get them kosher food via the Red Cross.[20] Pressure had to be brought on Britain, Germany, and Switzerland, all of whom had nationals taken hostage, not to strike separate deals with the hijackers that would increase the vulnerability of the remaining hostages. And a line of com-

---

19. Shortly after the hijacking, Elky met her husband, Moshe Yaakov (Robert) Goldschmidt, and became engaged. Rabbi Sherer always told her that her engagement was her reward for her efforts to locate him during the *peduyim shevu'im* (redemption of hostages) crisis.

20. Though no kosher food ever reached the hostages, extensive efforts were made in this regard. A list of the names of 14 observant Jews submitted to the Vatican was found in the Agudath Israel files. At one point, a U.S. consular official walked over the Allenby Bridge from Israel to Jordan hoping to find someone on the other side who would transmit kosher canned goods for Rabbi Hutner via the Jordanian Red Crescent. He was unsuccessful, and the observant Jews had to make due with the few foods available that did not pose kashrus issues. Raab, op. cit., pp. 161-62.

munication had to be established to the government of Israel, whose negotiating position would be a key factor. All the threads of information gleaned from various contacts had to be combined and analyzed.[21]

As the Orthodox leader with the widest web of connections, both nationally and internationally, Rabbi Sherer had a crucial role to play in all these various strands of action. Through Rabbi Menachem Porush, he kept constantly updated on the thinking of the Israeli government. And through his contacts in Europe, chiefly Aba Dunner of the British Agudah, he attempted to maintain pressure on European governments. With Dunner, he discussed organizing a committee of top religious leaders, including Chief Rabbi Immanuel Jakobovits and the Archbishop of Canterbury, to request the president of the International Red Cross to seek the immediate release of hostages over 60 (which would have included Rabbi Hutner) and under 18. They also discussed organizing influential British Jews and all the yeshivos to pressure the British government not to make any separate deals.

Protecting the Jewish Passengers

FROM THE BEGINNING, THE HIJACKERS SHOWED PARTICULAR interest in Jewish and Israeli passengers. Two days after the hijacking, six passengers on the TWA plane were taken away by the hijackers: three Orthodox Jews and three United States Defense Department and State Department employees. In that group were Rabbi Avraham Harari-Raful and Rabbi Yosef Harari-Raful, both of whom held Israeli, as well as American, citizenship.

At the end of the first week, the hijackers released a group of passengers from the TWA plane for "humanitarian reasons." But none of

---

21. As if all the complications of the hijacking of four planes were not enough, much of the hostage crisis was played out in the midst of a civil war in Jordan, which had the potential to explode any moment into a confrontation between the United States and the Soviet Union. King Hussein of Jordan was humiliated by the hijackers' use of the desert airstrip for their own purposes, without any prior consultation. The hijacking was, in many respects, the final straw that convinced him that he had no choice but to uproot the PLO from Jordan, as his generals and advisers had long been urging. The Palestinian strongholds and refugee camps in which the last 54 hostages, including Rabbi Hutner, were held came under both artillery fire and aerial bombardment in the course of that fighting.

Meanwhile two carrier groups from the U.S. Sixth Fleet took up positions off the coast of Lebanon, where they were soon joined by dozens of Soviet battleships. Syria, at the Soviets' prodding, invaded Jordan on the side of the PLO. Israel transmitted a warning to the Syrians that it was prepared to send its air force into the fray to protect Jordan's territorial integrity. As a result, Syria never introduced its air force into the battle, which allowed Jordanian planes to stop the advance of Syrian tanks.

the approximately 80 Jews, including children and the elderly, were among those released. A second group of 10 hostages was then separated from the rest and taken to a separate hiding place. Of that group, nine were Jewish, including Rabbi Yonoson David. Even after most of the women and children from the TWA flight were released, a group of five American Jewish women, including Rebbetzin David, were taken away to be held separately.

It was crucial to the safe return of all the identifiably Jewish passengers on board the TWA plane that the British, Swiss, and German governments not negotiate separate deals for their nationals and planes by agreeing to release the Palestinian terrorists then in their jails. Were such a deal to be struck, the pressure on Israel to release hundreds of *fedayeen* held in Israeli jails in return for the release of the remaining Jewish and American hostages would increase dramatically.

But Israel had little inclination to release Palestinian terrorists. First, there were no pure Israeli nationals — i.e., holding exclusively Israeli citizenship — among the hostages. Second, if taking Jewish hostages proved successful, the already great threat of hijacking to any flight to or from Israel would rise sharply. And Israel might find itself cut off from civilian aviation.

From the start, both the Swiss and German governments agreed in theory to strike separate deals with the PFLP. Only strong American pressure prevented them from doing so. By September 23, Shelby Davis, the United States ambassador to Switzerland — where the discussions between the United States, Britain, Switzerland, Germany, and (sometimes) Israel were taking place in Bern — concluded that the Europeans were prepared to act to get their nationals out and leave the American Jewish captives to their fate.[22] The British, Germans, and Swiss were stepping up their pressure on Israel to commit, at least theoretically, to releasing terrorists, even in the absence of any formal demands from the PFLP or the receipt from the PFLP of a list of the Israeli nationals it claimed to be holding.

In addition to its support for a united negotiating position among the nations whose citizens were being held, it was also crucial that the United States make no distinctions between dual nationals and those holding exclusively American citizenship, and that it allow no distinction between Jewish and non-Jewish American citizens. In the latter

---

22. Raab, op. cit., p. 202.

respect, a number of careless statements by State Department spokesman Robert McCloskey raised concerns. At a September 9 news conference, McCloskey was asked how the United States would respond if the guerillas were to offer a deal based on distinctions between gentile and Jewish American citizens. Rather than answering forthrightly that the United States would never countenance any such distinction, McCloskey responded that hypothetical questions are difficult to answer, and expressed his hope that such a thing would never happen.[23]

In a September 14 press conference, McCloskey made a potentially disastrous mistake, when he stated that among the hostages were 23 American citizens and 19 others holding possible dual American-Israeli citizenship. He based himself on information from the International Committee of the Red Cross (ICRC), which believed that any Jew who visited Israel automatically became an Israeli citizen. That position was virtually identical to that of the Palestinian hijackers, who viewed all Jews of military age — i.e., between 16 and 35 — as de facto Israeli citizens.[24]

The classification of American Jews as Israeli nationals clearly increased the danger to them. For one thing, it encouraged the hijackers to up the demands on Israel, which was little inclined to accede to those demands. Nathan Lewin, who had held a senior position in the State Department until a few years earlier, pushed McCloskey hard to correct his erroneous statement as to the status of the hostages. And a volunteer lawyers group that Lewin assembled quickly went to work debriefing the first American hostages released from the TWA flight after their return to the United States. On the basis of that debriefing, it was possible to thoroughly refute the claim that there might be as many as 19 dual nationals among the American hostages. A memo dated September 14, which had undoubtedly been transmitted to the State Department, was found in Agudath Israel's files. It concluded:

> [Of thirty-two of thirty-nine hostages with American addresses] none ... is currently an Israeli citizen. Only three of thirty-two, who had been residents of Israel at one time, might under Israeli law be considered Israeli citizens, but these three persons had subsequently become naturalized in the United States and thus

---

23. A written transcript of this exchange was found in the files of Agudath Israel of America.
24. Raab, op. cit., p. 86.

renounced their Israeli citizenship.

Of the five women being kept as hostages, four were born in the United States and are full American citizens, who had never at any time taken up residence in any [other] part of the world. The fifth woman was born in Sudan, was naturalized in the United States in 1964 as a citizen, and was now returning from her very first trip to Israel as a tourist.

The other seven were from various far-flung parts of the United States, and were unlikely by names or addresses to be Israeli or even Jewish.

The United States government was from the very beginning extremely solicitous of the fate of the Jewish hostages. Rabbi Ahron Schechter, the senior Chaim Berlin rosh yeshivah; Rabbi Reuven Savitz, a *musmach* of Chaim Berlin; and Nathan Lewin met with Secretary of State William Rogers on Monday, September 7, one day after the hijacking, even though it was Labor Day weekend.[25] There was a continual back-and-forth between the Orthodox parties and the State Department working desk on the hostages. For instance, toward the end of the first week, someone in Chaim Berlin received a report, supposedly from Lebanese radio, that an elderly rabbi among the hostages had suffered a heart attack. That led to a quick dialogue with the State Department to ascertain whether they could confirm or deny that report.[26]

The American position remained firm throughout the hostage crisis on the need for a united negotiating front between all the nations whose citizens were held captive. Nor is there any evidence that the United

Decades later, Rabbi Sherer with Rabbi Ahron Schechter at the *siyum Sefer Torah* in Rabbi Sherer's honor

---
25. That meeting was arranged by Lewin, who had excellent connections in the State Department, from his time there in a senior position.
26. Rabbi Reuven Savitz.

States ever contemplated making any distinction between its citizens on the basis of religion or dual nationality. A little less than three months before the hijackings, Rabbi Sherer met with Yitzchak Rabin, Israel's ambassador to the United States. At that meeting, Rabin expressed his opinion that President Nixon, for whom only 8 percent of American Jews had voted, would be more supportive of Israel than President Kennedy had been. That prediction was fully borne out during the hostage crisis. President Nixon and his administration remained stalwart. Secretary of State William Rogers told Israeli Prime Minister Golda Meir at a September 18 meeting in Washington, D.C. that there should be no deal without a release of all prisoners and that Israel should do nothing under pressure, including agreeing to a prisoner exchange in principle, without knowing exactly what the PFLP was demanding.[27]

On September 15, Rabbi Sherer sent President Nixon a letter commending him for having made Washington's position so clear on the two major issues. He thanked the president for "the unequivocal position that you have taken in protecting the interests of the innocent American citizens who are being kept as hostages by a terrorist group in Jordan." In particular, he commended President Nixon for his leadership in "assuring that all the free governments concerned should unite in negotiating with the terrorist hijackers, thus eliminating the possibility of seriously harmful unilateral action on the part of each individual government." He also expressed his appreciation to Nixon for "clearly indicating that our Government has not fallen into the trap of the terrorist hijackers, who attempted to hoodwink the public into believing that our American citizens, simply because they are of the Jewish faith or had paid a visit to Israel, were automatically 'dual citizens.'"

For all the frenetic activity devoted to the hostage crisis over more than three weeks, it would be hard to argue that any particular action of private individuals contributed directly to the hostages' eventual release. Ultimately, the key factor in their release was the defeat of PLO forces by the Jordanian army. On Friday, September 25, the Jordanian army discovered and freed 16 European hostages being held in one location. The next morning, President Nasser's closest confidant told the British ambassador to Cairo that all the American hostages would be released in return for seven Palestinian terrorists in European jails. Israel would not have to release anyone. The prospect of the Jordanian

---

27. Raab, op. cit.., p.163.

army's imminent discovery of the remaining hostages apparently convinced the PLO, which had taken control of the negotiations from the Palestinian side, that they would be better off settling for a goodwill gesture and freeing the remaining hostages. On Shabbos, September 26, the 32 American hostages being held in Amman were set free, without any quid pro quo.[28]

That evening both the British and American ambassadors to Cairo were informed by leading Egyptian officials that all the remaining hostages were now in control of the Egyptian agency in Amman. The next morning the Jordanian prime minister also informed the British that all hostages had been released.

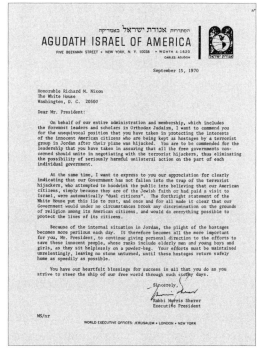

Rabbi Sherer's letter to President Nixon

Bringing Home the Harari-Raful Brothers

AMERICAN NEWS BROADCASTS ON SHABBOS REPORTED THAT ALL the American hostages, 32 in all, had been freed. Among those listening to the radio (left on before Shabbos) were Nathan Lewin and Rabbi Reuven Savitz, who had been told by Rabbi Yaakov Kamenetsky that anything to expedite the release of hostages fell into the category of *pikuach nefesh* (danger of life). Lewin quickly realized that 32 was not the total number of American hostages being held, and that still unaccounted for were the first six to be

---

28. Even though the hijackers released the 32 hostages without conditions, Britain, Germany, and Switzerland eventually released all the Palestinian terrorists in their jails. They feared that their continued presence only made it more likely that more of their citizens or planes would be hijacked in the future. Britain also whisked Leila Khaled, who had already participated in a least one prior hijacking, to Cairo, despite an extradition treaty with Israel that required her to be extradited to Israel for trial.

Rabbi Yitzchak Hutner, Rabbi Moshe Feinstein, Rabbi Yaakov Yitzchak Ruderman

removed from the plane, who were known to be held separately. He called the desk officer at the State Department to alert him to the mistake.

The last six hostages were being held in Irbid in northern Jordan, where the Palestinians were more solidly entrenched. As of the early hours of Monday morning, their release had still not been secured. At 4 a.m., the Egyptian president, Nasser, who had served as the guarantor for the release of the first 32 hostages, dropped dead. When Jerry Berkowitz, one of the last six hostages, heard from his captors the news that Nasser was dead, he thought to himself that he and his fellow captives would soon be dead as well.[29] The mourning for Nasser at the Egyptian Embassy in Amman complicated matters further, since there was no one to focus on the final six captives. Nevertheless, at midday Tuesday, an Egyptian intelligence official, who had been involved in the first release of American hostages, set out from Amman to Irbid to bring back the remaining hostages.

Not until 2 p.m. Tuesday (New York time) did the State Department confirm to Rabbi Sherer that the last six hostages were safely in Amman. He immediately conveyed the message to Rabbi Hutner, who was by then back in Brooklyn. The latter was overjoyed at the news.[30] Rosh

---

29. Raab, op. cit., p. 205.
30. Upon his return to the United States, Rabbi Hutner had specifically called Rabbi Sherer to tell

Hashanah was to begin less than 30 hours later. Everything had to fall into place for the three Orthodox hostages to make it home to New York for the holiday.

Now began the final stage of the hostage crisis, in which Rabbi Sherer and the other activists in New York and Washington, D.C., played an important role. The first key was making sure that the Harari-Raful brothers and Jerry Berkowitz got the first possible flight back to the United States. Rabbi Porush in Jerusalem had picked up a rumor that the International Committee of the Red Cross (ICRC) planned to first bring the hostages to Beirut, which would have likely made it impossible for them to arrive home before Rosh Hashanah. He called Rabbi Sherer to mount pressure on the Red Cross to take the hostages immediately to Nicosia, Cyprus instead. Rabbi Sherer told him to call Aba Dunner in England to push the Red Cross in Geneva.

Less than an hour later, Dunner called Rabbi Sherer and told him that his contacts in Geneva had told him that cables from high-level officials in Washington, D.C. would have the most influence on the Red Cross. Rabbi Sherer immediately enlisted Senator Jacob Javits and the Harari-Raful brothers' congressman in the cause. The next step was to work out with TWA the best plane to bring the hostages home. At 12:30 a.m. on Tuesday night, Rabbi Sherer was on the phone with TWA's chief of operations. He urged TWA to put the freed hostages on the first flight from Athens on Wednesday morning, which would arrive in New York by 3:30 in the afternoon on Erev Rosh Hashanah. But the president of TWA vetoed that idea, as it was the same flight, 741, that had originally been hijacked out of Frankfurt, and he feared a repeat, especially as airport security in Frankfurt remained weak. It was decided to place them on a later TWA flight from Athens. At 5:30 a.m. the next morning, Rabbi Sherer was back on the phone with TWA's chief of operations for further discussions.

The arrangements on Erev Rosh Hashanah included discussions with the Federal Aviation Administration to ensure that the TWA flight was given landing priority; gaining the agreement of the U.S. Customs Service to allow the hostages to skip customs and immigration entirely; and talks with the Lindsay administration over how they would be

---

him that the pace must not slacken until all the hostages were safely home. He also had a message that he wanted to convey to the top echelons of the Israeli government concerning his captivity, and he asked Rabbi Sherer to do so. The latter called Ambassador Rabin in Washington, D.C. to inform him, and asked Rabbi Porush in Jerusalem to pass this information on to Prime Minister Golda Meir.

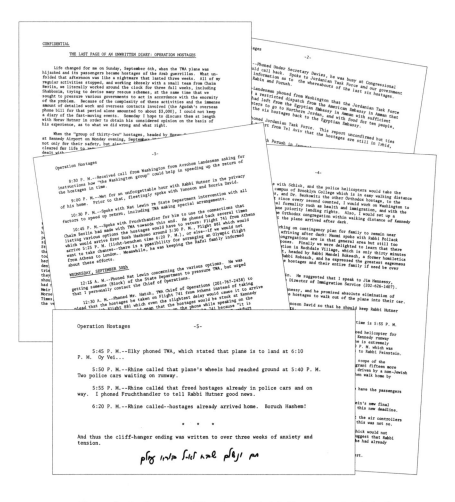

transported to their homes. The latter initially promised helicopters to take the Harari-Raful brothers to the campus of Brooklyn College, within short walking distance of their home, but later retracted the offer because of safety concerns. In the end, it was decided that they would be met by a police car on the runway.

All the while, Rabbi Sherer was receiving continual updates as to the projected landing time, especially after the plane encountered strong headwinds and had to stop for refueling in Lisbon, Portugal. When word was received that the plane would not land until 6:10 p.m., contingency arrangements were made with a shul near the airport (whose rav was a former homiletics student of Rabbi Sherer's). Meanwhile Rabbi Moshe Feinstein was consulted as to any possible halachic leniencies if the hostages could not make it to walking distance of their homes by sunset, which was 6:40 p.m.

In the end, the TWA flight touched down at 5:40 p.m. and the police car, its lights flashing, sped them through the rush hour traffic to their homes. Chacham Yosef Harari-Raful and Chacham Avraham Harari-Raful walked into their homes 40 minutes after landing, well before sunset. The bottom of Rabbi Sherer's aide-mémoire on the hectic last day and a half read in his handwriting: "תם ונשלם שבח לא-ל בורא עולם" — Finished and completed, all praise to the A-lmighty, Creator of the World."

EXECUTIVE ORDER 50[31]

A Brutal Choice

THE LEGAL BATTLE OCCASIONED BY EXECUTIVE ORDER 50 WOULD prove a defining moment for Agudath Israel of America and its president Rabbi Moshe Sherer. Almost as soon as Mayor Edward Koch moved into Gracie Mansion in 1977, he initiated a series of steps designed to end employment discrimination against people with deviant lifestyles. His first executive order as mayor, issued in 1977, barred any city governmental body from engaging in such discrimination. Three years later, the city issued Executive Order 50, which extended Executive Order 1 to the private sector by prohibiting any person or institution doing business with the city from discriminating on the basis of "sexual orientation or affectional preference." Executive Order 50 went into effect despite the City Council's repeated rejection of legislation to write the mayor's policy into law.

Despite the promulgation of Executive Order 50 in 1980, no panic buttons were pressed at Agudath Israel headquarters, because both New York City and New York State had already passed legislation specifically allowing religious institutions to make employment decisions designed to promote the religious principles for which the institutions had been formed. Agudath Israel remained confident that it was protected from Executive Order 50 by that legislation.

That confidence remained in place even when the city Bureau of

---

31. The account of Agudath Israel's response to Executive Order 50 is drawn almost entirely from Chaim Dovid Zwiebel's article "Fighting City Hall: When Gay Rights Collide With Religious Rights: Agudath Israel's Decision to Challenge New York City's Mayoral Executive Order 50," *The Jewish Observer*, March 1985, pp. 28-31 and from a speech delivered by Rabbi Zwiebel at the Melaveh Malkah at the annual Agudath Israel Convention, 15 *Kislev* 5765/December 27, 2004.

Labor Service promulgated a series of regulations to go into effect June 21, 1982 ostensibly pursuant to Executive Order 50, but in fact going far beyond anything hinted to in Executive Order 50. The new regulations not only barred any discrimination in hiring, but further required any beneficiary of city contracts to actively recruit individuals with these deviant lifestyles for employment and to undergo a compliance review before the award of any city contract.

In early 1984, it became clear that the city did not accept the premise that the hiring decisions of religious organizations were not subject to the strictures of Executive Order 50. In a highly publicized confrontation, Mayor Koch informed the Salvation Army, a Protestant relief organization, "There can be no exception to Executive Order 50." Both the Salvation Army and the New York archdiocese publicly announced that they would rather forfeit any municipal contracts rather than comply with Executive Order 50. They also girded themselves for legal battle. Meanwhile no Jewish organization, including Agudath Israel of America, had yet gone on record. *The New York Times* stressed the contrast for all to see in a June 24 editorial stating, "Orthodox Jewish groups have acquiesced in the city's policy."

Agudath Israel of America confronted a brutal choice. On the one side, it faced the loss of nearly $2 million of city funding for a host of crucial social service programs. The loss of the funding would have forced the closure of most of those programs, and the beneficiaries would have had to seek similar services from non-Orthodox agencies. And it could have been argued that there were unlikely to be adverse consequences from playing along with the city: After all, not many open deviants were ever likely to apply for jobs at Agudath Israel of America or any of its affiliates. Finally, Agudath Israel could likely have consoled itself that both the Torah's position and that of Agudath Israel itself on deviancy were sufficiently clear to the general public that there was no need to go to war with the city to clarify that position.

And, in fact, many of Agudath Israel's lay leaders counseled that it avoid a potentially expensive, even ruinous, confrontation with the city and Mayor Koch. And that position might well have prevailed had it not been for the actions of the Salvation Army and the New York archdiocese, combined with *The New York Times* editorial. Those two factors combined to create a situation, in the words of Chaim Dovid Zwiebel, that could only lead an outside observer to conclude that either the Torah did not condemn such relations, at least not to the same extent as the Christian Bible, or, alternatively, that Orthodox Jews are more willing to sacrifice their Torah values when money is at stake.

Neither view could be allowed to gain credence. Despite the costs involved, the Rabbinic leadership of Agudath Israel directed the professional staff to enter into a head-to-head battle with Mayor Koch over Executive Order 50. Agudath Israel filed suit against the city on June 24, 1984, just three days after the *Times* editorial, and three days before the deadline announced by the city beyond which no municipal contracts would be renewed with non-compliant religious institutions was to go into effect.

The next day Rabbi Sherer received a phone call from Deputy Mayor Stanley Brezenoff, with whom he enjoyed a particularly close relationship. He feared that Brezenoff was calling to tell Rabbi Sherer that their relationship was over. He did not.

Brezenoff told Rabbi Sherer, "Rabbi, we were sitting around the table when we issued this executive order, and we asked ourselves, 'Will we have any problems in the Jewish community?" We concluded: 'No, probably not. With the exception of Rabbi Sherer. He may fight us."

The deputy mayor had read his friend correctly. In a letter to *The New York Times* published on July 2, Rabbi Sherer set the record straight: "Agudath Israel, if faced with the choice between remaining faithful to religious principles and administering social service programs to the needy, will have no choice …. We would violate the trust of constituents and the religious tenets that are at the very core of our movement were we to close our eyes to a practice described by the Torah as an 'abomination.'"

AGUDATH ISRAEL, TOGETHER WITH THE SALVATION ARMY AND the archdiocese of New York, sued New York City. The case presented

Agudath Israel Sues City Hall

a fascinating constitutional issue: Did the Free Exercise rights of the plaintiffs to act in accord with their own religious beliefs entitle them to an exemption from a general government regulation that would apply to other contractors with the city? The traditional view had been that the government can place whatever conditions it wants on the benefits it provides and that the unwillingness of parties to comply with those conditions does not constitute compulsion by the governmental body in question. But as the magnitude and scope of government benefits has grown — the so-called "new property" — that doctrine has been called into question.

Still the constitutional issue was anything but clear cut. The other parties challenging Executive Order 50 did not even raise the issue, and left it to Agudath Israel to deal with it in its brief. The Salvation Army and the Catholic diocese focused only on the question: Did the mayor of New York have the power to issue Executive Order 50 and the accompanying regulations? Since the executive order was indistinguishable from any piece of normal legislation, the question was whether the New York City Council had delegated such law-making authority to the mayor. Both the City Council and the New York State legislature had repeatedly rejected "gay rights" legislation, and those challenging the city accused Mayor Koch of attempting to do by executive order what the legislative branches had refused to do.

Plaintiffs prevailed at the trial court level, and Executive Order 50 was struck down. But the trial court decision was reversed by the appellate court. Plaintiffs then announced their intention to appeal to the New York Court of Appeals, the state's highest court. At that point, Rabbi Sherer took Chaim David Zwiebel aside.[32] He did not want to indicate any lack of confidence in the conduct of the case so far. But with so much at stake he wanted to make sure that the best legal guns at Agudath Israel's disposal were all deployed. Thus he told Zwiebel that he wanted him to show the Court of Appeals brief to Nathan Lewin and to Professor Aaron Twerski for their comments.

It is doubtful that Zwiebel was in any way hurt by the request. At any major law firm, such as his former employer Paul, Weiss, Rifkind, Wharton, and Garrison, every brief in a case of such magnitude would have been reviewed by numerous lawyers, including a senior partner. Rabbi Sherer's request was certainly nothing other than a fourth-year associate would have routinely expected in such a case. Nevertheless, Rabbi Sherer went out of his way to reaffirm his confidence in Zwiebel and to assure him that he would still be the principal draftsman on the brief. (When the case was argued before the Court of Appeals, however, Professor Twerski made the oral argument.)

In late June, Zwiebel received word from the clerk of the Court of Appeals that a decision had been reached and that by a vote of 6-1 the Court of Appeals had found in favor of the parties challenging Executive Order 50. He rushed to share the good news with Rabbi

---

32. Zwiebel had only been working at Agudath Israel of America for a few months when he was thrown into the maelstrom of the legal battle over Executive Order 50.

Sherer. Rabbi Sherer wanted to savor the victory by reading the Court of Appeals decision. But in the era before fax machines and e-mails, that meant waiting for it to arrive by mail.

Rabbi Sherer had no patience for that, and put in a call to Alan Davitt, the Catholic Conference's chief lobbyist in Albany, and asked him if he could go over to the Court of Appeals and obtain a copy of the decision. An hour later, Davitt called back with the decision in hand, and began reading the opinion, though his reading was frequently interrupted by interjections from Rabbi Sherer, like *Gevaldik! Moiradik!*, that left Davitt more than a bit puzzled.

Even though the Court of Appeals never reached the constitutional issue, Zwiebel heard later from attorneys in the city legal department that when they received the briefs of the archdiocese and the Salvation Army they had not been concerned. But when they received the Agudath Israel of America brief, they started to worry.

Flush from victory in the biggest case of his legal career, Zwiebel could not resist telling Rabbi Sherer, "See, Rabbi Sherer, I told you it was a good brief." Rabbi Sherer, however, offered another explanation for the result: "What good brief? It was the *berachah* [blessing] from the Steipler."

Not until years later, while listening to a eulogy for Rabbi Sherer delivered by his son Rabbi Shimshon Sherer, would Zwiebel understand the full import of those words. Reb Shimshon related how in early June, before the Court of Appeals decision was announced, he had picked up his father at Kennedy Airport on his return from Israel. As he hugged his father and wished him *Shalom Aleichem*, the first words out of Rabbi Sherer's mouth were: "Shimshie, we won!" As his son probed to find out who had won and what they had won, Rabbi Sherer only told him, "I went to the Steipler, and he gave us a *berachah*. We won."

Rabbi Sherer's *emunah* (faith) was such that as soon as he heard the Steipler Gaon's blessing, he was confident of victory. In his mind, the *berachah* was the key to victory, and all the brilliant briefs and superb oral arguments were nothing but the necessary *hishtadlus*.

THE SECOND NEW YORK STATE *"GET LAW"*

THE 1992 NEW YORK STATE *"GET LAW"* PROVIDES ANOTHER EXAMple of Rabbi Sherer's unhesitating fealty to *gedolei Yisrael*, even when the costs were high. The 1992 legislation was the New York State legislature's second foray into the area of encouraging recalcitrant husbands to give their wives *gittin* (bills of divorce). Agudath Israel played a leading role in the passage of the first *"get* law" in 1983. That legislation required a husband seeking a civil divorce to file an affidavit that he had removed all bars to his wife's remarriage.[33]

Helping Protect Women

Passage of the 1983 *"get* law" represented a considerable triumph for Agudath Israel of America and its allies in the Orthodox world, and there is evidence that the law played a role in convincing hundreds of husbands to grant *gittin*.[34] In securing passage of the law, all Orthodox groups had signed off on the principle laid down by Rabbi Moshe Feinstein, then head of the Moetzes Gedolei HaTorah, that any legislation with a direct impact upon *halachah* must enjoy a broad consensus of support from all segments of the Torah community.

Despite the benefits of the 1983 law, its utility was limited to a relatively small range of cases — i.e., those in which it was the husband who sought a civil divorce. In 1992, a New York State lower court ruled in a civil divorce proceeding that a woman's inability to remarry because her husband refused to give a *get* could be taken into consideration in making an equitable distribution of the marital property, under a catch-all legislative directive that allowed trial court judges to take into account any factor they found to be "just and proper."

Legislation was introduced in the State legislature to codify that state court decision. While the bill provided a powerful tool to force recalcitrant husbands to give *gittin*, it raised potential halachic issues not present in the 1983 *"get* law."

Somehow wires were crossed and the legislation was introduced before Agudath Israel had obtained an opinion from the leading halachic authorities in Israel about the propriety of the law. Agudath Israel thus found itself caught by surprise when the bill was passed, while it

---

33. See Chapter 18, pp. 455-458. This section draws almost entirely from Chaim Dovid Zwiebel's article, "Tragedy Compounded," *The Jewish Observer*, September 1993, pp. 26-39.
34. Ibid., p. 31.

Consulting with Rabbi Shlomo Zalman Auerbach

was still waiting for an opinion on its halachic propriety.[35]

Even more problematic, when the opinion of the leading halachic authorities arrived, it was negative. Rabbi Yosef Shalom Elyashiv and the late Rabbi Shlomo Zalman Auerbach of Jerusalem concurred that the bill raised serious halachic problems of a *get meusah* (a coerced get). A *get* issued under improper coercion is invalid, and if a woman remarries pursuant to such a *get*, any subsequent children would be under a cloud of *mamzeres* (illegitimacy).

Based on the opinions of Rabbis Auerbach and Elyashiv, the Moetzes Gedolei HaTorah directed Agudath Israel to request the bill's sponsor to introduce a new bill to cure the problems with that just enacted. In effect, he was asked to introduce a bill diametrically opposite to that just passed. Instead of codifying the decision of the New York State Supreme Court (a lower court in New York), the new bill would specify that failure to issue a *get* cannot be taken into consideration by a court when making its equitable distribution of marital property.[36]

Thus the directive of the Moetzes Gedolei HaTorah placed Agudath Israel at complete loggerheads with most important friends in the New York State legislature. To make matters worse, the bill's lead sponsor had consulted with a rabbinic authority prior to introducing the legislation; thus he had acted in good faith.

---
35. Ibid., p. 35 fn. 7.
36. Ibid., p. 38 fn. 8.

Rabbi Sherer realized immediately that Agudath Israel had no choice but to seek repeal of the 1992 "*get* law" once the leading halachic authorities in the world had determined, after twice considering the matter at length, that the law had the potential to cause grave damage.

The second "*get* law" also placed Agudath Israel at loggerheads with what had been its primary outlet for news stories until then. *Jewish Press* publisher Rabbi Shalom Klass was the strongest advocate of the new "*get* law." After Agudath Israel took the opposite side, it became a virtual non-organization as far as the *Jewish Press* was concerned. In addition, Agudath Israel's stance came with a heavy public relations cost for the organization. The plight of the *agunah* (literally, a chained woman), a woman unable to remarry because of her husband's refusal to give a *get*, had attracted considerable attention in recent years. Any initiative that purports to provide a solution to the problem inevitably gains wide public support, even within a wide swath of the Orthodox world and even when the proposed solutions are halachically problematic. Indeed, the Rabbinical Council of America endorsed the 1992 "*get* law," on the grounds that individual *batei din* would be able to determine whether a *get* was given as a consequence of improper coercion.

The risk of alienating important allies and the adverse publicity were, however, a necessary price to be paid for total subservience to the guidance of the *gedolei Torah* — and a welcome price, at that.

THE CROWN HEIGHTS RIOTS

IF EVER URBAN-DWELLING ORTHODOX JEWS NEEDED A DEFENDER whose influence reached to high places, it was the Crown Heights community of Brooklyn during and in the aftermath of four days of pogromlike black rioting beginning August 19, 1991. Those riots traumatized not only the Jews of Crown Heights but those of every other Jewish neighborhood in New York City.

Champion of the Urban Jews

New York city police stood by passively, even after Yankel Rosenbaum, an Australian scholar in America doing research for his doctorate in Jewish history, was stabbed to death. For three days and nights angry black mobs controlled the streets of Crown Heights, while Jews cowered in their homes.

At the time of the Crown Heights riots, Rabbi Sherer already had a quarter-century of experience as one of the leading spokesmen on behalf of the city's Jewish population. He describes in an aide-mémoire a September 17, 1968 meeting at City Hall with leading representatives of the Lindsay administration. At that meeting, Rabbi Sherer demanded that the Lindsay administration put an end to the daily "beatings of innocent people by black terrorists" in Williamsburg and Crown Heights.

When Deputy Mayor Robert Sweet interjected that blacks also view themselves as victims, and suggested increased dialogue between the black and Jewish communities, Rabbi Sherer would have none of it. The mayor should not think he could salve his conscience with a little dialogue, Rabbi Sherer warned. Rather he needed to use his pull with black leaders to end the violence.

Following that meeting, Rabbi Sherer wrote to David Love, another Lindsay aide who had been present, the "blame is placed squarely on the mayor" for not taking more vigorous steps to use his influence with the black community to stop the wave of "terrorism" against urban Jews and for "coddling extremist black elements, who consider this mood of permissiveness as a license to act without restraint."

Two days later, on September 19, another meeting was held at City Hall, with representatives of a number of mainstream Jewish groups and the Urban Coalition, a city agency charged with finding jobs for black workers, also present. When a leader of one of the mainstream Jewish organizations called for increased efforts by Jewish organizations to help blacks, Rabbi Sherer responded that the primary concern of his constituents was bringing a halt to violence against Jews. Matters came to a head when Samuel Haber, one of the mainstream leaders, accused Rabbi Sherer of basing his depiction of black attacks on Jews on unfounded rumors. Arthur Jacobs, publisher of the *Morgen Journal*, replied that Haber could only speak like that because he and everyone else he knew lived in affluent Westchester County and had lost all contact with urban Jews.

The same divisions between Jewish organizations on display during the Lindsay administration remained in place at the time of the Crown Heights riots.[37]

---

[37]. Another issue that set Agudath Israel apart from some mainstream Jewish organizations was affirmative action. Rabbi Sherer consistently fought against any breach in the merit principle. Though New York State Merit Scholarships for college studies might not at first glance have seemed a major issue for the constituency of Agudath Israel, Rabbi Sherer worked hard and successfully to defeat a 1973 bill that would have required one Merit Scholarship per 40 students in a graduating

A Modern-Day Pogrom

THE RIOTS WERE TRIGGERED WHEN ONE OF THE CARS IN A police-escorted motorcade of the Lubavitcher Rebbe fell behind and while attempting to catch up was involved in a traffic accident. After being struck from the side, the car jumped a curb and hit a 6-year-old West Indian black child named Gavin Cato and his 7-year-old cousin. Two Hatzolah ambulances quickly arrived at the scene and administered treatment to the injured, until police instructed one of the Hatzolah ambulance drivers to take away the driver of the car for his own safety. Gavin Cato was declared dead on arrival at hospital. At his funeral, professional race huckster Al Sharpton worked up the crowd against "diamond dealers" and apartheid ambulance services (i.e., Hatzolah).

Rioting broke out almost immediately after the funeral, with chants of "Let's go to Kingston Avenue and get a Jew." Within a few hours of the tragic accident, a mob had surrounded Yankel Rosenbaum, who stood out by virtue of his 6'5" height, and he was stabbed a number of times. At the hospital, Rosenbaum, who was still fully lucid, identified his assailant, Lemrick Nelson, to police.

As news of the rioting spread, Rabbi Sherer immediately got on the phone with Abe Biderman, who by virtue of a series of senior positions in the previous administration had excellent connections in City Hall. Biderman had relatives living in Crown Heights and he was getting eyewitness accounts of the events there. Over the next four days, Rabbi Sherer and Biderman would speak on the phone at least 10 times a day, as each worked his connections in City Hall, and at the state and federal level.

The initial police response to the rioting was to do little. A subsequent investigation by Richard Gigenti, the New York State Director of Criminal Justice, concluded, "Many police officers, while being pelted with rocks and bottles, were told by their immediate superiors to hold the line. They were told to take no action unless given orders. Residents of the area watched as police officers stood passive in the

---

high-school class rather than allocating them on a district or county basis. He told Stanley Steingut, then the minority leader in the State Assembly, that there could be "no compromise [because] we must always oppose any quota system that goes against the merit system that has been responsible for Jewish achievement in this country." Upper middle-class Jews, whose children could afford to pay full tuition and would likely attend private colleges and universities, could afford to be "liberal" about such scholarships. That was not an option for poorer, mostly city-dwelling Jews, for whom Merit Scholarships were crucial, and Rabbi Sherer was their defender.

A police car overturned by rioters

face of lawlessness. They heard superior officers restrain those under their command." Mayor David Dinkins, New York City's first black mayor, and his police commissioner Lee Brown gave the word, "Let them vent."[38]

Rabbi Sherer's and Abe Biderman's increasingly frantic calls to City Hall elicited no satisfactory response. Herb Block, Mayor Dinkins' Jewish liason, kept telling Biderman that there had been a problem, but things were under control, when Biderman was receiving direct reports from Crown Heights that the rioting continued unabated. Jews in the Crown Heights community did not dare leave their homes to *daven* or for any other reason. Many had their cars torched and businesses ransacked. Rabbi Sherer later reported in a letter to David Singer on a "heated exchange" he had with Deputy Mayor Milt Mollen, who held the public security portfolio in City Hall and was the senior Jewish official in the Dinkins administration. Rabbi Sherer urged him "in the strongest terms imaginable" to put an end to the "pogrom atmosphere" and stop the rioting, looting, and destruction. Mollen promised him that the police would become more forceful.[39]

Meanwhile Rabbi Sherer also reached out to Governor Mario Cuomo

---

38. Mayor Dinkins, an avid tennis fan, remained at Forest Hills watching the U.S. Open tournament when the rioting broke out.
39. Rabbi Sherer to David Singer, September 4, 1991.

in Albany. Mayor Dinkins first refused Governor Cuomo's offer of National Guard troops, but at some point Cuomo told Mayor Dinkins that he would have no choice but to send in the National Guard. For Dinkins, who feared angering his political base in the black community with a forceful response to the rioting, bringing in the National Guard was the worst of all possible situations. Finally on August 22, the fourth day of rioting, 1,800 police, including mounted and motorcycle units were dispatched to the scene, and the rioting was brought under control.[40]

While the Agudath Israel offices had the air of a crisis control center, the attitude of the mainstream Jewish organizations was very much the same as it had been during the meetings with Lindsay administration officials a quarter-century earlier. The leaders of those organizations felt little identity with the *Chassidim* under siege and no sense of urgency in coming to their rescue. They viewed the events in Crown Heights as if they were taking place on a distant planet to members of some exotic sect. Abe Rosenthal, the former executive editor of *The New York Times*, would later pillory their attitude in a withering op-ed: "Are the Hasidim a little too Jewish for them? Maybe they think only a certain kind of Jew gets beaten up. Sweethearts,

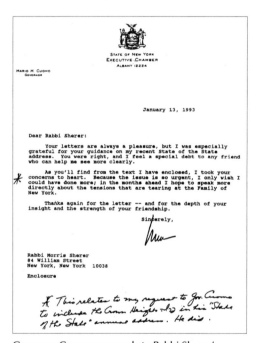

Governor Cuomo responds to Rabbi Sherer's request that he address the Crown Heights riots in his State of the State address

---

40. Rabbi Sherer never claimed that his harsh conversation with Deputy Mayor Milt Mollen or his approach to Governor Cuomo had led directly to the city's change in policy. And it is impossible to know. In such matters, a change in policy is generally a response to cumulative pressures from many directions. Both the mayor and the governor were undoubtedly receiving calls from numerous parties, and the Lubavitch community of Crown Heights was not lacking in its own political connections. Rabbi Sherer explicitly wrote to Singer, "I do not mean in the slightest to take credit for the city's shift in policy."

by you, you are Park Avenue, by your wife you are Park Avenue, but by an anti-Semite you are a Hasid."[41]

Besides the immediate issue of pressuring City Hall to take action, Rabbi Sherer was busy on a number of other fronts. As soon as the rioting broke out, he contacted Rabbi Shmuel Butman, the spokesman for the Lubavitch community. He also spoke to Joseph Katz, executive director of the Crown Heights Community Relations Council, several times to put Agudath Israel at the service of the community in any way in which it could be helpful. He also discussed with both men certain strategic points that they should be making in their own contacts with public officials and the media.

Rabbi Sherer also reached out to the media. When Agudath Israel board member Mr. Mendy Pollack was punched in the eye on a Manhattan subway by a black man who shouted, "That's for killing our children," Agudath Israel put out a press release decrying the spreading violence and arguing that the passive response of authorities to the rioting in Crown Heights would only encourage future incidents of a similar nature. Rabbi Sherer was also behind an editorial in the *Jewish Press* calling upon black leaders to distance the community from anti-Semitic rabble-rousers.

Support for the Rosenbaum Family

IN THE MIDDLE OF THE CRISIS, A FAX ARRIVED IN THE AGUDATH Israel offices from Norman Rosenbaum, the older brother of Yaakov Rosenbaum. The Rosenbaum family in Australia could barely comprehend the news that their son and brother, whom they had seen just a month earlier, had been murdered, Rosenbaum was seeking the phone number of Rabbi Chaskel Besser, to whom his brother had grown close in the course of his research on rabbinical leadership in pre-war Eastern European communities. Rather than simply respond to the fax with Rabbi Besser's phone number, Rabbi Sherer called Rosenbaum.

He gave the latter a summary of the rapidly changing events, as well as the contacts that had already been made with the Brooklyn District Attorney's office about prosecution of Yankel Rosenbaum's murderer.

---

41. Menachem Lubinsky, "Crown Heights: An Aberration? A Timely Warning? Or a Portent of Things to Come?," *The Jewish Observer*, 1993, p. 48. Abe Biderman, who had developed a friendly relationship with Rosenthal when he was in City Hall and the latter served as executive editor of *The New York Times*, consulted with Rosenthal on that July 18, 1993 op-ed.

He told Rosenbaum that Agudath Israel would be available to the Rosenbaum family whenever and in whatever capacity they desired. He emphasized that Rosenbaum should not hesitate to call him directly at any time. That conversation was the beginning of a relationship that would last until Rabbi Sherer's passing.

In October, Norman Rosenbaum traveled from Melbourne to New York. The Rosenbaum family had been told that without a family member present in the United States it would be much more difficult to pursue justice against the murderer, as well as against the hospital. The hospital had completely failed to realize the seriousness of Yankel Rosenbaum's multiple stab wounds, as a consequence of which he bled to death without receiving proper treatment.

On that trip, he met personally with Rabbi Sherer for the first time. Rabbi Sherer began, as usual, by asking Rosenbaum all about himself and about his emotional state and that of his parents. He reiterated once again Agudath Israel's desire to do whatever it could, and to stress the point, he invited Chaim Dovid Zwiebel into the meeting. After effusively singing Zwiebel's praises as a lawyer, Rabbi Sherer emphasized that those legal abilities would be at the service of the Rosenbaum family. The meeting with Zwiebel was of great interest to Rosenbaum, himself a leading Australian barrister, law professor, and former federal prosecutor.

Rabbi Sherer asked Rosenbaum what the family's goals were, and was relieved when he told him that their primary goal was that some form of *Kiddush Hashem* should emanate from his brother's murder. The family, he said, had no interest in doing anything that might adversely affect the already frayed relations between the black and Jewish communities by encouraging violence or vigilantism. Rabbi Sherer was relieved at Rosenbaum's sense of responsibility for the New York City Jewish community, which was very much in tune with the instructions he had received from the Moetzes Gedolei HaTorah. The Moetzes had opposed any demonstrations in front of Mayor Dinkins' residence, Gracie Mansion, or any calls for Dinkins' resignation or recall.[42]

Rosenbaum found Rabbi Sherer to be "the most astute person [he had] ever met." In his words, "Rabbi Sherer understood the big picture and the necessity to pay attention to every little detail. He was genuinely wise, combining intellect, experience, and maturity, which gave

---

42. Rabbi Sherer to David Singer, September 4, 1991.

him an ability to view a situation from every possible angle. And his perspective took into account the entire Jewish world."

But even more than his wisdom, Rosenbaum was struck by the fact that he "really, really cared." In the course of their relationship, Rabbi Sherer did not just wait for Rosenbaum to call him with some request, but often initiated a call, sometimes just to ask how the Rosenbaum family was holding up. He always made time for Rosenbaum on the latter's visits to New York or when he called, no matter how busy he was. Agudath Israel did not wait to be asked by the Rosenbaum family to take action on their behalf, but often took the initiative on its own.

Unfortunately, justice was very long in coming for the Rosenbaum family, and even then only partially. On October 29, 1992 a Brooklyn jury acquitted Lemrick Nelson of charges of having murdered Yankel Rosenbaum, despite the testimony of 10 police officers. Even before that acquittal, however, Chaim Dovid Zwiebel had raised the idea of prosecuting Nelson under federal civil rights statutes, in an August 12, 1992 meeting with Attorney General William Barr.[43] He followed that up with a formal request for a Justice Department investigation of the circumstances of Yankel Rosenbaum's murder the day after Nelson's acquittal on state charges.[44]

That request was followed by a November 16 call from Zwiebel to John Dunne, the head of the Civil Rights Division, in which Zwiebel urged that the investigation should not be limited to the issue of violations of Rosenbaum's civil rights, but should also include an investigation into police failures. In a follow-up letter on the subject, Zwiebel argued that a resolution of the New York City Council commending the Justice Department for launching a "comprehensive investigation" demonstrated the public interest in such an investigation.[45] Dunne, however, rejected the idea of a federal investigation over "general policy questions," involving errors in judgment, and noted that New York Governor Mario Cuomo had already appointed a blue-ribbon panel to examine the failures of the police and political echelons.[46]

But Zwiebel persisted, and eventually prevailed. He met with Attorney General Barr in Washington in January 1993, just two weeks

---

43. David Zwiebel to Attorney General William P. Barr, August 13, 1992.
44. David Zwiebel to Attorney General William P. Barr, October 30, 1992.
45. David Zwiebel to Assistant Attorney General for Civil Rights John R. Dunne, November 16, 1992.
46. Assistant Attorney General for Civil Rights John R. Dunne to David Zwiebel, November 23, 1992.

before the inauguration of a new president. In the meantime, he had found a new basis for a federal investigation of the riots: a statute making it a federal crime to interfere with law enforcement officers involved in controlling an outbreak of civil disorder, such as a riot.[47] Before leaving office, Barr wrote to U.S. Attorney Mary Jo White in the Eastern District of New York, "[Y]our investigation is not necessarily limited to the killing of Yankel Rosenbaum. Rather, you should follow the evidence wherever it leads, including any evidence that the community was deprived of its rights for discriminatory reasons." [48]

That victory, however, turned out to be short lived. Soon rumors started flying that the new Clinton administration Justice Department was not interested in pursuing the civil rights actions. Zwiebel wrote to the new Attorney General Janet Reno, July 13, 1993, urging her to take personal control of the investigation in light of the fact that the Civil Rights Division was still without a head. He was gratified when Reno announced a few days later that she would do so.

Finally, in August 1994, the Civil Rights Division announced the filing of an indictment not only against Lemrick Nelson, but also against Charles Price, who had incited the mob that surrounded Yankel Rosenbaum. Nelson was eventually convicted of having violated Yankel Rosenbaum's civil rights and was sentenced to the maximum sentence of almost 20 years in prison.[49]

An Iron Fist in a Velvet Glove

WHILE CHAIM DOVID ZWIEBEL WAS WORKING TO ENSURE THAT Yankel Rosenbaum's killer would not go scot free, Rabbi Sherer was attending to the broader communal issues growing out of the aftermath of the Crown Heights riots. Two letters that he wrote to Mayor Dinkins serve as classic examples of the diplomat's art of covering an iron fist in a velvet glove. In the first, written a month after Lemrick Nelson's acquittal in state court, Rabbi Sherer begins gently enough, with a

---

47. That description could have applied both to rioters themselves and to anyone in a position of authority who ordered police not to act forcefully to quell the riot.
48. David Zwiebel to Attorney General Janet Reno, July 13, 1993.
49. Nelson's federal conviction was overturned by the Second Circuit Court of Appeals in 2002, on the grounds that the jury had been improperly selected, and a retrial ordered. At the 2003 retrial, Nelson was convicted of violating Yankel Rosenbaum's civil rights, but acquitted on the more serious charge of having caused his death, despite his attorney's admission that he had stabbed Rosenbaum. Nelson had already served most of the 20-year sentence imposed by the trial judge, and on June 3, 2004, he was released from jail, nearly 13 years after he stabbed Yankel Rosenbaum.

An iconic image from the riots: The terror and violence were so pervasive that a *chassid* and his son huddled for protection, even with police standing by.

prayer that "we will all come through this difficult period with our capacity for mutual respect and tolerance intact." He then disassociates himself entirely from those "who have hurled epithets and offensive personal charges in your direction." "The notion that a man who has over the years demonstrated his friendship and support for the Jewish community ... is a 'Jew-hater,'" he continues, " ... would be extremely offensive if it were not so absurd."

But he then goes on to question the "soundness" of the mayor's judgment on four points. First, after the announcement of the Nelson judgment, Dinkins had stressed the sanctity of the jury system. But, Rabbi Sherer points out, after police officers in California were acquitted in the videotaped beating of Rodney King, a black man, the mayor had not hesitated to condemn the jury's decision. So why now treat the Nelson verdict as somehow sacrosanct? Second, the mayor's long delay in admitting that the Police Department made serious mistakes in its handling of the riots "had about it the aura of stonewalling." And even that admission had not been accompanied by any commitment to identify and hold accountable those responsible for the police failure.

Next Rabbi Sherer takes the mayor to task for having publicly warned of a potential backlash against the Jewish community if its members continue to harp too strenuously on the Nelson verdict or the failures of the black mayor and police commissioner. Rabbi Sherer notes that he too is aware of the danger, and has cautioned his constituents not to express their complaints in ways likely to exacerbate the conflict. But to warn publicly of such a backlash, he tells the mayor, "is almost to

Chapter Sixteen: Six Crises □ 413

invite the very reaction about which you warn. Self-fulfilling prophecies are dangerous things."

Finally, Rabbi Sherer rejects the mayor's rush to condemn the beating of a black man behind Lubavitch headquarters as a "bias crime," given that the man was carrying burglar tools in the middle of the night and had a criminal record. That, not any racial prejudice, likely explains why he was set upon. Rabbi Sherer then contrasts the mayor's quickness to label the matter a bias crime with his claim that the necessity of preserving public neutrality prevented him from condemning the mob that attacked and killed Yankel Rosenbaum.

Having delivered the stiletto, Rabbi Sherer closes with his typical politesse. The only reason he permitted himself to speak so freely, he writes, is that "I have so much respect for you as a great humanitarian, I believe I can speak to you openly and that you will understand what I have to say."[50]

On September 10, 1993, with new mayoral elections fast approaching, Rabbi Sherer wrote Mayor Dinkins another letter, in which he subtly suggested that it would be in Dinkins' best interest to support a full federal probe of those who obstructed law enforcement officials in their attempts to deal with the riots. Urging a federal prosecution under the Civil Disorders statute, he wrote, "could go a long way toward at long last healing some of the terrible wound created by the Crown Heights incident …. I see this as a potential win-win approach that should enjoy universal support" — a hint that Dinkins might be able to win back some Jewish voters by supporting more federal prosecutions.

Dinkins did not take Rabbi Sherer's advice, and in the next mayoral election, he was defeated by Rudy Giuliani, in part because of backlash from his inept handling of the Crown Heights riots. The Giuliani administration subsequently issued a formal apology to the citizens of Crown Heights for the police failure to respond adequately during the riots, bringing a measure of closure to the matter.

As a consequence of the riots, black and Jewish leaders in Crown Heights did reach out to one another and establish a number of joint communal bodies. That effort succeeded in part because of the path set by Rabbi Sherer and others at the height of the tensions: forcefully insisting on the right of Jews to live in an urban environment not

---

50. Rabbi Sherer to Mayor David N. Dinkins, December 4, 1992.

plagued by violence, on the one hand, while always maintaining a tone of respect and civility to other groups sharing that same urban setting.

The "Six Crises" described in this chapter illustrate several essential aspects of Rabbi Sherer's leadership and of the role of Agudath Israel. He was unswervingly loyal to the guidance of the *gedolei Yisrael*. His astuteness and integrity earned the respect of powerful people and institutions that one would not expect to be impressed by the principles of a relatively small religious organization. He was not fazed by the "logic" of skeptics who confidently predicted that he had not the slightest chance to succeed. And he had the courage to oppose the powerful when principle called for it. In short, his public life was a textbook for Torah activism.

Part V
AGUDATH ISRAEL

Chapter Seventeen

AN INDEPENDENT ORTHODOXY

A Painful Setback

THE 1970S BEGAN WITH A MAJOR DISAPPOINTMENT FOR Orthodox Jewry and Rabbi Sherer personally. Two major Supreme Court decisions dramatically limited the possible scope of state assistance to parochial schools or tax relief to parents of parochial-school children. In June 1971, in *Lemon v. Kurtzman*, a majority of the United States Supreme Court struck down a Rhode Island program of salary supplements for non-public school teachers and a Pennsylvania program of reimbursement of non-public-schools for teachers' salaries, textbooks, and instructional materials used in teaching specific secular subjects. Two years later, on June 25, 1973, the Supreme Court ruled in *Committee for Public Education and Religious Liberty v. Nyquist* that three types of aid to non-public schools were unconstitutional: (1) small grants to parents paying tuition at non-public schools; (2) income tax reductions for tuition-paying parents; and (3) payments to inner-city non-public schools to help maintain health and safety facilities.

That same year the court, in *Levitt v. Committee for Public Education*, also struck down a New York statute that reimbursed non-public schools for performing various services mandated by the State, including the administration, grading, and reporting of the results of state-prepared and teacher-prepared tests, as a violation of the Establishment Clause of the First Amendment.[1]

Taken together, those decisions represented the end of a nearly 13-year dream for Rabbi Sherer. Ever since his 1961 testimony before the House Education Committee, the major focus of his public activity had centered on efforts to secure some form of tax relief or school vouchers for Orthodox parents faced with the often crushing burden of providing their children with a Torah education. Rabbi Sherer played a leading role nationally in this area as the president of C.R.E.D.I.T.(Citizens Relief for EDucation through Income Tax [Credit]), a coalition of Jewish, Catholic, and other private schools representing five million non-public-school children. By the time of the Supreme Court decision in *Lemon v. Nyquist*, C.R.E.D.I.T. had already gained the support of a majority in both houses of the U.S. Congress for tax credits for parents of non-public-school children. That legislation was now a dead letter; in Rabbi Sherer's words, "a casualty of the Supreme Court decision."[2] In Rabbi Sherer's analysis of the case, the foreclo-

A C.R.E.D.I.T. brochure

---

1. The Supreme Court's chief concern seems to have been with the reimbursement of the costs associated with teacher-prepared exams. In response to the decision, New York State enacted another statute that provided for reimbursement for certain state-mandated services, excluding teacher-prepared examinations, and included a means for auditing the application of state funds. That statute was upheld in *Committee for Public Education and Religious Liberty v. Regan* (1980).
2. Rabbi Moshe Sherer, "The 'Victors' and the 'Vanquished'," *The Jewish Observer*, September 1973, p. 5.

sure of tax relief for parents of children in non-public schools was only part of the damage. By, in effect, rewriting its own previous "primary effect" test for unconstitutionality under the Constitution's Establishment Clause, to mean "'the direct and immediate effect of advancing religion' or a 'direct and substantial advancement of religion' — regardless of whether it is *primary* or not, ... [the Court had] erected a barrier which no meaningful non-public-school aid bill could ever hurdle," Rabbi Sherer wrote.³

As soon as the Supreme Court's decision was announced, Rabbi Sherer reported, "The condolence calls began ..., and they did not stop for many days. From every walk of life and every part of the world, friends and strangers phoned to console me on the loss of the U.S. Supreme Court case on non-public-school aid."⁴

Contempt for the Mainstream Leadership

NO AMOUNT OF REFRAMING COULD REMOVE THE BITTER STING of the court's 1973 decision. Rabbi Sherer could console himself that "courts change, justices are replaced, and decisions can be reversed," but nothing could hide the fact that, for the time being, all avenues of relief for overburdened parents intent on providing their children with a day-school education were dead ends.

And because Rabbi Sherer saw farther than most, his pain was greater. Consequences of the decisions that would have been of very secondary concern to the average Orthodox Jew in the street were paramount for him. One of those was the *chillul Hashem* caused by "the spectacle of 'respectable' Jewish 'spokesmen' publicly combating religious education" and the publicity mills of mainstream Jewish organizations trumpeting their great "victory" in the Supreme Court.⁵

Rabbi Sherer saw what the leaders of the American Jewish Congress did not: Their victory was a Pyrrhic one. By diminishing the potential of the yeshivos to reach beyond the hard-core Orthodox community — which would continue to provide its children with a Torah education no matter how great the financial strain — the secular leaders, wrote Rabbi Sherer, "may have lost the only hope for their own grandchildren to remain Jewish." He mourned "over the Jewish children whom we

---

3. Ibid., pp. 3-4.
4. Ibid., p. 3.
5. Ibid., p. 3.

would lose from the Jewish fold because the yeshivos were deprived of these dollars."[6]

He could scarcely contain his disdain for the secular Jewish organizations, spearheaded by the American Jewish Congress. They had embarked on the "'mission impossible' of creating Jews without Judaism" by dragging the school-aid laws into court, knowing full well that the only result would be the loss of millions of dollars for Jewish education. Their actions were that much more irksome for being accompanied by the "usual pious call" for the Jewish community to increase its support for Jewish schools, "even though this litany has not brought *one* dollar into the yeshivos' coffers." And this at a time when two-thirds of American Jewish children had no Jewish education, and less than 4 percent had any past the age of bar mitzvah.[7]

The disdain for the mainstream leadership that Rabbi Sherer expressed over the issue of school aid harkened all the way back to the failures of many of those same organizations during the Holocaust. He frequently contrasted the actions of a small band of dedicated youth led by Mike Tress to the total lack of urgency shown by the mainstream Jewish organizations. In *Bishtei Einayim* he quoted a question asked by the Klausenberger Rebbe, after the Sabra and Shatilla massacres led to the appointment of a governmental commission of inquiry in Israel: "If the killing of 300 Arabs [by other Arabs] in Lebanon justifies an investigation, is there not justification for investigating the actions of Jews over a period of time when six million [of their fellow] Jews were murdered?"[8]

All Rabbi Sherer's pent-up frustrations with the mainstream leadership came through in his review essay of Dr. Nachum Goldman's book, *The Jewish Paradox*. Goldman, the longtime head of the World Jewish Congress and the World Zionist Organization, acknowledged that Israel would not ensure the continuity of the Jewish people and that only faithful adherence to *Shulchan Aruch* had preserved the Jews as a people, yet he refused to carry those insights to their logical conclusion. He took it as axiomatic that no more than a small percentage of the Jewish people would ever again commit their lives to mitzvah observance. The only thing he could recommend to preserve Jewish identity was for Jews in all countries to ally themselves with the "pro-

---

6. Ibid. pp. 3-4.
7. Ibid., p. 6.
8. Rabbi Sherer, *Bishtei Einayim,* "A Story That Keeps Repeating Itself," p. 294.

gressive" movements in those countries.[9]

Rabbi Sherer expressed his amazement that any Jewish leader could write in such a fashion 60 years after the Bolshevik Revolution, which declared war on religion, 40 years since the Spanish Civil War, and a mere decade after so many Jews championed the civil rights movement only to be rewarded with new waves of hatred directed at them. Written in 1978, those words turned out to be prescient today, when chants of "Death to the Jews" are most likely to come from denizens of the "progressive" Left.

The low level of mainstream Jewish leadership was a subject to which Rabbi Sherer returned the same year in a piece on the opposition of Marc Tanenbaum, head of interreligious affairs for the American Jewish Committee, to legislation passed by the Israeli Knesset banning missionaries from offering any material inducement to conversion.[10] Tanenbaum had criticized Agudath Israel for pushing the legislation in the Knesset, and had accused Israel of doing to Christians what Christians had once done to Jews.

Those were fighting words for Rabbi Sherer. He recalled visiting then-Prime Minister Moshe Sharett in 1954, with a delegation from the Knessiah Gedolah headed by Rabbi Aharon Kotler. Reb Aharon had begged the prime minister to do something about missionary activity among confused and impoverished immigrants. Sharett had refused on the grounds that most of the missionaries were French and France was then Israel's closest ally. Within little more than a decade, France had become one of Israel's greatest enemies, Rabbi Sherer noted ironically, and its aid had come to a halt. But the missionaries still remain

Rabbi Sherer quoted, with amazement, Tanenbaum's comparison of the Knesset statute forbidding material inducements to convert with blood libels, autos-da-fé and the Inquisition directed at Jews. He accused Tanenbaum of a slave mentality that led him to libel his fellow Jews and accuse them of trying to harm Christians. The "modern Jew," he concluded may project a proud and free appearance, but, in reality, he is "chronically insecure, his inner eye darting about all the time in a desperate search for approval from the non-Jew, for some hint of a gentile smile."

---

9. Ibid., "The Jewish 'Paradox,'" pp. 222-226.
10. Ibid., "Servants to Themselves," pp. 258-261.

THE 13-YEAR BATTLE FOR AID FOR NON-PUBLIC SCHOOLS AND TAX relief for parents of children in those schools, over which Rabbi Sherer

Moving Ahead

broke so sharply with the mainstream Jewish organizations, was not for naught. It brought a general recognition in Orthodox circles that the Orthodox must forge their own path rather than rely on secular organizations. The core *hashkafah* of Agudath Israel "that Orthodoxy must break its shackles of domination by the secular Jewish Establishment" had been accepted by the vast majority of Orthodox organizations. As Rabbi Sherer put it, "Now everyone knows that there exists a historic Jewish community which is essentially distinctive from all others who bear the name Jews ... , and which speaks for itself."

In his final assessment of what had been gained and what lost, Rabbi Sherer was reminded of the interpretation of a great sage to the well-known *Gemara* (*Megillah* 6a): "If someone tells you 'I tried but did not find,' do not believe him." Explained the Sage, "Don't believe him because even if he did not find what he set out for, the very act of trying, of making a mighty effort, in itself is most rewarding." Applied to

American Orthodoxy, wrote Rabbi Sherer, the rewards of the struggle on behalf of Orthodox education were already evident in an emerging "independent Orthodoxy ... capable of representing its own interests in keeping with Torah precept and tradition."[11]

Rabbi Sherer took to heart Rabbi Hutner's advice that his task was "to do and not worry about accomplishments." So while he mourned the setbacks in the Supreme Court, he did not grow despondent. Instead he began looking for another way to advance the cause of an independent Orthodoxy in America. He decided to expand Agudath Israel's involvement into social services, an area that hitherto had been the exclusive province of the Jewish Federations.

Most of the Federation money, he realized, came from federal, state and local governments, and there was no reason that Agudath Israel could not apply for those same government funds to service the needs of Orthodox Jews without being dependent on the Federations.

Government funding of social services had greatly increased under the Great Society programs introduced by President Lyndon B. Johnson. Rabbi Sherer's crucial insight was that many of those programs could be utilized for the benefit of the Orthodox community. The extensive web of connections that he had built up in Washington, D.C. — in the course of lobbying for tax relief for parents of parochial-school children and other assistance to financially strapped Torah schools — would prove no less useful in the decade to come.

In steering Agudath Israel in the direction of social services for the Orthodox community, Rabbi Sherer saw himself as also making an important statement about Torah. "What can a young man think of the Torah," he explained to his staff members, "when he has to resort to the 'Liberal Jewish Establishment' to train for a career? If Torah is to be the true way of life, then the Torah community must provide the answers and the help needed at all phases of a person's life, providing solutions at every step." Rabbi Sherer termed that outlook "an ideology of activism."[12]

The Great Society programs proved in time to be the vehicle for the rapid expansion of Agudath Israel in the '70s.[13] Those programs

---

11. Ibid., p. 7.
12. Rabbi Shmuel Bloom, "Rabbi Moshe Sherer ל״צז: *Parnes Hador*," *The Jewish Observer*, Summer 1998, p. 42.
13. The first chairman of the Agudath Israel Commission on Social Services was Rabbi Sherer's close friend Louis (Leuchu) Glueck. Glueck's vice chairman and later successor as chairman was Rabbi Yitzchok Katzenstein. Rabbi Katzenstein also served as one of Rabbi Sherer's set of eyes and ears to

allowed Rabbi Sherer to bring in new young talent into the organization. Menachem Lubinsky was the first. For the two years prior to beginning full-time work for Agudath Israel, Lubinsky had been editing the *Zeirei Forum,* the publication of Zeirei Agudath Israel.

His first task at Agudath Israel was to write and edit a weekly newspaper called *Jewish Times,* which was fully subsidized by Julius Klugman, a German Jew with the passion for ideology typical of those who grew up in the German Agudah movement. Mr. Klugman and Rabbi Sherer each contributed $100 a week to Lubinsky's salary.

The first area of social services in which Agudah became involved was senior citizens' homes. Rabbi Sherer described the purpose of the new initiative in a letter to Mendy Shayovich, who became the first chairman of the Commission on Senior Citizens: "It is our intention to demonstrate that independent Orthodoxy, through Agudath Israel, can run model programs with government funds to benefit senior citizens. It will not only be a service for the elderly, but a *Kiddush Hashem*."[14]

Lubinsky wrote grant proposals for federally funded senior citizens' homes to be run by Agudath Israel in Boro Park and Washington Heights. (At one point, Agudath Israel ran five senior citizens' centers, of which three — Boro Park, Flatbush, and Washington Heights — remain open today.) Lubinsky himself became the director of the Boro Park home in 1973, with his salary paid under the terms of the grant.

There were those within the Agudah community who were wary of accepting government funding. Rabbi Sherer, however, viewed the programs as excellent training for talented young men whom he eventually hoped to bring into the offices of Agudath Israel on a full-time basis. Others criticized Rabbi Sherer for not being more aggressive in exploiting the potential of government programs. Rabbi Sherer was insistent, however, that Agudath Israel only involve itself in programs in which it could fulfill all the government requirements to the last dot. He made sure, for instance, that those drawing salaries under the terms of government grants were performing all the tasks required of them, and that there could be no question of their doing work for Agudath Israel on the government's tab.[15]

Rabbi Sherer never allowed himself to become captive to government grants. Agudath Israel once won a sizable grant to help with immigrant

---

the Washington Heights community.
14. Rabbi Sherer to Menachem Shayovich, January 16, 1974.
15. Menachem Lubinsky.

At the inauguration of the Boro Park Senior Citizens' Center
Above: Rabbi Sherer with Menachem Shayovich and Governor Carey
Left: Rabbi Sherer with New York Attorney General Louis Lefkowitz

absorption. Rabbi Sherer discovered, however, that under the terms of the grant, Agudath Israel could not limit itself to providing assistance to Russian Jewish immigrants, but would have to offer its services to other communities of immigrants as well. He decided that providing such services was too far afield from Agudath Israel's mandate and turned down the grant.

PROJECT COPE (CAREER OPPORTUNITIES AND PREPARATION FOR Employment) provides the best example of the way that government **Project COPE** programs were used by Agudath Israel to provide a training ground for promising young talent and to offer badly needed services to the community. The employment programs run by COPE represented a dramatic move of Agudath Israel into new areas in response to the developing needs of the Orthodox community.

In mid-1974, Rabbi Sherer asked staff member Joel Schnur to work together with Professor Bernard Fryshman on drafting a proposal for New York City funding of an on-the-job training program. Fryshman drafted the proposal, for which he refused to be compensated. Once the proposal was submitted in August, Rabbi Sherer met with Mayor Abe Beame, who responded positively, and then left it to Schnur to negotiate the terms of the grant with Lucille Rose, the city commissioner of employment.

In January 1975, Project COPE received a $670,000 grant from the New York City Department of Employment, as administrator of a CETA (Comprehensive Employment Training Act) grant from the Department of Labor. Under the terms of that grant, employers were reimbursed half the employees' first six months of salary while the employee received on-the-job training. The second grant was for $230,000 from the State of New York for vocational training.

The two programs were run under the auspices of Project COPE, which maintained separate offices from Agudath Israel for between 10 and 12 employees. All salaries were paid under the terms of the various government grants. Menachem Lubinsky was the director of Project Cope and ran the on-the-job training program: Rabbi Shmuel Bloom was brought in from Yeshiva Gedola of St. Louis to head the vocational training program. Their top assistants were David Seeve and Rabbi Yerachmiel Barash. Bloom, Lubinsky, and Seeve would go on to hold senior positions in Agudath Israel of America, and Rabbi Barash would head the COPE Institute.

After two years, Project COPE's on-the-job training program had the highest number of job placements of any organization in the city working under comparable grants. The first graduate of Project COPE's vocational education program was a Russian dentist, Dr. Leonid Gizunterman, who had been reduced to doing janitorial work. Project COPE paid for his retraining as a dental hygienist. While retraining, he began spending Shabbos with an Orthodox dentist, in large part as a consequence of the fact that an Orthodox organization had been the first to help him.[16]

Rabbi Barash's first task in the vocational education division was to survey the available vocational educational programs to determine which ones might be suitable for Orthodox job seekers and to establish relationships with the State Department of Education. Eventually, he recommended significantly downsizing the vocational educational program because of the poor quality of offerings available to the Orthodox public. Rabbi Bloom, however, had another idea. He approached the

---
16. Rabbi Shmuel Bloom to Rabbi Sherer, February 21, 1975.

State Department of Education with the idea of Project COPE opening its own vocational school. Impressed with what Project COPE had already achieved, the relevant state officials supported the idea.

Following the recommendation of the State Department of Education that Project COPE open its own vocational training school, COPE Institute was created in 1977, under the direction of Rabbi Barash. It began offering a secretarial course, and subsequently opened a program in computer programming. At its height, COPE Institute produced 500 graduates with computer certification every seven or eight months. Those graduates found themselves not only competing with graduates of four-year colleges in the marketplace, but winning.

At one point, AT&T was letting go many of its upper and middle-management personnel and replacing them with entry-level employees. The company had previously lost an employment discrimination suit, and as a consequence instituted a color-blind hiring policy, with no interview. Under that color-blind hiring policy, COPE Institute graduates were winning 75-80 percent of the new openings, even in competition with college graduates.

One day, Rabbi Barash heard that IBM was offering a number of old mainframe computers to non-profit organizations. Thinking that the name Agudath Israel of America would carry more cachet than COPE Institute, he identified himself as calling from Agudath Israel, only to be told that the computers were only available for educational institutions. At that point, he told the IBM representative that COPE Institute was a wholly owned affiliate of Agudath Israel, but was exclusively involved in educational programs. The person on the other end replied, "Oh, you don't have to tell me about COPE Institute. We have lots of your graduates, and they are first-rate."

Although Rabbi Sherer played little role in the day-to-day affairs of COPE Institute, his vast web of contacts and the repository of good will that he had built up over the years in Washington, D.C. and Albany was at its disposal. COPE Institute once had a $150,000 grant contingent on receiving certain accreditation from the federal Department of Education. Though the accreditation forms were filed in time, Barash was told that they could never be processed in time for the grant distributions. He went to Rabbi Sherer to discuss the problem and to seek his intervention with the Department of Education.

But Rabbi Sherer refused to intervene based on his longtime policy of not seeking any special dispensations for Agudath Israel. The only thing he would do was to give Rabbi Barash the name of a crucial figure at the Department of Education. "Tell him that you represent COPE Institute and that it is a subsidiary of Agudath Israel. Describe your problem, and ask for advice, but do not under any circumstances ask for a special favor on our behalf," Rabbi Sherer instructed him. "If he does not offer to help, just thank him for the advice and hang up."

Barash placed the call without too much hope for success. But as soon as he mentioned that "COPE Institute is a subsidiary of Agudath Israel of America," the official blurted out, "Agudath Israel, that's Rabbi Sherer's organization." Then he added for good measure, "I never met a more dedicated public servant in my life. Be in my office by 9 a.m. tomorrow."

The next morning, Rabbi Barash flew down to Washington, D.C. in time for the 9 a.m. appointment. At the start of the meeting, the official called in his assistant, and told him, "This rabbi is here for his school, and you're going to accompany him to make sure his application is processed today." He then proceeded to outline every desk through which the application had to pass. At the end of the day, with the application approved, the senior official told Rabbi Barash, "Give Rabbi Sherer my regards and respect."

COPE Institute bore the stamp of Rabbi Sherer's philosophy of an independent Orthodoxy. Instead of having to turn to the Jewish Federation or non-Jewish agencies for vocational training, thousands of Orthodox Jews received top-level vocational training under the umbrella of Agudath Israel of America. And like all the many branches of Agudath Israel, COPE Institute was run under the supervision and with the input of *gedolei Torah*. Rabbi Yaakov Kamenetsky was consulted frequently on tricky questions, such as whether COPE Institute should accept yeshivah students into its program if the student had not previously informed his rosh yeshivah and secured his approval.

The Southern Brooklyn Community Organization

IN THE '60S AND EARLY '70S, JEWS FLED IN LARGE NUMBERS FROM neighborhoods throughout New York City, including many Bronx neighborhoods, Washington Heights, and Crown Heights. In each case, at some point the neighborhoods began to "tip" ethnically, and Jewish flight ensued.

In the '40s and '50s, Crown Heights was considered by many the most desirable religious neighborhood in Brooklyn, and probably in all of New York City. When

Crown Heights began to decline, many former residents moved to Boro Park, which gradually became the center of Torah life in Brooklyn.

By the mid-'70s, however, Boro Park too was threatened. While the core of the neighborhood remained attractive, there were pockets of decline on the peripheries of the neighborhood that were all too reminiscent of the way that other neighborhoods had begun their descent. Fifteenth Avenue between 38th and 44th streets was beginning to look like the notorious Southern Bronx. A number of buildings had been abandoned by their owners as too dangerous or too non-remunerative to justify continued payment of municipal property taxes. Confrontations between the Jewish Defense League and Puerto Rican gangs became a regular feature of life on the borders of Boro Park.

Rabbi Sherer, himself a decades-long resident of Boro Park, was not prepared to witness another case of gradual neighborhood decline leading to mass flight a few years down the line. He felt strongly that as neighborhoods declined, the Jewish population had to hold their ground. "We are not going to run anymore. We are not going to repeat Crown Heights," he told those closest to him.[17]

Declarations that Jews would not run again were one thing; making it so, quite another. Fortunately, the concept of "neighborhood preservation" was then much in the air, with both the federal government and private foundations involved in the prevention of "white flight" from urban neighborhoods. Among the private foundations with an interest in neighborhood preservation, the Ford Foundation was one of the largest.

Dr. Seymour Lachman, the former president of the New York City Board of Education in the Lindsay administration, was then working as a consultant for the Ford Foundation. And he interested his friend Mitchell Swerdloff, one of the Ford Foundation vice presidents and a former senior official in the administration of Mayor John Lindsay, in the possibility of working with Agudath Israel of America to save Boro Park from rapid decline.

Rabbi Sherer made it a point to cultivate every Orthodox Jew in a position of prominence, and he and Dr. Lachman had grown close during the latter's tenure as president of the Board of Education. Not surprisingly, then, a good deal of Dr. Lachman's sales pitch to the Ford Foundation had to do with the sterling reputation of Agudath Israel of America and its president.

---

17. Naftoli Hirsch.

Before the Ford Foundation could provide a grant, however, it first needed to see a concrete grant proposal from Agudath Israel. The task of preparing the grant proposal fell to Menachem Lubinsky, who spent an entire year researching the field. In the end, the model chosen for emulation in Brooklyn was based on that developed in Baltimore by a local priest, Msg. Gino Berene, who later served as an assistant secretary in the Department of Housing and Urban Development under President Carter.

As the proposal was in the process of being drafted and approved, Rabbi Sherer tapped Rabbi Shmuel Lefkowitz to head the proposed organization to be called the Southern Brooklyn Community Organization (SBCO). Rabbi Lefkowitz was just the sort of young man for whom Rabbi Sherer was always on the lookout: He combined a first-rate yeshivah background — learning in the Mirrer *Kollel* until he was 26 — with the ability to function comfortably in the larger world.

After leaving *Kollel*, Rabbi Lefkowitz earned his master's degree in psychology from the New School of Social Research, and went to work for the Jewish Federation in the East Flatbush YMHA. There were, in those days, few Orthodox Jews working within the Jewish Federation, and Rabbi Lefkowitz's talents were soon noted by his superiors. The Federation sponsored his earning a Masters in Social Work degree with the expectation that he would continue working for the organization.

Rabbi Lefkowitz was still only 31 when Rabbi Sherer offered him the position heading SBCO. The selection process included not only an interview with Rabbi Sherer, but also several rounds of interviews with officials in the Ford Foundation, culminating in perhaps the only glatt-kosher luncheon in the history of the foundation, with Rabbi Sherer, Dr. Lachman, and Menachem Lubinsky all in attendance. Even after winning the approval of the Ford Foundation, Rabbi Lefkowitz still had one more hurdle to clear, securing the permission of the Jewish Federation to take the job. Fortunately, his boss at the Federation, a secular Jew, decided that heading such a major neighborhood project was sufficiently important that the Federation could console itself that it had recouped its investment.

A $62,000 grant from the Ford Foundation provided SBCO with most of the initial $75,000 needed to open an office and hire staff. From the beginning, it was clear that SBCO was a project of a different order of sophistication from anything previously undertaken by Agudath Israel of America, and Rabbi Sherer made sure to provide Rabbi Shmuel

Lefkowitz with a highly talented Board of Directors to assist him. That board included some of the finest young professionals active in Agudah ranks: Shmuel Krieger, an attorney; accountants David Singer and Naftoli Hirsch; and Mendy Shayovich, who was just a few years away from assuming a senior position in the administration of New York's governor, Hugh Carey.

In addition to loading the board with sophisticated professionals, Rabbi Sherer made sure that Rabbi Lefkowitz could call on businessmen with financial clout. So the board also included Louis Glueck and Mendel (Max) Berg, two of Rabbi Sherer's closest friends. Glueck had formerly lived in Crown Heights, and could be counted on to devote himself to preventing Boro Park from going the way of his former neighborhood.

To this mix, Rabbi Sherer added a number of local businessmen with a strong interest in preserving the Boro Park community. (Only those involved in real estate were excluded from the board to avoid any potential for conflicts of interest.) The SBCO Board even included non-Jewish residents of the Boro Park area, whose inclusion could only give SBCO more clout with the various government agencies — city, state, and federal — with which it would have to deal. In time, SBCO would be the subject of a laudatory editorial in *The New York Times* praising SBCO's cooperation with a Puerto Rican group working to strengthen the nearby Sunset Park neighborhood, and even win a grant from the Astor Foundation for its work with Puerto Rican organizations.

The first thing that SBCO had to do was buy time. The long-range

With Leuchu Glueck (l) and Mendel Berg (r)

Chapter Seventeen: An Independent Orthodoxy □ 433

plan was to identify deteriorating or abandoned buildings, and purchase them from banks holding the mortgages for a nominal sum. The next step would be to either renovate the buildings or demolish them and build decent housing on the site. That, however, would require both substantial financial resources and time.

In the meantime, it was crucial to keep the periphery of Boro Park from declining further and the decay from expanding toward the heart of the neighborhood. To that end, SBCO began by creating block associations of residents for the purposes of convincing people not to flee. Those block associations included both Jewish and non-Jewish residents.

Meanwhile the fund-raising had commenced. At the first fund-raising meeting, Mel Warrenbrand, the owner of G and Sons on New Utrecht Avenue, got the action rolling by declaring his willingness to put down $5,000. Others soon followed suit, and by the end of the evening $75,000 was raised. When Rabbi Shmuel Lefkowitz reported back to Rabbi Sherer on the success of the meeting, the latter was amazed.

At the opening ceremonies for Fifteenth Avenue Gardens. From right: Leuchu Glueck, Rabbi Shmuel Lefkowitz, Mayor Koch, Menachem Shayovich, Rabbi Sherer, Rabbi Paysach and Devora Konstam (residents of the building), Edward Rappaport, Mr. Klein (a resident), and Mel Warrenbrand.

Over time, the two largest contributors to the project were Eli Feldman, president of Metropolitan Geriatric Center, the neighborhood's largest employer, and Morly Neinkin, chairman of the board of Maimonides Medical Center, who prevailed upon a number of the hospital's board members to contribute generously. Maimonides Medical Center feared that if Boro Park deteriorated greatly it would ultimately face a situation in which its entire patient population consisted of uninsured individuals. Together Feldman and Neinkin brought $600,000 into SBCO coffers.

The renovation of a small apartment building on the corner of 15th Avenue and 42nd Street to create larger apartments for Orthodox families was SBCO's first building project. Mayor Edward Koch attended the opening ceremonies, which were marred by Puerto Rican protesters claiming that they had been dislocated. Rabbi Sherer was taken aback by the protests, but the more confrontational mayor took matters in stride. He requested the microphone from "my friend, Moses" and proceeded to tell the protesters that the city would be happy to help them emulate SBCO's success in their own neighborhoods.

Eventually, SBCO put up 56 housing units on both sides of 15th Avenue between 38th and 40th streets. When the organization began, the lots on which those units were built could not be given away. Soon, however, the abandoned apartment buildings were replaced by multi-family housing, with one-family units selling for $80,000, and which today are worth $400,000-$500,000. In time, SBCO put up 203 units of senior citizen housing under Section 202 of the National Housing Act, and another 130 units of low-income housing under Section 8.

After securing the weakest flank of Boro Park, SBCO expanded its activities to other areas in Boro Park, and to the adjacent Kensington neighborhood and the area around Yeshiva Torah Vodaath. At one time, the block surrounding Torah Vodaath had buildings filled with members of the Rastafarian cult. Today those buildings are almost entirely occupied by Orthodox Jews.

Much of this transformation was done in conjunction with private real estate developers, with SBCO in an advisery role, helping developers with such issues as financing and tenant relocation.

Rabbi Sherer did not involve himself in the day-to-day management of SBCO. That he left to Rabbi Shmuel Lefkowitz and the Board of Directors. He attended most board meetings, but was content to let Rabbi Lefkowitz chair them. When it came time, however, for crucial decisions to be made, the board instinctively turned to him. At one point, for instance, SBCO bought a church on 18th Avenue to build a center to deal with the problem of youth drifting aimlessly on Ocean Parkway. The question arose as to whether to build a pool. Rabbi Sherer took the issue to the Moetzes Gedolei HaTorah, which rejected the idea, on the grounds that Agudath Israel should not take on the responsibility for the supervision that goes with a pool. Rabbi Sherer urged the SBCO board to make sure that the church was torn down as rapidly as possible, lest the sight of a church being torn down to make way for a Jewish institution create resentment toward the Orthodox community.

More importantly, in the words of Rabbi Shmuel Lefkowitz, Rabbi Sherer was the one who "connected all the dots." Soon after Rabbi Lefkowitz took the helm of SBCO, for instance, Rabbi Sherer introduced him to the leading figure in the office of Senator Jacob Javits, who assured Rabbi Lefkowitz that he would have as much help as he needed from the senator.

Much of SBCO's success owed to the quality of the people prepared to get involved in its work, many of them non-observant. And in virtually every case, it was a personal relationship with Rabbi Sherer, or his and Agudath Israel's reputation for probity that was the key to attracting outside talent to the cause.

Of the latter, none was more crucial to SBCO's success than Richard

Schifter, who was a senior partner at the law firm of Fried, Frank, Jacobson, and Kampelman when he began working with SBCO. In December 1977, Agudath Israel hosted its third annual breakfast on social concerns, with a focus on housing. Rabbi Sherer sent out word that a major new initiative would be announced at the breakfast. That initiative was SBCO.

The New York Times sent reporter Peter Kihss to cover the breakfast, and his write-up in the Monday paper caught the eye of attorney Richard Schifter. At the time, Schifter's practice focused heavily on representing the Navajo Indians. As he read the article, Schifter, whose parents had sent him to the United States from Vienna just after Kristallnacht, thought to himself, *I've been using my expertise in housing law on behalf of other tribes, why not do it for my tribe?* He asked Mel Richey, an Orthodox partner of his, whether Agudath Israel of America was a reputable organization with which he should consider getting involved. Richey told him that Agudath Israel was the gold standard as far as Orthodox organizations are concerned.

With that, Schifter arranged to meet Rabbi Sherer. The two men found an instant rapport. Schifter explained to Rabbi Sherer that there were a plethora of federal programs that could be utilized by SBCO, including housing for the elderly and partially subsidized home mort-

Vice President George Bush presenting an award to SBCO for its achievements.
L-r: Rabbi Sherer, Leuchu Glueck, Vice President Bush, Rabbi Shmuel Lefkowitz

gages. For his part, Rabbi Sherer offered Schifter the chance to make a significant contribution to the Jewish community.

The idealistic motive is clear from the fact that Schifter agreed to take only the attorney's fees permitted under the various government programs from which SBCO benefited, fees which were, in most cases, 40 percent or less of his normal billing rates at Fried, Frank. Rabbi Shmuel Lefkowitz estimates that over the years, Schifter probably wrote off more than $3 million in legal fees to SBCO, a step that did not always meet with the hearty approbation of his partners.

In addition to his own considerable expertise in housing law, Schifter also placed at the disposal of SBCO a group of very bright young lawyers in the firm, including Douglas Feith, later the number-three man in the Defense Department under President George W. Bush. (Schifter himself became a high-ranking State Department official in the Clinton administration, in which capacity he continued to render many important services to Agudath Israel on behalf of Jews in Eastern Europe.)

Schifter identified two major programs that could be of immediate use to SBCO. The first was Urban Action Development Grants, which were designed to stimulate development. SBCO eventually received a $2 million grant under this program. The second relevant program was Section 235 low-interest mortgages, which could help large Orthodox families pay for the housing SBCO was building.

There was, however, a catch. The Section 235 mortgages were based on a complex formula, under which no purchases in New York City would ever be eligible because the apartment prices in the New York metropolitan area are too high. Schifter, however, discovered that the law also allowed for the Department of Housing and Urban Development to waive the formula in appropriate cases, and that the HUD official with the authority to waive the formula was a Jewish real-estate man from Denver named Phil Winn.

Rabbi Lefkowitz called Rabbi Sherer and asked him whether he knew anyone in Denver who might know Winn. Rabbi Sherer mentioned Sheldon Beren, a successful oil-man and a major Orthodox philanthropist. But before calling Beren, he asked Rabbi Lefkowitz once again whether Beren's intervention was crucial since he did not want to ask for a favor if it was not absolutely necessary. Rabbi Lefkowitz replied that it was.

In the meantime, Rabbi Lefkowitz and Schifter prepared an elaborate presentation for Phil Winn, in preparation for what they anticipated would be a long meeting the next morning in Washington, D.C. As it turned out, however, they never had a chance to make that presentation. Winn began the next day's meeting, "Rabbi, I have a friend from Denver named Sheldon Beren. He never calls me. But he called me about this. So it must be important."

Winn then turned to Richard Schifter and asked him one question, "Do I have the authority to do this?" Schifter assured him that he did. With that Winn announced, "If so, I'll do it." The entire meeting lasted no more than 10 minutes. Once more Rabbi Sherer had connected the right dots. Over time, the waiver of the Section 235 formula resulted in $4.2 million being made available to purchasers of units in SBCO buildings.

Judah Gribetz was another talented and politically connected attorney whom Rabbi Sherer brought on board for SBCO. He and Gribetz first came to know each other well when the latter served as deputy mayor of New York City under Mayor Abe Beame. And that relation-

The leadship of SBCO meets with the U.S. Department of Housing and Urban Development. Left to right: Rabbi Chaim Israel, Tom Bauer, Rabbi Yaakov Lonner, Louis Krawiecz, Housing Secretary Samuel Pierce, Unknown, Rabbi Shmuel Bloom. (circa 1985)

Chapter Seventeen: An Independent Orthodoxy □ 439

ship only deepened when Gribetz served as chief counsel to Governor Hugh Carey from 1975-78. As soon as he learned that Gribetz was leaving Albany, Rabbi Sherer called him up to offer his congratulations on Gribetz's planned move to the law firm of Mudge, Rose and to ask Gribetz to represent SBCO with New York City on a pro bono basis. Gribetz agreed.

Rabbi Lefkowitz will not soon forget a meeting of SBCO — himself, Naftoli Hirsch, and attorneys Gribetz and Schifter — with a number of members of the city housing commission. Gribetz opened the meeting by observing that the SBCO representatives were not distinguished by their ethnic diversity. But then looking at the housing commissioners, each of whom was a liberal Jew, Gribetz observed, "But then again neither are you." Someone who could talk in that easy fashion with city officials was a valuable asset for SBCO, and another one of the important dots that Rabbi Sherer connected for SBCO.

When SBCO began operations, Boro Park could easily have gone the way of Crown Heights. The boundaries of the neighborhood were increasingly becoming no-go zones, and those areas were growing. SBCO not only stopped that gradual deterioration on the edges of the neighborhood, but reversed the trend entirely. Over the last 28 years, Boro Park has expanded rapidly in every direction. Boro Park might have become the last stand of Orthodox Jewry in New York City. Today it anchors the vibrant Jewish life of Brooklyn.

AARTS

THE NOVOMINSKER REBBE WROTE TO RABBI SHERER IN 1980 urging him to fully document the creation of the Association of Advanced Rabbinical and Talmudic Schools (AARTS). Though "the full extent of your role in the esablishment of AARTS, and all that you have done for the yeshivos will probably never be known or appreciated by the public, ... [and] must be left to the *sefer zikaron* ... where it really and ultimately counts ....," the Rebbe wrote, "[n]onetheless I strongly urge you to record and keep all pertinent documents on contemporary events for future historical use .... "

Fortunately, the Novominsker's advice was heeded. No aspect of Rabbi Sherer's public career is so thoroughly documented as the nine years that he spent working to create a national accreditation agency for *yeshivos gedolos* in America. No single project commanded so much of his personal attention and over so long a period of time. And it is arguable that no project ultimately had such a profound impact. Because of

With the Novominsker Rebbe

AARTS, tens of millions of dollars have flowed from the federal government to *yeshivos gedolos* over the last 30 years.

Finally, no project so clearly demonstrates the profound impact of the personal relationships that Rabbi Sherer created with politicians and government officials for the benefit of the Orthodox Jewish community. The respect, bordering on awe, that John Proffitt — Director of the Accrediting and Institutional Eligibility Division of the United States Office of Education — had for Rabbi Sherer led him to exercise his discretion repeatedly over many years to the benefit of the *yeshivos gedolos* of America.

Prior to the creation of AARTS, *yeshivos gedolos* were recognized by the federal government only as institutions of higher learning, and their students eligible for student loans under various federal programs, under the so-called three-letter rule. That rule required the yeshivos to show that three accredited institutions awarded transfer credits for their course of study.

In June 1967, Rabbi Sherer heard from his friend Samuel Halperin, a former aide to Senator Jacob Javits and then Deputy Secretary of Health Education and Welfare, that the future of the three-letter rule was very much in doubt, and that legislation would soon be introduced in Congress to limit federal funding to accredited institutions. Halperin also informed him that his efforts to secure an exemption rule for yeshivos had been rejected.

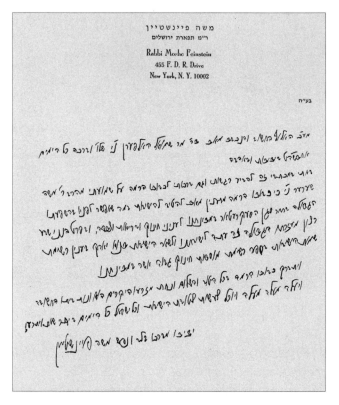

A letter of thanks from Rabbi Moshe Feinstein to Samuel Halperin for his efforts to help the yeshivos

Besides pressure to end the three-letter rule within the federal education bureaucracy, the New York State Education Department was waging a determined campaign against the inclusion of yeshivos located in New York State in the federal registry of recognized institutions of higher learning. Some of those institutions, state education officials charged, were entirely bogus, with names like Yeshivos Yaakov Avinu. Unfortunately, those charges could not be dismissed out of hand. The rapid expansion of federal education spending under President Johnson's Great Society program had attracted many unscrupulous operators. Much of the purpose of AARTS, as it would develop, was to prevent legitimate yeshivos from being tarred by the inevitable scandals caused by bogus institutions.

As warnings of the demise of the three-letter rule grew, Rabbi Sherer gathered a team to work with him on the issue. The other members included: Rabbi Naftoli Neuberger, Executive Director of Yeshiva Ner Israel; Rabbi Shmuel Yosef Labkovsky, who held the same position at Mesivta Tifereth Jerusalem's Yeshivah of Staten Island; and Rabbi

Samuel Halperin writes to Rabbi Labkovsky following a meeting in Washington: "Rabbi Sherer was magnificent in his presentation, truly irresistible."

Yaakov Weisberg of Beis Medrash Govoha of Lakewood. Each brought unique talents. Rabbi Neuberger was a brilliant strategist; Rabbi Weisberg could masterfully analyze statutory language. In time, Rabbi Labkovsky would undertake the first major feasibility study for establishing an accreditation agency.

The group had their first telephone conference in September 1968, and the next day Rabbi Sherer asked Samuel Halperin to send him all the regulations relevant to starting an accreditation agency. In the course of the conversation, Rabbi Sherer heard, for the first time, the name John Proffitt, who was the official in charge of accreditation.

On January 1, 1969, many of the major roshei yeshivah met at the office of Rabbi Moshe Feinstein to discuss the threat of a federal government clampdown on all yeshivos posed by the proliferation of requests for federal recognition by bogus yeshivos. Not until November of that year, however, did the roshei yeshivah specifically take up the question of an accreditation agency, after Rabbi Sherer received word that the entire eligibility of rabbinical seminaries was coming up for review.

The roshei yeshivah appointed Rabbi Sherer and the three executive directors previously mentioned to draft recommendations. The committee began by establishing a set of criteria for an association of major Rabbinical colleges. And in January 1970, Rabbi Labkovsky was appointed to commence a feasibility study for an accreditation agency.

Meanwhile New York State officals continued to argue in Washington that yeshivos lacked "legal authorization" to act as institutions of higher learning. A meeting was arranged between Rabbi Sherer, Congressman Carey, and John Proffitt. At that meeting, Rabbi Sherer told Proffitt that the State Education Department (SED) was attempting to use the federal government to force the yeshivos to submit to their jurisdiction.

Proffitt said that he had already sent a question about the eligibility of the New York State yeshivos to the office of the legal counsel of the Office of Education. But since he was fully persuaded by Rabbi Sherer's arguments, he would sound out the chief legal counsel, who was a friend of his, as to his likely determination.[18] If the chief legal counsel told him that his, conclusion would likely be negative, Proffitt said, he would simply withdraw the request for a legal opinion and enter his own administrative determination. In a subsequent memorandum about the meeting, Rabbi Sherer wrote, "Carey and I were extremely moved by this extraordinary gesture, which seemed unprecedented in our experience."

At the same meeting, Proffitt also showed Rabbi Sherer an advanced copy of a new federal regulation on the three-letter rule. Now each unaccredited institution would have to show three graduate schools that each accepted credits from the yeshivah in question for three students.

Rabbi Sherer showed the new regulations to Nathan Lewin, his top legal adviser at the time. Lewin saw no legal basis to challenge them. A call to Samuel Halperin was equally discouraging. Halperin told him that there were scandals brewing over the three-letter rule, and that he had been told by a senior official in John Proffitt's office that yeshivos would no longer be in the next federal registry of institutions whose students are eligible for federal funding.

Though John Proffitt had repeatedly pressed upon Rabbi Sherer the

---

18. In subsequent communication with the New York State Department of Education, Proffitt quoted almost verbatim the arguments that Rabbi Sherer had made to him. He began by noting that the yeshivos were chartered by the state, albeit under religious proviso rather than an educational one. He added, "It cannot be denied that these institutions attain their educational objectives efficiently and effectively. The scholarship of the rabbinate attests to this without equivocation."

idea that an accreditation agency was the only satisfactory long-term solution, Rabbi Sherer had remained noncommittal. Progress, however, had been made on that front. At a May 11, 1970 meeting of the committee, Rabbi Labkovsky presented a report in which he concluded that it would be technically feasible to create an accreditation agency. The only question was whether the yeshivos would be willing to agree to the high standards it would require. Despite that misgiving, at a meeting of the roshei yeshivah the next week, it was decided to take out a charter for an accreditation agency.

Two months later, the committee met at LaGuardia Airport and came up with a set of criteria to weed out bogus institutions: (1) 80 percent of the student body had to be involved in at least eight hours a day of studies; (2) there must be at least five full-time rabbanim; and (3) students must have completed four years of Talmudic high school or demonstrated an equivalent competence in tests.

By November 11, 1970, Rabbi Sherer felt confident enough to write Proffitt that steps had been set in motion that he hoped would lead to "the ultimate satisfactory solution to this problem." He invited Proffitt to make a visit to Ner Israel in order to provide him with an understanding of what a yeshivah is. Not only was Ner Israel the yeshivah closest to Washington, D.C., but it also boasted of an extremely impressive campus. Most important, Rabbi Sherer knew that he could count on Rabbi Neuberger to impress the visitors with his broad knowledge and old-world charm.

Two senior officials in Proffitt's office — Dr. Leslie Ross and Ron Pugsley — visited Ner Israel, and came away extremely impressed, as Rabbi Sherer had known they would. They urged upon Rabbi Sherer the importance of an accreditation agency to replace the doomed three-letter rule, and recommended the former executive head of the National Commission on Accreditation as a consultant, adding that his name would add luster to any proposal.

On December 9, 1971, the roshei yeshivah appointed a Study Commission to prepare the proposal for AARTS official recognition. A few weeks later, Rabbi Sherer met with his friend Sam Halperin, and the latter offered to serve on the Advisery Board. From Halperin's office, he went to visit John Proffitt and his top assistants. Proffitt pronounced what had been done so far a "miracle." Then he made two extraordinary offers.

Rabbi Sherer estimated that the cost of the Study Commission would be $85,000 for the first year. Proffitt said he believed he could obtain funding for that within the Office of Education. In addition, he too offered to serve on the Advisory Committee to AARTS. The next day Rabbi Sherer wrote him, "[W]hat you are doing ... is a major contribution toward allowing the entire Jewish faith community to obtain the proper recognition for the schools which are the fountain of their entire leadership."

All was not smooth sailing, however. In June 1972, members of the committee met at Ner Israel with Dr. Marvin Fox of Brandeis University. They concluded that yeshivos did not really fit into any existing categories for accreditation agencies. Dr. Fox was charged with describing the workings of yeshivos in the vernacular of the educational establishment. His 13-page working paper was presented to John Proffitt in November 1972. After reading the paper line by line together with Rabbi Sherer, Proffitt agreed to treat the yeshivos as a special category.

As the initial steps were being taken toward the creation of an accreditation agency, Rabbi Sherer was eager to create the same kind of special relationship with New York State higher-education officials that he had succeeded in creating in Washington. His first goal was to lessen the heat directed at the yeshivos from Albany. In addition, the Nixon administration had indicated its desire to funnel more federal higher-education spending through the states, which made it imperative to establish a good relationship with the State Education Department (SED). Rabbi Sherer's big break came in the form of an invitation to a dinner in Albany at which the top officials of SED and 15 leading figures in the non-public-school sector would be present.

Rabbi Sherer found himself sitting together with State Commissioner of Education Ewald Nyquist and Deputy Commissioner Gordon Ambach. He offered to do the same thing for them that he had done for federal officials: provide them with a list of yeshivos whose bona fides were beyond question. Both Nyquist and Ambach were receptive to the idea.

About a week later, Rabbi Sherer received a call from the State Commissioner for Higher Education, Edward (Ted) Hollander. Hollander told him that he had been discussing his lack of relationship with the yeshivos with Dr. Leslie Ross of John Proffitt's office, and the latter told him that if he wanted to understand the rabbinic schools he had to meet Rabbi Sherer.

Hollander quickly launched into a discussion of state licensing of rabbinical schools, an unchartered area into which Rabbi Sherer was not eager to venture. He asked Hollander to outline his thoughts in writing, and reminded him that his office had adopted a highly aggressive stance toward the yeshivos over the years.

At a May 16, 1973 meeting of the roshei yeshivah, the general sense of the roshei yeshivah was that Rabbi Sherer should adopt a very cautious stance toward the SED, and certainly not agree to state accreditation of yeshivos. A few days later, one of Hollander's assistants called Rabbi Sherer and read a very hostile letter that he planned to send Proffitt concerning the fact that the *yeshivos gedolos* were advertising that they offer advanced degrees. Rabbi Sherer told him that if the letter was sent in that form it would end any chance of a rapprochement between the SED and the yeshivos.

In the end, the letter sent from Hollander's office to Proffitt lacked any of the inflammatory language in the original draft. Still, Rabbi Sherer wanted to defuse the charges from Albany and discussed the issue with the other members of his brain trust. Rabbi Weisberg explained that the so-called "degrees" were largely a function of statisticians in Washington, D.C. trying to describe yeshivah learning in terms of familiar categories. Rabbi Sherer then wrote Proffitt putting the onus on the "feds" for trying "locking everything in life into a set of statistical patterns."

He assured Proffitt that the yeshivos had no desire to advertise themselves as offering advanced degrees, and the mention of those degrees in the federal registry was not at their initiative. He pointed to that clarification as "an example of how problems can be cleared up in the spirit of good will."

Commissioner Hollander kept pressing for a personal meeting, and Rabbi Sherer found it harder and harder to push him off. He too was convinced that such a meeting was necessary before the fraud being perpetrated by fake institutions lead to an explosion that would drag the yeshivos along with them. But only when the roshei yeshivah too were convinced that building a personal relationship with Hollander was crucial did he proceed with building one.

The clock continued to tick for the yeshivos. In July 1973 a two year-grace period they had been granted, after the expiration of the three-letter rule, was scheduled to expire. And so Rabbi Sherer headed for Washington, D.C. again. Even by his standards, May 16, 1973 was an exceptionally busy day. He began the morning chairing a meeting of C.R.E.D.I.T., the umbrella organization seeking tuition tax credits for families with children in private schools. Then he met with Senator Jacob Javits about restoring $80,000 in government funding for a particular yeshivah. Next came a talk with Congressman Carey about a contemplated run for mayor of New York. The two men also discussed funding for a new emergency room in Brooklyn's Maimonides Medical Center.

But the most crucial meeting of the day was with John Proffitt. Rabbi Sherer was able to present him a three-page preliminary report from Professor Avraham Tanenbaum of Columbia University, the director of the Study Commission appointed by the roshei yeshivah to make a recommendation on whether an accreditation agency was doable and desirable. The preliminary answer to both questions was affirmative.

As usual, Proffitt was extremely forthcoming with Rabbi Sherer. He told him that he would waive the normal requirement that the application for recognition as an accreditation agency must be filed 90 days before any meeting of the Advisery Committee that makes the final recommendation. Even more important, he told Rabbi Sherer that if the new agency were approved by the Advisery Committee, he would waive the normal rule requiring that the agency be in operation two years before gaining official government recognition. He also suggested that he and Rabbi Sherer set up a schedule of visitations to yeshivos by officials in his office, prior to the meeting of the Advisery Council, so that if the Advisery Council approved AARTS, he would be able to convince them to waive the normal requirement of a one-year probation period at the start of operations.

On September 19, 1973, the roshei yeshivah — Rabbi Moshe Feinstein, Rabbi Yaakov Yitzchak Ruderman, Rabbi Yaakov Weinberg, Rabbi Gedaliah Schorr, and Rabbi Mordechai Gifter — voted to accept the recommendation of the Study Commission to create an accreditation association. Rabbi Sherer suggested that the Accreditation Commission should include Rabbis Schorr, Gifter, and Weinberg representing the yeshivos; Professor Yisroel Meir Kirzner of New York University, Professor Jacob Landynski of the New School of Social Research, and Dr. Seymour Lachman, president of the New York City Board of Education representing academia; and law professor Larry Katz of Baltimore as the public representative.

Two months later, on November 21, 1973, the first official meeting took place between the heads of AARTS and officials in Proffitt's office, when Rabbi Sherer escorted Dr. Avraham Tanenbaum and Dr. Bernard

Fryshman, a physics professor at the New York Institute of Technology and Brooklyn College, to Washington, D.C.

At that meeting, Proffitt's staff established a timetable for the application process for recognition as an accreditation agency. The only dark cloud in the meeting came when Ron Pugsley told Dr. Fryshman that he could not see how to justify the waiver of the general rule that an accreditation agency must be operating for two years before obtaining federal recognition.

That cloud cleared the next week when John Proffitt made a special trip to New York City to meet with Rabbi Sherer. He assured Rabbi Sherer that he would waive the requirement. The rule, he explained, was designed to put a brake on doubtful applications, but was unnecessary in the case of "reliable" organizations such as AARTS. Rabbi Sherer prodded Proffitt for his impressions of the AARTS personnel he had met, and the latter replied that they were "far superior to many who run large accrediting agencies … first-rate highly professional people, who do honor to [your] association."

But at that meeting, just as all Rabbi Sherer's labors seemed to be coming to fruition, Proffitt dropped a bombshell. He told Rabbi Sherer that he was involved in a major intradepartmental battle with those who wanted the federal government to take over all accreditation from private associations. If he lost — and at present it appeared he was losing — he would have no choice but to resign. "The very thought that Proffitt would ever leave his position gave me the shudders," Rabbi Sherer wrote to the roshei yeshivah. "Let's pray."

Fortunately, he was able to do more than just pray. Proffitt called him on December 20, 1973 distraught over the way the battle was going, and told Rabbi Sherer that the only person who could help him was Senator Javits, who would be able to sway Secretary of Health, Education and Welfare Caspar Weinberger. Rabbi Sherer immediately arranged for Proffitt to speak to Roy Millenson, Senator Javits's senior aide on education matters, and by the next day an ebullient Proffitt called him to say the crisis had passed.

The news for which Rabbi Sherer had been waiting so many years finally arrived in a conversation with John Proffitt on October 4, 1974. Rabbi Sherer had inquired about the findings of the Advisory Council, and Proffitt replied that the official findings would not be available in writing until November 1. Nevertheless, "on the basis of our friendship," Proffitt confided to Rabbi Sherer that the final decision was posi-

Rabbi Mordechai Gifter addressing an Agudah Convention. At the dais, l-r: Rabbi Ahron Schechter, the Bostoner Rebbe of Boston-Har Nof, Rabbi Elya Svei, Rabbi Zelik Epstein, Rabbi Avrohom Pam, Rabbi Sherer, Rabbi Chaskel Besser, Rabbi Henoch Lebowitz, the Novominsker Rebbe, Rabbi Shimon Schwab. Visible in the background: Rabbi Yosef Meir Kantor, Rabbi Gavriel Bodenheimer, Rabbi Shlomo Carlebach, Rabbi Yisroel Belsky, Rabbi Avrohom Teichman, Rabbi Dov Eichenstien, Rabbi Elazar Yonah Ginsberg, Rabbi Moshe Heinemann, Rabbi Yaakov Reisman, Rabbi Chaim Grozovsky.

tive, and that AARTS had been granted recognition for a period of two years, as opposed to the normal one-year provisional period. The good news must, however, be kept absolutely secret, Proffitt warned.

A letter from Proffitt to Rabbi Sherer dated November 28, 1974 made clear precisely how crucial the personal relationship between the two men had been to the creation of AARTS. Rabbi Sherer had written to Proffitt thanking him profusely for his role in bringing AARTS into existence. Proffitt responded in kind: "My efforts should be simply considered as a small partial acknowledgment of the value which I place upon your friendship and that of many other persons of the Jewish faith who have befriended me in the past. *I do especially prize your friendship, and regard you as one of the small group of superior persons I have come to know*" (emphasis added).

That admiration was mutual. At a meeting July 1, 1975, Proffitt confided to Rabbi Sherer that he was convinced that the development of AARTS was "one of the best things that could have every happened to the Jewish community in this country." In his private aide-mémoire,

Rabbi Sherer confided, "As usual it was a very hearty and intimate chat between friends, running a broad gamut of subjects too numerous to record." Proffitt, Rabbi Sherer opined, was "one of the most high-minded men I have ever met in all my years working with government officials."

Shortly after the official recognition of AARTS, Rabbi Sherer wrote a letter to Rabbi Mordechai Gifter that reveals how he viewed the many years he had devoted to solving the accreditation problem of the yeshivos. He pointed out that Agudath Israel had been "the chief factor in accomplishing the historic tearing of the shackles of the recognition and accreditation of yeshivos from their links to secular graduate schools (and all the resultant chicanery)."

Rabbi Sherer had devoted nine years to the creation of an independent accreditation for yeshivos. Yet when someone suggested to him that Agudath Israel should take a fee from the yeshivos for the services rendered on their behalf, Rabbi Sherer rejected the suggestion out of hand. Agudath Israel exists to serve the yeshivos, he said. He saw the creation of AARTS, which saved the yeshivos from the loss of tens of millions of dollars in direct and indirect federal aid (via student loans), as one of his crowning achievements. But that reward, he often said, was one he was saving for *yenner velt* (the World to Come).

Chapter Eighteen

EXPANDING CAPACITIES

RABBI SHERER WAS ALWAYS AMBITIOUS TO EXPAND THE influence of Agudath Israel. From the early 1970s, he started hiring new personnel to take over primary responsibility in areas he had previously handled by himself. Gradually, he assumed the role of a chief executive of a major corporation with numerous divisions. In effect, Rabbi Sherer began metaphorically cloning parts of himself: new employees were hired, and sometimes new divisions created, to handle one of the many tasks that he had previously done by himself.

Chief Executive Officer

Thus in the early 1970s, the Division of Government and Public Affairs came into existence, and Rabbi Sherer shared his rolodex of governmental contacts with Menachem Lubinsky. Similarly, in 1984, Yitzchok Brandriss, a *musmach* (ordained rabbi) of Yeshivas Chafetz Chaim, was hired to become the first full-time Director of Public Affairs.

Rabbi Sherer continued to read every press release or article that went out of Agudath Israel's offices, but he was no longer the primary draftsman.

In October 1980, Rabbi Sherer hired Shmuel Prager, a recent law-school graduate, as the first attorney employed full-time by Agudath Israel of America. Though the original advertisement for the position specified that it would be a half-time position, after Prager had gone through a rigorous interview process, the decision was made to extend him a full-time offer.[1] Rabbi Sherer

Shmuel Prager (l) and Rabbi Sherer with Gordon Ambach, New York State Commissioner of Education

likely realized that no talented young lawyer would remain in the position for long on a part-time basis.

Prager's primary task was to serve as the liason for New York's yeshivos and Jewish girls' schools with the New York City and New York State governments. (Rabbi Sherer maintained the education portfolio at the federal level.) Prager's duties involved providing general legal advice to yeshivos and girls' schools in their dealings with the government. He also maintained close ties with various institutions of the Catholic Church, the largest provider of non-public education in the state.[2] In the latter capacity, Prager was the beneficiary of the close ties built up by Rabbi Sherer with the Catholic hierarchy over a period of decades.

Prager also held the seat formerly reserved for Rabbi Sherer on the State Education Commissioner's Advisery Council for Non-Public

---

1. Among the interviewers were Mendy Shayovich, Professor Bernard Fryshman, and Professor Aaron Twerski.
2. Among the Catholic bodies with which Prager was in frequent contact were the archdiocese of New York, the Brooklyn and Queens dioceses, and the New York State Catholic Conference.

Schools. Joan Arnold Bourgeois, a former nun, who served as the assistant state commissioner for non-public schools, was a great fan of Rabbi Sherer, and that esteem for Rabbi Sherer went a long way to smoothing Prager's path in Albany.

Prager describes Rabbi Sherer as the best law professor that he ever had. "He had an unparalleled ability to analyze a statute, take it apart, and redraft it," he remembers. In addition, he was a superb mentor when it came to dealing with government officials.

The hiring of Chaim Dovid Zwiebel in 1983 gave Agudath Israel of America its own independent litigation capability for the first time. Zwiebel was then a fourth-year litigation associate at Paul, Weiss, Rifkind, Wharton, and Garrison, one of New York's premier law firms, with a bright career in private practice ahead of him. Rabbi Sherer, however, had other plans for him. In the years to follow, Rabbi Sherer would frequently list bringing Zwiebel to Agudath Israel to head the Division of Government Affairs[3] as one of his greatest accomplishments.[4]

Rabbi Sherer's appeal to Zwiebel was the one he always used to attract high-caliber talent to Agudath Israel: "I just don't think that you'll ever be satisfied using your skills [on behalf of clients with whom you do not necessarily identify]," he said. Unbeknownst to him, Rabbi Sherer had a major assist in his efforts to persuade Zwiebel to join Agudath Israel from the latter's young son. The preceding Rosh Hashanah, when Zwiebel asked his oldest son what he had *davened* for in the coming year, the young boy replied, "That *Mashiach* come and that your office [at Paul, Weiss] burns down so that you'll be at home more."

Rabbi Sherer was acutely aware of the enormous financial sacrifice Zwiebel would be making by leaving private practice. Over the years, Rabbi Sherer, whose children were by then fully grown, deferred raises in his own salary from Agudath Israel of America in order to increase Zwiebel's. He also tried to make sure that the Zwiebel children would have occasion to celebrate his change of jobs, and frequently sent his young protégé home at night and told him not to emulate his example of coming into the office on Sundays.

---

3. The term "public affairs" was dropped from the name of the division as means of assuring Zwiebel that he would not bear responsibility for any public relations work, as his predecessor Menachem Lubinsky had, but could focus exclusively on legal and governmental work.
4. Rabbi Yaakov Perlow, the Novominsker Rebbe and Rosh Agudath Israel of America. Nathan Lewin, a leading member of Rabbi Sherer's legal brain trust, remembers Rabbi Sherer's delight when he succeeded in persuading Zwiebel to join Agudath Israel of America.

RABBI SHERER'S DECISION TO DEVELOP HIS OWN IN-HOUSE LEGAL team must be understood in the context of his three-year battle for passage of the first New York State *Get* Law." At a crucial juncture in that battle, he found himself literally begging for high quality legal assistance and unable to attain it. He never wanted to be in that situation again.

The First New York State "*Get* Law"

The tragedy of *"agunos,"* women unable to obtain a *get* (divorce decree) from their husbands, had long troubled Rabbi Sherer. In August 1979, he wrote to Rabbi Dovid Cohen, in response to the latter's earlier communication, "I have had much personal *agmas nefesh* [anguish] from some of the individual cases that I'm fully aware of. If you could have the *zechus* of getting *Klal Yisrael* beyond 'square one' where this problem has been for so many years, it will be one of the greatest accomplishments of this generation."

That communication with Rabbi Cohen convinced Rabbi Sherer to take the initiative and convene a meeting of leading lawyers and rabbinical scholars to consider possible approaches to the *agunah* issue. Over the years, Rabbi Sherer had succeeded in enlisting some of the United States' top legal talent on behalf of the Orthodox community. And that entire "legal team" was all lined up in the effort to find at least a partial legislative solution to the daunting "agunah problem," which brought not only untold suffering to many Jewish women and their families, but also constituted an ongoing *chillul Hashem*. The members of Rabbi Sherer's dream legal team included Nathan Lewin, the first Orthodox Jew to clerk for the United States Supreme Court and the son of Isaac Lewin, World Agudath Israel's longtime representative to the United Nations; Professor Aaron Twerski of Hofstra Law School, one of the country's leading experts in products liability and chairman of Agudath Israel's Commission on Legislation and Civic Action; and Judah Dick, a former New York City corporation counsel.

Rabbi Sherer also sent out an invitation to one of America's most famous public lawyers, Harvard Professor Alan Dershowitz, who had been raised in an Orthodox home in Brooklyn. "This complex issue, beyond the Halachic considerations, has serious legal and social aspects. In all probability it can only be solved through an in-depth evaluation of all its aspects simultaneously …. I realize that you are extremely busy, but I trust that you will understand that this type of meeting, long overdue, is of paramount importance [and that] *you* are needed," Rabbi Sherer wrote. Dershowitz accepted the invitation.

In addition to the aforementioned legal experts, Rabbi J. David Bleich, a law professor at Cardozo School of Law and a rosh yeshivah at Rabbeinu Yitzchak Elchonon Theological Seminary, joined the initial meeting on June 11, 1980 at the Agudath Israel's 5 Beekman Street headquarters. Also arrayed around the table were a number of leading halachic authorities including Rabbi Dovid Feinstein, Rabbi Yaakov Perlow (the Novominsker Rebbe), and Rabbi Dovid Cohen. At that initial meeting, the basic concept of the first "*get* law" took shape.

Involving the state in coercing a husband to grant a *get* was deemed inappropriate for both halachic and constitutional reasons. But in cases where the husband is the moving party in a civil divorce action — admittedly not the majority of "*agunah*" cases — it was suggested that the state could condition the granting of a civil divorce on the moving party removing any bar to remarriage on the part of his or her spouse. In the case of a Jewish man seeking to divorce his wife, those steps would include the grant of a valid *get*. That approach secured the support of a wide spectrum of the leading contemporary *poskim*, including Rabbi Moshe Feinstein, Rabbi Yaakov Kamenetsky, Rabbi Moshe Stern, the Debrecziner Rav, Rabbi Shimon Schwab, and Rabbi Yechezkel Roth, the Satmar *dayan*.

One of the major hurdles to the passage of such a bill was the constitutional objection that a law conditioning a civil divorce on the performance of a religious act — i.e., the granting of a *get* — would constitute an impermissible establishment of religion. Professor Dershowitz wrote to Sheldon Silver, an Orthodox Jew and one of the most powerful Democrats in the New York State Assembly, on May 26, 1981 stating that he supported the bill "both as a matter of policy and constitutionality."

Dershowitz's letter of approbation cleared the way for a year of intense lobbying in the New York State legislature by Menachem Lubinsky and Shmuel Prager. Armed with the letters of support of such organizations as the New York City Commission on the Status of Women and individuals like New York City Council President Carol Bellamy, the bill sailed through the New York State Assembly with only five negative votes, and was unanimously approved by the Senate.

All that remained was to attain Governor Carey's signature on the bill, which should have been a formality given the overwhelming support for the legislation in the legislature and the governor's close relationship with Rabbi Sherer. The catch, however, was that the governor's chief counsel felt the act constituted an unconstitutional establishment of religion, and Governor Carey, an attorney himself, agreed. In a July 26, 1982 phone conversation with Rabbi Sherer, Carey indicated that though he would be very pained to do something that would displease the Orthodox Jewish community and Rabbi Sherer, he would have to veto any such legislation.[5]

Rabbi Sherer had no choice but to ask the legislative sponsors to withdraw the bill. He realized that there was little chance of a Democratic legislature overriding the veto of a Democratic governor, and he had no wish to damage his relationship with Carey. He preferred instead to try to convince Governor Carey that the bill was constitutional. To that end, he was left scrambling for the requisite memorandum from a recognized legal authority. In an August 25, 1982 letter to Professor Dershowitz, Rabbi Sherer found himself "literally pleading" that Dershowitz join Rabbi Sherer at a meeting of several top constitutional experts to see whether the bill could yet be "rescue[d]." That meeting, however, never took place. Not until December of 1982 was Rabbi Sherer able to send to Governor Carey a memorandum authored by Professor Robert Sedler of Wayne State University defending the constitutionality of the "*Get* Law."

A redrafted "*Get* Law"[6] was ultimately signed into law by Governor Carey's successor Governor Mario Cuomo in September 1983, after Nathan Lewin personally defended the constitutionality of the law to Alice Daniel, the governor's chief counsel.[7] In a personal letter to Governor Cuomo on September 5, 1983, Rabbi Sherer wrote, "Dear Mario, I shall never forget how you acted as a *mentsch*, and you gave

---

5. At least one member of Rabbi Sherer's team of legal advisers, Nathan Lewin, was inclined to agree with Governor Carey that the law as drafted was unconstitutional. The original bill provided for a mediation panel in the event that all bars to remarriage were not removed. Such a panel would likely have had to interact with various *batei din*, which would have arguably constituted an impermissible "entanglement" of state and religion.
6. Nathan Lewin did the primary redrafting. He simplified the bill to require the moving party to file an affidavit that he had removed all barriers to remarriage, while dropping the whole concept of a mediation panel. He also had to satisfy concerns of the Catholic Church that the bill could be construed to require Catholics who sought a civil divorce to file for a religious annulment of their marital vows.
7. Nat Hentoff fiercely criticized Governor Cuomo for signing the "*Get* Law." He reported in his *Village Voice* column of September 20, 1983 of the meeting between Lewin and Daniel. The *New York Law Journal* published a front-page editorial by Madeline Kochen of the New York Civil Liberties Union on October 23 also attacking the legislation, and Lewin again drafted a response.

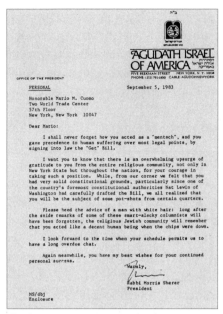

Thanking Governor Cuomo for signing the 1983 *"Get* Law"

precedence to human suffering over moot legal points, by signing into law the *'Get'* Bill .... Please heed the advice of a man with white hair: long after the snide remarks of some of these smart-alecky columnists will have been forgotten, the religious Jewish community will remember that you acted like a decent human being when the chips were down."

Despite the happy ending to the saga of the first *"Get* Law," the experience of repeatedly pleading for help in preparing the necessary legal memorandum undoubtedly strengthened Rabbi Sherer's resolve to acquire such in-house legal expertise for Agudath Israel of America.

THE PROMULGATION OF TORAH VALUES TO A WIDER PUBLIC — *Kiddush Hashem* — was one of the central themes of Rabbi Sherer's life.

Promoting Kiddush Hashem

High-quality *amicus curiae* (friend of the court) briefs of the type drafted by Chaim Dovid Zwiebel became another type of arrow in Rabbi Sherer's quiver for *Kiddush Hashem*. The 1989 Supreme Court case of *Webster v. Reproductive Health Services* provides a classic case in point. In agreeing to hear the case, the Supreme Court explicitly said that it would be considering whether to overrule its earlier abortion decision in *Roe v. Wade*.[8]

Until that point, Agudath Israel had never taken a high-profile public profile in the abortion debates. For one thing, the debate could have at most an indirect impact on the ability of observant Jews to live according to halachah. While *Roe v. Wade* gave a woman the right to terminate

---

8. The discussion that follows draws heavily on two articles by Chaim Dovid Zwiebel: "Symposium: Orthodoxy and the Public Square," *Tradition* Vol. 38, No. 1, Spring 2004; "Combatting Abortion Distortion: Agudath Israel Goes it Alone. Again," *The Jewish Observer*, May 1989, pp. 4-10.

an unwanted pregnancy, it did not force her to do so. And so there was little reason to think that Orthodox Jewish women would be having abortions as a result of the decision. Second, given the huge number of citizens demonstrating and lobbying on both sides of the abortion issue, there was little reason to believe that Orthodox Jewry would have any impact on the outcome of the debate.

Yet in the *Webster* case, the Moetzes Gedolei HaTorah instructed Agudath Israel to file an *amicus* brief arguing that *Roe v. Wade* was wrongly decided.[9] What changed the calculation of the Moetzes was the highly publicized intervention of other Jewish groups in the debate. Thus the president of the National Council of Jewish Women stated, "Our passion for choice is rooted in Jewish law and ethics …. In Judaism the mother's rights always come first." The American Jewish Congress, an old and familiar nemesis, took out a full-page ad in *The New York Times* in support of *Roe v. Wade*. The organization's president explained the group's decision: "To assume that only those who oppose abortion are 'pro-life' is a gross injustice …. The life of the mother, the life of the family — the quality of existing life — also has great value and that is something Jewish tradition recognizes."

These sophistic citations of "Jewish law and ethics" in support of positions diametrically opposed to Torah necessitated, in the view of the Moetzes, a response clarifying the Torah view. Confusion about the Torah view became only more acute when an *amicus* brief was filed in Webster supporting the result in *Roe v. Wade*, with a prominent Orthodox group listed on the brief by virtue of its membership in National Jewish Community Relations Advisory Council (NJCRAC). (If a powerful demonstration were needed of why Rabbi Sherer had hammered away at Orthodox participation in umbrella Jewish groups, this was surely it.) The apparent split within Orthodoxy over the "abortion issue" was quickly picked up by the press.[10]

---

9. Even while defending a state's right to regulate abortion, the Agudath Israel brief sought to ensure that those cases in which halachah mandates the destruction of fetal life be protected from state regulation. It maintained that there are a limited number of cases when the right to terminate a pregnancy does deserve protection as a "fundamental right," such as where the mother's life is in danger. The brief also took a rare step for Agudath Israel and argued that the Establishment Clause rendered impermissible the legislative "finding" that fetal life begins at conception, with which the Missouri legislature began the law in question. The Agudath Israel brief maintained that the question of when life begins is essentially religious in nature, and thus beyond the scope of what a secular government may determine. That argument was designed to ensure that a "fetus" not be accorded the status of a full-fledged person with a claim to life equal to the mother's.

10. The Union of Orthodox Jewish Congregations subsequently requested the NJCRAC to file an amended brief noting its dissent from the "pro-choice" position advocated by the NJCRAC's *amicus*

Though Agudath Israel might have contented itself with issuing statements and press releases refuting the claims of secular and heterodox Jewish groups, the Moetzes felt that a well-crafted *amicus* brief would gain the widest exposure for the Torah view. "The reality is ...," Chaim Dovid Zwiebel explained, "that these issues tend to be fought out in legislative and judicial arenas, and that media attention typically follows those battlegrounds."

Thus if heterodox and secular Jewish groups attempted to "prove" that Judaism sanctions same-gender unions from the fact that all men are created in the Divine Image, it behooves the Orthodox to point out that "*Leviticus* is part of the Jewish Bible too." And if those same groups sought "to convert the narrow halachic exception that permits or perhaps requires abortions under certain exceptional circumstances into a general rule endorsing 'reproductive choice' as an affirmative Jewish value," it is the duty of Orthodox groups to point out that they have transformed the exception into the rule.[11]

Through such means as *amicus* briefs and legislative testimony, Agudath Israel removed the stain on the Torah created when Jewish groups ripped Jewish texts out of context from the Torah in support of abortion on demand or same-gender marriage. In addition, it actually helped lessen the heat of anti-Semites enraged by "Jewish abortion doctors" and the like, and countered the stigma of Jews as purveyors of immorality.[12]

Part of Rabbi Sherer's lifelong *Kiddush Hashem* agenda included rebutting the image of Torah Jews as hopeless primitives. A sophisticated legal team headed by a skilled and articulate advocate, who was also a full *ben Torah*, had much to offer in that regard.

Rabbi Sherer took pride in the fact that Agudath Israel now possessed its own expert in First Amendment jurisprudence to place against the American Jewish Congress's Professor Leo Pfeffer, the nation's foremost academic opponent to any form of aid to parochial schools.[13] Many readers of *The Jewish Observer* probably could not follow the subtleties of Zwiebel's analysis in an area of the law in which the Supreme

---

brief. "Combatting Abortion Distortion," p. 10.
11. "Combatting Abortion Distortion," p. 7.
12. Ibid. p. 9.
13. Rabbi Sherer himself had expert command of Supreme Court's jurisprudence dealing with the Free Exercise and Establishment Clauses. He had famously clashed swords with the American Jewish Congress's Leo Pfeffer in his 1961 congressional testimony before the Senate Education Committee.

With Supreme Court Justice Antonin Scalia

Court had itself confessed that it could "only dimly perceive the lines of demarcation" and had frequently seemed to contradict itself. But there was a subliminal message in such an article: Agudath Israel and, through it, the Orthodox world, now possesses talent equal to any mainstream Jewish organization. We are second-class citizens no more.

RABBI SHERER'S DECISION TO ACQUIRE A LITIGATION CAPACITY for Agudath Israel of America began to pay dividends almost immediately. The legal battle against Mayor Koch's Executive Order 50 (see Chapter 16), which commenced almost immediately after Chaim Dovid Zwiebel joined the staff of Agudath Israel, would have been far more difficult without accomplished in-house counsel to fight the combined legal resources of New York City.

Large Dividends

Though, as we have seen, the primary purpose of the *amicus* briefs filed by Agudath Israel of America was usually to highlight the Torah position on the issue at hand, those briefs also made sophisticated legal arguments. In at least one case, an argument advanced in one of Agudath Israel's briefs was picked up by the Supreme Court in a rare reversal of a recent precedent. In the 1985 decision in *Aguilar v. Felton*, the Supreme Court ruled that public-school teachers could not provide remedial education on private-school property. That decision drastically cut the remedial education available to children in

Chapter Eighteen: Expanding Capacities □ 461

Orthodox educational frameworks, under various federal and state programs.

In response, the village of Kiryas Yoel, in New York's Orange County, incorporated itself as a separate public-school district, in order for children in Kiryas Yoel to receive desperately needed special education. That action was challenged in federal court as an unconstitutional establishment of religion, and the case eventually reached the Supreme Court. Agudath Israel filed an *amicus* brief in the case, on behalf of Kiryas Yoel. The brief argued that New York State had been forced to find a solution for the children of Kiryas Yoel desperately in need of special education in large part because of the Supreme Court's ruling in *Aguilar v. Felton*.

The Supreme Court ruled in the *Kiryas Yoel* case that New York State could not create a school district whose boundaries were exactly coterminous with the entirely Orthodox village of Kiryas Yoel. But three years later, the Supreme Court took the extraordinary step of overturning *Aguilar v. Felton* in *Agostini v. Felton*, which was essentially the position advocated by Agudath Israel's *amicus* brief in the Kiryas Yoel case.

Agudath Israel's legal team rendered another significant benefit to Torah education in a matter involving the Lakewood Cheder school. The Cheder, with approximately 1,000 students, desperately needed to expand in 1991, and the only way that it could fund the project was the issuance of a $3.5 million tax-exempt bond by the New Jersey Economic Development Authority (EDA). The EDA's lawyers, however, took the position that it was constitutionally barred from issuing the bond sought. A legal memorandum on the subject prepared by Chaim Dovid Zwiebel and Abba Cohen of Agudath Israel's Washington, D.C. office convinced the EDA's bond counsel to reverse its position and issue the bond. That bond led to the Cheder receiving another million dollars in private philanthropy, and being able to rebuild the entire physical plant and build a simchah hall as well.

Twice in the early '90s, Agudath Israel was successful in convincing the United States Department of Justice to either bring suit or intervene in a suit already brought. Without top-level legal talent of its own, it is highly unlikely that Agudath Israel would have been able to make a compelling legal argument to the Justice Department. The Justice Department's decision to bring criminal charges against Lemrick Nelson Jr., under federal civil rights statutes, for stabbing Yankel Rosenbaum

Rabbi Sherer and Rabbi Chaim Dovid Zwiebel (l) present an award to New York City Council Speaker Peter Vallone.

shortly after the start of the Crown Heights riots in the summer of 1991 has already been discussed (see Chapter 16).

Just a few months prior to the Crown Heights riots, in June 1991, Chaim Dovid Zwiebel met with then-Deputy Attorney General William Barr and the head of the Justice Department's Civil Rights Division John R. Dunne, and urged the department to intervene in a civil suit brought by private plaintiffs against the Village of Airmont, in New York's Rockland County. The private plaintiffs charged that Airmont had been incorporated, from a previously unincorporated area of Ramapo Township,[14] primarily for the purpose of keeping out Orthodox Jewish homeowners and had used its zoning powers to make it almost impossible to establish private *minyanim*, in order to render residence in Airmont untenable for Orthodox Jews.

Shortly after meeting with Zwiebel, William Barr was appointed attorney general, and one of his first actions was to announce, on December 17, 1991, that the Justice Department was bringing suit against the Village of Airmont.[15] "This kind of conduct — creating a new community with the intent to exclude groups because of their religious beliefs and practices — is wholly antithetical to the basic freedoms upon which this nation was founded," he declared.

---

14. Ramapo Township permitted prayer services of up to 50 in private homes.
15. Attorney General Barr was honored the following May at Agudath Israel's annual dinner.

The Airmont suit was the first time the Justice Department had ever filed a case under the federal Fair Housing Act alleging religious discrimination, and also the first Justice Department discrimination case of any type filed on behalf of Orthodox Jews. The trial record showed that the refusal to permit private *minyanim* or grant zoning variances was permeated with blatant anti-Orthodox sentiment.

After the jury returned a verdict on behalf of the Orthodox residents of Airmont, the trial judge Gerard L. Goettel vacated the jury's verdict. His opinion was spiced with more than a few negative comments about the Orthodox plaintiffs and their responsibility for the animosity directed at them. The Justice Department appealed, with the New York State attorney general, the Anti-Defamation League, and Agudath Israel of America all filing *amicus* briefs seeking to have the jury verdict reinstated. The Second Circuit Court of Appeals found that the trial record contained more than enough material to sustain the jury's finding that the Village of Airmont's actions resulted from a "discriminatory animus toward Orthodox and Hasidic Jews."

If there was ever an occasion for justified triumphalism, the victory in the Airmont litigation was it. Yet even flush from such an emotionally satisfying victory, Chaim Dovid Zwiebel chose to end his account of the litigation in *The Jewish Observer* not on a triumphal note celebrating Agudath Israel's role in seeing justice vindicated. Rather he issued a gentle reminder that not all government regulation is motivated by anti-Orthodox animus. "We do ourselves no favor when, for example, we seek to cut corners on legally mandated safety precautions and then scream 'Anti-Semitism,' when government officials move in to enforce the law," he wrote. Similarly, it behooves us to recognize the desire of existing suburban communities to preserve their rural character.[16]

In that gentle reminder to Orthodox readers to take into account the needs of gentile neighbors, he was showing himself to be Rabbi Sherer's devoted protégé. For one of Rabbi Sherer's basic *shtadlanus* principles (as we shall see) was to always take into account the interests and point of view of those with whom one was negotiating.

---

16. Chaim Dovid Zwiebel, "Foiling the Master Plan: The Airmont Case and its Implications for Expanding Torah Communities," *The Jewish Observer*, Nov. 1995, pp. 6-12.

Chapter Nineteen

THE WASHINGTON, D.C. OFFICE

THE NEXT MAJOR EXPANSION OF AGUDATH ISRAEL OF America's *shtadlanus* capacities came with the opening of a full-time office in Washington, D.C. in September 1988. It was the first full-time Orthodox lobbying office. The Washington office was Rabbi Sherer's "baby" from the start, and he took great interest in every aspect of its operations. The fund-raising burden for the new undertaking fell squarely on his shoulders, and he sent out regular letters updating the "patrons" of the office on crucial developments and achievements. He saw the Washington office as a means both for serving the *Klal* and assisting "Reb Yisrael," who might need assistance in dealing with the government bureaucracy.

The dedication of the office was an emotional event for Rabbi Sherer and the culmination of a 40-year dream. When speaking of the

Washington, D.C. office, he often said, "Just imagine if we had had an office in Washington during the Holocaust." He remembered when Washington, D.C. had been largely closed territory to Orthodox Jews. When, for instance, 400 Orthodox rabbis marched on Washington, D.C. in October 1943, three days before Yom Kippur, President Roosevelt thought it more important to slip out of the White House for a celebration of 40 Yugoslavs joining the United States Air Force than to receive the rabbis.[1]

Rabbi Nesanel Kasnett was the first director of the office. Even though he would return nine months later to his real vocation writing and editing *sifrei kodesh*, Congressman Stephen Solarz paid tribute to Kasnett in the *Congressional Record* of June 27, 1989 for having "shattered the stereotypes that so many persons in positions of power have had about Orthodox Jews."

Shattering stereotypes was, in fact, one of Rabbi Sherer's purposes in opening the office. He wanted to introduce a new Orthodoxy to the nation's policymakers: an Orthodoxy that was politically mature, fully engaged, and committed to working not only for the betterment of the Orthodox community but on behalf of all Americans. The Washington office met that test. Jeff Ballabon, legislative counsel to then-Missouri senator John Danforth, described Agudah's reputation for "effective advocacy for its constituency, as well as for its firm stances on many social/ethical issues in American society at large."[2]

In Abba Cohen, who has headed the Agudath Israel Washington office since early 1989, Rabbi Sherer found someone well suited to convey precisely the image that Rabbi Sherer wanted. A *musmach* of Yeshivas Ner Israel, Cohen also holds a law degree from Georgetown Law Center and a master's degree from the Columbia School of International Affairs. In addition, he worked for two years in the law firm of Nathan Lewin, the Orthodox world's premier public advocate, on several key Jewish community issues, and as assistant director of the Middle East desk of the Anti-Defamation League. Cohen brought to the job expertise in the nuts and bolts of public policy.

The biennial Washington visits of communal leaders from around the United States were another aspect of Rabbi Sherer's project of

---

1. David Wyman, *The Abandonment of the Jews*, pp. 152-53.
2. Jeffrey H. Ballabon, "A View of *Tikkun Olam* From Capitol Hill," in *Tikkun Olam: Social Responsibility in Jewish Thought and Law,* David Shatz, Chaim I. Waxman, and Nathan Diament, eds., p. 228.

L-r: Rabbi Chaim Dovid Zwiebel, Rabbi Sherer, and Rabbi Abba Cohen

changing perceptions of Orthodox Jews. He referred to these National Leadership Missions as unique opportunites *"liros v'liraos* — to see and be seen." At the first such National Leadership Mission, Agudah activists from 30 cities in 16 states heard from Vice President Dan Quayle, Attorney General Richard Thornborough, White House Chief of Staff John Sununu, Secretary of Education Dr. Lauro Cavazo, Deputy Secretary of State Lawrence Eagleburger, and First Lady Barbara Bush.

No less important, from Rabbi Sherer's point of view, was the time spent by Agudah activists visiting key congressional offices about matters of concern to them. One of Rabbi Sherer's lifetime missions was to make the broader world aware of Agudath Israel's "active and intelligent constituency." And, in his judgment, the visits to Washington were an excellent means of doing so.[3]

AN ONGOING PRESENCE IN THE NATION'S CAPITAL PROVIDED Agudath Israel with an opportunity to influence the crafting of legisla-

Achievements in the Halls of Power

tion to a degree previously unimaginable, and it led to government officials reaching out more to the Orthodox community. The legislative achievements of the office's first decade fully confirmed Rabbi Sherer's wisdom in pushing for full-time representation in the

---

3. Rabbi Moshe Sherer to patrons of the Washington office, July 7, 1989.

capital. The greatest legislative achievement of the decade was the passage of the 1990 Early Childhood Education and Development Act (often referred to as the ABC Child Care Bill), which remains to this day the only major federal program to rely heavily on the use of parental vouchers.

Abbie Gordon Klein, an academic researcher, gives pride of place to Agudath Israel of America in the lobbying efforts that resulted in crucial amendments to the ABC Child Care Bill.[4] As originally drafted, the bill would have allowed government grants to sectarian child-care providers, but only if there was no religious content to the day care being offered.

A series of amendments to the original bill, known collectively as the "Zwiebel amendments" after their principal draftsman, however, completely changed the structure of the bill and paved the way for Orthodox child-care providers to receive tens of millions of dollars, in the form of parental vouchers, under the act. The key amendment provided for certificates or vouchers that could be used by parents at sectarian child-care facilities, without restriction as to whether the content offered is predominantly religious, a major boon to large Orthodox families.[5]

Abba Cohen, the principal lobbyist for the amendments, spent hundreds of hours attending meetings, preparing legal memoranda, and drafting language for various versions of the Child Care Bill. Significantly, Agudath Israel of America, represented by Cohen, was the only Jewish group present at a crucial White House meeting with President George H.W. Bush to discuss legislative strategy.[6]

The final legislation, in Klein's words, constituted a "major victory" for Agudath Israel and the United States Catholic Conference, "after having expended two years of concentrated lobbying efforts for the purpose of securing the inclusion of a sectarian child-care option for parents and provider."

Agudath Israel and Rabbi Sherer also played a significant role in the

---

4. Abbie Gordon Klein, *The Debate Over Child Care 1969-1990: A Sociohistorical Analysis* (1992). Though Ms. Klein makes clear that she feels the amendments to the Early Childhood Education and Development Act, which resulted in greater participation of child-care providers offering specifically religious content, are poor public policy, she repeatedly describes the pivotal role of Agudath Israel in securing passage of those amendments.
5. Another amendment drafted by Agudath Israel of America permitted sectarian providers to hire only those who adhere to the religious tenets and teaching of such organization.
6. Ibid. p. 139 fn. 15.

Vice President Walter Mondale addressing Agudath Israel leaders at the White House. Seated (l-r) are: Alfred Moses, special assistant to the president; Stuart Eizenstadt, the president's chief assistant for domestic affairs; Zbigniew Brezinski, the president's chief adviser on foreign affairs; Rabbi Sherer

passage of the Religious Freedom Restoration Act (RFRA).[7] In the 1990 case of *Smith v. Oregon*, the so-called peyote case, the United States Supreme Court overturned decades of settled interpretation of the First Amendment's free exercise clause, and ruled that as long as a law is neutral on its face, and not specifically designed to prevent the exercise of any particular religion, the Constitution offers no protection to those whose observance of their religion might be impeded.

The implications of that ruling for Orthodox Jews were staggering. Regulations concerning animal slaughter, laws authorizing postmortem examinations by coroners, laws against gender discrimination were but a few of those "neutral" statutes that might have a potentially large impact on the religious observance of Torah Jews. Soon after the Supreme Court decision, Brooklyn congressman Stephen Solarz introduced the Religious Freedom Restoration Act. Solarz's bill essentially mandated that the government show a "compelling state interest" whenever a law placed a burden or impediment to the practice of a par-

---

7. The strongest proof of Agudath Israel's crucial role in advancing the RFRA in Congress was the choice of Chaim Dovid Zwiebel as one of the principal speakers at the March 1993 press conference called by Senator Edward Kennedy (D.-Mass.) and Senator Orrin Hatch (R.-Utah) announcing the introduction of the legislation in the Senate.

ticular religion: the constitutional standard prior to the *Smith* decision.

Though the RFRA bill enjoyed widespread congressional support, its chances of passage were seriously threatened by the opposition of the Catholic Church, which feared that it would bar any state legislative limitations on abortion.[8] Congressman Christopher Smith of New Jersey introduced his own version of the RFRA that included a specific exception to the general rule for abortion. That exception, however, would have cost the bill the support of all pro-abortion congressmen and senators. And it was problematic for Orthodox Jews because there are certain limited circumstances in which halachah requires an abortion.

In early February 1991, Rabbi Sherer met with John Cardinal O'Connor of New York, the most powerful voice in the American Catholic hierarchy at that time, to attempt to overcome the impasse. He emphasized that a failure to pass the RFRA posed a danger to the religious freedom of all religious groups in America. He also told Cardinal O'Connor that the position adapted by the Catholic Church imperiled all that Agudath Israel and the Catholic Church had been able to achieve in years of working together.

The force of Rabbi Sherer's presentation took Cardinal O'Connor aback. He assured Rabbi Sherer that the Catholic bishops would look closely at the legislation and also reexamine its position with respect to those cases in which halachah requires an abortion to save the mother's life.[9] That meeting with Cardinal O'Connor was the first of several.

Over the next two years, Rabbi Sherer and Chaim Dovid Zwiebel met again with Cardinal O'Connor. In addition, Rabbi Naftoli Neuberger and Abba Cohen met several times with William Cardinal Keeler, archbishop of Baltimore, who was the United States Catholic Conference liason to the Jewish community, and Nathan Lewin and Zwiebel met with Catholic Conference representatives in Washington. Zwiebel also circulated a lengthy refutation of charges of the National Right-to-Life Committee, which also opposed the bill.[10] Those meetings bore fruit.

---

8. The Church was afraid that if anti-abortion legislation were ever enacted and upheld by the Supreme Court, it would be rendered of little or no consequence by those claiming their "religion" required them to have an abortion. That concern was, in any event, more theoretical than practical, since by that time the Supreme Court had already struck down most legislative restrictions on abortion.
9. The Catholic Church's concerns about the RFRA's impact on anti-abortion legislation were more theoretical than practical, as mentoned in the previous note.
10. In a lengthy letter to Congressman Christopher H. Smith, Chaim Dovid Zwiebel noted the irony that Smith's bill to protect religious expression would end up by denying freedom of religious

Eventually statutory language was found that allowed the Catholic Church to withdraw its opposition.[11]

Another challenge to the legislation arose in the form of states' attorneys general. A number of states' attorneys general opposed the bill because they considered requirements of complying with the religious needs of state prisoners too onerous. With respect to Jewish prisoners, those requirements included providing kosher food, allowing Shabbos and Yom Tov observance, and permitting time for *davening*. Here too Agudath Israel's longstanding political connections proved of great assistance when New York State's Attorney General Robert Abrams, a longtime ally, came out in support of the legislation.[12]

On November 16, 1993, nearly three years after Congressman Solarz first introduced the RFRA in the House, President Clinton signed the bill into law. Chaim Dovid Zwiebel and Abba Cohen were invited to the signing ceremony in recognition of their contributions to the passage of the RFRA.[13]

In 1990, the Senate passed an immigration bill that removed for the first time the exemption from quota restrictions for religious workers. When the bill came up in the House, Agudath Israel, working through Congressman Charles Schumer — another young Brooklyn congressman with whom Rabbi Sherer had established a close relationship — introduced a number of crucial amendments. The amendments introduced by Schumer into the House legislation reaffirmed the existing exemption of "religious workers" from immigration quotas and expanded the category of "religious workers." The amendments also

---

expression to Jews, in those cases where halachah mandates an abortion. Zwiebel to Congressman Smith, February 14, 1992.

11. Because Agudath Israel was both "pro-life" and supported RFRA it was able to serve as an important bridge between supporters of RFRA and supporters of the Smith alternative.

12. Abrams' successor Dennis Vacco subsequently broke with most states' attorneys general and defended the RFRA in the Supreme Court. Rabbi Naftoli Neuberger and Abba Cohen also succeeded in persuading Maryland's attorney general to support RFRA.

13. Unfortunately the history of the RFRA did not end with its signing into law. Little more than three years after passage of the RFRA, the Supreme Court ruled that Congress had overstepped its authority in imposing the "compelling state interest test" on states and localities. The ruling in *City of Bourne v. Flores* was a major blow.

But it hardly meant that the effort expended on passage of the RFRA had been wasted. For one thing, the act still applied at the federal level. Nor did anything in the Supreme Court decision prevent states from enacting their own versions of the RFRA. Some states promptly did so using RFRA as a model. In addition, the Religious Land Use and Institutionalized Persons Act (RLUIPA), passed in 2000, did address two of the most pressing issues that concerned the proponents of RFRA: facially neutral zoning regulations that could severely impinge on religious interests and the treatment of federal prisoners asserting religious claims. Agudath Israel was one of the groups invited to the signing ceremony, in acknowledgment of its contributions to passage of the act.

provided that foreign religious workers — e.g., *rabbanim, shochtim, mohelim*, etc. — would be granted visas to work in the United States, not limited by any quota restrictions, for the purpose of serving American communities.

Rabbi Sherer had the foresight to anticipate that the exposure to the American rabbinate and institutions might be very beneficial for those religious workers who would return to serve in their native lands. That insight was borne out when the Jewish community of the former Soviet Union emerged from 80 years of anti-Jewish persecution, and there was a great need for trained religious functionaries to rejuvenate religious life in the FSU.

The 1990 Immigration Act that emerged from the House-Senate Conference, and which was eventually signed into law by President George H.W. Bush, incorporated the position advocated by Agudath Israel and other groups, and represented a considerable advance on the previous immigration law.[14]

But as often happens in government, the regulations issued by administrative agencies charged with administration of a law can take away hard-won legislative victories. When the Immigration and Naturalization Service (INS) published a set of proposed regulations pertaining to the law in the Federal Register, an alert Cohen caught the fact that the regulations had been drafted in language that would have effectively excluded Jewish religious workers. The regulations appear to have been drafted using the hierarchical structure of the Catholic Church as the model for defining religious workers. For instance, religious workers had to belong to a religious denomination defined by "having some form of ecclesiastical government," something that has not existed in Judaism since the Sanhedrin.

So important was the issue to Rabbi Sherer that he broke with his normal procedure of not writing directly to administrative agencies after Agudath Israel had filed formal written comments to the proposed federal regulations. Only the "far-reaching — and potentially disastrous — implications of the rules the INS has recently proposed," Rabbi Sherer wrote to INS Commissioner Gene McNary, led him to deviate from his normal protocol. He assured McNary that he knew that the impact of the proposed regulations of excluding Jewish functionaries was "certainly unintentional."

---

14. David Grunblatt, a prominent immigration attorney and chairman of Agudath Israel's Immigration Task Force, testified in Congress on the bill.

In a handwritten note at the bottom of the letter, Rabbi Sherer expressed his confidence that McNary would "find the way to solve [the problem]." And he proved right. The regulations were subsequently amended to reflect Agudath Israel's concerns.[15]

When the Clinton administration made government support for a wide range of volunteer activities, under the National and Community Service program, one of the centerpieces of its legislative agenda, Abba Cohen was quick to note that the proposed legislation explicitly excluded religious organizations and institutions from participation, and began raising objections to the bill as written. At stake were tens of millions of dollars of potential government funding to Orthodox schools and charitable institutions involved in volunteer activities.

Once again, Rabbi Sherer proved to be Cohen's trump card in negotiations with the House and Senate committees involved. Rabbi Sherer

With Senator Edward Kennedy and Governor Hugh Carey

---

15. The religious worker's exemption provides an interesting example of how the Washington office could frequently find itself involved in an issue on the legislative, administrative, and individual level. Even after Agudath Israel succeeded in having the proposed INS regulations modified, a consular official in Moscow refused to issue a "religious worker's" visa to the mother of Pinchas Bobrovski, a young Russian immigrant who had spoken in flawless Yiddish at the 1993 Agudath Israel dinner and was then learning at Novominsk Yeshiva. Mrs. Bobrovski was a religious studies teacher in the FSU. After the Washington office's intervention with the American Embassy in Moscow, she was granted her visa.

spoke to Senator Edward Kennedy, chairman of the Senate Labor and Human Resources Committee, with whom he had a long relationship, and Kennedy helped make sure that the final Senate legislation made provision for the participation of religious groups and schools. Agudath Israel's lobbying efforts in the House were similarly successful.

IN WASHINGTON, THE REGULATORY PROCESS OFTEN PROVES AS important as the legislative. That was the case when the U.S. Department of Agriculture's (USDA) Food Service and Inspection Service (FSIS) undertook a comprehensive review of the meat industry, after a 1994 outbreak of food poisoning from contaminated meat at several West Coast fast-food chains. Though none of the reported cases of food poisoning involved kosher meat, the proposed regulations issued by the FSIS would have had extremely serious consequences for all production of kosher meat and poultry in the United States.

Saving Shechitah

Monitoring any developments touching on *shechitah* or any other aspect of kosher food production had long been part of the Washington office's mandate. When Abba Cohen started reading the regulations, he did so not only as an attorney, but as a rabbi with *semichah* in precisely those areas most relevant to the subject at hand. And what he read worried him greatly.

Cohen quickly identified several potentially problematic areas, and consulted with Rabbi Moshe Heinemann of Baltimore, the rabbinic coordinator of Star-K Kosher Certification. The proposed regulations required the application of an antimicrobial solution to all slaughtered meat and poultry and also imposed strict cooling requirements on the carcasses. Those requirements raised two broad areas of concern. First, the likelihood that application of the antimicrobial solution would, in Rabbi Heinemann's words, "compromise" the subsequent *melichah* (salting) process. Second, the requirement to quickly cool the meat to specified temperatures would make it impossible, in many instances, to complete the *melichah* process within the halachically mandated 72-hour period, since colder, harder meat absorbs the salt much more slowly. Taken as a whole, the regulations could have made kosher meat production in the United States impossible, and significantly increased the price of imported kosher meat.

Abba Cohen quickly alerted Rabbi Sherer to his concerns. The latter responded with a sense of urgency. He told Cohen that the first thing he must do is to assemble the broadest possible coalition of Orthodox groups, particularly experts involved in kashrus certification, to discuss all the issues raised by the proposed regulations. On such an issue, he stressed, it is absolutely essential that the Orthodox world speak with one unified, authoritative voice.

The second assistance Rabbi Sherer provided was a key contact. Somehow Rabbi Sherer knew that Denver philanthropist Sheldon Beren, a major supporter of Agudath Israel's Washington office and the president of Torah Umesorah, had a personal connection with Dan Glickman, the secretary of agriculture and a former congressman from Kansas. Beren grew up in Wichita, Kansas, and had even attended Glickman's bar mitzvah.

Once he had outlined a strategy and provided a contact, Rabbi Sherer left the execution to Abba Cohen and Chaim Dovid Zwiebel, while asking to be updated continuously on an issue of such potentially major impact on the Jewish community.

Cohen now faced the unenviable task of having to explain some of the intricacies of the laws of kashrus and the processing of kosher meat to government officials with absolutely no background in these areas. In early July 1995, Agudath Israel submitted a detailed response to the proposed regulations, after extensive consultation with the kashrut experts of virtually every major kashrus certifying agency. Of the 7,000 comments filed, those of Agudath Israel were the only ones that touched on kashrus concerns.

The next step was to arrange a private meeting with Secretary of Agriculture Glickman to make sure that the kashrus concerns were highlighted among the multitude of comments being received. Here Sheldon Beren's connection proved invaluable. On August 22, Abba Cohen, Chaim Dovid Zwiebel, Nathan Lewin, and a half dozen of the America's leading kashrus experts met with Glickman and Undersecretary of Agriculture Michael Taylor. In preparation for that meeting, Cohen convened a two-and-a-half hour conference call with a dozen kashrus experts at which all the possible ramifications of the proposed regulations were discussed in depth.

Experienced advocate Nathan Lewin made the formal presentation of the halachic and practical impact of the proposed regulations at the meeting. Secretary Glickman listened attentively throughout and asked a number of questions. Though USDA administrative rules did not permit Secretary Glickman to make any formal response to the points raised, he assured the Agudath Israel delegation that the USDA under his direction would not allow the kosher meat and poultry industry to be eliminated or severely damaged. He instructed his staff to arrange for a separate hearing on the kashrus issue, at which a number of experts in the field testified.

The focus now shifted to finding alternative solutions to the public health issues that the new regulations sought to address. Those issues were by no means trivial. Nor were they treated lightly by Agudath Israel of America, in keeping with one of Rabbi Sherer's key principles of *shtadlanus*: Always keep in mind the viewpoint and interests of those with whom you are negotiating. Throughout the process, Agudath Israel made it clear that it was not seeking to exclude the consumer of kosher meat from protection against salmonella and E. coli bacteria.

In his original written submission, Cohen raised the possibility of an exemption for kosher meat and poultry on religious grounds, like the exemption for meat destined for export. That approach was partly based on the suggestion of some of the kashrus experts that *melichah* itself offers antibacterial protection. Throughout the process, Cohen made clear that the kosher meat producers and consumers were eager to find accommodations that would address the public health concerns. One alternative he suggested was that instead of mandating a uniform production process, the FSIS should institute performance standards for slaughterhouses buttressed by testing for bacterial content, while leaving it to individual plants to find the most efficient manner to meet those standards.

Little more than a year after the proposed regulations first appeared in the Federal Register, Abba Cohen was able to inform patrons of the Washington office that none of the requirements that had raised such concerns were incorporated in the final regulations. In the accompanying comments to the FSIS's promulgated regulations, the contributions of the kosher meat and poultry industry were explicitly acknowledged.

It is safe to say that no other intervention of the Washington office in the federal regulatory process in Rabbi Sherer's lifetime had a greater impact on the ability of observant Jews to live full Jewish lives in America than that to protect producers of kosher meat and poultry.

Sharing a light moment with then-Vice President George Bush

A FULL-TIME PRESENCE IN WASHINGTON, D.C. ALSO MADE IT possible for Agudath Israel to establish more ongoing relationships in the White House and the labyrinth of executive departments, where many government officials remain in place from one administration to another. On two issues of crucial importance to Agudath Israel — affirmative action in employment and school-choice reform — a close working relationship was formed during the first Bush presidency.

Working the Executive Branch

New civil rights legislation had been on the congressional agenda for a full two years before passage of the 1991 Civil Rights Act, as a result of several Supreme Court decisions. Many of the proposed versions of new civil rights legislation would have effectively imposed upon employers a racial quota system in hiring. Quotas almost inevitably work to the disadvantage of Jewish employees, and Agudath Israel strongly opposed the imposition of quotas.

Fortunately, the Bush administration also opposed employment quotas, and Agudath Israel representatives were invited to a number of high-level strategy sessions within the administration. Chaim Dovid Zwiebel was one of a small group of people invited to discuss the issue with President Bush himself, and Abba Cohen attended a strategy session presided over by White House Chief of Staff John Sununu. Cohen also submitted written testimony to the various congressional committees considering the issue. The final bill was free of any requirements on employers that would have pressured them to adapt racial quotas, and it also contained provisions protecting the rights of religious employees. Agudath Israel was the only Jewish group represented when President Bush signed it into law.

The Bush administration favored the concept of "school choice," i.e. providing parents with the means to remove their children from failing schools and place them in better ones, either public or private.[16] School vouchers — long a cause dear to Agudath Israel of America and its constituency of parents weighted down by the high costs of providing their large families with a Torah education — were widely discussed as one of the means of facilitating school-choice, especially in the wake of passage of the ABC Child Care Act, which provided for the extensive use of vouchers.[17]

So it was no surprise that when President Bush announced his AMERICA 2000 pro-school-choice educational initiative, Cohen was the only Jewish representative invited to a small, private briefing by Deputy Secretary of Education Ted Sanders. He later participated in a series of high-level meetings to promote educational choice with White House Chief of Staff John Sununu and Secretary of Education Lamar Alexander. When the Senate Labor and Human Resources Committee held hearings on educational reform in June 1991, Chaim Dovid Zwiebel was one of only four witnesses invited to testify. The others were Secretary of Education Lamar Alexander, Albert Shanker, the president of the American Federation of Teachers, and Theodore Sizer, a prominent educational reformer.

With the election of Bill Clinton in 1992, school choice was off the radar screen. Public-school teachers' unions were among his strongest supporters, and they fiercely opposed anything that might encourage parents to choose private or parochial schools. Agudath Israel now had to begin establishing relationships with the new administration and seeking other avenues of assistance to private schools. And, in fact,

---

16. Agudath Israel's support for school choice is by no means limited to parents of children in failing schools, which formed the focus of the Bush administration's initial initiatives in the area. But the Agudath Israel was nevertheless eager to see any use of educational vouchers to parents.

17. In *Zelman v. Simmons-Harris*, the Supreme Court vindicated Agudath Israel's longtime position that indirect aid to religious schools via vouchers does not violate the Establishment Clause of the U.S. Constitution.

during the Clinton years, a number of federal programs were made available for the first time to private schools, and the Department of Education consulted closely with private-school groups as to the impact of initiatives on them.

Shortly after the new administration came into power, the new Secretary of Education Richard Riley sent a questionnaire to Agudath Israel seeking its input on the Elementary and Secondary Education Act (ESEA), which was coming up for reauthorization. Agudath Israel responded in writing and in a series of meetings with Secretary Riley and other high Department of Education figures. In those meetings, Abba Cohen pointed out the difficulties faced by Torah educational institutions and ways that those problems could be solved in the context of ESEA. A number of those suggestions were subsequently included in the Department of Education's legislative proposals.

Cohen arranged for a getting-acquainted meeting on October 27, 1993 between the new Secretary of Education Richard Riley and the leaders of Agudath Israel of America. Rabbi Sherer and Chaim Dovid Zwiebel traveled to Washington, D.C. for the meeting. Secretary Riley quickly realized that he had in front of him a precious resource in the form of Rabbi Sherer, who had played a major role in the enactment of the original ESEA, the government's major education-funding bill, in 1965.

Rabbi Sherer regaled the secretary of education at length with the story of how he had helped hammer out the original clause allowing for equitable funding of non-public schools. Secretary Riley sat there transfixed and taking notes, as Rabbi Sherer laid out all the arguments that he would face from those opposed to funding of private and parochial schools.

The meeting also addressed rumors that the Department of Education was about to eliminate the Title II program of the ESEA, under which yeshivos and day schools had received computers and classroom and library supplies. Riley told the Agudath Israel representatives that he had not been aware of the impact that elimination of the program would have, and said he was eager to hear suggestions from Agudath Israel about how the program could be restructured to do away with certain inefficiencies without being scrapped entirely.

In the end, the Washington office had a major impact on the final shape of the $13 billion reauthorization of ESEA. Agudath Israel and other groups subsequently succeeded in removing language from the

With President George Bush

bill that would have barred children in parochial schools from participation in government programs for remedial education ("Title I") and the provision of library and computer materials ("Title II"). The Washington office also played a lead role in drafting language incorporated into the final legislation aimed at ensuring the more equitable participation of private-school children in ESEA programs.

After the breakup of the Soviet Union, the United States began to distribute hundreds of millions of dollars in humanitarian aid to projects in the newly independent countries formed from the FSU. Rabbi Sherer immediately organized a consortium of Jewish groups working in the Ukraine and other parts of the FSU, under the auspices of Agudath Israel, to apply for grants. Those efforts bore immediate fruit in the form of a $575,000 grant to Agudath Israel of America acting on behalf of the consortium.

In the wake of that success, Abba Cohen scheduled a meeting between Rabbi Sherer, together with Rabbi Shmuel Bloom and Chaim Dovid Zwiebel, and Ambassador Thomas W. Simons, the coordinator of American assistance to the New Independent States and the person in charge of disbursing hundreds of millions of dollars for humanitarian, educational, and economic purposes.

Ambassador Simons made clear that he was quite familiar with the work of Agudath Israel of America and of the close relationships that Rabbi Sherer had forged with leading officials in previous administrations, including former secretaries of state Cyrus Vance and Henry Kissinger.

Summing up the meeting, Cohen wrote that it had helped cement Agudath Israel's relationship with those in the new Clinton administration who would be most important in ensuring the success of various Orthodox groups working in the FSU. In Ambassador Simons, Cohen concluded, another high-level contact had been made, who could keep Agudath Israel apprised of important new developments in the FSU, and their possible implications for the large Jewish populations in the newly impendent states. Cohen's verdict on the meeting was: "When *hatzolas nefashos* is at stake, every contact counts." Indeed, that might well have been the motto of the Washington office itself: Every contact counts.

In a June 2, 1993 letter to Rabbi Sherer, Jerrold Nadler — another New York congressman representing a district with a large Orthodox population — wrote to Rabbi Sherer, "But for the existence of your Washington office, the perspective of the Orthodox community in America would not receive the highly visible and skillful representation it now enjoys."[18] A heartier confirmation of Rabbi Sherer's vision in establishing the office can hardly be imagined.[19]

---

18. Subsequent to the opening of the Agudath Israel Washington Office, both the Orthodox Union and Lubavitch have established their own offices.

19. Congressman Nadler had introduced legislation aimed at protecting the rights of Sabbath-observant employees, which had been whittled away by a string of judicial decisions. Even though that legislation did not ultimately pass, Nadler credited Abba Cohen with having developed the winning formula for stating the appropriate test for employer exemptions from the anti-discrimination provisions. A broad coalition of religious and civil rights groups had coalesced around Cohen's formulation.

Chapter Twenty

SHTADLANUS: THEORY AND PRACTICE

Setting Priorities

SHTADLANUS, WORKING WITH THE GOVERNMENT FOR the benefit of *Klal Yisrael*, was a subject about which Rabbi Sherer thought deeply for decades. He was the beneficiary of nearly daily tutorials on the topic from Rabbi Aharon Kotler for the last 13 years of Reb Aharon's life. And he continued to refine the lessons he absorbed from Reb Aharon as long as he lived.

In a 1983 letter to Professor Bernard Fryshman, Rabbi Sherer set forth in distilled form his priorities in *Klal* work.[1] The first priority, he wrote, "is what affects our ability as Orthodox Jews to live on the face of this earth. Therefore anything that relates to Torah study must be on the

---

1. Rabbi Sherer to Dr. Bernard Fryshman, May 2, 1983.

With Rabbi Aharon Kotler (l) and the Bostoner Rebbe

top of our agenda at all times, since Torah is the only 'medicine' that Hashem gave us for life itself."

The second priority was to fight anything "which violates our religious rights or which infringes upon our ability to live as observant Jews." Here the focus was primarily defensive — protecting Jews in their ability to live as Jews — rather than on trying to positively change society in the direction of Jewish values.

Toward this end, Agudath Israel might support consumer protection statutes seeking to protect Jews from fraud in the sale of religious items like *tefillin* or kosher meat. But Agudath Israel had no interest in "persuading government to make halachah the law of the land, thereby converting the police power of the state into an enforcement arm of the *Shulchan Aruch*," as Chaim Dovid Zwiebel put it in a 1987 *Jewish Observer* article.[2] That is why abortion and same-gender "marriage" were not issues to which Agudath Israel devoted a great deal of its energies until forced to counteract the falsifications of the Torah view put forth by other Jewish groups.

---

2. Chaim Dovid Zwiebel, "Using Secular Government to Promote Religious Interests: What Are the Boundaries?," *The Jewish Observer*, February 1987, pp. 27-32.

Chapter Twenty: *Shtadlanus*: Theory and Practice ☐ 483

At the same time the dividing line between promoting halachah and concern with general societal values is not a bright one. Agudath Israel actively opposed various "gay rights" legislation, the Equal Rights Amendment, and supported legislation placing limitations on abortion after *Roe v. Wade*. And Zwiebel testified before the Senate Judiciary Committee in support of the Defense of Marriage Act, which provided that no state is required to give "full faith and credit" — i.e., recognize — same-gender "marriages" performed in other states.[3]

Rabbi Sherer also knew that moral pollution could eventually take its toll on observant Jews as well. Lewd advertisements on public transportation, for instance, constituted a direct assault on Orthodox riders, and, accordingly, Agudath Israel fought the issue hard (see Chapter 11). In a less direct and immediate fashion, legislation or judicial decisions that embodied a declining belief in the sanctity of life could have implications for Torah Jews in such areas as end-of-life healthcare.

Thus Agudath Israel filed an *amicus curiae* brief in *Vacco v. Quill* (1996), the assisted-suicide case, strongly expressing its concerns about the declining emphasis on the "sanctity of life." The brief pointed out that even before World War II, the Nazi regime put to death 200,000 mentally ill or physically disabled people, on the grounds that they were "mouths not worth feeding." Scholars of the topic had drawn a direct line between recognition of the right to dispose of one's life as one sees fit by committing suicide and the sanction of euthanasia. Both flew in the face of the traditional concept of the "sanctity of life." The brief quoted Dr. Leo Alexander, the chief medical consultant to the prosecution at the Nuremburg War Trials Tribunal:

> Whatever proportions these crimes finally assumed, it became evident to all who investigated them that they had started from small beginnings. The beginnings at first were merely a subtle shift in emphasis in the basic attitude of the physicians. It started with the acceptance of the attitude, basic in the euthanasia movement, that there is such a thing as life not worthy to be lived .... Gradually, the sphere of those to be included in this category was enlarged to encompass the socially unproductive, the ideologically unwanted, the racially unwanted and finally all non-Germans.

---

3. These issues were not without a potential direct impact on Orthodox Jews. The ERA, for instance, might have resulted in the withdrawal of tax-exempt status for same-gender institutions — i.e., Torah educational institutions. And "gay rights" legislation might impede the ability of parents to shield their children from flagrantly deviant teachers.

In his letter to Professor Fryshman, Rabbi Sherer listed a third priority: Agudath Israel must never forget that it was created "to perpetuate authentic *Yiddishkeit* and create *Kiddush Hashem* for the classical Jewish people."

Perpetuating "authentic *Yiddishkeit*" included resisting any government action that might make it harder for the vast majority of American Jews to reconnect to Torah observance. As a consequence, Agudath Israel broke with many of its traditional religious allies over the issue of a constitutional amendment to permit school prayer.[4] While sympathetic to the view that a truly non-denominational prayer in school could have a positive impact, the Moetzes held that the danger was simply too great that children who were members of a minority faith would find themselves pressured "into joining their classmates in a religious exercise specifically identified with a majority denomination."

Agudath Israel, at the direction of its rabbinic leadership, lobbied strongly against 1984 "Equal Access" legislation that was pushed by many of the same religious groups who were promoting the school-prayer amendment. That legislation required schools who made available space for after-school clubs to provide equal access to religious or any other kind of student-led club. Agudah's primary concern was that Jewish public-school children could find themselves facing aggressive and active student missionary groups in school. Here too Agudath Israel's concern extended far beyond Orthodox Jewish children, few of whom attend public schools.[5]

Assisting Jonathan Pollard

AS AGUDATH ISRAEL'S CONCERN WITH THE THREAT OF SECULAR Jewish children being subjected to religious pressure in a majority Christian environment makes clear, the organization's area of concern extended to every Jew, not just the already Orthodox. Agudath Israel, for instance, consistently opposed affirmative action quotas in employment and education as a threat to middle-class and lower middle-class Jews.

Discrimination or attacks against Jews anywhere in the world inevitably made it to Rabbi Sherer's radar screen. The sentence meted out to

---

4. Ibid.
5. Once the "Equal Access" legislation was enacted, Agudath Israel urged the Torah community to take advantage of the legislation to form after-school Torah clubs in schools where there was a sufficient Jewish population to support such a club.

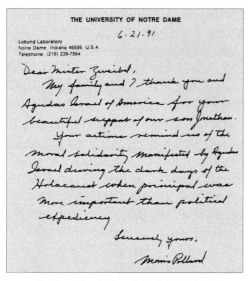

A note of thanks from Morris Pollard, father of Jonathan, for the Agudah's support

Jonathan Pollard for passing classified documents to Israel is a case in point. There is, as yet, no happy ending to the Jonathan Pollard saga, now well into its third decade. But the failure to secure Pollard's release from prison was not for want of effort on Rabbi Sherer's part.

In 1991, Rabbi Sherer invited Jonathan Pollard's parents, Dr. Morris and Molly Pollard, to make a personal appeal to the Nesius of Agudath Israel on behalf of their son. Their presentation left the members of the Nesius deeply moved. Later that year, Agudath Israel was one of three organizations to sign on an *amicus curiae* brief in support of Jonathan Pollard's 1991 petition to remove his guilty plea, and Chaim Dovid Zwiebel was one of the principal draftsmen of that brief.

After the District of Columbia Circuit Court of Appeals denied that petition by a 2-1 vote, Pollard petitioned President Bush for a commutation of sentence. Pollard's petition was endorsed by the national board of Agudath Israel. Rabbi Sherer twice wrote to President George H.W. Bush in support of Jonathan Pollard's petition, the first time during the heat of the 1992 election campaign.[6] He pointed out that Jonathan Pollard had entered into a "plea bargain" with the government that had turned out to be no "bargain" at all, because the judge in effect refused to recognize it, after Secretary of Defense Caspar Weinberger urged him to impose an extremely harsh sentence. As Rabbi Sherer eloquently summed up the matter, "He ... relinquished his right to a trial, cooperated with government investigators, pleaded guilty — all with the reasonable expectation that some leniency would be shown in his sentence. The expectation was reasonable, but it proved illusory. The 'bargain' was all one-sided."

---

6. Rabbi Sherer to President George H.W. Bush, October 23, 1992.

His second point was that Pollard's life sentence was wildly disproportional. He had received the maximum allowed under the law even though he had never been accused of giving classified information to an enemy of the United States. In addition, that sentence was far, far longer than those meted out to many who had been convicted of transferring highly sensitive information to enemy countries.

On behalf of Pollard, Rabbi Sherer did not hesitate to call in all his political chits with President Bush, who had always shown great affection for him. He reminded President Bush that Agudath Israel had worked closely with him on the America 2000 Education initiative to increase school-choice options, had supported his stand against affirmative-action quotas in civil rights legislation, and backed his nominees to the Supreme Court.

Two months later, on December 28, 1992, after President Bush had lost his contest for a second term, and was now in a position to commute Jonathan Pollard's sentence without any risk of political fallout, Rabbi Sherer wrote him again, urging him to reconsider the "extraordinarily harsh effusive that Pollard received" and commute it to time already served as a "humanitarian gesture." He prefaced his request with sincere and effusive praise to President Bush for having made the world "a safer place than it was four years ago," for "empowering parents to choose the most appropriate education for their children," and refusing to buckle under to "those who would sacrifice considerations of merit for arbitrary quotas in the workforce," and expressed his pride in having been associated with the president over the preceding 12 years. While the praise was undoubtedly heartfelt, it was also a prelude to a request for a major favor from the outgoing president.

His first opportunity to speak to President Bush's successor about Jonathan Pollard, after President Clinton invited him to participate in a White House breakfast for religious leaders, Rabbi Sherer wrote to express his delight with the president's strong support for the Religious Freedom Restoration Act.[7] Then he expressed his thoughts about the "tragic case of Jonathan J. Pollard." Since President Clinton had already committed himself to personally review the case, Rabbi Sherer confined himself to the two points he had made in his initial letter to President Bush.

But a few months later, after *The New York Times* reported that

---

7. Rabbi Sherer to President William J. Clinton, October 12, 1993.

Secretary of Defense Les Aspin had recommended that the president not commute Pollard's sentence, Rabbi Sherer wrote a forceful letter refuting Aspin's arguments — at least as those arguments were reported by the *Times*. Aspin had written that it did not matter that Pollard had handed information to Israel, a staunch American ally, for no holder of classified information has the right to transfer it "to a government the holder considers friendly." The secretary of defense, Rabbi Sherer pointed out, had created a straw man only to knock it down. No one denied that Pollard was guilty of espionage or that the crime was "reprehensible."

Aspin had pointed out that "a nation considered friendly today may have divergent interests tomorrow." But to jump from there to the conclusion that there is no difference between providing information to a staunch ally of America and an enemy nation was, Rabbi Sherer argued, a non sequitur. The United States, he pointed out, regularly distinguishes between friendly and non-friendly governments with respect to the sharing of information, technology, and equipment.

The decretary of defense's major point was that Pollard had done grave damage to American security. That claim had also been the thrust of a secret government memorandum submitted to the trial judge who sentenced Pollard. But if so, wrote Rabbi Sherer, the American people had a right to know why Pollard had only been charged with having passed information "to the advantage of a foreign nation" and not on the alternative statutory ground of "to the injury of the United States." There was something "fundamentally" unfair about charging him with one offense and then sentencing and evaluating his case on the basis of another, with which he had never been charged, said Rabbi Sherer.[8]

Finally, Aspin had argued that Pollard remained a security risk, as classified information had been found in 14 of his letters from 1989 to 1992. While being careful to stress Aspin's high reputation for integrity, Rabbi Sherer noted that Pollard would have to be insane to have done so knowing that every letter he sent was carefully scrutinized by the government. He also pointed out that not one of the government's legal papers submitted during this period in response to Pollard's efforts

---

8. See David Zwiebel, "Why Jonathan Pollard Got Life," *Middle East Quarterly*, June 1997. There Zwiebel argued at length that: "In making its case against Pollard, the government traveled a great distance: from choosing in its indictment not to charge Pollard with injuring the United States, to listing in the Victim Impact Statement allegations of damage to American interests, to raising in Secretary Weinberger's declaration the specter of danger to American lives, to accusing Pollard of 'treason' in Weinberger's eve-of-sentencing supplemental declaration."

to withdraw his guilty plea had made any mention of his continuing security breaches. Rabbi Sherer concluded with a "strong protest" against "what is obviously a series of carefully orchestrated public leaks by some of the opponents of leniency for Pollard."

Ultimately the greatest service Rabbi Sherer rendered Jonathan Pollard was personal not political. One day, during one of their periodic phone conversations, Rabbi Sherer said to Pollard, "Jonathan, I want you to promise me three things. You will keep Shabbos, eat only kosher, and never grow to hate *HaKadosh Baruch Hu*, despite whatever happens to you." Years later, Pollard told Rabbi Aryeh Zev Ginzberg, who visited him in prison, that if Rabbi Sherer were to return, he would be able to tell him, "Rabbi Sherer, I kept my promise to you on all three."⁹

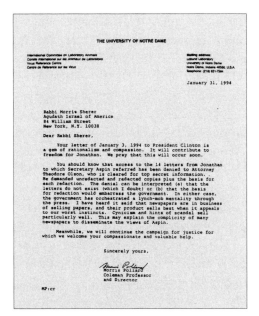

Morris Pollard thanks Rabbi Sherer for his letter to President Clinton

The Practice of Shtadlanus

THE FIRST OF RABBI SHERER'S PRACTICAL PRINCIPLES OF *shtadlanus* was: Wherever feasible create a broad-based coalition. The battle to retain the draft exemption of divinity students is a case in point. While the yeshivos had by far the biggest stake in the legislative outcome of that issue, the legislative battle could never have been won as an "Orthodox Jewish" issue. Success depended on the yeshivos waging the war under the banner of a credible interdenominational committee (see Chapter 16).

Rabbi Sherer's 30-year alliance with the Catholic hierarchy on aid to parochial and private schools brought enormous benefit to the

---

9. Rabbi Aryeh Zev Ginzberg, "A Mitzvah Rabba: The Plight of Jonathan Pollard," *The Jewish Observer*, January 2007, p. 53.

Orthodox community. Together they developed the concept of "mandated services," under which the state reimburses private schools for those activities that the state mandates — e.g., taking attendance, administering state-required tests. New York yeshivos and girls' schools received over $30 million in such payments in 2008.

Rabbi Sherer was one of the pioneers in the development of government programs benefiting Orthodox educational institutions and parents. The effort began with his alliance with the Catholic Church to secure passage of Title I of the 1965 Education Act. Under Title I, various forms of federally funded programs were made available to "educationally disadvantaged students," even if they were attending parochial schools.[10]

The second of Rabbi Sherer's *shtadlanus* principles was a decided preference for keeping public confrontation to a minimum. *Shtadlanus*, in his view, depended on establishing and nurturing long-term relationships, and even successful confrontation could come at a cost somewhere down the line when dealing with the same officials. A third principle was always to understand and keep in mind the point of view of those with whom one is dealing.

All his practical rules for *shtadlanus* came into play in combating the New York State Regents Action Plan announced in July 1983 to rectify the failures of the New York State educational system. The Regents Action Plan was doubly problematic. It contemplated an unprecedented degree of regulation of non-public schools, particularly those whose educational results were below par, and would have required content that might have been deemed inappropriate by Torah institutions.

In mapping out a strategy to respond to the Regents Plan, Rabbi Sherer began by gathering the broadest possible coalition within the Orthodox world: *shtadlanus* principle number one. The first step was to alert all affected Torah institutions of the potential threat, and to

---

10. Out of recognition of Rabbi Sherer's outstanding abilities in the area of government relations, Agudath Israel of America became, in his lifetime, the major intermediary, at both the state and federal level, between the government and the Orthodox community, and remains so until today. Agudath Israel, for instance, is the principal liaison for K-12 schools, yeshivos, and seminaries, with the federal, state, and local governments. That entails keeping Orthodox educational institutions constantly up-dated about the government aid and services to which they are entitled, and how to go about securing that governmental assistance. Monthly, or even more frequent, newsletters from Agudath Israel's Division of Yeshivah Services notify yeshivos and seminaries of all new government regulations and their various reporting requirements. That work today requires three full-time staff members to deal with various government programs that bring to Orthodox K-12 schools, yeshivos, and seminaries close to $100 million annually in government aid and services.

call them together to hammer together a strategy that would take into consideration the specific needs and concerns of all aspects of the community. The second was to solicit the support of other groups, particularly within the non-public-school community, that might share similar concerns with Orthodox Jews.

Though Shmuel Prager did raise questions about the Regents Action Plan in public hearings convened by the Regents themselves, in general, Agudath Israel's concerns were conveyed privately to the Board of Regents in private meetings and behind closed doors: *shtadlanus* principle number two. And finally, Agudath Israel never denied that the educational failure addressed by the Regents Action Plan was real and well within the ambit of the Regents' legitimate concerns: *shtadlanus* principle number three. Indeed, the Agudah coalition sought ways to address the Regents' concerns without impinging on the autonomy of Orthodox schools.

Agudath Israel's *shtadlanus* efforts paid off in a dramatically revised Action Plan. Whereas the initial plan had called for mandatory hours of certain subjects, which would have necessitated many institutions cutting back on their *limudei kodesh*, the revised plan focused on measurable test results in those subjects, not a specific number of learning hours. Even where the standardized test results fell below the targets, the revised plan left the initial responsibility for addressing those deficits with the institutions themselves. In addition, a failing institution would not be required to undergo a complete curricular overhaul, but only to address the specific deficit in question. Finally, the revised Action Plan allowed for "equivalent" courses to be offered as alternatives to courses whose content might have offended the sensibilities of Orthodox parents and educators.[11]

End-of-Life Issues

AS MEDICAL SCIENCE AND TECHNOLOGY HAVE ADVANCED AND made it possible to dramatically extend the lives of people who would have died in former times, end-of-life issues, including the rationing of medical resources, have gained ever greater prominence. Those policy debates are fraught with implications for Torah-observant Jews. Not surprisingly, then, such issues occupied a good deal of Rabbi Sherer's time in the last two and a half decades of his life.

---

11. Chaim Dovid Zwiebel, "The Yeshivos' Educational Independence Under Threat: Responding to New York's 'Regents Action Plan,'" *The Jewish Observer*, May 1984, pp. 4-6.

Traditionally, death was defined as the cessation of breathing and heart function, but with advances in the ability to maintain patients for long periods of time on respirators, many doctors began pushing for a new definition of death based on the cessation of brain activity or cessation of spontaneous breathing. Advances in transplants of vital organs gave further impetus to the push for redefinition of death, as many of those organs cannot be transplanted unless they are harvested while the "deceased" is still breathing with the aid of a respirator and his heart is still beating.

The challenge for Torah Jews, however, is that many halachic authorities do not endorse the concept of "brain death," defined as the irreversible cessation of the entire brain function, including the brain stem. Even for those authorities who do accept brain death in theory, it is questionable whether the testing required to establish brain death in terms of halachah is embodied in statute or employed by doctors. Furthermore, there remains the issue of whether doctors can be relied upon to apply the stringent standards required by halachah. A final problem is that some of the tests required to establish brain death would be forbidden to perform on a patient with the status of a *goses* (someone whose death is imminent), who may not be touched lest death thereby be hastened.[12]

In 1975 a "brain death" statute was introduced into the New York State legislature late in the term. Only a message of necessity from the governor would have made it possible for the legislation to be debated and passed before the legislature recessed. Though Rabbi Sherer convinced Governor Carey not to issue such a message of necessity (see Chapter 13), Dr. Kevin Cahill, Carey's closest friend and health czar, told Rabbi Sherer at the time that the issue would not go away.

And indeed "brain death" legislation was introduced again the following term. Rabbi Sherer focused his efforts on obtaining a "religious exemption" in the bill for those patients who for religious reasons reject

---

12. In a November 6, 1991 letter to *The Jewish Observer*, Dr. Joseph S. Jeret, an Orthodox neurologist, described an experiment on 50 patients given apnea tests, a standard part of the determination of a patient's ability to breathe spontaneously. That experiment showed that roughly one-third developed a drop in blood pressure, which carries a risk of mortality. Dr. Jeret discussed the issue with Rabbi Avrohom S. Abraham, M.D., who conferred with Rabbi Shlomo Zalman Auerbach. And the latter ruled the apnea test would be *assur* since most such patients have the status of a *goses*.

In Rabbi Sherer's diary entry of May 12, 1976, he recorded a conversation with Rabbi Moshe Feinstein, in which he asked whether a "blood flow" test has any significance for a patient breathing through a respirator. Rabbi Feinstein replied, "Definitely not, ... the test could not be performed altogether since the person is after all a *goses*."

"brain death" as the proper standard. Those efforts were frustrated, however, by a report that Rabbi Moshe Feinstein supported the "brain death" bill.

On May 17, Rabbi Sherer received a call from Assemblyman Leonard Silverman, who was the legislative point man on Agudath Israel's request for a religious exemption. Silverman said that the head of the Assembly Health Committee, Assemblyman Miller, had told him that Rabbi Sherer was wrong: Rabbi Feinstein accepts "brain death" as a definition of death. A week later, May 24, Silverman called again to inform Rabbi Sherer that Dr. Veith, a member of the doctors' committee advising Dr. Cahill on the bill, claimed that Rabbi Feinstein does not support a religious exemption.

Quite apart from the importance of the issue itself, the legislative deliberations had become a personal crisis for Rabbi Sherer: His stature in Albany derived in large part from the fact that he spoke as the undisputed voice of the Moetzes Gedolei HaTorah, and his integrity was unquestioned. Now, for the first time, his credibility had been publicly challenged. Insinuations that he had misled legislators about Rabbi Feinstein's position threatened to undermine his credibility in Albany, and had they remained unrefuted, would have greatly tarnished his reputation and undermined his standing as the spokesman for the Torah leadership.

Rabbi Sherer reported to Rabbi Feinstein, who responded with a letter to Assemblyman Miller, in whose committee the bill was pending. He wrote, "The bill, as written, is and always has been unacceptable." Rabbi Feinstein described the cessation of spontaneous respiration as the sole criterion of death, and added the crucial caveat that it is forbidden to remove a patient from a respirator to ascertain whether there is spontaneous respiration.

If all his specific requirements were not introduced into the bill, Rabbi Feinstein wrote, "I strongly endorse and support the religious exemption clause ... a concept which is in keeping with religious rights and social ethics." Rabbi Feinstein expanded on the phrase "religious rights and social ethics," in a *teshuvah* (responsum) dated 8 *Shevat* 5737 (1977):

> In accordance with the Law of the Torah it is impossible under any circumstances for even a great Torah scholar to compel any person to accept his opinion with regard to matters pertaining to [said person's] body or soul, [and particularly,] with regard to the deter-

mination of death because in accordance with [the scholar's] opinion [the patient] is already dead. Nor may any state or government declare that its opinion must be accepted. Rather the patient and his relatives must determine this, upon consultation with a great scholar who is competent in this matter, that is, provide that their [determination] is not contrary to the Torah.

Therefore, since our country, the United States of America, does not wish, Heaven forfend, to force any person to violate his religion, [i.e.,} the Torah, [the legislators] should incorporate a specific section in whatever [legislation] they may enact for themselves [which shall provide] that the patient himself and his relatives shall not be bound, if they do not so desire, with regard to whatever [the government] may establish with regard to this [matter] since this is [a matter] which pertains to [a person's] body and soul.

By 1986, almost every state in the United States had accepted a "brain death" standard. New Jersey was one of the few exceptions. In 1984, Governor Thomas Kean vetoed a "brain death" bill because of its failure to include the religious exemption, for which Agudath Israel's New Jersey representative Rabbi Yaakov Dombroff had lobbied. Eventually, New Jersey would be the first state to enact a full religious exemption to the use of the "brain death" standard.[13] In New York, brain death became the standard of death in 1984 by virtue of a decision of the Court of Appeals, the state's highest court.

In 1987, the New York State Department of Health promulgated a regulation requiring health-care providers to establish written policies for the determination of death that would include "a procedure for the reasonable accommodation of the individual's moral or religious objection to the determination .... " While in certain respects the regulation fell far short of the absolute exemption that Chaim Dovid Zwiebel had urged upon the State Task Force on Life and the Law in testimony the previous year, it contained a number of salutary provisions.[14]

---

13. That legislation was based on the recommendations of the New Jersey Task Force on Life and the Law. Chaim Dovid Zwiebel testified before the Task Force.

14. Just such an exemption was embodied in a bill that passed the legislature in 1987, with the sponsorship of Assemblyman Sheldon Silver, Assemblyman Sam Colman, and State Sen. Eugene Levy. That bill provided that "no decision or decisions with respect to an individual to commence or terminate life support treatment ... shall employ a definition of death that would be contrary to the religious beliefs ... of such individual." But Governor Cuomo let the legislation die without signing it.

In a meeting in the Agudah offices with Rabbi Sherer, Rabbi J. David Bleich, and Chaim Dovid

On the other hand, the regulation did contain certain provisions for which Agudath Israel had long lobbied. One was that health care providers make reasonable attempts to contact next of kin prior to the determination of death to enable them to express their objections. The timing was crucial, for if the objection were only expressed after a determination of death, insurance companies would likely not cover any subsequent treatment.

The Supreme Court's 1990 *Cruzan* case, involving a woman who was in a permanent vegetative state as a result of a car accident, triggered a new flurry of activity concerning end-of-life issues. Nancy Cruzan's parents had sued the state of Missouri to have her food and water cut off, arguing that she would never have wanted to live for such a pro-

---

Zwiebel, State Health Commissioner David Axelrod promised that the regulation he would draft on the subject would be better than the legislation that did not pass. Under the bill, insurance providers might have argued that a brain dead patient has "died," and is therefore no longer covered by insurance, and that the statute only grants an exemption, for religious reasons, from the hospital terminating life support. Axelrod, whose parents came from the same town in Ukraine as Rabbi Sherer's and who had a very close relationship with him, promised to remove that ambiguity, and to make clear that such a patient is not considered "dead" under state law.

longed period of time in her current condition. By a narrow 5-4 vote the Supreme Court ruled for the state and against Ms. Cruzan's parents.

The *Cruzan* case brought the macabre term "the right to die" to the forefront of public discourse and focused the nation on the issue of who should make decisions about the preservation of life for those unable to do so themselves. A national movement came into being to encourage people to specify while still fully competent their wishes as to a wide range of treatment issues that might one day arise. That could be done either through a "living will," in which the person attempted to anticipate a series of end-of-life medical decisions that might arise and express his or her wishes in advance, or by virtue of a "health care proxy," in which a person appoints an agent to make those decisions in the event of incapacity.

When New York State was deliberating a Health Care Agents and Proxies Act, Chaim Dovid Zwiebel testified against the proposed legislation on the grounds that it conferred on third parties appointed as health care proxies too much discretion to decide that a patient should die. But after passage of the Act, Agudath Israel immediately began working on its own Living Will/Health Care Proxy as a means of protecting the rights of Orthodox Jews to ensure that their end-of-life medical treatment and the post-mortem treatment of their bodies conform with halachah.[15]

The basic health care proxy developed by Agudath Israel is elegant in its simplicity.[16] In its basic outline, the Agudath Israel health care proxy directs the designated agent to make all the relevant health care and post-mortem decisions in accordance with halachah, as determined by the rabbi(s) designated on the health care proxy. In theory, the Agudath Israel proxy is perfectly suitable for any Orthodox Jew no matter what his or her position on any disputed halachic issue, such as the standard to be applied in determination of death, because it takes absolutely no stand on any such issue.

It makes no effort to anticipate all the questions that may arise in the treatment of terminally ill patients. As Zwiebel explained in his *Jewish Observer* article outlining the Agudath Israel proxy, the Moetzes Gedolei HaTorah concluded "that the range of halachic issues was too great, the changes in medical technology too rapid, the *sheilos* (halachic

---

15. Chaim Dovid Zwiebel, "The 'Halachic Health Care Proxy': An Insurance Policy With Unique Benefits," *The Jewish Observer*, September 1990, pp. 11, 17 fn. 5.
16. The Health Care Proxy has been adopted on a state-by-state basis to comply with the various legal requirements of the state in question.

questions) too dependent upon individual circumstances, to presume to identify in advance the precise course of action to be taken under all future hypothetical situations."[17]

Nor did the Agudath Israel health care proxy take any stand on the myriad of halachic issues about which there is considerable disparity between recognized halachic authorities. Rather, it sought to ensure only that the relevant halachic decisions are made by the same rabbi with whom the patient would have consulted had he or she been competent to do so.

Indeed when Rabbi Sherer first discussed the Agudath Israel health care proxy with Rabbi Marc Angel, then president of the RCA, the latter expressed great enthusiasm for what Agudath Israel had done. Rabbi Angel wrote to Rabbi Sherer on December 10, 1990 that the RCA would like to circulate the Agudath Israel proxy. Subsequently, Rabbi Angel informed Rabbi Sherer that Rabbi Moshe Tendler, the chairman of the RCA's Medical Ethics Committee, was preparing his own form that would be circulated by the RCA, but not as a document officially endorsed by the RCA.[18]

At its 1991 convention, however, the RCA released and endorsed a proxy written by Rabbi Tendler. In both form and substance, the RCA proxy differed greatly from the Agudath Israel proxy. Most notably, the RCA proxy endorsed in no uncertain terms "brain death," as the standard for determination of death.[19] In addition, the RCA proxy specifically encouraged those using the form to declare their desire to donate their life-saving organs for transplant in the event of "brain death." It thus assumed, as a matter of settled halachah, that the existing tests for the determination of brain death for patients on respirators were sufficient for purposes of halachah, that doctors could be trusted to administer the necessary tests, and that the tests could be administered without any danger of hastening the death of a *goses*.

In another radical departure from the Agudath Israel health care proxy, the RCA Proxy included a general directive that described four possible scenarios and ten different treatments for each scenario that the holder of the proxy could declare I Want/I Do Not Want. Those boxes thus allowed

---

17. Chaim Dovid Zwiebel, "The 'Halachic Health Care Proxy': An Insurance Policy With Unique Benefits," *The Jewish Observer*, September 1990, pp. 11, 18.
18. Rabbi Moshe Sherer to Rabbi Marc D. Angel, 9 *Tammuz* 5751 (June 21, 1991).
19. The following discussion of the RCA health care proxy draws on Chaim Dovid Zwiebel's article, "A Matter of Life and Death: Organ Transplants and the New RCA 'Health Care Proxy,'" *The Jewish Observer*, Summer 1991, pp. 11-14.

the proxy holder to declare in advance that he declines virtually all life-sustaining procedures in certain circumstances. And the proxy states baldly, "a quality of life that is burdensome to the patient may justify passive euthanasia … [i.e., the denial of life-sustaining food or treatment]."

The RCA health care proxy was subsequently critiqued in *The Jewish Observer* by Chaim Dovid Zwiebel, with its author Rabbi Tendler afforded an opportunity to respond,[20] and a final response by Zwiebel. Zwiebel repeatedly emphasized that the Agudath Israel Living Will/Health Care Proxy took no position on the hotly disputed issue of "brain death," and thus was suitable for any observant Jew. His second piece did, however, contain a *psak*, from the two greatest *poskim* then living, Rabbi Shlomo Zalman Auerbach and Rabbi Yosef Shalom Elyashiv, rejecting the brain death standard as a basis for organ transplantation.

The second prong of Zwiebel's critique was aimed at the RCA proxy's endorsement of "passive euthanasia," in certain circumstances, based on the patient's quality of life. That position was in starker contrast to the traditionally accepted principle that "sanctity of life" supersedes "quality of life" as the key halachic determinant. Zwiebel noted — and Rabbi Tendler agreed — that at least some of the procedures that the RCA form allowed a person to decline in advance would be required by halachah, according to every recognized *posek* in the world.

Zwiebel's critique of the RCA proxy drew a predictable avalanche of responses. The next issue of *The Jewish Observer*[21] carried a letter from Dr. Yoel Jakobovits, a physician and son of Rabbi Immanuel Jakobovits, the then-chief rabbi of the British Commonwealth and himself a world-recognized expert in the area of medical ethics. The thrust of Dr. Jakobovits's letter was to critique the "living will" aspect of the RCA proxy, which encouraged perfectly healthy people to anticipate a number of health scenarios that might one day arise.

Dr. Jakobovits described the whole concept of living wills as arising directly "from contemporary secular notions of personal autonomy, individual rights, and self-determination …," and encouraged Jewish doctors, lawyers, and rabbis to do everything possible to discourage such trends. In particular, he found the whole concept of making blanket halachic statements "well before the circumstances of the *she'eilah*

---

20. Rabbi Sherer had earlier afforded Rabbi Tendler an opportunity to present his views in support of brain death as the standard of death and against a religious exemption to brain death statutes, on public policy grounds, to the Moetzes Gedolei HaTorah in October 1987.
21. "'A Matter of Life and Death' — Revisted," *The Jewish Observer*, October 1991, pp. 14-15.

have occurred, let alone been asked" to undermine the proper decision-making authority of both rabbis and physicians. The proper solution, he urged, was the simplest possible health care proxy, like that developed by Agudath Israel, in which the document directs the agent and physicians to the rabbi or rabbis to be consulted with regard to issues involving a terminal patient.

Subsequently, the RCA recognized that its health care proxy was not universally accepted. Its president Rabbi Marc Angel sent a letter to its membership acknowledging that "there are great rabbinic authorities — including members of the current RCA Va'ad Halachah Commission — who do not accept brain death and who do not allow organ transplants," and he offered to make the Agudath Israel form available to RCA members.[22]

Though Chaim Dovid Zwiebel was the public face of the health care proxy debate, Rabbi Sherer was heavily involved at every stage. Even after the public debate ended, he continued to be besieged by increasingly vitriolic attacks on his protégé. Rabbi Sherer adamantly defended Zwiebel and cut off any further correspondence on the issue. Such staunch support was something that Agudath Israel employees could always count on, especially those thrust into the crossfire of public debate.

Agudath Israel was not able to find solutions to all the end-of-life issues raised by advances in medical technology, and indeed the issues have only become more complicated and pressing in the years since Rabbi Sherer's passing. It did, however, succeed in obtaining some form of "religious exemption" in a number of states with large Jewish populations and in passing a variety of health care statutes mandating that the religious beliefs of the patient be taken into consideration when health care decisions are being made by others on the patient's behalf. And finally, with the development of the Living Will/Health Care Proxy, Agudath Israel provided Torah Jews with a powerful tool to ensure that end-of-life decisions concerning them would be made in accordance with halachah.

In short, Agudath Israel fulfilled Rabbi Sherer's second priority in *shtadlanus:* protecting the ability of religious Jews to live in accord with halachah.

---

22. Rabbi Angel, however, erroneously characterized the Agudath Israel form as not accepting either brain death or organ transplants. In fact, one of the crucial features of the Agudath Israel form was that it studiously avoided adopting any halachic position on disputed matters, but rather required each individual to designate the halachic authority who would make those decisions for him in the event of his incapacity.

Chapter Twenty-One

ON THE INTERNATIONAL SCENE

FROM HIS EARLIEST YOUTH, RABBI SHERER WAS ENCHANTED with the idea of Agudath Israel: all world Jewry united under the banner of the Torah and led by *gedolei Torah*. Though the Torah luminaries present at the founding of Agudath Israel at Kattowicz were almost all European — a reflection of Europe's dominance as a center of Torah learning at the beginning of the 20th century — the movement was, in theory, an international one from its inception.

In 1980, Rabbi Sherer would assume the leadership of World Agudath Israel, in addition to his duties as head of Agudath Israel of America, but from the beginning his perspective was international in scope. *Shalom*, unity, was one of Rabbi Sherer's most cherished values, and his excitement over the idea of a united world Jewry necessarily gave him an internationalist perspective.[1]

---

1. Rabbi Sherer's emphasis on unity came especially to the fore in his last decade when a great deal

NO PROJECT IN WHICH RABBI SHERER WAS INVOLVED IN THE international arena had a greater impact than the rescue of Iranian Jewry. Hashem, our Sages tell us (*Megillah* 13b), puts in place the cure before He brings the disease, but rarely has this been so clear as in the case of Iranian Jewry.

Iranian Rescue

The story of the Iranian rescue begins with Rabbi Sherer's lifelong friend and colleague, Rabbi Naftoli Neuberger. In 1975, Rabbi Neuberger received a call from his wife's nephew, Rabbi Yosef Leib Schuchatowitz, who was then heading the Otzar Hatorah institutions in Iran. Rabbi Schuchatowitz described the decline in religious life under the Shah, who had decided to abolish all private schooling and ban religious education as part of his modernization drive. The impetus for the decree was the reports produced by the Shah's secret services that the Islamic religious schools, madrassas, were the principal hotbeds of anti-Shah indoctrination and ferment. But as formulated, the Shah's decree would have had a devastating effect on Jewish religious life.

Rabbi Neuberger accepted an invitation from Rabbi Solomon Sassoon, one of the leading patrons of Otzar Hatorah, who was then living in Jerusalem, to travel to Iran to negotiate with the Shah to reverse the ban on all religious schooling. At the time of their visit to Iran, most Iranian Jews, particularly outside of Teheran, were still somewhat traditional in their religious observance. But apart from the community in Shiraz, led by Rabbi Yitzchak Baal Haness, religious life lacked vitality.

While in Iran, Rabbi Neuberger conceived the idea of bringing a small group of young men from Iran to America for rabbinical training. The intention was that the young men thus trained would return to Iran where they would revitalize Jewish life.

Rabbi Reuven Khaver

The first group of Iranians arrived at Ner Israel in Baltimore in 1977; the second group arrived a year later. Altogether there were no more

---

of his time was spent preventing the divisions that had divided the Agudah movement in Israel into two rival parties from gaining a foothold in America.

than 25 *bachurim* in both groups. In the second group, there was a young man, Reuven Khaver, who would be a crucial cog in all efforts on behalf of Iranian Jewry for decades to come. Between 19 and 21 years of age, the Iranians were far behind their American contemporaries in their level of religious knowledge, and most lacked English. As a consequence, they had to begin their studies in Ner Israel's high-school program.

Meanwhile, the situation in Iran was growing increasingly tense, as the Shah's grip on power grew more tenuous by the day. In December 1978, a meeting took place in the Agudath Israel offices at 5 Beekman Street, between the rabbinic and lay leaders of the Sefardic community of Brooklyn and leading officials of Agudath Israel and members of the Nesius. At that meeting Rabbi Mordechai Maslaton reported, based on his own visit to Iran, that the more traditional community was now willing to send their children to the United States to study in yeshivah. At that meeting, it was decided to immediately open an office at 5 Beekman Street for screening young people from Iran who might be suitable for study in Torah institutions in America. The new office was jointly funded by the Sefardic community and Agudath Israel, and Rabbi Maslaton was given a six-month leave of absence from his yeshivah duties to serve as executive director.

In addition to the screening process, the new office had to enlist various Torah institutions in the United States in filling out the forms for I-20 student visas. Ner Israel alone could not possibly meet the entire need. By the end of December, the new office had already completed I-20 forms for 45 boys and 30 girls, and had received commitments from both yeshivos and seminaries to accept at least 200 Iranians.[2]

It was also necessary to make sure that consular officials in Iran acted expeditiously on the visa applications. Both Rabbi Sherer and Rabbi Neuberger put to work their extensive web of contacts in the State Department to that end. Those efforts proved successful. Eventually, Rabbi Sherer secured through State Department counsel Matthew Nimitz, a letter from Secretary of State Cyrus Vance to all consular officials in Iran that they should honor any student visa requests sent by a list of specified Orthodox institutions. He also received from Nimitz a

---

2. Among the participating institutions were: Hebrew Theological College (Skokie Yeshiva), Yeshivah Chofetz Chaim of Baltimore, Mirrer Yeshiva, Yeshivah Rabbi Samson Raphael Hirsch, Yeshivas Chaim Berlin, Telshe Yeshiva, Bais Yaakov Academy of Brooklyn, Bais Yaakov of Brooklyn, Bas Torah Academy of Suffern, Stern College, Yeshivah Rabbi S.R.H. for Girls.

promise that the I-20 student visa requests would be eligible for transmission to Iran via diplomatic pouch.[3]

As the situation worsened in Iran, the question arose as to whether Agudath Israel should be primarily focused on *kiruv* work or should it expand its operations to *hatzalah* (rescue). If the former, then work on student visas would be confined to Torah institutions; if the latter, Agudath Israel would have to expand its scope of operations to enlist non-Torah institutions. A question was presented to the Moetzes Gedolei HaTorah of America as to whether Persian Jews should be encouraged to escape or not. On the one hand, in Iran their observance was likely to remain traditional and the young people were almost sure to marry Jews. Anyone who intermarried was completely ostracized by the community. On the other hand, no one could know what to expect under a radical Muslim regime.

As the Moetzes considered the issue, the Bluzhover Rebbe began to tremble. "I see 1939 before me again. I had one daughter and one granddaughter. We asked a *shailah*, and were told to stay, and I lost my only daughter." He refused to *pasken*. Rabbi Yaakov Kamenetsky gave the final *psak*: Those who will come to yeshivos should be encouraged to leave. With respect to the others, no advice should be offered one way or the other.[4]

The Islamic Revolution of early 1979 overthrew the regime of the pro-Western Shah and replaced it in April 1979 with a fundamentalist and aggressive Shiite Muslim regime led by the Ayatollah Rubollah Khomeini. The Jews of Iran immediately felt themselves under immense threat.

Rabbi Sherer was suddenly thrust back into the rescue work of the World War II years. When an Iranian Jew by the name of Albert Danielpour was sentenced to death by the Khomeini regime on charges of Zionism, contact with Israel, and murder, Rabbi Sherer asked the archbishop of New York, Cardinal Terence Cooke, to seek the Vatican's intervention on his behalf. He stressed that the execution on trumped-up charges would place every Jew in Iran under threat. Cardinal Cooke succeeded in securing the pope's intervention with Iranian authorities.

Rabbi Sherer wrote to Cardinal Cooke May 2, 1980 with the happy news that Agudath Israel had been informed via the International Red Cross that Mr. Danielpour's sentence had been commuted to three

---

3. Rabbi Sherer to Deputy Assistant Secretary of State William Crawford, January 19, 1979.
4. Rabbi Shmuel Bloom.

A meeting of the Moetzes Gedolei HaTorah and Rabbanim in the home of Rabbi Moshe Feinstein. Clockwise from l: Rabbi Feinstein, the Bluzhover Rebbe, Rabbi Sherer, Rabbi Elya Svei, Rabbi Chaskel Besser, Rabbi Shmuel Bloom, Rabbi Avrohom Pam, the Bostoner Rebbe, Rabbi Yaakov Yitzchak Ruderman

years in prison. That commutation, wrote Rabbi Sherer, served as proof of the "good results which can be achieved, despite impossible odds, when good people pool their resources with great determination." Unfortunately, a month later he had to write Cardinal Cooke again with the news that Mr. Danielpour had been executed, despite the original report that his sentence had been commuted.

Meanwhile Rabbi Sherer found himself criticized for having solicited the help of the Vatican on behalf of Iranian Jews. He responded that in seeking the assistance of foreign leaders to save a Jewish life, "One has to plead, and not 'demand' as you suggest." He continued: "In accordance with halachah, there is nothing that I would personally not do, even if means demeaning myself to the lowest extent, if there is the slightest chance to save a Jewish life from being snuffed out for his 'sin' of being a Jew. As to whether it is helpful or useful, I would not make any such *'cheshbon'* [accounting] if the life of my child was at stake, and I would like to treat every Jew in danger with this same approach."[5]

---

5. Rabbi Sherer to Mrs. Ernest Grossberger, August 7, 1980.

That was exactly the attitude toward rescue he had learned from Rabbi Aharon Kotler.

With the Islamic Revolution, Agudath Israel's involvement in all forms of immigration work on behalf of Iranian Jews expanded greatly. Rabbi Sholom Steinberg was hired to work full-time on immigration matters. He and Rabbi Shmuel Bloom were in frequent contact with State Department and Immigration and Naturalization Service officials in Washington, D.C. over individual cases. Meanwhile Rabbi Sherer worked with senior officials over changes in American immigration policy to meet the needs of Iranian Jews.[6]

Of immediate concern were the 8-10,000 Iranian Jews, mostly students, then in the United States. Rabbi Sherer scored a major breakthrough in an April 15, 1980 meeting in the White House, with President Carter's chief domestic policy adviser Stuart Eizenstadt. At issue was the status of Iranian Jews already in America on student or visitors' visas whose visas were about to expire. The only existing route for them was to apply for political asylum. But that path was fraught with the danger that the Khomeini government might take revenge on relatives of those applying for political asylum still in Iran or on the entire Jewish community.

To meet those concerns, David Crosland, the acting head of Immigration and Naturalization Service, agreed at that meeting that the names of all applicants for political asylum and their ethnic identity would remain confidential. In addition, the applications would be sent directly to the assistant secretary of state, who would not process them further, in order to avoid any public hearings. Finally, from the moment of applying for political asylum, the applicant would be permitted to work, even without a green card, unless the application was explicitly denied.[7]

The numbers of Iranian Jews fleeing the country swelled after the onset of the Iraq-Iran War in 1980. The Iranian Revolutionary Guard

---

6. In December 1979, he wrote to Lucien Magnichever of Agudath Israel of France, who had arranged places in various institutions for 100 Iranian Jews, pending American action on their visa requests. He expressed his gratitude to Magnichever for undertaking what he knew to be a very difficult task, with the only consolation being that "there can be no greater mitzvah than Hatzolos Nefoshos." While he could not assure Magnichever that every refugee would be granted an American visa, Rabbi Sherer could at least assure him that the State Department had promised "sympathetic understanding" and "to speed up the processing procedure out of consideration for their special plight."
7. Interoffice Memorandum from Rabbi Sherer to the Iranian Task Force of Agudath Israel, April 15, 1980.

drafted even young children to the front, where they were treated as human cannon fodder and sent unarmed on suicide missions against the Iraqi invaders. Jews desperate to save their children looked for ways to smuggle them out of the country.

Rabbi Sherer worked continuously to make it easier for Iranian Jews fortunate enough to have made it out of Iran to gain entry to the United States. One of those means was to expand the use of humanitarian parole, which could be issued in cases of family reunification or upon showing that the applicant was a member of a persecuted minority in Iran.

In September 1980, Rabbi Sherer met with Ralph Goldman, the executive vice-president of the Joint Distribution Committee and Gaynor Jacobson, executive vice president of the Hebrew Immigrant Aid Society (HIAS), the organization most involved in processing visa requests for the Iranians. Rabbi Sherer proposed a joint mission to the State Department to try to cut through some of the red tape that was slowing down the process, but Jacobson argued that it was pointless, as the consular officials in each locale did what they wanted in any event. (The independence of consular officials had also been one of the major impediments to rescue work during World War II.) Jacobson suggested instead preparing a list of individual cases requiring special attention for presentation to the State Department.

Nevertheless, substantial progress was made. In an October 24, 1980 memo from Rabbi Bloom to Rabbi Sherer, the former summarized his discussion the previous day with Boruch Muller, the Agudath Israel World Organization representative in Zurich. Muller reported that he had met the U.S. Consul-General in Zurich, and that it was obvious from their talks that State Department instructions to take a lenient stance on applications for humanitarian parole, which Rabbi Sherer had arranged, had effected a decisive change in attitude. Rabbi Bloom concluded on a very upbeat note: "With the efficiency and effectiveness of Boruch Muller in Zurich, we have been able to put in place a smoothly operating system that ensures that every Jewish Iranian [who manages to make it out of Iran] has the opportunity to come to the United States."

The efficiency of that system, however, required constant direct contact with senior State Department officials, as well as pressure via faithful allies in Congress such as Stephen Solarz. In September 1983, Rabbi Sherer and Rabbi Neuberger met with seven government officials, including H. Eugene Douglas, the U.S. Coordinator for Refugee Affairs, and

Richard D. English, Deputy Assistant Secretary of State, to discuss "the shock waves" in the Jewish community in Iran created by the fact that many of those who had escaped found themselves "stranded in Europe for lengthy periods of time." Part of the problem of those stranded was that their relatives in the United States had themselves not had their applications for political asylum granted and thus lacked status to help bring in those in Europe.[8] Rabbi Sherer and Rabbi Neuberger urged special consideration for those stuck in Europe before "the screws become too tight" for the Iranian Jews still in Iran.

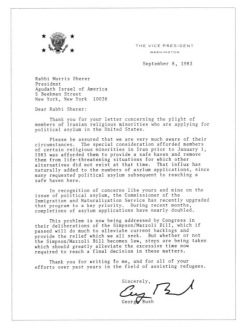

Eventually, the continual pressure on the State Department to speed up the processing of visas to America paid off. On July 23, 1985, Richard Krieger of the U.S. State Department called Rabbi Sherer to report on lengthy negotiations with the American Immigration Service officials in Vienna. The result of those discussions was an assurance to Rabbi Sherer that future arrivals would be able to leave Vienna for the United States within 30 days, and in no event after more than three months. "I know how much this means to you and your organization, and I'm happy to give you this good news," Krieger concluded.

In order to maximize the number of Jews able to flee Iran, the cooperation of the countries adjacent to Iran was essential. If those countries

---

8. Rabbi Sherer had continually pushed for more lenient treatment of political asylum applications by Iranian Jews who were already in the United States. On December 30, 1981, the State Department's Bureau of Human Rights and Humanitarian Affairs, acting on instructions of the incoming head Elliot Abrams, issued a bulletin to INS officials that in light of the changing position of Jews in Iran the previous guidelines for grants of political asylum were being loosened. And no deportation proceedings should go forward against those who had their petitions denied under previous guidelines.

In September 1983, Vice President George H.W. Bush wrote to Rabbi Sherer that "steps are being taken which should greatly alleviate the excessive time now required to reach a final decision on [political asylum requests]."

repatriated Jews who succeeded in crossing the border, and thereby doomed them to death or life imprisonment at the hands of Iranian authorities, the number of Jews attempting to find ways out of Iran was bound to slow drastically. Turkey and Pakistan were the two countries into which Jews could be most easily smuggled. Over the years, sometimes one was easier and sometimes the other. At one point, word was received that Turkey had repatriated to Iran several Jews who had successfully made their way to Turkey. That action by the Turkish government could have effectively ended any hopes for smuggling out more Jews at that juncture.

Rabbi Sherer, however, was able to take advantage of the close relationship he had forged with Congressman Stephen Solarz, a member of the House Foreign Affairs Committee and Chairman of the Subcommittee on Asia and the Pacific, which had jurisdiction over Turkish affairs. Solarz was also one of the few congressmen who had not adopted a strongly pro-Greek tilt in the dispute between Greece and Turkey over Cyprus. As a consequence, he had immense influence with the Turkish government.

Rabbi Sherer asked Solarz to set up a meeting with the Turkish ambassador to the United States. The date of the scheduled meeting happened to be the day that the Iran-contra scandal broke, and Solarz had every reason to reschedule in order to be on Capitol Hill. But out of deference to Rabbi Sherer, he went ahead with the scheduled meeting. Also in attendance were Rabbi Neuberger, Reuven Khaver, Shlomo Berger of the Iranian Rescue Committee, and Chaim David Zwiebel, representing Agudath Israel of America. Solarz's presence proved the key, and the Turkish ambassador made a commitment that his government would not repatriate any more fleeing Jews.

Apart from the concerns about the physical safety of Iranian Jews, there was a no less important worry about the spiritual status of those who found themselves stuck in Vienna or other European cities as they waited for their visa requests to be processed. Those most likely to be smuggled out were usually young men and women in their late teens or early 20's, who were in particularly parlous spiritual danger the longer they lingered, with little to do, in Europe.

Agudath Israel had already begun to get involved in the spiritual side of the Iranian rescue in the early 1980s. Groups of Iranian Jewish students, who had arrived in the United States, had gathered on university campuses in some unlikely places, like Oklahoma City, Oklahoma and Lafayette, Lousiana. Reuven Khaver, who carefully tracked the movements of Iranian Jews while continuing his studies in Ner Israel, proposed running a series of *kiruv* programs on these campuses and presented the proposal to Rabbi Sherer, who immediately agreed to fund the programs.

But the major *kiruv* work did not begin until 1985, when Rabbi Mechel Gruss traveled to Vienna at the request of Rabbi Elya Svei, to observe the state of the Iranian Jewish refugees there. Prior to his trip, Rabbi Gruss was briefed by Rabbi Shmuel Bloom on the major organizations involved in Vienna and what he would find there. Rabbi Gruss reported back that the situation in Vienna was very grave from a spiritual point of view: almost all the refugees were single boys and girls, who had come from a traditional, conservative society and suddenly found themselves thrust into the middle of a modern European city, without any adult supervision. At the same time, Rabbi Gruss said, the situation in Vienna also presented some unique opportunities for *kiruv*, as the young people in Vienna had a great deal of time on their hands and very little to do.

That report led to the formation of the Iranian Rescue Committee under the auspicies of Agudath Israel of America. Rabbi Sherer played a decisive role in the creation of the Iranian Rescue Committee and con-

With members of the Iranian Rescue Committee: (l-r) Dovid Dembitzer, Dovid Weldler, Rabbi Shlomo Berger, Benzion Fishoff, Rabbi Mechel Gruss, Rabbi Sherer, Dov Hertz, and Dr. Moshe Ruzhorsky. Shia Markowitz, a key member of the committee, is not in the photo.

tinued to render crucial assistance throughout the four-year life of the Committee. He patiently assembled the pieces needed to get the Iranian Rescue Committee off the ground. Among those pieces was a rabbinical board that included Rabbi Elya Svei, Rabbi Yosef Harari-Raful, and Rabbi Ahron Schechter. Rabbi Yitzchok Feigelstock subsequently took an active role.

A top-level rabbinical board was crucial. By 1986 the Iranian Rescue Committee was involved in the smuggling of Jews out of Iran, and the life-and-death decisions involved could not be taken without rabbinical guidance. One time, for instance, the committee received information that the father of one of a group of youths about to be smuggled out of Iran was threatening to reveal the smuggling operation if his son insisted on leaving. The question then arose whether the father would actually act upon his threat. If yes, then the entire operation had to be canceled; if not, it could proceed.[9]

The central figure in the smuggling operation was Rabbi Reuven Khaver in Baltimore, who had long been pushing for Agudath Israel to get involved. He would receive names of Jews wishing to escape from Iran, usually from relatives already in the United States, and make contact with a network of smugglers in Iran. Over the years, Rabbi Khaver arranged for approximately 2,500 Jews to be smuggled out of Iran,[10] with the committee picking up the bill when there were no relatives to do so.

Rabbi Sherer had so much respect for the *mesiras nefesh* of Khaver that he stood for the young man when he entered the room.[11] Once Rabbi Khaver was visiting Rabbi Sherer in the Agudath Israel offices, and he commented about some matter, "We should get somebody to do this." Rabbi Sherer promptly escorted him to the copy machine where he had posted the saga of four brothers named Somebody, Anybody, Everybody, and Nobody: Everybody said, "We should get Somebody to do it." Somebody said, "Anybody can do it." In the end, Nobody did it.

Rabbi Sherer tapped Rabbi Shlomo Berger to head the Iranian project and provided him with offices in Agudath Israel's Manhattan head-

---

9. In the end, the operation went forward, and the father did not inform the authorities. There were Jews who lost their lives attempting to escape from Iran, but not one whom was smuggled out under the auspices of the Iranian Rescue Committee.

10. The price for smuggling Jews out of Iran dramatically shot up over time, from a few hundred dollars in the beginning to several thousand dollars. The Iranian Rescue Committee provided the money to pay the smugglers only when the families of those leaving could not afford to pay the smugglers.

11. Rabbi Shmuel Bloom.

quarters. In the summer of 1985, Rabbi Neuberger had gotten word that it would be possible to smuggle a group of schoolgirls out of Iran into neighboring Kurdistan, under the guise of going on a school outing. Rabbi Neuberger and Rabbi Sherer[12] hired Berger to oversee that mission, which had to be canceled at the last moment due to inclement weather on the day for which the outing had been scheduled. But in the meantime, Berger had earned the confidence of Rabbi Sherer. Rabbi Sherer told Berger at the very outset that the Iranian rescue was his "baby," as he had begun his career in Holocaust rescue work. He promised Berger that he would have ready access to him whenever he needed.

Meanwhile Rabbi Sherer had assembled the committee of committed *baalebattim* upon whom the spiritual rescue depended. Rabbi Sherer had a keen eye for untapped or underutilized talent, and it was employed to the selection of the Iranian Rescue Committee. The obvious choice to head the Committee was Rabbi Mechel Gruss, who had already gone to Vienna as Rabbi Svei's emissary. Over the next four years, Gruss would spend on average at least half his day involved in Iranian rescue work. The other leading members of the committee were Dovid Weldler, Shia Markowitz, and Dr. Moshe Ruzhorsky. Though the members of the committee barely knew one another in advance, they soon meshed into a close-knit team. It was not unusual for members of the committee to spend 30 hours in a week on fund-raising and other matters connected to Iranian rescue. Some even took Iranian Jewish children into their homes and raised and married them off like their own children.

The dedication of the members of the committee was total. "I could call any one of them up and say, 'We are flying to Vienna tomorrow,' and they would be there," remembers Berger. In a letter to major donors to the Iranian Rescue Committee in England, Rabbi Sherer offered his own assessment of the Rescue Committee: "In my 45 years of public life I have rarely seen a project conducted with such dedication by young *bnei Torah*."

Shortly after the committee was formed, its leading members and Shlomo Berger traveled to Vienna to observe the situation firsthand. The sight of hundreds of Jewish youngsters, plucked from a highly traditional society and thrust into a modern one, without any adults or family members to guide them as they prepared for an uncertain future, was a wrenching one. Shia Markowitz kept thinking of the stories of his

---

12. Rabbi Berger first came to Rabbi Sherer's attention when the latter heard him lecture on Holocaust education.

father-in-law, a Holocaust survivor, surviving the war all alone.

The committee members quickly realized that the project they had undertaken was going to require lots of money. Though none of the committee members had any particular experience in fund-raising, they would raise millions of dollars during the second half of the 1980s. The projected budget for 1988 alone was close to $2 million. Here too Rabbi Sherer helped by identifying those who would respond to the call for *hatzalas nefashos*. A generous check of $36,000 from Rabbi Ezriel Tauber, at the first meeting of the Iranian Rescue Committee, got matters off to an auspicious beginning. In Europe, where the committee also raised funds, Rabbi Sherer's connections were invaluable.

Rabbi Sherer put the Iranian Rescue Committee on the Friday program at the Agudath Israel convention, and provided the committee with the rare privilege of doing his own fund-raising at the convention. Shia Markowitz's speech electrified those in attendance. "This time we will not be able to say we did not know what was happening," he challenged the crowd.

The Novominsker Rebbe held a meeting of Brooklyn *rabbanim* in his home. Getting the *rabbanim* on board was crucial, as it opened the way for members of the committee to speak about the project in shuls on Shabbos, sometimes as many as five or six times — at an early and later *Maariv minyan* on *leil Shabbos*, two different *Shacharis minyanim*, and again in the afternoon. At one parlor meeting, an old Jew approached one of the committee members and asked him, "Where were you guys in the '40s?"

At one point, when the committee was deeply in debt for the meals they were providing in Vienna, the members flew to Toronto to meet with Moshe Reichmann, someone whose respect for Rabbi Sherer was almost unlimited. His check for $180,000 saved the project at that point, and over the years, he would give many times that amount.

Rabbi Sherer also gave the Iranian Rescue Committee access to the web of connections and goodwill he had built up over decades. In every organization — the JDC, HIAS — he instantly knew whom the committee would be able to work with. "He did not just know the top person in each organization," remembers Shlomo Berger. "He knew the organizational chart of the entire organization." He could tell Berger what organization or individual would be interested in a particular aspect of the committee's work. And he could convene a meeting in Switzerland, for instance, with all the relevant parties, in an instant.

The Iranian Rescue Committee provided kosher meals for all who wanted them. At its height, it was preparing 500 hot lunches a day, and breakfast for anyone who attended the learning programs. Among the beneficiaries of the free meals were Iranian Jews who were being sponsored in Vienna by other organizations. Given the financial burden on the committee, the question arose whether to continue providing meals for those being sponsored by other organizations. But Rabbi Sherer adamantly opposed charging for the food or placing any conditions on its provision. Food was sacrosanct in rescue work, he stated, and that was the end of the matter.[13]

In addition to providing meals, the committee also obtained a building to serve as a women's dormitory for between 60 and 100 young women (and apartments for five couples who were in Vienna to teach) in a supervised setting. The building was obtained through the intervention of Rabbi Sherer's friend Richard Schifter, the former attorney for SBCO, who was then serving as Assistant Secretary of State for Human Rights and Humanitarian Affairs.[14] Schifter, a native of Vienna, who had fled as a teenager, pressured the Austrian government to provide a building for the Jewish refugees. Shlomo Grusgot, a local diamond merchant, who was well connected in governmental circles, helped with negotiations from the Austrian side. The Austrian government refused to sell the building outright, preferring to rent it for $120,000 per year. The Rescue Committee had to spend twice that amount to provide security against the very real threat of a terrorist attack.[15]

Even at the last moment, the lease almost fell through. Mr. and Mrs. Michoel Jacobovits, a middle-aged couple from Washington Heights, flew to Vienna in early 1988 to take up residence as dorm parents. (Mrs. Jacobovits was also a veteran educator) Vienna city officials required a local organization to provide a guarantee for the lease and against any damages to the building. A local rabbi had assured Rabbi Sherer that his shul would do so. But at the final meeting with city authorities

---

13. Rabbi Mechel Gruss.
14. Schifter's help in obtaining the building was only one aspect of his assistance to Rabbi Sherer with regard to the Iranian refugees. Shortly after he assumed his duties as Assistant Secretary of State, Rabbi Sherer asked Schifter to work out with the Immigration and Naturalization Service an arrangement whereby a group of 25 Iranian girls would be allowed to study in a Jewish school in Strasbourg, France, even though they were registered for immigration purposes in the American consulate in Vienna. Schifter, Rabbi Sherer recorded in a memo for his files dated October 17, 1985, was "very elated" with his successful resolution of the matter and told Rabbi Sherer that he would personally follow up if he needed any further help.
15. Rabbi Sherer to Messrs. Benzion and Shlomo Freshwater, April 5, 1988.

to sign the lease, the rabbi in question suddenly developed cold feet and refused to sign the guarantee. The city officials refused to proceed without a guarantor. At that point, Jacobovits called Rabbi Sherer, even though it was 5 a.m. in New York.

Rabbi Sherer was then sick with the flu and had been out of the office for a couple of days. Nevertheless, he greeted Jacobovits as if it were the middle of the morning and asked him how he could help. Jacobovits explained the problem and put the local rabbi on the phone. The two men spoke for about 20 minutes, and when they finished the rabbi emerged from the room and signed the guarantee. Rabbi Sherer had told him, "Agudath Israel is responsible," and that had quelled all his fears. A letter to that effect was subsequently signed by Rabbi Sherer, Louis Glueck, Rabbi Mechel Gruss, and Shia Markowitz.

The kosher meals and dormitory were important in their own right. But they were also instruments of the most ambitious aspect of the Iranian Rescue Committee's efforts in Vienna: teaching Torah to those who found themselves stuck in Vienna with time on their hands. The committee sponsored young couples in Vienna. At a minimum, there were always at least two young couples — one native-born Americans, the other of Iranian origin — in Vienna at any one time, and sometimes as many as five. The couples offered Torah classes throughout the day for both men and women. Rabbi Yisroel Szyf, a graduate of Chevron Yeshiva, who had been the head of all the Otzar Hatorah institutions in Iran for 20 years, and who spoke fluent Farsi, supervised all the learning programs.

There was even a *beis medrash* in which a group of 30 or so students learned *Gemara* all day, with an Iranian-born rabbi who had learned for nine years in Ner Israel. Though many of the youth who passed through Vienna came from traditional homes, this was for most of them their first exposure to *Gemara* learning.[16] While they were in Vienna, every effort was made to convince the young people that they should attend yeshivos and seminaries when they reached America. And many did.

In a 1988 letter to two major supporters of the program in England, Rabbi Sherer reported that in the preceding 18 months, 200 boys and girls had been placed in Torah institutions in America. Another 75 were living with Orthodox families while they started to work. Fifty girls were training in Agudath Israel-sponsored programs and 80 had

---

16. In "Two Paths Through Vienna," *The Jewish Observer*, January 1987, Rabbi Shlomo Berger describes one such young man.

already been placed in jobs.[17] The projected budget for 1988 allocated nearly $340,000 to absorption of the refugee youth in America.

As a result of the efforts that began with Rabbi Neuberger's 1976 trip to Iran, there are in America today dozens of yeshivah-trained Iranian rabbis and 500 couples of *bnei Torah*. More than 20 Iranian congregations and educational institutions have been created by the early yeshivah graduates and by those who were won over to Torah study during their time in Vienna.

When the first young men came from Iran to study at Ner Israel, Persian Jewry was in a state of decline and no signs of revival were on the horizon. The great irony is that as a result of being uprooted from their ancient homeland, Persian Jewry is stronger and more vibrant in America today than it was in Iran.

Russian Jewry

WITH THE BOLSHEVIK REVOLUTION OF 1917, THE SECOND LARGEST Jewish community in the world was cut off from the rest of world Jewry. It would remain so until the first stirrings of Jewish consciousness among Russian Jews after Israel's dramatic victory in the 1967 Six-Day War. Those stirrings coincided with the beginnings of an active movement on behalf of Soviet Jewry in the West.

The millions of Jews trapped in the Soviet Union were a source of great interest to Rabbi Sherer, but there was little in the way of tangible help that he or Agudath Israel was able to offer until the late 1970s. Prior to that time Agudath Israel's principal activity on behalf of the Russian Jewish community consisted of sending matzos to Soviet Jews. Soviet officials did not permit any large-scale shipments. Rather, each box of matzos had to be sent to a specific individual. Money collected by Agudath Israel of America for sending matzos was transferred to Agudah activists like Alexander Schweid in London, who then prepared the individually mailed packages to the Soviet Union. Thousands of boxes of matzos were sent in this fashion every year.

In the mid-'70s, the Soviets suddenly decided to stop the shipments of matzos. Rabbi Sherer met several times with Secretary of State Cyrus Vance on the issue. He also approached the Russians directly. On a trip to Albany with Rabbi Bloom, Rabbi Sherer returned a call from the Russian Embassy in Washington, D.C. from an airport pay phone. He

---

17. Rabbi Sherer to Messrs. Benzion and Shlomo Freshwater, April 5, 1988.

asked to speak to the long-time Soviet ambassador to the United States, Anatoly Dobrynin, and identified himself to the operator as the president of Agudath Israel of America. Dobrynin took the call and began, "I know about Agudath Israel of America, and I know about your Council of Torah Sages."

Dobrynin's knowledge of the Council of Torah Sages derived from the early 1970s, when members of the Jewish Defense League had harassed Soviet diplomats in New York City. Shots were even fired at Soviet diplomats in the Riverdale section of the Bronx. Secretary of State Henry Kissinger called Rabbi Sherer at the time and told him that the shootings were endangering the Nixon administration's entire policy of détente with the Soviet Union. Kissinger, a former Pirchei boy in Germany, asked Rabbi Sherer to arrange for him to make a presentation to the Moetzes Gedolei HaTorah to explain the potential consequences of the attacks on Soviet diplomats.

Rabbi Sherer was unwilling to arrange such a meeting. He asked Kissinger, however, to provide him with all the arguments, and told him that he would personally present them to the Moetzes. The secretary of state told Rabbi Sherer that the Russians knew that those who were shooting at their diplomats wore yarmulkes, and that they might well respond with greater severity toward the small number of religious Jews in the Soviet Union.[18]

The Moetzes did, in fact, issue a public statement that castigated the shootings as "not the way of the Torah." Immediately thereafter, the shootings stopped. Whether the cessation of the shootings had anything to do with the proclamation there is no way of knowing. But the Russians believed that they did. Thus, this was Dobrynin's reference to the Council of Torah Sages at the beginning of his discussion with Rabbi Sherer.

Dobrynin explained to Rabbi Sherer why the Soviets had decided to stop the shipment of matzos from abroad. He candidly admitted that it made the Soviet Union look bad that it could not produce enough matzos of its own to satisfy the demand. In addition, he said, the sale of matzos was the major source of revenue for the state-authorized synagogues, and the government wanted to increase

---

18. That concern about reprisals against religious Jews in the Soviet Union had long been paramount for Rabbi Sherer. In a January 19, 1971 letter to Dr. Gordon Meyerhoff, for instance, he advised against *davening* with a *minyan* outside the Soviet mission as a form of protest. The Russians, he warned, might come to see a *minyan* as a form of revolutionary activity and place further restrictions on public prayer in the Soviet Union.

that revenue. Finally, he told Rabbi Sherer that matzos had become a political not a religious issue, and specifically referred him to ads that had appeared in *The Jewish Press* and elsewhere under the heading "Do not be silent," which showed a crying Jew reaching out from behind barbed wire for matzos. "Is this religion or is this politics?" Dobrynin asked.

There was a brief spike in Jewish emigration from the Soviet Union between 1971 and 1973. Most of the Jews leaving the Soviet Union in those years, however, went to Israel. Thus when the question of what could be done on behalf of Russian Jews was first raised at the annual convention of Agudath Israel of America in the early '70s, the first answer was the creation of a committee of *baalebattim* in Israel to deal with the issues raised by the influx of tens of thousands of Jewish immigrants who had been cut off from virtually any knowledge of their Jewish heritage for more than half a century. Such a committee was established, under the leadership of Meyer Dovid Lewenstein. Rabbi Sherer remained involved in its work, and frequently wrote to Rabbi Shlomo Lorincz for information on the committee's activities and to urge it to become more active.

Only in the late '70s, when Jewish immigration from Russia to the United States increased greatly, did Agudath Israel of America open

Rabbi Sherer meets with former Soviet refuseniks Zev and Carmela Raiz after their release.

up its own American operation.¹⁹ Project RISE (**R**ussian **I**mmigration **S**ervices and **E**ducation) was the response. As was often the case with a new project, Rabbi Sherer began by looking for a *baalebos* who would take overall responsibility and undertake to raise much of the funding and for top talent to direct the project. He found the former in Mr. Willie (Zev) Wiesner, who threw himself into Project RISE with single-minded devotion, and was involved in every aspect of its activities.

Rabbi Sherer's search for the proper person to run the project took him to Israel to meet with Rabbi Ephraim Oratz, the founding principal of Bais Yaakov Academy of Brooklyn.²⁰ Rabbi Oratz had already been living and teaching in Israel for many years. He told Rabbi Sherer that he was very happy living in Israel, and had no intention of returning to America.

The next day, Rabbi Sherer called again. "The least you can do is ask a *shailah*," he told the surprised Rabbi Oratz. The latter agreed, and was even more surprised when Rabbi Yosef Shalom Elyashiv told him, "When the *tzibbur* [public] needs a *yachid* [individual], the individual has no choice but to do the bidding of the public."

When Rabbi Oratz, who was roughly Rabbi Sherer's contemporary, joined Agudath Israel to head Project RISE, Rabbi Sherer told him, "With respect to this project, Ephraim Oratz is Moshe Sherer. When anyone calls me about Russian immigration, I will refer them to you, and tell them that you speak for me." He added, however, that Rabbi Oratz should not hesitate to consult him whenever he needed: "Don't wait until the light turns red. When it starts to turn to yellow, come to me."

One of the many difficulties that Rabbi Oratz faced was that by the time the Russian immigrants reached America their primary focus was on making a living, and they had little time or energy to think of anything else. Moreover, the cultural gap was very wide. For instance, Project RISE developed a program for religious families to adopt new

---

19. The Soviets first allowed a very limited Jewish emigration in 1967. That ended with the Six-Day War. During the period of détente, there was another spike in emigration between 1971 and 1973. Passage of the Jackson-Vanik amendment, which conditioned favorable trade status on Soviet emigration policy, in 1974, and the beginnings of the Helsinki Human Rights Watch in 1975 brought pressure on the Soviet Union to permit Jewish emigration. From 1977 to 1979, there was another increase, culminating in the exodus of 51,000 Jews in 1979. The latter emigration, however, was accompanied by the show trials of leading Jewish activists like Natan Sharansky, Yosef Begun, and Ida Nudel. Only in 1990 did the floodgates of emigration open, with more than 100,000 Jews leaving the former Soviet Union and its successor states each year from 1990 through 1994.
20. It was Rabbi Oratz who had previously introduced Rabbi Sherer to Mr. Wiesner.

immigrant families, and there was a great response from the religious community. But the new immigrants proved to be very suspicious of the proffered help. They did not want to let anyone into their homes for fear that they might be KGB agents. A program to help find jobs with Orthodox employers also floundered on cultural differences and the work habits developed working for the State in the Soviet Union.

In the end, it was decided that education of the young offered the greatest potential for having any impact on the community of Russian-speaking immigrants, and Rabbi Oratz, who had been an educator all his professional life, turned his efforts in that direction. Rabbi Yaakov Kamenetsky, a native of Russia, took a great interest in the project, and answered the many difficult questions that arose — e.g., should boys who were reluctant to undergo a *bris* be allowed to put on *tefillin*.[21]

The difficulties experienced by Project RISE suggested that Agudath Israel's potential impact upon Jewish observance might be far greater among Jews still living in the Soviet Union, as compared to those who were struggling to get started in new countries. Rabbi Sherer would soon have direct evidence for that proposition from Yosef Mendelevich, a young Jew who was arrested by the Soviets in 1970 for his part in a plan to take a small Soviet plane and fly it to Israel.

In the late 1970s, Mrs. Rivka Drori, Yosef Mendelevich's sister, visited America in an effort to raise support for her brother, who had languished nearly eight years in Soviet prison camps. All those who had been arrested together with Mendelevich had already been released from jail. His mitzvah observance while in prison made Mendelevich particularly anathema to his Soviet jailers, and he had been sentenced to three years under far more restrictive conditions, as a consequence of his evasion of all prison labor on Shabbos.

Rabbi Sherer was one of the Jewish leaders whom Mrs. Drori contacted on her trip to the United States, and thus it was natural that she should call him in 1978 when she required intervention with the Soviet government at the highest level. She explained that her father and stepmother had been given exit visas after many years of waiting. But on the very night of their scheduled flight to Israel, her father had passed away.

Her father's dying wish had been to be taken for burial in *Eretz*

---

21. When the question was raised in a meeting of the Moetzes Gedolei HaTorah, Reb Yaakov said that the opposition to *bris milah* probably came from the boys' mothers. If it is winter, they will say it was too cold. And in the spring, they will find some other excuse. So, Reb Yaakov *paskened*, we'll give them a full year, and if at the end of that time the boys still have not undergone *bris milah*, they will be told that they have to find another school.

Yisrael, where Mrs. Drori and another sister were already living. But the Soviets would only let the body out if it were first cremated. Meanwhile, Mrs. Mendelevich had only a few days left on her exit permit before it expired. *Could Rabbi Sherer do anything to help get permission for Mr. Mendelevich's intact body to be flown to Israel?* Mrs. Drori wanted to know.

Rabbi Sherer contacted Henry Kissinger, who had just recently resigned as secretary of state, but who had more pull with the Soviets than any American. Kissinger promised that if an appropriate memorandum were on his desk the next day, he would personally deliver it at the Soviet Embassy. Kissinger called Rabbi Sherer the next day and told him, "The Russians never say yes. But they didn't say no either." He advised that Mrs. Mendelevich should once again request permission to leave with her husband's *aron*.

Her requests were turned down. But a few days before the exit permit was to expire, Rabbi Sherer again called the former secretary of state, who told him that he had done all that he could. Nevertheless, the next time that Mrs. Mendelevich went to request permission to take her husband's body with her, the attitude of Soviet officials had completely changed. She was told that she could take her husband's body and even extend her permit if she wished.

After that initial success, Rabbi Sherer became involved, along with many others, in efforts to obtain the release of Yosef Mendelevich himself. Mendelevich, however, was not released until Purim Kattan of 1981. After first going to Israel, Mendelevich traveled to America to meet with President Reagan and all those who had worked on his behalf, and to give a boost to the Soviet Jewry movement.

Rabbi Sherer was among those with whom he met. At that first meeting, Rabbi Sherer told the young hero, "Think of me as your uncle. I want to help you in any way I can." Those were no idle words. At that first meeting, Rabbi Sherer noticed that Mendelevich seemed very tense, and asked him why. He told Rabbi Sherer that he had decided to go on a hunger strike in order to pressure the Soviet Jewry movement in America to intensify its activities. Rabbi Sherer told him, "You can't decide something like that on your own. I'm your driver. We are going to Rabbi Moshe Feinstein."

Upon arriving at Rabbi Feinstein's, Reb Moshe immediately drew everybody into the kitchen. He told Yosef that there is no such thing as a "protest fast" in the Torah, and so fasting in his case would be a

Rabbi Shmuel Bloom, Rabbi Sherer, and Rabbi Chaim Dovid Zwiebel meet with Yosef Mendelevich on his visit to America.

prohibited endangering of his life. Just to make sure that his *psak* was accepted, Reb Moshe immediately offered his guest a drink of juice and asked his wife to prepare some eggs for him.

Rabbi Sherer also took Mendelevich to meet Rabbi Yaakov Kamenetsky. Reb Yaakov told him that now that he was free, he must take the opportunity to begin learning *Gemara*, and advised him that he should review every *sugya* with the commentary of the *Rif*. It was the first of a number of meetings between the venerable, Russian-born *gadol* and Mendelevich.

On that first trip to America, Mendelevich spoke at Agudath Israel's annual dinner. He held up the *tzitzis* that he had worn during 11 years in captivity and described how he had obtained everything needed to make his own Pesach Seder. Tears could be seen rolling down Rabbi Sherer's cheeks as he spoke, and Rabbi Yaakov Kamenetsky, usually the epitome of calm, cried openly.

In the late '60s, Reb Yaakov had visited Russia, in part to see two younger siblings. He came back from that trip extremely discouraged about the future of Russian Jewry. Even his younger brother, who had learned briefly in Slabodka Yeshiva, retained almost nothing of his *Yiddishkeit*. Listening to Yosef Mendelevich speak, Reb Yaakov realized that he had despaired too quickly of anything being saved of Russian Jewry.

Introducing Yosef Mendelevich to Rabbi Shneur Kotler at the Agudah Dinner.

That visit to America would be the first of many for Yosef Mendelevich, and Rabbi Sherer continued to play the role of the wise "uncle" for him. One piece of advice he gave him was to steer clear of all those who would try to get him involved in Israeli politics. If he chose to do anything of a public nature, it should be in the area of working with Soviet Jews, where he had something special to offer.

In one of their talks, the young man mentioned that he wanted to learn full-time, but he also wanted to marry, and he had no means of supporting himself. Rabbi Sherer immediately wrote out a $1,000 check to help support him while he learned in Yeshivat Mercaz HaRav. He also arranged over the years for many yeshivos in America to invite Mendelevich to be the guest speaker at dinners and relate the riveting story of his mitzvah observance in Soviet prisons. Those speeches were an important source of income during the seven years that Mendelevich learned full-time until he obtained *semichah*. (Today he teaches *Gemara* in the Russian-language program of Machon Meir.)

Of his relationship with Rabbi Sherer, Rabbi Mendelevich says today, "I never felt that there was any self-interest on his part, or even that he had any ideological agenda. He just wanted to help me. I felt he loved me, and I loved him."

From Yosef Mendelevich, Rabbi Sherer received something more than inspiration. He learned of an underground movement of Jews in the Soviet Union who were returning to Jewish observance and learning Torah in clandestine circumstances. That information was to lead to an entire transformation of Agudath Israel's activities with Russian-speaking Jews.

At the Knessiah Gedolah of the World Agudath Israel in Jerusalem in 1980, just a few months after Yosef Mendelevich's release from prison, Rabbi Sherer declared, "Yosef Mendelevich wants to learn Torah. But he also feels he has an obligation to start an organization to help Jews trying to live as Jews in the Soviet Union. We are going to take on that organizational work so he can learn." He pledged $50,000 toward a program sending *shluchim* (emissaries) to the Soviet Union to meet with the underground cells of Jews drawing closer to religious observance.

At the same Knessiah Gedolah, Rabbi Pinchos Teitz of Elizabeth, New Jersey, who had been traveling regularly to the Soviet Union since

Addressing the Sixth Knessiah Gedolah. Seated at the dais (l-r): Rabbi Moshe Porush, Rabbi Pinchos Levin, Rabbi Shlomo Zalman Auerbach

1973, also described the phenomenon of young Soviet Jews learning Torah with great *mesiras nefesh*. As a consequence of these reports, the Vaad HaPoel HaOlami of World Agudath Israel decided to create a Vaad L'Hatzolas Nidchei Yisrael to address the needs of the Jews still in the Soviet Union. Rabbi Mordechai Neustadt, who had been a young activist in Zeirei Agudah Israel in *Eretz Yisrael* prior to moving to the United States, was tapped to head the new project, and he has continued to do so for nearly three decades.

The Vaad would send approximately 500 *shluchim* prior to the breakup of the Soviet Union in 1991. The *shluchim* brought with them kosher food, *sefarim*, religious articles, and items of value that could be sold on the black market. The black market price of one sophisticated camera was almost enough, for instance, to finance an entire summer-camp program in one of the Baltic Republics. But the most important gift the *shluchim* brought was one that even the ever-watchful KGB could not uncover: the stored-up Jewish knowledge that they imparted in *shiurim* to Jews eager to soak up every crumb of knowledge.

Initially, Rabbi Shmuel Bloom assisted Rabbi Mordechai Neustadt in helping to find the *shluchim*. The first to go were Rabbi and Mrs. Neustadt together with Rabbi and Mrs. Herschel Lieber, followed by Rabbi and Mrs. Mendel Goldberg and Rabbi and Mrs. Chaim Septimus. Rabbi Shlomo Noach Mandel of Toronto was in the third pair of emissaries, which turned out to be the start of his extensive work in Eastern Europe on behalf of the Albert Reichmann family.[22]

The primary destination for these *shluchim* to the Soviet Union was the underground learning group in Moscow, headed by a brilliant, young mathematician by the name of Eliyahu Essas. Essas was one of the many numerous Prisoners of Zion and refuseniks, including Yuri Edelstein and Natan Sharansky, whom Rabbi Sherer attempted to help through his close contacts with former Secretary of State Henry Kissinger and through Senator Edward Kennedy.[23] Essas was eventual-

---

22. The *shluchim* were but one aspect of the continuing work of the Vaad L'Hatzolas Nidchei Yisrael over the years. Through the efforts of Rabbi Mordechai Neustadt and the Vaad, a number of yeshivos were established in the former Asiatic republics. The Vaad also made it possible for a number of immigrants from the FSU to learn for many years upon their arrival in Israel, thereby making possible the development of a group of Russian-speaking *talmidei chachamim*, who would become some of the primary Torah teachers to Russian immigrants, after the opening of the floodgates of the FSU in 1991.

23. Rabbi Sherer wrote to both in 1980, urging them to use their influence with the Soviets on behalf of Essas.

ly freed in 1986. His was one of three names of prominent refuseniks on a list President Reagan presented to Soviet leader Mikhail Gorbachev at a summit in Geneva in November 1985. Soviet Foreign Minister Andre Gromyko, appropriately nicknamed "Mr. Nyet (Mr. No)," looked at the list and told President Reagan he could have Essas as a goodwill gesture.[24]

Long before Rabbi Essas's release, his father had met with Rabbi Sherer, while he was in America together with Natan Sharansky's wife Avital to arouse American support for their loved ones. The senior Essas found in Rabbi Sherer someone with an open ear, who was eager to consider all practical steps that might help gain the release of refuseniks and Prisoners of Zion. He was, the elder Essas reported to his son, not content only to organize the recitation of *Tehillim*, though Agudath Israel did call many solidarity prayer gatherings as well. Until his dying day, the senior Essas recalled the compliment he had received from Rabbi Sherer for giving new impetus to the cause of the refuseniks by his visit to America.

Rabbi Sherer had worked together with Israel Singer and the latter's boss at the World Jewish Congress, Edgar Bronfman, on securing Rabbi Essas's exit visa, and had sent Rabbi Essas a number of letters via emissaries. So it was natural that Rabbi Sherer was one of the first addresses for Rabbi Essas when he visited America after his release. Rabbi Essas was the guest of honor at the Agudath Israel convention that year.

Rabbi Essas, who had developed a keen ability to size up Jewish leaders in advance, was taken aback by Rabbi Sherer at their first meeting. He was unprepared for the breadth of Rabbi Sherer's perspective. "He wanted to make the whole world better from the perspective of Torah. His perspective was not that of someone running a *kreml* [a small grocery store] or a *shtiebel*," Rabbi Essas remembers. In particular, Rabbi Essas was surprised by how little of Rabbi Sherer's conversation focused on Agudath Israel.

Essas was prepared for questions about the learning circles in Moscow, Leningrad, and other Soviet cities, and what could be done to help them. But when Rabbi Sherer began asking what could be done to preserve or foster the connection of the mass of non-observant Soviet

---

24. Rabbi Essas was the third on a list that included famous refuseniks Yosef Begun and Ida Nudel, and thus the "cheapest" in Soviet eyes. Making it to such a list at all required the combined efforts of numerous parties exerting pressure from different directions.

Dancing with Rabbi Eliyahu Essas at an Agudah convention. Among those in the background are Rabbi Mordechai Neustadt, Hirsch Wolf, and Yossi Ashkenazy.

Meeting with Rabbi Eliyahu Essas and Rabbi Mordechai Neustadt

Jews to their Judaism, Rabbi Essas was surprised. He had not expected that to be a particular concern of the president of Agudath Israel.

"When Rabbi Sherer asked, 'What can we do?,'" Rabbi Essas felt, he was not asking what could Agudath Israel do, but rather what the entire religious community could do together. He sensed that Rabbi Sherer was deeply pained by the divisions between Orthodox Jews and eager to find ways of overcoming some of those divisions in common, goal-oriented projects.

At the establishment of the Moscow office of Agudath Israel World Organization in 1991. L-r: Rabbi Mordechai Neustadt; Rabbi Sherer; Rabbi Yaakov Bleich, Chief Rabbi of Ukraine; Sender (Sasha) Rubinonvich, director of the office

Journey South

TWO ARDUOUS TRIPS TO SOUTH AMERICA IN THE 1970S REFLECTED Rabbi Sherer's commitment to world Jewry.[25] His arrival in Buenos Aires, Argentina in August 1970 was treated as a state visit by a major dignitary by the entire Jewish *kehillah*. Shortly after his arrival, he conducted a press conference for the Jewish press: two Yiddish dailies and two or three Spanish-language Jewish papers. Much of the press conference centered on the governmental work of Agudath Israel of America. Of particular interest to the reporters was the fact that Agudath Israel of America included in its membership ranks those with a university education and university professors.

Rabbi Sherer's visit created waves even beyond the Jewish community. The press conference with the Jewish press was followed the next day by one with the Argentinian press — including the country's most prestigious paper, *La Prensa* — radio, and television. The American ambassador John Lodge, a former governor of Connecticut and brother of Richard Nixon's running mate in 1960, Henry Cabot Lodge Jr., hosted a large reception for Rabbi Sherer. The *La Prensa* story about Rabbi Sherer's visit and his analysis of current events in the United States, accompanied by a photograph, added greatly to the prestige of Agudath Israel in the eyes of the local Jewish community.

So did the elaborate reception at the American Embassy, at which Ambassador Lodge read letters of greetings from two politicians with

---

25. This section is based on two lengthy aide-mémoires: (1) Memo: Argentine Diary; (2) Argentine Diary: South America Revisited, July 1976. These were written by Rabbi Sherer after his August 20-26, 1970 and and July 8-14, 1976 trips.

At a reception for Rabbi Sherer at the American Embassy in Buenos Aires. L-r: Yisroel Gutwirth, Dr. Yerachmiel Kugielsky, Rabbi Zelig Privalsky, Rabbi Sherer, United States Ambassador John Davis Lodge, Isaac Tawil

whom Rabbi Sherer was very close: Governor Nelson Rockefeller of New York and Senator Jacob Javits. The local Agudah head, Dr. Raphael Kugielsky, widely publicized that the embassy relied only on the strictest local *hashgachah*, not the standard *Kehillah hashgachah*, for the smorgasbord at Rabbi Sherer's reception. The local Agudists were, in Rabbi Sherer's words, "thrilled beyond expression" by their increased status in the eyes of the local Orthodox community as a result of the honor shown to Rabbi Sherer. Among other things, they expected that increased status to open up doors for local fund-raising and to make affiliation with the local Agudah more prestigious.

One of Rabbi Sherer's main goals was to bolster the local Agudah in Buenos Aires, and that he did in a number of ways. The first was lending his organizational expertise. His visit was timed to coincide with a Latin-American conference of Agudath Israel. After an opening banquet, Rabbi Sherer insisted that the subsequent sessions dispense with all speech-making so as to leave all the available time for in-depth organizational work. Rabbi Sherer quickly came to view the local Agudah leader Dr. Kugielsky as "an extraordinary person whose work for Agudah is hardly duplicated by any non-professional anywhere else in the world."

At the same time, he identified a major problem with the local Agudah as the lack of any organizational structure, which left Dr. Kugielsky effec-

A reception for Rabbi Sherer at the offices of the Buenos Aires Kehillah. Seated: Zvi Seingersh, President of the Kehillah; Rabbi Sherer; Rabbi Dov Kahan, Chief Rabbi of Argentina. Standing: Mr Schwartzman, Mr. Eisenberg, Dr. Yerachmiel Kugielsky, Dr. Gorenstein, Mr. Nathan Guttentag, Rabbi Zelig Privalsky, Dr. Asher Schnurman, Mr. Fleischmann

tively doing almost everything by himself. One of the keys to the success that Rabbi Sherer was just beginning to see in the American Agudah was his ability to mobilize large numbers of *baalebattim* to the cause, and for that a more formal organizational structure was required. Rabbi Sherer described in detail how a Vaad Hanhalah Hametzumzam functioned to encourage the active involvement of *baalebattim* in the organization. He recommended that the Latin American organization adopt a similar format and that the youth movements, Ezra and Bnos Ezra, be represented on the new council. The next day Rabbi Sherer was delighted to hear a report that everyone elected to the new Vaad Hametzumzam had attended the first meeting, and that the "enthusiasm was unparalleled, with everyone [agreeing] to take different tasks."

Everywhere he went Rabbi Sherer stressed the importance of focusing on improving the level of Torah learning. Even in the Agudah-sponsored elementary school, *limudei kodesh* only commenced at 2 p.m. in the afternoon. Rabbi Sherer urged that the situation be immediately reversed, but every place he did so, he was immediately met with the response that the government would never permit such a thing. Rabbi

Sherer, however, insisted that was not necessarily the case, and continued to harp on the importance of placing the emphasis on *limudei kodesh*. Eventually, by stressing the issue, he was able to "cut through all the layers of habit and indifference that paralyzed [local] thinking until now." By the end of his visit, a number of local educators had assured him of their intention to switch over all *limudei kodesh* to the morning.

Perhaps Rabbi Sherer's greatest impact on the future of Argentinian Jewry came from his insistence that the community needed to engage a top-level Torah leader. He tapped Rabbi Shmuel Aryeh Levine, a native of Argentina, who had been learning in Ponevezh Yeshivah in Bnei Brak for seven years. The 30-year-old *talmid chacham* possessed, in Rabbi Sherer's analysis, "the Torah knowledge, appearance, dedication, as well as the knowledge of Spanish" necessary to lead the community and to establish a genuine yeshivah in Buenos Aires, and would add that special "Torah flavor" that the community lacked. Rabbi Sherer spent a good deal of time with Rabbi Levine and his wife convincing them of the importance of his returning to his native land, and with the community leaders persuading them to meet Rabbi Levine's requirements for doing so.

Rabbi Sherer also took the opportunity to connect with the local youth. On *Motza'ei Shabbos*, 150 members of the Agudah youth movements gathered for a lavish Melaveh Malkah, at which Rabbi Sherer

Rabbi Sherer, Rabbi Shmuel Aryeh Levine (l), and young men from the Buenos Aires Yeshivah

made a brief speech and then took questions. The event did not end until 2 a.m. (as did almost every evening event for the week of Rabbi Sherer's visit, in the Argentinian custom), and could have gone on for another hour and a half had Rabbi Sherer not insisted on trying to catch a bit of sleep. Rabbi Sherer was pleasantly surprised by the "incisive" nature of the questions, and viewed the session as one of the more constructive of his entire visit. He repeatedly stressed Torah must serve as the "underpinning of one's personal life and Agudah life."

The next evening Rabbi Sherer met with a group of non-religious univeristy students in the penthouse apartment of Mr. and Mrs. Boruch Mehl, among the wealthiest Jews in Buenos Aires and "penthouse Agudists." The Mehls' two sons learned in university and in an evening yeshivah program. They brought home 60 of their classmates to meet Rabbi Sherer. While impressed with "the sincerity of these kids," Rabbi Sherer "was deeply depressed by [their] total lack of identification [with] or minimal knowledge about *Yiddishkeit*." He emphasized to them that there can be no genuine understanding of *Yiddishkeit* based on "abstract philosophical talks." Understanding can only come from experiencing a life of mitzvos. He invited them to be guests of Agudath Israel if they ever visited the United States and promised to set them up with either young religious college people their own age or religious college professors for Shabbos if they did so. The students responded with enthusiasm to his offer to experience authentic Jewish life and, at the same time, to be able to ask any question they wanted.

One signature theme that Rabbi Sherer emphasized in many venues was the danger posed to Argentinian Jewry by the growth of the Conservative movement in South America, led by Spanish-speaking rabbis. He spoke on "Who is a Jew?" at a speech open to the general community. While the capacity crowd of 600 was primarily composed of Orthodox Jews, he was surprised by the number of non-religious Jews who came to hear him. At an evening event hosted by the general *kehillah*, Rabbi Sherer "hammered away" at the dangers to the *kehillah* from any recognition of the Conservative and Reform movements. The chief rabbi of the *kehillah*, Rabbi Kahane, was present, and Rabbi Sherer was eager to get him firmly committed in front of a large gathering to opposing any recognition of the heterodox movements.

The issue was then a hot one in the community, as a Conservative convert had applied for membership in the *kehillah*, which up until that point was officially Orthodox. Over the objections of the local Agudah, the *kehillah* did not refer the issue for rabbinical decision but instead had referred it to the *kehillah* presidium, which had approved the application.

As he headed for the airport at the end of his six-day whirlwind tour, Rabbi Sherer was filled with many conflicting thoughts. He saw tremendous opportunities to have a major impact on the 350,000 Jews of Buenos Aires. "I know of no other area where we could obtain such tremendous results and spiritual profits from the most minimal investment," he wrote on the plane ride home. Among the many ideas going through his mind was sending two of the American Agudah's better youth leaders during summer vacation, where they would "be treated like kings and would not cost [the American Agudah] anything." Even a *kollel* could be started with a little encouragement and seed money from America, he felt.

On a personal note, Rabbi Sherer hoped that the trip would prove to be the "beginning of our being given the ability by *Hashem Yisbarach* to broaden our horizons to help communities that could use some charging of their spiritual storage batteries." Not wishing to sound like a "sob sister," he still wished that some way could be found to lift from his shoulders the "paralyzing responsibility for the daily expenses of the entire Agudah operation" so that he could "use whatever *kishronos* Hashem gave him in the right way."

Almost six years after his first trip to Argentina, Rabbi Sherer returned for a second visit. That visit provided him an opportunity to view the fruits of his first trip. On that earlier visit, he had pushed hard to bring an Argentinian-born *talmid chacham* to Buenos Aires to establish a *yeshivah gedolah* and *kollel*, and had handpicked Ponevezh-trained Rabbi Shmuel Aryeh Levine for the task.

What had been considered a "wild dream" six years earlier had come to pass. The *yeshivah gedola* and *kollel*, under Rabbi Levine's guidance, had come into existence, and the effects were evident everywhere. Rabbi Sherer found "a mini-Boro Park" in Buenos Aires that brought tears to his eyes. The level of *Yiddishkeit* of the local Bais Yaakov girls was, in his opinion, equal to that of their peers in New York and Jerusalem.

But his greatest "*nachas*" of all came from the visit to the *yeshivah gedolah*, where he met with 30 young men learning from early morning until late at night. He saw these local *bnei Torah*, "who could compare to [their] peers in Bnei Brak and Jerusalem," as the key to the future of Argentinian Jewry.

Addressing a conference of the Latin American Agudah. Seated l-r: Mordechai Erps; Rabbi Dov Kahan, Chief Rabbi of Argentina; Rabbi Yosef Tzvi Oppenheimer, Yisroel Gutwirth, Rabbi Berman.

The local Agudath Israel was now the second largest group in the local *kehillah* and had garnered almost 10 percent of the vote in the most recent elections. And Agudath Israel had shown itself a major player on the local scene. By creating an independent, not-for-profit *shechitah*, Agudath Israel had managed to lower the price of kosher meat by 18 percent and that of kosher chickens by 25 percent, thereby bringing kosher meat within the price range of many Jews who were not sufficiently committed to bear the tremendous disparity between kosher and non-kosher meat and chickens.

In keeping with the deep respect that he always showed for dedicated *baalebattim*, Rabbi Sherer attributed much of the development of the Argentinian Agudah to the head of the local branch, Dr. Kugielesky, whose *"mesiras nefesh"* had made him the major architect and builder of Torah in Argentina. Dr. Kugielesky was the dentist of the rich and famous in Buenos Aires, and yet he saw patients only from 3 p.m. to 10 p.m. in order to leave his mornings free for Agudah fund-raising and administration.

Rabbi Sherer took time for a private meeting with the newly appointed director of Agudah branches in Latin America. He shared with him one of the secrets of success in public life — good human relations —

Chapter Twenty-One: On the International Scene   □   533

and stressed the importance of working closely with the Agudah veterans on the scene: Dr. Kugielsky and Rabbi Levine.

As always, Rabbi Sherer showed little interest in resting on what had been achieved so far. He saw much potential for the expansion of Torah in Argentina. Secular Jewish youth on university campuses had drifted toward the Left, and as a result many had disappeared in the "dirty war" between the ruling junta and anyone suspected of left-wing sympathies.

Ever alert to the local political situation, Rabbi Sherer quickly picked up that the fears of parents of losing their children could serve as an impetus to putting them in religious educational frameworks. At his opening press conference with the Jewish press, Rabbi Sherer laced into the World Zionist Organization for sending left-wing emissaries to Argentina, who would only poison the minds of Jewish children and perhaps put them in mortal danger.

Rabbi Sherer returned to related themes at the reception in his honor at the American Embassy. Ambassador Robert Hill was so impressed by his discussion of Agudath Israel's work with local youth and of religious education that he asked Rabbi Sherer for a memorandum on the subject that he could present at his next meeting with the president of Argentina.

Rabbi Sherer always dreamed big, and South America was no exception. He heard from many in the community that the first priority, as he saw it, was the completion of a large dormitory for the *yeshivah gedola* so that the yeshivah could draw students from outlying areas, where the Conservative movement had made significant inroads. As a consequence he devoted a good deal of his visit to raising money for the new dormitory. He added a day at the end of the trip to go to Brazil, together with Dr. Kugielesky, to present a special plaque to Mr. Guertzenstein, who had dedicated the new building of the yeshivah and *kollel* in the name of his father, the first rabbi in Brazil.[26] He succeeded in convincing Mr. Guertzenstein to contribute an additional $36,000 toward building a new dormitory. That was the second large donation he successfully solicited on his trip. He also told Dr. Kugielesky that the American Agudah would promise the final 10 percent when the rest of the money for a dormitory was collected.

In addition to the potential that he saw in expanding the yeshivah

---

26. Rabbi Sherer had arranged for special messages of greeting from New York Governor Hugh Carey and New York City Mayor Abraham Beame to Mr. Guertzenstein.

in Buenos Aires and attracting *talmidim* from a wider area, Rabbi Sherer reported on the opportunities available to open new yeshivos in Uruguay, Brazil, and even Peru.

But if the past six years had witnessed the great strengthening of the yeshiva-oriented community in Buenos Aires, the Conservative movement in Argentina, led by Spanish-speakng rabbis, had also attracted many young people. Everywhere he went, Rabbi Sherer inveighed against the dangers of the Conservative movement. A special conference took place at the local Agudah headquarters, with all the local rabbis, except the "official rabbi" of the *kehillah* and one or two others, to develop a strategy to deal with large infusions of money coming to the Conservative movement from the United States.

At a reception in his honor tendered by the local *kehillah*, Rabbi Sherer stressed the importance of the *kehillah* placing its focus on Torah education, and warned strongly of the dangers of continued flirtation with the Conservative movement.

As draining as Rabbi Sherer found the rush of social events in Argentina — they inevitably started at least an hour after the scheduled time and frequently lasted past 2 a.m. — he finished the trip elated that he once again had the *"zechus* to encourage thousands of Jews in Buenos Aires to strive for 'big things' in *Yiddishkeit* and to concentrate on intensive Torah study." He returned home more convinced than ever that North American Jewry had a special responsibility to help build Torah in the spiritual desert of South America, "especially since the possibilities of success are so much greater than in our own country."

Forging a Foreign Policy

DEMONSTRATING THAT COMPLETE FEALTY TO THE TORAH IS NO contradiction to running an office with the highest level of professionalism was one of Rabbi Sherer's life missions. Thus he was delighted when Agudath Israel World Organization (AIWO) became the first major Jewish organization to have an expert on international law on its staff with the 1995 hiring of Professor Moishe Zvi Reicher.[27] Reicher replaced

---

27. Professor Reicher, formerly a leading Australian barrister, teaches Law and the Holocaust at the University of Pennsylvania law school. He did his graduate work in law at Harvard Law School under Professor Louis Sohn, the leading expert on United Nations-related law and worked as a consultant for the International Monetary Fund. Professor Reicher's father, a Sanzer *Chassid*, served in the diplomatic corps of the Polish-government-in-exile during World War II. Professor Reicher's

Dr. Isaac Lewin, who passed away in the summer of 1995 after serving with distinction as AIWO's United Nations representative for nearly 50 years.[28] Subsequently, he was appointed Director of International Affairs of AIWO.

Rabbi Sherer and Reicher set out to create a pro-active foreign policy for AIWO. Instead of reacting to each new crisis as it arose, the new policy sought to build ongoing relationships between Agudath Israel and foreign countries based on mutuality of interests.[29] The new republics carved out of the former Soviet Union, for instance, were desperate for foreign currency and thus eager to encourage tourism. For them, favorable publicity, even in the *chareidi* press, a seemingly small niche market, was very important. The families of many religious Jews have their roots in those countries, which makes them a natural draw for Orthodox Jews eager to visit the gravesites of their ancestors and the great *tzaddikim* of previous generations.

These republics soon learned that Agudath Israel could provide them with all the positive publicity they wanted, as long as they were forthcoming on the issues of greatest importance to the Jewish people, particularly the preservation of Jewish cemeteries and the restitution of former Jewish properties.

The preservation of Jewish cemeteries was not a new area for Rabbi Sherer. In 1987, for instance, he enlisted Congressman Stephen Solarz, a leading member of the House Committee on Foreign Affairs, to write to the Czechoslovakian Ambassador to the United States about the building of a playground on the Jewish cemetery in Lipnik, in which

---

rich Yiddish proved very useful when working with Holocaust survivors on issues relating to Eastern Europe.

28. Dr. Lewin's life spanned almost the entire 20th century. He was the son of Rabbi Aharon Levine, Rav of Reisha, who represented Agudath Israel in the Polish Sejm. Dr. Lewin was an active member of the Lodz City Council prior to the war and a major presence on behalf of Agudath Israel World Organization at the United Nations from its creation. He gained for AIWO consultative status at the United Nations, the highest level of affiliation for non-governmental bodies. Dr. Lewin played an active role in the drafting of the Universal Declaration of Human Rights in 1948, particularly Article 18 guaranteeing religious freedom, and was considered the architect of the 1981 General Assembly Declaration on the Elimination of All Forms of Intolerance and Discrimination Based on Religion or Belief.

29. A classic case of how this mutuality of interests worked took place after Rabbi Sherer's passing, in 2000, when the Ukraine sought UN Security Council membership, and asked AIWO to support its candidacy. After consulting with Rabbi Besser, Reicher called Rabbi Menachem Porush in Jerusalem to explain the various issues of Jewish significance on the table with the Ukraine, and asked him to use all his connections to secure Israeli government support for the Ukraine. Reicher spoke with Rabbi Porush on a Monday, and already by Wednesday, Israel's UN Ambassador Dore Gold had been instructed to vote for the Ukraine. The rapid flow of events was not lost on the Ukraine.

Rabbi Baruch Frankel-Teomim (known as the Baruch Taam after his most famous work) was buried. That intervention eventually proved successful, and Rabbi Sherer himself traveled to Czechoslovakia to speak at the rededication of the cemetery in 1992. With the addition of Professor Reicher to the staff, the work of cemetery preservation could be pursued in a more systematic fashion.

AIWO also developed relationships with the United States government in such a way that formerly "Jewish issues" became transformed into American issues.[30] The U.S. Commission for the Preservation of America's Heritage Abroad played a major role in that respect.[31] By law, the commission is charged with working together with the Department of State to obtain from foreign governments in Eastern and Central Europe guarantees of the protection of cemeteries and other holy sites in areas from which American citizens emigrated. Rabbi Chaskel Besser was one of the commissioners, and Professor Reicher was appointed international legal counsel to the commission by its Chairman Michael Lewan, who enjoyed a long and especially warm relationship with Rabbi Sherer. Another Agudah connection to the State Department developed when Professor Reicher was chosen to brief State Department officials — about to be posted to one of the new republics carved out of the former Soviet Union — about the religious issues they would face.

In pursuing its foreign policy, AIWO benefited from the belief of many Eastern European governments that Jews wield inordinate

Congressman Solarz intervenes to help preserve the Lipnik cemetery.

---

30. An example of turning Jewish issues into American issues occurred when the Moldovian government began privatization proceedings to take over a former shul in Kishinev. The shul was then hosting a yeshivah of the Vaad L'Hatzolas Nidchei Yisrael. Professor Reicher prevailed upon the Senior Adviser for Property Restitution in the State Department to raise the matter with Moldovian officials. Shortly thereafter, the yeshivah was returned to the Vaad.

31. The Commission was created by an Act of Congress in 1985 for the express purpose of protecting the cultural heritage of those Central and Eastern European countries from which Jews and other American citizens emigrated. The initiative for the legislation came from Rabbi Zvi Kestenbaum of Brooklyn

Rabbi Sherer addressing the ceremony at the restored Lipnik cemetery, burial site of the Baruch Taam

power. As a consequence, the names Agudath Israel and Moshe Sherer definitely meant something to them. At one point, Professor Reicher arranged a meeting between Agudath Israel representatives and top Ukrainian officials. The first question asked by the Ukrainian Foreign Minister Gennadi Udovenko was, "Where's Rabbi Sherer?" (The meeting took place *Chol HaMoed Succos*, and Rabbi Sherer was out of town.)

Agudath Israel's foreign policy began to pay dividends almost immediately. In 1996, a serious threat developed to the Jewish cemetery in Mliniv, in which the Bais Aharon, founder of the Karlin-Stolin dynasty, is buried. (The issue was particularly important to Rabbi Sherer because of his family roots in Stolin.) Professor Reicher arranged for a meeting *Erev Shavuos* with the Ukrainian ambassador to the United Nations. When he told Rabbi Sherer that he and Rabbi Besser would be going, Rabbi Sherer gave him a piece of advice: "It's the *shadchan* (matchmaker) that counts." At that point, he called Michael Lewan, and asked him to write a letter, as chairman of the U.S. Commission for the

Expressing gratitude to the mayor of Lipnik for his assistance, at a reception in New York City Hall. L-r: Rabbi Naftali Tzvi Halberstam, future Bobover Rebbe; the mayor of Lipnik; New York's Mayor Rudolph Giuliani, Rabbi Sherer, Rabbi Chaskel Besser

Preservation of America's Cultural Heritage Abroad, introducing the AIWO delegation.

That meeting contributed significantly to averting the threat to the Mliniv cemetery, and also marked the beginning of a more than two-year process of negotiating with the Ukrainian government toward an administrative decree banning the privatization of and construction on cemeteries, as a preliminary to comprehensive national legislation on the subject. That executive order of the cabinet of ministers was presented by Ukrainian President Leonid Kuchma to United States Vice President Albert Gore, Jr. in Kiev in July 1998.[32] (The Ukrainian executive order became the model for similar legislation in Romania.)

In time, Professor Reicher also began to work with Rabbi Sherer on restitution issues and had an opportunity to watch him in action from close quarters. Over the years that Rabbi Sherer represented Agudath Israel on the Conference on Jewish Material Claims Against Germany (the Claims Conference), between 15-20 percent of the money distrib-

---

32. By that time, Rabbi Sherer had passed away, without living to see to fruition the negotiations in which he had been involved for over two years.

At the next meeting of the U.S.-Ukraine Joint Cultural Commission, after presentation of the executive order to Vice President Gore, comprehensive legislation on the subject of cemeteries was discussed. The head of the United States delegation proclaimed that the legislation would be known as the Novohatko-Reicher Act, after Professor Reicher and the head of the Ukrainian delegation.

uted by the Claims Conference went to Orthodox institutions.[33] Rabbi Sherer was working against formidable odds. Apart from the Chairman of the Claims Conference Rabbi Israel Miller, he was one of the few Orthodox members on the allocations committee. In addition, the Orthodox community awakened very slowly to the potential funding available from the Claims Conference, and was not yet well versed in the grant application process. The appointment of Professor Reicher to work on restitution issues was designed, in part, to remedy that lack of awareness of how the grant process worked.

Finally, many of the members of the conference harbored a barely concealed distrust of Orthodox institutions. Many of them were born in Orthodox homes, and their contempt for anything Orthodox was part of a process of self-justification for their life choices. Traveling to meetings of the Claims Conference, Rabbi Sherer would give Reicher thumbnail sketches of everyone who would be at the meeting, including familial background, and predict with nearly unerring accuracy how they would vote on the issues likely to arise.

Despite these obstacles, Rabbi Sherer maintained good relations with the other members of the Claims Conference and commanded their respect. Of particular note was his relationship with Alexander Schindler, head of the Union of American Hebrew Congregations (Reform). During breaks in the discussion, the two could be seen discussing their respective heart-bypass surgeries. Schindler confessed to Rabbi Sherer that he was under attack in Reform circles for being too "palsy" with him.[34]

And, in truth, that criticism is not hard to understand, for Rabbi Sherer never held back from flaying the heterodox movements for their failures at every possible opportunity. On the other hand, his attitude was always one of hating the sin not the sinner. As a consequence, he did not let his revulsion at falsifications of Judaism prevent him from maintaining proper relationships with those whose religious views were repugnant to him. That ability served him in good stead on the Claims Conference and in other bodies dealing with restitution issues.

---

33. These figures were calculated by Rabbi Boruch Borchardt, who carefully reviewed the Claims Conference allocations every year in order to categorize them.

34. After Rabbi Sherer's passing, Schindler submitted a eulogy of him to *The New York Times*.

Chapter Twenty-Two

FOR THE LAND AND HER PEOPLE

ERETZ YISRAEL WAS NEVER FAR FROM RABBI SHERER'S thoughts from the very outset of his public life. His passionate love of the Land comes through clearly in his account of his first visit to Israel after the recapture of the *Kosel* (the Western Wall) by Israeli forces in the Six-Day War.

> Before I had even unpacked my suitcase, I was drawn, like iron to a magnet, to the site from which the *Shechinah* never departed, the Wall that I had stood before so often, but only in my heart ....
>
> Walking down the street leading to the *Kosel HaMa'aravi*, one begins to tremble ... out of pure happiness [like] a lost little boy who has suddenly spied his mother. Unexpected tears gush forth, hot, holy, and sublime.[1]

---
1. Rabbi Sherer, "The Call of the *Kosel*," *Bishtei Einayim*, pp. 281-85.

His first visit to the *Kosel*, in 1967

The *Kosel* summoned up for him all the emotions of Jewish history: both the tragedy of Exile, the awareness that we "are children who have been driven from their father's table" (*Berachos* 3b), and the hope symbolized by the *Kosel*, the knowledge that "no matter how many times we have been decimated, a remnant has always survived to carry on."[2]

His love of the Land was not something abstract or expressed only in words. It was he who turned Keren Ha'Shvi'is, the support fund for *Shmittah*-observant farmers in *Eretz Yisrael*, into a multimillion-

---

2. On every visit to Israel, Rabbi Sherer would always make some form of *kabbalah ruchanis* (spiritual resolution) at the *Kosel*. One year, for instance, he took upon himself the custom of always reciting the chapter of *Tehillim* with the same number as his next birthday at the end of *Shacharis*.

His final visit to the Kosel, while leading the Am Echad mission to Israel months before his passing.

dollar project. In an early *Jewish Observer* essay on *Shmittah*, Rabbi Sherer began by relating how at the beginning of one *Shmittah* year, the Ponevezher Rav had once gone out to the fields of Kibbutz Chofetz Chaim, prostrated himself on the earth, kissed it, and called out, "*Gut Shabbos*, Mother Earth." It was clearly a gesture with which he identified fully.

Still, Rabbi Sherer asked: What is so fundamental about *Shmittah* that the *Mishnah* (*Pirkei Avos* 5:11) lists it together with the three cardinal sins — murder, immorality, and idol worship — as one of the causes for which Israel is sent into *galus* (exile)? He answered that the basic lesson of Jewish belief contained in the observance of the *Shmittah* year is

Chapter Twenty-Two: For the Land and Her People □ 543

Visiting *Shmittah*-observant farmers. Rabbi Moshe Kliers is to the right of Rabbi Sherer.

even more important today when mankind "having gained some small insight into the secrets of Creation is intoxicated with his newfound power, and lays claim to mastery of the Earth .... " Then especially do we need to know, "The earth is the Lord's, and all that it contains."

For Jews, *Shmittah* contains another message as well: We are subject to a metaphysical Law "over and above the laws of nature [and] of history that govern other peoples and other lands." When we place our faith solely in the "laws and principles of military science, of economics, of political science, which may be valid for other peoples," and therefore outside the metaphysical system that governs our existence, we jeopardize our very existence. For according to the former laws and principles, there is no way that a nation whose every border is occupied by enemies could survive at all.[3]

Even before the creation of the State of Israel, Rabbi Sherer was involved in the affairs of the fledgling Jewish settlement. A pair of young rabbis, Rabbi Menachem Porush and Rabbi Shlomo Lorincz, made trips to the United States from Palestine in order to collect money to build the infrastructure of Torah life in the holy land. Rabbi Sherer was heavily involved in the behind-the-scenes logistics of their visits. When Rabbi

---

3. Rabbi Sherer, "The Earth is Mine: The Fallow Earth of *Shmita* Yields a Rich Spiritual Harvest," *The Jewish Observer*, October 1965, pp. 16-7.

Yitzchak Meir Levin, the son-in-law of the revered Imre Emes of Ger, visited America in the early '50s, drawing tumultuous crowds in every city, Rabbi Sherer again helped handle the logistics of his visit.

From those early fund-raising trips, Rabbi Sherer forged a personal bond with Rabbis Lorincz and Porush. Both men ended up representing Agudath Israel in the Knesset for over three decades. During their time in the Knesset, Rabbi Sherer was in touch with each of them on a constant, often daily, basis. His correspondence with Rabbi Porush alone fills numerous file cabinets.

Security for the Jews of *Eretz Yisrael*

RABBI SHERER WAS A LIFELONG OPPONENT OF ZIONIST IDEOLOGY. He rejected the view that the age-old yearnings of the Jewish heart could be content with "nothing more than a country of our own and a unifying language." That view, he argued, was nothing but a pale imitation of 19th-century European nationalism, and a betrayal of the traditional vision of "a unique nation — *am levadad yishkon* — with a unique history and a unique Torah." All his life, he fought to uproot from the Jewish consciousness the Second Zionist Congress's declaration that religion is a purely private matter.

And yet his fervent opposition to Zionism never lessened his concern for the Jewish settlement in *Eretz Yisrael*. In a piece entitled "Zion, Yes — Zionism, No!" he critiqued, on the one hand, Zionism for having reduced the Jewish religion to a purely private matter unconnected to national identity.[4] But at the same time, he rejected those groups who "consider any positive remark concerning *Eretz Yisrael*, or even the Jewish *Yishuv* within it, to indicate support for Zionism."

Concern with the "affairs of *Eretz Yisrael* and the Jewish *Yishuv*, efforts to maintain and secure its physical and spiritual existence" have nothing to do with Zionism, he insisted, but are a fulfillment of the verse, "*U're'ei betuv Yerushalayim* — May you gaze upon the goodness of *Yerushalayim*" (*Tehillim* 128:5).[5]

Rabbi Sherer's summary of a confidential June 17, 1970 meeting with Israel's Ambassador to Washington Yitzchak Rabin reflects his lifelong approach to Israel's security needs. Rabbi Sherer began the meeting by describing Agudath Israel's areas of influence on Capitol Hill. He

---
4. Rabbi Moshe Sherer, *Bishtei Einayim*, pp. 230-233.
5. Ibid.

emphasized that many of his contacts were outside the channels of the general "Jewish Establishment," and told the new Israeli ambassador that those contacts would always be at Israel's disposal whenever needed.

Rabbi Sherer summed up the meeting with Ambassador Rabin as follows: "I believe that this type of informal, off-the-record ... rapport is extremely important for our organization, for our spiritual aims, as well as actually being of help to Israel in its physical and material problems."[6]

The offer of political support Rabbi Sherer made to Yitzchak Rabin was one he would repeat on many occasions to Israeli leaders. In a 1981 letter to Israeli Ambassador Ephraim Efron, for instance, he described Agudath Israel's grassroots constituency as a "reservoir of manpower which is totally committed to the safety and security of Israel." After an Agudath Israel delegation met with Israel's UN Ambassador Professor Yehuda Blum, Rabbi Sherer explained in a follow-up note that it was important for Orthodox Jewish leaders "with yarmulkes," who strongly support Israel's stance, "to be seen in the corridors of the United Nations, if only to offset the false impression left by other anti-Israel demonstrations."

Yisrael Katsover, the longtime military reporter for the Hebrew *Hamodia* and the dean of Israeli military correspondents, wrote after Rabbi Sherer's passing, that he was one of the few North American leaders who "closely followed the nitty-gritty of the security situation of the State of Israel and the Jewish nation [in Israel]." After any security incident, especially if there was any loss of Jewish life, Katsover could always count on Rabbi Sherer to be on the phone to find out: "How did it happen? Why did they act this way and not this way? Who gave the orders? Who will investigate the incident so that failures should not happen again?"

---

6. Many of Rabin's private observations to Rabbi Sherer were very interesting. He was aware that Rabbi Sherer had been one of a small group of Jewish leaders who had met with President John F. Kennedy on the Tishah B'Av prior to his assassination, and that JFK had commented, "I know that 80 percent of the Jews voted for me, and I have a long memory." Rabin, however, felt that President Nixon, who knew that only 8 percent of Jews voted for him, had done more for Israel, including supply it with badly needed planes. Rabbi Sherer reported: "[Rabin] feels that Nixon really believes and understands Israel's cause, but it is his hunch that the famed evangelist Billy Graham deserves great credit ...."

When Rabbi Sherer spoke of his close relationship to New York Senator Jacob Javits, Rabin told him that he thought it was much better for Israel's pleading to be left to non-Jews, "who are much more effective."

The questions revealed not only a deep knowledge of Israel's military situation, but also his own pain and worry. During the 1991 Gulf War, Rabbi Sherer spoke on the phone to Katsover almost every day: "He didn't sleep. Every missile that fell was a cut in his own skin."

For all his concern with Israel's defense, Rabbi Sherer did not allow himself to become carried away by military victories. In a fascinating letter to Rabbi Menachem Porush, written half a year after Israel's dramatic victory in the Six-Day War, Rabbi Sherer agreed "that what transpired were great miracles." Nevertheless, he warned Rabbi Porush against the danger "in our intoxication over these miracles into believing ... that the entire Israeli ... population has suddenly become religious minded." He labeled such a view "an oversimplification that can lead to poor judgment ...." His own view was that "anyone who sees things clearly in this age of *hester panim* is merely deluding himself." "The only clear thing to me is that there is no clarity on anything ...," he concluded.[7]

When Rabbi Sherer felt he had important information to convey to Israeli leaders, he did not hesitate to do so, often via Rabbi Lorincz or Rabbi Porush both of whom commanded great respect in government circles. After the Sabra and Shatilla massacres, at the end of Israel's 1982 military campaign to clear the PLO from Lebanon, Rabbi Sherer sent an urgent telegram to all Agudath Israel's Knesset representatives.[8] The Moetzes Gedolei HaTorah had instructed Agudath Israel Knesset members to vote against a governmental committee of investigation of Sabra and Shatilla. Such a committee of investigation would have served as a ploy to unseat Prime Minister Menachem Begin, for whom both the Moetzes Gedolei HaTorah of America and that of *Eretz Yisrael* had great respect.[9]

---

7. Rabbi Moshe Sherer to Rabbi Menachem Porush, January 4, 1968.
8. The massacres were carried out by Christian Phalangists between September 15 and 16 in two Palestinian refugee camps outside Beirut in revenge for the assassination of Phalangist leader Bashir Gemayel the preceding day. At least 324 Palestinians were killed. Even though Israeli troops had no involvement in the killings or any advanced warning of the Phalangists' intentions, Israel bore the brunt of international opprobrium for not having anticipated those intentions, at a time when it was in effective control of Beirut.
9. Part of Agudath Israel's coalition agreement prior to entering the second Begin government was that El Al, the national air carrier, would not fly on Shabbos. The Prime Minister told Agudath Israel MK Menachem Porush that for him Shabbos is a very personal matter ..., and the source of blessing for Jews. "The fact that El Al would ostensibly lose money because of closing on Shabbos and Yom Tov is meaningless," Begin told Rabbi Porush. When Rabbi Porush conveyed these sentiments to Rabbi Shach, the later responded, "We must pray for the health of Begin. Please phone Begin immediately and tell him that I pray for him constantly." Internal Memo re: Begin's Attitude

Prime Minister Menachem Begin meets with members of the Moetzes Gedolei HaTorah at the home of Rabbi Moshe Feinstein. Clockwise from left: Rabbi Sherer, Rabbi Yaakov Kamenetsky, Rabbi Yitzchak Hutner, Rabbi Feinstein, Prime Minister Menachem Begin

Rabbi Sherer fully understood the stance of the Moetzes Gedolei HaTorah. Nevertheless, Rabbi Sherer felt it was crucial to address the political fallout in America. He described the shocking photographs of the massacres as having fueled "the strongest wave of anti-Israel feeling in my memory." Rabbi Sherer warned, "I sense the wall of reliable support upon which Israel depends crumbling. Even [her] best friends are deserting Israel." He urged the Agudath Israel MKs to convey news of the emergency "from a true friend" to Prime Minister Begin immediately so that he could begin formulating a response designed to reverse the trend.

Nor was that the only time Rabbi Sherer conveyed an important message to Israeli leaders. After reading in *The New York Times* that Prime Minister Begin intended to tell President Carter that Israel objected to American aid to Jewish refugees from the Soviet Union coming to America, Rabbi Sherer sent an urgent telegram to Rabbi Lorincz. He urged Rabbi Lorincz to tell Prime Minister Begin that any attempt to involve the United States government in cutting off humanitarian aid to Russian Jews would set a dangerous precedent. In the end, either

---

Toward Shabbos, April 30, 1982.

Christian missionary groups would fill the vacuum left by the removal of American government assistance or the American Jewish community would do so, with the result that American Jews would give less to Israel. Prime Minister Begin assured Rabbi Lorincz that he had never contemplated doing so, and that the story had been planted by Aryeh Dulzin of the Jewish Agency.

Rabbi Sherer's constant concern with the physical well-being and safety of the Jews of *Eretz Yisrael* was a direct outgrowth of everything he had learned from Rabbi Aharon Kotler during the wartime rescue work. In a letter to Professor Seymour Siegel of the Jewish Theological Seminary (Conservative), Rabbi Sherer spelled out the philosophy of rescue that had guided Agudath Israel of America since its early wartime rescue work. Siegel had accused Rabbi Sherer of spending all his "time and effort fighting other Jews" in response to Rabbi Sherer's public condemnation of the views of the Conservative Movement as "fraudulent."

Rabbi Sherer rejected the charge of spending most of his time fighting other Jews. While reiterating Agudath Israel's refusal of cooperation on any religious or educational matter with heterodox groups, Rabbi Sherer drew the distinction where it came to issues of Jewish lives: "On the other hand, when the security of Jews in Israel or in the *Gola* (Exile) is on the agenda, we believe that a Jew is a Jew is a Jew, and we seek to work [together] under proper guidelines."

The position that in matters of life and death "a Jew is a Jew is a

With Prime Minister Menachem Begin and Governor Hugh Carey

Jew" is one that Rabbi Sherer heard directly from Rabbi Aharon Kotler during the Holocaust, when the Orthodox were criticized for their willingness to enter into ransom negotiations with the Nazis, even for Jews who had converted out. In comments to a report by Professor Seymour Maxwell Finger to the Goldberg Commission, which was convened for the purpose of assessing the performance of American Jewish leadership during the Holocaust, Rabbi Sherer expressed his firm conviction that a Torah perspective necessarily leads to a greater concern with one's fellow Jews:

> The Orthodox Jew is inculcated from early childhood with a special sense of *"areivus"* (responsibility) of one Jew for the other and for all mankind. When one's heart is overflowing with love for G-d, then that love naturally flows over to man who was created in the image of G-d. The tighter one clings to his roots as a Jew, the more profoundly one thinks and acts as a Jew.

Agudath Israel's participation in a protest rally against the United Nations' decision to grant observer status to Yasir Arafat's Palestine Liberation Organization provides a good example of putting aside ideological and theological differences in the face of threats to Jewish lives. Rabbi Israel Miller, the chairman of the Conference of Presidents of Major Jewish Organizations, reached out to Rabbi Sherer to encourage Agudath Israel to participate in the rally.[10]

In response to that invitation, Rabbi Sherer worked out a formula, which was endorsed by the Moetzes Gedolei HaTorah, that permitted Agudath Israel to participate in the rally without submerging its identity with groups coming from a very different ideological perspective. For that reason, Agudath Israel was not listed as a sponsor. Rabbi Sherer requested and was granted a special area at which there would be separate sections for men and women.

The proclamation issued by the Moetzes Gedolei HaTorah stressed the importance of Jewish solidarity in the face of the threat to Jewish life posed by the PLO: "Despite the differences which separate us from

---

10. Rabbi Israel Miller and Rabbi Sherer worked together closely in many contexts over the years, including in the Claims Conference, which Rabbi Miller headed until the end of his life. The two men shared an ability to win the favor and respect of non-religious Jews and non-Jews alike that derived from the dignity with which they always conducted themselves. Prior to heading the Presidents Conference and subsequently the Claims Conference, Rabbi Miller, who was a vice president and dean of students at Yeshiva University, also served as head of the American Zionist Federation and as chairman of the American Jewish Council on Soviet Jewry, neither of which were religious organizations.

> ## A PROCLAMATION
>
> The United Nations decision to grant recognition to the terrorist Palestine Liberation Organization makes a mockery of basic humanitarian concepts, and is a throwback to the "values" of World War II, when the nations of the world witnessed with cruel complacency the slaughter of six million innocent Jews.
>
> This callous act by the U.N. should serve to open the eyes of all Jews to the bankruptcy of world civilization, to perceive the unique position of "Jewry among the nations," to understand that hope and deliverance cannot come forth from the great powers, and that "we can depend on no one but Avinu Shebashamayim."
>
> Therefore, at this critical time, we call upon all Jews to return to our sacred heritage, with prayer and renewed allegiance to Torah, our eternal wellspring of life and source of strength to withstand all our enemies.
>
> Coupled with our supplications, we feel duty-bound to express to the world our deep anguish over the shameless act of the UN to give encouragement to a band of murderers and to recognize the spurious claims of terrorists to our Holy Land. Despite the differences which separate us from other groups, we are together, in solidarity, with all Jews in this expression of outrage and shock.
>
> We therefore summon our members and all Jews to participate in the forthcoming RALLY AGAINST TERROR...
>
> **Agudath Israel of America**
>
> Please note: For the reserved separate sections for men and women, please come 11:30 A.M. to the right side of the Plaza, entering from Second Avenue.

other groups, we are together, in solidarity, with all Jews in this expression of outrage and shock." The proclamation termed the UN's recognition of the PLO, an organization with the "avowed intention to wipe out the *Yishuv* of 3,000,000 Jews," a throwback to the complacency the world showed to the slaughter of six million innocent Jews during the Holocaust.

An accompanying press release explained why Agudath Israel could not, however, join in sponsoring the rally, lest it be misconstrued as an endorsement of the concept of "secular Judaism" shared by most members of the Presidents' Council. In addition, it reiterated Agudath Israel's commitment to the concept of a Torah nation based upon Torah and mitzvos, whose destiny is exclusively determined by Divine Providence, and even pointed out that the religious policies of the Israel government "endanger the security and survival of our People." The last line of the release reminded all Jews that the ultimate solution to terror against Jews could only come from *Hashem Yisbarach* Himself — the Guardian of Israel."

The release concluded with numerous other examples of instances where dangers to the security of Jews had lead Agudath Israel to put aside "that which divides us [to] join all of Jewry in a cry of outrage": the Arab pogroms of 1929-1936, laws to ban *Shechitah* in pre-war Poland, and during the crisis periods prior to and during the Israeli-Arab Wars of 1948, 1956, 1967, and 1973.

Defending Religious Interests in Israel

BECAUSE SECULAR ISRAELI OFFICIALS VIEWED RABBI SHERER AS one of the major American Jewish leaders, and highly valued his eagerness to assist Israel, on many issues he had more influence with Israeli politicians than did religious politicians in Israel. For that reason, the Israel Torah leadership often asked him to intervene with Israeli secular politicians. For instance, at one point the Jewish Agency instituted a sort of loyalty test for institutions receiving funding from the Jewish Agency. Any institution that did not prove itself sufficiently Zionistic — e.g., encouraging army service — could find its funding cut off. Among the institutions affected were residential educational institutions for underprivileged children, some of which had been been in existence since the mass immigration from Moslem lands in the early years of the state.

In a sharp letter to Aryeh Dulzin, chairman of the Jewish Agency, Rabbi Sherer expressed his profound shock that the Jewish Agency would punish "needy children on the sole basis of the religious convictions of their families and the charitable organizations [in which they are resident]."[11] He strongly urged the Jewish Agency to reverse its resolution, which was sure to provoke "worldwide revulsion by compassionate people of all beliefs, ... [and which] can only exacerbate tensions when we are all working to still them."

The same year Rabbi Sherer again presented himself as one always seeking to quiet religious/secular tensions, this time to Israeli Justice Minister Yitzchak Modai. With Modai, however, his tone was the opposite of the confrontational one he had adopted with Dulzin. After meeting the minister, together with the Novominsker Rebbe, while Modai was in the United States on government business, Rabbi Sherer wrote how "heartened" he and the Rebbe were by his undertaking to bring a halt to lewd advertising on bus stops. "Your positive reaction ... left us with the hope that *b'ezras Hashem* you will take a leadership role to shore up the crumbling religious status quo agreement .... If the current tensions do not abate, one shudders at the consequences for Israel and all world Jewry." [12]

On a number of occasions, Rabbi Sherer also used his extensive American-government connections to defend religious interests in Israel. The most notable example concerned autopsies that were

---
11. Rabbi Moshe Sherer to Aryeh Dulzin, June 27, 1986.
12. Rabbi Moshe Sherer to Justice Minister Yitzchak Modai, June 12, 1986.

routinely performed in Israeli hospitals without the consent of the families of the deceased and even over their strenuous religious objections. Rabbi Sherer met with the Surgeon General of the Public Health Service to win his support for a proposal to deny American-government research funding to Israeli hospitals that did not require familial consent for autopsies. He simultaneously directed a public relations campaign to embarrass the Hadassah Women's organization into adopting a different policy in its two Jerusalem hospitals.[13]

But when fervently anti-Zionistic groups wanted to demonstrate against Israeli Prime Minister Levi Eshkol over the autopsy issue, Rabbi Sherer strongly opposed any involvement of Agudath Israel. He recognized that Jews attacking the Israeli prime minister while the latter was in the United States seeking the replenishment of vital weaponry lost in the 1967 War could only blacken Orthodoxy in the eyes of the broader American Jewish public and set back the battle against autopsies.[14]

Rabbi Sherer was ever alert to the implications of events in America for the Israeli Torah world. In 1980, for instance, the Carter administration proposed a revision of the Selective Service Act to require compulsory registration of women, apparently on the theory that they might be needed in civilian service in the event of a major national disaster. Rabbi Sherer immediately realized that the issue had immense implications for Torah Jews in Israel as well as the United States. All the greatest Torah leaders in Israel had strongly rejected compulsory national service for women in the 1950s. Were the United States to institute even a registration requirement, Rabbi Sherer felt, it would remove one of the arguments against compulsory national service for women in Israel: i.e., that no other country in the world had either compulsory military service or a compulsory national-service requirement for women. Rabbi Sherer had Senator Jacob Javits write to the incoming Secretary of Defense Harold Brown alerting him to the problem of "Orthodox Jewish women who had deep religious objections and who may feel compelled to refuse to comply with a registration requirement." Toward the end of his letter, Senator Javits noted that this issue had "caused a considerable amount of turmoil in Israel," clearly an indication of Rabbi Sherer's thinking about the Israel angle.

Rabbi Sherer met personally with Secretary of Defense Brown about the issue. Prior to that meeting, Secretary Brown, whom Rabbi Sherer

---
13. See Chapter 12.
14. Rabbi Sherer to Rabbi Menachem Porush, January 4, 1968.

described as a man of "unusual intelligence and quick grasp," had not been aware of Agudath Israel's opposition to compulsory civilian service for women. Rabbi Sherer told Brown that his strong preference was against any registration requirement for women, but if the administration was unwilling to go that far, at least the new statute should include a religious exemption clause. The second course, however, was fraught with difficulty, as Rabbi Sherer well knew from his close attention to Israeli politics. Claiming an absolute exemption for Orthodox young women to avoid serving in any capacity in times of emergency would have negative consequences for the public image of the Orthodox community and, Rabbi Sherer wrote in a memo, "would have to be dealt with at the highest levels of Torah authority." While others professed not to be very concerned about the draft issue, Rabbi Sherer's "sixth sense" told him that the women's draft issue might develop into "one of the most vexing problems to have faced Orthodox Jewry in recent times, if *chas v'chalilah* any emergency arises."

One of the most intense lobbying campaigns Rabbi Sherer ever ran was against a bill introduced in Congress that would have done away with the 4-D, or divinity school exemption (see Chapter 16). Here too one of his principal considerations was the potential impact on the draft deferment for yeshivah students in Israel if the exemption for yeshivah students in America were removed.

Relations With the Israeli Agudah

RABBI SHERER'S RELATIONS WITH AGUDATH ISRAEL IN ISRAEL were highly ambivalent for the entire period that he headed Agudath Israel of America. On the one hand, he enjoyed a close personal relationship with the leading figures in the Israeli Agudah movement and with members of the Israeli Moetzes Gedolei HaTorah. As the leader of the Agudah movement in America, and from 1980 onwards the co-chairman of Agudath Israel World Organization, Rabbi Sherer was often called upon to explain the position of the Torah leaders of *Eretz Yisrael* to the broader public. It was a task he fulfilled with relish. Indeed, much of his correspondence with Agudah activists in *Eretz Yisrael* consisted of requests for more detailed information on the thinking of the leading Torah authorities on various issues, in part so that he could faithfully represent their views to the Moetzes Gedolei HaTorah of America and to the American public.

At an Agudath Israel World Organization conference in Jerusalem, 1981. L-r: Rabbi Sherer, Rabbi Moshe Shmuel Shapiro, the Slonimer Rebbe, the Modzitzer Rebbe, the Vizhnitzer Rebbe, the Gerrer Rebbe, Rabbi Elazar Menachem Man Shach (speaking). Among those visible in the background are Agudath Israel Knesset members Rabbi Menachem Porush, Rabbi Avrohom Yosef Shapiro, Rabbi Shlomo Yaakov Gross, and Rabbi Shmelke Halpert.

Chapter Twenty-Two: For the Land and Her People □ 555

For instance, when the Israeli government proposed extending compulsory education with secular studies to the ninth grade (instead of 8th grade), Rabbi Sherer wrote to Rabbi Porush eager to hear the thinking of the *gedolei Torah* on the issue. On the one hand, 9th grade had always been the first year of full-day yeshivah studies in what are called *yeshivos ketanos* in Israel. On the other hand, if the *yeshivos ketanos* did not comply with the requirement of secular studies in ninth grade, there was a great danger that "the overwhelming majority of Chinuch Atzmai eightth grade graduates [would be lost] to Mizrachi-oriented high schools."[15]

Similarly, when a Mizrachi-backed proposal to draft yeshivah students came before the Knesset, Rabbi Sherer wrote to Rabbi Itche Meyer Levin seeking his assessment of the seriousness of the proposal. At the same time, he took the initiative of meeting with the Israel consul general in New York Michael Arnon, with whom he had "an extremely cordial and intimate relationship," to explain the opposition of Agudath Israel to the proposal, but more importantly to learn from him the Israeli government's position on the Knesset legislation. He ended his letter to Rabbi Levin with an oft-repeated complaint that the lack of regular information from Israel hampered his ability to explain events in Israel "to the public and to the American Agudah."

When major issues to be decided by the *gedolei Yisrael* in *Eretz Yisrael* were on the agenda — e.g., how Agudath Israel Knesset members should vote on the Camp David Accords with Egypt — Rabbi Sherer was in constant phone contact with *Eretz Yisrael* to ensure that the positions expressed by the Moetzes Gedolei HaTorah in America faithfully reflected the views of the *gedolei Torah* of *Eretz Yisrael*. During the 1982 Lebanon War, for instance, he called Rabbi Shach directly to discuss the speech that the latter had given on the subject in Ponevezh Yeshiva.[16]

Yet as much as Rabbi Sherer served as a faithful spokesman for the Torah leaders of Eretz Yisrael, he was nevertheless a frequent critic of the organizational structure of the Israeli Agudah. The Israeli Agudah was plagued by internal division, which resulted in long periods during which the Moetzes Gedolei HaTorah rarely, if ever, met. Those internal divisions culminated in the movement splitting in 1988 into two separate political parties, Agudath Israel and Degel HaTorah, each with its own Moetzes Gedolei HaTorah. (Earlier, most of the Sephardi members of Agudath Israel had departed to form the Shas party, with the explicit

---

15. Rabbi Sherer to Rabbi Menachem Porush, February 5, 1968.
16. Rabbi Sherer's personal notes of his conversation with Rabbi Shach, July 27, 1982.

support of some members of the Moetzes Gedolei HaTorah of Agudath Israel.)

In addition, the Israeli Agudah also suffered from what Rabbi Sherer once called the "blot"[17] of being primarily a political organization. The party was often torn by strife between various official factions over such issues as the placement order on election lists. (In Israel's system of proportional representation system, in which voters vote for a party, rather than for a particular candidate, placement on the party list determines the likelihood of entering the Knesset.) Since each Knesset member was granted a certain amount of money to distribute to institutions, the placement of each faction's representatives on the Knesset list could determine which institutions received more government funding and which less.

During one particularly tense pre-election period, Rabbi Sherer was invited to Israel to attempt to negotiate some form of modus vivendi between the different factions. During one lengthy, late-night session over which faction would receive which placement on the upcoming Knesset list, he could not help sharing a *vort* he had once heard. The *Gemara* in *Berachos* (28a) relates that on the day that Rabban Gamliel was deposed as Nasi, they had to add a large number of *benches* in the *beis medrash:* according to one opinion 400 benches and according to the other 700. Why does the *Gemara* refer to the additional numbers who entered to learn in terms of the *benklach (benches)* and not in terms of the number of new students who were added?

He answered that the great increase in the numbers learning was because of the rescission of Rabban Gamliel's decree that only those who were *tocho k'boro (who are the same on the inside as the outside)* could enter. And when you are dealing with those who are not *tocho k'boro*, they will end up fighting over *benklach*. Thus the *Gemara* refers to the increased numbers in terms of the greater number of benches in the *beis medrash*.

Because the structure of the Israeli Agudah was based on official factions, and almost all Agudah personnel were paid functionaries of one or another faction, the Israeli Agudah movement was, in effect, a coalition, rather than a cohesive, professional organization serving the needs of the entire Torah community. And due to the very nature of the party, it did not produce a large group of committed lay supporters.

---
17. Rabbi Sherer to Daniel Tropper, December 21, 1983.

In short, it was very different from what Rabbi Sherer envisioned for the American Agudah and also very different from what Agudah had been in Europe prior to the war, where Reb Yaakov Rosenheim ran a large professional organization. The focus of all activity in Israel on the Knesset, Rabbi Sherer felt, was misplaced, and prevented any role for laymen developing.[18] In many of his letters to colleagues in Israel, he wondered why various committees established to deal with different issues — e.g., Youth Aliyah, Russian immigration — seemed to be so inactive.[19] And when one of the Agudath Israel MKs with whom he was close also took a seat on the Jerusalem City Council, Rabbi Sherer was quick to point out that such a concentration of responsibility in one person's hands made it impossible to develop new talents in the organization.

The divisions within the Israeli Agudah movement were a source of constant anguish to Rabbbi Sherer. For one thing, he felt they hurt the image of Agudah in America, and thereby made it more difficult to build the large grassroots movement he envisioned. The damage done by strife in Israel to the image of Agudah in America is a constant theme of his letters to his colleagues in Israel.[20] To Agudah activists in Europe he wrote that the divisions in Israel prevented the development of a vibrant international movement.[21]

Though Rabbi Sherer was a fervent believer in Agudath Israel as an international movement, he refused for many years to assume the lead role in Agudath Israel World Organization (AIWO) because of his feeling that the lack of unity in the Israeli Agudah would inevitably stymie any effective action by AIWO. He refused the entreaties of Aba Dunner of the British Agudah to take a lead role in AIWO on the grounds that the world organization could not be separated from "the impossibly bad structuring of the Israeli Agudah."[22] In 1974, he wrote to Avraham Hirsch of AIWO that there was little point of the meeting of the Vaad HaPoel of AIWO as long as the divisions within the Israeli Agudah persisted.[23] And two years prior to the last Knessiah Gedolah

---

18. Rabbi Moshe Sherer to Rabbi Menachem Porush, January 7, 1970.
19. See e.g., Rabbi Sherer to Rabbi Yitzchak Meir Levin, Rabbi Menachem Porush, and Rabbi Shlomo Lorincz, February 16, 1968, Rabbi Sherer to Rabbi Lorincz, September 12, 1972.
20. See, e.g., Rabbi Moshe Sherer to Rabbi Shlomo Lorincz, January 25, 1968 (internal disputes of the Israeli Agudah have greatly tarnished the image of Agudah in the United States).
21. Rabbi Sherer to M. Springer, a British Agudah activist, January 25, 1968.
22. Rabbi Sherer to Aba Dunner, October 2, 1972.
23. Rabbi Sherer to Avraham Hirsch, May 17, 1974.

Rabbi Sherer at an Agudath Israel World Organization conference with his co-chairman, Rabbi Yehudah Meir Abramowitz. Rabbi Shlomo Lorincz is speaking.

of AIWO in 1980, Rabbi suggested to Hirsch that none of the preparatory meetings take place in Israel "where there are always so many distractions."

Rabbi Sherer's concerns were fully shared by the Moetzes Gedolei HaTorah of America. As early as 1967, Rabbi Yitzchak Hutner wrote a letter to Rabbi Shach, in which he expressed his fear that a failure of the Moetzes Gedolei HaTorah of *Eretz Yisrael* to meet for a prolonged period had drained all enthusiasm for the movement from supporters and activists around the world.[24] When Rabbi Sherer was approached about assuming the chairmanship of AIWO, Rabbi Yaakov Kamenetsky made it an absolute condition of his acceptance that he would not have any responsibility for the internal affairs of the Israeli Agudah.[25] During the 1973 election campaign in Israel, the Nesius of Agudath Israel of

---

24. Rabbi Yitzchak Hutner to Rabbi Elazar Menachem Man Shach, 4 Av 5727.
25. There were rumors that as head of AIWO, Rabbi Sherer would be pressured to move to *Eretz Yisrael* and to grow a beard, and Rabbi Sherer went to discuss the matter with Reb Yaakov in case the rumors materialized. Reb Yaakov replied that with respect to the first matter he felt confident replying in the name of the entire Moetzes Gedolei HaTorah that it would never permit Rabbi Sherer to leave America. About the beard, he could not answer on behalf of anyone besides himself. But in his opinion, it was at least arguable that an element of Rabbi Sherer's immense success with secular political figures was his distinguished appearance, and that even the possibility that growing a beard would lessen his effectiveness was a risk not worth taking.

Chapter Twenty-Two: For the Land and Her People

America sent two representatives to ensure that all the various factions in Agudah conducted themselves properly and without rancor toward one another during party primaries.

Above all, Rabbi Sherer feared the importation of division from Israel to the United States. After the formal split of the Israeli movement into two rival parties, he expressed his determination, in a 1988 memo prepared for the Moetzes Gedolei HaTorah of America, to keep "the tragic fire of *machlokes* [division] away from the American shores." No subject occupied more of his attention in the last decade of his life than preventing any rifts in the American Agudah like that which split the Israeli Agudah movement. No *chareidi* Knesset members were invited to the conventions of Agudath Israel of America in that period.

Though he largely avoided trips to Israel in that period to avoid being drawn into the political battles there, he did make at least one trip in an effort to heal the breaches. Upon his return, he joked that he had, in fact, succeeded in achieving a rare unity among the various factions. Each told him, in almost identical language: "Rabbi Sherer, we very much appreciate your efforts, but this is not your affair."[26]

For someone who had thrilled to the ideal of a unified Agudah movement under the leadership of the *gedolei Torah*, however, it was not a laughing matter.

The Am Echad Delegation

NO SUBJECT CONNECTED TO *ERETZ YISRAEL* OCCUPIED MORE OF his time than preventing any inroads by the heterodox movements.[27]

Fittingly, that was the subject of his last trip to Israel.

In November 1996, Binyamin Netanyahu was elected prime minister of Israel, and formed a government coalition that included the religious parties. The coalition guidelines contained an undertaking by the new government to pass a law clarifying that conversion for purposes of the Israeli Law of Return must be according to halachah. That announcement set off alarms in the inner sanctums of the heterodox movements in America and around the world. For the next year, a steady stream of heterodox dignitaries visited Israel to express their great dismay over the coalition agreement, and to threaten Prime Minister Netanyahu with a massive loss of support for Israel among American Jewry if the so-called Conversion Law were passed.

---

26. Rabbi Eliezer Horowitz.
27. See Chapter 5, pp. 141ff.

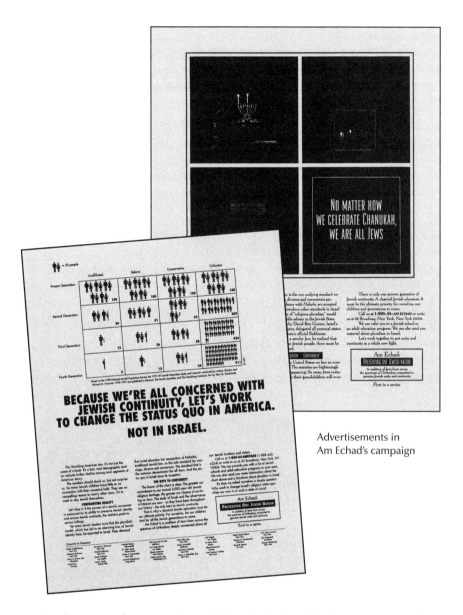

Advertisements in Am Echad's campaign

At the annual convention of Agudath Israel of America, in late November 1997, Rabbi Sherer announced a major initiative to counter the ongoing Reform and Conservative pressure. He declared a goal of raising $2 million dollars to counteract the Reform and Conservative propaganda campaigns, and announced that he would be personally leading a mission to Israel, under the banner Am Echad, to push Israeli lawmakers for passage of the Conversion Law.

By the time that Rabbi Sherer made his dramatic announcement, it was probably too late to reverse the loss of momentum on passage of the Conversion Law. While the Netanyahu government might have been strong enough to push the measure through the Knesset immediately after the formation of a new government, the non-stop campaign by the heterodox movements and the threats of a loss of American Jewish support quickly destroyed whatever enthusiasm the new prime minister had ever possessed for passage of the law. In addition, the Netanyahu government had been greatly weakened in the intervening period by further territorial concessions, under the Oslo Accords, which cost it much of its right-wing support, and the Palestinian rioting that erupted, with a heavy loss of life, after the opening of the Temple Mount tunnels in September 1996.

But even if there was little chance of reversing the effect of the campaign by mainstream Jewish leaders against the Conversion Law, Rabbi Sherer was determined to launch a major campaign to alert Israelis to the dangers of the heterodox movements and to describe their impact on the spiritual health of the American Jewish community.

The mission's schedule was a grueling one, including meetings with President Weizmann, Prime Minister Binyamin Netanyahu, a delega-

Addressing the Am Echad meeting with Prime Minister Netanyahu. Avrohom Biderman is seated at left.

The Am Echad delegation meets with Rabbi Aharon Leib Shteinman. Seated beside Rabbi Shteinman are Rabbi Chaskel Besser and Zev Schlesinger. Standing l-r are Rabbi David Avigdor, Efraim Nierenberg, Rabbi Yisroel Lefkowitz, Rabbi Shimshon Sherer, Rabbi Shlomo Friedman, Rabbi E.B. Freedman, Rabbi Chaim Dovid Zwiebel

tion of the Labor opposition, headed by Ehud Barak,[28] a luncheon with *chareidi* Knesset members, and audiences with *gedolei Yisrael*. Because of his general weakness, Rabbi Sherer turned over responsibility for leading various meetings to trusted lieutenants: Chaim Dovid Zwiebel, Rabbi Chaskel Besser, and Avrohom Biderman. But even when he was not the one presenting the Orthodox world's viewpoint, he was clearly the one running the show and the person upon whom the politicians focused their remarks.

One of the highlights of the mission was a graphic presentation to Prime Minister Netanyahu of a study showing how many Jewish offspring a cohort of 100 Orthodox Jews will produce over three generations compared to a similar cohort of 100 Conservative Jews and one of 100 Reform Jews. Richard Horowitz of Los Angeles, one of the study's authors, made the presentation. The prime minister sat transfixed throughout, and asked a number of questions that showed he had been paying full attention.

---

28. After Barak replaced Netanyahu as prime minister, he told Avraham Biderman that he wished he had an Orthodox leader in Israel like Rabbi Sherer with whom to speak.

After the completion of the mission, Rabbi Sherer was accompanied to the airport by a number of well-wishers. He asked his son Shimshon to help him find a *mezuzah* to kiss. As he did so, he told Shimshon, "This may be the last time I'll ever kiss a *mezuzah in der heiliger Eretz Yisrael.*"[29] It was. But it was fitting that his last great public undertaking was one on behalf of the holy Land he loved so much.

---

29. Rabbi Sherer used to explain the custom to touch the *mezuzah* both when we enter and leave our private abode (see Rema to *Yoreh Deah* 285:2). The two chapters included in the *mezuzah* begin with the acknowledgment of the unity of Hashem, which is one of the six constant commandments. It is introduced with the words *Shema Yisrael*, Hear O Israel, which address all Jews equally. To Rabbi Sherer, these words also imply a call to all Jews to recognize that we are members of *Klal Yisrael* and are responsible for one another: a concept that is symbolized by the *mezuzah* itself. By touching the *mezuzah* with our hand — the organ of action — as we enter our home, we express our commitment to remember and act on behalf of our fellow Jews (even the ones far from our sight, just as the summons *Shema Yisrael* is hidden under the *mezuzah* cover), even as we enter our own private sphere. Privacy does not absolve us of our responsibility for our brethren. And when we leave our homes to enter the active, workday sphere of our lives, we touch the *mezuzah* again, as a reminder to work on behalf of our fellow Jews in the public sphere. Not only do we *touch* the *mezuzah*, many have the custom to kiss the fingers that touch it (*Chayei Adam* 15:1), for we cherish the responsibility to help. The Am Echad mission was Rabbi Sherer's expression of his abiding love and concern for the Jews of *Eretz Yisrael*.

Part VI
THE MAN

Chapter Twenty-Three

IN PRIVATE

RABBI SHERER LIVED HIS ENTIRE LIFE ON THE PUBLIC stage. There was scarcely a moment that he did not inhabit the larger-than-life persona of Rabbi Moshe Sherer, president of Agudath Israel of America.[1]

Yet he was by nature an intensely private man. For all the many people with whom he shared bonds of deep affection, there were very few to whom Rabbi Sherer ever fully unburdened himself. Of the latter group, none was closer than Wolf (Volvie) Friedman, whom Rabbi Sherer respected as both a *talmid chacham*[2] and an astute business man. Friedman was the only person he ever eulogized, beginning, "Volvie, Volvie, Volvie .... "

His preferred location for his annual summer vacation with his

---
1. Despite his apparent ease in the public limelight, a certain *eimasah d'tzibura* (fear of the public) (see *Sotah* 40a) never left him. He never ate, for instance, before delivering a public address.
2. Prior to World War II, Friedman was considered the outstanding student in Yeshivas Tiferes Habachurim in Budapest.

Presented with a token of appreciation by Volvie Friedman as Menachem Shayovich and Chaim Hertz look on.

wife Debby (Devorah) was a rustic cabin somewhere in New England, where he would be unlikely to meet anyone he knew.[3] On vacation, he delighted in doing those little things that he never had time for during the year, like shopping in the local supermarket with Mrs. Sherer. She remembers, with a smile, how fascinated he was the first time he saw an automated price checker.

RABBI SHERER WAS NOT ONE OF THOSE POSSESSED OF A SURFEIT OF charm for the outside world, but with nothing left for those closest to him. He was the same person at home as in public. He often quoted the words of the Reisher Rav, Rabbi Aharon Levine,[4] on the verse in *Shir HaShirim* (1:15), "הִנָּךְ יָפָה רַעְיָתִי הִנָּךְ יָפָה עֵינַיִךְ יוֹנִים — Behold you are beautiful, My beloved; behold,

Tocho K'Boro

---

[3]. Connecticut was a frequent venue. Connecticut Senator Joseph Lieberman once related at a convention of Agudath Israel how Rabbi Sherer would drop him one of his handwritten notes after vacations in Connecticut telling him that he had polled his constituents and he was, in their opinion, "doing a great job!"
[4]. The Reisher Rav, who represented Agudath Israel in the Polish Sejm, was the father of Dr. Isaac Lewin, the longtime representative of Agudath Israel World Organization in the United Nations, and the grandfather of Nathan Lewin, the Washington, D.C. superlawyer with whom Rabbi Sherer worked closely over decades.

you are beautiful, your eyes are doves." The *Midrash* interprets the verse, "Behold you are beautiful in the house; behold you are beautiful in the field." The Reisher Rav explained the *Midrash* to mean that a Jew must display the same *middos* in the confines of his house that he displays in public.

Rabbi Sherer lived those words. His *middos* were the deeply ingrained result of years of hard work, and thus equally on display at home as at work. He never rose from the dinner table without thanking his wife Debby for preparing such a delicious meal. And he would not leave for shul on *Erev Shabbos* until she had lit the Shabbos candles and he could wish her a good Shabbos.

The same sensitivity to the feelings of others that helped make him so successful in the public realm was on full display in private as well. He once approached a high school-age yeshivah student at a *simchah*. After introducing himself, he asked the young man his name and who his parents were. Only then did he point out to the young man that something was amiss in his dress. When he related the story years later, the young man was convinced that Rabbi Sherer had wanted to be sure he was neither an orphan nor from a divorced home, before offering what might be construed as a criticism, no matter how slight.

More typically, especially with young people, Rabbi Sherer looked for opportunities to offer encouragement. Rabbi and Mrs. Sherer once spent Shabbos at the Galei Sanz Hotel in Netanya, at the same time that Rabbi Moshe Jacobson was there with his 16-year-old son Tzvi. Due to the long connection between the Sherer and Jacobson families, they decided to eat their meals together. Rabbi Sherer noted how attentive Tzvi was to the conversation, particularly anything to do with public activities, and at the end of Shabbos, he told Rabbi Jacobson, "This one is going to be an *askan*." As usual, he was right.[5]

Pinchos Lipshutz was the younger *chavrusah* (study partner) of Shimshon Sherer in the Philadelphia Yeshiva. From the first time that Shimshon introduced him to Rabbi Sherer, the latter always encouraged the young man, who was already orphaned from his mother, to do great

---

5. Rabbi Moshe Jacobson was the longtime rav of Be'er Yaakov in central Israel and the director of a dormitory school for girls in the town. His father, Rabbi Binyamin Zeev Jacobson, served as a top assistant to Moreinu Yaakov Rosenheim, the first head of Agudath Israel World Organization, and established a home in Sweden for girls who survived the horrors of the Holocaust., together with Rabbi Shlomo Wolbe.

Tzvi Jacobson did, become a prominent *askan*, as Rabbi Sherer had predicted, as well as one of the leading writers in the Israeli *chareidi* press.

things with his life and never forget his distinguished *yichus* (lineage).⁶

That habit of approaching young people whenever the opportunity presented itself was a lifelong one. At a wedding in Toronto, Rabbi Sherer noticed that one of the friends of the *chassan* was obviously undergoing some kind of intense therapy. He introduced himself, and inquired about the young man's condition. The *bachur* told him that his name was Eli Werther, he learned in Long Beach Yeshiva, and he was undergoing radiation treatment for Hodgkin's disease at home in Milwaukee. Rabbi Sherer shared with his new friend that he had survived intense chemotherapy for lymphoma at well past 70.

Rabbi Sherer wrote down Eli's Hebrew name and told him that he would pray for his complete recovery. He asked him for two promises in return: the first, that he would invite Rabbi Sherer to his wedding; the second, that he would remember how healthy and robust Rabbi Sherer looked, despite having battled an even more serious cancer at an advanced age. Rabbi Sherer then embraced Eli and gave him a warm kiss on the cheek. He placed the note with Eli's name on it into his wallet, where it remained until Rabbi Sherer passed away three years later.

The next *Erev Pesach* and *Erev Shavuos*, Eli received a call at home in Milwaukee from Rabbi Sherer, who inquired about his progress and wished him a good Yom Tov. Around Rosh Hashanah, Rabbi Sherer was speaking to Eli's Rosh Yeshivah, Rabbi Yitzchak Feigelstock, and learned that Eli was back in the yeshivah and doing well. *Erev Yom Kippur*, Rabbi Sherer shocked Eli by calling him on a pay phone in the yeshivah to wish him a *Gmar Chasimah Tova* and tell him how overjoyed he was to hear that he was back in the yeshivah learning. He reminded Eli of his promise to invite him to his wedding. Rabbi Sherer did not live to dance at Eli Werther's *chasanah*, but as it turned out he had a hand in it nevertheless.⁷

---

6. Rabbi Sherer had great respect for Pinchos Lipshutz's maternal grandfather, Rabbi Eliezer Levin of Detroit, a *talmid* of the Chofetz Chaim in Radin, and worked closely over the years with three of his maternal uncles, Rabbi Avrohom Chaim Levin and Rabbi Chaim Dov Keller, roshei yeshivah of Yeshivas Telshe Chicago, and Rabbi Berel Wein. Lipshutz's paternal great-grandfather, Rabbi Yaakov Lipshutz, was the right-hand man of Rabbi Yitzchok Elchonon Spektor of Kovno and author of *Zichron Yaakov*.

7. Rabbi Shimshon Sherer spoke in Los Angeles at an Agudath Israel Shabbos of Chizuk shortly after his father's passing. He told the story of how his father had kissed Eli Werther on the cheek, while taking care to change all the pertinent details: Eli's name, the yeshivah in which he learned, and his hometown. Rabbi Sherer concluded his story by saying that his father was undoubtedly praying in Heaven for Eli. In the audience that Shabbos afternoon was a young woman named Yehudis Eidlitz who had come into the city proper that Shabbos from her home in the Valley for a friend's Shabbos *Sheva Berachos*. Her brothers learned in Long Beach Yeshivah with Eli Werther, and

Rabbi Sherer fully inherited his mother's love of doing *chesed* for others. He never felt that his public activities on behalf of *Klal Yisrael* constituted an excuse not to be involved in private *chesed* activities. His help extended far beyond those who were connected to Agudath Israel. He not only responded to requests for help, but actively sought out opportunities to assist people. "When you had a problem," says Rabbi Lemel Ehrenreich, "Rabbi Sherer was the person you went to."

Rabbi Yerucham Pitter, the Mashgiach in the Yeshivah had already suggested Eli as a *shidduch* to Yehudis's parents. Rabbi and Mrs. Eidlitz, however, were understandably nervous because of Eli's previous bout with Hodgkin's disease. Inspired by Rabbi Sherer's speech, Yehudis Eidlitz convinced her parents to let the *shidduch* proceed.

Four months later — two weeks after Rabbi Sherer's first *yahrtzeit* — Eli Werther and Yehudis Eidlitz were engaged. On a trip to Los Angeles, Eli brought a photograph of himself, Rabbi Sherer, and Rabbi Shimshon Sherer taken at the wedding in Toronto to show his *kallah*. He was about to tell her how the picture came to be taken when she interjected with the story she had heard Rabbi Shimshon Sherer tell about the boy his father had kissed on the cheek and the role it played in their *shidduch*. Eli waited until she was finished, and then said, "I'm that boy, and this is right where he kissed me on the cheek."

Joining Eli and Yehudis at their *chasanah* was Rabbi Sherer's grandson Mendy Sherer, a friend of Eli's from Long Beach. He and Eli were convinced that Rabbi Sherer was indeed dancing there with them. The Werthers live in Lakewood today and have four children.

We wish to thank the Werther and Eidlitz families for permission to include these personal details in this biography.

Chapter Twenty-Three: In Private

Rabbi David Winter, then Director of the New York Council of Mizrachi, was shocked to receive a call one day from Rabbi Sherer. Mizrachi had just opened a Zionist-oriented high school, in which the language of instruction was modern Hebrew. Rabbi Sherer told Rabbi Winter that he was acquainted with a young man who needed the type of education the Mizrachi school offered, and that he personally undertook to raise the boy's tuition from among his Agudah supporters.

Rabbi Winter informed him that the school required parents to pay Mizrachi membership dues as well as tuition. Even that did not cause Rabbi Sherer to flinch, despite the historic antagonism between Agudath Israel and Mizrachi. The next day Rabbi Winter received a check from Rabbi Sherer for Mizrachi membership dues (which he promptly had copied and framed for his wall). For the next five years, Rabbi Winter received the check for membership dues at the beginning of every school year. To this day Rabbi Winter marvels at what "an unusually great man Rabbi Sherer" was and how far he would go to save one Jewish soul.[8]

Mordechai Friedman once received a call from a highly respected rabbi in Williamsburg about a teacher in his Talmud Torah who was living in extremely cramped quarters with a large family. A single large apartment remained to be allocated in a new housing project, and the rabbi wanted to know whether Friedman, whom he knew to be very friendly with Rabbi Sherer, could ask him to use some of his political pull to secure the apartment for the teacher. The rabbi added that he knew Rabbi Sherer as someone "who does kindnesses for everyone, regardless of political affiliation."

When Friedman called Rabbi Sherer, the latter asked first whether there was any question of the apartment having already been assigned to another Jew; if so, he would not get involved on behalf of one Jew at the expense of another. Assured that was not the case, he went to work, and within two weeks the young man — who was affiliated with the anti-Agudah Satmar — had received his apartment. He went around after that singing the praises of Agudath Israel for helping everybody without asking any benefit in return.

Just as political affiliations placed no limits on Rabbi Sherer's acts of kindness, neither did he bear any grudges when it came to doing favors

---

8. Rabbi Sherer's analysis of what the young boy needed was borne out by subsequent events. Today he is a successful attorney and, much more important from Rabbi Sherer's point of view, a *ben Torah*.

for others. Someone with whom Rabbi Sherer had a number of sharp differences on institutional matters once wanted to send his son to Camp Agudah. Even though the camp was already filled, Rabbi Sherer told Meir Frischman to find the boy a place. Another time someone whom Rabbi Sherer had once fired, and who, as a consequence, carried a bitter grudge against Rabbi Sherer, fell on hard times and needed a favor from him. "I know he despises me. But he's a Jew, and I have to help him," Rabbi Sherer said.[9]

Upon entering the old Agudath Israel of America offices at 5 Beekman Street, Rabbi Sherer would always knock on the door of the building superintendent to wish him good morning on his way to the elevator. One day he noticed that the superintendent looked overwrought about something. Rabbi Sherer stopped to ask him what the problem was, and the superintendent told him that he had lost his immigration case and he and his family were about to be deported back to South America. Rabbi Sherer asked him to bring him all his legal papers.

Using all his political connections, Rabbi Sherer achieved a "miracle" and the deportation order was rescinded. Even then, Rabbi Sherer refused to allow the superintendent to thank him. "Just continue doing such a good job taking care of the building," he said. "This is my thank-you to you."[10]

Rabbi Sherer heard a young man in his early 20's reciting *Kaddish* one Shabbos in the Fourteenth Avenue Agudah *minyan*. After *Mussaf*, he called over the young man and inquired about his loss and the particulars of his family situation. For the next eight years, Rabbi Sherer spoke weekly with that young man, Rabbi Yaakov Feitman, to share a story or some point of guidance, and introduced him to many people who were helpful to him in both his life and career.[11] After Volvie Friedman passed away in 1982, Rabbi Sherer talked with his son David every week. There was nothing perfunctory about the

---

9. Rabbi Ephraim Oratz.
10. Mr. Rubin Schron heard this story from the superintendent himself. Once Schron was surveying the building with the superintendent when they arrived at what had once been Rabbi Sherer's corner office. The superintendent turned to Schron and told him, "This is a holy room because this is where the holy Rabbi worked."

Rabbi Sherer's habit of warmly greeting the building personnel when he entered invariably made a strong impression on those greeted. Manny, a Hispanic security guard at 84 William Street, told senior Agudah employee Mordechai Biser how grateful he was to Rabbi Sherer for the respect he always showed him and the time he took to speak to him about his problems. He had even brought his children to Rabbi Sherer for a blessing.
11. Rabbi Yaakov Feitman, "Rabbi Moshe Sherer, Z"L: A Personal Tribute," *Young Israel Viewpoint*, Fall 1998.

calls; they were real conversations, in which Rabbi Sherer undertook to fill some of the void left in Friedman's life by his father's passing.[12]

Protecting His Family

RABBI SHERER WORKED HARD TO PRESERVE THE DIVIDING LINE between his public life and his family and to protect his children's privacy. He did not want his children to feel that they were living in the same fishbowl that he did.

There were times — particularly the weddings of his children — when his public duties and family life overlapped. Prominent politicians and public figures with whom Rabbi Sherer dealt on a regular basis had to be invited to the weddings. His daughter Elky's wedding fell in the midst of an intense lobbying campaign to preserve the draft exemption for yeshivah students,[13] and Rabbi Sherer spent much of the *chasanah* huddled with Senator Jacob Javits discussing strategy, for instance, before breaking away to dance with the *chassan*. Both before and after the wedding, Rabbi Sherer asked Elky's forgiveness for the fact that he was so preoccupied with the crisis over the draft exemptions. But he knew he did not need to worry, because of Elky's easygoing nature.

With Senator Jacob Javits at the wedding of his daughter Elky to Moshe Yaakov (Robert) Goldschmidt. Rabbi Sheah Brander is standing off to the right.

---

12. David Friedman had developed his own relationship with Rabbi Sherer as national president of Zeirei Agudath Israel in the late '60s and early '70s.
13. See Chapter 16, pp. 369ff.

Members of the Moetzes Gedolei HaTorah, roshei yeshivah, and dozens of leading rabbis also graced his children's weddings. Looking over the wedding pictures from Shimshon's wedding, Rabbi Sherer commented on the large number of "kings" present. When Shimshon looked at him quizzically, he replied, "Don't *Chazal* say, 'Who are the kings? The great rabbis'" (*Gittin* 62a).

Apart from weddings, however, other *simchos* were confined to his closest friends and family. Benzion Fishoff, whose statesmanlike qualities Rabbi Sherer greatly admired, and Rabbi Chaskel Besser singing *grammen* (entertaining poems) were usually the only speakers outside the family. At those *simchos*, he was not Moshe Sherer, the famous leader of world Jewry, but a father or grandfather enjoying the company of family and friends.[14] He did not seek to add luster to those *simchos* by inviting the *gedolim* to whom he was close, though they would have attended out of respect for him. He had too much awe for *gedolei Torah* to turn them into adornments.

At the wedding of his daughter Elky to Moshe Yaakov (Robert) Goldschmidt.
L-r: The Novominsker Rebbe, Moshe Yaakov Goldschmidt, Rabbi Sherer, Rabbi Shneur Kotler, Rabbi Moshe Feinstein, Rabbi Gedaliah Schorr, and Rabbi Yitzchak Reich

---

14. Rabbi Nosson Scherman and Rabbi Meir Zlotowitz, "The Man in the Corner," *The Jewish Observer*, Summer 1998, p. 46.

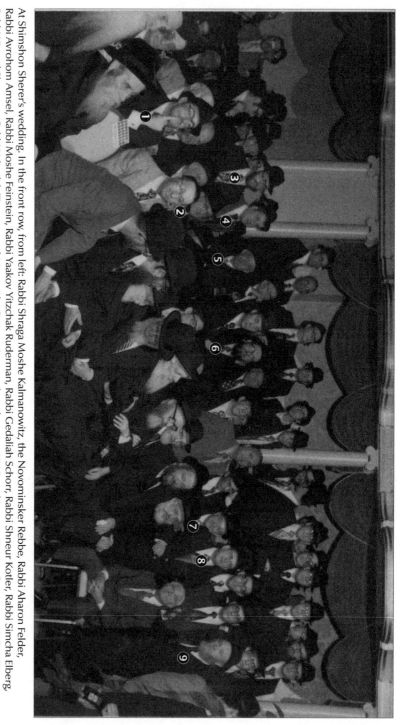

At Shimshon Sherer's wedding. In the front row, from left: Rabbi Shraga Moshe Kalmanowitz, the Novominsker Rebbe, Rabbi Aharon Felder, Rabbi Avrohom Amsel, Rabbi Moshe Feinstein, Rabbi Yaakov Yitzchak Ruderman, Rabbi Gedaliah Schorr, Rabbi Shneur Kotler, Rabbi Simcha Elberg, Rabbi Yisroel Shemano, Rabbi Yehudah Tirnauer, and Mayor Abe Beame. Among the others are (1) Yisroel Langer, (2) Max Grossman, (3) Tzvi Tress, (4) Getzel Segal, (5) Itche Meir Cymerman, (6) Rabbi Yitzchok Kerzner (7) Emil Adler, (8) Moshe Braunfeld, (9) Rabbi Shlomo Gruenbaum

A Happy Home

RABBI SHERER OFTEN WORRIED THAT HIS DEDICATION TO Agudath Israel had been at the expense of his children, and would frequently urge staff members to spend more time with their families than he had with his.

His guilt feelings on this score were greatly exaggerated. His two daughters, Rochel and Elky, reached maturity at a time when Agudath Israel was still a relatively small organization, and never felt deprived of their father's attention. He personally investigated every *shidduch* suggestion for his daughters, and when a young man called for the first time, he was almost always at home to chat with him, and tried to be home for subsequent meetings as well.[15]

The Sherer children recall growing up in a happy home. For all the many pressures on him, Rabbi Sherer always conveyed an upbeat, positive air. "If life deals you a lemon, make it into lemonade" was not just a favorite family refrain, but the way he taught his children to live.[16] And he gave them confidence that they had the talents to make lemonade. For many years, a little wooden sign that read, "Today is the tomorrow you worried about yesterday," hung in the kitchen.

Only once do his children remember seeing him "down," and even then for only a few days, when he was subjected to a campaign of anonymous vilification on posters and leaflets by those whose bidding he refused to do. He feared that his effectiveness in the public realm might be adversely affected by the accusations.

The Sherer children never heard their father shout, except on long-distance calls to Israel in the early days of transatlantic calls. If he was angry with one of the children, he would bite his lip and count to 10 before offering his reproof in a modulated tone.

Early Shabbos morning, Rabbi Sherer would entertain his children with a gallery of characters of his own creation: Pinchikel, his sister

---

15. Ironically, one of the very few times he could not be home for a first meeting was when his future son-in-law, Moshe Yaakov (Robert) Goldschmidt, met his daughter Elky for the first time. Rabbi Sherer found some consolation for those times he could not be home in a comment of the Netziv in *Parashas Chayei Sarah (Haemek Davar, Bereishis* 24:1). The Netziv explains that Avraham Avinu sent Eliezer to find a spouse for Yitzchak, because Avraham was busy healing the sick with a precious stone that hung around his neck (*Bava Basra* 16b). Avraham was confident that the merit of helping so many people would help him to find the right match for Yitzchak, and in a similar vein, Rabbi Sherer hoped that the merit of his efforts on behalf of the public would aid his children in *shidduchim* and on their path in life.

16. *Turn "lemon" situations into "lemonade"* was a constant admonition to those with whom he worked as well. Rabbi Shmuel Lefkowitz, Agudath Israel's vice president for community affairs, once heard from him that if one does not face difficulties at the beginning of a worthwhile project that is just an indication that he is not yet working.

Entertaining grandchildren with stories of Pinchikel and Channah Fufeleh.
Top, l-r: Yehuda Langer, Daniel Langer, Chavie Langer (Galinsky), Suri Goldschmidt (Schoenbrun), Bashie Langer (Sova)
Bottom, l-r: Chavie (Galinsky), Bashie (Sova) and Levi Langer

Channah Fufeleh, his rebbi Rabbi Goldberg, and Channah Fufeleh's teacher Miss McGuire. These characters came along with songs and special effects — the magical matzah, flying yarmulkes, a *succah* like a flying saucer, and chocolate-covered menorahs. The productions were presented with the same verve as a speech for tens of thousands at Madison Square Garden, and each came with an educational lesson as well. (In subsequent years, the Sherer grandchildren sat entranced by the same cast of characters and special effects at birthday parties and family Chanukah gatherings.)

Singing was a major part of every Shabbos meal. Rabbi Sherer had a beautiful voice and loved to harmonize. In general, he favored the *harztige*, emotion-laden melodies of his youth. One of the highlights of Succos was Rabbi Sherer's rendition of *A Succaleh a Kleiner* on the first night of the *chag*.

Singing *zemiros* with his son Shimshon and Abish Brodt.

Rabbi Sherer liked to share stories of his interactions with *gedolei Yisrael* with his children and later, with his grandchildren, when those stories could bring out a point about the true nature of the Torah leaders. One such story, involving Rabbi Moshe Feinstein, demonstrated how the *gedolim* live for the public, not for themselves. Reb Moshe called Rabbi Sherer one day and told him that he had a problem with which only he could help. A young woman had called Reb Moshe's home. Though he was no longer taking his own calls, on that particular occasion Reb Moshe answered himself. The caller explained that she had been orphaned of her father many years earlier, and had just recently lost her mother as well. She was getting married, and told Reb Moshe that it would add greatly to her *simchah* if he would attend. Reb Moshe had agreed, despite his advanced years and frail health, but in her excitement, the young woman had forgotten to tell him her name or where she was getting married. Now Reb Moshe was calling Rabbi Sherer in the hope that he could locate the wedding hall and the *kallah* (bride).

Unlike his older sisters, Rochel and Elky, Shimshon's childhood coincided with dramatically increased demands on Rabbi Sherer's time, and the guilt feelings Rabbi Sherer often expressed about not having spent enough time with his children related most to his youngest child. Whenever he expressed those guilt feelings in latter years, Shimshon would protest vociferously that he had never felt deprived in any way.

Rabbi Sherer once told Shimshon about a meeting that he had had with Secretary of State Henry Kissinger. It was a time of high international tension, and as Rabbi Sherer waited for his meeting, he saw a phalanx of top State Department and military men coming out of the secretary of state's office. Yet after ushering Rabbi Sherer into his office, Kissinger focused totally on him, which impressed Rabbi Sherer immensely. Upon returning from Washington, D.C., Rabbi Sherer told Shimshon that a parent must develop that ability to focus completely on his child when the child needs his attention, despite all the other pressures under which he might be laboring.[17] He had that ability.

Rabbi Sherer learned regularly with Shimshie, and was never satisfied to let his son just mumble the *Gemara*, without verve or understanding. From a young age, he developed Shimshie's skills as a *darshan* (speaker). He would throw various wordplays of *Chazal* or *ma'amrei Chazal* (sayings of the Sages), and challenge his son to think of ways to use them in a speech.

He called Shimshie often when he was learning in the Talmudical Yeshiva of Philadelphia (Philadelphia Yeshiva).[18] The conversations were not confined to pro forma inquiries about how Shimshie was learning. Rabbi Sherer would usually share a *vort* from his homiletics class and often a story about a Torah giant that demonstrated his sharpness of understanding or *ahavas Yisrael* (love of the Jewish people). Often he included a *Chassidishe ma'aseh* (story) as well to develop Shimshie's appreciation of all different expressions of authentic *Yiddishkeit*.

When Shimshie was about 8, he asked for permission to cross the street in front of the Sherer's apartment himself. The other boys in his class, almost all of whom were older than Shimshie, were already crossing the street. Only reluctantly did Rabbi Sherer agree. Many years later, he told Shimshie that he had been peeking out from the venetian blinds as he crossed the street. He cited the verse that we recite in *Kiddush Levanah* (*Shir HaShirim* 2:8-9), "הִנֵּה זֶה עוֹמֵד אַחַר כָּתְלֵנוּ מַשְׁגִּיחַ מִן הַחֲלֹנוֹת מֵצִיץ מִן הַחֲרַכִּים — He was standing behind our wall, observing through

---

17. In truth, he applied the lesson learned from Henry Kissinger to every person with whom he met.
18. The last two decades of Rabbi Sherer's life the two spoke every day when Rabbi Sherer was at home.

A young Shimshon Sherer delivers greetings from Pirchei Agudath Israel to the 1964 Agudah dinner. Seated l-r: Volvie Friedman, Rabbi Sherer, Rabbi Moshe Feinstein, Rabbi Yaakov Kamenetsky.

Rabbi Sherer would often quip to his son that he should always bear in mind the responsibility of his father and Rav Moshe looking up to him.

the windows, peering through the lattices" — a perfect description of Rabbi Sherer watching from afar.

The verse is often interpreted as a metaphor for Hashem's Divine Providence, which accompanies the Jewish people in Exile, even when He seems far away. But it also applies to parents and children: A parent can be fully occupied with his child, even though the child is completely unaware of his presence. "When you were crossing that street," he told Shimshie, "I was concentrating on you more completely than when I'm holding your hand and talking to someone else on the way to shul, even though you didn't even know I was watching you."

Lessons of the Home

CERTAIN PRINCIPLES WERE VERY MUCH PART OF THE AIR OF THE Sherer home. Chief among them was the insignificance of money. One frequently repeated rule was: No crying about anything that money can fix. *Farginning* others and rejoicing in their successes was a trait Rabbi Sherer cultivated in his children.[19] He encouraged his children to recite the

---

19. Mrs. Elky Goldschmidt.

famous prayer of the Noam Elimelech before *davening* in which we ask Hashem to be spared from all jealousy — "neither should jealousy of others be found in our heart nor should we incite jealousy in others" — and granted the power for the power "to see the *ma'alos* [virtues] in others and not their defects."[20]

He interpreted the verse in *Tehillim* (147:13), "כִּי חִזַּק בְּרִיחֵי שְׁעָרָיִךְ בֵּרַךְ בָּנַיִךְ בְּקִרְבֵּךְ — For He has strengthened the bars of your gates, and blessed your children in your midst," to mean that one must reinforce the bars of one's home to produce healthy, successful children. Teaching them not to look outside all the time at what others possess constituted an important aspect of that reinforcement.

A constant theme in the Sherer home was the necessity of showing *hakaras hatov*. Rabbi Sherer's personal example played a large role in that. He never forgot a favor done for him, no matter how small, or stopped expressing his appreciation to the one who had helped him. Among the principal beneficiaries of his gratitude were his childrens' teachers and rebbeim, to whom he continued to express gratitude long after his children had moved up to the next grade.[21] On his annual visits to Camp Bnos and Camp Agudah, he always made a special point of going into the kitchen and thanking the chief cooks, Mrs. Uhr and Mrs. Lankry. Mrs. Lankry credits the *chizuk* he gave her with the fact that she is still in Camp Agudah.[22] He would also make sure to express his gratitude to

---

20. When Rabbi Sherer taught Shimshie to recite the *tefillah* of the Noam Elimelech, he connected it to the laws of *borer* (separating) on Shabbos: Just as it is only permitted to separate if one takes the *"ochel"* (the desired object) from the *"psoles"* (the undesired object), so, too, when one looks at another, he must learn to see the *"ma'alos"* and not the *"chesronos"* (failings). But there is a difference, he noted: *Borer* is forbidden only on Shabbos; whereas when it comes to judging people, we must focus on their *ma'alos*, not their *chesronos*, even during the week.

21. One rebbi to whom he showed special gratitude was Rabbi Yehoshua "Josh" Silbermintz, the long-time national director of Pirchei Agudath Israel and Shimshie's third-grade rebbi. In particular, he was grateful to Rabbi Silbermintz for teaching Shimshie Yiddish, though it had created a problem in the Sherer home, since Rabbi and Mrs. Sherer could no longer speak in Yiddish when they did not want their children to understand.

Rabbi Sherer never haggled over tuition, even when living on very limited means. Reb Shraga Feivel Mendlowitz had often quoted the *Gemara* (*Beitzah* 16a) that Shabbos and Yom Tov expenses and those connected to one's children's learning are not deducted from one's yearly income. And those words continued to resonate with him.

22. On one of his annual visits to her kitchen, Mrs. Lankry wondered whether she had perhaps been in the same place for too long, and should be thinking about doing something new. Rabbi Sherer responded with a story from the Beis Halevi's days as rav of Brisk. Two townspeople consulted with the Beis Halevi around the same time as to whether they should change their employment. The Beis Halevi told one to change and the other to remain where he was, and explained his different advice with a *vort* from the waving of the Four Species during Hallel.

When we call out *"Ana Hashem Hoshiyah Na* — Please, Hashem, save us," we wave the Four Species. But when we call out, *"And, Hashem Hatzlichah Na* — Please, Hashem, grant us success,"

Rebbetzin Shonnie Perr for her decades of leadership in Camp Bnos.

In part, the Sherer children's sensitivity to issues of *hakaras hatov* came from having a father who was "in the business of doing favors for people," as Mrs. Langer puts it, and watching the way that some people failed to show gratitude. Rabbi Sherer used to joke that he always carried a bag of small pebbles with him to give to those for whom he had rendered some service, in the hopes that they would content themselves later with throwing a pebble rather than a large boulder at him. Yet whenever a child would point to some instance of ingratitude, or wonder why he extended himself to such an extent on behalf of individuals who would not show sufficient appreciation, he would brush off their objections. "Do you have a problem with that?" he would ask. "I don't have a problem with that. I know why I was put in the world."[23]

The importance of *davening* was something else that Rabbi Sherer never failed to emphasize. No prayer goes unanswered, he would say, but "No" is also an answer. He also stressed including others in one's prayers. He would often quote the *Gemara* (*Bava Kamma* 92a) that one who beseeches Hashem on behalf of his friend, if he needs the same thing himself, he will be answered first. He explained that to mean that if one *davens* for one's friend as if for oneself, he will be answered first.

The *Gemara* (*Berachos* 34b) says it preferable to pray in a room with windows, and Rabbi Sherer linked the *Gemara's* use of the plural "windows" to the Zohar's statement that ideally each person should pray in a *beis haknesses* with twelve windows. Those twelve windows, said Rabbi Sherer, represent the Twelve Tribes, and the meaning of the *Gemara* is that when one *davens* one should do so with all the needs of *Klal Yisrael* in mind. One cannot *daven* to Hashem as "*avinu* — our

---

we do not. In the first case, the Beis Halevi explained, we are beseeching Hashem to rescue us from a desperate situation, a situation that requires action on our part as well, and so we wave the *dalet minim*. But in the case of "*Hatzlichah Na*," we are basically asking for continued success, and so we hold the Four Species in place without movements. "You are doing well," the Beis Halevi told the person whom he had advised to stay put, "and so I did not suggest that you switch employment." After telling Mrs. Lankry the story, Rabbi Sherer said that the same principle applied to her. She was far too successful in Camp Agudah to consider moving. She heeded his advice.

23. In the course of learning the Maharal's commentary on Rashi, *Gur Aryeh* (*Bereishis* 2:5), Rabbi Sherer was once troubled by a statement of the Maharal: "It is forbidden to do a favor for someone who will not show proper appreciation." He even asked Rabbi Elya Svei how he should conduct himself in light of the Maharal's statement. In the end, however, he continued doing favors for people, even where he knew that they would show minimal gratitude. The Maharal, Rabbi Sherer explained, is speaking where a person feels he is doing a favor for someone else. But if he views the favor as for himself, he need not concern himself with the likelihood of ingratitude. As he used to say when people would thank him for some favor rendered, "Would you thank me for putting on *tefillin* this morning or for keeping kosher?"

father," unless one views one's fellow Jews as one's brothers and sisters, he would say.

He was strict about praying in his *makom kavua* (fixed place), unless a guest in shul had inadvertently taken his place. For him a *makom kavua* meant not only a physical place, but also making sure that one's thoughts during *davening* were firmly on the words of *Shemoneh Esrei*.

Sharing the secrets of his success one day with his granddaughter Chavie Galinsky, he started with prayer. "I wake up early in the morning, and I think about what I have to do that day. Then I ask Hashem for help. Many people make the mistake of thinking that one only *davens* when things are not going well," he told his granddaughter.

Rabbi Sherer's example affected each of his children, according to their individual personalities. The Sherers' oldest daughter, Mrs. Rochel Langer, is a teacher. One day she called her father to express her frustration over a classroom project on which she was working. She had torn up stencil after stencil because of some nearly imperceptible imperfection. After describing her problem, she told her father in mock, accusing fashion, "You know, it's your fault."

Rabbi Sherer's reply to the accusation of having passed on his own perfectionism was both an admission of guilt and acceptance of the consequences: "I'm not sorry." As a parent, Rabbi Sherer did not expect or demand that his children would always bring home perfect report cards. But he did insist that they work to the best of their abilities.

Mrs. Langer's choice of history as her major subject of teaching was also influenced by Rabbi Sherer. Lack of knowledge of Jewish history — not his-story, but my-story, he would say — pained him greatly. The *Gemara* (*Shabbos* 31a) tells us that one of the questions that a person will be asked in the World to Come is: *Kavata itim l'Torah* — Did you establish fixed times for Torah study? Rabbi Sherer offered a homiletical twist: Did you know the times (i.e., dates) in the history of Torah and the Jewish people? He prepared long charts of well-known dates in the secular calendar with the crucial events in Jewish history that were taking place at the same time. Every Jewish child should know, for instance, that 1492 is not only the year that Columbus discovered America, but also the year of the expulsion of the Jews from Spain.

Each of Rabbi Sherer's descendants can cite examples of frequently repeated insights, and the effect of his personal example. Rabbi Shimshon Sherer recalls a typical example of the messages that his father conveyed. Rabbi Sherer once asked him, "Shimshie, do you think

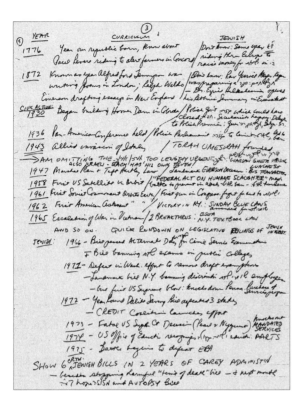

One of Rabbi Sherer's charts correlating world events with events in Jewish history

that the *Ribbono shel Olam* is smarter than Henry Ford?" Though bewildered by the question, the young boy responded that Henry Ford's intelligence cannot be compared to Hashem's infinite wisdom. "Then why didn't Hashem create man with a rearview mirror?" Rabbi Sherer asked. The message he wanted to convey is that while one must consult the past to prepare for the future,[24] but if one spends all one's time looking backward through a rearview mirror, he will never forge ahead in life, just as someone who spends all his time looking in the rearview mirror on his car will ultimately crash.

A Doting Grandfather

RABBI SHERER WAS INTIMATELY INVOLVED IN THE LIVES OF HIS grandchildren. The relationship between grandparents and grandchildren, he felt, holds the key to the continuity of *Klal Yisrael*. He used to buttress this point with an insight from his father-in-law, Rabbi Shimshon Zelig

---

24. He did not, of course, deny the great value of experience, both one's own and that of others. One of the hand-written quotations found after his passing contained a quotation from Winston Churchill: "The farther backward you can look, the farther forward you are likely to see."

Holding his first great-grandchild, Leah Galinsky (Senft)

Fortman. Rabbi Fortman asked: Why are the Jewish people referred to as *Klal Yisrael*, rather than as *Klal Avraham* or *Klal Yitzchak* or *Klal Yaakov*? He answered that nowhere in the Torah do we find a dialogue between Avraham and his grandchildren or Yitzchak and his grandchildren. Only after Yaakov Avinu received the additional name Yisrael do we find an explicit reference to a strong connection between a grandfather and grandchildren, when Yaakov says of Yosef's sons, "Ephraim and Menashe shall be mine like Reuven and Shimon" (*Bereishis* 48:5).[25] Only once such a strong connection between the generations was established, with grandchildren treated as sons, was the continuity of the Jewish people secure, and thus the name *Klal Yisrael*.

Rabbi Sherer made time to attend the birthday parties of grandchildren and even great-grandchildren, as well as family Chanukah parties. In the course of a summer at camp, the grandchildren could count on receiving a least two long letters from him signed, "Your grandfather, who loves you *b'lev v'nefesh* [heart and soul]."

The grandchildren had ample opportunity to know how much they were in their grandfather's thoughts. Rabbi Sherer purchased *tefillin* for all his grandsons. On one of his last trips to *Eretz Yisrael*, he not only purchased *tefillin* for the upcoming bar mitzvah of Shimshon's son Yisroel Shneur (Sruly), but also for Shimshon's next son Matis, whose bar mitzvah was still 10 years away.[26] If he knew that one of his mar-

---

25. Though the blessing is given in the name of Yaakov, Rabbi Fortman's point was that only after Yaakov Avinu was given the additional name Yisrael do we find the first instance in the Torah of one of the *Avos* interacting with a grandchild.

26. He feared that he would no longer be alive to present Matis with his *tefillin*, and when he arrived

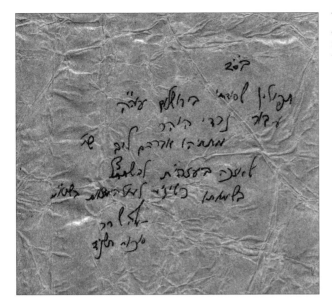

The inscription accompanying the *tefillin* he purchased for his grandson Matis

ried grandchildren was traveling on *Erev Shabbos*, Rabbi Sherer would remind them to leave plenty of time for traffic, and asked to be called when they arrived at their destination.

He was available for consultations about the choice of schools for children, and even great-grandchildren, and actively investigated *shidduch* suggestions for his grandchildren. Avi Schoenbrun was the counselor of Rabbi Sherer's grandson Shragie Goldschmidt the summer he began dating Shragie's older sister Suri. When Rabbi Sherer made his annual visit to Camp Agudah, he told Shragie that he would like to speak to his counselor. The two chatted, but Rabbi Sherer did not interview Avi or make him feel uncomfortable. Indeed, he reminded him that a number of years earlier, he had made a *shivah* call at the Schoenbrun house, and Avi had shown him the way to get back on the Brooklyn-Queens Expressway by driving in front of him onto the highway.

His grandchildren knew that they could call him on the phone if they needed his advice, and they did. When Suri (Goldschmidt) Schoenbrun was in the process of obtaining licensing for a playgroup, he made him-

---

back in the United States, he asked Shimshon to put the *tefillin* for Matis in safekeeping until his bar mitzvah, something which Shimshon refused to do on the grounds that Rabbi Sherer would yet live to present the *tefillin* himself. Unfortunately, Rabbi Sherer's premonition was correct. When Matis received his bar mitzvah *tefillin*, he found a note Rabbi Sherer had written in Hebrew: "I arranged these *tefillin* in *Yerushalayim Ir HaKodesh* for my beloved grandson Matisyahu Avrohom Leib. May I merit to be present at his bar mitzvah ...."

Chapter Twenty-Three: In Private ☐ 587

With Rabbi Yaakov Yitzchak Ruderman and grandchildren on his annual visit to Camp Agudah. Standing l-r: Shragie Goldschmidt, Levi Langer, Yehuda Langer, Daniel Langer.

self available to her to discuss the procedures to be followed. Another granddaughter, Chavie (Langer) Galinsky, called him one *Erev Shabbos* to seek his guidance about an educational project in which she was involved that was being stymied by too much politics and infighting among those responsible. "So you'll just have to be *mekarev kulam* [draw everyone close]," he told her.

Rabbi Sherer was not the type of grandfather to just sit back and savor his offspring. He also guided them and sought to instill some of his most cherished values. He spent time teaching his grandchildren the art of public speaking. He might stop them in the middle of a *dvar Torah*, just as he would a student in his homiletics class at Torah Vodaath, if he had a point he wanted to make.

Shragie Goldschmidt was the grandchild who lived closest to his grandparents and thus spent the most time with Rabbi Sherer. He sat next to his grandfather during *davening* every Shabbos morning, and would accompany him home from shul. When Shragie was a young boy, it was Rabbi Sherer who insisted that he go to a speech therapist for a very minor lisp. And the latter had the *nachas* from that decision years later when Shragie gave the valedictory address at his Touro College graduation. Rabbi Sherer went over that speech in advance and wrote extensive notes on a draft.

Greeting Rabbi Mordechai Gifter with family members on his annual visit to Camp Agudah. L-r: Mendy Sherer, Rabbi Shimshon Sherer, Yudi Sherer, Yehuda Langer, Shragie Goldschmidt, Rabbi Gifter, Rabbi Sherer, Sruly Sherer, Daniel Langer, Levi Langer

Rabbi Sherer's life mission was *Kiddush Hashem*, in all its forms, and his children and grandchildren were always acutely aware that they had to be exemplars. The worst possible failing, they knew, was that someone should ever say, or even think, that any of the Sherer progeny felt themselves entitled to special privileges by virtue of their relationship to Rabbi Sherer.

When his grandsons went to learn in *Eretz Yisrael*, Rabbi Sherer had two requests. The first was that they stay away from all demonstrations. The second was that they should conduct themselves at all times with the gravitas appropriate to students of Torah and not as if they were on vacation. He told them to never forget that their cabdriver might have a son at the battlefront and to conduct themselves accordingly.[27]

That sensitivity was deeply engrained in him. On the second day of the Yom Kippur War, Shimshie returned from the Philadelphia Yeshiva

---

27. Rabbi Sherer had good precedent for these instructions. During World War II, Reb Shraga Feivel Mendlowitz would not allow students in Torah Vodaath to go in large groups to perform *Tashlich*. He feared that the sight of large numbers of Orthodox young men not in uniform might cause animosity to Orthodox Jews among those who had sons or loved ones serving overseas or who had lost family members in the war. Yonoson Rosenblum, *Reb Shraga Feivel*, p. 234 fn. 7.

to find a large emergency meeting taking place in the Sherer family dining room. Rabbi Sherer had never been reticent about kissing his son in public, and so Shimshie approached his father for his anticipated greeting kiss. To his great surprise, Rabbi Sherer indicated that it was not the time. A few minutes later, after Shimshie had gone into the kitchen to greet his mother, Rabbi Sherer entered. He realized that Shimshie might have been hurt by his failure to kiss him hello, and wanted to explain the reason.

"Yesterday many Jewish parents did not even have a chance to say goodbye to their sons as they rushed off to the battlefront to defend *Eretz Yisrael*. Those parents are frantic right now with worry over whether they will ever again kiss their sons. How could I kiss you today when so many of our brothers and sisters are worried that they may never have this opportunity again?" he told Shimshie.[28]

Rabbi Sherer also told his grandsons that he was *makpid* (strict) they should not smoke. Reminiscing in his *succah*, he once related to Yudi and Sruly Sherer how he had been a heavy smoker. On a visit to the United States Surgeon General to enlist his assistance in the battle against indiscriminate autopsies in Israel hospitals (some of which received U.S. government funding), the Surgeon General, after learning that Rabbi Sherer was a smoker, took him aside and told him, "If you are so important to Senator Javits [who had arranged the meeting], I'm going to save your life." He proceeded to show Rabbi Sherer photographs of healthy lungs and the lungs of smokers. From the time that he walked out of the room that day, Rabbi Sherer never smoked another cigarette.

Rabbi Sherer took the responsibility for welcoming new members to the Sherer family, beginning with his two son-in-laws, Yisroel Langer and Moshe Yaakov (Robert) Goldschmidt, both *musmachim* of Torah Vodaath. Langer was a close *talmid* of Rabbi Gedaliah Schorr in Bais Medrash Elyon, and later graduated from Columbia Law School. Goldschmidt is Dean of Students at Touro College. Rabbi Sherer took enormous pride in both.

Both of his sons-in-law were orphaned from their fathers long before marriage. Their mothers, Pessel Leah Langer and Leba Goldschmidt, had to work very hard to provide their sons a yeshivah education, and

---

28. A story told about Rabbi Isser Zalman Meltzer reflects the same sensitivity. Rabbi Isser Zalman Meltzer refused to accompany his grandson Rabbi Shneur Kotler more than a few steps upon the latter's departure from *Eretz Yisrael* for his *chasanah* in America, out of deference to all the Jews murdered by the Nazis who would never have the opportunity to accompany their children to the *chuppah*.

At the *Hachnasas Sefer Torah,* sharing the *simchah* with his family. From left: Rabbi Sherer, Yisroel Langer, Moshe Yaakov (Robert) Goldschmidt, Rabbi Shimshon Sherer

Rabbi Sherer often expressed his admiration for their *mesiras nefesh* (self-sacrifice) for Torah.[29]

Shimshon's wife Shifi, according to one family joke, inherited from her father-in-law the organizational skills and discipline that by rights should have gone to his son. Not only did Rabbi and Mrs. Sherer enjoy a close relationship with her parents, Mr. and Mrs. Meyer Thurm, but also with Mr. Thurm's older brother Leo, and with Mrs. Thurm's two brothers from Toronto, Henik and Hatzik Mandelbaum and their families.

New additions to the family were soon made to feel like full-fledged members. The first Pesach after Avi Schoenbrun married Suri Goldschmidt, Rabbi Sherer insisted that Avi sit next to him at the Seder table and that the family sing Avi's favorite *niggunim,* as well as their own.

The mother of the Goldschmidts' *machutenesta* Mrs. Laya Leshkowitz is from the town Sighet, where the recently deceased Satmar Rebbe, Rabbi Moshe Teitelbaum, was the rav before World War II. The Leshkowitz family had a tradition of drinking a *l'chaim* in the Rebbe's home to cel-

---

29. Mrs. Goldschmidt was the granddaughter of the Rabbi Yaakov Koppel Reich, the Chief Rabbi of Budapest for 37 years. She had managed a successful export-import business prior to World War II in Europe. After her husband Shraga Goldschmidt's premature passing in 1964, some kindhearted people offered to find jobs for her two sons as diamond-cutters. But she insisted on taking a menial job in a tool factory, which required her to leave home at 6 a.m. every morning, so that her two sons could remain in yeshivah.

At the *l'chaim* of Shragie Goldschmidt and S'Rivky (Sara Rivka) Leshkowitz at the home of the Satmar Rebbe. Seated clockwise from left: Moshe Yaakov (Robert) Goldschmidt, Rabbi Sherer, the Satmar Rebbe, Shragie Goldschmidt, Chaim Leshkowitz.

ebrate family *simchos*. At the time of the engagement of the Leshkowitz's daughter Sarah Rivka (S'Rivky) to Shragie Goldschmidt, the anti-Agudah Satmar paper *Der Yid* was busy attacking Agudath Israel of America. That created a potentially embarrassing situation for the *kallah's* parents, who hesitated about inviting Rabbi Sherer to the *l'chaim* at the home of the Satmar Rebbe out of fear that he would be uncomfortable.

When Chaim Leshkowitz finally summoned up the courage to explain his predicament to Rabbi Sherer, the latter responded immediately that he would be thrilled to come. He confided to Leshkowitz that the Rebbe had paid him *bikur cholim* visits in his home both after his open-heart surgery and during his treatment for lymphoma.[30] The Satmar Rebbe was standing to greet Rabbi Sherer on the night of the *l'chaim*, and the two gave each other big smiles and embraced.

RABBI SHERER TOOK GREAT PRIDE IN THE ACHIEVEMENTS OF HIS offspring. Whenever some one complimented him on one of his descen-

A Proud Father and Grandfather

dants, he was wont to respond, *"Zeh schari mikol amali* — That is the reward for all my labors." During one of his last hospital stays, Rabbi Sherer's granddaughter Chavie Galinsky went to visit him. As

---

30. After Rabbi Sherer's passing, the Satmar Rebbe made a *shivah* call, at which he said that he and Rabbi Sherer had enjoyed a special friendship. He told how Rabbi Sherer had done many favors for Satmar, even though, for ideological reasons, these had never been publicized.

always, he turned the conversation to her and a presentation that she had recently made to a group of teachers about how to build a positive relationship with their students. He wanted to hear every detail of her presentation, why she had chosen to make her points in that particular fashion, and what the response had been. Though he had been very weak at the outset of the conversation, and his voice almost inaudible, the longer he and his granddaughter spoke, the stronger he became. By the end of the conversation, his voice was animated, and he physically looked like another person. Rabbi Sherer always enjoyed hearing of other people's successes, but those of a beloved granddaughter were particularly sweet.

Dancing with his youngest grandson, Matis Sherer, at the *Hachnasas Sefer Torah*.

Nothing filled Rabbi Sherer with more pride than his descendants' attainments in Torah learning. Those who were in the Agudath Israel offices the day his grandson Rabbi Levi Langer[31] won the Memorial Foundation prize for the best *chaburah* on a Talmudic topic for an unprecedented third time will never forget Rabbi Sherer's beaming smile.

From the moment that a fledgling Flatbush congregation offered his son Shimshon the position as its first rav, Rabbi Sherer pushed Shimshon to accept the position, despite his initial reluctance. When Shimshon saw how important his acceptance of the *rabbanus* was to his father, he agreed to accept the position for a trial period of one year, on condition that if he did not enjoy it, his father would not push him to remain. Before Shimshon assumed his new position, Rabbi Sherer offered him two pieces of advice. Because he was so confident that Shimshon would succeed in his new position, he warned him not to

---

31. Rabbi Langer is currently the Rosh Kollel of the Pittsburgh Kollel.

take himself too seriously. "You have to take the authority of your position very seriously, but not yourself," Rabbi Sherer warned. "If I find out that you are, you'll hear from me."

The second piece of advice was even more important than the first: Remember that the *rabbanus* is not a popularity contest; any rav who is properly doing his job must stir opposition. He buttressed his point by citing the blessing that Hashem promised Avraham Avinu at the beginning of his mission: וַאֲבָרְכָה מְבָרְכֶיךָ וּמְקַלֶּלְךָ אָאֹר — I will bless those who bless you, and he who curses you I will curse" (*Bereishis* 12:3). Would it not have been a greater blessing, Rabbi Sherer asked his son, if Hashem had simply told Avraham that he would have no detractors? He answered his own question: A rav who has no detractors is not properly performing his duties. In short, the desire for short-term popularity is antithetical to leadership.[32]

A few months after accepting the *rabbanus* on a trial basis, Reb Shimshon called his father on *Motza'ei Shabbos* to tell him that his halachic *shiur* that Shabbos had riled at least one member of the congregation. When Rabbi Sherer heard that, he fairly shouted into the phone, "*Baruch Hashem*, my son is now on the road to success."

Though Rabbi Sherer tried not to be overly involved in his son's new *Klal* role, he was looking through the lattices, just as he had those many years earlier when Shimshie crossed the street by himself for the first time. Every *Motza'ei Shabbos*, Rabbi Sherer would call his grandson-in-law Avi Schoenbrun, who *davened* in Shimshon's shul, to cross-examine him about Shimshon's *derashah* that Shabbos: What had he said? How did the congregation respond? How many people were in shul? And most important, how long was the *derashah*?[33] When Reb Shimshon

---

32. No less a great leader than Rav Shach once made this point to Rabbi Sherer, citing an insight from the Maharil Diskin. In *Parashas Zos Haberachah*, the Torah describes the mourning for Moshe Rabbeinu, "וַיִּבְכּוּ בְנֵי יִשְׂרָאֵל — and *Bnei Yisrael* cried" (*Devarim* 34:8). But earlier, when describing the mourning for Aharon HaKohen, the Torah says, "וַיִּבְכּוּ אֶת אַהֲרֹן שְׁלֹשִׁים יוֹם כֹּל בֵּית יִשְׂרָאֵל — And the entire Jewish people cried for Aharon" (*Bamidbar* 20:29). The contrast suggests that the crying for Aharon was more inclusive — i.e., everyone cried for Aharon, but not for Moshe.

Even if that was the case, the Maharil Diskin asked, why did the Torah emphasize the lesser degree of mourning for Moshe Rabbeinu? He answered that the less-inclusive mourning was, in fact, praiseworthy for Moshe Rabbeinu in his role as leader of the Jewish people. Aharon's role was to be a "maker of peace, a pursuer of peace." And the Torah tells us that he successfully fulfilled his task: everyone mourned his passing. Moshe's role, by contrast, was to be a leader. And in that task, he often had to act contrary to popular opinion. And the Torah tells us that he too fulfilled his mission to perfection, as proven by the fact that not everyone mourned his passing.

33. A longstanding family joke has it that Shimshon must have been adopted. The ability to speak briefly and to the point seemed almost part of Rabbi Sherer's DNA, but the "speak short" gene had skipped Shimshon entirely.

called him after Shabbos, his first question was invariably, "*Nu*, how long did you speak?" Even before Shimshon could reply, he would invariably answer his own question: "Too long."

Toward the end of his life, Rabbi Sherer lamented that he had so little to leave his children in the way of a material inheritance and even asked his son for *mechilah* (forgiveness) on that score.[34] Shimshon brushed aside his concerns and responded immediately that he had provided his children with the greatest inheritance of all: the privilege of being his child. He spoke for the whole family.

For his part, Rabbi Sherer had a one-line oral *tzavaah* (ethical will) for his descendants, one which fully reflected his commitment to family: "*mi'besarecha al tisalam* — from your own flesh and blood do not hide yourself."[35] All he asked is that his children remain close and never forsake one another.

---

34. The late Satmar Rebbe, Rabbi Yoel Teitelbaum, once told Moshe Yaakov (Robert) Goldschmidt that his father-in-law was one of the great *ba'alei tzedakah* of the generation. He could have been a millionaire several times over, the Rebbe said, but instead he dedicated his life to *Klal Yisrael*.

35. That is how the phrase is generally quoted based on the Rosh (*Orchos Chaim* 78). But Rabbi Sherer was careful to note that the actual verse (*Yeshayahu* 58:7) from which this instruction is drawn reads "*lo tisalam*" rather than "*al tisalam*."

Chapter Twenty-Four

DEALING WITH ADVERSITY

RABBI SHERER ONCE POSED THE FOLLOWING QUESTION: Why does the subject of *eruchin* (the valuation of human beings for purposes of vows to the *Beis HaMikdash*) follow immediately after the terrible *tochachah* (curses) of *Bechukosai*. He answered, in the name of an *adam gadol* (great man),[1] that the juxtaposition teaches us that we can only know the true worth of a person after having seen how he reacts to adversity. By that standard, Rabbi Sherer's value was very great indeed.

The last decade of Rabbi Sherer's life was marked by repeated medical crises: open-heart surgery, lymphoma, and, finally, acute leukemia. Those medical crises revealed the true mettle of the man. He never succumbed to despair, and throughout each of his illnesses was driven

---
1. Rabbi Shmuel Alter, *Likutei Basar Likutei*.

by the desire to regain his health so that he could continue serving *Klal Yisrael*.

Intimations of Mortality

IN NOVEMBER 1993 RABBI SHERER WAS FLYING FROM ANTWERP to New York when he bent down to pick up his watch, which had fallen off, and felt a sharp pain in his chest. Even prior to his trip to Antwerp, his cardiologist Dr. Edgar Lichstein had detected something amiss and scheduled an angiogram immediately upon his return. As soon as he looked at the results of the angiogram, Dr. Jacob Shani told Rabbi Sherer he would not be going home, but required immediate open-heart surgery. The major artery to his heart was 99 percent occluded. The sharp pain he had experienced on the plane, it turned out, was likely an indication of the heart shutting down.[2]

After receiving the news, Mrs. Sherer, his daughter Elky Goldschmidt, and son Shimshon were ushered into the room at Maimonides Medical Center where he was being prepared for surgery.[3] They found Rabbi Sherer looking surprisingly upbeat for someone who had just been told he would soon be undergoing open-heart surgery. Noticing the fear on his wife's face, he told her, "Devoraleh, you'll see it will be for the best. Remember my mother's *fleshele* [bottle] of medicine." When that still failed to calm her, he added, "You don't understand. I asked the surgeon[4] what the prognosis is, and he told me that I will come out feeling 10 years younger. That's 10 more years to serve *Klal Yisrael*."

Rabbi Sherer's optimism turned out to be well founded. The operation was a success. The day after surgery, while still in considerable pain from the surgery, Rabbi Sherer was already at work with his daughter Elky on the "State of Agudath Israel" speech to be delivered that *Motza'ei Shabbos* at the upcoming Agudah convention. He dictated numerous drafts of the speech, which his son Rabbi Shimshon Sherer delivered in his stead.

As soon as his doctors permitted, he began exercising seriously to work himself back into shape. Yisrael Lefkowitz, one of his closest

---

2. Two members of the Maimonides Medical Center administration were particularly dedicated to Rabbi Sherer during his stays there: Douglas Jablon, Vice President for Patient Relations and Special Assistant to the President, and Dr. Marcel (Mosie) Biberfeld, Vice President for Psychiatry and Community Services, who is a longtime Agudah activist.
3. As soon as she heard that her father would be undergoing surgery, his daughter Rochel Langer rushed to the hospital from Monsey.
4. Dr. Israel Jacobowitz performed the surgery.

Rabbi Sherer speaking at the *seudas hoda'ah* celebrating his recovery from open-heart surgery. Rabbi Elya Svei is beside him.

friends and supporters, sent an exercise cycle to Rabbi Sherer's house, as soon has he heard that Rabbi Sherer had been cleared for exercise. He pedaled away many hours on the cycle while listening to Torah tapes.

Rabbi Sherer had never walked much, except on Shabbos, because he was always accosted by someone as soon as he went out into public. But now, his doctors told him to walk, and walk he did. Every morning around 8 a.m. his granddaughter Suri's husband, Avi Schoenbrun, would pick him up at his home and they would go for a walk together. The Kings Plaza Mall was a frequent venue for their exertions. When the weather permitted, they also walked along the Belt Parkway. Rabbi Sherer told Avi that there were times in his life when he had walked in solitude along the Belt Parkway.

Rabbi Sherer always arrived for his morning workout wearing a hat, jacket, and tie. As he explained to Avi, "You never know who you are going to meet." He took very seriously the task of regaining his past energy levels. Even in the period immediately after the surgery, he never complained and stuck to his prescribed exercise regime.

On those walks, he was open to answering any questions his grandson-in-law posed to him, but, in general, he steered the conversation to Avi. He did not initiate conversation about himself. On one of their walks through the Kings Plaza Mall, Avi got a taste of what made Rabbi Sherer tick. It was December, and there was a boys' choir singing carols on the level below in the mall. Rabbi Sherer's eyes began to swell with tears at the sight. When Avi asked why he was so emotional, he answered, "I'm sure that there are Russian Jewish children in that choir." As a former public-school student, Rabbi Sherer could remember the pressure to sing carols and their impact on the other Jewish students.

Rabbi Sherer recovered fully from his heart surgery, and was able to resume his pre-surgery schedule within two months. Little more than a month after the surgery, he delivered the invocation at Mayor Rudolph Giuliani's first inauguration while still recuperating from his surgery. Giuliani had pressed him very hard to speak, despite his recent surgery. He told Rabbi Sherer that he had no specific need for a rabbi to deliver the invocation, but that he wanted the best the clergy had to offer, and that was Rabbi Sherer.

In his invocation, it is clear that the trauma of the Crown Heights riots was still very much on his mind. He began: "*Avinu she'baShamayim* — Our Father in Heaven. Our hearts overflow with gratitude to thee for this diverse assemblage of New Yorkers, wonderful people of good faith and of all faiths, *committed to healing the divisions that have tragically arisen in the city*"(emphasis added). And he concluded with another veiled reference to the riots, in praying that "we may witness the fulfillment of the vision of the Psalmist — they that sow in tears shall reap in joy — so that the tensions that torture our society today will be replaced by a renewal of civic pride, *of cherished family values, and of neighbors living congenially in safe streets, which was once so common among New Yorkers*, for the glory of G-d and all mankind" (emphasis added).[5]

In between, he prayed that the incoming administration, made up of "men and women who love to serve and who will serve with love," would demonstrate for all to see that beneath the cold outer veneer of a city's bureaucracy, there beats a warm heart in which the anguished

---

5. The reference to family values was very much in keeping with a letter Rabbi Sherer wrote to Governor Mario Cuomo December 28, 1993 in which he urged Cuomo to use the platform of his next State of the State address to address the "moral component" of so many of the quality of life issues facing society. Governor Cuomo wrote back a warm personal note with the text of his State of the State address, which he hoped would demonstrate that "I took your concerns to heart." He expressed gratitude for Rabbi Sherer's guidance and "special debt to any friend who can help me see more clearly." He concluded by thanking Rabbi Sherer for the "the depth of your insight and the strength of your friendship." *Governor Mario Cuomo to Rabbi Moshe Sherer,* January 13, 1994.

cry of the depressed, the deprived, and the disadvantaged strikes a responsive chord."

A New Crisis

FOLLOWING THE OPEN-HEART SURGERY, RABBI SHERER WAS SO careful about what he ate that no one suspected anything was amiss when he began to lose a great deal of weight. That sharp weight loss, however, turned out to be the harbinger of his next life-threatening illness. A little more than two years after his heart surgery, a CAT scan revealed swelling of his lymph nodes.

As soon as the diagnoses was known, Rabbi Sherer's close friend Leuchu Glueck, called Dr. Michael Bashevkin, one of New York's leading experts on lymphoma and an Orthodox Jew, and told him that he would like him to meet a very important patient the following Monday, which was *Taanis Esther*. The call from Glueck, who was on the Board of Maimonides Hospital and president of the Boro Park Bikur Cholim, alerted Dr. Bashevkin that this would be no ordinary patient.

Not wishing to alarm his family members, Rabbi Sherer went to the appointment alone. (His son Shimshon, after calling the Agudath Israel offices and learning that his father had left the office for the day, suspected that he might be at Dr. Bashevkin's office and drove over from his office nearby.) Dr. Bashevkin was immediately impressed by Rabbi Sherer's mental organization, even in such a highly stressful situation. Dr. Bashevkin described to Rabbi Sherer the likely treatment — eight courses of chemotherapy over 24 weeks — and Rabbi Sherer's short and long-term prognosis. Despite the grim news, Rabbi Sherer was perfectly calm. He took notes throughout the conversation, asked all the right questions, and immediately understood the import of the information he was being given, remembers Dr. Bashevkin.

At the end of that first meeting, Rabbi Sherer had a request for Dr. Bashevkin. "I want you to do me a huge favor," he began. "In a day or two, I'll bring my wife to meet you. Please be as optimistic as possible with her. She has to hear the positive."

By the time the appointment was over, it was almost time for the reading of *Megillas Esther*. Rabbi Sherer permitted himself one tear, as he told his son, "I have to get better. I have so much still to do. But we can't cry. It's Purim." He made Shimshon promise not to share the news with anyone so as not to dampen the joy of the next day's Purim *seudah* (meal). At the Purim *seudah*, at his daughter Elky Goldschmidt's home,

Rabbi Sherer was in his usual festive mood. None of those present had any clue as to his situation. Mrs. Sherer even commented, "Daddy looks the best he's looked in a long time."

Eventually Rabbi Sherer switched from Dr. Bashevkin to Dr. Morton Coleman, one of the world's leading oncologists, while continuing to come to Dr. Bashevkin's clinic for blood tests. Rabbi Sherer changed doctors only reluctantly. He had full confidence in Dr. Bashevkin, whose office wall is filled with awards attesting to his eminence in the field, and he feared hurting his feelings. At the same time, he was being pressured by a number of those close to him to go to Dr. Coleman, who had previously treated Rabbi Feinstein. Rabbi Sherer explained to Dr. Bashevkin that he was sparing him the hassle of a celebrity patient, and that if he remained as his patient, Dr. Bashevkin would be subjected to endless inquiries about Rabbi Sherer's progress from well-wishers and would find himself working under a communal microscope.

Now it was Dr. Bashevkin's turn to put Rabbi Sherer at ease. He assured him that Dr. Coleman was the top doctor in the field, adding that Dr. Coleman had trained him. If Dr. Bashevkin was disappointed in any way, it did not affect his relationship with Rabbi Sherer. The two continued to enjoy a close relationship. In the course of his examinations, Rabbi Sherer would, characteristically, ask Dr. Bashevkin about himself.

For his part, Dr. Bashevkin found Rabbi Sherer to be someone with whom one was "able to forge the kind of bond that does not develop easily with others." He sought out the opinion and input of others, and enjoyed making friends, Dr. Bashevkin recalls. During Rabbi Sherer's final illness, Dr. Bashevkin visited him in the hospital a number of times, and always found him delighted to see him. To this day, he calls Mrs. Sherer every *Erev Rosh Hashanah.*

By the time of Rabbi Sherer's first appointment with Dr. Coleman at Cornell Medical Center, the latter was already filled with anticipation. He had been called by Mrs. Miriam Lubling, president of the Rivka Laufer Bikur Cholim organization, who runs a medical referral organization from her office at NYU Hospital.[6] She told Dr. Coleman that his new patient was "the world's greatest rabbi."

At their first meeting, Dr. Coleman repeated Mrs. Lubling's description and added, "I'd like to believe her, but she's told me the same thing

---

6. At an Agudath Israel convention Rabbi Sherer once described Mrs. Lubling as *Klal Yisrael's* Angel of Mercy.

too many times in the past. Time will tell." Rabbi Sherer laughed and told him, "All Jews are great. All rabbis are great. We are a great people."

About one thing Rabbi Sherer was surely right: Being his doctor was not without its unique pressures. Dr. Coleman received calls from the office of both New York City Mayor Rudolph Giuliani and Cardinal John O'Connor urging him to be especially careful in his treatment of Rabbi Sherer. The message in both cases was virtually identical: "Take good care of Rabbi Sherer. He's my rabbi."

Rabbi Sherer's lymphoma was already at an advanced stage, and Dr. Coleman expressed concern as to whether a man of his age would be able to survive the heavy doses of chemotherapy that would be needed to cure him. As he cheerily put it to Rabbi Sherer, "I'll have to kill you to save you." Rabbi Sherer replied, "Kill me, as long as you save me. I have too much to do for our people."

Dr. Coleman wanted to run a battery of heart tests on Rabbi Sherer to ascertain his ability to withstand the debilitating chemotherapy treatments he would be facing. But there were then no beds in the oncology ward, and so Dr. Coleman told Rabbi Sherer that he would have to wait until the tests could be administered.

Rabbi Sherer, however, was eager to begin treatment. He asked Dr. Coleman if he had a piece of stationery with the names of the board of directors of the hospital on it. He quickly scanned the list, and told Dr. Coleman he would come back first thing the next morning. Dr. Coleman assured him that not even a director of the hospital could create a space where none existed.

As soon as he left the meeting with Dr. Coleman, Rabbi Sherer called his friend Avrohom Biderman and asked him whether he was still friendly with a certain member of the board of directors. Biderman assured him that he was, and Rabbi Sherer asked him to make sure that a bed was available the next morning. The next morning, upon his arrival in the hospital, Rabbi Sherer was greeted like a visiting president. Biderman had obviously done his work well, something for which Rabbi Sherer remained ever grateful in the years to come.

After receiving the results of Rabbi Sherer's heart tests, Dr. Coleman told Rabbi Sherer, "You have some heart." He asked Rabbi Sherer, "What is your regimen?" Rabbi Sherer replied, "I'm a disciplined man. I watched what I ate and exercised, just as my heart doctor told me." "Because of your discipline," Dr. Coleman told him, "You have the heart of a 45-year-old. As a consequence, I can save you." When he heard that, Rabbi Sherer turned to his wife and told her triumphantly, "Remember when I had heart surgery and I told you that it would all be for the best." His rigorous exercise regimen recovering from open-heart surgery had paid off.

Now, the chemotherapy could begin in earnest. Shimshon drove his father to the hospital for the first of his treatments. The mood in the car was somber. Rabbi Sherer suggested that they listen to a tape. Shimshon put on a tape that neither had ever heard, and the words seemed tailor-made to the situation: *"Avinu, Av HaRachaman. Tatte, oy Tatte, Avinu, Av HaRachaman ...."* Both Rabbi Sherer and Shimshon started crying. Rabbi Sherer stopped first, telling his son, "Shimshie, we're not allowed to cry because there is a *Tatte in Himmel* [a Father in Heaven], Who is a *Rachaman* [Merciful One] and will watch over me." He kept asking Shimshon to rewind the tape to that *niggun* (song), with Rabbi Sherer interjecting from time to time, "No crying."[7]

The chemotherapy treatments proved to be as grueling as predicted. Rabbi Sherer had always been impeccably groomed, and now suddenly he lost all his hair and his skin turned yellow. During his initial hospital stay, he saw no one besides his wife and children. When he eventually returned home, there was a message on the answering machine from the Telshe Rosh Yeshivah Rabbi Mordechai Gifter calling to wish him a *refuah shleimah* (speedy recovery). Rabbi Gifter was crying. "This can't be. *Klal Yisrael* needs you too much," Rabbi Gifter said. Listening to the message, Rabbi Sherer commented, "What a *zechus* it is for me to have such a good friend."

Even upon returning home, Rabbi Sherer preferred not to see people in person. He conducted whatever business he could primarily by telephone. During the course of his chemotherapy, he made only two public appearances. The first was in late May for the annual dinner of Agudath Israel of America. His presence had not been announced, and was totally unexpected by those gathered for the dinner. While the lights in the hall were dimmed, Rabbi Sherer walked to the podium via a staircase from the balcony. When the lights came on, the audience saw him standing at the podium.

That dinner coincided with the publication of *From Ashes to*

---

7. In time that Yitzy Bald composition sung by Srully Williger became known as Reb Moshe Sherer's *niggun*. Rabbi Sherer asked Srully Williger to sing it at the Tenth *Siyum HaShas*. When the camera at the event panned the auditorium, as Williger sang, and came to rest on Rabbi Sherer, the tears were streaming down his face.

Rabbi Gifter addressing an Agudah convention

Renewal, an Agudath Israel-produced volume chronicling the path of the survivors of the European inferno to spiritual and material renewal in America. In his speech, Rabbi Sherer pulled from his wallet a copy of an order, issued November 23, 1940, from the German High Commander I.A. Eckhardt to the German Army of Occupation on Poland, which he always carried with him. In it Eckhardt commands that the *Ostjuden*, the Eastern European Jews, must not be allowed to escape because they comprise the majority of the rabbis and "Talmud teachers." If the "Talmud *lehrer*" escape, warns the Nazi commander, they can bring about the spiritual regeneration of world Jewry, even American Jewry."[8] Those words would prove as prophetic as those

---

8. On a 1991 visit to Camp Agudah, Rabbi Sherer told a story that he had heard from the famous Holocaust historian Reb Moshe Prager. In the small Polish town of Zdunska-Wola, the Nazis assembled all the Jews in the town square on the first day of Shavuos. They built 10 gallows — one for each commandment — and placed 10 of the most prominent Jews of the town on the gallows, each with a noose around his neck. Before the chair on which he was standing was kicked away, one of the Jews shouted, "*Breider Yidden, nemts nekamah far unzer blut* [Jewish brothers, avenge our blood]!"

Rabbi Sherer told his young listeners, "When I see *Yiddishe kinderlach* [Jewish children] here in Camp Agudah observing Torah and mitzvos, I see the blood of those *kedoshim* [martyrs] being avenged. When I see children in Camp Agudah from Russia, who, according to the Nazi master plan, were never supposed to have been born, and according to the Communist master plan were never supposed to exist again, [these children] are avenging the blood of the *kedoshim* in that *shtetl* in Europe and all the others martyrs murdered in Europe."

The directive by German High Commander Eckhardt

Rabbi Sherer's moving tribute to his family, all murdered in the Holocaust, in the *Ashes to Renewal* memorial volume, including a note written from his hospital bed

uttered by another great hater of the Jews, the gentile prophet Bilaam.[9] When Rabbi Sherer had finished speaking, he quickly left the hall without greeting any of his friends and admirers. Because of his weakened immune system he was not allowed to shake anyone's hand.

A Visit to the Agudah Camps

IN THE SUMMER OF 1995, JUST AFTER RABBI SHERER HAD completed his fifth round of chemotherapy, he called his daughter Mrs. Rochel Langer and told her that he wanted to make his annual trip to the various Agudath Israel-run camps in the Catskills. She knew how reluctant her father had been to be seen by anyone looking as he did, and asked him why he was so determined to make this particular journey.

"I've spoken for 25 years," he replied, "and I have a message that I believe is important." Then he asked his daughter whether she had a problem with his decision. She replied that she did not, but she did have a request: she wanted to accompany him. In particular, she wanted to know what her father had to say that was so important for him to strain himself to such a degree.

Rabbi Sherer began the day speaking at the two Agudah camps for girls: Bnos and Camp Chayl Miriam[10] (Chayil), and finished it at Camp Agudah for boys. The staff at each of the three camps were acutely aware of his medical condition and that he had not been seen in public in months, and they were petrified at the responsibility of hosting him now.

The message remained the same throughout the day, though it changed form according to the age of the audience. He told his rapt young audiences that their purpose in the world is to improve the lives of others, and urged them to find ways to take responsibility for helping those others than themselves. At one point, he cried out, "As long as I have air in my lungs, I will scream to whoever will listen that we have

---

9. In his speech, Rabbi Sherer also made reference to the photograph of his uncle Reb Avrohom Leib Moruchnik and his children and grandchildren, which he had placed in the *Ashes to Renewal* volume. The entire Moruchnik family was wiped out by the Nazis, and, as Rabbi Sherer wrote in the volume, that photograph was all that remained of his mother and father's large families.

10. The camp was dedicated in the name of Mrs. Miriam Klein, who devoted herself to the camp every summer, by her husband Reb Ephraim (Frank) Klein. The Kleins' son, Reb Avraham Noach Klein, continued his parents' dedication to Camp Agudah and their loyalty to Rabbi Sherer. He dedicated the intensified learning division of Camp Agudah, Machaneh Ephraim, in the name of his father.

to live for the next person and not just for ourselves."

"Don't say, I'm just a kid, what can I possibly do?" Rabbi Sherer told his audiences. And then he proceeded to provide them with concrete examples of how they could help others. At Camp Bnos, for instance, he described a scene on a playground where a number of girls are playing together and another little girl is sitting by herself on the side. He told the girls to consider the merit of the one in the group who invites the outsider to join their play.

He illustrated with vignettes from the lives of contemporary Torah giants what it means to live for *Klal Yisrael*. One of those stories concerned the Steipler Gaon. An older yeshivah student came to the Steipler seeking a *berachah* (blessing) that he should soon find a wife. The Steipler's hearing was very poor, and all communication with him had to be in writing. After looking at the student's request, the Steipler took out a pen and began circling words in the note. He returned the note with every "*Ani* (I)" circled. "If you want to know your problem in finding a *shidduch* [match]," the Steipler told him, "it's that you have too much *Ani*." That too fit well with Rabbi Sherer's message of the necessity to think beyond oneself.

He told another story of the impact of a brief encounter with Rabbi Yaakov Kamenetsky on an 8-year-old boy. The parents of the boy in question had brought him to the *Motza'ei Shabbos* keynote session of the Agudah convention, and he waited patiently by the door with his camera to take photos of the *gedolei Torah* as they entered the hall. But each time, he was pushed aside by a throng of people seeking a closer look. As he entered, Reb Yaakov noticed what was happening to the boy. He stopped, fixed his tie, and motioned to the boy that he should come over and shoot the photograph. That boy told Rabbi Sherer years later how Reb Yaakov's small kindness had dramatically affected his life.

Prior to the trip, Rabbi Sherer was told by Dr. Coleman that he should not shake hands with anyone. Despite that warning, Rabbi Sherer hugged Rabbi Simcha Kaufman, the head counselor at Camp Agudah. And he insisted on shaking hands with each of the special-needs campers. Rabbi Sherer had been a strong early supporter of providing a program for special-needs children at Camp Agudah, in part to teach the other campers that the Jews with special needs are also part of *Klal Yisrael*. And he always felt a special connection to this particular group of campers.

When his son Shimshon, who had driven from the city to join his father at the boys camp, remonstrated with Rabbi Sherer for ignoring his doctor's orders, the latter replied, "These are my children. You can't deprive a father of hugging his children. I couldn't help myself." Shimshon, who had not been allowed to hug his father for months, told him, "In that case, give me a hug too." As they embraced, Rabbi Sherer added, "Don't worry *mein kindt* [my child], there is an *Av HaRachaman* in Heaven, and on the merit of having founded this special-needs program, I'm going to be cured."

By the time that he spoke at Camp Agudah, Mrs. Langer could see that her father was straining himself greatly. He had to have the microphone moved closer in order that he could even be heard. When he finished at Camp Agudah, he looked, in her words, "as bad as a person can look and still be upright."

After the long day of speeches, Rabbi Sherer went with Shimshon to the latter's bungalow nearby to recuperate. Soon afterward he received a call from the *gabbai* (attendant) of a Rebbe, who said that the Rebbe wanted to speak with Rabbi Sherer. Rabbi Sherer told his son, "I'm very sick. I just can't." Shimshon told the *gabbai* that his father was too drained to speak, but apparently the man did not hear him, and continued to importune him. Finally, Rabbi Sherer instructed his son to tell the *gabbai* that he would come to visit the Rebbe on his way back to Brooklyn from the Catskills.

"I know what he wants, and I don't think I can help him," Rabbi Sherer told his son. The latter wondered why his father was placing additional strain on himself if there was nothing he could do to help. "Perhaps I can be of assistance in some other way," Rabbi Sherer answered.

The Last Hurrah

THE LAST GREAT MISSION OF RABBI SHERER'S LIFE WAS TO counteract the concerted Reform and Conservative pressure on the Israeli government to recognize their conversions. Under the banner of Am Echad, he embarked on a large-scale public relations campaign in America to explain why there can be only one standard for conversion and undertook a major mission to Israel in early 1998.[11]

The night before the official Am Echad mission was to begin, a small group convened at Jerusalem's Central Hotel, to plan strategy. Normally Rabbi Sherer would have chaired such a meeting and run it with a iron

---

11. See Chapter 22, pp. 560ff for more on the Am Echad mission to Israel.

hand and a clear focus. That night, however, he barely participated. At one point, he even dozed in his chair while others went on talking.

After the meeting, Yonoson Rosenblum (the author of this book), one of those present at the meeting, accompanied Rabbi Sherer back to his room. Rabbi Sherer confided that he was sick, perhaps with pneumonia, and that his doctors had strongly advised him against making the trip. Rabbi Sherer's listlessness throughout the meeting and the slowness with which he made his way back to his room only confirmed the wisdom of his doctors' judgment.[12]

After escorting Rabbi Sherer to his room for the night, Rosenblum returned home and told his wife, "I can't see any way that Rabbi Sherer can lead the delegation tomorrow." He silently prayed that the heavy snow forecast might force the cancellation of the entire mission.

On the Am Echad mission.
Seated beside Rabbi Sherer are Chief Rabbi Yisrael Meir Lau and Rabbi Chaskel Besser. Standing behind him are Avrohom Biderman; Rabbi Pesach Lerner, Executive Vice President of Young Israel; Rabbi Shlomo Gertzulin; and Rabbi Shmuel Bloom

---

12. In his *hesped* for Rabbi Sherer, Rabbi Elya Svei related that he had advised Rabbi Sherer to reconsider the trip in light of his poor health and his doctors' concern about the likely strain of the trip and whirlwind mission. Rabbi Sherer, however, insisted that he must go if there was any chance that his going might have an impact. Rabbi Svei described the battle against legitimacy for the heterodox movements as the great mission that Rabbi Sherer had received from Rabbi Aharon Kotler.

Despite the heavy snows that fell overnight, the mission began the next morning with a press conference at Jerusalem's Renaissance Hotel. If Rabbi Sherer was feeling sick, it was in no way evident. He spoke with his customary force, and handled questions from the press with aplomb. Haim Shapiro, the *Jerusalem Post's* religious affairs reporter, asked a hostile question designed to prove that the Am Echad delegation did not represent a cross-section of American Orthodoxy, as claimed, but was rather a de facto subsidiary of Agudath Israel of America. Rabbi Sherer did not blink for a second, but quickly pointed to the presence behind him on the podium of Rabbi Pesach Lerner, Executive Vice President of Young Israel, and to Rabbi Ronald Greenwald of the Orthodox Union in the audience.

Throughout the grueling day of meetings with top Israeli political figures, Rabbi Sherer was repeatedly interviewed by the Israeli press. After a meeting with President Ezer Weizman, Israel TV interviewed Rabbi Sherer. Despite his poor health and the fact that the interviews were conducted in Hebrew, a language he rarely had the chance to speak, he had no trouble putting forth his case. Had the mission itself not been so important in his eyes and the strain on his health so great he might even have enjoyed the opportunity to show off his Hebrew.[13]

Interviewed by the Israeli press

---

13. On his first trip to Israel in 1954, Rabbi Sherer spoke in Yiddish at a rally in Jerusalem. He noticed that there were those in the crowd who were not paying attention, and resolved on the spot to master spoken Hebrew.

Rabbi Sherer, cold and bundled in a coat, leaving the home of President Ezer Weizman with members of the Am Echad delegation. L-r: Rabbi Avrohom Berkowitz, Rabbi Chaskel Besser, Yoel Ehrenreich, Rabbi Sherer, Chaim Leshkowitz, Tzvi Jacobson, Rabbi Shmuel Bloom, Rabbi Gedaliah Weinberger, Henry Lowenthal

Throughout the three-day mission, Rabbi Sherer was bothered by a persistent cough that he could not shake, and even consulted a doctor in Israel. The final day of the mission was devoted to meetings with *gedolei Yisrael*. After an audience with the Belzer Rebbe, Rabbi Sherer could no longer ignore how sick he felt. He nearly fainted, and Dr. Paul Rosenstock, one of the members of the delegation, examined him in a special room set aside for that purpose in the Belz complex. Rabbi Sherer's lungs did not sound right, and Dr. Rosenstock was concerned about the possibility of pneumonia.

Nevertheless, Rabbi Sherer insisted on continuing to the home of Rabbi Ovadia Yosef. "I can't disappoint Rav Ovadia," he told those who advised him that he should return immediately to his hotel. He remained fully attentive during the entire visit, even as younger and healthier members of the delegation had difficulty forcing their eyes open. Immediately after the audience with Rabbi Yosef, Tzvi Jacobson, who had handled the logistics for the entire trip, insisted on taking Rabbi Sherer, along with Dr. Rosentock, to the nearby Terem emergency clinic,

His final meeting with Rabbi Ovadia Yosef. Blood tests taken moments later showed that his white blood count had risen to extremely high levels.

where he knew the blood test results would be immediately available.

The blood test revealed that Rabbi Sherer's white blood cell count was an astronomical 100,000, ten times the normal count. The Israeli doctor who read the results took Jacobson aside and told him that Rabbi Sherer must immediately return home and enter the hospital. He could not understand how a person could still be standing with such a white blood count. Dr. Rosenstock too realized that the white blood cell count was a clear sign of acute leukemia, an aftereffect of chemotherapy in about 8 percent of those treated for lymphoma.

Dr. Rosenstock knew something else: A white blood count of 100,000 does not develop overnight. Rabbi Sherer had been a very sick man for the entirety of the mission. For Dr. Rosenstock, the recognition of Rabbi Sherer's heroism was a life-changing event. Until then, he had "never understood the full extent of how much a person can sacrifice for *Klal Yisrael*." And that recognition filled Dr. Rosenstock with inspiration to become even more actively involved in *Klal* activities.

Dr. Rosenstock did not immediately share with Rabbi Sherer the full seriousness of his elevated white blood cells. But Rabbi Sherer was far too sharp not to know from the look on Jacobson and Dr. Rosenstock's faces that the situation was bad. Dr. Rosenstock accompanied Rabbi Sherer to his room at the Central Hotel, and together they called Dr. Coleman in New York. After speaking to Dr. Coleman, Dr. Rosenstock arranged for the head of the oncology department at Hadassah Hospital to come to Rabbi Sherer's room.

The Israeli doctor at first attempted to play down the results of the blood test in light of the fact that Rabbi Sherer's outward appearance remained good. A further meeting was scheduled at Hadassah Ein Kerem for the next morning at 11 a.m. Dr. Rosenstock accompanied Rabbi Sherer, while Shimshon went to *daven* at *Kever Rachel*. At Hadassah Hospital, Rabbi Sherer asked the head of oncology what his prognosis was. The doctor replied, "I only give my patients good news," meaning that he had nothing to say because there was no possible good news. Rabbi Sherer was devastated by the apparent finality of the verdict. His white blood cell count was now up to 120,000, raising the danger of internal hemorrhaging. Dr. Rosenstock told him that he must fly home immediately.

Rabbi Sherer had intended to remain in Israel over Shabbos, and then fly to Switzerland for a meeting of the World Jewish Restitution Organization (WJRO). Even after receiving the initial news at Terem, he had still insisted that he would go to Switzerland. But that was now clearly impossible. He had to return to America as soon as possible.

Rabbi Sherer's mood on the flight home was somber but not despairing. He asked Dr. Rosenstock the same question that he had asked the head of oncology at Hadassah Hospital: "Is this it?" Dr. Rosenstock assured him that there was still much that could be done. Rabbi Sherer's only comment was, "I have so much more to do."

When he was not resting, Rabbi Sherer spent much of the trip reminiscing with his colleague of almost 50 years, Rabbi Chaskel Besser. Rabbi Besser had been shocked when he saw Rabbi Sherer, Mrs. Sherer, and Shimshon board the flight. He knew that Rabbi Sherer's original plan had been to stay in Jerusalem for Shabbos and then fly to Switzerland for a meeting of the WJRO. Rabbi Sherer explained that he was gravely ill, and could not possibly make the trip to Switzerland. Apologetically, he asked Rabbi Besser, who had long been involved in restitution issues, to fly from New York to Switzerland on *Motza'ei Shabbos*, and replace him at the WJRO meetings. Though the subject of Rabbi Sherer's health was not far from either man's thoughts, Rabbi Sherer and Rabbi Besser took advantage of the 12-hour flight for the type of long, meandering conversation that would have been impossible in Rabbi Sherer's office, with constant interruptions from secretaries and callers. [14]

---

14. Rabbi Chaskel Besser, "My Last Flight With Rabbi Sherer," *The Jewish Observer*, Summer 1998, p. 32.

The Am Echad delegation meets with Rabbi Yosef Shalom Elyashiv.
L-r: Yoel Ehrenreich, Chaim Leshkowitz, Rabbi Pesach Lerner, Rabbi Sherer, Rabbi Shmuel Bloom, Rabbi Shlomo Gertzulin, Rabbi Yisroel Lefkowitz

Rabbi Sherer's grandson Shragie Goldschmidt picked up the Sherers at the airport at 6 a.m. His first question was naturally about his grandfather's health. Rabbi Sherer responded, "I just don't know. We will have to see." Rabbi Sherer went home for a few hours to freshen up from the long flight, and from there was driven to Maimonides Medical Center.

Rabbi Pinchos Lipshutz, the publisher of *Yated Ne'eman* in America, was shocked when his wife summoned him to the phone that morning and told him that Rabbi Sherer was on the line. Rabbi Lipshutz had already heard that Rabbi Sherer's disease had reappeared and he would be going straight to the hospital. "Pinnaleh, this is Moshe Sherer. I came back from *Eretz Yisrael* last night. I am in the hospital. I don't know if I will leave here alive. I want you to listen to me."

Rabbi Sherer spoke and Rabbi Lipshutz listened. The former covered everything: how to run the paper, general rules for success in public and private life, how to balance the demands of family with public duties. "It was if," Rabbi Lipshutz wrote later, "he was exactly in my situation and knew exactly what I was dealing with. He pierced my inner thoughts and responded to the types of fears a person doesn't divulge to others .... No one had ever taken such an interest in me before or since .... Not a day goes by that some facet of what he told me in that conversation does not come into play."

When he had pulled himself together, Lipshutz called his rebbi, Rabbi Elya Svei, and described what had happened. He told Rabbi Svei that he had felt like Rabbi Sherer was giving him a *tzaavah*. Rabbi Svei confirmed that is exactly what he had been doing, and asked to hear everything Rabbi Sherer had said. "I thought I knew him. I thought I had a special relationship with him. But I never realized *how* smart he really is," Lipshutz confided to his rebbe.

"Now that you found out," Rabbi Svei told him, "you should be clever enough to remember what he said and to follow his every word."

One of his first calls in the hospital was from Rabbi Yosef Shalom Elyashiv in Jerusalem. Rabbi Elyashiv told him, *"Ihr muzt veren gezunte* [You must return to health]," because the *Gemara* (*Pesachim* 8b) says that those who are involved in a mitzvah do not come to harm.[15]

As the call to Rabbi Lipshutz demonstrates, Rabbi Sherer was far too perceptive not to have known that his time was likely limited. But he did not sink into despair and remained focused, as always, on his agenda for the future. When Joseph Lobenstein, a longtime pillar of the British Agudah movement, called before Pesach to wish him a good Yom Tov and a *refuah shleimah* (full recovery), he replied with a discussion of the "huge agenda" of projects he still hoped to undertake. The need to get better, in order to realize his agenda, was a constant refrain with all his visitors.[16]

Most people battling a life-threatening illness find it difficult to think about anything besides their own struggle. Not so Rabbi Sherer. Mrs. Miriam Grossman, a family friend, provided him with *Tehillim* tapes for those times when he was too ill from his treatments to read or work. He arranged for a similar set to be delivered to the father of

---

15. What Rabbi Elyashiv did not know was that Rabbi Sherer was already gravely ill when he arrived in Israel. The trip, while very draining for someone in his condition, probably did not worsen his prognosis appreciably.
16. Dr. Michael Bashevkin.

Rabbi Elya Svei in his *hesped* (eulogy) for Rabbi Sherer linked him to Rabbi Aharon Kotler in his relentless drive to keep achieving for *Klal Yisrael*. Rabbi Svei described how Reb Aharon had once been in *Eretz Yisrael* when some bombs had fallen and everyone lay down on the floor. Reb Aharon was overheard praying, *"Ribbono shel Olam,* I still have so much to do."

Shlomo Gertzulin, who was then nearly blind. He even remembered to call Tzvi Jacobson in Israel to apologize for not having paid for his visit to the Terem clinic, and to assure him that he would reimburse him at the earliest opportunity.[17] When he heard that the young grandchild of close friends was very ill, Rabbi Sherer took the time to call both sets of grandparents. And he penned the same kind of beautiful bar mitzvah note for the son of Dr. Irving Lebovics, the driving force behind the West Coast branch of Agudath Israel, he would have in better days. He found the strength to dictate warm letters of appreciation to a class of young boys who had each sent him a get-well card, and to their rebbi.

Mrs. Rochel Langer was amazed one day to hear her father asking the nurse who was administering a painful shot about the results of a job-placement exam her son had taken. Similar shows of concern and respect earned Rabbi Sherer the affection of all the hospital staff down to the cleaning ladies. After Rabbi Sherer's *petirah* (passing), the sadness was etched on the faces of all the nurses on the ward, and a woman on the maintenance staff on the floor was seen crying openly.

His Last Pesach at Home

RABBI SHERER WAS ABLE TO RETURN HOME FOR PESACH FOR A brief interlude between his first and second round of treatments. He had always recited the *Shechiyanu* blessing with great fervor at the beginning of each holiday, and this time more than ever. At the end of the Seder, the family danced briefly in a circle, during which Rabbi Sherer was visibly emotional. He then offered his traditional wish: *"Iber a yahr* — Next year, again." But this time the words had a special poignancy. In return for the *afikoman*, his grandson Shragie Goldschmidt asked his grandparents to join him and his wife for a Shabbos meal. Rabbi Sherer agreed, and came to Shragie's home the last Shabbos before he returned to the hospital. He was in good spirits, eating heartily and singing harmonies with his grandson.

Rabbi Sherer's last time *davening* in the Fourteenth Avenue Agudah was on *Shevi'i shel Pesach*. Yisroel Lefkowitz left shul in the middle of *davening* to accompany Rabbi Sherer to shul from his home. The congregation waited until Rabbi Sherer arrived to begin

---

17. Jacobson had naturally told Rabbi Sherer that there was no need for him to refund the minimal payment the clinic had taken, but Rabbi Sherer was insistent, telling Jacobson, "I have never let others pay for me."

Hallel, a gesture that moved him greatly. Mordechai Eisenberg purchased what would turn out to be Rabbi Sherer's last *aliyah*.[18] At the end of *davening*, he took leave of his fellow *mispallelim* (congregants), some of whom, like Rabbi Elias Karp and Rabbi Meir Lamet, were lifelong friends.[19]

While home, Rabbi Sherer asked Shlomo Chaimovits, one of the younger *baalebattim* in the Fourteenth Avenue Agudah with whom he was especially close, what was happening with the *shidduchim* of his daughter Miri. In particular, he wanted to know why Chaimovits had not availed himself of his services as an investigator, as he had with his older children. When Chaimovits confessed that he and his wife had not wanted to bother him in the hospital, Rabbi Sherer remonstrated with him.

As he walked into Cornell Medical Center after Pesach for his second round of chemotherapy, he told his son, "I don't know why, but this is the very first time I've ever felt afraid to enter." Yet he never gave up hope. When he learned that the Chaimovits's daughter had become engaged, he called to apologize for not having arranged an audio hookup of the *vort*. At that time, he could barely lift his head from the pillow. In the course of speaking to Mrs. Chaimovits and the new *kallah*, he asked when the wedding would be. Told that it was scheduled for July 9, he replied, "Good, that's a few days after my last treatment. I'll have time to recuperate, and be ready to dance at the *chasanah*." He called the Schick brothers from the hospi-

With Rabbi Eli Teitelbaum

---

18. The penultimate *aliyah* that morning contained the words, "I am Hashem your Healer" (*Shemos* 15:26), which surely buoyed Rabbi Sherer's spirits.
19. Also in shul that day was Rabbi Eli Teitelbaum, whose activism on behalf of a host of causes made him greatly beloved to Rabbi Sherer. Rabbi Teitelbaum used to speak to him after *davening* every Shabbos morning.

tal, when they were sitting *shivah* for their mother, even though by that point his voice was barely audible.

Nor did he lose his sense of humor. When informed about all the people who were davening for him, he replied with a *vort* from Rabbi Shlomo Zalman Auerbach. Reb Shlomo Zalman noted that in the *Mi'she'beirach* for those who are involved in the needs of the *Klal*, we first ask that Hashem should, "וְיִרְפָּא לְכָל גּוּפָם — heal their entire body" and then we ask, "וְיִסְלַח לְכָל עֲוֹנָם — forgive all their sins." Yet in our own thrice-daily *Shemoneh Esrei*, the blessing for forgiveness precedes that for healing. Reb Shlomo Zalman explained that when the public prays for an important activist, its primary concern is that he be able to continue serving, and therefore it prays first for his return to full health. But when we *daven* for ourselves, our first concern is to clear our spiritual state, and so we pray for forgiveness for our sins. Based on this *vort*, Rabbi Sherer would say, since so many people were *davening* for his physical recovery, he better focus on seeking forgiveness for his *neshamah*.

Until near the end, he continued to receive visits from those with whom he had worked, like Mayor Rudolph Giuliani, and from friends, young and old. Moshe Reichmann flew in from Toronto for a 10-minute visit. George Klein walked over to the hospital every Shabbos morning, and Shmuel Yosef (Ralph) Rieder every Shabbos afternoon. A family member was in the hospital around the clock. When Rabbi Sherer fretted about the amount of time his wife and children were spending at his bedside, they reminded him that he had always expressed his regret at

With George Klein

not having more years to perform the mitzvah of *kibbud av v'eim* (honoring one's parents) with his own parents.

Rabbi Avrohom Pam could not come to visit in the hospital because he was a Kohen. But he sent Rabbi Sherer a letter that brought tears to his eyes. He told his children that of the thousands of letters he had received in his life, Rabbi Pam's was one of the most meaningful. It read:

> This past Shabbos, before *Mussaf*, when we read the *Mi'she'beirach* prayer for all those who faithfully attend to the needs of the public [and ask] *HaKadosh Baruch Hu* to provide their reward and remove from them all illness and heal their entire bodies .... I said in my heart, "*Ribbono shel Olam*, to whom do these words apply and are more suitable than to Your faithful servant, Moshe ben Basya Bluma, You have no one who is more faithfully involved in the needs of the public than he.
>
> "Therefore our eyes and the eyes of all Yisrael are lifted toward You that You will remove from him every illness and send him a complete cure from Heaven, speedily, among all the other sick in Yisrael." Until here, my thoughts and whispered prayers on *Shabbos Kodesh*.
>
> I once heard from the Gaon HaRav Chaim Kreiswirth ... that it is written in the *Yerushalmi*, "אַל תְּהִי בִּרְכַּת אוֹהֵב קַלָה בְּעֵינֶיךָ — Do not view the blessing of one who loves you as something light in your eyes."[20] And therefore, I am sending you my blessing from the depths of my heart that *Hashem Yisbarach* should return you to your watch, with a complete healing and physical health for lengthy days and years, for your sake and the sake of the entire House of Israel.

Above all, he kept working with his devoted secretary, Mrs. Debby Jacobs, both in person in the hospital and over the phone. During the last weeks of his life, he was instrumental in obtaining a $400,000 grant for Hatzolah, the vaunted volunteer ambulance service, through the

---

20. After absorbing the letter, Rabbi Sherer told his son that he did not think there is any language in the *Yerushalmi* like that which Rabbi Pam quoted in the name of Rabbi Kreiswirth because, as someone who had given so many *derashos* over his life, he would certainly have known such a *ma'amar Chazal*. He also noted that Rabbi Pam also doubted that such a language exists in the *Yerushalmi* or he would not have quoted it in the name of Rabbi Kreiswirth.

The next time Rabbi Shimshon Sherer met Rabbi Kreiswirth, he asked him about the *ma'amar Chazal*. Rabbi Kreiswirth replied that Rabbi Pam must have misunderstood him, for the language, as far as he knows, appears in the name of a *Kadmon* (early commentator).

The letter from Rabbi Pam

Claims Conference,[21] and even had his hand in a few *shidduchim* for a dear friend's children. He told his son Shimshon that if Hashem granted him more time, the three top items on his agenda would be the problems of "children at risk," the growing number of young men and women not finding a spouse, and developing a Torah response to feminism. He planned to speak to Rebbetzin Zehava Braunstein about heading the last project. Eight days before the annual dinner of Agudath Israel of America, he was still working on the speech he hoped to deliver.

Rabbi Sherer worried that disease would deprive him of his mental faculties prior to taking his life. That never happened; his mental acuity remained undiminished until he lost consciousness. But he did tell Rabbi Elya Svei on the latter's last visit that he was having great difficulty concentrating, even in *davening*. He felt that he had nothing left with which to serve Hashem: not *tefillah* (prayer), not Torah learning, and not work on behalf of the *Klal*.

---

21. Hatzolah subsequently named a new ambulance purchased for the Catskills after Rabbi Sherer.

With Rabbi Chaim Kreiswirth of Antwerp and Rabbi Betzalel Rakow of Gateshead at a conference of the European Agudah

Reb Elya related that Rabbi Elazar Menachem Man Shach had also complained of his lack of ability to concentrate in his later years. Rabbi Shach had found that reciting the phrase, *"ein od milvado* — There is nothing besides Him,"* provided him a measure of relief. Hearing this piece of advice from Reb Elya, he began repeating those words, as he lay in bed, He found they did give him a measure of peace, so that the next time Shimshon entered the room, he asked to go for a walk in the hall for the first time in days. On that walk, he sang a tune to himself based on the words *"ein od milvado."*

Rabbi Sherer's final hospital stay coincided with the nightly counting of the *Omer*. The counting of the *Omer* provided him with an opportunity to ask his son Shimshon if he still remembered the bar mitzvah *derashah* Rabbi Sherer had written for him, which also related to the counting of the *Omer*.[22] That *derashah* dealt with an oft-asked question: Why do we count the *Omer* in ascending order rather than backward toward Shavuos, which would force us to continually think about how many days remain to Shavuos and *Mattan Torah* (the Giving of the Torah)? The Belzer Rebbe answered: If we counted the days left toward Shavuos, human nature is such that we would tell ourselves, "I still

---

22. Shimshon's bar mitzvah was on *Parashas Emor*, which contains the mitzvah of counting the *Omer* and falls during the *Omer*.

have time." By counting forward we remind ourselves of how much time has elapsed and we still have not begun to prepare to receive the Torah anew. Rabbi Sherer had never taken time for granted, and especially now, with so little remaining.

On the last Shabbos morning before Rabbi Sherer lapsed into a coma, a Jew who was staying in the hospital with a relative came to wish him *"Gut Shabbos."* Though he did not know the man, Rabbi Sherer insisted on telling him a *dvar Torah* before he left, citing the *Gemara* (*Berachos* 31a; *Eruvin* 64a) that one should not part from a friend without sharing a halachic thought by which to be remembered.

Rabbi Sherer pointed out that at the end of every *Shemoneh Esrei*, we take three steps backward prior to reciting the verse, "He makes peace in Heavens ...." The three steps back teach us that before one can achieve true peace, one must first strive to remove one's subjective perspective. Stepping back represents the effort to achieve greater objectivity. But even that is not enough. One must also know that the achievement of peace requires action; thus the bending to the left and right. The bowing represents our commitment to compromise for the sake of peace.[23]

The following Monday evening Rabbi Sherer called Rabbi Shmuel Bloom, Chaim Dovid Zwiebel, and Shlomo Gertzulin, to discuss preparations for the upcoming Agudah dinner at which Vice President Al Gore, Jr. would be honored. He told them that he was counting on them, in the event he could not be present. The next evening, he counted the *Omer* for the last time, having reached 32 in the count,[24] and shortly thereafter lost consciousness.

For the next five days, Rabbi Sherer remained unconscious.

---

23. The subject of *shalom* (peace) and how to attain it was one of Rabbi Sherer's favorites. He often repeated something he had heard in the name of the Sar Shalom of Belz on the subject. The verse in *Mishlei* (27:19) כַּמַּיִם הַפָּנִים לַפָּנִים כֵּן לֵב הָאָדָם לָאָדָם, tells us that just as water reflects the face of one who looks into it, so is one's heart reflected back to him by another. The feelings that we show to others will be reflected in their feelings to us. The Sar Shalom asked, however: If that is the lesson, why does the verse choose the metaphor of a face reflected in the water and not just one reflected in the mirror? He answered because one who looks in the water does something that the one who looks in the mirror does not: He bends over and lowers himself. To achieve peace with others, the Sar Shalom taught, it is also necessary to lower oneself and remove any tendency to haughtiness.

24. Thirty-two corresponds to the numerical value of the Hebrew word לֵב (heart). The Rambam (*Hilchos Melachim* 3:6) describes the heart of a Jewish king as the *heart* of the whole community of Israel because his concern encompasses the entire community. Rabbi Shlomo Wolbe once told his son-in-law Rabbi Ezriel Erlanger, after Rabbi Sherer had come to visit him, that the latter's regal bearing and demeanor helped him imagine what a *"melech b'Yisrael* — Jewish king" must have looked like.

Dr. Coleman did not want to place him on a respirator. He told Rabbi Shimshon Sherer that his father was among the most dignified men he had ever met, and as such should not be subjected to the indignity of being placed on a respirator. Shimshon replied, however, that his father's dignity, like everything else, is defined by the Torah. The only true dignity comes from complying with the Torah's dictates, and that the matter would be decided by a halachic authority.

As the moment of his *petirah* drew near, Rabbi Sherer was surrounded by all his male descendants and his two sons-in-law. They stood by his bed reciting the traditional verses from the *Yigdal* prayer. As his son Shimshon read the words, "גּוֹמֵל לְאִישׁ חֶסֶד כְּמִפְעָלוֹ" — The *Ribbono shel Olam* pays back a person in proportion to his deeds in this world," he imagined the preparations being made for his father in Gan Eden.

Just before *yetzias neshamah* (the departure of the soul; demise) Shimshon lead the singing of his father's favorite *niggun* — "*Avinu, Av HaRachaman ... Tatte, oy Tatte* — Father, merciful Father Who is compassionate, have mercy on us" — the same *niggun* he and his father had sung over and over in the car on the way to the hospital for Rabbi Sherer's first chemotherapy treatment. And he remembered what his father had said then, "Always remember, *mein kindt,* there is a *Tatte in Himmel,* Who is an *Av HaRachaman.*"

From the hospital, Shimshon returned to his parents' home to look for a *tzavaah* (will) of any kind that his father might have left and might be relevant for the next day's *levayah*. In his father's desk, he found one locked drawer. Thinking that it might hold the *tzavaah,* he asked his mother for the key. When he opened the drawer, however, he did not find a *tzavaah*. But at the top of the drawer was a photo of Rabbi Aharon Kotler and a cut-out pull quote from an old *Jewish Observer*. The

The photo of Rabbi Aharon Kotler found in Rabbi Sherer's drawer

quote read: Rabbi Baruch Ber Lebovitz instructed his son-in-law [Rabbi Reuven Grozovsky]: *"When you go to a conference for Klal, you must pack your tachrichim* [shrouds] .... A Jewish leader must put his life on the line for his people."[25]

Those words might well serve as a *tzavaah* for Rabbi Sherer. In going to *Eretz Yisrael*, on the Am Echad mission, against the strong advice of his doctors, he had indeed put his life on the line for the Jewish people.

---

25. Rashi at the beginning of *Parashas Mishpatim* (*Shemos* 21:1) explains the connection between the end of the preceding *parashah, Yisro,* which discusses the Altar, and the laws enumerated in *Mishpatim*. This teaches us, writes Rashi, that the place where the Sanhedrin sat (and applied the laws) is adjacent to the Temple, in which the Altar was located. Rabbi Sherer would add, in the name of an *"adam gadol,"* that only one who was prepared to sacrifice himself on the Altar was worthy to sit as a judge on the Sanhedrin.

Chapter Twenty-Five

FAREWELL

MANY OF THOSE WHO GATHERED FOR THE 76TH annual dinner of Agudath Israel of America had entertained hopes that Rabbi Sherer would make a surprise appearance, as he had at the annual dinner three years earlier, after months of not appearing in public while undergoing chemotherapy.

This time it was not to be. Rabbi Sherer passed away just four hours before the dinner, on Sunday afternoon, May 17, 1998, 21 *Iyar* 5758.

News of Rabbi Sherer's passing spread quickly through the Agudah community. *Somber* would be far too mild a term to describe the mood prior to the dinner. People avoided one another's gazes, fearful that to exchange glances with one another would lead to the topic on the mind of everyone in the room, and that would lead to tears.

Out of deference to Rabbi Sherer, the dinner program was radically shortened.[1] Rabbi Hillel David led the recitation of *Tehillim* for the soul

---
1. The special honorees for the dinner each quickly agreed to forgo presentation of their awards.

of Moshe ben Chaim Yehudah. He was followed by Rabbi Shmuel Bloom, who was unable to restrain his tears, as he mourned the loss to *Klal Yisrael* of Rabbi Sherer. The Novominsker Rebbe emphasized Rabbi Sherer's gift for creating *achdus* (unity) out of all the divergent strands of Torah Jewry, and implored the community to particularly honor that aspect of his legacy. Rabbi Shmuel Kamenetsky, the chairman of the Nesius of Agudath Israel, paid brief tribute to Rabbi Sherer's *mesiras nefesh* for *Klal Yisrael*.

Chaim Dovid Zwiebel then introduced Vice President Albert Gore, Jr., the highest-ranking government official ever to address an Agudath Israel dinner. The vice president had intended to praise Rabbi Sherer; now he came to eulogize him. Gore described Rabbi Sherer as a pioneer "in promoting understanding. He came to dispel stereotypes. He came to share knowledge and, humbly, wisdom. He came to spread understanding. And he came to demand freedom."

He recounted how on a recent visit to the White House, President Clinton had offered Rabbi Sherer a choice of two types of kosher meals.

Vice President Albert Gore, Jr. addresses the Agudah dinner just hours after Rabbi Sherer's passing

---

They were: Saul Kamelhar, recipient of the HaGaon Rav Aharon Kotler Award for service to Torah; Yosef Davis, recipient of the Moreinu Yaakov Rosenheim Award for service to Agudath Israel; Rabbi Dovid Grossman, Shearis HaPleitah "Man of the Year" Award; and Shimon Lefkowitz, the Wolf Friedman "Young Leadership" Award

Rabbi Sherer had commented about the remarkable change in attitudes toward Orthodox Jews from those that prevailed during the Holocaust, when access to the corridors of power was so limited and so many doors had been shut in the faces of those who came to plead on behalf of the Jews of Europe. How many lives might have been saved, Rabbi Sherer had mused.

On that occasion, Rabbi Sherer had said, "That's how far we have come." That formulation, however, was far too passive, Vice President Gore pointed out. For the changes between 1941 and 1997 had not just happened. They were the result of much effort. The distance between then and now, said the vice president, was not just a matter of how far Orthodox Jews had come, but of "how far Rabbi Sherer himself brought us."

"By explaining the Orthodox community to America, Rabbi Sherer awakened members of Congress and members of the administration, members of the Supreme Court, and citizens of this Republic to how much the interests of American and Orthodox Jewry coincide," Gore said.

Vice President Gore pointed to a host of initiatives promoted by Rabbi Sherer and Agudath Israel to which the Clinton administration had signed on: the Religious Freedom Restoration Act, designed to remove barriers to worship; a class-action suit filed by the Equal Opportunity Employment Commission against a store that required employees to work on their Sabbath; an argument by the solicitor general before the Supreme Court in favor of allowing funding of remedial education for disadvantaged students attending parochial schools; and the provision of ready-to-eat kosher meals to U.S. combat troops in the field.

Much of his speech focused on the *Siyum HaShas* that had taken place little more than half a year earlier. The gathering of 70,000 people at Madison Square Garden, the Nassau Coliseum, and dozens of other venues around the world by satellite hookup on September 28, 1997/26 *Elul* 5657 was the crowning triumph of Rabbi Sherer's final year.

The vice president noted that "55 years ago when Rabbi Sherer was in rabbinical school and the world was in the fourth cycle of *Daf Yomi*, most Jews who came to America thought that they might not be able to keep the Sabbath anymore." Jews of that era assumed that America was an inhospitable environment for the observance of Torah, and that observance of their religious faith would not "harmonize with the common patterns of weekly life. [U]nder the guidance of Rabbi Sherer, you proved them wrong," said the vice president.

Speaking at the 10th *Siyum HaShas* of Daf Yomi. Seated: Rabbi Mechel Silber, Rabbi Mattisyahu Salomon, Rabbi Levi Krupenia, Rabbi Shmuel Kamenetsky, Rabbi Yaakov Weinberg, Rabbi Yisroel Perkowski, Rabbi Ahron Schechter, Rabbi Elya Svei, Rabbi Avrohom Chaim Feuer, Rabbi Zelik Epstein, Rabbi Binyomin Paler, the Skulener Rebbe, the Rachmastrivka Rebbe, the Novominsker Rebbe, the Klausenberger Rebbe, the Mattesdorfer Rav, Rabbi Naftoli Halberstam (future Bobover Rebbe), Rabbi Malkiel Kotler, Rabbi Dovid Feinstein, Rabbi Reuven Feinstein, Rabbi Zecharia Gelley

THE MOST IMPORTANT SPEECH OF THE DINNER, HOWEVER, WAS the one that no one heard. On Friday afternoon, just over a week prior to the dinner, Rabbi Sherer's doctor told him that he was looking so well that he could reasonably expect to once again surprise the guests at the Agudath Israel dinner.

A Speech Not Given

As soon as he heard that, Rabbi Sherer asked his son Shimshon for a pad of paper and a pen. He wished Shimshon a *"Gut Shabbos,"* and went to work on his speech for the dinner. (He would never permit Shimshon to remain with him in the hospital over Shabbos because of his responsibilities to his congregation.)

Shimshon found the notes from the speech that Rabbi Sherer had intended to give while collecting his father's personal effects after his passing. It would be wrong to view the speech that was never given as Rabbi Sherer's valedictory address or as his *tzavaah* (ethical will). For one thing, it is doubtful that he was capable of leave-taking or looking backward. If he had succeeded in making it to the dinner, he would have immediately begun looking forward.[2]

Indeed, in point #8 of those he jotted down, Rabbi Sherer was already looking forward to the next *Siyum HaShas*. Referring to a news item that he had clipped from *The New York Times,* he noted that one of New York's baseball teams was planning to build a domed stadium. And, wrote Rabbi Sherer, "In about seven years, we will be the first ones to lease this new domed stadium for the next *Siyum HaShas."*

Still, the awareness of his own mortality and the precious gift of every moment that Hashem grants a person were obviously very much on Rabbi Sherer's mind, as he began to organize his thoughts. In his intended introduction, Rabbi Sherer recalled having spoken at the previous year's dinner of the upcoming *Siyum HaShas*, and the fact

---

2. In his address at the 1994 convention, Rabbi Sherer began by relating how someone had asked him whether he had yet sat down to write his memoirs. (He had missed the previous year's convention due to his open-heart surgery.) He answered, "I'm not ready to write memoirs of the past. But, *b'ezras Hashem*, I would like to start a new beginning for the future."

He then continued with one of his favorite *vertlach*, from the brother of the Maharal, Rabbi Chaim ben Betzalel. After completing almost all of *sefer Tehillim*, David Hamelech concludes Psalm 145 (which we recite three times a day as part of the *Ashrei* prayer): "תְּהִלַּת ה' יְדַבֶּר פִּי וִיבָרֵךְ כָּל בָּשָׂר שֵׁם קָדְשׁוֹ לְעוֹלָם וָעֶד — My mouth will speak Hashem's praise. And all flesh will bless His holy Name, forever." Rabbi Chaim asks why after all the praises of the entire *sefer Tehillim*, David Hamelech still refers to speaking Hashem's praise in the future tense — וִיבָרֵךְ ... יְדַבֵּר. He answered that David Hamelech is teaching us that no matter how much one praises Hashem he has only begun, and there are far more praises yet to be sung. So too, said Rabbi Sherer, would he and Agudath Israel be seeking to make a fresh start.

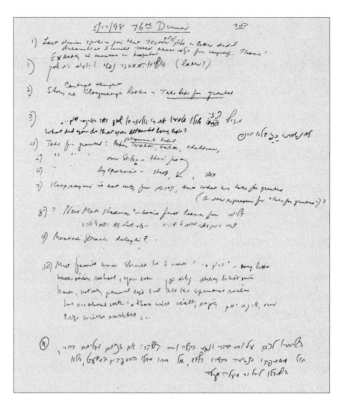

Rabbi Sherer's notes, written from his hospital bed, for the speech he hoped to deliver at the dinner

that nearly a hundred thousand Jews would be simultaneously reciting *Tehillim* for all the *cholei Yisrael* (ailing Jews).

"Little did I dream that I would need those *tefillos* for myself.," he wrote. "As David Hamelech says in *Tehillim* (142:8): הוֹצִיאָה מִמַּסְגֵּר נַפְשִׁי לְהוֹדוֹת אֶת שְׁמֶךָ — 'Release my soul from confinement to acknowledge Your Name'— I thank the *Ribbono shel Olam* for allowing me to come out of the hospital to praise the *Ribbono shel Olam* ...." The necessity of expressing gratitude to Hashem for every thing that we receive in life was the focus of Rabbi Sherer's intended words. In his notes, he had written out in full a poignant story once told him by the Klausenberger Rebbe. In the final days of the war, the Rebbe was placed on a train with other inmates. Jews were dying right and left in the suffocating conditions, and dead bodies began to pile up in the corners. Occasionally, the train would stop, and the guards would put jugs of water in the middle of the cars, but in the prisoners' rush to get to the water, much of it spilled out. Other times, the guards opened the doors near springs of water, and then turned vicious attack dogs on the parched prisoners who had run to the water, with many killed in that fashion.³

As he contemplated his situation, the Klausenberger Rebbe concluded that Hashem was showing him that sometime in the past he had taken for granted the ready availability of water to drink. And he promised that if he somehow managed to live until liberation, he would never again take a glass of water for granted. The walls would shake from the force of his shouting, *"Shehakol nihiyeh b'dvaro,"* every time he drank.

And so it was, the Rebbe told Rabbi Sherer, with the first *berachah* after liberation. It had a *Yiddishe taam*. "But now it's 40 years later," the Rebbe confessed. "Occasionally, I do remember those days … and the vow I made. But more often than not, when I have a glass of water, I'm not even sure if I made the blessing."

Rabbi Sherer linked, in his notes, the Klausenberger Rebbe's story with a statement of Rabbi Elazar ben Shamua in the *Gemara* (*Megillah 27b*). Asked by his *talmidim* to what merit he attributed his long life, Rabbi Elazar ben Shamua replied with three things, the third of which was that he never lifted his hands without a *berachah*.

Rabbi Elazar ben Shamua was a Kohen, and the literal meaning of his statement was that he never lifted his hands to perform *Bircas Kohanim* (the Priestly Benediction) without making the requisite blessing. But a *gadol* once offered another explanation of Rabbi Elazar ben Shamua's message to his students: He was referring not to *Bircas Kohanim,* but to every activity in life: whatever we lift our hands to do, even something as simple as taking a drink of water. If one wants to be *zocheh* to longevity, one must realize that even for the seemingly effortless, insignificant acts that we all take for granted, one must express gratitude *to Hashem*. When He sees us expressing gratitude even for such things, the *Ribbono shel Olam* grants long life. Our favorite expression, Rabbi Sherer wrote, "should be two words: *Baruch Hashem. Baruch Hashem* for all that we have; yes, even for the ability to lift one's hands."

The last words that Rabbi Sherer ever wrote were a clarion call for ever greater striving in the spiritual realm. He noted that the annual dinner of Agudath Israel usually falls just before Shavuos. When

---

3. When Rabbi Sherer repeated this story, he invariably added that *Pirkei d'Rebbe Eliezer* (30) describes death from thirst as the most degrading form of death. The Imrei Emes explains why: At the holiest moment of a person's life, when all his thoughts should be focused on *teshuvah* (repentance) and the realization that he will soon be standing before the Holy Throne, all the person who is dying of thirst can think about is somehow obtaining a cup of water.

Hashem told Moshe Rabbeinu how to prepare the Jewish people for the receipt of the Torah, He commanded Moshe to set boundaries for the nation around the mountain and to warn the people, saying, "הִשָּׁמְרוּ לָכֶם עֲלוֹת בָּהָר וּנְגֹעַ בְּקָצֵהוּ כָּל הַנֹּגֵעַ בָּהָר מוֹת יוּמָת — Be careful of ascending the mountain or touching its edge; whoever touches the mountain shall surely die" (*Shemos* 19:12).

The Kotzker Rebbe, however, offered a homiletic interpretation of the words: "הִשָּׁמְרוּ לָכֶם עֲלוֹת בָּהָר וּנְגֹעַ בְּקָצֵהוּ" — If you have been privileged to have climbed the mountain, to have achieved success in spiritual realms, don't satisfy yourself with touching the edge of the mountain. Do not be one of those who contents himself with small attainments, who is content as long as he has reached the base of the mountain. One must work on oneself to climb higher and higher, to strive for and reach greater attainments.

We will never know for certain whether Rabbi Sherer meant those words to be a coda for his life's work. What is certain, however, is that he always viewed Agudath Israel as a *d'var she'bekedushah*, as something holy, and that in his over half a century in Agudath Israel he was never once content with what had been achieved but was always looking for new vistas to conquer. The Vilna Gaon's words, quoted in *Even Shleimah* (4:9) — "If a person does not constantly strive to go higher and higher, he will necessarily decline lower and lower" — applied, in Rabbi Sherer's view, to organizations as well as individuals.

The Levayah

AS SOON AS THE DINNER WAS OVER, THE STAFF OF AGUDATH Israel sat down to plan the next day's *levayah*. Almost everyone around the table had worked together with Rabbi Sherer for decades. Beyond an occasional soft *krechtz* (groan), they had no time now to reflect on what Rabbi Sherer had meant to them or the impact of his passing.

Tomorrow would bring one of the largest *levayos* New York City had seen in a long time. All the worlds within which Rabbi Sherer had moved so effortlessly would be represented: roshei yeshivah from all over the country, government dignitaries, and thousands of Jews from every walk of life. The staff had only a few hours to work out all the myriad details. And for the first time, they would be doing so without the firm hand of Rabbi Sherer to guide them. Each person sitting around the table had only one goal: i.e., that the *levayah* should be a *kavod* for Rabbi Sherer, and it should run exactly as he would have wanted. They

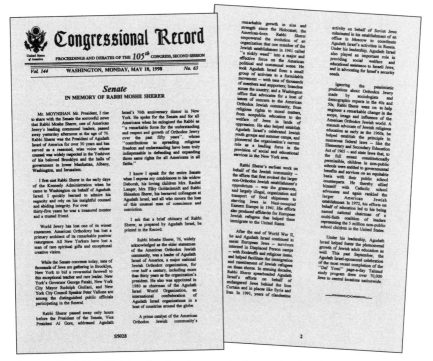

Senator Daniel Patrick Moynihan's eulogy on the floor of the Senate

all had countless memories of the lessons that Rabbi Sherer had taught them, but now they did not have him.

The *levayah* took place at 2:30 the next afternoon, on a sweltering day, in the 14th Avenue Agudah shul, between 45th and 46th street, where Rabbi Sherer had *davened*. Even though it was the beginning of the workweek, 14th Avenue was packed from 44th to 56th Street — one continuous sea of people. Despite the size of the crowd — estimated by police at between 20,000-25,000 — there was little jostling or shoving, as if Rabbi Sherer had personally trained those in attendance in the proper decorum for the occasion. In attendance were leading New York officials, including Governor George Pataki

Mayor Rudolph Giuliani, Governor George Pataki, and George Klein at the funeral.

Chapter Twenty-Five: Farewell □ 633

Among the rabbanim at the *levayah*, seated l-r: Rabbi Yisrael Perkowski, the Bluzhover Rebbe, Rabbi Reuven Feinstein, the Klausenberger Rebbe, Rabbi Mattisyahu Salomon, Rabbi Ahron Schechter, Rabbi Dovid Feinstein, Rabbi Dovid Schustal, Rabbi Elya Svei, Rabbi Yerucham Olshin and Mayor Rudolph Giuliani. During the *levayah*, New York Senator Daniel Patrick Moynihan held a lengthy address about Rabbi Sherer on the floor of the United States Senate.

A broad cross-section of America's Torah leadership eulogized Rabbi Sherer. Though the *maspidim* obviously had no opportunity to coordinate their remarks in advance, they each touched on a different aspect of Rabbi Sherer. Rabbi Hillel David once again led the recitation of *Tehillim*. Rabbi Chaskel Besser, so often tapped by Rabbi Sherer to be the chairman at major events, introduced the speakers.[4] Rabbi Eliezer Horowitz, rabbi of the Fourteenth Avenue Agudah, where Rabbi Sherer *davened* for decades, described the personal loss for himself and each member of the shul. He was followed by Rabbi Mattisyahu Salomon, the Mashgiach of Bais Medrash Govoha, who said that Rabbi Sherer's loss would be felt by Torah Jews the world over, not just those in America.

Rabbi Elya Svei, Rosh Yeshivah of the Talmudical Yeshiva of Philadelphia, and a friend of Rabbi Sherer's since they were students together in Yeshiva Torah Vodaath, described Rabbi Sherer as "our general," who consistently devised winning strategies on behalf of the Torah community. He emphasized Rabbi Sherer's superhuman efforts to protect Agudath Israel of America from any *machlokes*, and expressed the hope that the same spirit of *achdus*, uniting Jews from widely varying backgrounds, would continue to prevail.[5]

The greatest testament to Rabbi Avrohom Pam's respect for Rabbi Sherer came before he had even opened his mouth. Rabbi Pam, the senior member of the Moetzes Gedolei HaTorah, was gravely ill himself. Nevertheless, he made a supreme effort to attend. As a Kohen, he could not enter the shul, and so he spoke from the auditorium of the Bais Yaakov of Boro Park across the street. "That which we feared has happened," he said simply. He attributed Rabbi Sherer's ability to continue working 15 to 18 hour days for decades to his *kesher nafshi* (soul connection) with the *tzibbur* (public).

---

4. The summaries of the eulogies are drawn from the reporting of Mrs. Ruth Lichtenstein in *Hamodia*, May 22, 1998, pp. 1,8-10.
5. Rabbi Sherer himself always emphasized that the attainment of *shalom* (peace) requires more than good intentions; it must be actively pursued. He used to ask: Why when we sing *Shalom Aleichem* at the outset of the *leil Shabbos* meal are the accompanying angels referred to in the first stanza as *malachei hashareis* (angels of service) and only in the subsequent stanzas as *malachei hashalom* (angels of peace)? He answered that this teaches us that peace is only attained by those who are determined to work for it.

With (standing) Rabbi Shmuel Kamenetsky, Rabbi Elya Svei; (sitting) the Novominsker Rebbe and Rabbi Ahron Schechter

The Novominsker Rebbe, Rabbi Yaakov Perlow, declared that in addition to making a tearful *berachah* of "*Dayan HaEmes*" upon Rabbi Sherer's passing, we should all make a *berachah* of "*HaTov V'HaMeitiv*," for the special gift from Hashem to *Klal Yisrael* of Rabbi Sherer's 50 years of service elevating *Kavod HaTorah*. When he began his career in *askanus*, Rabbi Perlow said, respect for Orthodox Jews and Torah Judaism was at its nadir. Rabbi Sherer had completely reversed that situation, and brought unprecedented respect for Torah and its adherents.

Both the Novominsker Rebbe and the next speaker Rabbi Yaakov Weinberg, the Rosh Yeshivah of Ner Israel, emphasized Rabbi Sherer's complete subservience to *gedolei Yisrael*. But Rabbi Weinberg also described him as a *shlucha d'Rachmana*, an agent sent by Hashem to stand before "kings" — both temporal leaders and great rabbis, who are referred to by the Talmud as "kings." Rabbi Weinberg spoke of Rabbi Sherer as a confidant of the *gedolim*, whose views were valued and respected almost as an equal. The honor that the *gedolim* showed him, Rabbi Weinberg attributed to the fact they knew he lacked any personal *negios* (self-interest), and was motivated solely by the issue at hand, not advancing himself or Agudath Israel.

The Klausenberger Rebbe of America, Rabbi Shmuel Dovid Halberstam, whose *beis medrash* is opposite Rabbi Sherer's home and where Rabbi Sherer *davened Shacharis* every weekday morning, spoke of his ability to totally separate himself from all the pressures weighing on him when he *davened* and his ability to pray with complete serenity. He quoted the verse (*Shemos* 2:11), "… [A]nd Moshe grew up and went out to his brothers and saw their suffering," in just the same manner that Rabbi Sherer always had: The measure of a Jewish leader lies in his ability to feel the suffering of each and every fellow Jew.

Rabbi Naftoli Halberstam, the son of the Bobover Rebbe, spoke on behalf of his father, who despite his frail health remained for the entire *levayah*. He predicted that the full extent of Rabbi Sherer's loss would only be fully felt with the passage of time, as the community had a chance to absorb the impact of his absence. Rabbi Malkiel Kotler, Rosh Yeshivah of Bais Medrash Govoha of Lakewood, reflected on Rabbi Sherer's closeness to his grandfather Rabbi Aharon Kotler, whose image was ever before him, and his father Rabbi Shneur Kotler. The final, non-family member to speak was Rabbi Menachem Porush, who flew in from *Eretz Yisrael* specially to take part in the *levayah* and who worked closely with Rabbi Sherer for a full half-century. Rabbi Porush related how when he had taken leave of Rabbi Sherer for the last time at Ben Gurion Airport, his focus had not been on his own precarious health, but on the continuing battle to prevent the Conservative and Reform movements from gaining a foothold in the Holy Land.

Rabbi Sherer's oldest grandson, Rabbi Levi Langer, spoke on behalf of all the grandchildren. He reflected on the way that Rabbi Sherer always managed to find the time for his family. Despite the demands on his time from every direction, when his grandfather sang the family's traditional *niggun* of *Kol Mekadesh She'vii* on *leil Shabbos*, one could feel the *menuchah* of Shabbos permeating the home, Rabbi Langer said. The final speaker was Rabbi Shimshon Sherer, who shared a series of emotional vignettes from his father's life.[6] Reb Abish Brodt's[7] recitation of *Keil Malei Rachamim* and the announcement that only grandsons and staff members of Agudath Israel of America, Rabbi Sherer's "fourth child," should carry the *aron* (coffin) concluded the three hours of *hespedim* (eulogies) during which the mourners stood riveted.

After the eulogies, New York's finest stood at attention as the huge crowd accompanied the *aron*. A young *Chassidishe* mother standing on the sidewalk attempted to explain to the young children holding on

---

6. Those vignettes are found throughout this book.
7. Reb Abish's leading the singing into the wee hours of the morning at the *Motza'ei Shabbos tisch* at the annual Agudath Israel convention had long been one of Rabbi Sherer's favorite parts of the convention.

The *aron* being carried from the *levayah* by members of his family and Agudah staff. At far left are Rabbi Yerachmiel Barash and Rabbi Aharon Halpert. Around the *aron*, from left, Rabbi Mordechai Avigdor, Rabbi Yonah Feinstein, Rabbi Meir Frischman, Rabbi Daniel Langer, Rabbi Levi Langer, Rabbi Yossi Sova, Moshe Yaakov (Robert) Goldschmidt, and Shragie Goldschmidt

to her hand why such a huge crowd had gathered and who they were honoring. *"Ehr iz nisht geven a Rebbe; nisht a prezident. Nor an ish emes, a ta'yere Yid* — He was not a Rebbe, and not a president. But he was a man of truth and a precious Jew."

At 60th Street a motorcade of between 150 to 200 cars formed to accompany Rabbi Sherer to his final resting place at the Beth Moses Cemetery on Long Island. New York City police on motorcycles led the way and blocked off side streets and every entrance to the Belt Parkway to let the procession pass unimpeded. At the Nassau County line, they were replaced by Nassau County police.

A Wish Fulfilled

DURING RABBI SHERER'S LAST WEEKS, HIS DAUGHTER ELKY almost never left his bedside. In the week before he lapsed into a coma, she heard him repeating to himself in his sleep, "We must make a proper *kavod* for them. We must make a proper *kavod* for them." Once he even awakened and told his daughter that he must get dressed in order to greet the guests from *Eretz Yisrael*. He was referring to the upcoming visit to the United States of Rabbi Aharon Leib Shteinman, the leader of the Israeli yeshivah world, and the Gerrer Rebbe, head of the largest Chassidic group in *Eretz Yisrael*.

In the last decade of his life, no project was closer to Rabbi Sherer's heart than restoring the unity of the Agudah movement in *Eretz Yisrael* and preventing the divisions that plagued the Israeli Agudah movement from spilling over to America. Thus nothing could have given Rabbi Sherer greater satisfaction than the unprecedented visit to America of Rabbi Shteinman and the Gerrer Rebbe. Informed of Rabbi Sherer's passing before their departure from *Eretz Yisrael*, they specifically requested that the *levayah* be delayed sufficiently for them to participate in some way. They landed in America just as the *levayah* was leaving Brooklyn, and they headed straight from the airport to the cemetery.

At the *beis olam*, two of the most revered figures in world Jewry — one a great Rosh Yeshivah; the other the scion of the distinguished Gerrer dynasty — paid their final tribute to the man who had done more than any other to bring all the disparate elements of Torah Jewry together under the leadership of the *gedolei Yisrael*.[8] Their presence was

---

8. The importance of unity was one of the great themes of Rabbi Sherer's life. Every year at the Seder, when we lift the cup of wine and recite, וְהִיא שֶׁעָמְדָה, he would repeat a *vort* from the *Sfas Emes*. The *Sfas Emes* would explain the words "שֶׁלֹּא אֶחָד בִּלְבַד עָמַד עָלֵינוּ לְכַלּוֹתֵנוּ," which literally mean, "not just

a fulfillment of his own words at one convention of Agudath Israel, "Let us stay together, dream together, work together. Together, for that is what Agudath Israel is all about."⁹

IT IS POINTLESS TO SAY THAT RABBI SHERER'S LIFE WAS CUT OFF in the middle. No matter when the end came that would have been true,

Kasheh Preidasicha Aleinu

for he was always seeking new challenges to tackle. *Klal Yisrael* found it hard to part from him. Not only because there remained much more he could have done, but because he had so much more yet to teach. By continuing to speak about him, the lessons he spent a lifetime teaching in word and, more importantly, in deed became more deeply engrained.

Thousands poured into the Sherer home during the week of *shivah*, from the most renowned figures of the Torah and Chassidic worlds to those who did not personally know Rabbi Sherer or any of the family members. Rabbi Avrohom Pam somehow managed to gather the strength to make a *shivah* visit, despite his own perilous health. He sat between Rabbi Shmuel Kamenetsky and the Skulener Rebbe, repeating over and over, with tears in his eyes, "This is a nightmare. This is a nightmare." Shimshon told Rabbi Pam how much his letter in the hospital had meant to Rabbi Sherer and thanked him for his *mesiras nefesh* in speaking at the *levayah* and making a *shivah* call, but added that his father would have been upset to see Rabbi Pam jeopardize his health to come. "I just couldn't stay home," Rabbi Pam replied. He then went to the women's side and sat next to Mrs. Sherer, not saying a word, just crying and crying. Those tears brought more consolation than any words could have.

Many of those who came to pay their respects, including some whom no one in the family knew, mentioned how much Rabbi Sherer's warm "*Gut Shabbos*" greeting had meant to them. Some of those related how

---

one [enemy] has risen against us to annihilate us," as a powerful call for unity — only because we are not one — i.e., unified — are our enemies able to rise up to destroy us. But if we were unified, no power in the world could threaten the Jewish people.

9. That quotation appears on the last page of the beautiful commemorative volume prepared by Agudath Israel for Rabbi Sherer's first *yahrtzeit*. On the back of the slip-on cover appears another signature quote on the same theme: "We can only conquer all the evils facing *Klal Yisrael* when we join together, united *b'shalom v'achdus* [in peace and brotherhood], with one hand, one mind, one heart, one *neshamah*, one goal, one aspiration, *l'kadesh shem Shamayim b'rabbim* [to sanctify the Name of Heaven in public]."

they had been embarrassed to see Rabbi Sherer crossing the street to greet them and had hurried toward him, often meeting in the middle of the street.[10]

Within the *shloshim* (the first 30 days of mourning), memorial gatherings took place in approximately 40 locations worldwide, with the most sought-after speakers in the Torah world, his colleagues in Agudath Israel, leading communal *rabbanim*, and his son Rabbi Shimshon Sherer sharing their memories in order to extract every possible lesson from Rabbi Sherer's life.

For the first *yahrtzeit*, Agudath Israel produced a beautiful, glossy volume of pictures and documents touching on virtually every aspect of Rabbi Sherer's life and career, entitled *Rabbi Moshe Sherer: His Life and Legacy*, dedicated by Dovid Bodner and Murray Huberfeld, with many additional sponsors.. As a result of the visit of Rabbi Shteinman and the Gerrer Rebbe, an entire new system of schools for children from non-religious families in *Eretz Yisrael*, Keren Nesivos Moshe, was created and named after Rabbi Sherer.[11] No project could have delighted him more.

The national headquarters of Agudath Israel were rededicated as the Rabbi Moshe Sherer National Headquarters. And the Fourteenth Avenue Agudah *minyan*, in which Rabbi Sherer *davened* for decades, relocated to 50th Street between 15th and 16th Avenues in Boro Park, under the name Agudath Israel/Zichron Moshe.

For the 10th *yahrtzeit*, virtually every Orthodox publication dedicated entire sections to Rabbi Sherer. A second *sefer Torah*[12] was written in his honor, with Moshe Marx, one of the numerous sponsors, honored with writing the first and last letters. This volume is the final stage of the process of recording "a life worthy of being recorded for posterity."[13]

In the only *hesped* he ever delivered — for his dear friend Wolf (Volvie) Friedman — Rabbi Sherer explained the verse with which eulogies traditionally conclude:

---

10. The number of people who commented on how much Rabbi Sherer's "*Gut Shabbos*" meant to them attested to the truth of something that he told his children frequently when they were young. In a play on the *Gemara*, "There are those who acquire the World to Come in a single moment (*b'sha'ah achas*)" (*Avodah Zarah* 10b), he used to say, "We have no idea how much we can accomplish in the most fleeting moment: b'*Gut Shabbos achas*, b'*Good Morning achas*, b'*warm smile achas*, b'*compliment achas*, b' phone call achas, b'*note achas*."
11. One of the major supporters of Keren Nesivos Moshe is Shimon Glick, the son of Rabbi Sherer's old high-school classmate Louis Glick.
12. A first *sefer Torah* was presented to Rabbi Sherer by the officers of Agudath Israel as a surprise at the 1997 Agudath Israel annual dinner.
13. See Introduction for Benjamin Franklin's recipe for being remembered after one's passing.

"בִּלַּע הַמָּוֶת לָנֶצַח" — He will eliminate [literally, "swallow up"] death forever" (*Yeshayahu* 25:8), with a homiletical twist: If one seeks to conquer death, to swallow up its fearful power, there is only one way — לָנֶצַח (eternity). One must dedicate one's life to eternal matters and attach oneself to that which has eternal meaning and lives on after our bodies have perished.[14] He did.

---

14. Rabbi Sherer used the same *vort* in his written eulogy for Rabbi Yitzchak Meir Levin. *Bishtei Einayim*, p. 372.

INDEX

INDEX

A

"A Succaleh a Kleiner" (song)   72, 578
AARTS (Association of Advanced
   Rabbinical and Talmudic Schools)   260,
   188, 260 297, 375 (*fn*), 442, 445, 448
      and Novominsker Rebbe   440
      first official meeting   448
      official recognition of   450
ABC Child Care Bill   468
abortion issue   285, 459, 483
      and Supreme Court   458
      anti-abortion legislation   470, 470 (*fn*)
      limitations on   484
      Medicaid funds for   299
      where required by *halachah*   470
Abraham, Rabbi Dr. Avrohom S.   492 (*fn*)
Abramowitz, Rabbi
   Yehudah Meir   218 (*illus.*), 559 (*illus.*)
Abrams, Elliot   507 (*fn*)
Abrams, Attorney General Robert   471
Abzug, Bella   375
accreditation of yeshivos   445
      roshei yeshivos' attitude
         regarding 447
activism   195
Adas Yeshurun shul   54 (*fn*)
Adler, Emil   576 (*illus.*)
Adler, Nathan   83
      arranging a meeting with   83 (*illus.*)
advertising standards and MTA   283
Advisory Council   448, 449
affidavits of financial support   102
affirmative action   405
Agostini v. Felton   462
Agudas HaRabbonim   94, 109, 163
Agudath ideology, discussion of   53
Agudath Israel of California   252, 270
Agudath Israel of Great Britian   225
Agudath Israel World Organization
   (AIWO)   54, 112, 133, 217, 245 (*fn*), 275,
   500, 536-7 (*fn*), 558, 568 (*fn*)

Agudath Israel Youth Council
   a misnomer   108
   see also Zeirei Agudath Israel
Agudath Israel *and* Agudath Israel of
   America   99, 163, 181, 225
      and social service   425
      not merely a social service
         organization   175
      and Youth Council merger   108
      anti-nepotism policy in   183
      archivist of   27
      as a *davar she'be'kedushah*   195
      as an ideological movement   175
      both "pro-life" and supporter of
         RFRA   471
      branches   155
      convention 1941   (*illus.*) 87, 190
      debts   151*ff*, 155
      Division of Government and Public
         Affairs   452
      Division of Yeshivah
         Services   490 (*fn*)
      Humanitarian Award   258
      ideals declared at Kattowicz 178
      ideology   104, 331
      importance of to *yeshivah
         bachurim*   215
      in Atlantic City   157
      in Israel   132
      in the 1930s   51
      kiruv or *hatzalah*   503
      Management Committee   151
      mortgage bonds   150
      outposts   170
      Program of Activities   169
      salaries paid on time   157
      Washington office   474
      see also Washington, D.C.
Agudath Israel/Zichron Moshe   642
Aguilar v. Felton   461, 462
agunos, tragedy of   455

Index   □   647

ah menstch darf tun, nisht oiftun 313
Aharon HaKohen's garments fit
    Elazar   207 (*fn*)
aid to parochial and private schools   163, 158*ff*, 164, 311, 419, 489
aide-mémoire   292, 298, 300, 320, 527
AIDS education, in yeshivos   282, 302
AIPAC   191
Airmont, Village of   463
AIWO,
    see Agudath Israel World Organization
Akeidah   313
Albany   195
Albert, Carl   374, 376
Alexander, Lamar   477
Alexander, Dr. Leo   484
Alfih family   296, 296 (*illus.*)
aliyah to the Torah, Rabbi Sherer's last   617
almanos (widows), concern for   239
Alter of Slabodka   9, 68
Alter, Rabbi
    Pinchas Menachem   69 (*illus.*)
Alter, Rabbi Shmuel   596 (*fn*)
Am Echad   141, 169, 234, 338 (*illus.*), 542, 561, 562 (*illus.*), 563 (*illus.*), 564, 608-9 (*illus.*), 611 (*illus.*), 614 (*illus.*), 624
    advertisements   561 (*illus.*)
    delegation   560-564
Amalek and Sabbath   353
Ambach, Commissioner of Education Gordon   257, 297, 308, 323, 446, 452 (*illus.*)
America-Israel Public Affairs Committee, see AIPAC
American *baalebattim*   231
American Federation of Teachers   477
American Jewish Congress   160, 421, 459, 460
    oppose aid to day schools   164
    disdain for   422
American Jewish Council on Soviety Jewry   550 (*fn*)
American Mizrachi   94
    see also Mizrachi
American Rabbi, The (publication)   140
American Zionist Federation   550 (*fn*)
American-Irish society   325
amicus curiae brief   458, 459, 461-2, 484, 486
Amsel, Rabbi Avrohom   576 (*illus.*)
"An idealist without illusions"   255
"An Ideology of Activisim"   195 (*fn*), 196 (*fn*)
Andrusier, Rabbi Rafael   232 (*illus.*)
Angel, Rabbi Marc   497

angels,
    teachers resemble   69
    visited Yehoshua   69
Anglo-Jewish press   274
Ani, too much   607
anti-nepotism policy in the Agudath Israel   183
anshei emes — men of truth   141
anti-abortion legislation   470, 470 (*fn*)
Anti-Defamation League   464, 466
anti-Semitic cartoon   275
anti-Zionism   77, 553
Antwerp   621 (*illus.*)
Arab pogroms of 1929-1936   551
Arafat, Yasir   550
Archbishop of Canterbury   388
Archdiocese of Chicago   279
Archdiocese of New York   328
areivus   550
Argamon, Stephanie (Pearson)   28
Argentinian Jewry   530
Ark, Noach entered only after rain began   55
Army Postal Office (APO)   99
Arnon, Michael   556
aron being carried from the *levayah*   638 (*illus.*)
Aron, Herbert   67
ArtScroll Publications   237, 363-5
    Schottenstein Ed.Talmud   367
    staff   21
Aseres Yemei Teshuvah
    (Ten Days of Repentance)   239
Ashcroft, Sen. John   184 (*fn*)
Ashkenazy, Yossi   526 (*illus.*)
Ashrei, in future tense   629
askanim (activists)   223
askanus   177, 350
Askowitz, Dr. Shimon   176
Aspin, Les   488
assisted-suicide case   484
Association of Jewish Day Schools of Greater Baltimore   374 (*fn*)
Astor Foundation   433
AT&T and COPE Institute   429
at-risk teens   296
Auerbach, Rabbi
    Shlomo Zalman   403 (*illus.*), 403, 492 (*fn*), 498, 523 (*illus.*), 618
Austria   148
Austritt, community in Frankfurt   78, 78 (*fn*)
autopsies   210, 553, 590
    and informed consent   304
    California autopsy bill   251
    confidential memo   304 (*illus.*)
    Hadassah Hospital in Jerusalem   305
    nonconsensual, in Israel   303

avenging the blood of *kedoshim*   604 (*fn*)
Avigdor, Rabbi David   563 (*illus.*)
Avigdor, Rabbi
  Mordechai   276 (*illus.*), 638 (*illus.*)
"Avinu, Av HaRachaman …
  Tatte, oy Tatte" (song)   623
Avraham and Yitzchak,
  and mountain (*Midrash*)   173
Avraham's *chesed*   16
Avraham Avinu, seeking
  match for Yitzchak   577 (*fn*)
Axelrod, David   495

B

*B'mechitzasam:
  In Their Shadows*   204 (*fn*)
b'sha'ah achas   642 (*fn*)
baalebattim   221ff
    contibution of   240
    developing American   231
Badillo, Herman   375
Bais Aharon   538
Bais Medrash Elyon   590
Bais Yaakov   102, 243
Bais Yaakov Academy
  of Brooklyn   502 (*fn*), 518
Bais Yaakov D'Rav Meir   152 (*fn*)
Bais Yaakov of Baltimore   374
Bais Yaakov of Brooklyn   502 (*fn*)
Bais Yaakov of West Bronx   291
Bais Yaakov students   303
Bald, Yitzy   603 (*fn*)
Ballabon, Jeff   466
Baltimore Orioles   80
Barak, Ehud   563
Barash, Rabbi Yerachmiel   428, 638 (*illus.*)
Barnholtz, Zelick   67
Barr, Attorney General William   411, 463
Baruch Hashem   631
Baruch Taam   537
Baruchson, Rabbi Isaac   70 (*illus.*)
Bas Torah Academy of Suffern   502 (*fn*)
Basch, Eli   183, 227 (*illus.*)
Basel Convention   107
Bashevkin, Dr. Michael   600, 615 (*fn*)
Basic Educational Opportunity Grant   263
Basya, the daughter of Pharaoh   75, 129
Bauer, Tom   439 (*illus.*)
Baumol, Rabbi Yehoshua   54 (*fn*)
Bayley, Dr. Ned   383
Beame, Mayor Abe   251, 266, 299,
  320, 534 (*fn*), 576 (*illus.*)
beard, Rabbi Sherer growing a   559
"beautiful in the house; beautiful in
  the field"   569
Becker, Rabbi Labish   179, 202 (*fn*),
  245 (*illus.*), 264 (*illus.*), 331, 336, 338, 342

Be'er Yaakov   569 (*fn*)
Begin,
  Prime Minister Menachem   547,
  548 (*illus.*), 549 (*illus.*)
    and ill-fitting yarmulke   183
    and Rabbi Shach   547
    and U.S. aid to Soviet refugees   548
    attitude regarding Shabbos   547
    Sabra and Shatillah massacres   547
Begun, Yosef   518 (*fn*)
Beis HaLevi (Brisker Rav),
  Rabbi Yosef Dov Soloveichik
    advice on switching
      employment   582 (*fn*)
Beis Shammai and Beis Hillel,
  debate between   19
Beis Yisrael (Gerrer Rebbe)   217
Belkin, Dr. Samuel   138, 140, 141
Bell, Dr. Terence   306
Bellamy, Carol   456
Belsky, Rabbi Yisroel   450 (*illus.*)
Belzer Rebbe   291 (*illus.*), 611, 621
  green card   290
benches in the *beis medrash*   557
Bender, Rabbi Yaakov   261 (*fn*)
Bennett, Chaskel   28
Beren, Sheldon, and waiver of
  Section 235 mortgages   438-9, 474
Berene, Msg. Gino   432
Berg, Mendel (Max)   244 (*illus.*), 245
  (*illus.*), 433, 433 (*illus.*)
Berger, Moshe   227 (*fn*)
Berger, Ralph   67
Berger, Rabbi Shlomo   241,
  508-9 (*illus.*), 510
Berkowitz, Rabbi Avrohom   611 (*illus.*)
Berkowitz, Jerry   394. 395
Berman, Julius   179 (*fn*)
Berman, Rabbi   533 (*illus.*)
Bernholtz, Moshe   67
Bernstein, Rabbi Louis   378
Bernstein, Morris   67
Besser, Rabbi Chaskel   214, 215 (*fn*), 228
  229, 242, 258, 258 (*fn*), 282, 348 (*fn*), 409,
  536 (*fn*), 537, 539, 563, 575, 613, 613 (*fn*), 635
  (*illus.*) 131, 190, 205, 321, 450, 504, 563,
  609, 611
Besser, Rabbi Yisroel   28
Beth Medrash Govoha of Lakewood   130,
  192, 288, 289 (*fn*), 443
  see also Lakewood
Beth Moses Cemetery   639
Biberfeld, Dr. Marcel (Mosie)   597 (*fn*)
Biderman, Avrohom,   234 (*fn*), 240, 334,
  406, 409 (*fn*), 563, 602
  (*illus.*) 238, 562, 609

Biderman, Rabbi Avrohom
   (ArtScroll) 21, 27
Biderman, Sarah 238
Bienstock, Mollie 110
Bikur Cholim of Boro Park 243
Bilaam 606
binding with cords of love 342
Bircas Hamazon 194 (*fn*)
Bircas Kohanim
   (the Priestly Benediction) 631
   and supplications regarding
      dreams 125
Birnbaum, Lieut. Meyer 100, 101
Biser, Mordechai 573 (*fn*)
Bishtei Einayim 17, 71 (*fn*), 123 (*fn*), 156,
   173, 345, 350 (*fn*), 350 (*fn*), 351 (*illus.*),
   352 (*fn*), 368 (*fn*), 422, 422 (*fn*), 541 (*fn*),
   545 (*fn*), 643 (*fn*)
bitul Torah 69
Blaine Amendment 168
Blau, Rabbi Moshe 57 (*illus.*)
Bleich, Rabbi J. David 321, 456, 494 (*fn*)
Bleich, Rabbi Yaakov 527 (*illus.*)
Bloch, Rabbi Eliyahu Meir 84
Block, Herb 407
"blood flow" test 492 (*fn*)
Bloom, Jeff 27
Bloom, Rabbi Shmuel 27, 71 (*fn*),
   153 (*fn*), 161 (*fn*), 194 (*fn*), 235, 258,
   293 (*fn*), 308 (*fn*), 331, 333, 338, 339 (*fn*),
   364 (*fn*), 425 (*fn*), 428, 503 (*fn*), 505,
   510 (*fn*), 524, 622, 626
      (*illus.*) 182, 196, 216, 224, 235, 291, 373,
         439, 504, 521, 609, 611, 614
Blue Laws, and merchants 177
   repeal of 165
Blum, Prof. Yehuda 545
Bluzhover Rebbe 46 (*fn*), 155, 212, 228, 503
   (*illus.*) 157, 183, 198, 201, 506, 634
Bnos 83, 104
Board of Education 169
Board of Education v. Allen 168
Board of Estimate 286
Board of Health 210
Board of Regents 491
Bobover Rebbe 539, 628 (*illus.*)
Bobrovski, Pinchas 473
Bodenheimer, Dr. Ernst 202, 202 (*fn*),
   206 (*illus.*), 359
Bodenheimer, Rabbi Gavriel 450 (*illus.*)
Bodenheimer, Ludwig 67
Bodner, David 642
Bookson, State Senator Paul 43 (*illus.*)
Borchardt, Rabbi Boruch B. 36, 204, 205,
   226, 267, 329, 339, 540 (*fn*)
      (*illus.*) 154, 322, 340, 342

Boro Park 158, 238, 315
   Senior Citizens' Center, 426, 427 (*illus.*)
   preservation 431*ff*
Bostoner Rebbe
   (Boston-Har Nof) 372 (*illus.*), 350
Bostoner Rebbe (New York) 373 (*illus.*),
   190, 208, 216, 235, 292, 450, 483, 504
Bourgeois, Joan Arnold 452
Boyaner Rebbe 86 (*illus.*), 228 (*illus.*), 228
"brain death" 492, 497
   and insurance coverage 495
   legislation 492
   standard in New York, with some
      religious exemption 494, 498
Brandeis University 446
Brander, Rabbi Sheah 574 (*illus.*)
Brandriss, Rabbi Yitzchak 111, 452
Braunfeld, Moshe 287 (*illus.*), 576 (*illus.*)
Braunstein, Rebbetzin Zehava 620
Brazil 535 *ff*
Brennglass, Samuel Lawrence 145
Breslauer, Rabbi Dr. Leo 106
Breuer, Dr. Isaac 107, 107 (*fn*)
Brezenoff, Deputy Mayor
   Stanley 255 (*illus.*), 257, 269, 278,
   297, 399
Brezinski, Zbigniew 469 (*illus.*)
Brezovsky, Rabbi
   Sholom Noach 555 (*illus.*)
bridge figure between modern America
   and the eternal Jewish people 30
Brigham Young University 306
bris milah of Russian immigrants 519
Brisker Rav, Rabbi Yitzchak Zev
   (Reb Velvel) Soloveichik
      support for Agudath Israel 204
British Agudah 200
British Airways 385
British government 94
British Mandate in Palestine 131
Broadway Central Hotel 58
Broderick, Bishop 323
Brodt, Abish 233 (*illus.*), 579 (*illus.*), 637
Bronfman, Edgar 297 (*fn*), 525
Brooklyn Art Museum 285 (*fn*)
Brooklyn College 298
Brown, Harold 553
Brown, Lee 407
Buchenwald, liberation of 102
Budapest 567
Buenos Aires, Argentina,
   kehillah 529 (*illus.*)
   Rabbi Sherer visit to 527
   shechitah in 533
   yeshivah dormitory 534
   yeshivah gedolah and *kollel* 532

Bulman, Rabbi Nachman 359
Burak, Morris J. 67
bus stops, lewd advertising on 552
Bush, Barbara 467
Bush, President George H.W. 275, 468, 472
   support of Jonathan Pollard 486
   (illus.) 186, 271, 477, 480
Bush, Vice President
   George H. W. 437 (illus.), 507 (fn)
busing for New York City yeshivah students 203
Butman, Rabbi Shmuel 409
Byrne, Gov. Brendan 288
Byrnes, Congressman 378

C

C.R.E.D.I.T. (Citizens Relief for Education through Income Tax [Credit]) 420, 447
   brochure 420 (illus.)
Cahill, Dr. Kevin 324, 492
California, Agudath Israel of 252, 270
Camp Agudah 82, 83, 158, 188, 232, 232 (illus.), 237, 330, 573, 582, 587, 604 (fn), 606
   beginnings of 104-5
   inculcating campers with Agudah ideology 177
   mortgage bonds 150
   room in 237
Camp Bnos 158, 232, 330, 582
   inculcating campers with Agudah ideology 177
Camp Chayl Miriam (Chayil) 606
Camp David Accords 556
Canarsie, forced busing 292
cantor, *mechalel Shabbos* 53 (fn)
Cardozo, Justice 185
Cardozo School of Law 456
Carey, Gov. Hugh 240, 266-7, 334, 339, 375, 377, 444, 448, 492, 534 (fn)
   (illus.) 224, 315, 318, 319, 427, 473, 549
   and Catholic leaders 324
   and "*get*" law 456
   Humanitarian Award 323
   invocation at first inauguration 317
   personal letters to 267
   special closeness to Rabbi Sherer 314
Carlebach, Rabbi Shlomo 450 (illus.)
carols 599
Carter, President Jimmy 254, 261, 272, 295, 505, 553
   (illus.), 274, 294
Catholic Church 324 (fn), 325, 400, 472
   alliance with 279, 489
   and "*get*" law 457
   and Blue Laws 166

   a powerful ally 282
   of Baltimore 374 (fn) (illus.), 264, 303
Catholic Conference 324 (fn), 376 (fn), 470
Catholic New York (periodical) 284
Cato, Gavin 406
Cavazo, Dr. Lauro 467
Cellar, Rep. Emanual 375
cemeteries
   preservation of,
      in Soviet Union 536-9
   encouraged by Pope 282
   in Eastern and Central Europe 242, 281
Central Conference of American Rabbis 139
Central Hotel, Jerusalem 242 (fn), 608, 612
CETA (Comprehensive Employment Training Act) 428
Chai-Chi 143
Chaim Ozer, Reb 55
Chaimovits, Miri 617
Chaimovits, Shlomo 231 (fn), 237, 347 (fn), 617
Chananau Bill 167
changes, responding to 195
Chanukah candles 293
Chanukah parties 586
Charleston, South Carolina 356
Charney, Samuel 67
Chasam Sofer 39, 61 (fn)
Chasam Sofer shul 54 (fn)
chassan's Shas 116
Chashmonaim and Hellenizers 352
Chassidic courts, splendor of 192
chemotherapy 570, 600 ff
   for leukemia 31
cherem (ban of excommuncation) 354
chesed, act of 196
chesed and *gevurah* 16
Chevra Kadisha 44
Chevrah Tehillim in Stoliner *shtiebel* 40
chezkas kashrus
   (reputation for probity) 261
Chicago 165
Chiddushei HaRim 156
child care bill 468
"children at risk" 620
children, entertaining 577
children's Homes for Israel 132
children of the poor 68
chillul Hashem 210, 292
   vs. *pikuach nefesh* 309
Chinn, Rabbi Yitzchok 82
Chinuch Atzmai *see* Torah Schools for Israel
Chizkiyahu HaMelech 177
chochmah in creation 355

Index □ 651

Chofetz Chaim   55, 61, 128, 570 (fn)
Chortkover Rebbe   265
Christian Phalangists   547 (fn)
Churchill, Winston   585 (fn)
Chush   332
Chushim   75
City of Bourne v. Flores   471
Civil Rights Act   477
Civil Rights Division   412
Civil Rights Law   285 (fn)
Claims Conference   265, 277, 539, 550 (fn), 620
Clanton Park shul   347
classes, segregated by gender   298
Cleveland   165
Clinton, President William J.   254, 477, 487, 626
Clymer Street shul   62
Cohen, Rabbi Abba   175, 462, 466, 468, 471, 474, 475, 479, 480
Cohen, Rabbi Dovid   455, 456
Cohen, Rabbi Lawrence   67, 91 (fn)
coin, two sides   351
Coleman, Dr. Morton   601, 607, 612
college, varying approaches to   357
Colman, Assemblyman Sam   494 (fn)
Columbia Law School   590
Columbia School of International Affairs   466
Columbia University   448
Commission on Law and Public Affairs (COLPA)   288 (fn)
Commission on Senior Citizens   426
Commissioner of Education   257
Commissioner of Health   210
Committee for Public Education and Religious Liberty v. Regan   419, 420
communal service   232
community service, three aspects of   32
  see also askanus
compulsory civilian service by women   553
Conference of Catholic Bishops, and draft exemptions   371
Conference of Presidents of Major Jewish Organizations   272 (fn), 276, 550
Conference of World Synagogues in Jerusalem   201
Conference on Jewish Material Claims Against Germany, see Claims Conference
Congregation Kenesseth Israel, Far Rockaway   110, 113, 121
Congressional Hotel   375
Congressional testimony   159
Conservative movement in America, growth during 1950's   144
Conservative movement in South America   531
Conservative movement,
  ad hoc alliance with   371
  clergy   134ff
  draft exemption   370
  entry into Israeli schools   143
  Education Ministry,
    official recognition of   143
  synagogues   143
constructive suggestions   247
conversion according to
  halachah   362, 560, 562
  Reform and Conservative   608
Cooke, Cardinal Terence   503
COPE Institute   428, 429
Cornell Medical Center   601, 617
Council of Jewish Federations, convention in San Francisco   142
Council of Torah Sages
  and Soviets   516
  see also Moetzes Gedolei HaTorah
Council of Twelve Apostles, meeting with   307
count to 10, before offering reproof   577
Counterforce grant   287 (fn)
Cranston, Sen. Alan   196 (illus.)
Crawford, William   503 (fn)
"credit" or "clock hours" in yeshivah brochures   308
cries of Jews, falling on deaf ears   75
criticism
  by leaders, not ignoring   60
  constructive   246f
  listening to   60
  targets for   247
critique of "Holocaust Jewry"   353
Crosland, David   505
Crown Heights   430
  riots   404, 413 (illus.), 463
  backlash against Jewish community   413
crows, three   261
Cruzan case   495, 496
cultural pluralism through tuition tax credits   302
Cuomo, Gov. Mario   407, 494 (fn), 599 (fn) (illus.) 286, 337
  and abortion   285
  and blue ribbon panel   411
  letter to Rabbi Sherer about Crown Heights riot   408 (illus.)
cure before the disease   501
Cymerman, Reb Itche Meir   32, 240, 576 (illus.)
Cymerman, Boruch Moshe   223

cynical claims about Rabbi Sherer's "manipulations"   206
Cywiak, Rabbi Leibel   159 (*illus.*), 227 (*illus.*)
Czechoslovakia   287, 537

D

daas Torah   62, 63, 179, 197 ff
   public questioning of   201
Daf Yomi   48-9, 169, 192, 363
   on day of Rabbi Sherer's passing   19
Danforth, John   466
Daniel, Alice   457,
Danielpour, Albert   503
davar she'be'kedushah   195
David, Herbert   67
David, Rabbi Hillel   625, 635
David, Rabbi Yonoson   384, 389
   Rebbetzin Beruriah   385
Davis, Shelby   389
Davis, Yosef   626 (*fn*)
Davitt, Alan   256, 265, 279, 401
Dawson Field   385
day schools, federal aid, opposed by Reform   164
Day-Morning Journal   140
death from thirst   631 (*fn*)
death, time of   210, 321, 492
Defense of Marriage Act   484
Degel HaTorah   181, 556
Dembitzer, Dovid   509 (*illus.*)
Department of Agriculture   369, 382
Department of Education   253, 257, 339, 429, 479
Department of Health, Education, and Welfare   298
Department of Housing and Urban Development (HUD)   438
DePuy, Dr. Hadley S.   262 (*fn*)
Der Yid   591
derashah and public-speaking   345
   length of   594
Dershowitz, Professor Alan   455, 456
DeSalvio Bill   167
Dessler, Reuven   233 (*illus.*)
Detroit   570 (*fn*)
Deutsch, Rudolph   67
Diament, Nathan   466 (*fn*)
Diamond, Dr. David   44 (*fn*), 233 (*illus.*)
Diamond, Dr. Isaac (Yitzchak)   44 (*fn*)
Diaspora Affairs in the Education Ministry   143
Dick, Judah   168 (*fn*), 455
dina d'malchusa dina   59
Dine, Tom   191-2
Dinitz, Simcha   320
Dinkins, Mayor David, and Crown Heights riots   407-8, 413
Dinovitz, Benjamin   67
discrimination in the workplace   296
Dishon, Rabbi Shmuel   43 (*fn*), 350
disparaging fellow Jews   60
Displaced Persons camps   230
divinity student draft exemption   370, 379, 381, 554
   telephone campaign   375
   see also draft deferment
divinity students, outspoken criticism of   379
divrei Torah cited by Rabbi Sherer   35
Djerejian, Assistant Secretary of State Edward   295
Dobrynin, Anatoly   516
Dombroff, Rabbi Yaakov   494
domed stadium   629
Dominick, Sen. Peter   378
Dos Yiddish Tagblatt   53
Dos Yiddishe Vort   118, 169, 335 (*fn*), 358, 363
   Tishrei 5740   49 (*fn*)
doting grandfather   585
Douglas, H. Eugene   506
draft deferment (2-D) and exemption for yeshivah students   369-72ff, 554, 556, 574
   exemption, change to deferment   378
   final regulations   381
   in USA impacted on yeshivah student deferment in Israel   381 (*fn*)
   interfaith memorandum   377
   telephone campaign   375
"Dream all you want, but don't sleep"   125
dreams *see also* Bircas Kohanim
Drori, Mrs. Rivka   519
Dulzin, Aryeh   549, 552
Dunne, John R.   411, 463
Dunner, Rabbi Aba   170, 176, 200 (*fn*), 203, 223, 225, 247, 388, 395, 558

E

Eagleburger, Lawrence   467
Early Childhood Education and Development Act   468, 468 (*fn*)
East Flatbush, forced busing   292
Eckhardt, German High Commander,   604, 605 (*illus.*)
Economic Development Authority (EDA)   462
ecumenical service, rejected   280
Edelman, David   196 (*illus.*)
Edelstein, Yuri   524
Education Act   490

education, private and federal aid for 311
Egan, Bishop (today Cardinal) Edward M. 283
Ehrenreich, Rabbi Lemel 45 (fn), 571
Ehrenreich, Yoel 611 (illus.), 614 (illus.)
ehrlich, as a distinction 223
Eichenstein, Rabbi Dov 450 (illus.)
Eidlitz, Yehudis 570 (fn), 571 (fn)
Eiger, Rabbi Akiva 71 (fn)
  explanation of "veil" 297
84 William Street 58, 573 (fn)
eimasah d'tzibura (fear of the public) 567 (fn)
ein od milvado 621
Eisen, Shlomo 28
Eisenberg, Benno 67
Eisenberg, Mordechai 617
Eisenberg, Mr. 529 (illus.)
Eisenhower, President Dwight D. 149
Eisenstadt, Stuart 269, 272, 301, 505 (illus.) 254, 469
El Al 191, 385
  Shabbos flights 547
Elbaum, Rabbi Nachman 291 (illus.)
Elbaum, Rabbi Yechiel 93 (illus.)
Elberg, Rabbi Simcha 190 (illus.), 576 (illus.)
Eldad and Medad 96
elderly, housing for 189
Elementary and Secondary Education Act (ESEA) 163, 311, 315, 479
Elias, Rabbi Joseph 94 (fn), 227 (fn), 359
Elyashiv, Rabbi Yosef Shalom 403, 498, 518, 614 (illus.)
  call to Rabbi Sherer in hospital 615
emes and echad 355
employment discrimination 397
employment quotas 477
employment, switching 582 (fn)
employee's spouses, concern for 238
employees, Sabbath legislation 43
emunah that a disaster is really great berachah 46
Encyclopedia Judaica 287 (fn)
end-of-life issue 209, 369, 491-2
  medical treatment 496
English, Richard D. 507
Ephraim and Menashe 586
Epstein, Rabbi Zelik 23, 450 (illus.), 628 (illus.)
"Equal Access" legislation 485
Equal Opportunity Employment Commission 627
Equal Rights Amendment 484

Eretz Yisrael 246
  Agudah activities in 131
  building of Torah life in 130
  Rabbi Sherer's passionate love for 541
  requests to grandchildren learning in 589
Erev Yom Kippur 238, 239
Erlanger, Rabbi Ezriel 622 (fn)
Erps, Mordechai 533 (illus.)
Eruchin 596
"es past nisht" 40
escape of "Talmud lehrer" 604
ESEA programs 479
Eshkol, Prime Minister Levi 553
esrogim, importation of 369, 382-3
Essas, Rabbi Eliyahu 524, 526 (illus.)
Establishment Clause 311, 420, 460 (fn)
  and beginning of life 459 (fn)
  and school vouchers 478 (fn)
eternal matters, dedicate one's life to 643
ethical standards 193
eulogies, summaries of the 635 (fn)
euthanasia 211, , 409, 484
executive director of Zeirei Agudath Israel 92
  resignation by Rabbi Sherer 108
Executive Order 50 397, 400, 461
Executive Order 1 397
eyes, closed during Shema 174
eyes, one and two 350 (fn)
Ezer Associates 316

F

Faber, Peter 196 (illus.)
face of the generation resembling face of a dog 60
Fair Housing Act 464
Faivelson, Rabbi Shmuel Avigdor 216 (illus.)
falling as prelude to salvation 46
false rumors 263
familial consent for autopsies 553
Hadassah Women's organization 553
family values 599 (fn)
Far Rockaway 113
Farbstein, Congressman Leonard 304
farginning others 581
farsholtenne land 101
father's table, children driven from 542
favors, for people who lack gratitude 583 (fn)
federal aid to Jewish parochial schools 163, 311
Federal Education Act 167

Federation of Jewish Philanthropies   138, 272, 299
   oppose federal aid to Jewish education   165
Feigelstock, Rabbi Yitzchak   129, 208, 215, 216 (*illus.*), 245 (*illus.*), 510, 570
Feinberg, Sam   152
Feinstein, Rabbi Dovid   118, 456, 628 (*illus.*), 634 (*illus.*)
Feinstein, Faye   117 (*illus.*)
Feinstein, Rabbi Michel   117 (*illus.*)
Feinstein, Rabbi Moshe   85, 118, 139, 140, 148, 193, 200, 206 (*fn*), 212, 292, 322, 357, 378, 380, 396, 402, 443, 448, 456, 492 (*fn*), 520, 579
   (*illus.*) 51, 86, 117, 137, 190, 206, 213, 235, 292, 322, 394, 504, 548, 575, 576, 581, 601
   and moment of death   493
   and religious exemption clause   493
   letter to Samuel Halperin   442 (*illus.*)
   Syrian Jews exposed to   181
Feinstein, Rabbi Reuven   117 (*illus.*), 628 (*illus.*), 634 (*illus.*)
Feinstein, Rabbi Yonah   638 (*illus.*)
Feith, Douglas   438
Feitman, Rabbi Yaakov   29, 573, 573 (*fn*)
Feldafing DP camp   101 (*illus.*)
Felder, Rabbi Aharon   51 (*illus.*), 576 (*illus.*)
Feldman, Rabbi Aharon   68 (*fn*)
Feldman, Eli   435
Feldman, Rabbi Emanuel   80
Feldman, Yossi   194
Felt Forum   364
feminism, Torah response to   620
Ferber, Rabbi Yosef   218 (*illus.*)
Ferndale, New York   105
fetal life   459 (*fn*)
Feuer, Rabbi Avrohom Chaim   235, 628 (*illus.*)
final illness   611ff
final visit to the *Kosel*   542
Finger, Prof. Seymour Maxwell   550
Fink, Rabbi Anshel   51, 51 (*illus.*), 52 (*illus.*)
   friendship with Rav Schorr   51
Fink, Rabbi Yoel   51
Finkel, Rabbi Nosson Tzvi   68
Finkelman, Rabbi Shimon   162 (*fn*)
Finkelstein, Dr. Louis   138
First Amendment
   free exercise clause   469
   jurisprudence, expert in   460
First National Bank and Trust Company of Ellenville   150

Fisch, Isidor   67
Fischer, Rabbi Elya   215, 216 (*illus.*)
Fischmann, Emil   67
Fishman, Jeff   196 (*illus.*)
Fishman, Marty   196 (*illus.*)
Fishman, Rabbi Yehoshua   168
Fishoff, Benzion   331, 575 (*illus.*), 222, 224, 229, 243, 244, 358, 509
   as emissary to Bobover Rebbes   242
   as "*Malach HaShalom*" (Angel of Peace)   242
5 Beekman Street   133, 226, 231, 257, 215, 320, 456, 502, 573
Flatbush, senior citizens' center   426
fleshele (bottle) of medicine   46
food and clothing distributed to DP camps   100
Food for Jerusalem campaign   132
food packages   94
Food Service and Inspection Service (FSIS)   473
Ford Foundation   158, 432
Ford, President Gerald   274, 376, 377 (*illus.*)
forgotten matters, remembering   49
Fort Kilmer   149
Fort Oswego   99
Fortman, Debby (Devorah)   113
Fortman, Evelyn   122
Fortman, Henya Roshka   121
Fortman, Rabbi Shimshon Zelig   59 (*illus.*), 110, 113, 117 (*illus.*), 118 (*illus.*), 124 (*illus.*), 347 (*fn*), 585
   a *Kohen*   121
   a living link to old world   123
   learned English   121
Fortman, Rabbi Yisroel Tanchum   118, 120 (*illus.*)
Fortman, Rebbetzin   110
Forward (publication)   30
Four Cups   123
4-D draft deferment   554
Four Species, waving of   582 (*fn*)
Fourteenth Avenue Agudah *minyan*   47, 231, 237, 616, 642
Fourth Knessiah Gedolah   133
Fox, Dr. Marvin   446
Frankel, Max   275
Frankel, Rabbi Shabse   124 (*illus.*)
Frankel-Teomim, Rabbi Baruch   537
Franklin, Benjamin   33
fraud, protecting Jews from   483
Free Exercise Clause   460 (*fn*)
Freedman, Rabbi E.B.   563 (*illus.*)
Freedom National Bank in Harlem   278

Freshwater, Benzion   513 (fn)
Freshwater, Shlomo   513 (fn)
Fried, Rabbi Aharon   332
Fried, Frank, Jacobson, and
  Kampelman   188, 437
Friedenson, Mr. Yosef   112, 146 (fn),
  187 (fn), 216 (illus.), 226, 235 (illus.),
  291 (fn), 329-30, 335 (fn), 357,
  339, 358, 363
Friedman, David   573
Friedman, Mordechai   32, 32 (fn),
  186 (fn), 302 (fn), 572
    (illus.) 222, 229, 233, 243, 244, 245
Friedman, Rabbi Moshe
  (Murray)   287 (fn)
Friedman, Rabbi Shlomo   563 (illus.)
Friedman, Wolf (Volvie)   151, 225, 227,
  567, 573, 642
    (illus.) 224, 568, 581
    Wolf Friedman "Young Leadership"
      Award   626 (fn)
Frischman, Rabbi Meir   185, 188, 237,
  243 (illus.), 289 (fn), 573, 638 (illus.)
From Ashes to Renewal   103 (fn), 603,
  605 (illus.)
Fruchthandler, Avrohom   138, 386
Fryshman, Prof. Bernard   427, 482
FSU, humanitarian aid to   480-481
funeral   632ff

G

G and Sons   434
Galei Sanz Hotel   569
Galinsky, Chavie (Langer)   110 (fn),
  333, 348 (fn), 578 (illus.), 587,
  584, 592
Galinsky, Leah (Senft)   586 (illus.)
Gates of Tears   196
Gateshead   621 (illus.)
  Rosh Yeshivah   200
"gavra d'mistafina minai"   329
"gay rights" legislation   400, 484
  see also same-gender
    "marriages"/unions
gedolei Torah, advice of   199
  authority and dependability
    of the   199
  fealty to   359, 636
Geffen, Mr.   227 (illus.)
gelechter   158
Gelernter, Fishel   355
Gelley, Rabbi Zecharia   628 (illus.)
Gellman, Rabbi Aryeh Leib   94
Genuine Electric   108
Genuth, Sol   196 (illus.)
Georgetown Law Center   466

Gerrer Rebbe   55, 69 (illus.), 217,
  242 (illus.), 555 (illus.)
  Benzion Fishoff, emissary to   242
  visit to U.S.A.   639
    see also Werdiger, Shlomo
Gertzulin, Rabbi Shlomo   197, 205,
  205 (fn), 237, 338, 343, 622
    (illus.) 338, 609, 614
  father of   616
get law   167, 369
  and Catholic Church   457
  and Gov. Cuomo   458 (illus.)
  constitutionality of   457
  first New York State   455
  second, in 1992   402
get me'usah (a coerced get)   403
Gewirtz, Rabbi Seymour
  (Abba Zalka)   293 (fn)
Gifter, Rabbi Mordechai   135, 141, 177, 189,
  189 (fn), 364, 373, 378, 448, 451, 603, 604 (fn)
    (illus.) 198, 450, 589
  and The Jewish Observer   359
Gigenti, Richard   406
Gilman, Neil   378
Ginsberg, Rabbi Elazar Yonah   450 (illus.)
Ginzberg, Rabbi Aryeh Zev   489
Giuliani, Mayor Rudolph   251, 284 (fn),
  285 (fn), 414, 539, 599, 602, 618, 635
    (illus.) 244, 633
  Rabbi Sherer delivered the invocation
    at inaugural of   258
  thanking Rabbi Sherer for his
    invocation   259 (illus.)
giur k'halachah   362
Gizunterman, Dr. Leonid   428
Glenwild Hotel   364
Glick, Louis   56, 642 (fn)
Glick, Shimon   642 (fn)
Glickman, Dan   474
Glueck, Louis (Leuchu)   230, 240, 243, 255,
  425, 433, 514, 600
    (illus.) 233, 241, 244, 303, 433, 434, 437
Glueck, Dr. Nelson   138
Goettel, Gerard L.   464
going national   103
golah and ge'ulah   352
Gold, Dore   536 (fn)
Goldberg, Arthur J.   138
  Goldberg Commission   550
Goldberg, Rabbi Mendel   524
Goldberg, Pinchas   229 (illus.)
Golden, Howard   286, 315
Golden, Martha   324
Goldenberg, Rabbi Bernard   57 (fn)
Golding, Rabbi Yosef Chaim   186 (fn),
  340 (fn), 342, 363
    (illus.) 154, 330

Goldman, Dr. Nachum   165, 422
Goldman, Ralph   506
Goldschmidt, Elky (Sherer)   574 (*illus.*), 581 (*fn*), 600, 639
Goldschmidt, Leba   590
Goldschmidt, Moshe Yaakov (Robert)   27, 387 (*fn*), 577 (*fn*), 590, 595 (*fn*) (*illus.*) 574, 575, 591, 638
  and Elky   21
Goldschmidt, Shragie   591 (*fn*), 592, 587, 588, 616
  (*illus.*) 588, 589, 638, 638
Goldschmidt, S'Rivky (Leshkowitz)   592
Goldschmidt, Suri   587, 591
Goldstein, Rabbi Herbert   124 (*illus.*), 132
Goldstein, Rabbi Tuvia   60 (*fn*)
good deed, pain from doing   263
"good enough is not good enough"   335
Goodman, Rabbi Yosef   357 (*fn*)
Gorbachev, Mikhail   525
Gore Jr., Vice President Albert   539, 622, 626, 626 (*illus.*)
Gorelick, Rabbi Yerucham   291
Gorenstein, Dr.   529 (*illus.*)
goses
  (someone whose death is imminent)   492
Government Affairs   337
government interference in religion   298
government programs   188, 426
Graham, Rev. Billy   546 (*fn*)
grammen, at family simchos   575
grandchildren, shidduch suggestions   587
grandfather, doting   585
grassroots organization   223
gratitude, people's lack of   583 (*fn*)
grave of Rabbi Moshe Sherer (*illus.*)   26
grave of the Noda B'Yehudah   287
graves, Jewish, preservation of   242
  see also cemeteries
Great Society Program   157, 442
Green, Assistant Secretary of Labor Ernest   288
Greenwald, Rabbi Ronald   610
greeting, Reb Elchonon Wasserman, first to offer   58
Gribetz, Judah   266, 316, 321, 322, 439
Griffel, Dr. Jacob   97
Grodzensky, Rav Chaim Ozer   55
Gromyko, Andre   525
Gross, Chaim   244 (*illus.*), 291 (*illus.*)
Gross, Reuben   179 (*fn*)
Gross, Rabbi Shlomo Yaakov   555 (*illus.*)
Grossberger, Mrs. Ernest   504 (*fn*)
Grossman, Rabbi Dovid   626 (*fn*)
Grossman, Max   576 (*illus.*)
Grossman, Miriam   615

Grozovsky, Rabbi Chaim   450 (*illus.*)
Grozovsky, Rabbi Reuven   84, 109, 206 (*fn*), 624
Gruenbaum, Rabbi Shlomo   576 (*illus.*)
Grunblatt, David   472 (*fn*)
Grusgot, Shlomo   513
Gruss, Rabbi Mechel   509, 509 (*illus.*), 511, 513 (*fn*), 514
Guertzenstein, Mr.   534
Gulf War   547
Gurwicz, Rabbi Aryeh Leib   200
"*Gut Morgen*," said by Reb Elchonon Wasserman   58
Gut Shabbos   642 (*fn*)
Guttentag, Nathan   529 (*illus.*)
Gutwirth, Yisroel   528 (*illus.*), 533 (*illus.*)

H

Haber, Samuel   405
Hachnasas Sefer Torah   591 (*illus.*), 593 (*illus.*)
Hadassah Hospital, Jerusalem 612-3
  and autopsies   305
  anti-autopsy poster   305 (*illus.*)
HaDoar (periodical)   140
Hadran   367
Hafez al-Assad, Syrian dictator   295
hakaras hatov (trait of gratitude)   582
Hakhel gathering   365
Halabi community   180
Halberstam, Rabbi Naftali Tzvi   539, 628 (*illus.*), 637
Halberstam, Rabbi Shmuel Dovid   636
Hallel HaGadol, name   193
Halperin, Samuel   314 (*fn*), 441, 444-5
  letter from Rabbi Moshe Feinstein   442 (*illus.*)
  letter to Rabbi Labkovsky   443 (*illus.*)
Halpern, Avrohom   222 (*illus.*), 244 (*illus.*)
Halpern, Murray   67
Halpert, Rabbi Aharon   638 (*illus.*)
Halpert, Rabbi Shmelke   555 (*illus.*)
Hammer, Education Minister Zevulun   143, 271
Hamodia (newspaper)   44, 142, 261 (*fn*), 279, 546
  see also Lichtenstein, Mrs. Ruth
handbook for all future *askanim*   26
Handelsman, Ira   196 (*illus.*)
hands, lifting up   631
handwritten congratulations   334
  notes of recognition   236 (*illus.*)
Haness, R' Yitzchak Baal   501
Harari-Raful
  brothers, release of   395
  Chacham Avraham   385, 388

Chacham Yosef   179, 181 (*fn*), 215, 216 (*illus.*), 234, 295, 380 (*fn*), 385, 388, 510
   addressing the Ninth *Siyum HaShas* of *Daf Yomi*   180 (*illus.*)
Harman, Israeli Ambassador to the United States Avraham   304
HASC (Hebrew Academy for Special Children)   278
Hashem's will — nothing is *gelechter*   158
Hatch, Sen. Orrin   469 (*fn*)
Hatikva   107
hatzalah work   503
Hatzalah   619, 620 (*fn*)
   Crown Heights riot   406
Hausman, Nathan   104 (*illus.*)
healing of body and forgiveness of sins   618
health care proxy   210, 496
   and Rabbi Moshe Tendler   497
   and RCA   497
Heath, Tom   323
heavenly angels, description of in blessings of *Shema*   246
Hebrew Academy for Special Children (HASC)   278
Hebrew Immigrant Aid Society *see* HIAS
Hebrew Theological College (Skokie Yeshiva)   502 (*fn*)
Hebrew University   306
Heichal Shlomo   353
heiliger Rizhiner   49 (*fn*)
Heiman, Rabbi Shlomo   54 (*fn*), 59, 59 (*illus.*)
Heinemann, Rabbi Moshe   450 (*illus.*), 474
Hellenizers and Chashmonaim   352
Helsinki Human Rights Watch   518 (*fn*)
Hendeles, Rabbi Binyomin Zev   124 (*illus.*)
Hentoff, Nat   457
Hertz, Barry   335 (*illus.*)
Hertz, Chaim   224 (*illus.*), 568 (*illus.*)
Hertz, Dov   509 (*illus.*)
Heschel, Rabbi Sysche   177
Hess, John   191
heterodox movements, dangers of   141, 359, 368, 562
Hettleman, Julius   67
HIAS (Hebrew Immigrant Aid Society)   149, 370-1 (*fn*), 506
Hill, Robert   534
Hinckley, Gordon   307
Hirsch, Avraham   558
Hirsch, Joseph   67
Hirsch, Naftoli   431 (*fn*), 433, 440
Hirsch, Rabbi Samson Raphael   78, 107

Hirschberg, Manfred   67
Hodgkin's disease   570
Hoenlein, Malcolm   276 (*illus.*), 276
Holland, Dr. Jeffrey   306
Hollander, Rabbi David B.   121 (*fn*), 135 (*fn*)
Hollander, Edward (Ted), and yeshivah accreditation   446
Hollander, Rebbetzin Fay   121 (*fn*)
Holocaust   285 ff
   apathy of American Jewry during the   352
   cheapening of   286
   restitution   277
homiletics class   121, 232, 347ff
Horowitz, Rabbi Eliezer   47, 560 (*fn*), 635
Horowitz, Richard   563
Horowitz, Rabbi Yaakov   331 (*fn*), 336
hostages, 390 ff
   release of   393
House Armed Forces Committee   370, 374
House Committee on Foreign Affairs   295, 315 (*fn*), 508, 536
House Committee on Ways and Means   279, 302
House Education and Labor Subcommittee   158
House Education Committee   341
House of Representatives   225
housing for the elderly   189
Hatov V'HaMeitiv, on the gift of Rabbi Sherer's 50 years of service   636
Huberfeld, Murray   642
HUD *see* Department of Housing and Urban Development
Hungarian Rescue Campaign   148
Hungarian Revolution   147-9, 155
Hutner, Rabbi Yitzchak   110 (*fn*), 139, 187 (*fn*), 200, 313, 354, 378, 384, 386, 394, 425 (*illus.*) 201, 354, 386-7, 394, 548, 559
   hijacking, hostage in Jordan   369, 384
   letters to Rabbi Sherer   208, 210 (*illus.*), 220, 312 (*illus.*)
Hutner, Rebbetzin   384, 389

I

"I tried and did not find"   424
I-20 student visas   502
"*iber a yahr* — Next year, again"   616
IBM and COPE Institute   429
ideology and action   196
ideology of *daas Torah*   197ff
Iggeres HaRamban   61 (*fn*)
Igla, Rev. Salomon   85 (*illus.*)
ikvesa d'Meshicha   63
image of Torah Jewry   183

Immigration and Naturalization Service
   (INS)   290, 472, 505
immigration issues   96
   Immigration Act   472
   quotas lifted for Hungarian Jews   149
Imrei Emes of Ger   130, 207 (fn), 545
independent Orthodoxy   419 ff
Inter-Faith Committee on
   Selective Service Exemption
   of Seminarians   372, 377
interfaith dialogue, opposition to   280
intermarriage   142
Internal Revenue Service   288 (fn)
International Committee of the Red Cross
   (ICRC)   388, 390, 503
intimations of mortality   597-599
Iran
   helping Jews flee   295
   rescue work   241
   school girls smuggled
      to Kurdistan   511
Iran-contra scandal   508
Iranian Rescue Committee   508-513
Iranian Jewry   501
   and Turkey   508
   political asylum applications
      by   507 (fn)
Iranian Revolutionary Guard   505
Iranian Task Force   505 (fn)
Iraq war   297
Iraq-Iran War   505
Irbid (northern Jordan)   394
Iron Curtain, food distributed to Jews
   behind   100
Irvington Hotel   288
"ish matzliach," making others
   successful   344
Islamic Revolution   503, 505
"isms"   351
Israel
   Agriculture Department   383
   aid to   312
   Israeli Chief Rabbinate   353
   Education Law   133
   Israeli Law of Return   560
   last trip to   560
   Ministry of Agriculture,
      inspection of esrogim   384
   security needs   161, 321, 356
Israeli Agudah movement   133
   divisions within   556-558
   relations with   554
Israel, Rabbi Chaim   439 (illus.)

J

Jablon, Douglas   597 (fn)
Jackson-Vanik amendment   518 (fn)

Jacobovits, Michoel   513
Jacobowitz, Dr. Israel   597 (fn)
Jacobs, Arthur   405
Jacobs, Mrs. Debby   58, 185, 275, 331,
   336, 337, 340, 341, 619
Jacobson, Rabbi Binyamin Zeev   569 (fn)
Jacobson, Gaynor   506
Jacobson, Rabbi Moshe   569
Jacobson, Tzvi   569 (fn), 611,
   611 (illus.), 616
Jakobovits, Chief Rabbi Immanuel   388, 498
Jakobovits, Dr. Yoel   498
Javits, Sen. Jacob   158, 251, 286, 290,
   314 (fn), 315 (fn), 320, 341, 383, 395, 436,
   441, 448, 546 (fn), 553, 574, 590
   (illus.) 159, 287, 377, 574
   telegram to Rabbi Sherer about
      Dept. of Agriculture   373 (illus.)
jealousy, being spared from   582
JEP (Jewish Educational Project)   363
Jeret, Dr. Joseph S.   492
Jericho   174
Jerusalem bus stops, bombings of   362
Jerusalem City Council   558
Jerusalem Post   362
Jerusalem, food to besieged   132
Jewish Agency   549
   loyalty test   552
Jewish common interests   356
Jewish Community Relations Council
   (JCRC), Agudah membership in   212
Jewish cries   75
Jewish Defense League   289, 431, 516
Jewish Education Program (JEP)   330 (illus.)
Jewish education, opposition to federal
   aid for   165
Jewish establishment   273
Jewish graves, see cemeteries
Jewish history, knowledge of   584
   and world events   585 (illus.)
Jewish Home and Hospital for the
   Aged   299
Jewish Observer, The   138, 141, 163, 202,
   310, 366, 460, 492 (fn), 498
   birth of   169, 359
   December 1968   352 (fn)
   February-March 1977   165
   February 1987   483
   January 1965   164
   January 1987   514
   January 2007   489
   March 1985   397 (fn)
   May 1984   491
   May 1992   175
   mission statement   359
   November 1966   163

Index   ☐   659

November 1995   464 (fn)
November 1998   296 (fn)
October 1963   311
October 1965   544 (fn)
October 1991   498
September 1965   165
September 1973   311, 420, 421
September 1990   496 (fn), 497 (fn)
September 1993   192, 402 (fn)
spoke for diverse groups within Torah Jewry   361
Summer 1991   497 (fn)
Summer 1997   194 (fn), 195 (fn), 196 (fn)
Summer 1998   162, 167, 183, 184 (fn), 185 (fn), 195 (fn), 196 (fn), 197, 202 (fn), 205 (fn), 231 (fn), 235, 236 (fn), 239 (fn), 252, 258, 270 (fn), 282, 313 (fn), 331 (fn), 344 (fn), 425, 613 (fn)
Jewish Paradox   422
Jewish people compared to a "teabag"   270
Jewish Pocketbook Series   227 (fn)
Jewish Press, The (newspaper)   319, 379 (fn), 409, 517
and "*get* law"   404
Jewish religious workers   472
Jewish Servicemen's Bureau   99
Jewish Telegraph Agency (JTA)   274, 354
Jewish Theological Seminary   370, 378, 549
Jewish *yishuv*   545
Jewry, united under the banner of the Torah   500
Jews
   alleviating problems of   194
   crying out   129
   livelihood of   194
Jniv cemetery   539
Job Corps   288
Joffen, Rabbi Avraham   84
Johnson, President Lyndon B.   166 (*illus.*), 425
   and education act   163
   and Great Society   157
Joint Boycott Council   94
Joint Commission on Public Affairs (Baptist)   372
Joint Distribution Committee (JDC)   370 (fn), 506
Joint Chiefs of Staff   274
Jordan, hostage crisis   384ff, 388 (fn)
Joshua (Yehoshua) and angel   174
Judaism, "wings" of   356
   see also Synagogue Council

judging people   582 (fn)
Justice Department   464

K

Kahan, Rabbi Dov   529 (*illus.*), 531-533 (*illus.*)
Kahaneman, Rabbi Yosef Shlomo   115, 123
Kalisz, Poland   282
Kalmanowitz, Rabbi Shraga Moshe   378, 576 (*illus.*)
Kamelhar, Saul   626 (fn)
Kamenetsky, Rabbi Binyamin   71
Kamenetsky, Sam   67
Kamenetsky, Rabbi Binyamin   71 (fn)
Kamenetsky, Rabbi Shmuel   71, 293, 626, 636, 641
   (*illus.*) 216, 628
Kamenetsky, Rabbi Yaakov   23, 71, 126, 139, 176, 203, 206 (fn), 212, 219, 340, 354, 378, 393, 430, 456, 503, 519, 559, 607 (*illus.*) 111, 137, 190, 201, 204, 205, 213, 218, 219, 354, 521, 548, 581
   regarding *pikuach nefesh* and *chillul Hashem*   209
Kamin, Rabbi Dovid   110 (fn)
Kamin, Rabbi Ephraim   110 (fn)
Kaminetsky, Dr. Joseph   211 (fn)
Kantor, Rabbi Yosef Meir   450 (*illus.*)
Kaplan, Rabbi Mendel   60 (fn)
Kaplan, Rabbi Yisrael Chaim   84
Karlin-Stolin   41, 44, 538
Karp, Rabbi Elias   243 (*illus.*), 617
Kasheh Preidasicha Aleinu   641
Kashrus Magazine   366
Kasnett, Rabbi Nesanel   184, 184 (fn), 344, 344 (fn), 466
Katsover, Yisrael   545
Kattowicz   39, 175-8, 229 (fn), 361, 500
Katz family in New Orleans   145
Katz, Joseph   409
Katz, Prof. Larry   231, 448
Katz, Mordechai   84, 363
Katz, Rabbi Mordechai   84
Katz, Rabbi Nechemia   117 (*illus.*)
Katz, Yitzchok   117 (*illus.*)
Katzenstein, Rabbi Yitzchok   425
Kaufman, Rabbi Simcha   177, 607
"*Kavata itim l'Torah?*"   199, 584
Kean, Gov. Thomas   263, 337 (*illus.*)
   and religious exemption clause   494
Keap Street, early residence of Sherer family   41
Keeler, William Cardinal 470
Keller, Rabbi Chaim Dov   570 (fn)
Kellman, Wolfe   67

Kennedy, Sen. Edward (Ted)   184 (*fn*),
    266, 294, 373, 378, 469 (*fn*), 474, 524
    (*illus.*) 337, 473
Kennedy, Jackie   255
Kennedy, President John F.   161, 251,
    546 (*fn*)
Kennedy, Sen. Robert F.   266, 267 (*illus.*)
    letter to Rabbi Sherer   164 (*illus.*)
Keren Ha'Shvi'is   542
Keren Nesivos Moshe   642
Kerzner, Rabbi Yitzchok   347, 576 (*illus.*)
Kestenbaum, Rabbi Zvi   537 (*fn*)
Kever Rachel   613
Khaled, Leila   385 (*fn*), 393 (*fn*)
Khaver, Rabbi Reuven   501 (*illus.*), 502,
    508, 510
Khiss, Peter   437
Khomeini, Ayatollah Rubollah   503
Kibbutz Choftez Chaim   542
Kiddush Hashem   185, 193, 240, 460, 485
Kiev   539
King Hussein of Jordan   384, 388 (*fn*)
King, Rodney   413
"kings" at children's wedding   575
Kirkpatrick, Ambassador Jean   264
kiruv work   503
Kiryas Yoel   462
Kirzner, Prof. Yisroel Meir   448
Kishinev, shul in   537 (*fn*)
kissing in a *beis medrash*   51
Kissinger, Henry   481, 516, 520, 524, 580
klal work   223, 231
    not a burden   96
    priorities in   482
    reward for   95
    three rules of   313
Klal Yisrael   195
    and "Reb Yisrael"   18
    contributing to   231
    duty of every Jew to   107
    Klal Avraham, Klal Yitzchak,
       Klal Yaakov, not called   586
    preserving unity within,   71
    yeshivah *bachurim* responsibility
       to   177
Klass, Rabbi Sholom   319
    and "*get* law"   404
Klausenberger Rebbe   422, 628 (*illus.*),
    630, 634 (*illus.*)
Klavan, Rabbi Hillel   67, 71
Klavan, Rabbi Yehoshua   70 (*illus.*), 71
Klein, Abbie Gordon   468, 468 (*fn*)
Klein, Avraham Noach   606 (*fn*)
Klein, Ephraim (Frank)   224 (*illus.*), 606 (*fn*)
Klein, George   212, 274, 618
    (*illus.*) 233, 618, 633

Klein, Mrs. Miriam   606 (*fn*)
Kleinman, Rabbi Yaakov   122
Kliers, Rabbi Moshe   544 (*illus.*)
Kline, Oscar   67
Klugman, Rabbi Eliyahu Meir   183 (*fn*),
    185 (*fn*), 186 (*fn*), 196 (*fn*), 313 (*fn*)
Klugman, Julius   185, 426
Kneller, John   298
Knesset list, placement on   557
Knessiah Gedolah   50, 129, 133,
    363, 423, 523
    Second   50
Koch, Mayor Ed   255 (*illus.*), 265, 266,
    280, 397-8, 400, 434 (*illus.*), 435, 461
Kochen, Madeline   457
kol korei   355
Kollek, Jerusalem Mayor Teddy   306-7
Kolodny, Rabbi Moshe   27
Komarek, Thomas   288
Konigsberg, Jacob   67
Konstam, Rabbi Paysach   434 (*illus.*)
Koppel, Ted   341
Kopyczinitzer Rebbe   228 (*illus.*), 228
Kosel (the Western Wall)
    final visit to   543 (*illus.*)
    first visit to   542 (*illus.*)
    recapture of the   541
kosher food
    for Jewish prisoners   299, 471
    on airplanes   346 (*fn*)
kosher meat production,
    legislation affecting   474
Koslowitz, Rabbi Nota   371 (*fn*)
Kotler, Rabbi Aharon   11, 49, 84, 109, 110,
    112, 133, 134, 135, 152, 158, 161, 199, 202,
    206 (*fn*), 368, 423, 482, 549, 609 (*fn*), 615
    (*fn*), 637
    (*illus.*) 57, 111, 127, 137, 205, 483, 623
    an "*emese* Agudist"   126
    and young Shimshie   127f
    at 1961 *Siyum HaShas*   364
    pictures of   58
    sandek for   40
    took Rabbi Sherer under
       his wing   126
Kotler, Rabbi Malkiel   226 (*illus.*),
    628 (*illus.*), 637
Kotler, Rabbi Shneur   19, 61, 110 (*fn*), 217,
    288, 375, 378, 575, 590 (*fn*), 637
    (*illus.*) 62, 213, 224, 522, 576,
Kotler, Rebbetzin   152
Kotzker Rebbe   141, 339 (*fn*), 355
Kovno Rov   570 (*fn*)
Kowalsky, Rabbi Sholom   67-68, 70 (*illus.*),
    72, 77, 79
Kramer, Rabbi Joel   309

Index   □   661

Kranzler, Dr. David   41 (fn), 44, 47, 50
Kranzler, Gershon   82, 227 (fn)
   missive to   82 (illus.)
Kraus, Rabbi Yaakov   51
Krauss, Samson   67
Krawiecz, Louis   439 (illus.)
Kreisler, Seymour   67
Kreistman, Norman   67
Kreiswirth, Rabbi Chaim   619, 621 (illus.)
Krias HaTorah, always stood for   47
Krias Shema,
   blessings of   69 (fn)
   closing eyes during   174
Krieger, Richard   507
Krieger, Shmuel   433
Krohn, Rabbi Avrohom Zelig
   (Abraham)   67, 70 (illus.), 71
Krohn, Ben Zion   67
Krohn, Rabbi Paysach   71, 244 (illus.), 245 (illus.)
Krohn, Philip   67
Krupenia, Rabbi Levi   628 (illus.)
Kuchman, Leonid   539
Kugielsky, Dr. Raphael   528
Kugielsky, Dr. Yerachmiel   528 (illus.), 529 (illus.)
Kurland, Jacob   67
Kviat, Rabbi Dovid   71 (fn)
Kwestel, Shimon   43 (illus.), 224 (illus.)

L

l'chaim of Shragie Goldschmidt and S'Rivky Leshkowitz   592 (illus.)
La Prensa   527
Labkovsky, Rabbi Shmuel Yosef   67, 68 (fn), 71, 375, 376, 380, 442
   letter for Samuel Halperin   443 (illus.)
Labor Department   289
Lachman, Dr. Seymour   240, 269, 291, 282, 298 (illus.), 300, 317, 319 (illus.), 431, 448
Laizerson, Rabbi
   Avrohom Yosef   233 (illus.)
Lakewood   192, 288-9
   see also Beth Medrash Govoha
Lakewood Cheder School   462
Lamet, Rabbi Meir   617
Lamm, Rabbi Norman   140, 319
Lamport Brothers   225
Landau, David, JTA's Israel correspondent   191, 275
Landau, Rabbi Yechezkel   287 (fn)
Landau, Rabbi Yisrael Yonah   71 (fn)
Landynski, Professor Jacob   448
Langer, Rabbi Daniel   236, 243 (illus.), 578 (illus.), 588 (illus.), 638 (illus.)

Langer, Rabbi Levi   349 (fn), 593, 637 (illus.) 243, 578, 588, 589, 638
Langer, Pessel Leah   590
Langer, Rochel (Sherer)   577-9, 583-4, 597 (fn), 606, 616
Langer, Rabbi Yehuda   578 (illus.), 588 (illus.), 589 (illus.)
Langer, Yisroel   576 (illus.), 590, 591
   and Rochy   21
Langsam, Rabbi Naftali   135
Lankry, Mrs.   582
last Pesach at home   616ff
Latin American countries,
   Agudists in   170
Lau, Chief Rabbi Yisrael Meir   609 (illus.)
Laventhol, David   275
Law of Return   362
leader, quality of   194
   criticism   61
   popular opinion   594 (fn)
leadership by Torah scholars   107, 197
Lebanon War   556
Labkovsky, Rabbi Shmuel Yosef   67
leadership, not a popularity contest   60
Lebovics, Dr. Irving   196 (illus.), 252, 270 (fn), 616
Lebovics, Rabbi Yaakov   342 (illus.)
Lebovitz, Rabbi Baruch Ber   624
Lebowitz, Rabbi Henoch   450 (illus.)
Lefkowitz, Louis   427 (illus.)
Lefkowitz, Shimon   626 (fn)
Lefkowitz, Rabbi Shmuel   195, 241, 310, 432, 434, 436, 435, 438, 577 (fn) (illus.) 154, 434, 437
Lefkowitz, Rabbi Yisrael   563 (illus.), 614 (illus.), 616
Legislation   43
legislation and *halachah*   402
Leibovitch, Harry   67
Leibovitch, Hyman   67
Leibovitch, Walter   67
Leibowitz, Rabbi Dovid   72
Leibowitz, Hershel   72
Leibtag, Abraham   67
Leiser, Heshy   149
Leiter, David   67
"lemon into lemonade"   577
Lemon v. Kurtzman   419
Lemon v. Nyquist   420
Leningrad   525
Lerner, Rabbi Pesach   609 (illus.), 610, 614 (illus.)
Leshkowitz, Chaim   222 (illus.), 592, 611 (illus.), 614 (illus.)
Leshkowitz, Mrs. Laya   591
Leshkowitz, Sara Rivka (S'Rivky)   592

leukemia 596
levaya 632*ff*
Leventhal, Rabbi Dov 86 (*illus.*)
Levin, Rabbi Avrohom Chaim 215, 373, 570 (*fn*)
  (*illus.*) 216, 373
Levin, Rabbi Eliezer 570 (*fn*)
Levin, Rabbi Itche Meir 131, 217, 219, 545, 556, 643 (*fn*)
  (*illus.*) 130, 218
Levin, Rabbi Pinchos 523 (*illus.*)
Levine, Rabbi Aharon 536 (*fn*), 568
Levine, Rabbi Shmuel Aryeh 530, 530 (*illus.*), 532
"Leviticus (*Vayikra*) is part of the Jewish Bible too" 460
Levitt v. Committee for Public Education 420
Levovitz, Rabbi Pesach 117 (*illus.*)
Levovitz, Rabbi Reuven 117 (*illus.*)
Levovitz, Rabbi Simchah Zissel 84
Levy, State Senator Eugene 494 (*fn*)
Lewan, Michael 253, 256, 257, 281, 537, 538
Lewenstein, Meyer Dovid 517
Lewin, Dr. Isaac 124 (*illus.*), 218 (*illus.*), 455, 536, 568 (*fn*)
Lewin, Nathan 30, 288, 377 (*fn*), 390, 391, 393, 400, 444, 454, 455, 457, 457 (*fn*), 466, 470, 475
Lewis, State Sen. Al 43 (*illus.*)
Lichstein, Dr. Edgar 597
Lichtenstein, Mrs. Ruth 44, 142
  see also Hamodia
Lider, Mrs. Chaya 332 (*fn*), 336 (*fn*), 343
Liebb, Harry 67
Lieber, Herschel 524
Lieberman, Sen. Joseph 184 (*fn*), 253, 334, 568 (*fn*)
  (*illus.*) 184, 244, 264, 335
Liebowitz, Rabbi Hershel 70 (*illus.*)
Lieff, Jacob D. 67
life
  beginning of 459 (*fn*)
  see also brain death; death, time of; end of life; respirator
Liff, Rabbi Abba Yaakov 71
Liff, Albert 67
Lindsay, Mayor John 168, 405
Lipnik
  cemetery 537, 538 (*illus.*)
  mayor of 539
Lipshutz, Rabbi Pinchos 569, 570 (*fn*)
  final advice from Rabbi Sherer 614
  see also Yated Ne'eman
Lipshutz, Rabbi Yaakov 570 (*fn*)
Litvin, Baruch 145

livelihood of Jews 194
Living Will/Health Care Proxy 496-9
lobbyist 195
Lobenstein, Joseph 615
Lodge, John David 527, 528 (*illus.*)
Lodge Jr., Henry Cabot 527
Lodz 229 (*fn*), 536 (*fn*)
London Jewish Tribune (newspaper) 176
long life, merit of 631
longshoremen's strike 293
Lonner, Rabbi Yaakov 439 (*illus.*)
Lorincz, Rabbi Shlomo 132, 143, 153, 176, 179 (*fn*), 183, 185, 200 (*fn*), 204 (*fn*), 517, 544, 547
  (*illus.*) 131, 178, 559
Los Angeles 269
Lott, Trent 184 (*fn*)
Louis Glick 57 (*fn*)
Love, David 405
Lowenthal, Henry 611 (*illus.*)
Lubavitch 481 (*fn*)
  and Crown Heights riot 408 (*fn*)
Lubavitcher Rebbe 266
  motorcade of the 406
Lubinsky, Menachem 167 (*fn*), 183, 200, 201 (*illus.*), 226, 332, 337, 339, 341, 343, 346 (*fn*), 348 (*fn*), 349 (*fn*), 409 (*fn*), 426, 426 (*fn*), 428, 432, 452, 454, 456
Lublin 363
Lubliner Rav 153, 363
Lubling, Mrs. Miriam 601
Lvov, Rebbe Dovid 277
lymphoma 596

M

maalos (virtues), seeing in people 582 (*fn*)
Maariv, Israeli tabloid, threatened with libel suit 274
Machaneh Ephraim 606 (*fn*)
Machon Meir 522
Madison Square Garden 365, 627
  1990 *Siyum HaShas* after start of ArtScroll Talmud 364
Magnichever, Lucien 505 (*fn*)
Maharal 583 (*fn*)
Maharil Diskin 594 (*fn*)
Maimonides Medical Center 243, 255 (*illus.*), 435, 597 (*fn*), 614
mainstream Jewish organization, anti-Semitic view of Chassidic Jews 409
makom kavua (fixed place for prayer), praying in 47 (*fn*), 584
  and not asking a guest to relinquish his seat 47
malachei hashareis and
  malachei hashalom 635

Management Committee of
  Agudath Israel 151, 225, 227
mandated services 490
mandatory AIDS curriculum 302
Mandel, Rabbi Shlomo 177 (fn),
  373 (illus.)
Mandel, Rabbi Shlomo Noach 524
Mandelbaum, Henik and Hatzik 591
Mandelcorn, Samuel P. 67
Mandelkorn, Rabbi Harry 67, 70 (illus.),
Manhattan Center, 1975 Siyum
  HaShas 364
Mann, Theodore 272 (fn)
mantras 143
Markowitz, Shia 509 (illus.), 511, 514
marriage 113ff
Marx, Moshe 642
Maryles, David 52
Mase, Jacob 67
Mashiach, period before 60
maskilim 198
Maslaton, Rabbi Mordechai 502
master of the word 73ff
material inheritance 595
Mattesdorfer Rav 628 (illus.)
matzos to Soviet Jews 262, 515
McCloskey, Robert 390
McCormack, Speaker of the House
  John 158, 160 (illus.), 223, 251
McKeesport, Pennsylvania 82
McManus, Bishop 279
McNary, Gene 472
Meah Shearim neighborhood 362
mechitzah 144, 145
medical crises 596
Medical Ethics Committee 497
medical resources, rationing of 491
medication, spilled 45
Mediterranean fruit fly,
  and importation of esrogim 382
meetings, being fully prepared for 310
Mehl, Boruch 531
Mehlman, Rabbi Mordechai 226 (illus.)
Meir, Prime Minister Golda 392
Meltzer, Rabbi Isser Zalman 119, 152, 590 (fn)
Memorial Foundation 242, 593
memories and dreams 194
Mendelevich, Yosef 519, 520, 522
  (illus.) 521, 522
Mendlowitz, Reb Shraga Feivel 52 (illus.),
  55 (illus.), 56, 57, 64, 69 (fn), 95, 589 (fn)
  regarding tuition 582 (fn)
menorah, golden 352
merger of Agudath Israel and
  Youth Council 108
Merit Scholarship, New York State 405

Mermelstein, Rabbi Jacob 151
Meseches Avodas HaKlal 126
meshugener,
  leaders being referred to as 61
  Rabbi Sherer referred to as 61
Mesilas Yesharim 302
Mesivta Torah Vodaath, Brooklyn, article
  in Dos Yiddishe Tagblatt 53 (illus.)
  see also Yeshiva Torah Vodaath
Mesivta Tifereth Jerusalem, NYC 72,
  308, 442
mesorah (transmitted tradition) through
  gedolei Torah 195
Mesorah, see ArtScroll
Metropolitan Geriatric Center 435
Metropolitan Transport Authority
  (MTA) 283
Meyerhoff, Dr. Gordon 516 (fn)
mezuzah, custom of touching 564 (fn)
mezuzah, kissing on final Israel trip 564
mibesar'cha al tisalam 595
Miami, Florida 235
Michigan Supreme Court 145
Middle East Quarterly, June 1997 488
middos to be displayed privately as
  publicly 569
Milah Board 136
Millenson, Roy 314 (fn), 384, 449
Miller, Assemblyman 493
Miller, Rabbi Israel 540, 550
Miller, Mrs. Rochel 330, 333, 336 (fn)
Milwaukee, Wisconsin 570
minyan,
  always on time for 47
  waiting for tenth man 231
minyanim, private 463
Mirrer Yeshiva 331, 502 (fn)
  kollel in Jerusalem 254
missionary activity in Israel 307 f
  banning of 423
mistakes by leader, 220
mitzvah, reward for unfulfilled 313
Mizrachi 77, 85, 94, 572
  alliances with the Conservative or
    Masorti movement in Israel 143
  dominated Orthodoxy in
    the 1940s 77
  membership dues to 572
Mliniv, Jewish cemetery 538
Modai, Yitzchak 552
Modzitzer Rebbbe 555 (illus.)
Moetzes Gedolei HaTorah 12, 85, 127,
  139, 176, 179, 200, 205, 206, 212, 223,
  283, 306, 308, 343, 363, 402, 493, 496,
  516, 519 (fn), 547, 550, 556, 635
  (illus.) 201, 286, 548

and abortion   459
claims that Rabbi Sherer manipulated   206
criticism of the   202
regarding building a swimming pool   436
regularly scheduled meetings   211
younger roshei yeshivah on   206
Moetzes Gedolei HaTorah of *Eretz Yisrael*, failure to meet   559
Moldovian government   537 (*fn*)
Mollen, Deputy Mayor, Milt   407
Molloy, Monsignor Eugene   168 (*fn*)
Mondale, Vice President Walter   469 (*illus.*)
money, insignificance of   581
Monroe, NY   181
Monsey, NY   235
moral pollution   484
Mordechai, coin minted by   351
Morgado, Robert   324 (*fn*)
Morgen Journal (newspaper)   405
Moriah, Mount (*Midrash*)   173
Mormon Church   306
Moruchnik, Basya Bluma   40
see also Sherer, Mrs. Basya Bluma
Moruchnik, Reb Avrohom Leib   606 (*fn*)
Moruchnik, Morris (pseudonym)   75
Moscow   525
office of Agudath Israel   527 (*illus.*)
Moses, Alfred   273, 469 (*illus.*)
Moshe, name, and *mashuy*   39
Moshe Rabbeinu   96
and Aharon HaKohen, mourning for   594 (*fn*)
eved ne'eman (faithful servant)   17
"veil" of   297
Moskowitz, Dovid   233 (*illus.*)
Moskowitz, Heshy   132
Mount Clemens, Michigan, legal battle over *mechitzah*   145
Mount Kisco   310
Mount Scopus campus of Brigham Young University   306
mountain, edge of the   632
Moynihan, Sen. Daniel Patrick   184 (*fn*), 251, 263, 302 (*illus.*) 264, 303
eulogy by   633 (*illus.*)
m'reim, enemy or friend   60 (*fn*)
MTA and offensive advertising   283
Mudge, Rose   440
Muller, Boruch   506
Munk, Rabbi Michael   93 (*illus.*)
Muskin, Yaakov   67

N

n'ki kapa'im (financial rectitude)   229, 230
Nadler, Jerrold   481
Nassau Coliseum   365, 627
Nasser, President   394
National and Community Service program   473
National Association of Evangelicals   372, 373
National Association of Jewish Theological Seminaries   372
National Council of Churches, and draft exemptions   372
National Council of Jewish Women   459
National Guard and Crown Heights riot   408
National Housing Act   435
National Institute of Health (NIH) anti-abortion policy   306
National Jewish Community Relations Advisory Council (NJCRAC)   459
National Leadership Missions   467
National Religious Party   143
National Right-to-Life Committee   470
Navajo Indians   437
Nazis, comparison to   285
negdah, "presence of" or "against"   61 (*fn*)
Neinkin, Morly   435
"*nekamah far unzer blut*"   604 (*fn*)
Nelson, Lemrick   406, 511-2, 462
Ner Israel, *see* Yeshiva Ner Israel
Nerl, Martin (pseudonym)   75, 76, 77, 107 (*fn*)
Nesius of Agudath Israel   214, 486, 626
meeting of   216 (*illus.*)
role of   215
younger roshei yeshivah added to   215
Netanya   569
Netanyahu, Prime Minister Binyamin   560, 562 (*illus.*), 562
Neturei Karta   275
Neuberger, Rabbi Naftoli   24, 51 (*illus.*), 70 (*illus.*), 78 (*illus.*), 79, 91, 144, 322, 370, 374, 378, 380, 442, 470, 501, 508
Neumann, Yosef   291 (*illus.*)
Neustadt, Rabbi Mordechai   241, 524, 526 (*illus.*), 527 (*illus.*)
New Orleans, legal battle over *mechitzah*   144
New School for Social Research   310, 432
New York Archdiocese   398
New York Blue Law, repeal of   165
New York Board of Rabbis   138, 212
and Gov. Carey   318
psak against   134

New York Board of Regents 240
New York Catholic Conference 256,
　265, 279, 324 (fn), 375, 376 (fn), 470
　　see also Catholic Church, U.S.
　　　Catholic Conference
New York City Board of Education 167
New York City Council Committee
　on Transportation 283
New York City Jewish Federation
　budget allocation 165 (fn)
New York Federation 272
New York Magazine 273 (*illus.*), 284 (fn)
New York Post 191
　article impuning Rabbi Sherer's
　　integrity 189 (fn)
New York State Education
　Department 260, 262
New York State Regents Action Plan 490
New York State Textbook Bill 167-8
New York Times, The 110, 111, 142, 159,
　162 (*illus.*), 188, 191, 264, 275, 398, 408,
　433, 437, 459, 487
　　and SBCO 433
　　and Talmud study 365
Newsday (periodical) 275
Ney, Heinz 67
Nierenberg, Efraim 563 (*illus.*)
Nightline 341
Nimetz, Matthew 272 (fn), 502
ninth grade, compulsory education
　with secular studies 556
92nd Street Y 165 (fn)
Nitra Rav 97
Nitra Yeshiva 310
Nixon, President Richard 386, 369, 546 (fn)
　Rabbi Sherer letter to 393 (*illus.*)
Noach,
　and belief in cause 54
　entered Ark only after rain began 55
Noam Elimelech 582
Noda Bi'Yehudah 71 (fn)
Nolan, Don 265, 293, 308
non-public education
　advisory council 258
　aid to 163, 158ff, 164, 311, 419, 489
notes of recognition,
　handwritten 236 (*illus.*)
Notre Dame University 285
Novohatko-Reicher Act 539 (fn)
Novominsk Yeshiva 473 (fn)
Novominsker Rebbe 33, 208, 454, 456,
　512, 552, 626, 635, 636
　　(*illus.*) 86, 154, 208, 216, 286, 440, 441,
　　　450, 575, 576, 628, 636
N'shei Agudath Israel 132
Nudel, Ida 518 (fn)

Nunn, Sen. Sam 260
Nuremburg War Trials Tribunal 484
Nyquist, Edwald B. (Joe) 263, 323, 446

O

O'Connor, Cardinal John 266, 279,
　280, 281, 282, 284, 325, 470, 602
Odessa 41
Oelbaum, Eli 347
Oelbaum, Rabbi Yehudah 190 (*illus.*)
office "chats" 263
Office of Government Affairs 237
offspring comparison, Orthodox,
　Conservative and Reform 563
oil, contaminated by Greeks 352
Oklahoma City 508
Olshin, Rabbi Yerucham 634 (*illus.*)
omer, counting of 621
"one bird with three wings" 141
157 Rodney Street 48, 62]
113 W. 42nd Street 96
　on-the-job training program 427
　Beame, Mayor Abe 428
open-heart surgery 596, 597
Operation Hostages, memos 396 (*illus.*)
Oppenheimer, Rabb Yosef Tzvi 533 (*illus.*)
Oratorical abilities 57
oratory 183
Oratz, Rabbi Ephraim 335 (fn), 341,
　518, 573 (fn)
Orchos Tzaddikim 302
organ transplants 492, 497ff
Orthodox Jewish Archives 241 (*illus.*)
Orthodox Jews (*see also* ultra-Orthodox)
　federal employees 294
　and the Federation 299 (fn)
　animosity toward 589
　changing perceptions of 467
　independent 360, 419, 425
　new prominence of 274
　participation in the New York
　　Board of Rabbis 201
　represenation in the
　　public sphere 161
　responsibility for negative
　　image of, 193
　scandals in community 189
　servicemen 99
Orthodox lay leader, most influential of
　the second half of the 20th century 31
Orthodox Tribune (periodical) 75, 105,
　106 (*illus.*), 357
Orthodox Union 137, 199, 319, 370,
　481 (fn), 610
Orthodox Youth (periodical) 105, 132, 357
Oslo Accords 562

Ostreicher, Yossi   318 (*illus.*)
Otzar Hatorah   501, 514
Ouziel, Chaim   384
Oysher, Cantor Moishe   53
Ozeiry, Rabbi David   180, 180 (*fn*), 234

P

Packwood, Sen. Robert   263
paid vacation days, and Yom Tov   294
Paler, Rabbi Binyamin   260, 628 (*illus.*)
Palestine   101, 229 (*fn*)
Palestine Liberation Organization
   (PLO)   550
      UN's recognition of   551
Palestinian rioting   562
Pam, Rabbi Avrohom   213, 635, 641
      (*illus.*) 74, 214, 226, 238, 245, 286, 373,
      450, 504
   letter from   619, 620 (*illus.*)
Pan Am   385
parents, watching over children   581
parnassah   194 (*fn*)
parochial school aid   163, *158ff*, 164,
   311, 419, 489
passport, fake Latin American   155
Pataki, Gov. George   251, 633 (*illus.*)
Pattaschnick, Albert   67
Paul, Weiss, Rifkind, Wharton,
   and Garrison   338, 400
Pearl v. Nyquist decision   311
pebbles, bag of   583
Pell Grant scandals   260, 293
Pennsylvania program   419
Perkowski, Rabbi Yisrael   (*illus.*) 628, 634
Perl, Rabbi Avrohom Nissan   243 (*illus.*)
Perlow, Rabbi Yaakov
   see Novominsker Rebbe
Pernikoff, Aaron   67
Perr, Rebbetzin Shonnie   177, 583
Persian Jews   503
Peru   535
Pfeffer, Prof. Leo   160 (*illus.*),
   162 (*illus.*), 460
pharmacy and medication for
   young Moshe   45
Pheterson, Joseph   67
Philadelphia Yeshiva   176, 355, 569,
   580, 589
picketing   354
pidyon sh'vuim   148
Pierce, Samuel   439 (*illus.*)
*Piety and Power: The World of Jewish
   Fundamentalism*   191
pikuach nefesh vs. *chillul Hashem*   309
Pilchik, Rabbi Meir   40 (*fn*)
Pilchik, Rabbi Yisrael   40 (*fn*)

Pioneer Hotel   128
Pirchei Agudath Israel   104, 178 (*fn*), 582 (*fn*)
   Leadership Guide   237
Pirchei groups   50
Pirchei *Melaveh Malkah*   62
Pirkei d'Rebbe Eliezer 30   631 (*fn*)
Pitter, Rabbi Yeruchem   570 (*fn*)
Plagman, Herman   151, 225, 227 (*illus.*), 227
Plant Quarantine Division   382
Polish Sejm   568 (*fn*)
Polish-Hungarian border   98
Pollack, Mendy   409
Pollard, Jonathan, Rabbi Sherer's efforts
      on his behalf   486
   promise to Rabbi Sherer   489
Pollard, Dr. Morris and Molly   486
Ponevezh Yeshiva   357, 530, 556,
Ponevezher Rav   115, 123, 542
poor, children of   68
Pope John Paul II
   encouraged preservation of
      Jewish graves   282
   meeting with Kurt Waldheim   279
   visit to Poland   281
Popular Front for the Liberation of
   Palestine (PFLP)   385, 392
Porush, Rabbi Menachem   94, 132, 183, 354,
   354 (*fn*), 388, 395, 536 (*fn*), 544, 547, 637
   (*illus.*), 130, 131, 555
Porush, Rabbi Moshe   523 (*illus.*)
power of the media   183
Prager, Reb Moshe   604 (*fn*)
Prager, Shmuel   332, 452, 452 (*illus.*),
   456, 491
prayers, none go unanswered   583
praying
   for sustenance   194 (*fn*)
   in *makom kavua*   47 (*fn*), 584
   in room with windows   583
prescription medication, spilled   45
Presidents Conference
   see Conference of Presidents of
      Major Jewish Organizations
press releases, rules for writing and
   submitting   82
Price, Charles   412
Price, Rabbi Dovid   318 (*illus.*)
Prisoner of Zion   208, 524
Privalsky, Rabbi Zelig   (*illus.*) 528, 529
private sectarian schools, value of   315
"pro-choice"   459 (*fn*)
proclamation against UN recognition of
   PLO   551 (*illus.*)
Proffitt, Dr. John   253, 259, 260, 320, 441,
   443, 444, 446, 449
Project COPE   427*ff*

Index   □   667

Project RISE (Russian Immigrants Seniors and Education) 341, 518
Project Y.E.S. (Youth Enrichment Service) 331 (fn), 336
Prospect Park High School 310
protecting his family 574-575
Protestants and draft exemptions 372
Psak din, adherence to 202
psak of eleven roshei yeshivah 133
public aid for parochial schools 163, 158ff, 164, 311, 419, 489
public organ, need for 359
public school 54
public speaking
    eye contact 349
    focus on "the man in the corner" 349
    Rabbi Sherer's rules for 347
    Rabbi Sherer taught grandchildren 588
    3 B's of 348
public transportation, lewd advertisements on 484
Puerto Rican gangs 431-3
Pugsley, Ron 445, 449
Purim *seudah* 600

Q

Quayle, Vice President Dan 467
quotas, racial, impact on Jewish employee 477

R

R' Yehudah, main speaker 348
Raab, David 386 (fn)
Rabban Shimon ben Gamliel 368
Rabbi Jacob Joseph Mesivta 110 (fn)
Rabbi Moshe Sherer National Headquarters 642
Rabbinical Assembly 139
Rabbinical Council of America (RCA) 137, 139, 370, 375
    and synagogue council 134
    and "*get* law" 404
    and health care proxy 497
    Va'ad Halachah Commission, and brain death 499
rabbis,
    most powerful in New York 273 (*illus.*)
Rabin, Israeli Prime Minister Yitzchak 320, 321, 392, 396, 545
    offer of political support to 545
Rabinowitz, Rabbi Mordechai 72
Rachel Imeinu crying 344 (fn)
Rachmastrivka Rebbe 628 (*illus.*)
Radomsk Yeshiva 229 (fn)
Raful, *see* Harari-Raful

rainbow, as metaphor in speech 74
Raiz, Zev and Carmela 517 (*illus.*)
Rajchenbach, Yaakov 222 (*illus.*)
Rakow, Rabbi Betzalel 621 (*illus.*)
Ramapo Township 463
Ramaz 182
Rangel, Representative Charles 278
Rappaport, Dr. Avraham 135
Rapaport, Rabbi Berish 243 (*illus.*)
Rappaport, Edward 434 (*illus.*)
Rapps, Dennis 179 (fn)
Rastafarian cult 435
Rav Pappa 367
Rav who has no detractors 594
RCA, *see* Rabbinical Council of America
Reagan, President Ronald 252 (*illus.*), 525
rearview mirror, man not created with 585
Reb Elchonon's *hoiz bachur* 62
"Reb Yisrael" 465
Reb Yosef Hatzaddik 71 (fn)
Red Cross *see* International Committee of the Red Cross
Reed, George 381
"Reflections" column 75
Reform movement 265
Reform American Council of Judaism 77
Reform clergy 134ff
Reform movement, 265
    and draft exemption 370 (fn)
    toehold in Israel 143
    oppose aid to day schools 164
    propaganda campaigns, counteracting 561
Refugee Affairs 99, 506
Refugee and Immigration Division 96, 97
refugees, group of 103 (*illus.*)
refugees, Iranian, letter for Vice President Bush 507 (*illus.*)
refuseniks 524
Regan, Tom 317
Regents Action Plan 257, 490, 491
Reich, Rabbi Yaakov Koppel 590 (fn)
Reich, Rabbi Yitzchak 575 (*illus.*)
Reicher, Prof. Moishe Zvi 246 (fn), 329, 535, 540
Reichmann, Albert 524
Reichmann, Moshe 512, 618
Reid, Congressman 324
Reidel, Dovid 346 (fn)
Reisher Rav 536 (fn), 568, 569
Reisman, Rabbi Yaakov 450 (*illus.*)
Religious Freedom Restoration Act, *see* RFRA
Religious Land Use and Institutionalized Persons Act (RLUIPA) 471

"religious workers" and immigration
   quotas   471, 473
remedial speech therapy   299
remembering Amalek and Sabbath   353
remembering forgotten matters   49
Renaissance Hotel, Jerusalem   610
Reno, Attorney General Janet   412
rescue work   96
resignation of Rabbi Sherer   108
   letter of   109 (illus.)
respirator
   and time of death   492
   placing a patient on   623
   removing a patient from a   493
RFRA   469f, 487, 627
   Catholic Church's concerns
      about   470 (fn)
   problematic for Orthodox Jews   470
   supported by Agudath Israel   471
Rhode Island program   419
Ribicoff, Sen. Abraham   311
Richey, Melvin   188
Rieder, Rabbi Harry   364 (fn)
Rieder, Shlomo   243 (illus.), 364 (fn)
Rieder, Shmuel Yosef (Ralph)   618
   and Siyum HaShas   364
Rieder, Yaakov (Al)   364
"right to die"   496
   see also end of life
Riley, Richard   479
Rivka Laufer Bikur Cholim   601
Robertson, Dr. Pat   373
Robinson, Avraham   79
rock and cleft of the rock   277
Rockefeller, Gov. Nelson   42, 44 (illus.),
   251, 528
   and Sabbath observance
      legislation   42
Roe v. Wade   458, 459, 484
   see also abortion
Rogers, Secretary of State
   William   387, 391-2
Rohatyn, Felix   320
Romania   539
Roodman, Rabbi David   67, 70
Rooney, Congressman John   290
Roosevelt, President Franklin   98, 466
Rose, Lucille   428
Rosedale, Steven   28
Rosenbaum, Meyer   233 (illus.)
Rosenbaum, Norman   409
Rosenbaum, Yankel   406, 409, 414, 462
Rosenberg, Rabbi Yisrael   94
Rosenberger, Yosef   227 (fn)
Rosenblum, Chananya   28
Rosenblum, Elimelech Gavriel   28

Rosenblum, Elisha   28
Rosenblum, Judith   28
Rosenblum, Micha David and Elisheva   28
Rosenblum, Mrs. Miriam   28
Rosenblum, Naama and Moshe   28
Rosenblum, Paul (Feivel Yisroel)   28
Rosenblum, Rabbi Mattisyahu   28
Rosenblum, Rabbi Yonoson   12, 21,
   26 (illus.), 59 (fn.), 94, 362, 609
Rosenblum, Yaakov   28
Rosenblum, Yechezkel Mordechai and
   Tova Rina   28
Rosenblum, Zechariah   28
Rosenheim, Moreinu Yaakov   85,
   86 (illus.), 92, 112, 175, 558, 569 (fn)
Rosenstock, Dr. Paul   611, 612
Rosenthal, Abe   408
Rosh Agudath Israel of America   208
   see also Novominsker Rebbe
Rosh Hashanah greetings   101 (illus.)
roshei yeshivah
   younger than Rabbi Sherer   206
   added to the Nesius   215
Ross, Dr. Leslie   259, 445, 446
Ross, Labor Commissioner Phil   288
Roth, Rabbi Yechezkel
   (Satmar dayan)   456
Rottenberg, Rabbi Shlomo   107, 107 (fn),
   245 (illus.)
Rubinonvich, Sender (Sasha)   527 (illus.)
Rubinson, Beirach   102, 103 (illus.), 132
ruchiniyos, ascendancy in   195
Rudensky, Abraham   67
Ruderman, Rabbi Yaakov Yitzchak   65, 67,
   68, 71, 74, 75, 78, 80, 81, 139, 206, 212, 448
   (illus.) 69, 70, 73, 90, 182, 190, 198, 201,
   207, 213, 224, 348, 378, 380, 394, 504,
   576, 588
   phenomenal memory of   68
Rumsfeld, Secretary of Defense
   Donald   274
Russian Jewish immigrants   188, 427
Russian Jewry   515
Russian-speaking immigrant children   239
Ruzhorsky, Dr. Moshe   509 (illus.), 511
Ryzman, Zvi   222 (illus.)

S

Sabbath and Amalek   353
Sabbath desecration   53
Sabbath laws   312
   see also Blue Laws
Sabbath
   observance   43
   legislation   167, 481, 627
   see also Shabbos

Sabra and Shatilla massacres 422, 547
sacrifices for Klal Yisrael 624 (fn)
Sager, Sam 67
Salanter, Rabbi Yisrael 313
Salomon, Rabbi Mattisyahu 628 (illus.), 634 (illus.), 635
Salt Lake City, Rabbi Sherer's trip to 306 (fn)
Salvation Army 398, 400
same-gender "marriage"/unions 483, 460
  Torah position on 398
"sanctity of life" 484
Sanctity of the Synagogue, The 145
Sander, Ted 477
Sanhedrin, adjacent to the Temple 624 (fn)
Sar Shalom of Belz 622 (fn)
Sassoon, Rabbi Solomon 501
Satmar community 181, 370, 374, 572
Satmar Rebbe 97, 181, 183, 591, 592 (illus.), 595 (fn)
  shivah call by 592 (fn)
Savitz, Rabbi Reuven 371, 374, 375, 378, 391, 393
Saxbe, Sen. William 373
SBCO, see Southern Brooklyn Community Organization
Scalia, Antonin 461 (illus.)
scandals in the Orthodox community 189, 299
Schacter, Rabbi Herschel 373
Schechter, Rabbi Ahron 215, 391, 510 (illus.) 216, 245, 286, 391, 450, 628, 634, 636
Scherman, Rabbi Nosson 21, 23, 27, 187, 191 (fn), 236 (fn), 237, 348 (fn), 349 (fn), 365 (illus.) 226, 237
Scheuer, James 375
Schick brothers 617
Schick, Dr. Marvin 179 (fn)
Schiff, Dorothy 189
Schifter, Assistant Secretary of State Richard 188, 264, 273, 295, 437, 439, 513
Schlesinger, Zev 233 (illus.), 563 (illus.)
Schmelczer, Rabbi Chaim 150 (fn)
Schnur, Rabbi Chaim 196 (illus.)
Schnur, Joel 427
Schnurman, Dr. Asher 529 (illus.)
Schoenbrun, Avi 587, 591, 594, 598
Schoenbrun, Suri (Goldschmidt) 578 (illus.), 587
Schonberger, Avrohom 244 (illus.)
Schonkopf, Asher 222 (illus.)
school aid testimony, excerpts 162 (illus.)
"school choice" 477
school prayer 485
school vouchers 477
Schorr, Rabbi Gedaliah 48, 49, 50, 51, 54 (fn), 56, 95, 96, 98, 116, 365, 378, 380 (fn), 448, 590
  (illus.) 48, 49, 50, 52, 116, 189, 575, 576
  and Mike Tress, friendship between 50
  closeness to Rabbi Sherer 51
  delegate to Second Knessiah Gedolah 49
  natural modesty 49
  never taking credit or discussing his role in Zeirei or wartime rescue 49 (fn)
  Rabbi Sherer's personal rav 50
Schottenstein Edition of Talmud 364
Schron, Rubin 573 (fn)
Schuchatowitz, Rabbi Yosef Leib 501
Schumer, Sen. Charles (Chuck) 184 (fn), 234, 264, 265, 270, 278, 296, 301, 334, 471
  and Orthodox constituents 297
Schustal, Rabbi Dovid 634 (illus.)
Schwab, Moshe 72
Schwab, Rabbi Shimon 72, 78 (fn), 84, 148, 456
  (illus.) 74, 85, 104, 450
Schwartz, David 72
Schwartz, Rabbi Avraham 72
Schwartz, Rabbi Simon 150
Schwartz, Rabbi Vam 77
Schwartzman, Mr. 529 (illus.)
Schwebel, Yaakov 358 (illus.)
Schweiker, Sen. Richard 373
Sdunska-Wola 604 (fn)
Second Circuit 285 (fn)
Secretary of Health, Education, and Welfare 311
Section 235 mortgages 438
Section 8 435
secular studies, compulsory in Israel 556
security for Jews of Eretz Yisrael 545-551
SED, see State Education Department
Sedler, Robert 457
Seeve, David 428
Sefer Torah presented to Rabbi Sherer 243 (illus.)
Sefirah, symbolism of in Rabbi Sherer's passing 16
Segal, Rabbi Getzel 576 (illus.)
Segal, Rabbi Zev 375
Seif, Aaron 224 (illus.)
Seingersh, Zvi 529 (illus.)
Selective Service Act 553
Selective Service system 369
  see also draft
semichah, 90 (illus.)

Senate Armed Services Committee
  (SASC)   372, 373, 378, 379
Senate Committee on
  Education   302, 460 (*fn*)
Senate Committtte on
  Human Resources   288
Senate Finance Committee   263
senior citizens' centers   426
sensitivity to others' feeling   569
Sephardi members of Agudath Israel   556
Septimus, Chaim   524
Septimus, Louis J.   214-215 (*fn*), 358
Septimus, Solomon   108
seudas hoda'ah   598 (*illus.*)
Sefas Emes   639 (*fn*)
sh'nos and *shinuy*   195
Shaareti Teshuvah   61(*fn*)
Shabbasos, observance of two
  consecutive   122
Shabbos candles in Sherer home   44
Shabbos demonstrations   49, 351
Shabbos, El Al flights on   547
Shabbos HaGadol   122
Shabbos observance   94
Shabbos Shuvah   122
Shabbos, working on after prayers   42
Shach,
  Rabbi Elazar Menachem Man   119 (*illus.*),
  209 (*fn*), 555 (*illus.*), 559, 594 (*fn*), 621
    addressing political issues   198
    on Begin   547
    on Lebanon War   556
Shafran, Rabbi Avi   199, 362
Shah of Iran, decline in religious life
  under   501
Shalom Aleichem (song)   635 (*fn*)
shalom, attainment of   622 (*fn*)
Shamir, Prime Minister Yitzchak   275
Shapiro, Rabbi Avrohom Yosef   555 (*illus.*)
Shapiro, Haim   610
Shapiro, Rabbi Meir   48, 153, 363
Shapiro, Rabbi Moshe Shmuel   555 (*illus.*)
Sharansky, Natan   518 (*fn*), 524
Sharett, Moshe   423
Sharpton, Al   406
Shas   181
Shas party   556
Shatdlanus principles   464,476, 489
Shatz, David   466 (*fn*)
Shayovich, Menachem (Mendy)   138,
  179, 182, 217, 226, 267, 290, 315, 316, 317,
  318, 320, 334, 339, 426, 433, 568
    (*illus.*) 43, 233, 244, 245, 427, 434
Shazar, President Zalman   131 (*illus.*)
shearis hapleitah (survivors)   99, 100, 104,
  130, 227, 228, 229, 231, 339

Shearith Israel   74
shechitah   474
  banning of, in pre-war Poland   551
  in Argentina   533
  protection of   168, 312
Shechiyanu blessing   616
Shecter, Joseph H.   67
shem tov (good name)   261
Shema
  and *mezuzah*   564 (*fn*)
  closing eyes while reciting   174
  recital of   355
Shemano, Rabbi Yisroel   576 (*illus.*)
Shemoneh Esrei, stepping back   622
Sherer, Basya Bluma,   28, 39, 40 (*illus.*) 43,
  47, 115 (*illus.*), see also Moruchnik,
  Basya Bluma
    and Chevra Kadisha   44
    love of doing *chesed*   47
    piety of   43
Sherer, Chaim Yehudah   40 (*illus.*)
Sherer, Elky   387 (*fn*), 577, 579
  wedding of   574, 575 (*illus.*)
  see Goldschmidt, Elky
Sherer, Harry   41, 42, 48, 56
Sherer, Jenny   41
  lived with the Tress family   48
Sherer, Matis   593 (*illus.*)
  tefillin for   586
Sherer, Mendy   125, 571 (*fn*), 589 (*illus.*)
Sherer, Mrs. Debby (Devorah)   28, 113,
  114 (*illus.*), 568 (*illus.*), 601
Sherer, Rabbi Moshe   67, 70 (*illus.*),
  85 (*illus.*)
    a leader in moral value   284
    advice was untainted   256
    always considered *kiddush Hashem*
      implications of every action   185
    and criticism   60
    and Devorah (Debby) wedding photo
      and invitation 114 (*illus.*)
    and non-Orthodox world   301
    and Reb Elchonon   57
    and web of personal
      relationships   251
    as a young man (*illus.*)   56
    as "bridge builder"   278
    as advocate   301
    as *askan* bowing before *daas Torah*   208
    as young *darshan*   74
    at age 60   219
    at Giuliani inauguration   259 (*illus.*)
    avid student of Jewish history   123
    berachah from Steipler   401
    birth date   39
    birth of   39

builder of people   234
burial   242 (fn)
chassan and kallah photo   115 (illus.)
considered resigning   108
constitutional analysis, mastery of   310f
darshan   73
descriptions of   29
emphasis on detailed
    preparation   309
eye for talent   234
fully relied on gedolei Yisrael   205
fund-raising duties   150
greeted everyone   58
growing a beard   559
guilt feeling about not spending
    enough time with children   580
homiletics teacher   73
intensely private   567 (fn)
last Siyum HaShas   365
love of the Land   541
many levels of leadership   271
modus operandi   329
never stinted on his praise   341
New York Times, The   162 (illus.)
notes   630 (illus.)
oratorical skills   75
postcard to Mike Tress   81
prayers by   263
private side   73
punctuality   243
quoted father-in-law's vertlach   122
reaction to opinion rejected
    by Moetzes   206
read late into the night   79
referred to as "Jewish
    Godfather"   293
resignation and retraction   151f
secret of success   333
semichah   89
seudas hodaah following open-heart
    surgery   154 (illus.)
shtadlanus strategy   279
taken under Rabbi Aharon Kotler's
    wing   126
testimony to Congress   160
tombstone   230 (illus.)
uncompromising on ideological
    issues   297
"urbane, witty and insightful"   269
urged by Gedolei Torah to leave
    business   109
vulgarity never passed his lips   256
workaholic   333
would not accept payment for a
    favor   185
writing skills   75

Sherer, Rochel see Langer, Rochel
Sherer, Mrs. Shifi   21, 591
Sherer, Rabbi Shimshon Zelig   13, 24,
    55, 57 (fn), 60 (fn), 195, 195 (fn), 235, 239,
    239 (fn), 355, 401, 564, 569, 584, 589, 597,
    619 (fn), 623, 637, 642
    (illus.) 26, 51, 222, 243, 244, 245, 318,
        563, 579, 589, 591
    and fatherly kiss   590
    and Rabbi Aharon Kotler, 127f
    childhood   579
    greetings at Agudah dinner   581 (illus.)
    Jewish Observer, Summer 1998   56
    learned with father   580
    position as Rav   593
    visit to Rabbi Shach   119 (fn)
    wedding   576 (illus.), 318 (illus.), 324
Sherer, Ruby   41
Sherer, Yisroel Shneur (Sruly)   586,
    589 (illus.)
Sherer, Yudi   589 (illus.)
Sherman, Dr. David   196 (illus.)
shidduchim of children   577
Shiraz   501
Shisgal,
    Rabbi AvrohomYitzchok   117 (illus.)
Shisgal, Rabbi Eliyahu Moshe   117 (illus.)
shivah   641
Shkop, Rabbi Moshe   85
shloshim   642
shlucha d'Rachmana   95, 208, 220, 636
shmad (conversion from Judaism)   280
shmittah   542
    messages of   544
shmittah-observant farmers   542, 544 (illus.)
shochtim (ritual slaughterers),
    dispute with government inspectors
    in Iowa   287
Shomer Shabbos, see Sabbath
shtadlanus   465, 499
    principles of   280
    working with the government   482
Shteinman, Rabbi Aharon Leib   563 (illus.)
    visit to America   242 (fn), 639
Shulman, Harold   67
Shulman, Rabbi Shmaryahu   71, 72
Shulman, Sidney   67
Shurkin, Rabbi Yaakov Moshe   110 (fn)
Shuvalsky, Morris   67
SHUVU   239
Shweid, Alexander   515
"sickly weed" (reference to Orthodox
    Jews and Zeirei Agudath Israel)   9, 94
side income, avoiding   231
Siegel, Prof. Seymour   144, 549
Silber, Rabbi Mechel   628 (illus.)

Silbermintz, Rabbi Joshua 226, 226 (*illus.*), 582 (*fn*)
Silver, Aaron 67
Silver, New York State Assembly Speaker Sheldon 289, 456, 494 (*fn*)
Silver, Mendel 67
Silver, Rabbi Eliezer 72, 86, (*illus.*) 109, 111 (*illus.*), 124 (*illus.*), 214, 215 (*fn*)
Silver, Sam 67
Silverman, Assemblyman Leonard 493
Simchas Beis Hasho'eivah 368
simchos, confined to closest friends and family 575
Simons, Ambassador Thomas W. 480f
Singer, David 407, 433
Singer, Israel 276, 277, 297 (*fn*)
singing, 578
   in Sherer home 41
sisters, Basya Bluma Sherer and Henya Tress 41 (*fn*), 48
"sit and do nothing" 155
Sitren, Isaac 67
"Six Crises" 415
Six-Day War 518 (*fn*), 547
616 Bedford Avenue 52, 82, 96, 98, 227 (*fn*)
sixty and *ziknah* 219
Siyata d'Shmaya, in growth of Agudah 170
Siyum HaShas 180, 334, 363, 364, 603 (*fn*), 627, 628, 629
   Rabbi Sherer's last 365
   10th 30
Siyum Sefer Torah 391 (*illus.*)
Skulener Rebbe 32, 628 (*illus.*), 641
Slabodka, Alter of 9, 68 (*fn*)
slaughterhouse, performance standards for 476
Slonimer Rebbe 555 (*illus.*)
Small, Rabbi Isaac 117 (*illus.*)
Smith v. Oregon 469
Smith, Congressman Christopher H. 470
smoking 590
Snake, curse of 339
social services 193
societal moral decline 282
Sohn, Prof. Louis 535 (*fn*)
Solarz, Congressman Stephen 253, 255, 257, 262, 294 (*illus.*), 294, 265, 278 (*fn*), 281, 300, 301, 309, 315 (*fn*), 466, 469, 471, 506, 508, 536, 537
Solender, Sandford 299
Soloff, Reuven 63
Soloveichik, Rabbi Yitzchak Zev (Reb Velvel) *see* Brisker Rav
Soloveichik, Rabbi Yosef Ber 85

Soloveichik, Rabbi Yosef Dov see Beis HaLevi
Soltin 538
"Somebody," "Anybody," "Everybody," and "Nobody" 510
Sorasky, Rabbi Aharon 95, 153
Sorotzkin, Rabbi Boruch 177, 190 (*illus.*), 213 (*illus.*), 375, 380 (*fn*)
Sorotzkin, Rabbi Zalman 213
South Fifth Street shul 53
Southern Brooklyn Community Organization (SBCO) 158, 188, 241, 242, 264, 310
   subject of laudatory editorial in *The New York Times* 433
Sova, Bashie (Langer) 578 (*illus.*)
Sova, Rabbi Yossi 638 (*illus.*)
Soviet Union 241
   Jewish emigration from the 517
   Jews in 515
   shipment of matzos to 262
   underground movement of Jews 523
Special Emergency Visitors' Visas 97
Specter, Arlen 184 (*fn*)
speech for dinner, never delivered 629
speech therapy, funding for 300
Spektor, Rabbi Yitzchok Elchonon 71 (*fn*), 570 (*fn*)
spontaneous breathing, cessation of 492
   see also end-of-life issue,
   respirator 209, 369, 491
SS Marine Flasher 102
St. Louis Rabbinical College 258, 338
   accreditation 259
Stangl, Peter 283
Star-K Kosher Certification 474
Starobin (*shtetl*) 118
state aid 159ff, 167, 419
State Department 186
State Education Department (SED) and accreditation of yeshivos 444-447
State Educational Commissioner 263
state prisoners, religious needs of 471
State Regents 302
State Task Force on Life and the Law 494
Staten Island, NY 238
Statler Hilton Hotel, NY 374
Steinberg, Rabbi Sholom 505
Steingut, Stanley 406 (*fn*)
Steipler Gaon 607
   berachah from 401
   supported Rabbi Sherer as co-chariman of World Agudath Israel 185
Stennis, Sen. John 378

Steppin 41
Stern College 502 (fn)
Stern, Rabbi Moshe (Debrecziner Rav) 456
Stern, Rabbi Yosef Naftali 218 (illus.)
Sternbuchs in Switzerland 97-98
Stewart, Surgeon General
 Dr. William 303
Stolin Yeshiva 350
 see also Karlin-Stolin
Stoliner Rebbe, 44
 blessing of 40
Stoliner *shtiebel* 40
Stone, Robert D. 262, 300
Strasbourg, France 513 (fn)
Strauss Square 351
strep throat 45
Struma tragedy 77
Study Commission for AARTS 445 ff
submission to the judgment of
 the *gedolei haTorah* 220
success, Rabbi Sherer's secret of 333
suicide 484
summit in Geneva 525
Sunset Park neighborhood 433
Sununu, White House Chief of Staff
 John 466-7
Supreme Court 168, 299, 462, 270 (fn)
 aid and assistance to non-public
  education 311
 reversal of a recent precedent 461
surprise presentation of
 Sefer Torah 244 (illus.)
Svei, Rabbi Elya 24, 57 (fn), 213, 261 (fn),
 373, 375, 510, 583 (fn), 609 (fn), 615,
 615 (fn), 620, 635,
  (illus.) 154, 214, 244, 245, 286, 318, 450,
   504, 598, 628, 634, 636
Sweden, home for girls 569 (fn)
Sweet, Deputy Mayor, Robert 405
Swerdloff, Mitchell 431
SwissAir 385
"sympathy won't help — money will" 97,
 98 (illus.)
Synagogue Council 137, 138, 139, 140,
 141, 189, 199, 212, 370 (fn)
  Anniversary Dinner 140
  ad hoc alliance with 371
  psak against 134
  1966 dinner, statement of the roshei
   yeshivah regarding 139 (illus.)
Syria, helping Jews leave 295
Syrian dictator Hafez al-Assad,
 let Jewish girls leave Syria 295
Syrian Jewish community of Flatbush 179
Syrian Jewish community,
 visas for members 234

Syrian Jewish girls 295
Szyf, Rabbi Yisroel 514

T

talent, Rabbi Sherer's eye for 232-234
Taller, Reuben 67
Talmud, ArtScroll Schottenstein
 translation 363-4
Talmud study, and maintstream
 media 365
Talmud Torah, rabbis not observant 54
Talmud, unpacked 116
Talmudical Yeshiva of Philadelphia
 see Philadelphia Yeshiva
Tanenbaum, Professor Avraham 448
Tannenbaum, Bernice 305
Targum Yerushalmi 355
Tarnopol 277
Tarr, Curtis 373, 379, 380
tashlich, small groups 589 (fn)
Tawil, Isaac 528 (illus.)
tax relief to parents of parochial school
 children 163, *158ff*, 164, 311, 419, 489
 see also non-public education
Taylor, Michael 475
Tchebiner Rav 232
Tchortkover Rebbe 55
teabag, Jewish people compared to 270
teacher-prepared exams 420 (fn)
teachers, resemble angels 69
teaching out of love for students 69 (fn)
tefillin for all his grandsons 586
Teichman, Rabbi Avrohom 450 (illus.)
Teitelbaum, Rabbi Eli 617 (illus.)
Teitelbaum, Rabbi Moshe 591
 early morning meeting 182
 see also Satmar Rebbe
Teitelbaum, Rabbi Yoel 181
 see also Satmar Rebbe
Teitz, Rabbi Pinchas M. 54 (fn),
 190 (illus.), 375, 523
Telshe Yeshiva 79, 293, 355, 502 (fn)
 Kollel 235
 Rosh Yeshivah 141
Temple Mount tunnels, opening of,
 and rioting 562
Ten Commandments 194
Ten Plagues, compressed by
 R' Yehudah 348
Tendler, Rabbi Moshe,
 and health care proxy 497
Tenenbaum, Dr. Joseph 94
tenth man, waiting for at *minyan* 231
Tepler, Efraim 318 (illus.)
Terem emergency clinic 611
teref (driven mad), 62

Teshuvah 9
They Called Him Mike 36, 49 (*fn*), 59 (*fn*), 63 (*fn*), 88 (*illus.*), 94 (*fn*), 96 (*fn*)
3320 Garrison Boulevard 65
Thornborough, Richard 467
three aspects of community service 32
  see also askanus
three B's of public speaking 348
three rules of *Klal* work 313
three-letter rule for
  student funding 441, 444, 447
Thurm, Leo 591
Thurm, Meyer 318 (*illus.*)
Thurm, Mr. and Mrs. Meyer 591
Thurmond, Strom 184 (*fn*)
tiferes, and *emes* 15
  inherent quality of 15
Tiferes Israel shul 65
Tifereth Israel shul 65 (*illus.*) 65
Tikkun Olam 466 (*fn*)
time of death 300, 321ff
  see also end of life, respirator
Tirnauer, Rabbi Yehudah 576 (*illus.*)
Tishah B'Av, meeting at White House 161
Tishman, Peggy 356
Title I program 167, 190, 480
Title II program, reauthorization of 479f
Titlebaum, Rabbi Milton 67, 70 (*illus.*)
Tobin, Carley 375
tocho k'boro (who are the same on the inside as the outside) 557
tombstone of Rabbi Sherer 230 (*illus.*)
Torah, everything is found in 63
Torah guidelines, as interpreted by Torah sages 196
Torah institutions never collapsed solely because of a lack of money 124
Torah Jews, united under the banner of Torah 197
Torah lishmah 127
Torah leaders, trust in 18
Torah leadership, primacy secures future of *Klal Yisrael* 206
Torah scholars, as leaders 197
Torah Schools for Israel (Chinuch Atzmai) 132, 133
Torah Umesorah 168, 211 (*fn*), 356, 474
  restoration of $350,000 grant to 287
Torah Vodaath 51, 82
  see Yeshiva Torah Vodaath
  taught homiletics at 346
Torah, collective Jewish life must be based on 107
Toronto 570
Touro College 590
  valedictory address at 588

town *meshugener* 61
Tradition magazine 80
Travia, New York State Assembly Speaker Anthony 168
Treisser, Herman 109
Treitel, Eli 196 (*illus.*)
Treitel, Stanley 196 (*illus.*)
Tress, Elimelech Gavriel ("Mike") 11, 36, 41 (*fn*), 47, 48, 50, 51, 52, 56, 74, 81, 82, 83, 84, 85, 88, 89, 96, 132, 214, 225, 266, 276, 422
  (*illus.*) 87, 93, 103, 111, 137
  last public campaign 147
  deteriorating health 150
  letter to 84 (*illus.*)
  mettings with at Baltimore train station 85
  postcard to 81 (*illus.*)
  visits to Baltimore 88
Tress, Mrs. Henya 41, 43, 47, 48
Tress, Henya, aunt 48
Tress, Mrs. Hinda 88
  inscription to Rabbi Sherer in Mike Tress biography 88 (*illus.*)
Tress, Tzvi 576 (*illus.*)
Tropper, Daniel 271, 557 (*fn*)
truth, left unspoken 355
tuition tax
  credits 263, 279, 302, 341, 369, 447
tuition, Mrs. Sherer's difficulty paying 56
tuition, never haggle over 582 (*fn*)
Turkel, David 112, 151, 152, 224 (*illus.*), 225, 227 (*illus.*), 227
Turkey, smuggling of Iranian Jews to 508
TWA Flight 741, highjacking of 384
Twerski, Professor Aaron 179, 182 (*fn*), 237 (*illus.*), 400, 455
Twersky, Rabbi Chaim 159 (*illus.*)
tzavaah (ethical will) 595, 623

U

UN's recognition of the PLO 551
Udell, Lester 132
Udovenko, Gennadi 538
Uhr, Mrs. 582
UJA, see United Jewish Appeal
Ukraine 480, 536 (*fn*)
  Foreign Minister 538
ultra-Orthodox, 275
  derogatory description of 191
  see also Orthodox
umbrella groups, membership in 137
Union of American Hebrew Congregations 540
Union of Orthodox Jewish Congregations 459 (*fn*)
  see also Orthodox Union

United Jewish Appeal   191, 356
United Methodist Church   372
United Nations   161
United Nations Relief and Rehabilitation Agency (UNRRA)   94, 100
United States
   Catholic Conference   372, 374, 376 (fn), 470
     see also Catholic Conference
   combat troops, kosher meals   627
   Commission for the Preservation of America's Heritage Abroad   253, 281, 537
   Department of Agriculture (USDA)   473
   Department of Labor   316
   immigration to   101
     see also immigration
   Surgeon General, and autopsies   303
   Ukraine Joint Cultural Commission   539 (fn)
Universal Declaration of Human Rights   536 (fn)
Unsdorfer, Simcha   221
Urban Action Development Grants   438
Urban Coalition   405
Uruguay   535

V

Vaad Hapoel of World Agudah   240
Vaad Hatzalah   97
Vaad L'Hatzolas
   Nidchei Yisrael   241, 524, 537 (fn)
vacation interests   568
Vacco, Dennis   471
Vaccov v. Quill   484
Vallone, Peter   462
Vance, Secretary of State
   Cyrus, 261, 272 (fn), 357, 481, 502, 515
Vaughn, Auxiliary Bishop Austin   285
"veil of Moshe Rabbeinu"   297
Veith, Dr.   493
vertlach cited by Rabbi Sherer   35
Vienna   50, 363, 507, 511
   Hotel Continental   149 (*illus.*)
   Iranian refugees in   507
   underground railroad   148
Village Voice   457
violence in Crown Heights and Williamsburg   405
visas requests   96, 155
   for immigrant rabbis   104
   visas, Iranian, speeding up of   505ff
   visitors'   102
Vizhnitzer Rebbe   217 (*illus.*), 219, 302, 555 (*illus.*)
vows to Hashem 61 (fn)

W

Waldheim, UN Secretary General, Kurt   320
   meeting with Pope John Paul II   279
walking   598
war refugees   98
Warrenbrand, Mel   434, 434, (*illus.*)
Warsaw   246
Washington Heights   267, 426 (fn)
   senior citizens' centers   426
Washington, D.C.   158
   400 Orthodox rabbis marched by   466
   office   175, 465
Wasserman, Rabbi Elchonon   57-63 (*illus.*) 49, 55, 57
   accompanied by Moshe Sherer   57
   held back from smiling   59
   pictures of   58
Wasserman, Rabbi Simcha   63 (fn)
water, not to be taken for granted   631
water, reflection in   622(fn)
Waxman, Chaim I.   466 (fn)
Waxman, Congressman Henry   196 (*illus.*)
Waxman, Rabbi Nissan   117 (*illus.*)
Webster v. Reproductive Health Services   458
Wein, Rabbi Berel   183, 570 (fn)
Weinberg, Rabbi Chaim Aron   295, 296 (*illus.*), 302 (fn)
Weinberg, Rabbi Yaakov   448, 628 (*illus.*), 636
Weinberger, Secretary of Defense Caspar   449
   and Jonathan Pollard   486
Weinberger, Rabbi Gedaliah   348 (fn), 611 (*illus.*)
Weinberger, Judy   149
Weiner, Dovid   85 (*illus.*)
Weiner, Jacob   85 (*illus.*)
Weinreb, Israel   67
Weisberg, Rabbi Yaakov   289, 375, 380, 443
Weisel, Bernie   196 (*illus.*)
Weissmandl, Rabbi Michoel Ber   97, 118 (fn), 149, 310
Weiss, Isaac   196 (*illus.*)
Weiss, Rabbi Moshe Meir   238
Weiss, Rudolph   67
Weizman, President Ezer   562, 610, 611 (*illus.*)
Weldler, Dovid   509 (*illus.*), 510
Wendell, Steven   356 (fn)
Werdiger, Shlomo
   major role in bringing Gerrer Rebbe and Rabbi Aharon Leib Shteinman to America   242

Werther, Eli   570, 571 (*fn*)
West Side Institutional Synagogue   132
Westchester County   405
white blood cell count   612
White House
   meeting on *Tishah B'Av*   161
   signing of the Egyptian-Israel peace treaty   183
White Shul, Far Rockaway   110, 113, 121
White, U.S. Attorney Mary Jo   412
"Who is a Jew" issue   275
Wiener, Rabbi Gerd   70 (*illus.*)
Wiesner, Mr. Willie (Zev)   518
Wikler, Rabbi Yosef   366
Williams, Sen. Harrison   288
Williamsburg   48, 181, 405
Williger, Srully   603 (*fn*)
window, praying in a room with   583
Winn, Phil   438
Winter, Rabbi David   572
Wolbe, Rabbi Shlomo   569 (*fn*), 622 (*fn*)
Wolf, Hirsch   526 (*illus.*)
Wolf, Rabbi Ephraim (Freddy)   64, 67, 81, 82, 85 (*illus.*)
Wolfson, Rabbi Wilfred   67, 70 (*illus.*), 71
Wolpin, Rabbi Nisson   28, 237 (*illus.*), 342 (*illus.*), 359, 360 (*illus.*)
Wolpin, Rabbi Raphael   357 (*fn*)
women,
   compulsory civilian service by   553
World Agudath Israel,
   see Agudath Israel World Organization
World Conference of Synagogues   353
world events and
   Jewish history   585 (*illus.*)
World Jewish
   Congress   276, 277, 297 (*fn*), 422, 525
World Jewish Restitution Organization (WJRO)   613
World Zionist Youth Foundation   200
World Zionist Organization   422, 534
Wyman, David   466 (*fn*)

X-Y

Yaakov Avinu as Yisrael   586
Yaakov, blessing his grandchildren, mentioning himself first   15
Yaakov's *tiferes*   16
Yad Yisrael   350
Yahrzeit   642
Yahrzeit of Rabbi Sherer   16
yarmulke
   wearing at job   346
   wearing of a   265
yarmulkes, two red   200

Yated Ne'eman   336, 362, 614
   see also Lipshutz, Rabbi Pinchos
Yehoshua (Joshua)   96
   angels visited   69
   and angel   174
   and battle of Ai   69
Yericho (Jericho)   174
Yeser, one of the names of Yisro   246
Yeshiva Ateret Torah   295-6
Yeshiva Chachmei Lublin   153, 363
Yeshiva Chaim Berlin   110 (*fn*), 313, 502 (*fn*)
   central command setup during hostage crisis   386
Yeshiva Chofetz Chaim of Baltimore   502 (*fn*)
Yeshiva Chofetz Chaim on the West Side   262
Yeshiva Eitz Chaim in Slutsk   119
Yeshiva Emergency Committee   374-5
Yeshiva Gedola of St. Louis, see St. Louis Rabbinical College
Yeshiva M'kor Chaim   260
Yeshiva Ner Israel   64ff, 144, 203, 235, 338, 355, 445, 466
   group photo   66 (*illus.*)
   Iranians' arrival   501
   names of students in yearbook photo   67
   poor conditions in early dormitory   67
   student yearbook   66 (*illus.*)
   visit to campus   445
Yeshiva of Brooklyn   177 (*fn*)
   expansion plans   286
Yeshiva of Flatbush   182
Yeshiva of Staten Island   442
Yeshiva Rabbi Samson Raphael Hirsch   502 (*fn*)
Yeshiva Torah Vodaath   44, 51, 56, 82, 102, 121, 435
   homiletics class 121, 232, 347ff
Yeshiva University   140, 179, 319, 370, 374, 378, 550 (*fn*)
Yeshiva Telshe Chicago   570 (*fn*)
Yeshiva Tiferes Habachurim   567 (*fn*)
yeshivah bachurim identifying with Agudath Israel   176
yeshivah closings for fund raising   98
Yeshivas Chafetz Chaim   72
Yeshivat Mercas HaRav   522
yeshivos, accreditation of   444-5
   Agudath Israel service to the   203
   bogus   442, 443, 447
   independent accreditation of,   449-451
   offering advanced degrees   447
   tax-exempt status of   288 (*fn*)

yetzias neshamah (the departure of the soul; demise) 623
  see also death, time of
Yiddish, taught to Shimshie 582 (*fn*)
Yiddishe *chein* 270
"*Yiddishe shtub* — a Jewish home" 116
Yiddishkeit, to perpetuate authentic 485
Yiddish-speaking community 357
Yigdal prayer 623
Yisro 141
Yitzchak Avinu's name 158
Yitzchak's *gevurah* 16
YMHA
  games at 72
  of Boro Park 242
Yom Kippur War 589
Yom Tov, and paid vacation days 294
Yosef, Chief Rabbi Ovadia 144, 611
Young Israel 610
Young Israel Viewpoint, Fall 1998 573 (*fn*)
Youth Aliyah 558
Youth Council and Agudath Israel merger 108

Z

Zachai, Deborah (Jacob) 338
Zahn, Shammai 67
Zaks, Rabbi Mendel 84
Zeirei Agudath Israel 48, 84, 91, 99, 104, 132, 155, 200, 214, 227 (*fn*), 228, 305, 337, 357, 358, 364, 524
  a misnomer 108
  appointment as executive director 92 (*illus.*)
  minutes of meeting 93
  minyan at 157 Rodney Street 48
  participation of yeshivah *bachurim* 203
  referred to as a "sickly weed" 94
  Williamsburg branch of 225

Zeirei convention 1941 84, 86 (*illus.*)
Zeirei Forum 336
Zeirei *minyan* 98
Zelman v. Simmons-Harris 478 (*fn*)
Zemiros, singing 578, 579 (*illus.*)
  in childhood home 42
Zevulun and Yissachar, partnership between 220
Zichron Yaakov 570 (*fn*)
ziknah at age sixty 219
"Zion, Yes — Zionist, No!" 545
Zionism 77
Zionism and the establishment of a secular sphere 107
Zionist flag 107
Zionist Congress, Second 545
Zionist, ideology of 545
Zionist-oriented high school 572
Zionist religious movement Mizrachi 52
Zlotowitz, Rabbi Meir 21, 27, 187, 191 (*fn*), 194 (*fn*), 236, 236 (*fn*), 237, 237 (*illus.*), 348 (*fn*), 349 (*fn*), 363
  Rabbi Sherer's handwritten invitation to, 236 (*illus.*)
Zuccotti, John 262
Zuckoff, Murray 275
Zurich 506
"Zwiebel amendments" 468
Zwiebel, Rabbi Chaim Dovid 11, 161 (*fn*), 184 (*fn*), 205, 206 (*fn*), 211 (*fn*), 256 (*fn*), 261 (*fn*), 266, 279 (*fn*), 283, 284, 285, 310, 338, 343, 397, 398, 400, 402 (*fn*), 410, 411, 454, 458, 460, 461, 462, 464, 469 (*fn*), 470, 471, 475, 477, 479, 483 (*fn*), 488 (*fn*), 491 (*fn*), 494, 496, 496 (*fn*), 497 (*fn*), 499, 508, 563, 563, 622, 626
  (*illus.*) 154, 198, 222, 264, 463, 467, 521, 563
Zwienicki, Gerd 67

SCRIPTURAL INDEX (LISTING SOURCES FROM TANACH)

Bereishis
   12:3   192
   12:3   594
   39:12   344
   41:14   161 (fn)
   48:5   586
   48:16   15

Shemos
   2:6   75
   2:10   39, 129
   2:11   637
   6:6   123
   18:17   247
   18:21   246
   19:12   632
   21:1   624
   33:21-22   277

Vayikra
   4:22   219
   26:44-45   10

Bamidbar
   11:28   96 (fn)
   20:26   207 (fn)
   20:29   594
   7:9   96
   8:25   156

Devarim
   32:7   195
   33:18   220
   34:8   594

Yehoshua
   8:13   69 (fn)
   5:15   174
   25:8   643
   58:7   595

Yeshayahu
   25:8   643
   58:7   595

Yirmiyahu 31:14   344

Zechariah 4:2   352

Tehillim
   92:12   60
   111:5   61
   119:49-51   102
   118:13   46
   121:1   18
   128:5   545
   142:8   630
   145:21   629 (fn)
   147:13   582

Mishlei
   3:4   270
   17:6   15
   27:19   622

Iyov 22:29   61 (*fn*)

Shir HaShirim
   1:15   568
   2:8-9   580

Koheles 3:1-8   199

INDEX OF TALMUDIC AND RABBINIC SOURCES

Arachin 11a   96
Avodah Zarah 10b   642 (fn)
Bava Basra 16b   577
Bava Kamma
    17a   195
    92a   583
Bava Metzia 83b (fn)   128
Bechoros 44a   207 (fn)
Beitzah 16a   323
Beis Halevi   582
Berachos
    3b   542
    6a   313
    6b   47, 231
    17a   58 (fn)
    28a   557
    31a   622
    32b   196
    34b   583
    55b   125
    58a   187 (fn)
    63b   348
Chasam Sofer al HaTorah (Toras Moshe),
    Bereishis 41:14   161
Chayei Adam 15:1   564
Chiddushei HaRim   156
Daas Zekeinim MiBaalei HaTosafos,
    Shemos 32:2   71
Ein HaBedolach   71 (fn)
Eruvin 64a   622
Even Shleimah 4:9   632
Gittin 62a   575
Gur Aryeh, Bereishis 2:5   583
Haemek Davar, Bereishis 24:1   57
Horayos 10b   219
Iggeres HaRamban   61 (fn)
Imrei Emes   207 (fn), 631 (fn)
Kiddushin
    32b   219
    40a   313

Maharil Diskin   594
Magen Avraham Orach Chaim 224:4   187
Masechta Kallah 1:15   128
Megillah
    3a   69
    6a   424
    13b   501
    15a   122
    27b   631
Midrash Bereishis Rabbah
    1:1   198
    1:21   207 (fn)
    68:1   18
    Parashah 40   62
Midrash Shemos Rabbah parashah 1   129
Midrash Tanchuma, Ki Setzei   353
Moed Kattan 24a   329
Nedarim 81a   68
Pachad Yitzchak, Chanukah 9   187 (fn)
Pesachim
    8b   615
    117b   123
    118a   193
Pirkei Avos
    2:9   232
    4:17   261
    5:11   543
    5:25   219
    5:26   163
Pirkei d'Rebbe Eliezer 30   631
Rambam, Hilchos Melachim 3:6   622
Rema to Yoreh Deah 285:2   564
Rosh Hashanah 10b
Rosh, Orchos Chaim 78   595
Sanhedrin 94b   177
Sfas Emes   639
Shabbos
    31a   584
    88b   350
    92a   207 (fn)
    119b   122

Shabbos Shacharis Shemonei Esrei 17
Shaarei Teshuvah (Rabbeinu Yonah)
    1:29   61 (*fn*)
Shulchan Aruch, Yoreh Deah 149   317
Sotah
    12b   210
    13a   75
    13b   19
    40a   567
    49b   60
Succah 53a   368
Targum Yerushalmi, Bereishis 1:1   355
Teshuvos HaRema   367
Yalkut Shimoni, Parashas Yisro   194
Yam Shel Shlomo   367
Yevamos 105b   61 (*fn*)

This volume is part of
THE ARTSCROLL SERIES®
an ongoing project of
translations, commentaries and expositions
on Scripture, Mishnah, Talmud, Halachah,
liturgy, history, the classic Rabbinic writings,
biographies and thought.

For a brochure of current publications
visit your local Hebrew bookseller
or contact the publisher:

Mesorah Publications, ltd

4401 Second Avenue
Brooklyn, New York 11232
(718) 921-9000
www.artscroll.com